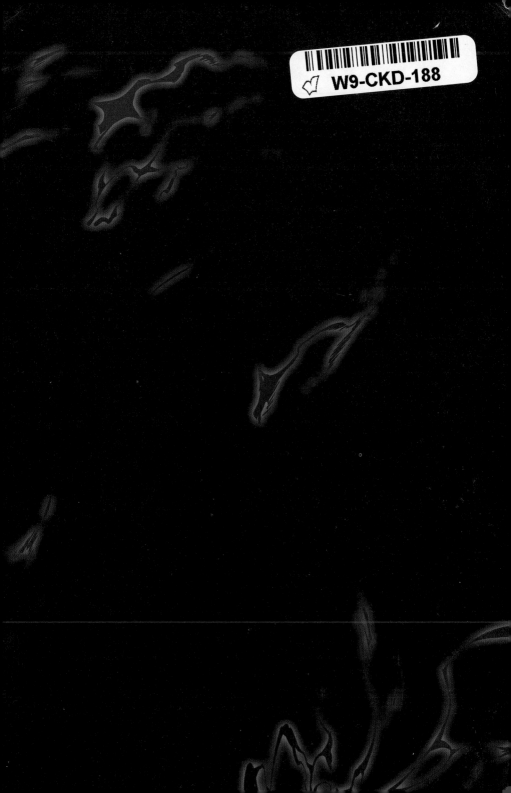

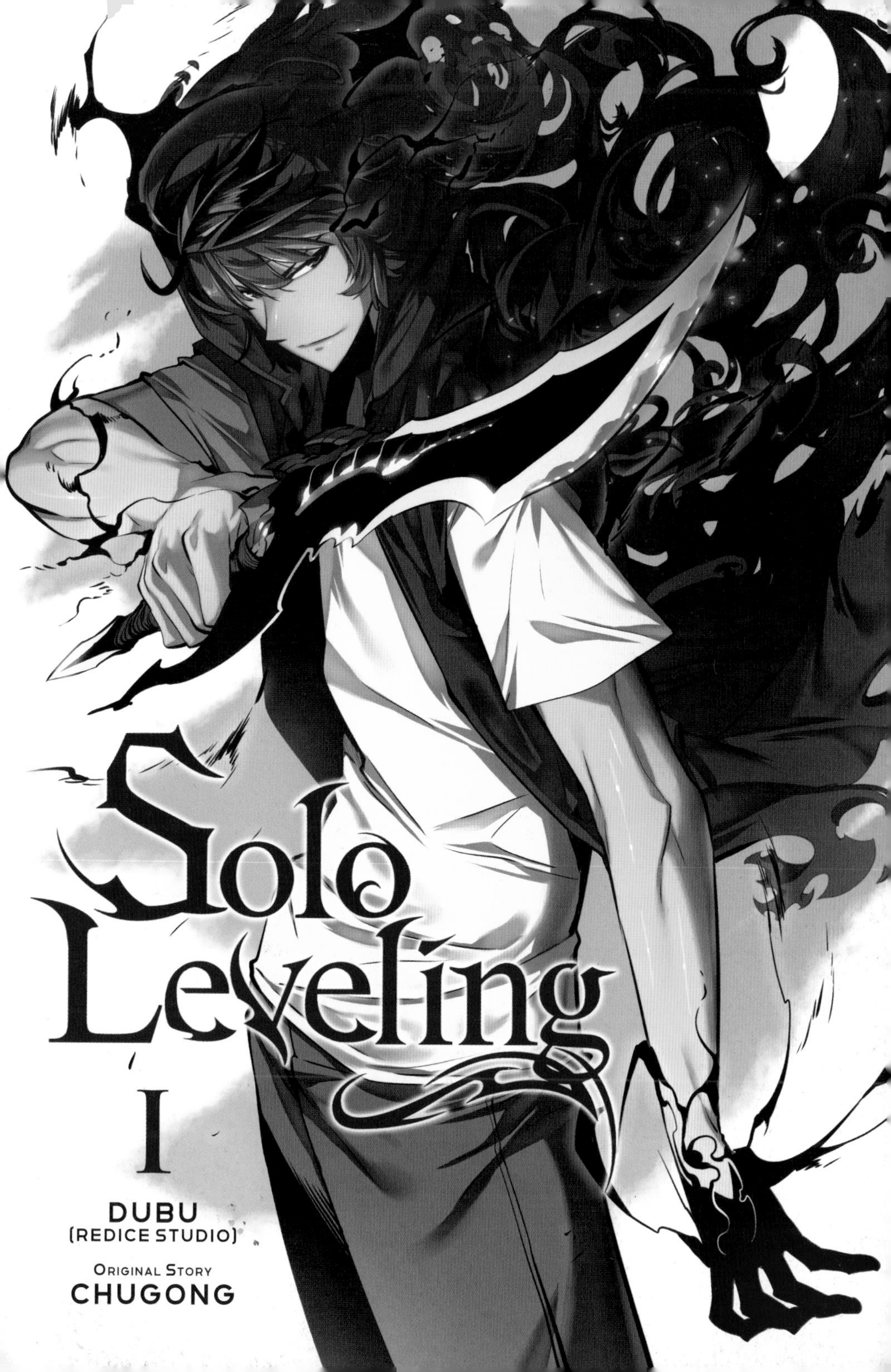
Solo Leveling
I
DUBU
(REDICE STUDIO)
Original Story
CHUGONG

CHARACTERS

Jinwoo Sung

E-rank Hunter

Chiyul Song

C-rank Hunter / Leader

Joohee Lee

B-rank Hunter / Healer

Sangshik Kim

D-rank Hunter

CONTENTS

Solo Leveling

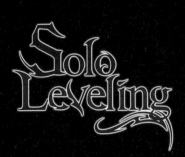

PROLOGUE

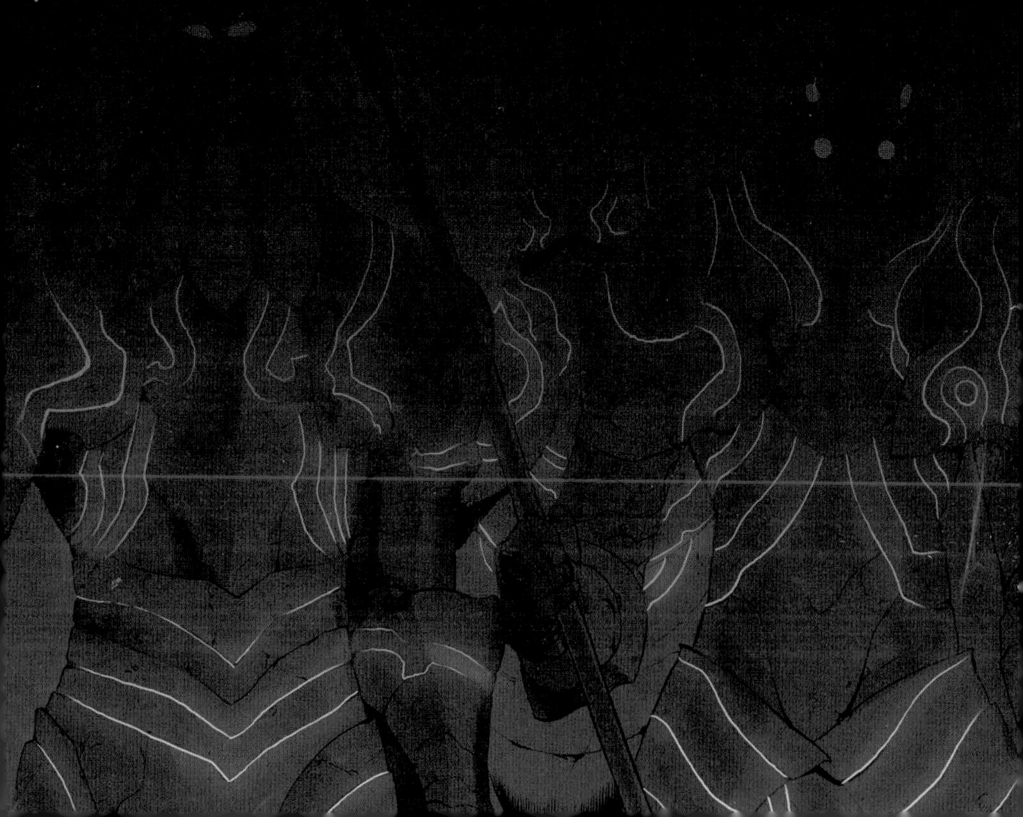

Solo Leveling

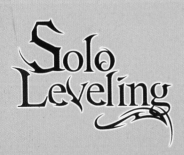

MY NAME IS
JINWOO SUNG.

HFF...

HUFF...

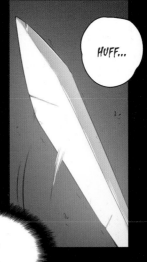

E-RANK
HUNTER.

THE LOWEST LEVEL IN THE HUNTER'S ASSOCIATION. THE WEAKEST OF THEM ALL.
HUFF!
HUFF!
THUD THUD

THUD
THUD
THUD
FOR SOMEONE LIKE ME TO BE IN A SITUATION LIKE THIS—

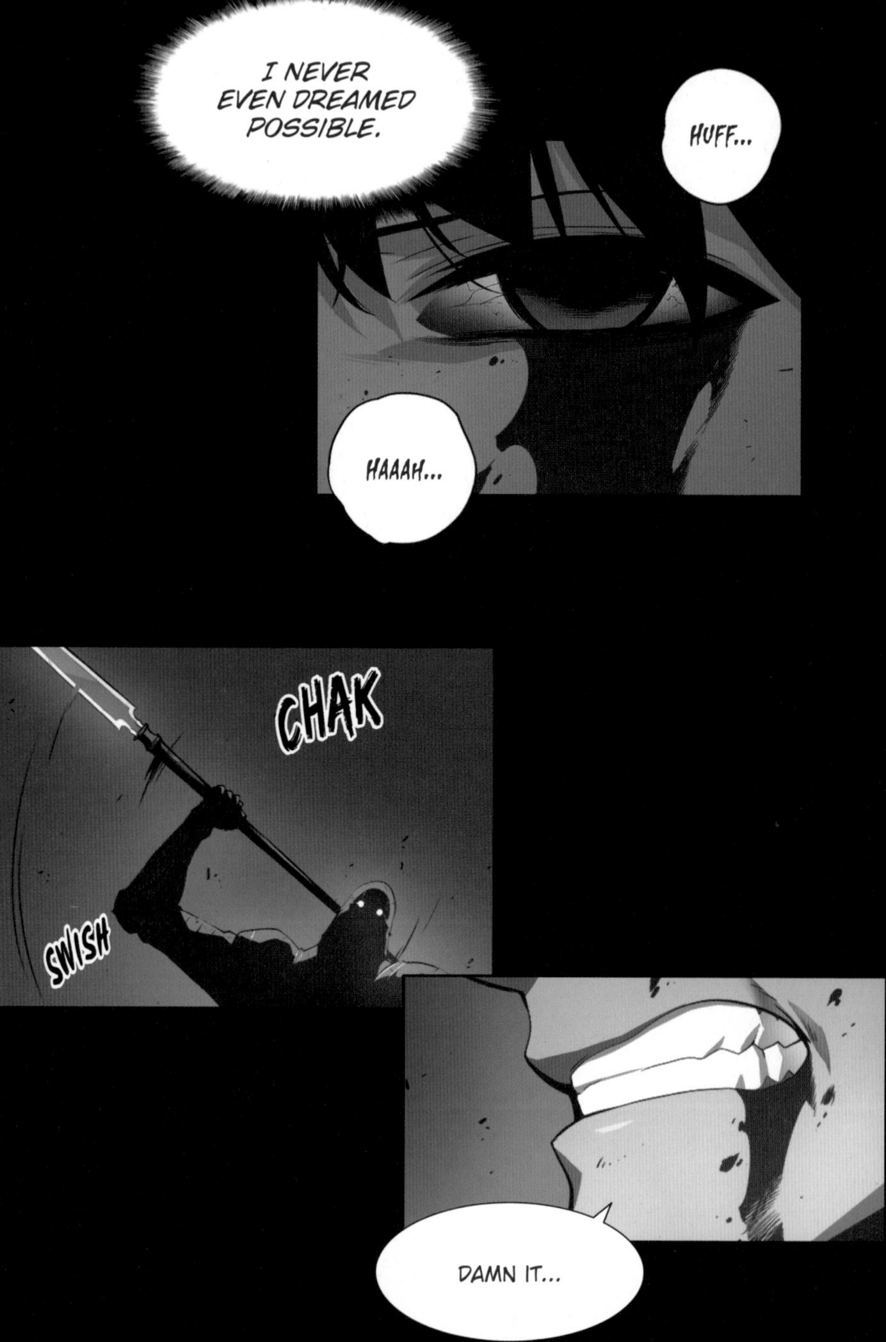
I NEVER EVEN DREAMED POSSIBLE.
HUFF...
HAAAH...
CHAK
SWISH
DAMN IT...

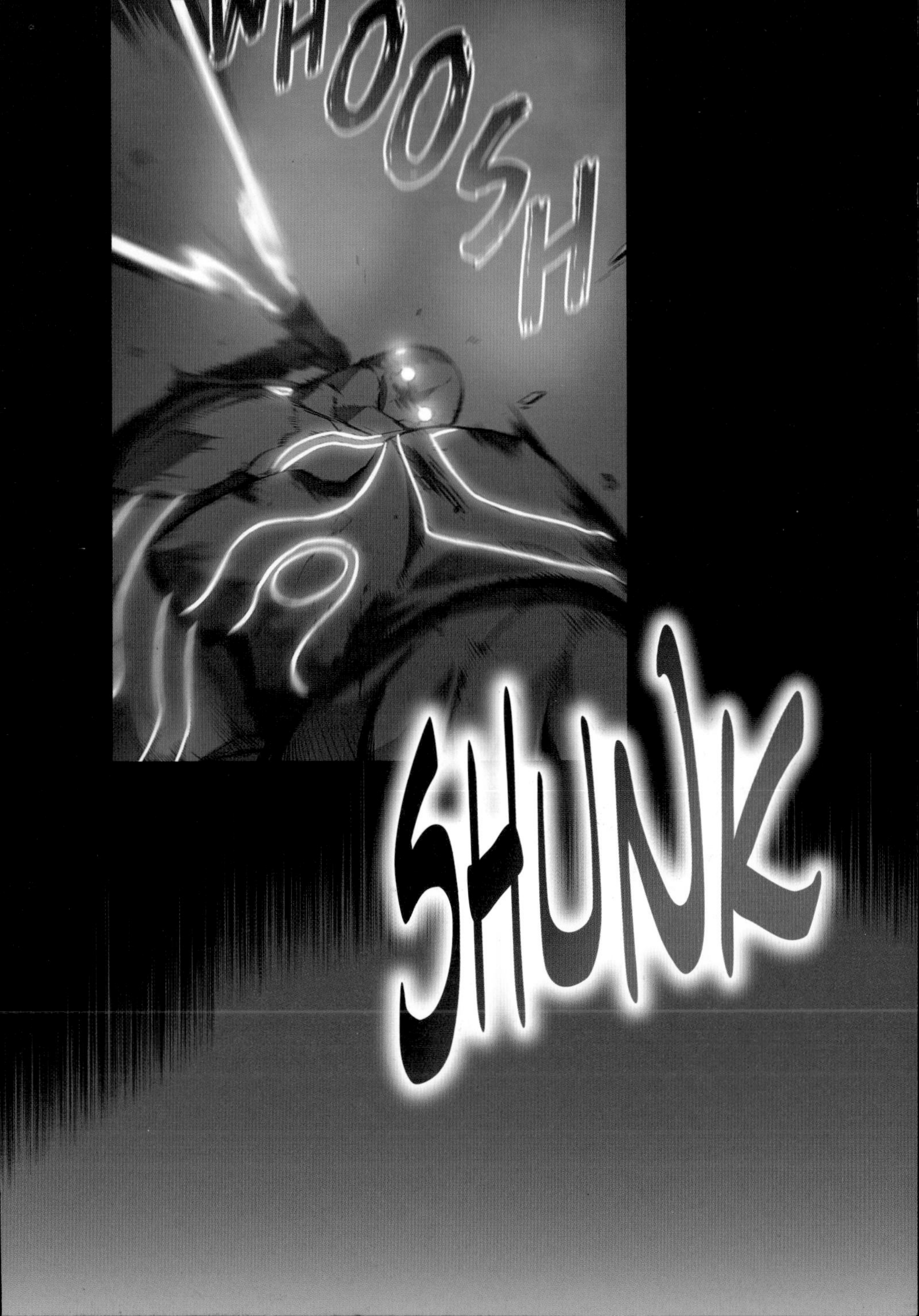
WHOOSH
SHUNK

Solo Leveling

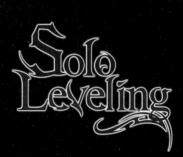

CHAPTER 1

Double Dungeon

Solo Leveling

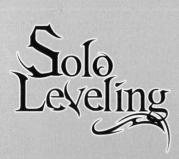

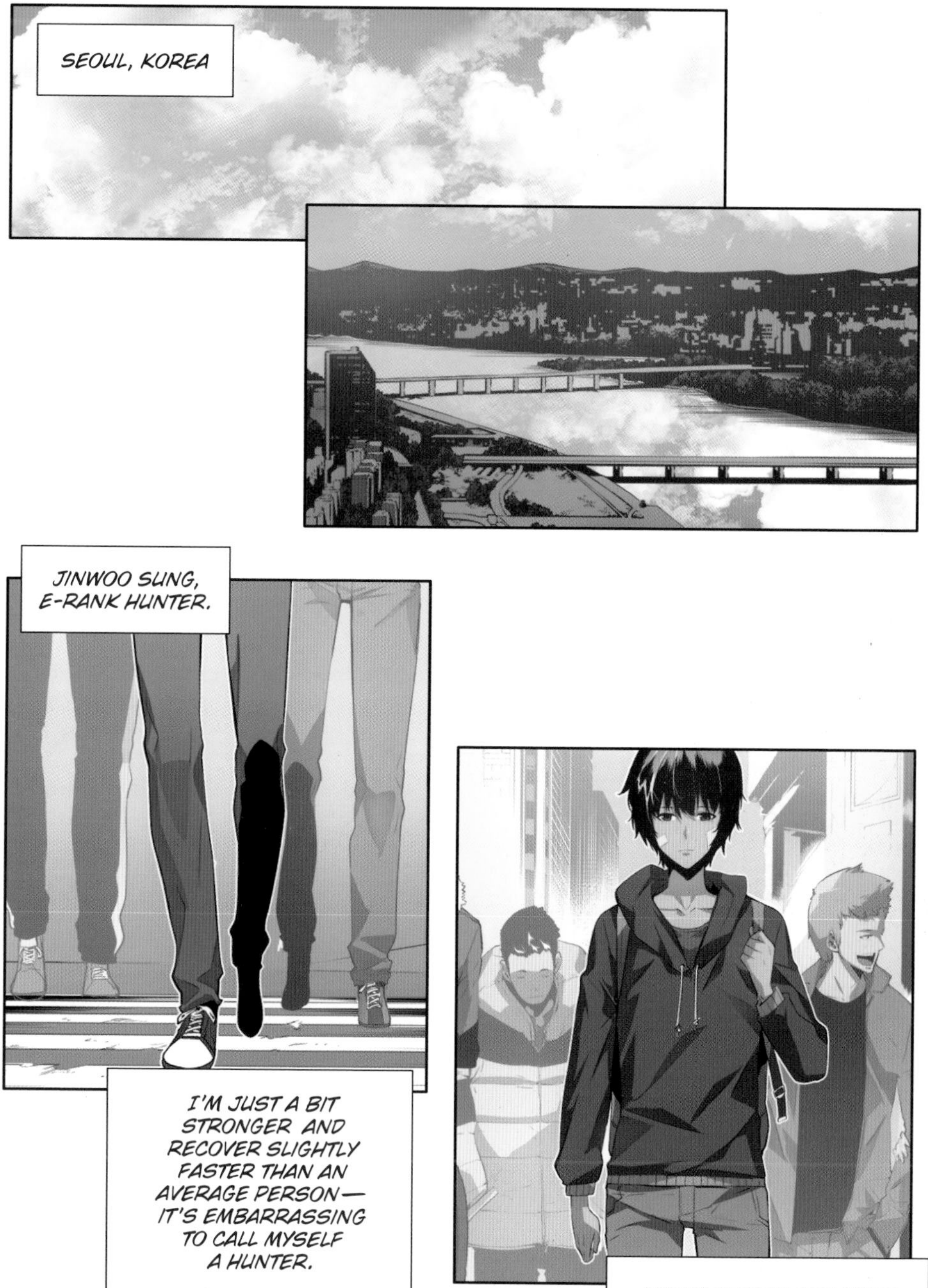
SEOUL, KOREA
JINWOO SUNG, E-RANK HUNTER.
I'M JUST A BIT STRONGER AND RECOVER SLIGHTLY FASTER THAN AN AVERAGE PERSON—IT'S EMBARRASSING TO CALL MYSELF A HUNTER.
NOT ONLY DO I GET HURT ALL THE TIME, NEAR-DEATH EXPERIENCES ARE NOTHING NEW TO ME.

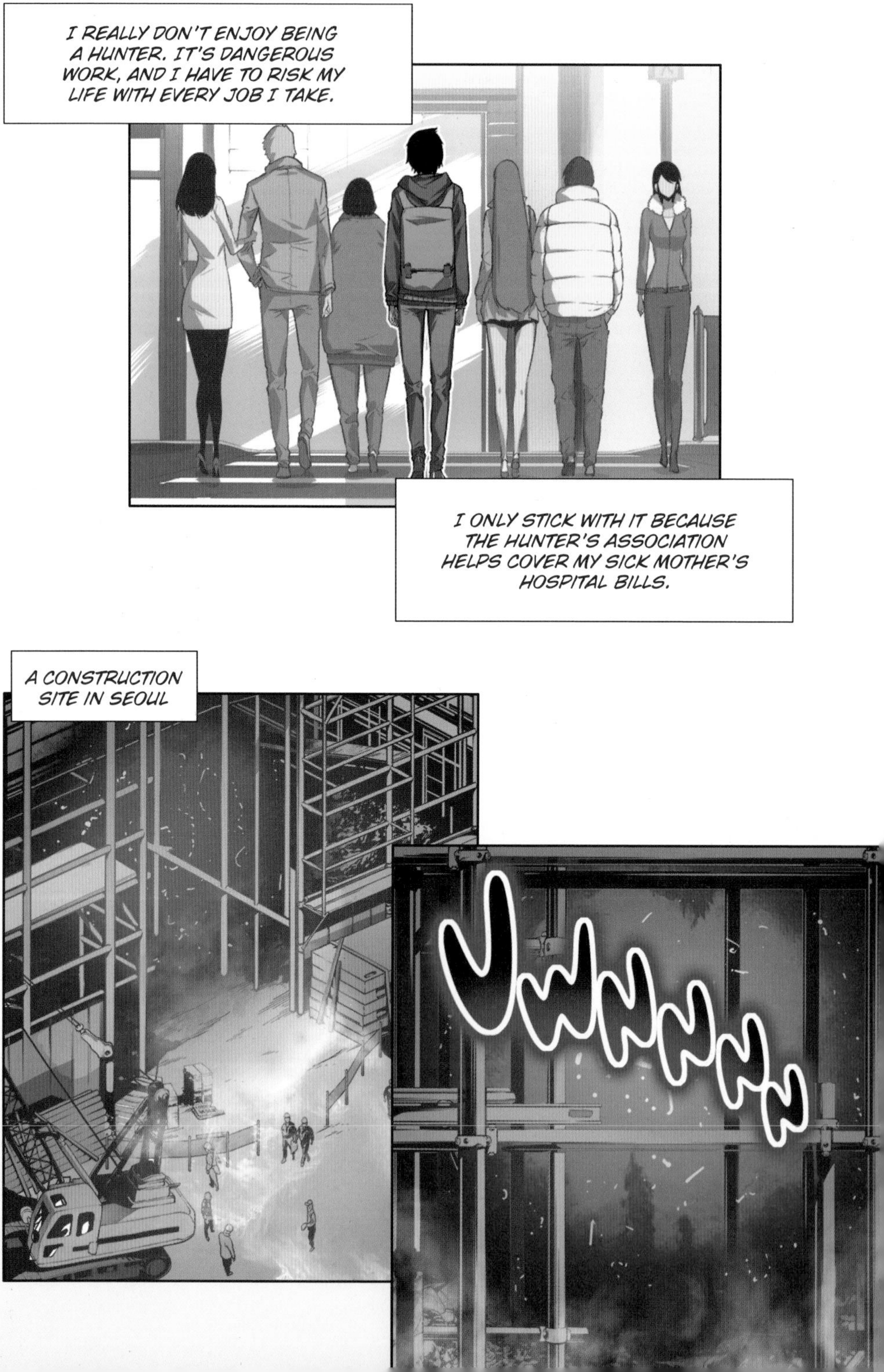
I REALLY DON'T ENJOY BEING A HUNTER. IT'S DANGEROUS WORK, AND I HAVE TO RISK MY LIFE WITH EVERY JOB I TAKE.
I ONLY STICK WITH IT BECAUSE THE HUNTER'S ASSOCIATION HELPS COVER MY SICK MOTHER'S HOSPITAL BILLS.
A CONSTRUCTION SITE IN SEOUL
VWHHHHH

AS A HIGH SCHOOL GRADUATE WITH
NO SPECIAL SKILLS OR TRAINING,
IT WAS THE ONLY OPTION LEFT TO ME.

HERE YOU GO.
GOOD LUCK WITH
TODAY'S RAID.

THANK
YOU.

HEY,
KIM!

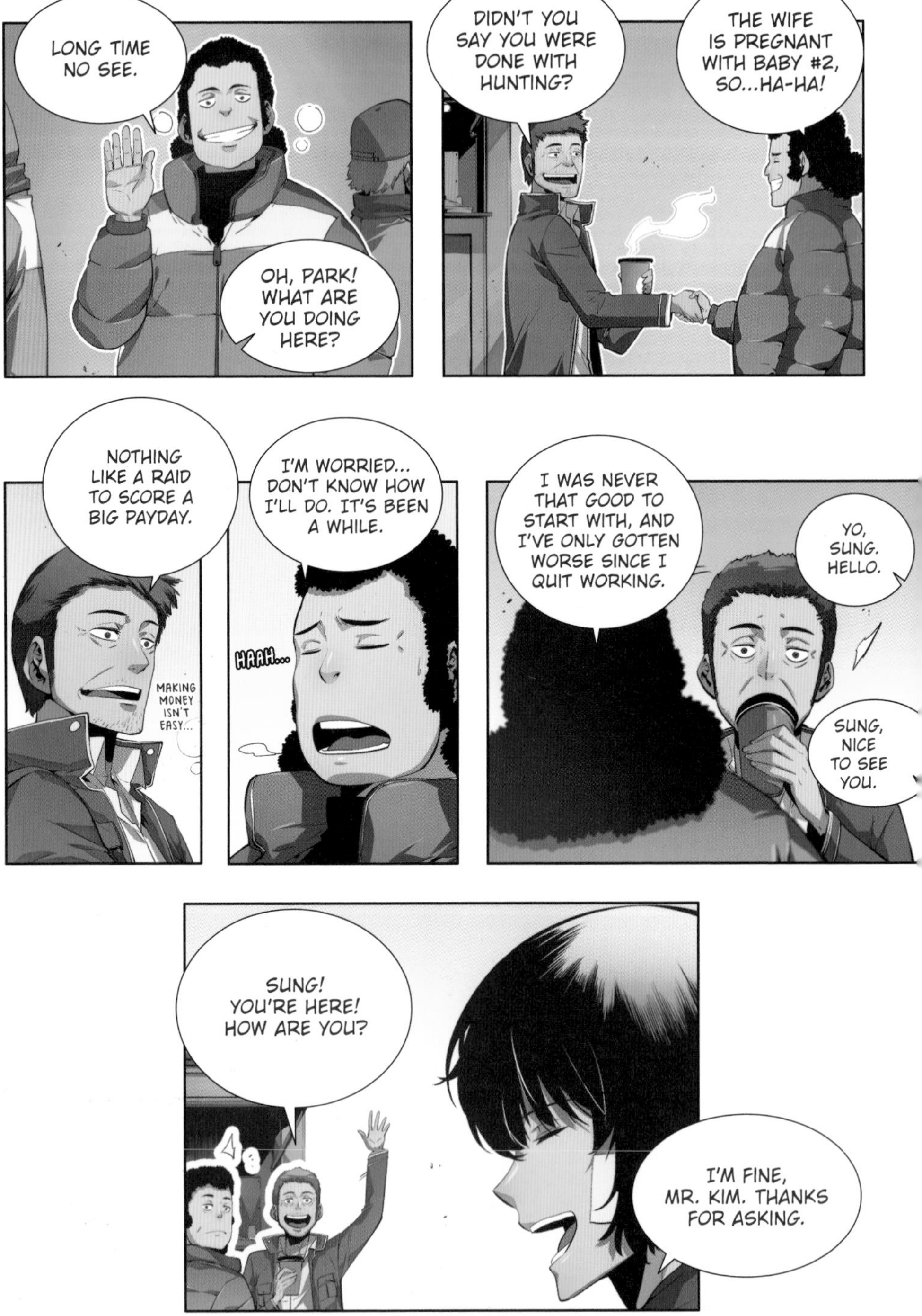
LONG TIME NO SEE.
OH, PARK! WHAT ARE YOU DOING HERE?
DIDN'T YOU SAY YOU WERE DONE WITH HUNTING?
THE WIFE IS PREGNANT WITH BABY #2, SO...HA-HA!
NOTHING LIKE A RAID TO SCORE A BIG PAYDAY.
MAKING MONEY ISN'T EASY...
I'M WORRIED... DON'T KNOW HOW I'LL DO. IT'S BEEN A WHILE.
HAAH...
I WAS NEVER THAT GOOD TO START WITH, AND I'VE ONLY GOTTEN WORSE SINCE I QUIT WORKING.
YO, SUNG. HELLO.
SUNG, NICE TO SEE YOU.
SUNG! YOU'RE HERE! HOW ARE YOU?
I'M FINE, MR. KIM. THANKS FOR ASKING.

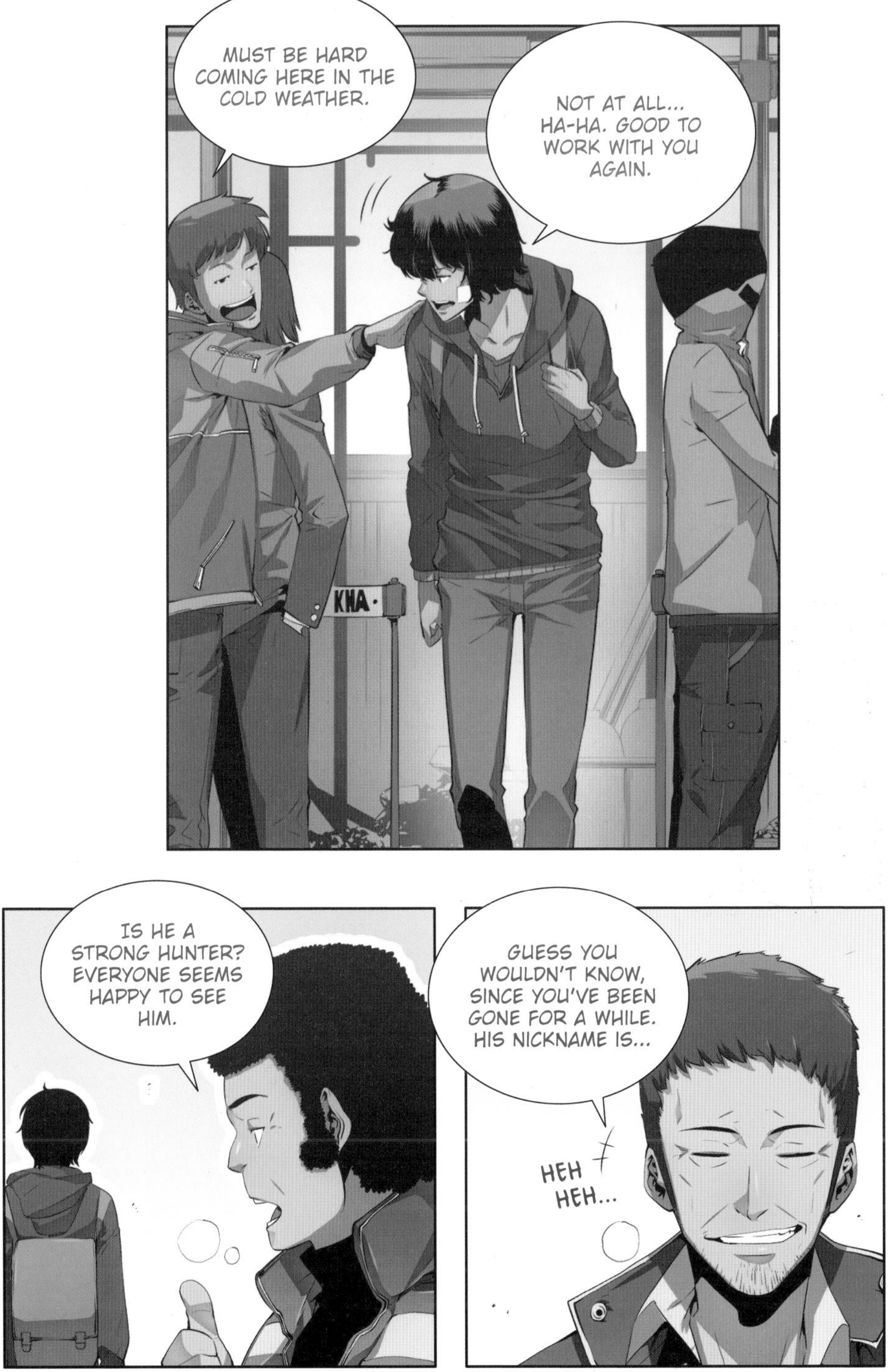
MUST BE HARD COMING HERE IN THE COLD WEATHER.
NOT AT ALL... HA-HA. GOOD TO WORK WITH YOU AGAIN.
KHA·
IS HE A STRONG HUNTER? EVERYONE SEEMS HAPPY TO SEE HIM.
GUESS YOU WOULDN'T KNOW, SINCE YOU'VE BEEN GONE FOR A WHILE. HIS NICKNAME IS...
HEH HEH...

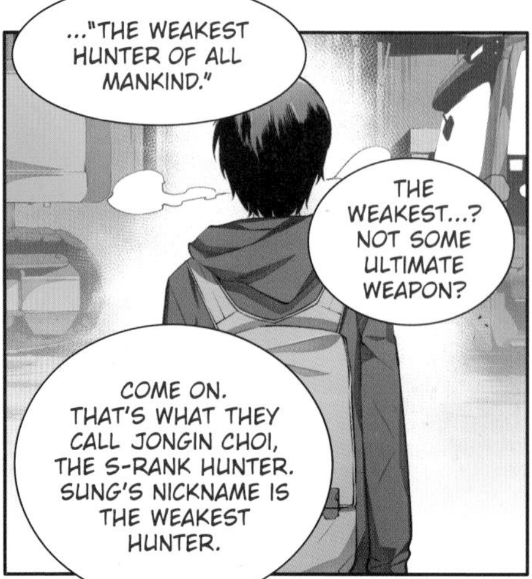
..."THE WEAKEST HUNTER OF ALL MANKIND."
THE WEAKEST...? NOT SOME ULTIMATE WEAPON?
COME ON. THAT'S WHAT THEY CALL JONGIN CHOI, THE S-RANK HUNTER. SUNG'S NICKNAME IS THE WEAKEST HUNTER.

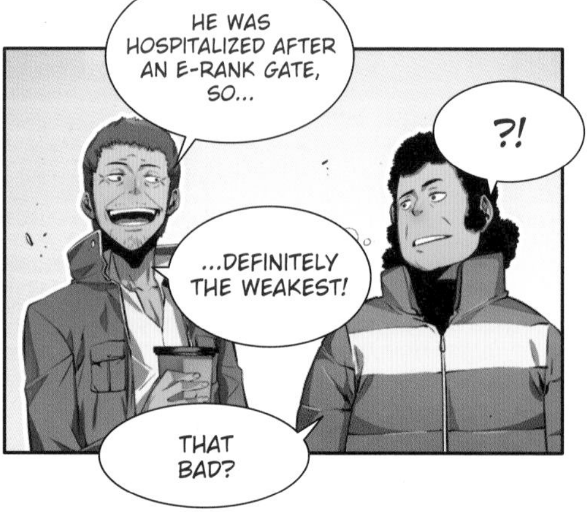
HE WAS HOSPITALIZED AFTER AN E-RANK GATE, SO...
?!
...DEFINITELY THE WEAKEST!
THAT BAD?

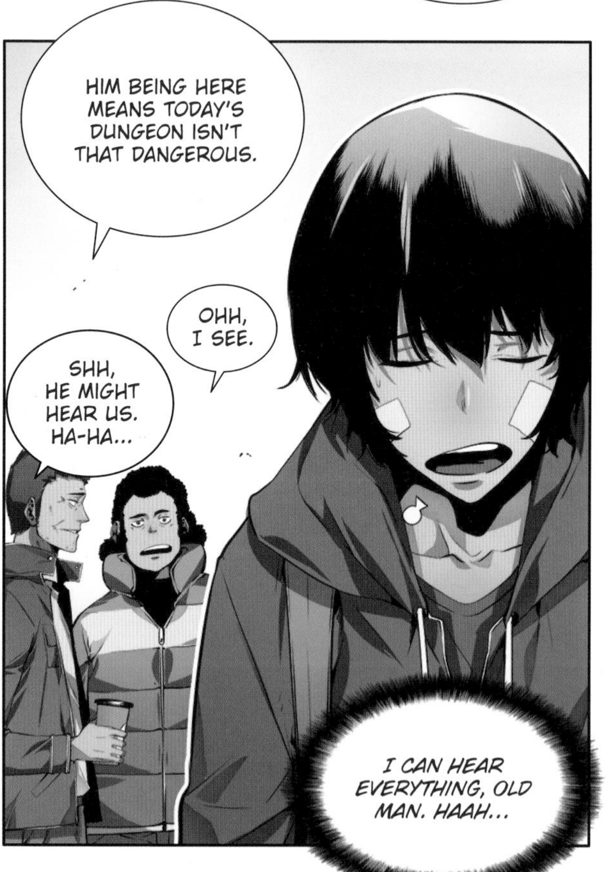
HIM BEING HERE MEANS TODAY'S DUNGEON ISN'T THAT DANGEROUS.
OHH, I SEE.
SHH, HE MIGHT HEAR US. HA-HA...
I CAN HEAR EVERYTHING, OLD MAN. HAAH...

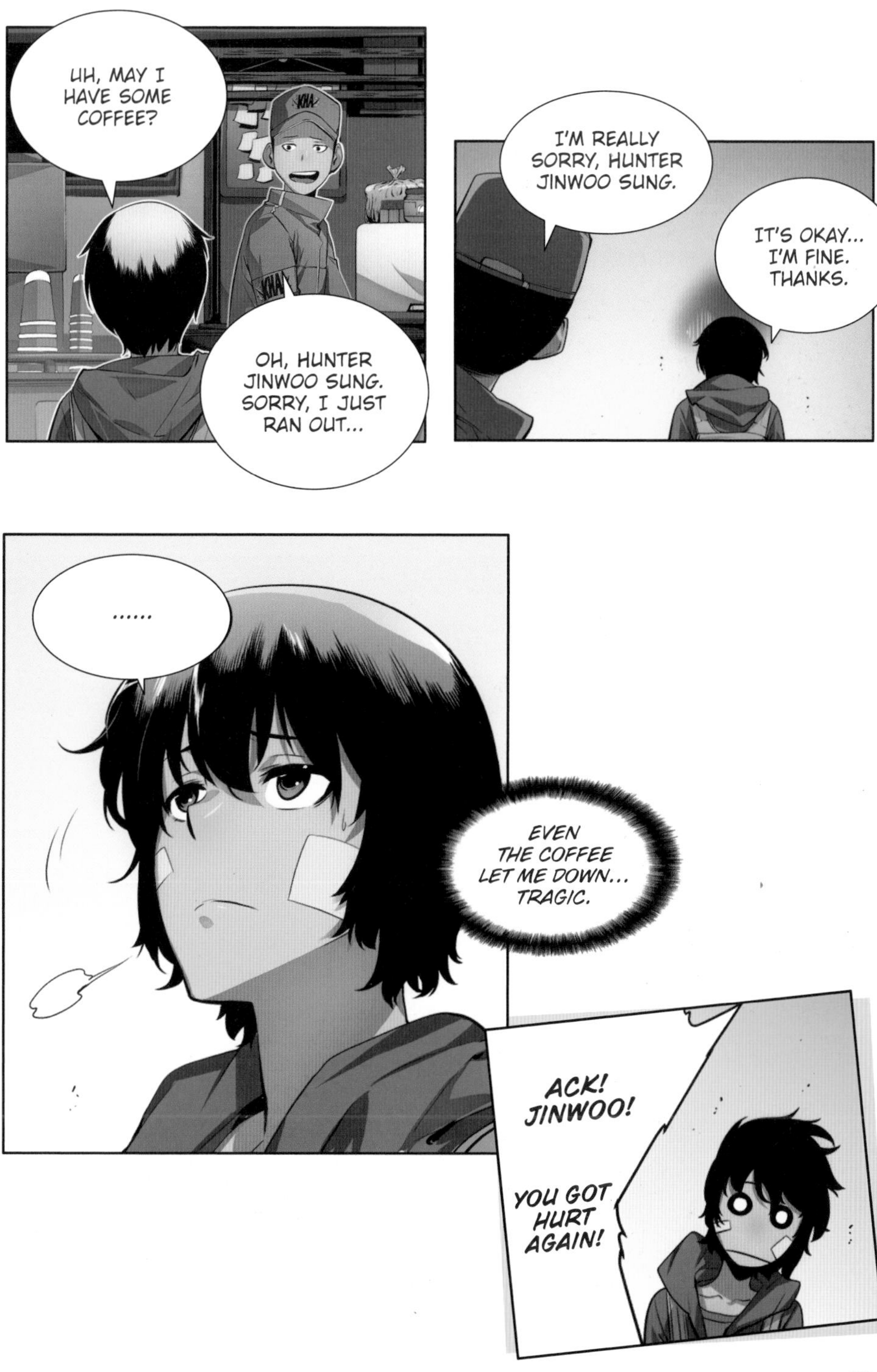
UH, MAY I HAVE SOME COFFEE?
OH, HUNTER JINWOO SUNG. SORRY, I JUST RAN OUT...
I'M REALLY SORRY, HUNTER JINWOO SUNG.
IT'S OKAY... I'M FINE. THANKS.
......
EVEN THE COFFEE LET ME DOWN... TRAGIC.
ACK! JINWOO!
YOU GOT HURT AGAIN!

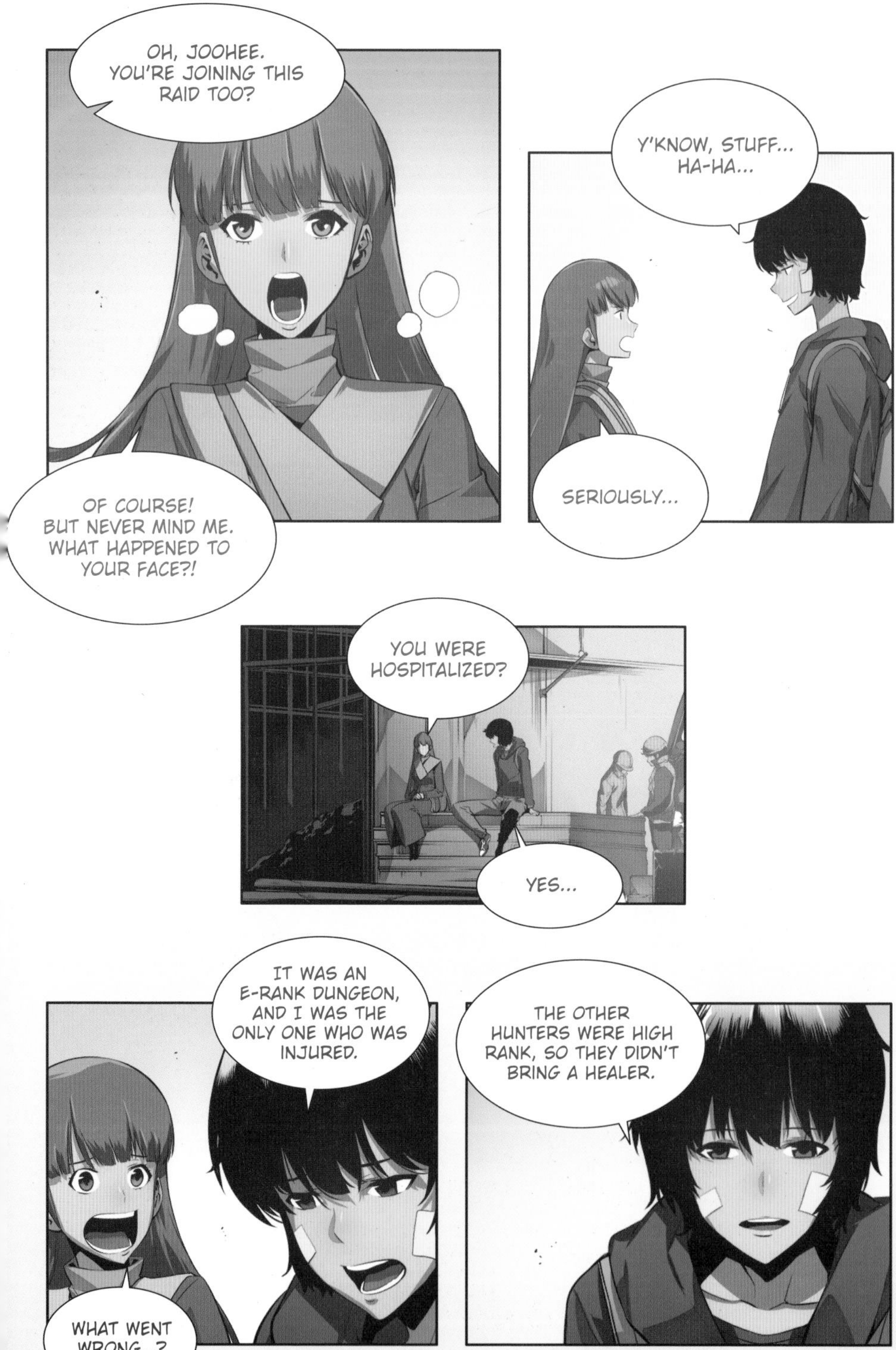
OH, JOOHEE. YOU'RE JOINING THIS RAID TOO?
OF COURSE! BUT NEVER MIND ME. WHAT HAPPENED TO YOUR FACE?!
Y'KNOW, STUFF... HA-HA...
SERIOUSLY...
YOU WERE HOSPITALIZED?
YES...
WHAT WENT WRONG...?
IT WAS AN E-RANK DUNGEON, AND I WAS THE ONLY ONE WHO WAS INJURED.
THE OTHER HUNTERS WERE HIGH RANK, SO THEY DIDN'T BRING A HEALER.

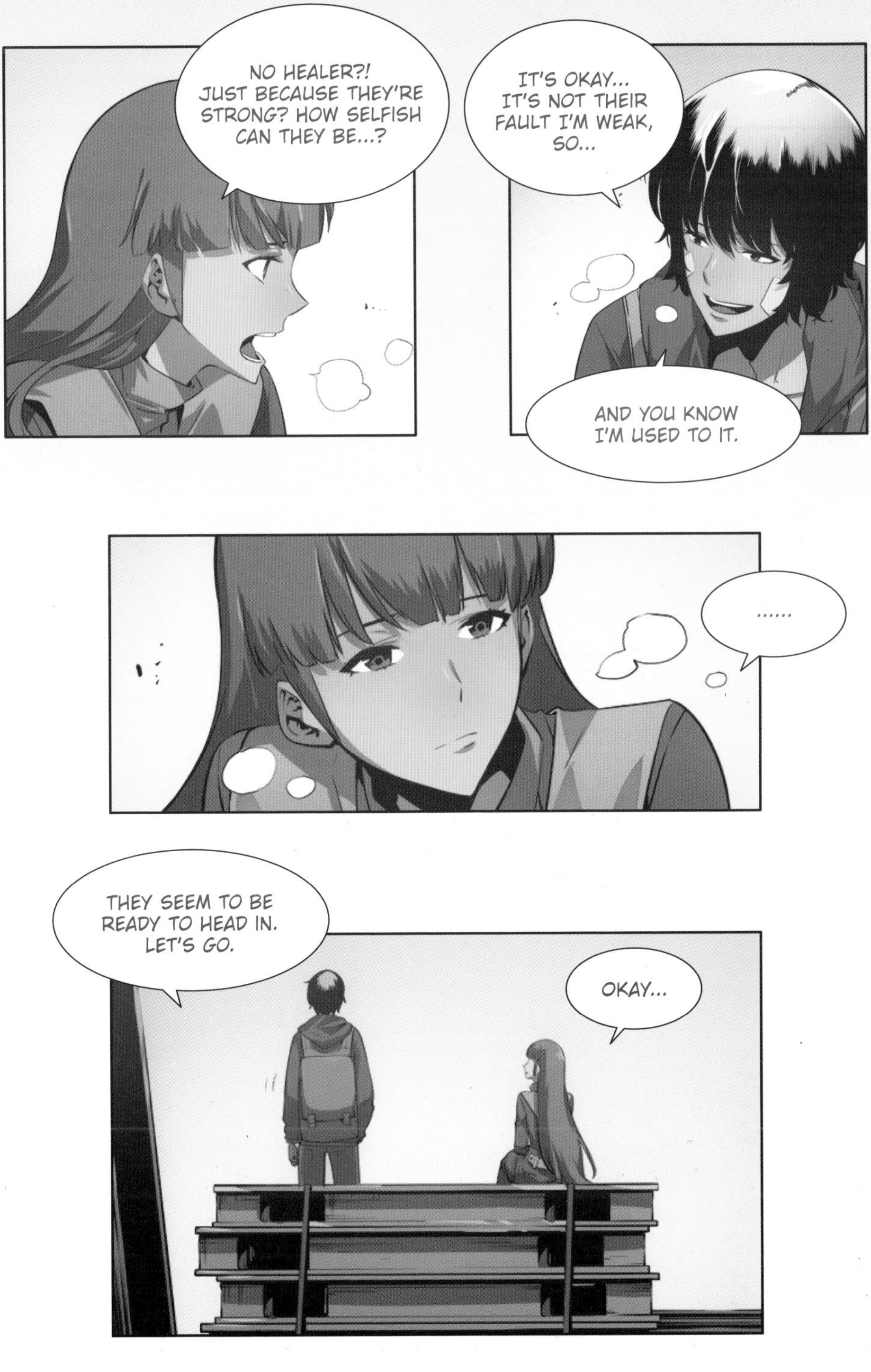
NO HEALER?! JUST BECAUSE THEY'RE STRONG? HOW SELFISH CAN THEY BE...?
IT'S OKAY... IT'S NOT THEIR FAULT I'M WEAK, SO...
AND YOU KNOW I'M USED TO IT.
......
THEY SEEM TO BE READY TO HEAD IN. LET'S GO.
OKAY...

ATTEN-TION PLEASE!

WE'RE ALL HERE FOR A BIG PAYOUT. AND IF I MAY BE SO BOLD...

...I WOULD LIKE TO LEAD THIS RAID. ANY OBJECTIONS?

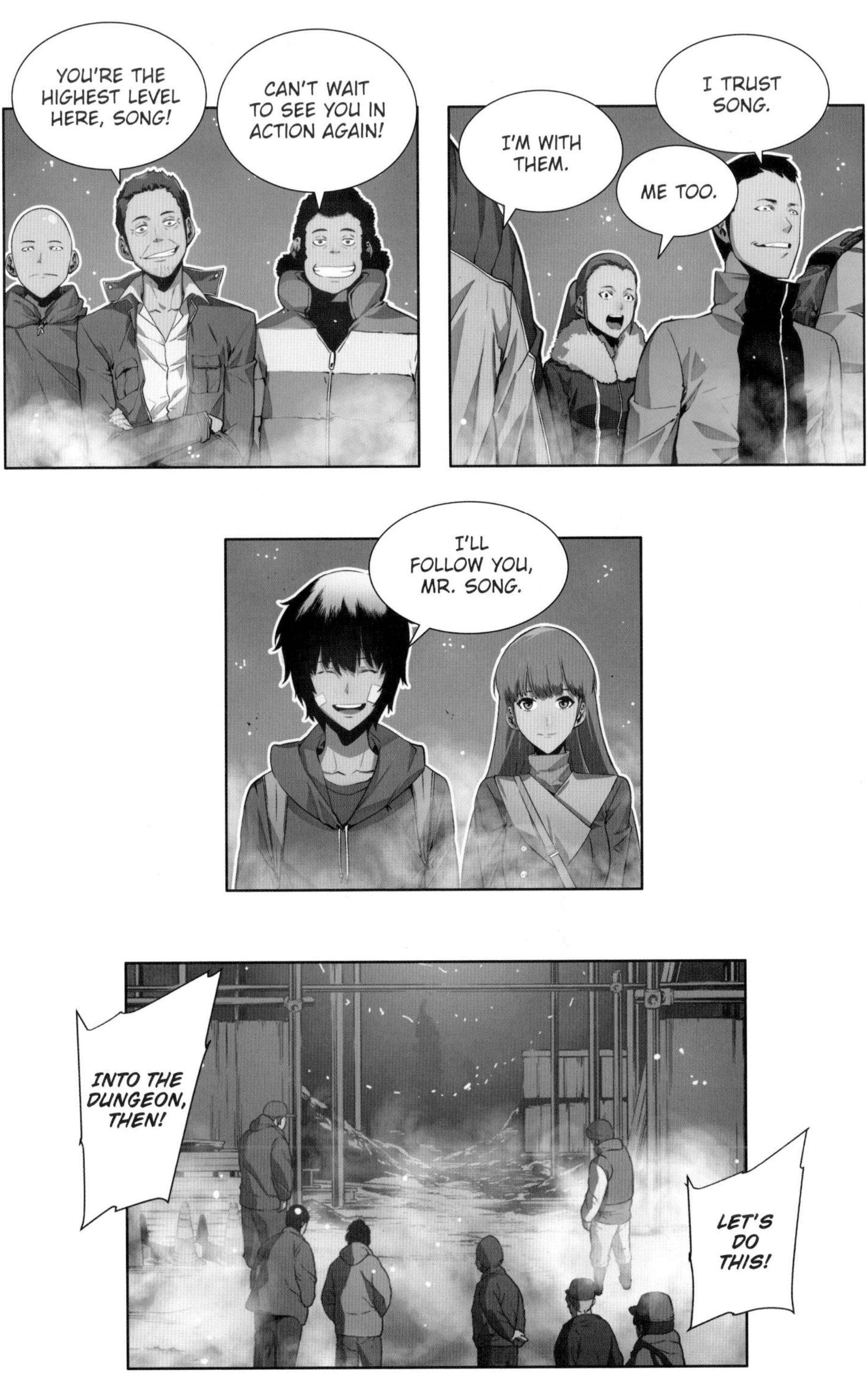
YOU'RE THE HIGHEST LEVEL HERE, SONG!
CAN'T WAIT TO SEE YOU IN ACTION AGAIN!
I'M WITH THEM.
I TRUST SONG.
ME TOO.
I'LL FOLLOW YOU, MR. SONG.
INTO THE DUNGEON, THEN!
LET'S DO THIS!

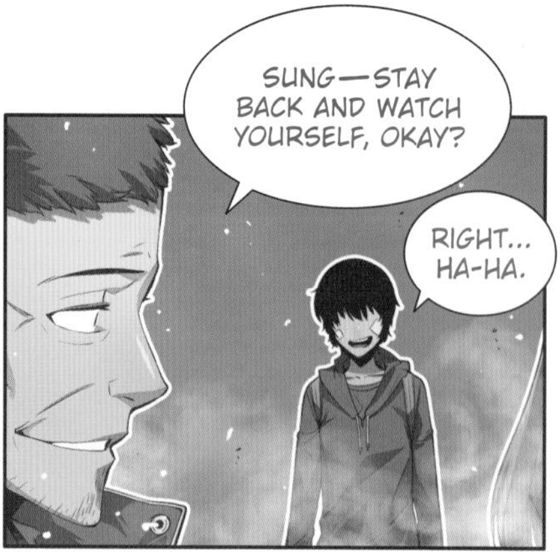
SUNG—STAY BACK AND WATCH YOURSELF, OKAY?
RIGHT... HA-HA.

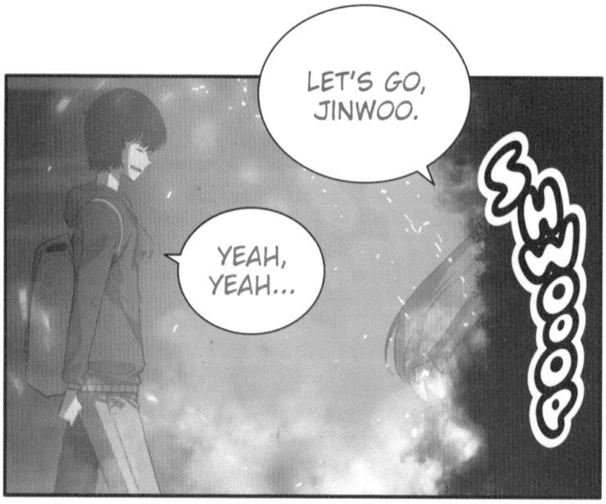
LET'S GO, JINWOO.
YEAH, YEAH...
SHWOOOP

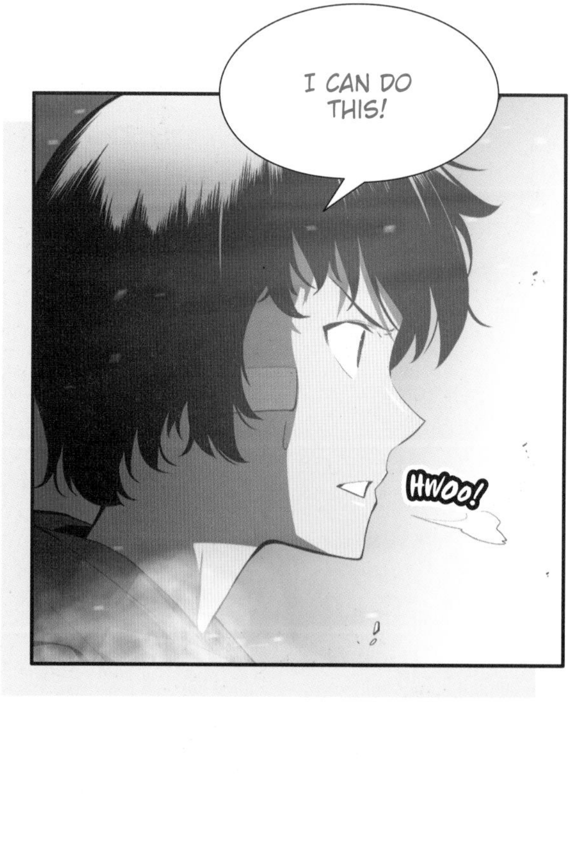
I CAN DO THIS!
HWOO!

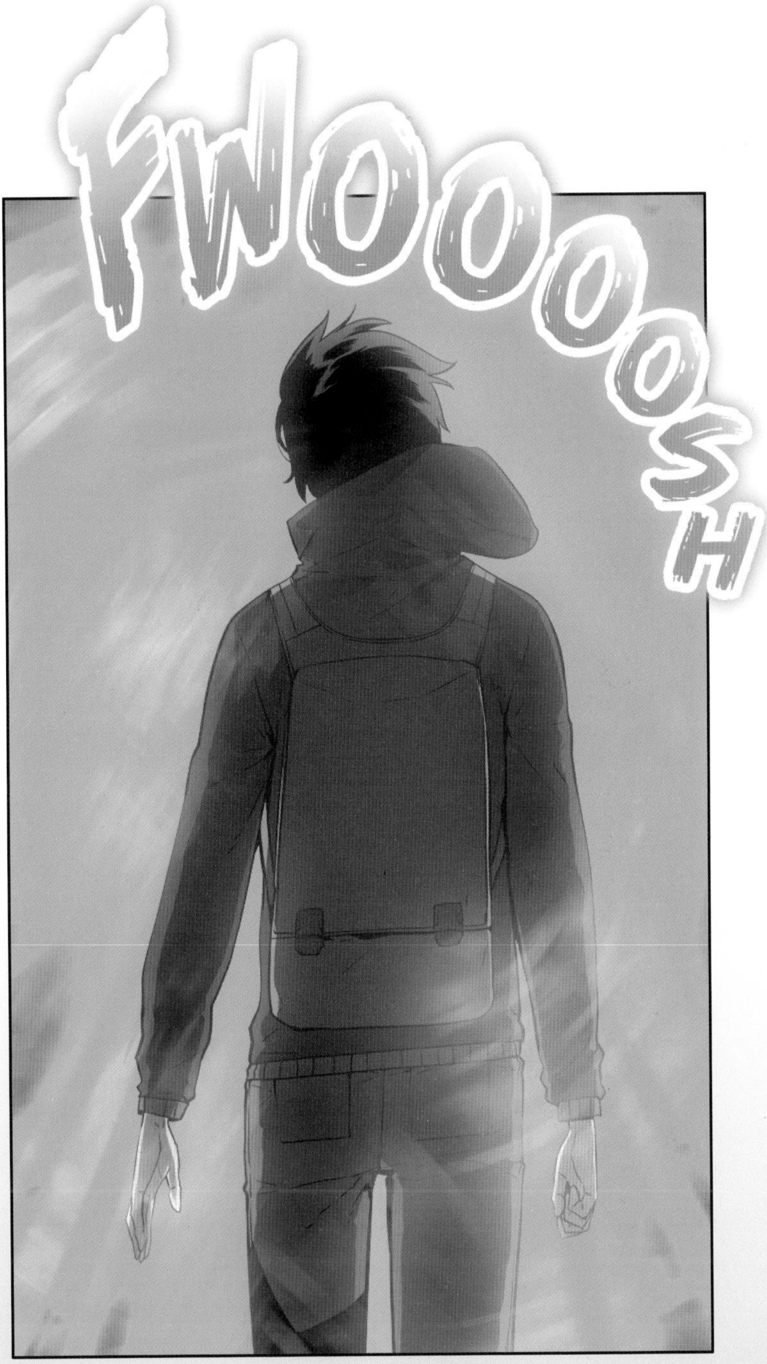
FWOOOOOSH

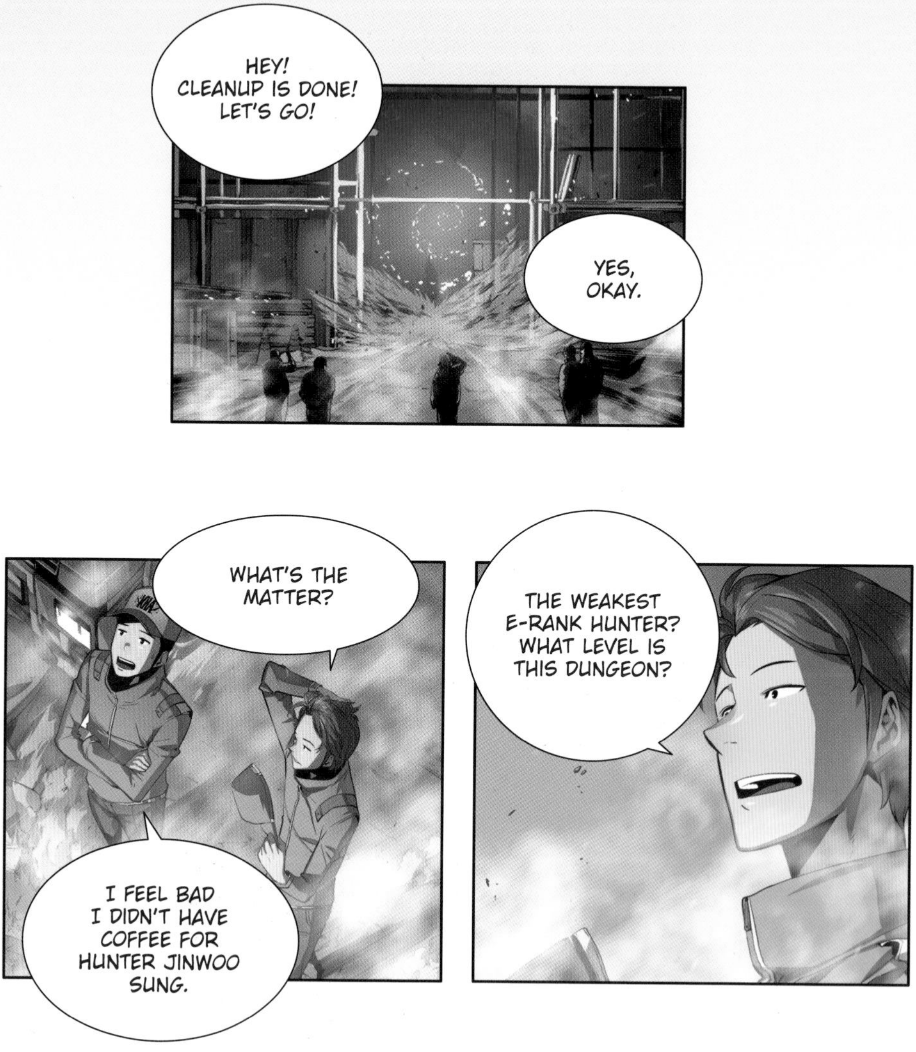
HEY! CLEANUP IS DONE! LET'S GO!
YES, OKAY.
WHAT'S THE MATTER?
I FEEL BAD I DIDN'T HAVE COFFEE FOR HUNTER JINWOO SUNG.
THE WEAKEST E-RANK HUNTER? WHAT LEVEL IS THIS DUNGEON?

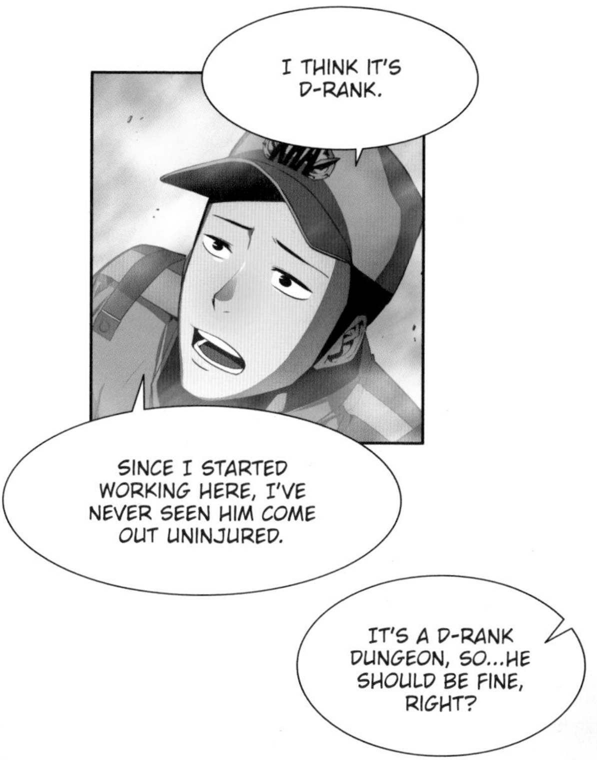
I THINK IT'S D-RANK.
SINCE I STARTED WORKING HERE, I'VE NEVER SEEN HIM COME OUT UNINJURED.
IT'S A D-RANK DUNGEON, SO...HE SHOULD BE FINE, RIGHT?

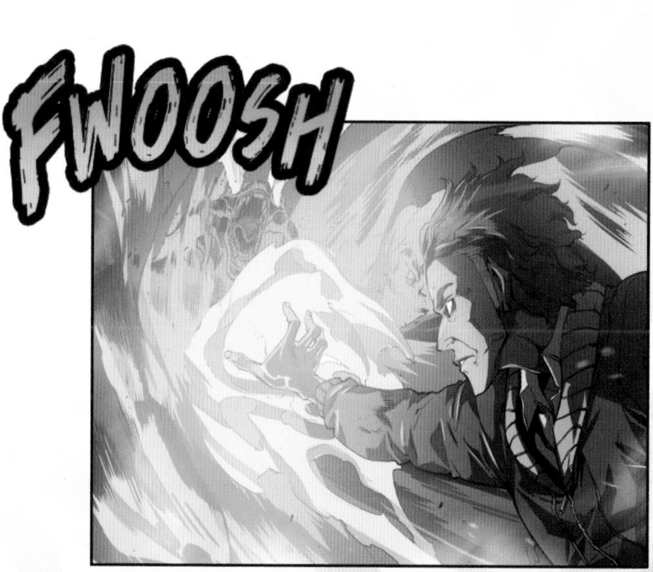
FWOOSH

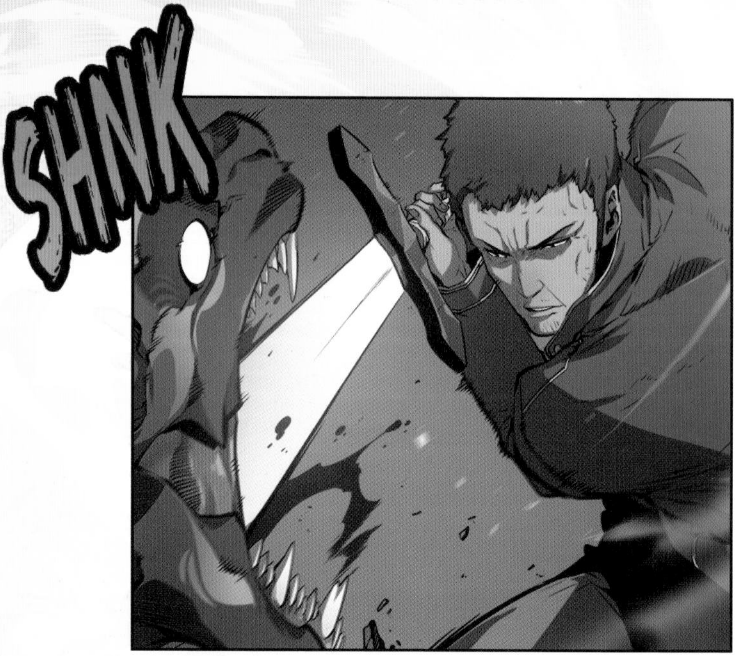
SHNK

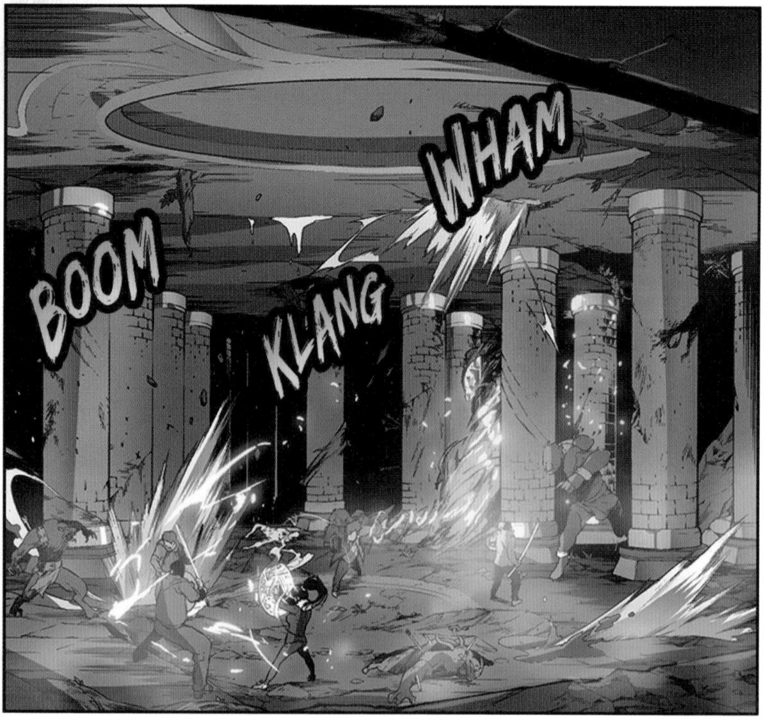
BOOM
KLANG
WHAM

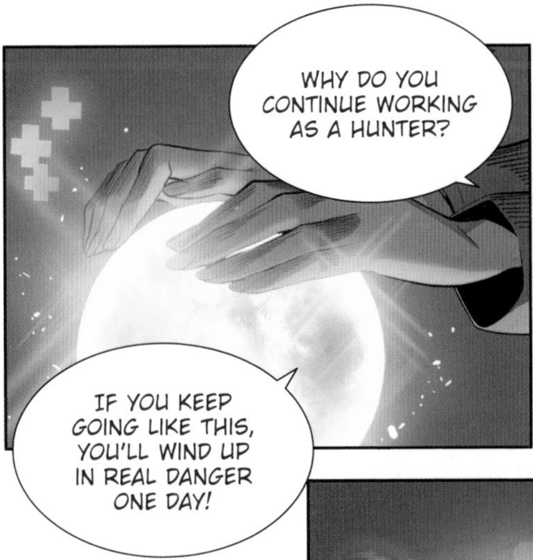
WHY DO YOU CONTINUE WORKING AS A HUNTER?
IF YOU KEEP GOING LIKE THIS, YOU'LL WIND UP IN REAL DANGER ONE DAY!

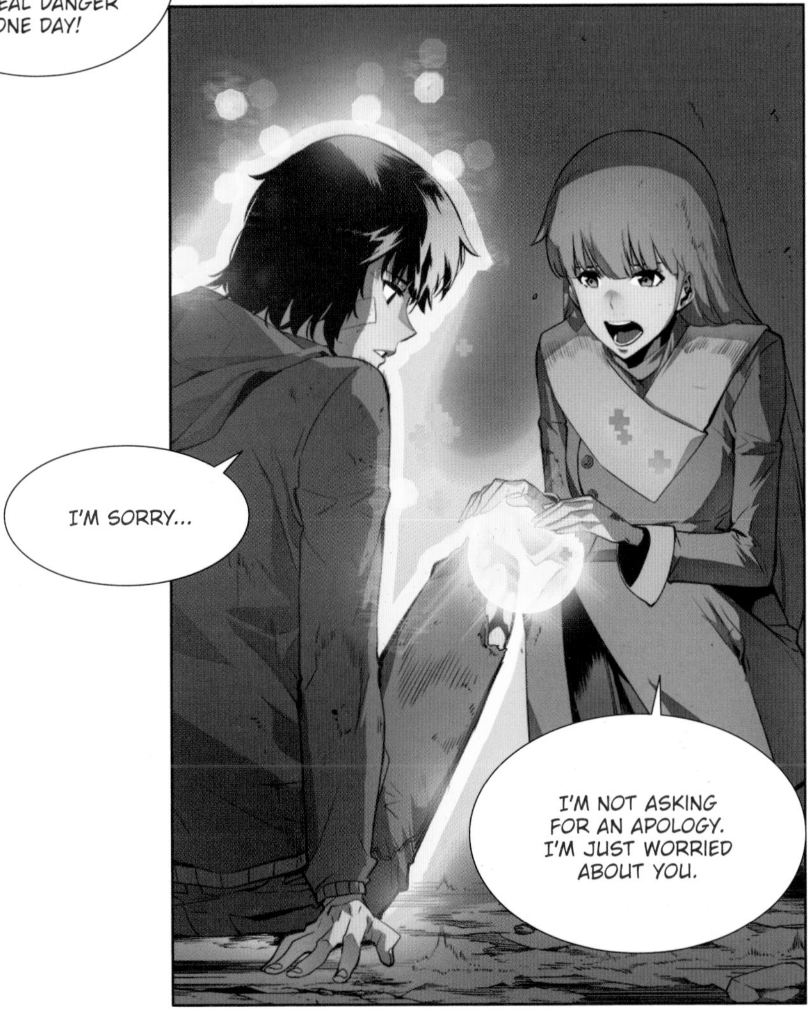
I'M SORRY...
I'M NOT ASKING FOR AN APOLOGY. I'M JUST WORRIED ABOUT YOU.

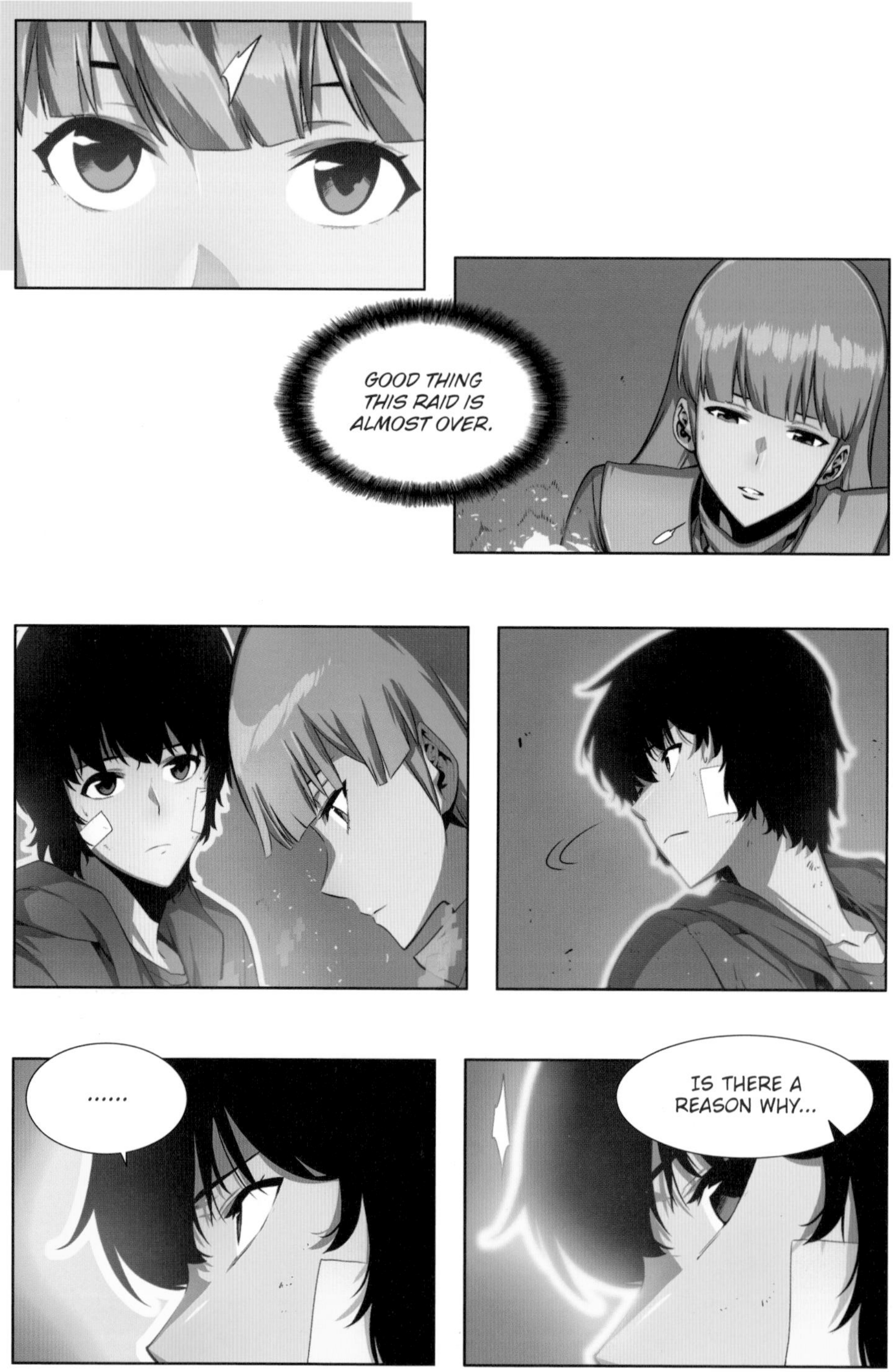

GOOD THING THIS RAID IS ALMOST OVER.
......
IS THERE A REASON WHY...

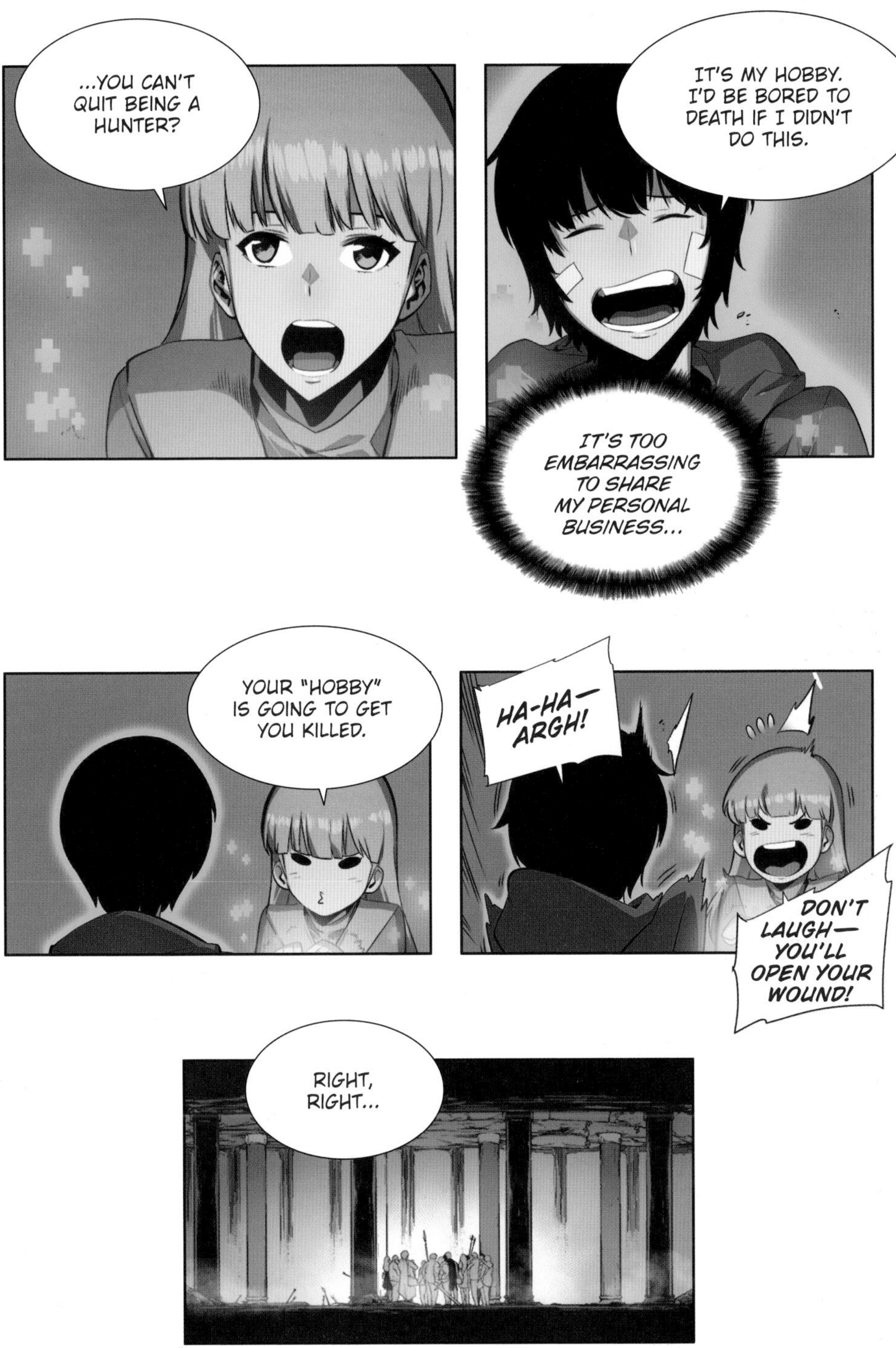

...YOU CAN'T QUIT BEING A HUNTER?
IT'S MY HOBBY. I'D BE BORED TO DEATH IF I DIDN'T DO THIS.
IT'S TOO EMBARRASSING TO SHARE MY PERSONAL BUSINESS...
YOUR "HOBBY" IS GOING TO GET YOU KILLED.
HA-HA—ARGH!
DON'T LAUGH—YOU'LL OPEN YOUR WOUND!
RIGHT, RIGHT...

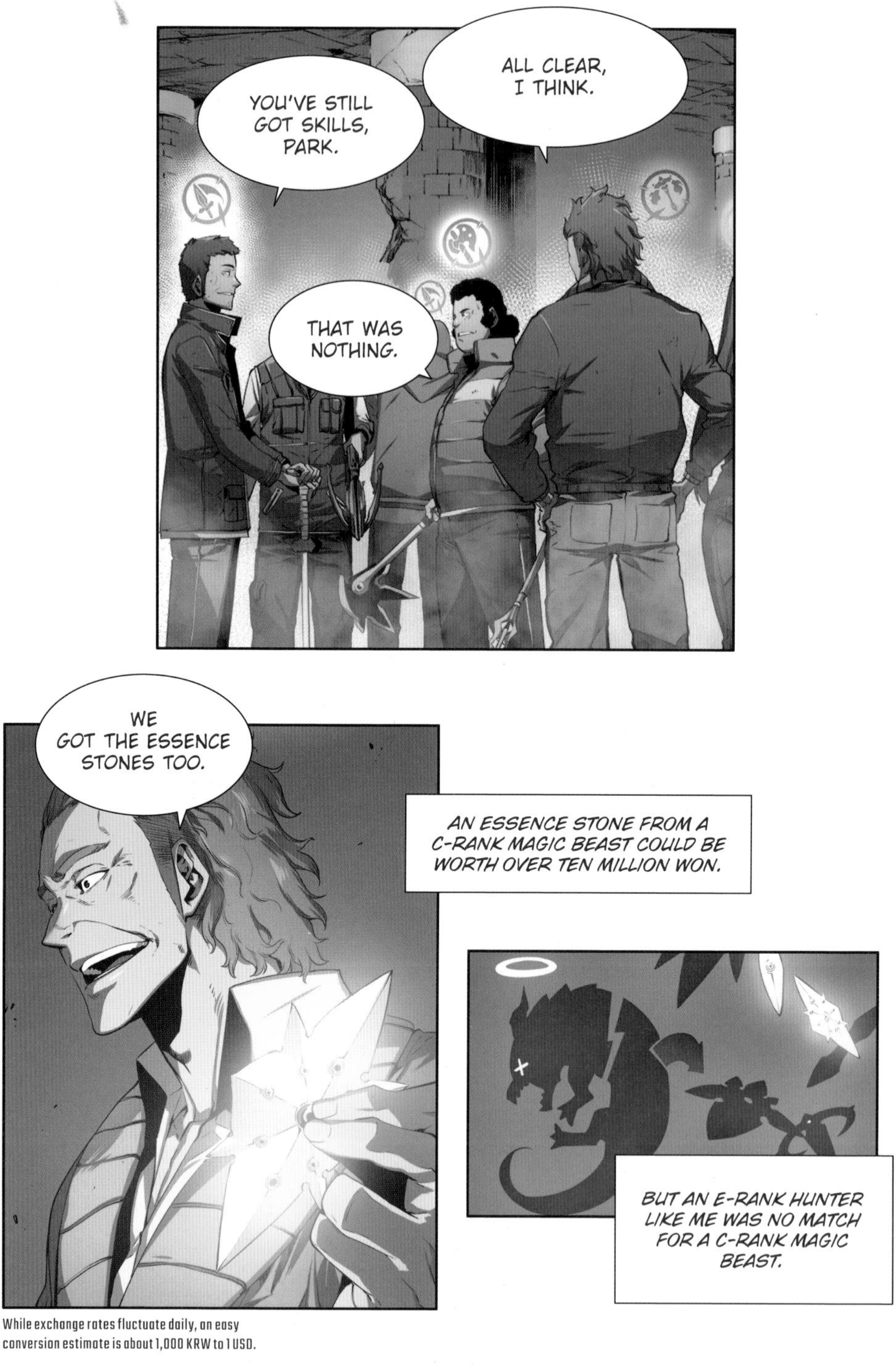
ALL CLEAR, I THINK.
YOU'VE STILL GOT SKILLS, PARK.
THAT WAS NOTHING.
WE GOT THE ESSENCE STONES TOO.
AN ESSENCE STONE FROM A C-RANK MAGIC BEAST COULD BE WORTH OVER TEN MILLION WON.
BUT AN E-RANK HUNTER LIKE ME WAS NO MATCH FOR A C-RANK MAGIC BEAST.

While exchange rates fluctuate daily, an easy conversion estimate is about 1,000 KRW to 1 USD.

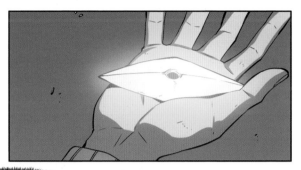

AFTER ALL THIS, ALL I GOT WAS AN E-RANK ESSENCE STONE.

WHAT A CRAPPY REWARD FOR RISKING MY LIFE.

AT THIS RATE, I'LL NEVER BE—

HEY! LOOK HERE! IS THIS ANOTHER ENTRANCE?

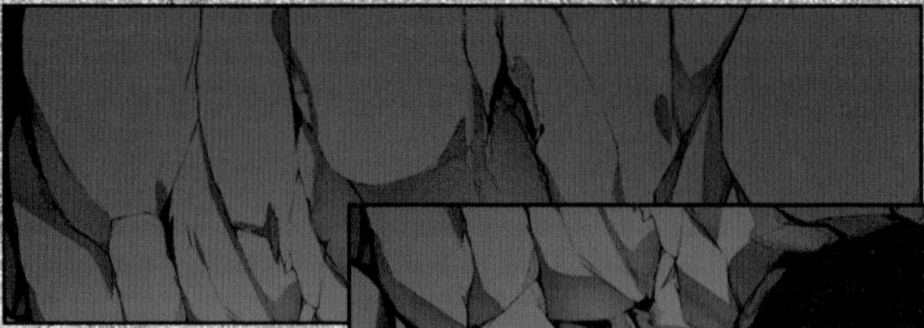

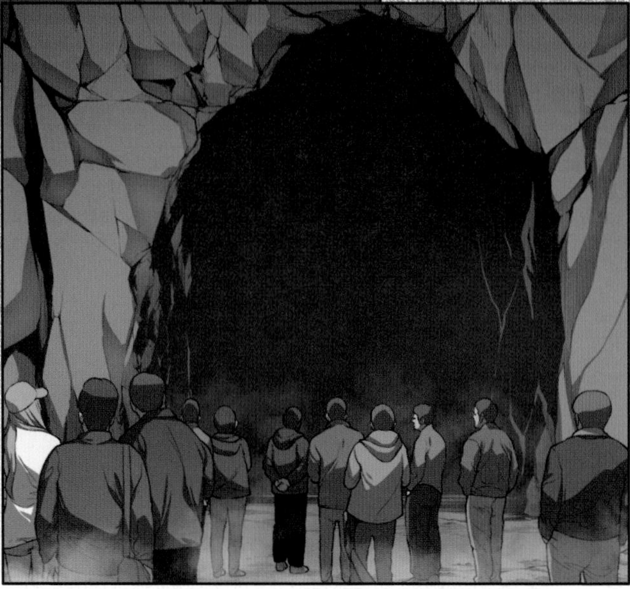

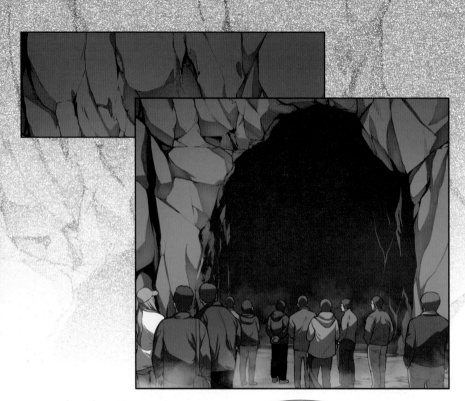

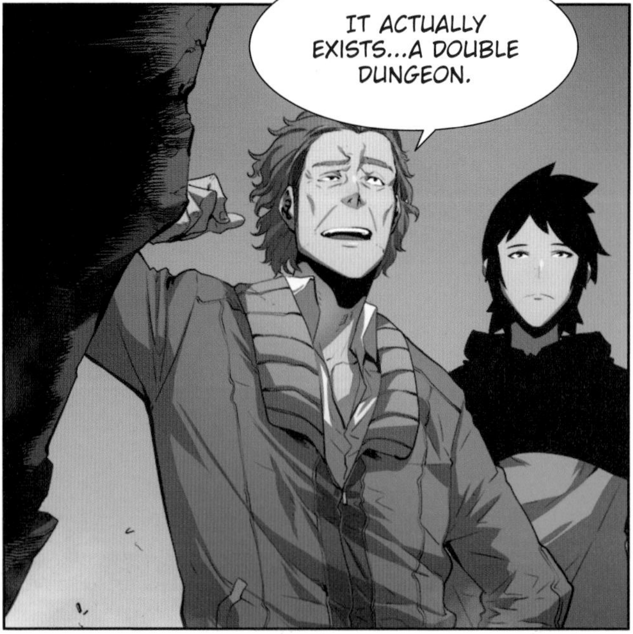
IT ACTUALLY EXISTS...A DOUBLE DUNGEON.

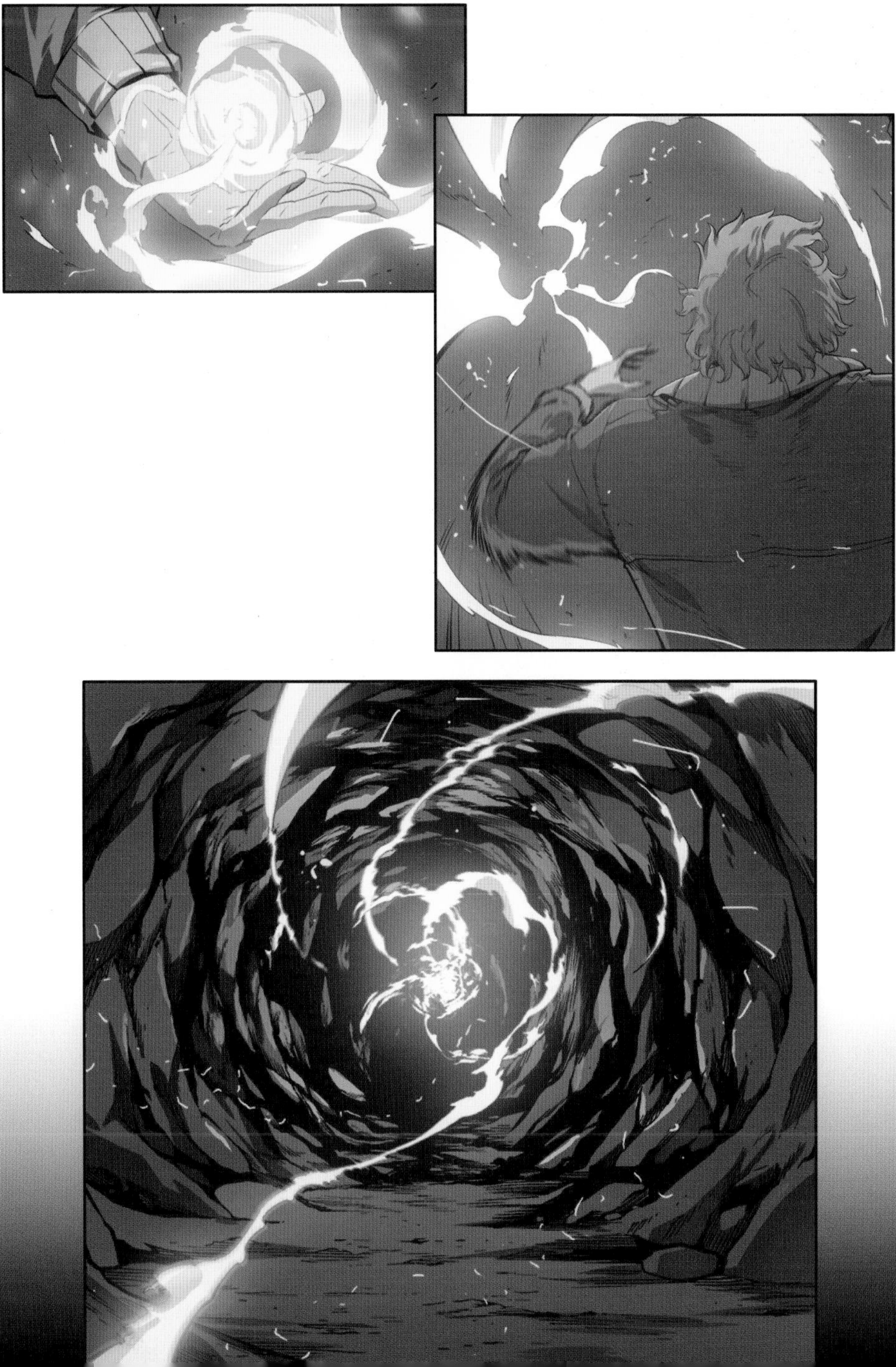

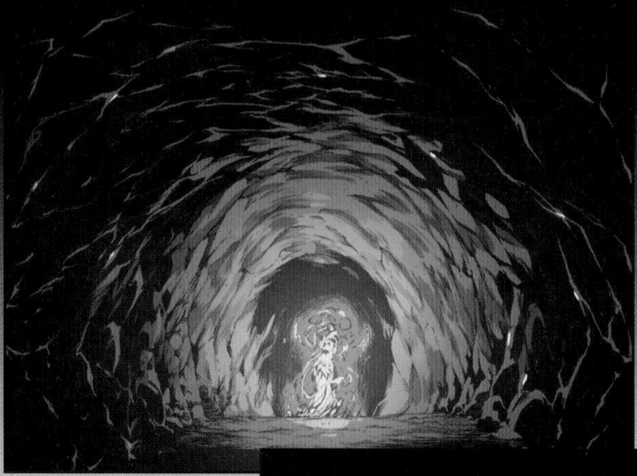

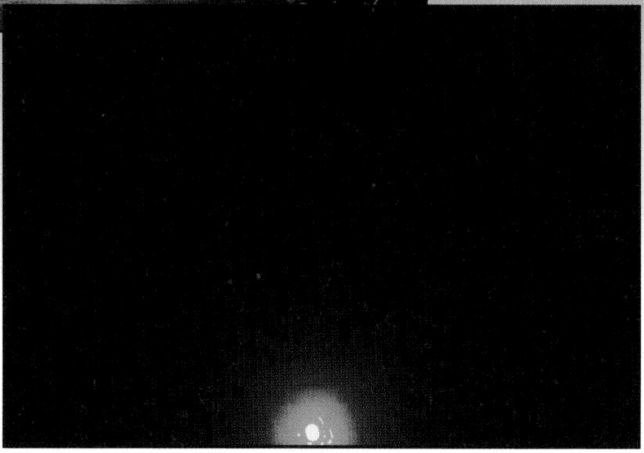

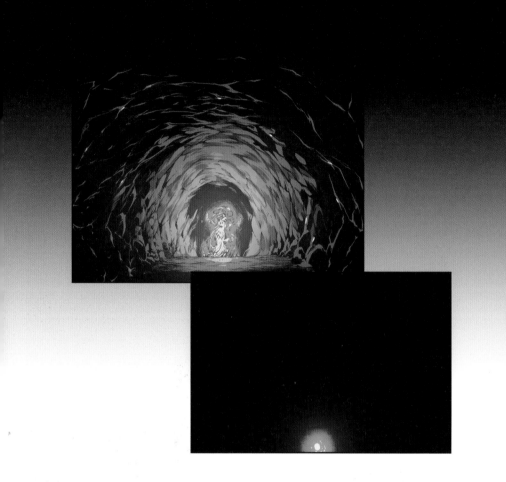

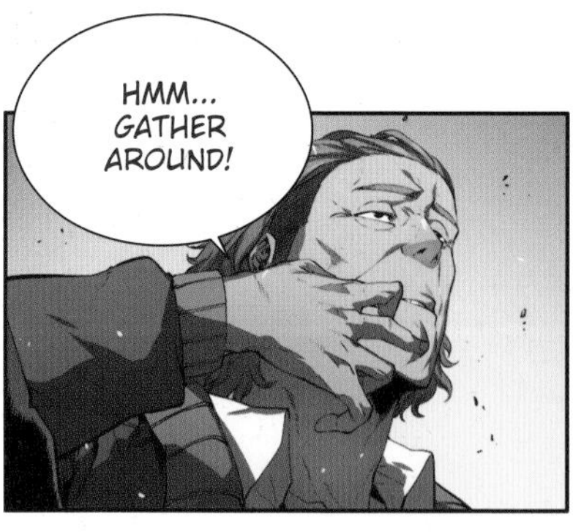
HMM... GATHER AROUND!

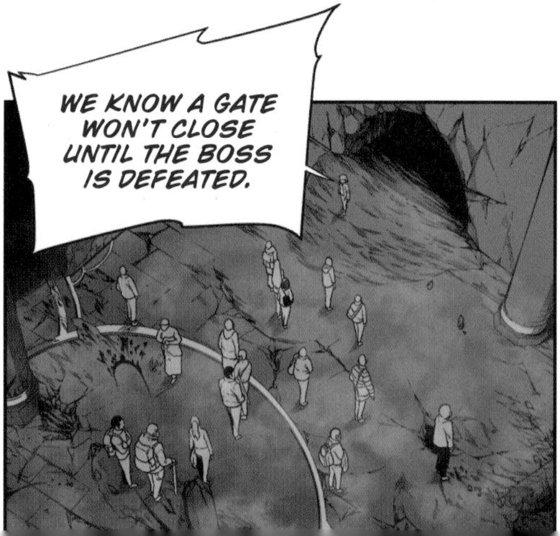
WE KNOW A GATE WON'T CLOSE UNTIL THE BOSS IS DEFEATED.

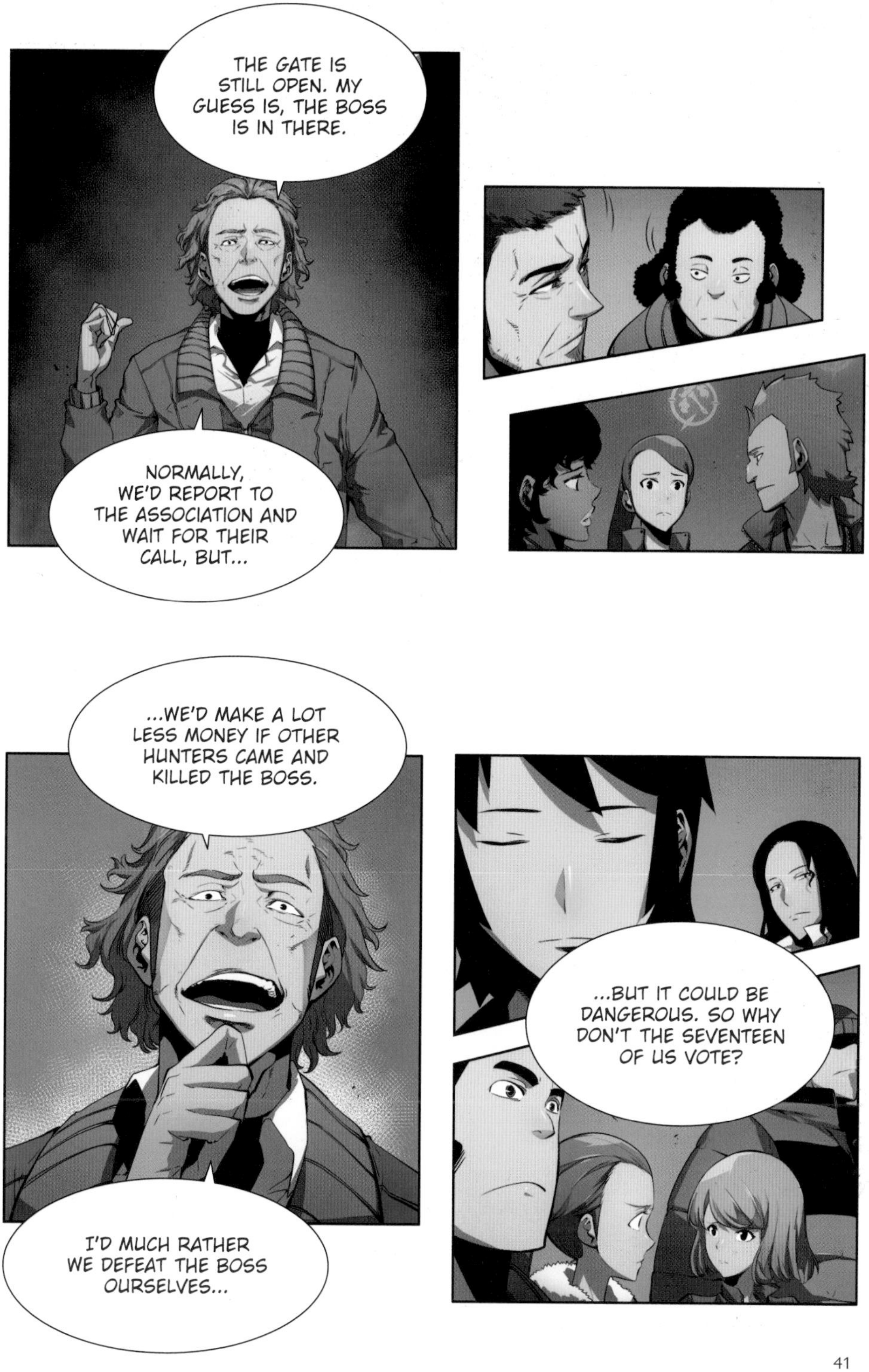
THE GATE IS STILL OPEN. MY GUESS IS, THE BOSS IS IN THERE.
NORMALLY, WE'D REPORT TO THE ASSOCIATION AND WAIT FOR THEIR CALL, BUT...
...WE'D MAKE A LOT LESS MONEY IF OTHER HUNTERS CAME AND KILLED THE BOSS.
I'D MUCH RATHER WE DEFEAT THE BOSS OURSELVES...
...BUT IT COULD BE DANGEROUS. SO WHY DON'T THE SEVENTEEN OF US VOTE?

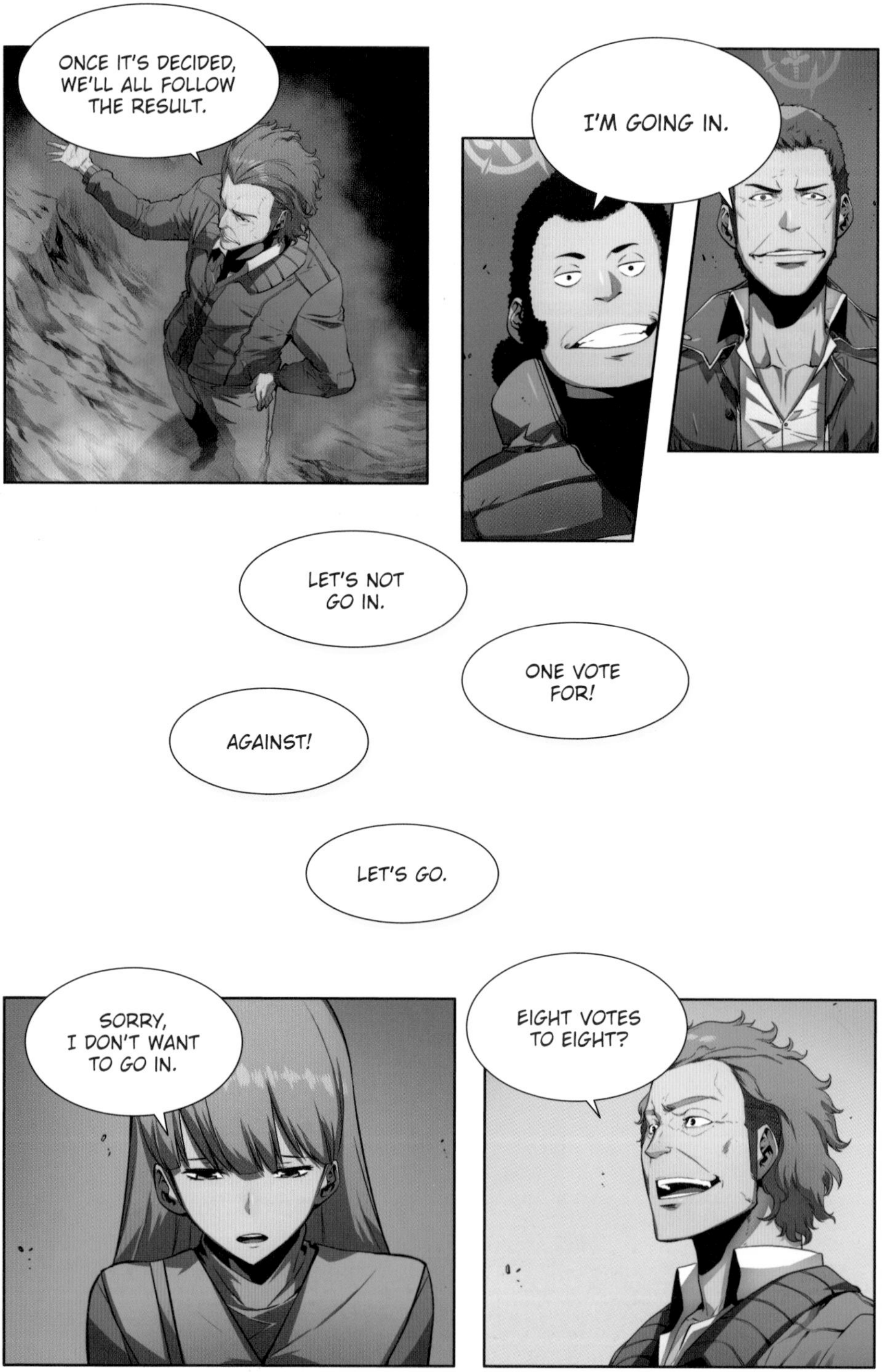
ONCE IT'S DECIDED, WE'LL ALL FOLLOW THE RESULT.
I'M GOING IN.
LET'S NOT GO IN.
ONE VOTE FOR!
AGAINST!
LET'S GO.
SORRY, I DON'T WANT TO GO IN.
EIGHT VOTES TO EIGHT?

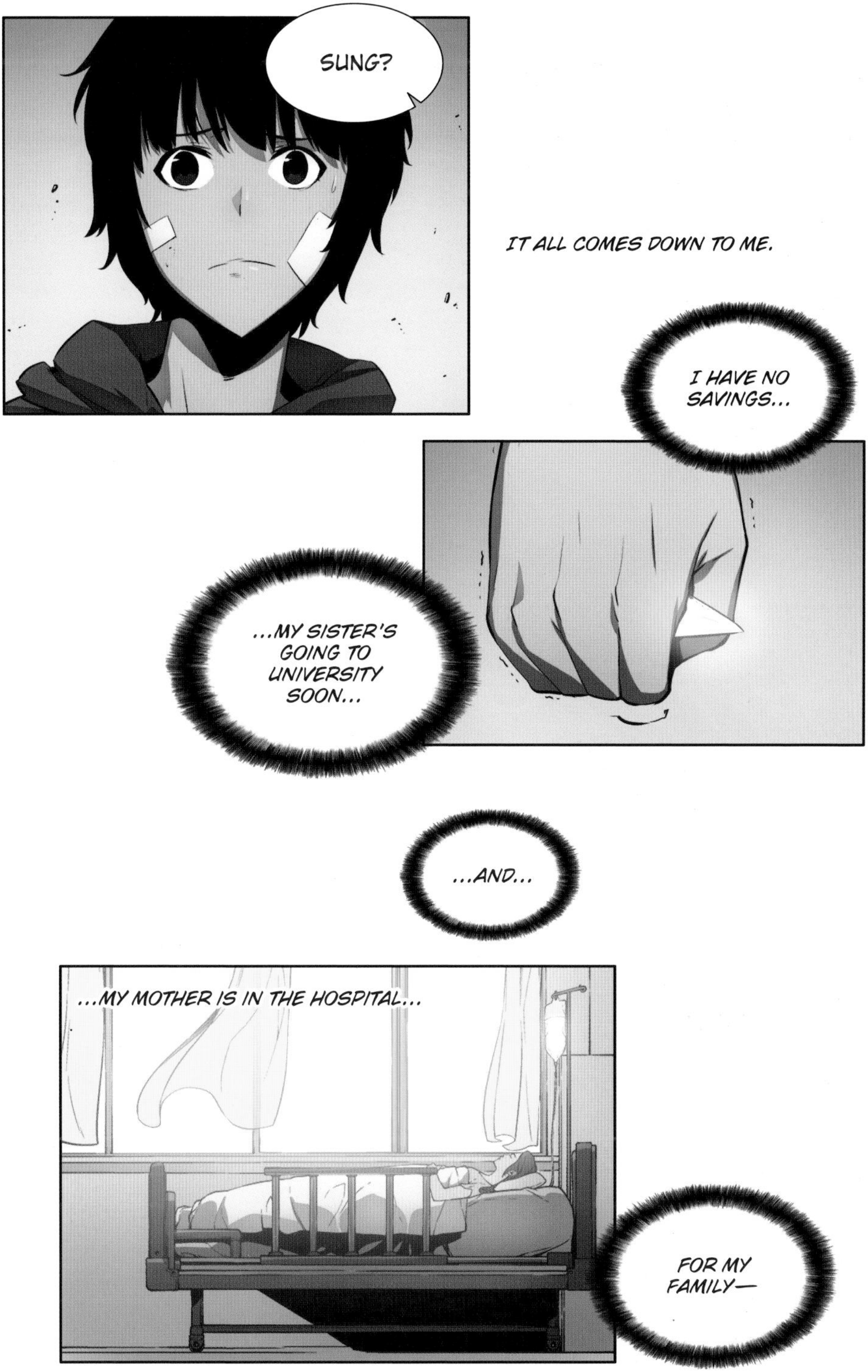
SUNG?
IT ALL COMES DOWN TO ME.
I HAVE NO SAVINGS...
...MY SISTER'S GOING TO UNIVERSITY SOON...
...AND...
...MY MOTHER IS IN THE HOSPITAL...
FOR MY FAMILY—

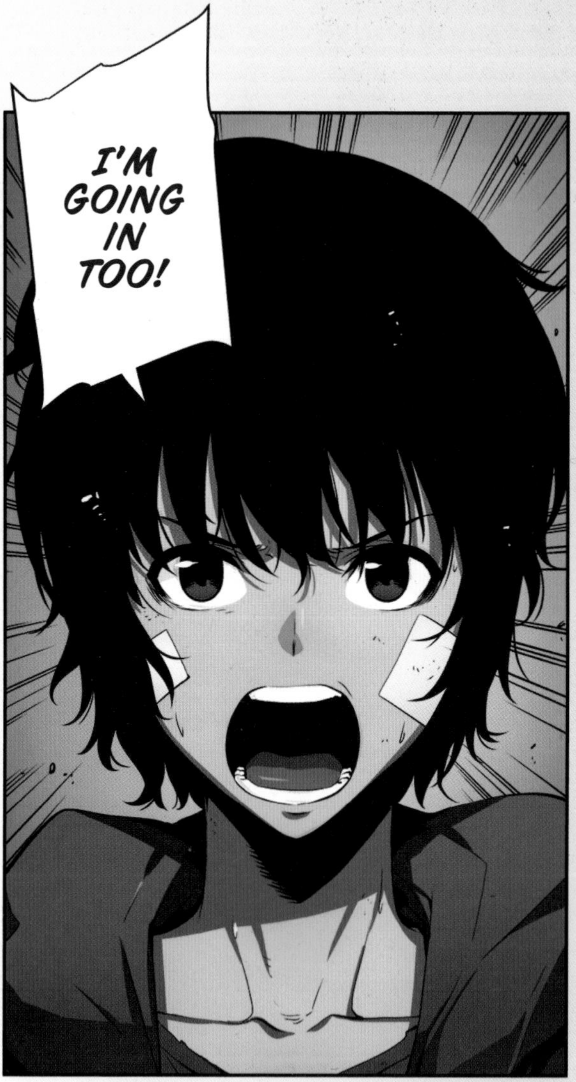
I'M GOING IN TOO!

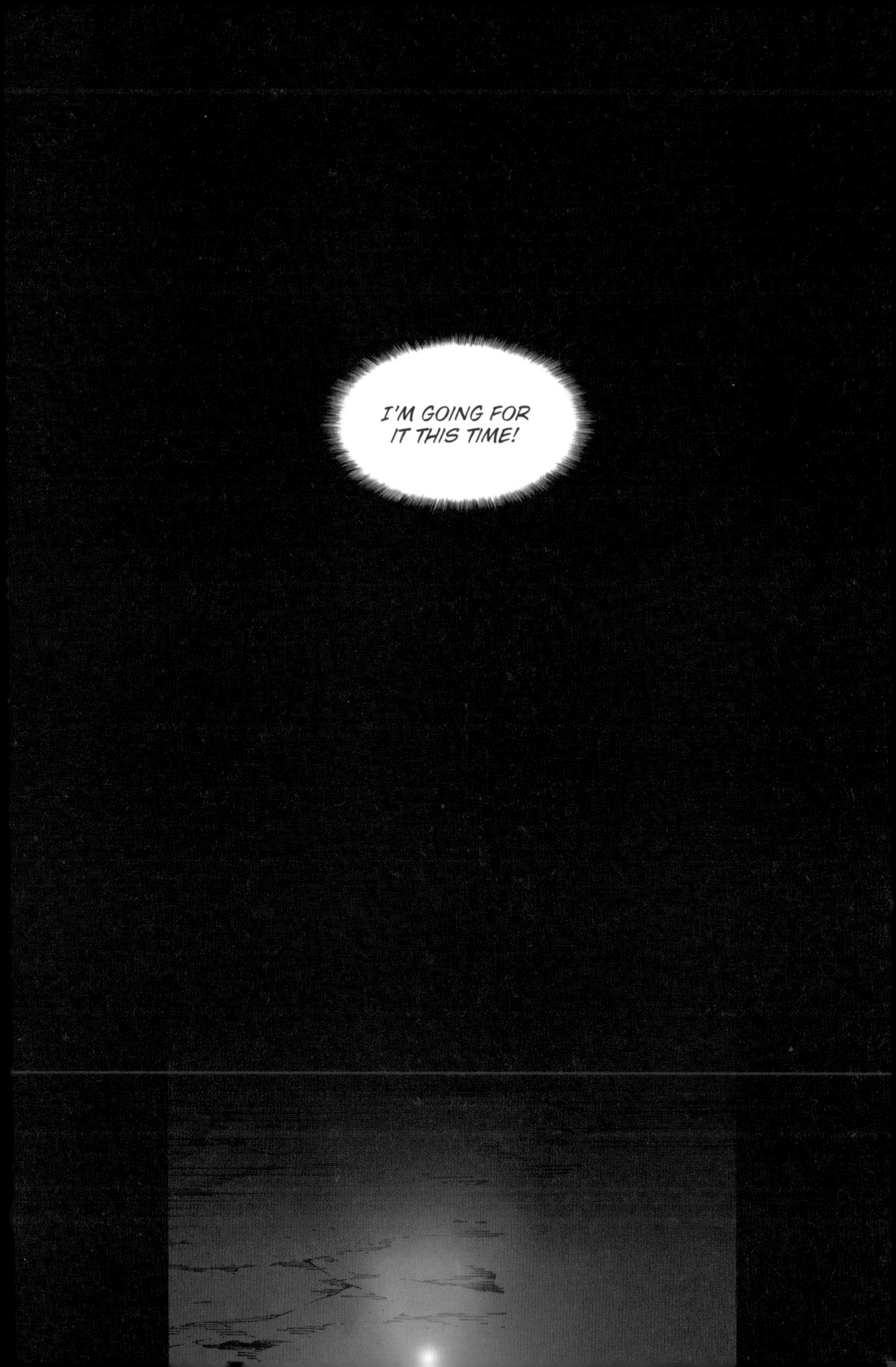
I'M GOING FOR IT THIS TIME!

DON'T YOU THINK WE'RE GOING IN TOO DEEP?
HOW LONG HAVE WE BEEN WALKING?
FOR ABOUT FORTY MINUTES.
GATES CLOSE AN HOUR AFTER THE BOSS IS DEFEATED, SO WE'RE GOOD FOR ABOUT TWENTY MORE MINUTES.

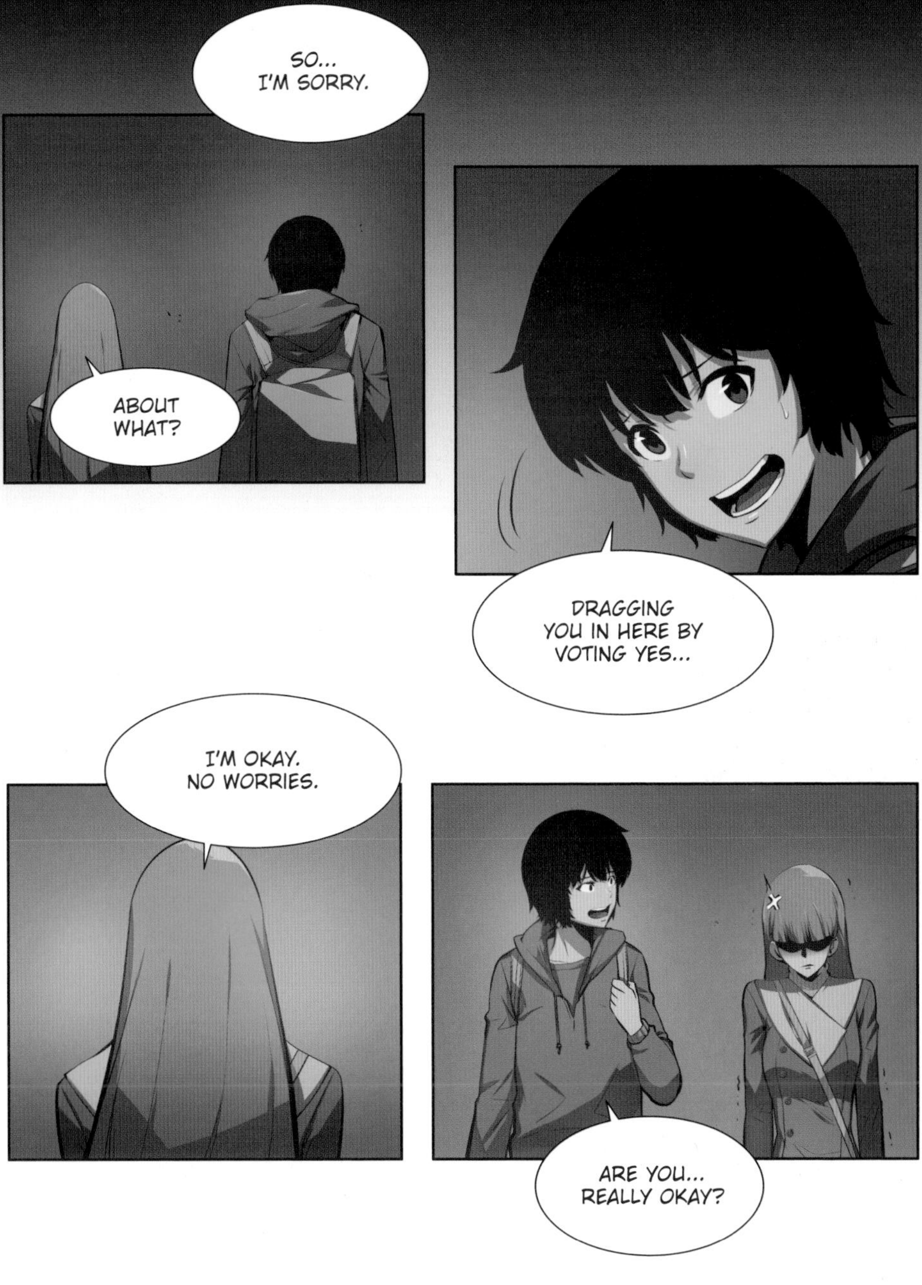
SO... I'M SORRY.
ABOUT WHAT?
DRAGGING YOU IN HERE BY VOTING YES...
I'M OKAY. NO WORRIES.
ARE YOU... REALLY OKAY?

HONESTLY... I'M TOTALLY NOT OKAY.

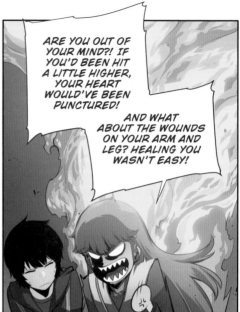

ARE YOU OUT OF YOUR MIND?! IF YOU'D BEEN HIT A LITTLE HIGHER, YOUR HEART WOULD'VE BEEN PUNCTURED!

AND WHAT ABOUT THE WOUNDS ON YOUR ARM AND LEG? HEALING YOU WASN'T EASY!

BUT YOU WANT TO GO INTO ANOTHER DUNGEON? DID YOU HURT YOUR HEAD?!

HUH?!

SORRY...

SHE HELPS ME EVERY TIME. I'D BE A GONER IF SHE WASN'T A B-RANK HEALER.

ARE YOU REALLY SORRY?!

YES...

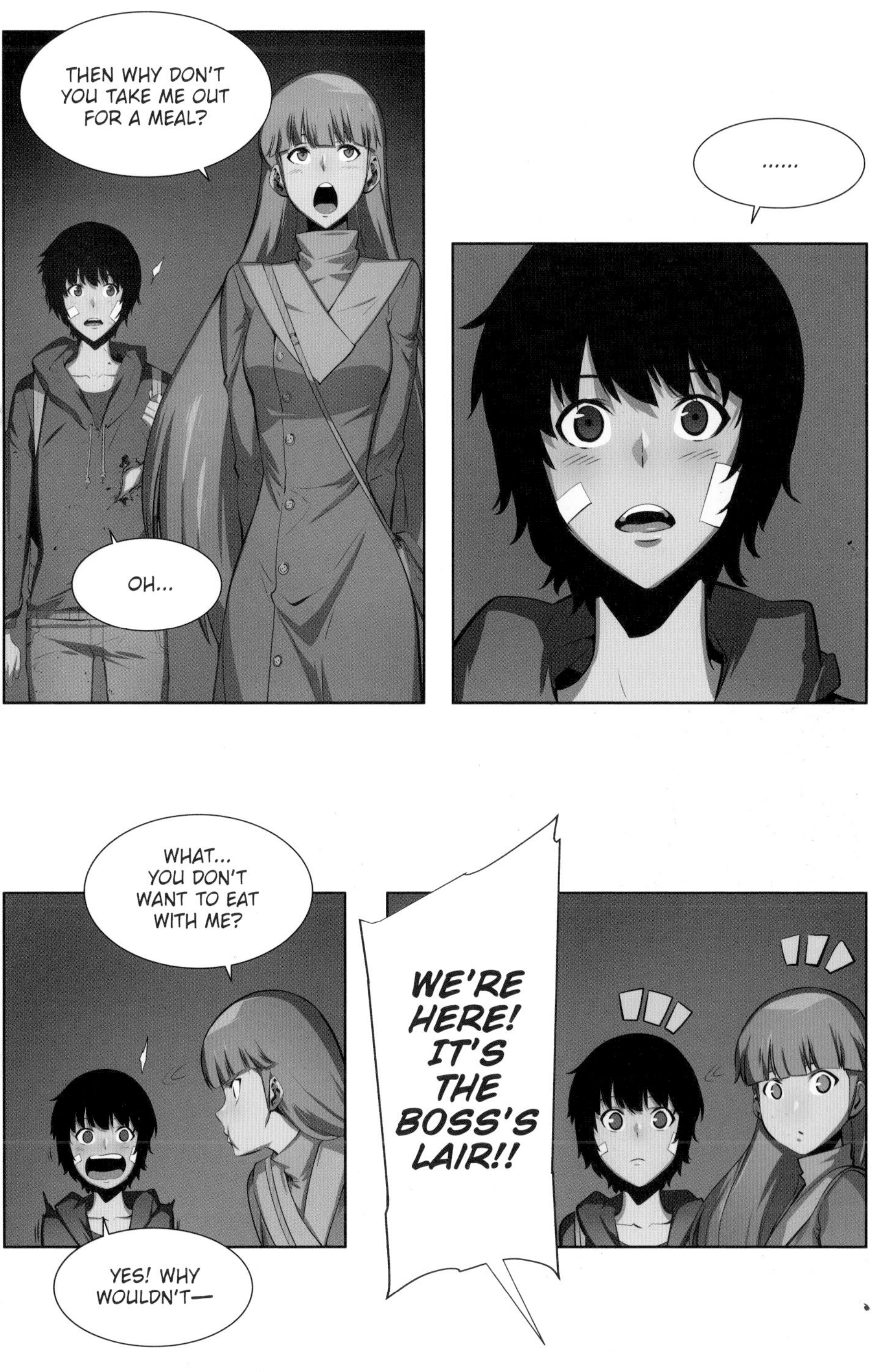
THEN WHY DON'T YOU TAKE ME OUT FOR A MEAL?
OH...
......
WHAT... YOU DON'T WANT TO EAT WITH ME?
YES! WHY WOULDN'T—
WE'RE HERE! IT'S THE BOSS'S LAIR!!

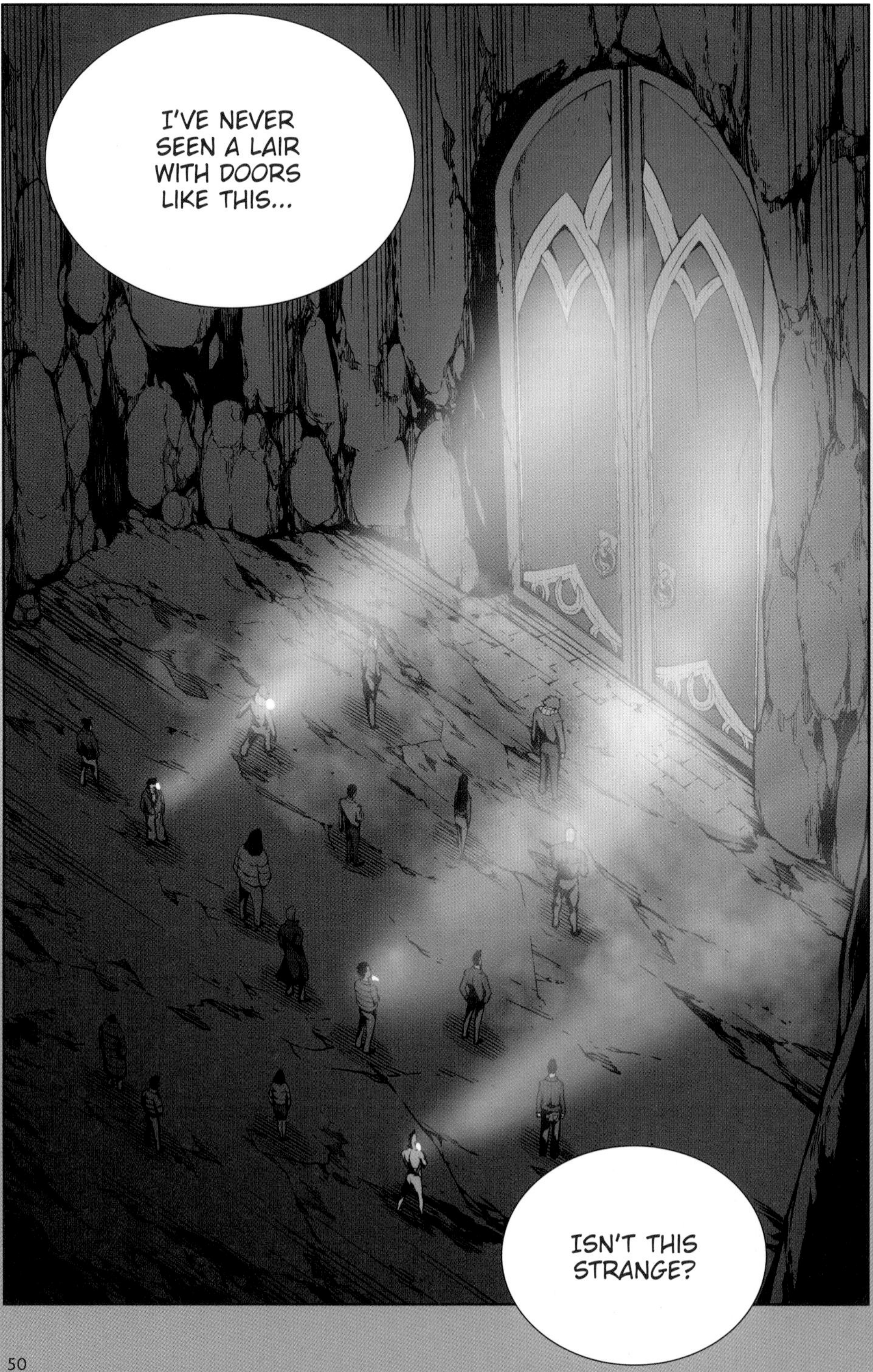
I'VE NEVER SEEN A LAIR WITH DOORS LIKE THIS...
ISN'T THIS STRANGE?

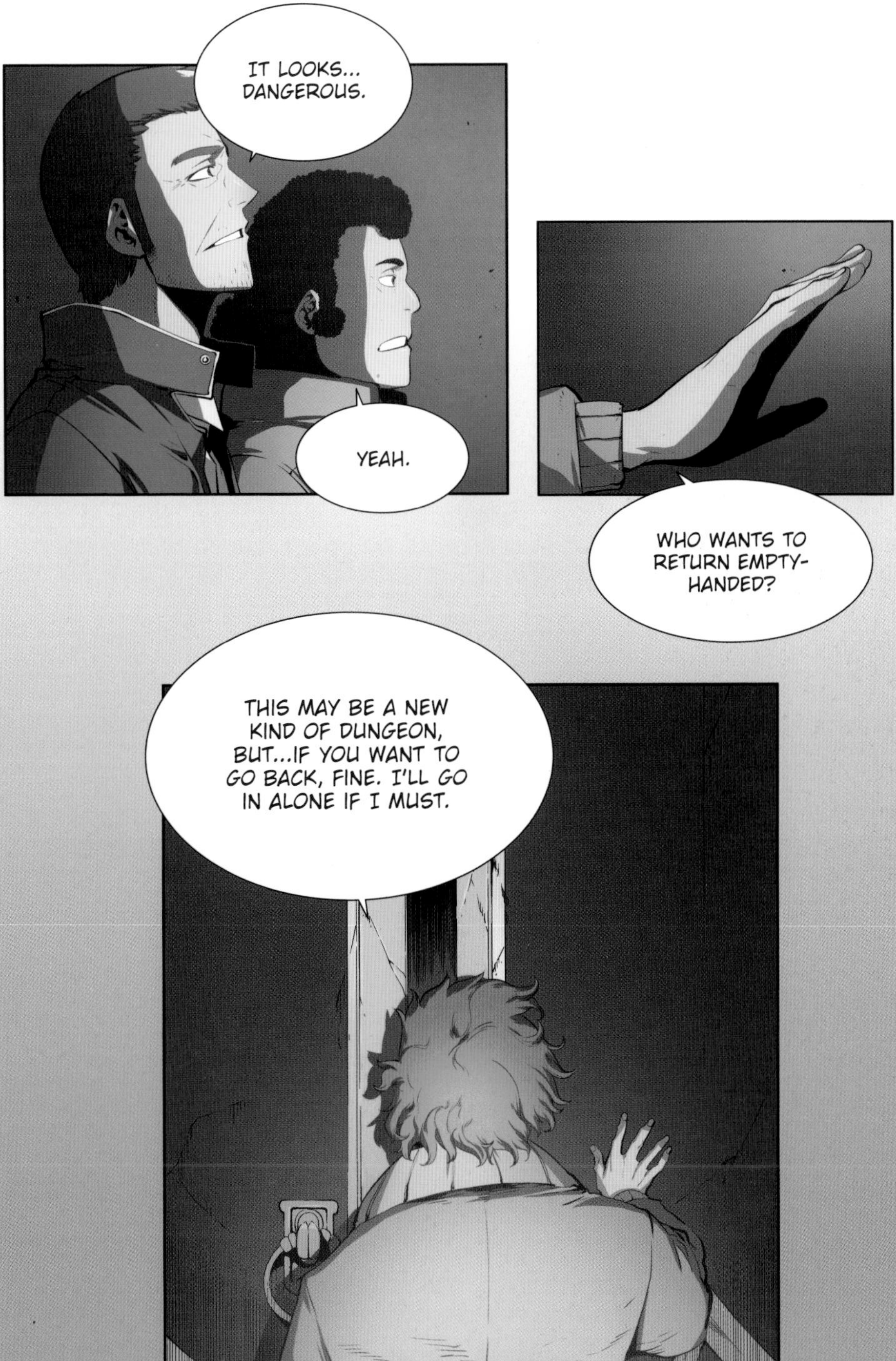
IT LOOKS...
DANGEROUS.
YEAH.
WHO WANTS TO RETURN EMPTY-HANDED?
THIS MAY BE A NEW KIND OF DUNGEON, BUT...IF YOU WANT TO GO BACK, FINE. I'LL GO IN ALONE IF I MUST.

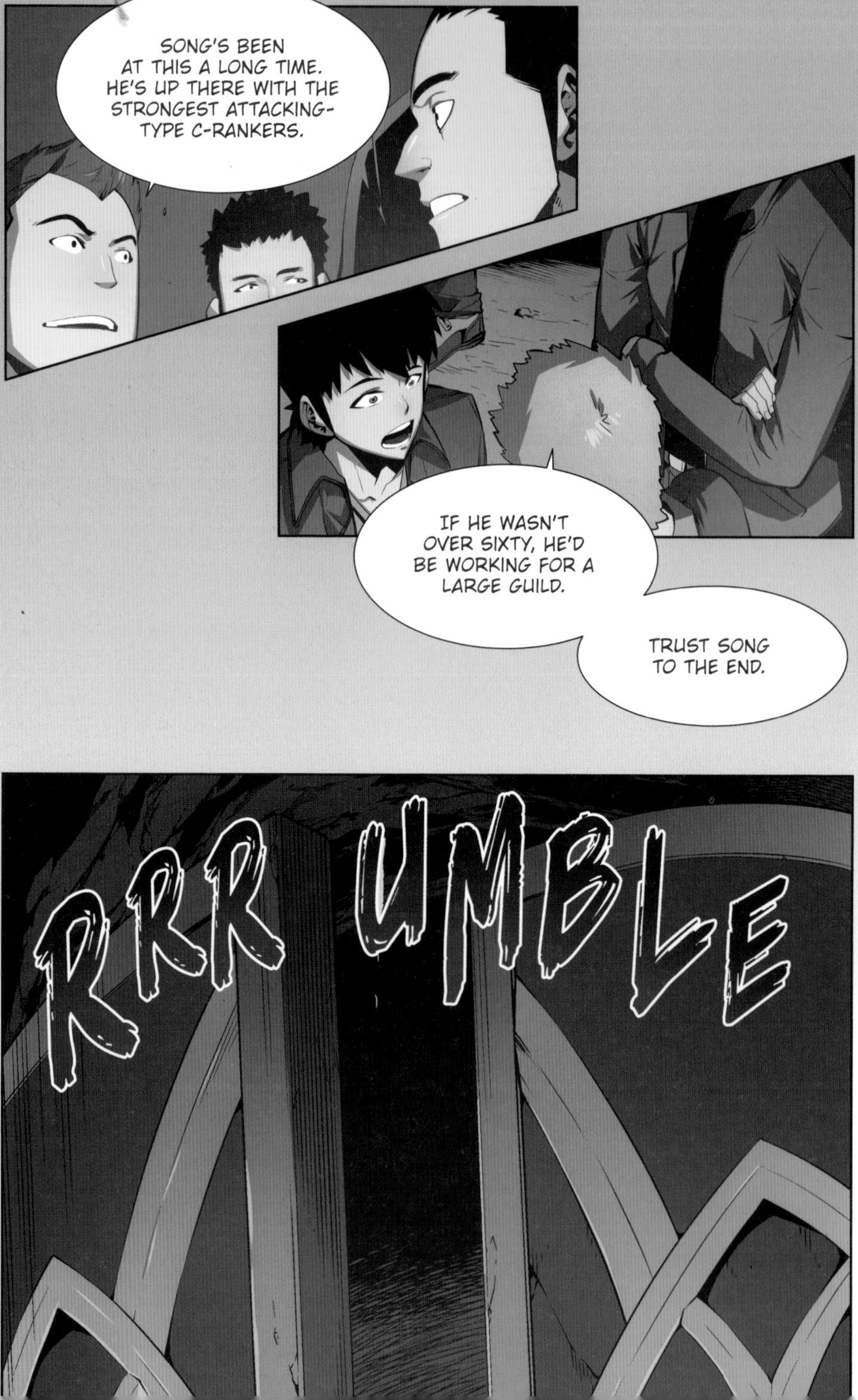
SONG'S BEEN AT THIS A LONG TIME. HE'S UP THERE WITH THE STRONGEST ATTACKING-TYPE C-RANKERS.
IF HE WASN'T OVER SIXTY, HE'D BE WORKING FOR A LARGE GUILD.
TRUST SONG TO THE END.
RRRUMBLE

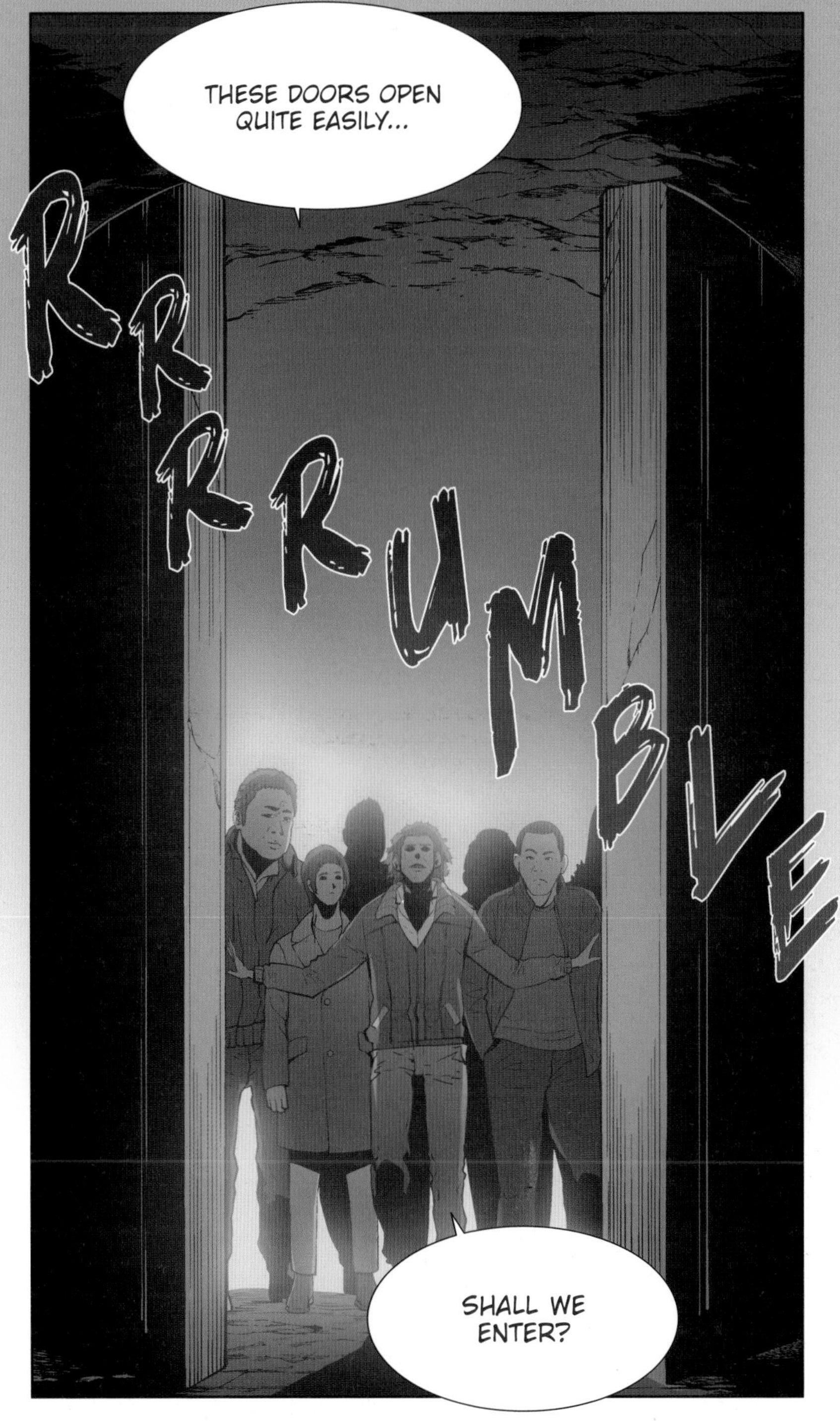
THESE DOORS OPEN QUITE EASILY...
RRRRRUMBLE
SHALL WE ENTER?

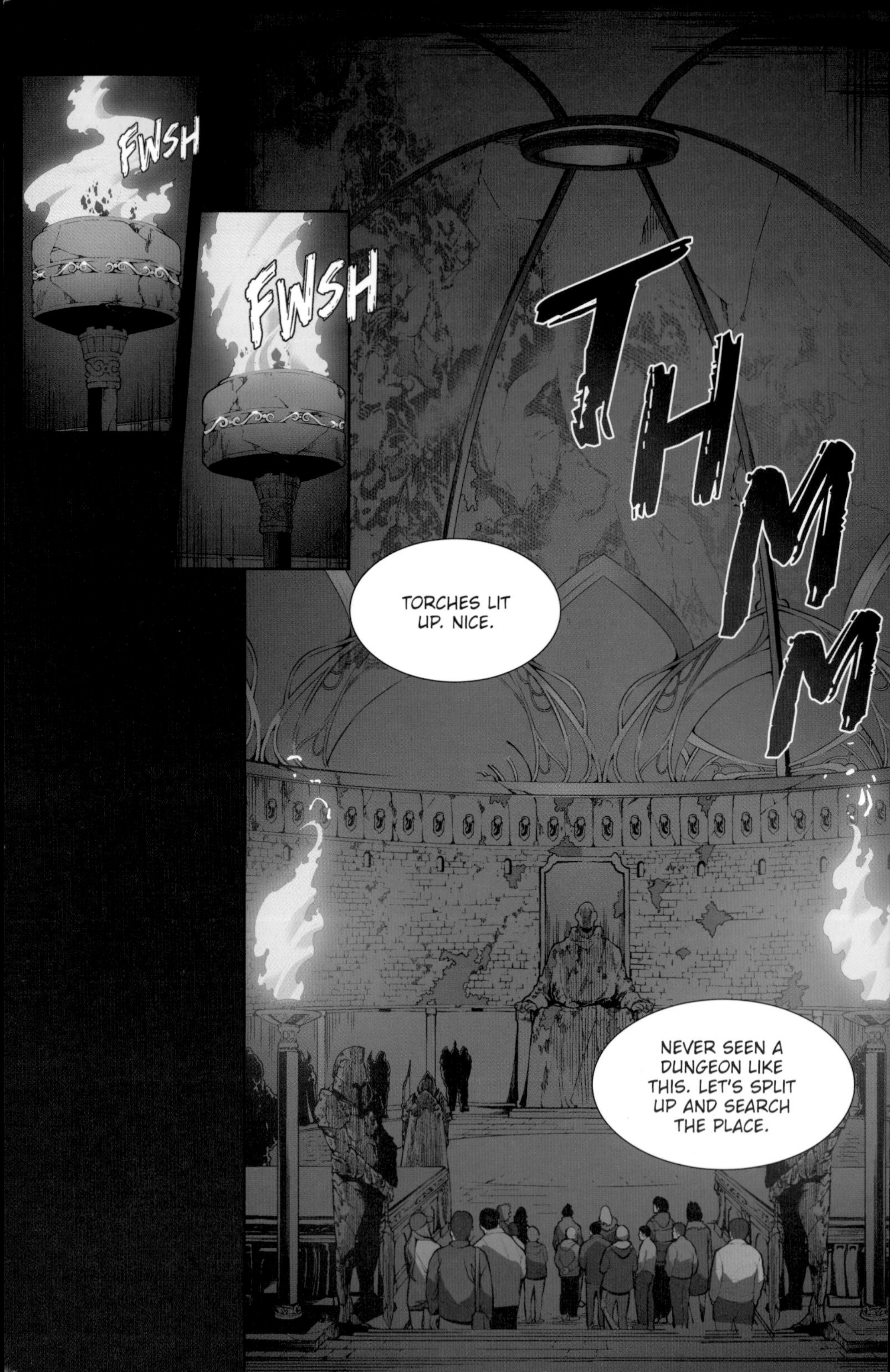
FWSH
FWSH
THMM
TORCHES LIT UP. NICE.
NEVER SEEN A DUNGEON LIKE THIS. LET'S SPLIT UP AND SEARCH THE PLACE.

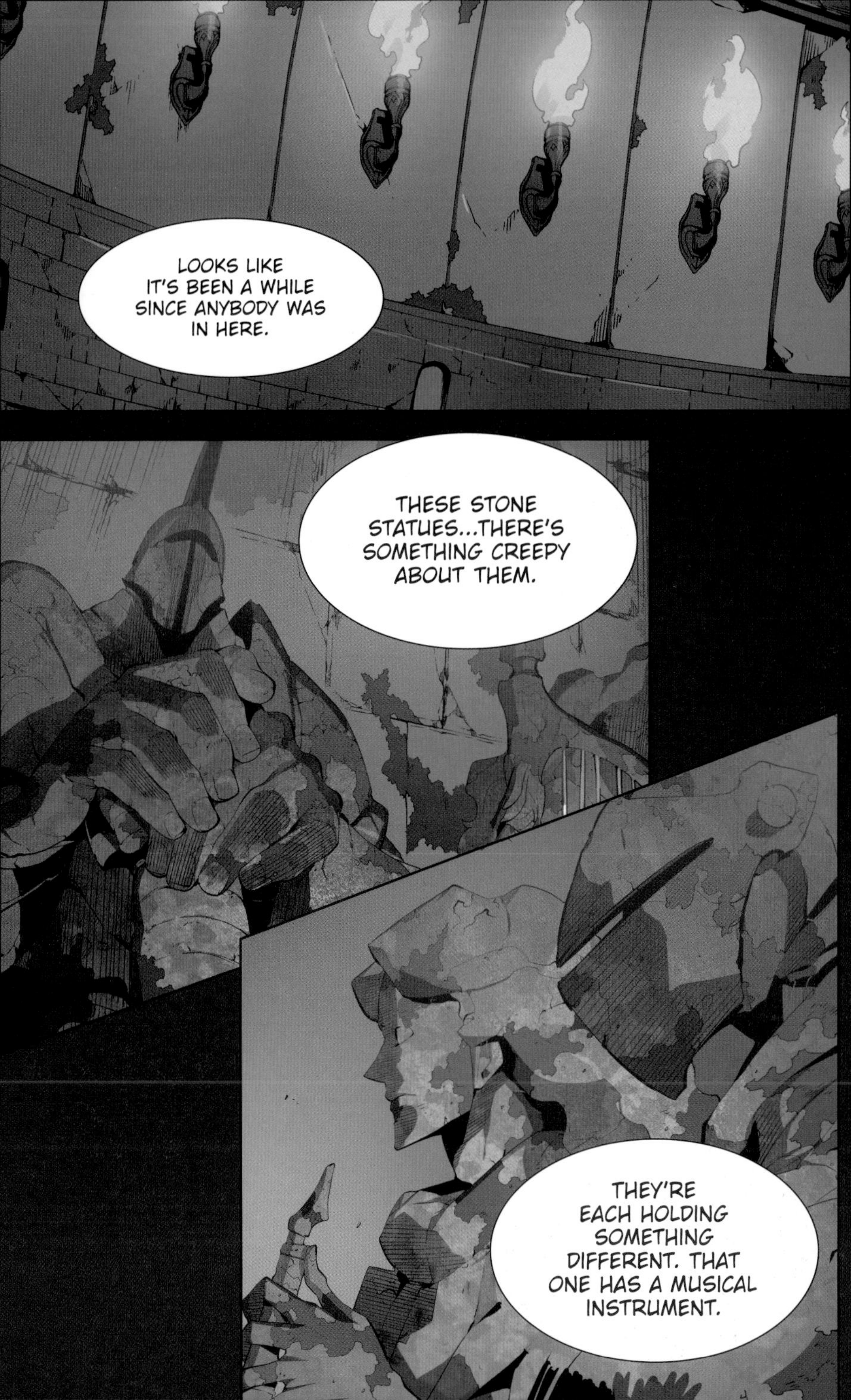
LOOKS LIKE IT'S BEEN A WHILE SINCE ANYBODY WAS IN HERE.
THESE STONE STATUES...THERE'S SOMETHING CREEPY ABOUT THEM.
THEY'RE EACH HOLDING SOMETHING DIFFERENT. THAT ONE HAS A MUSICAL INSTRUMENT.

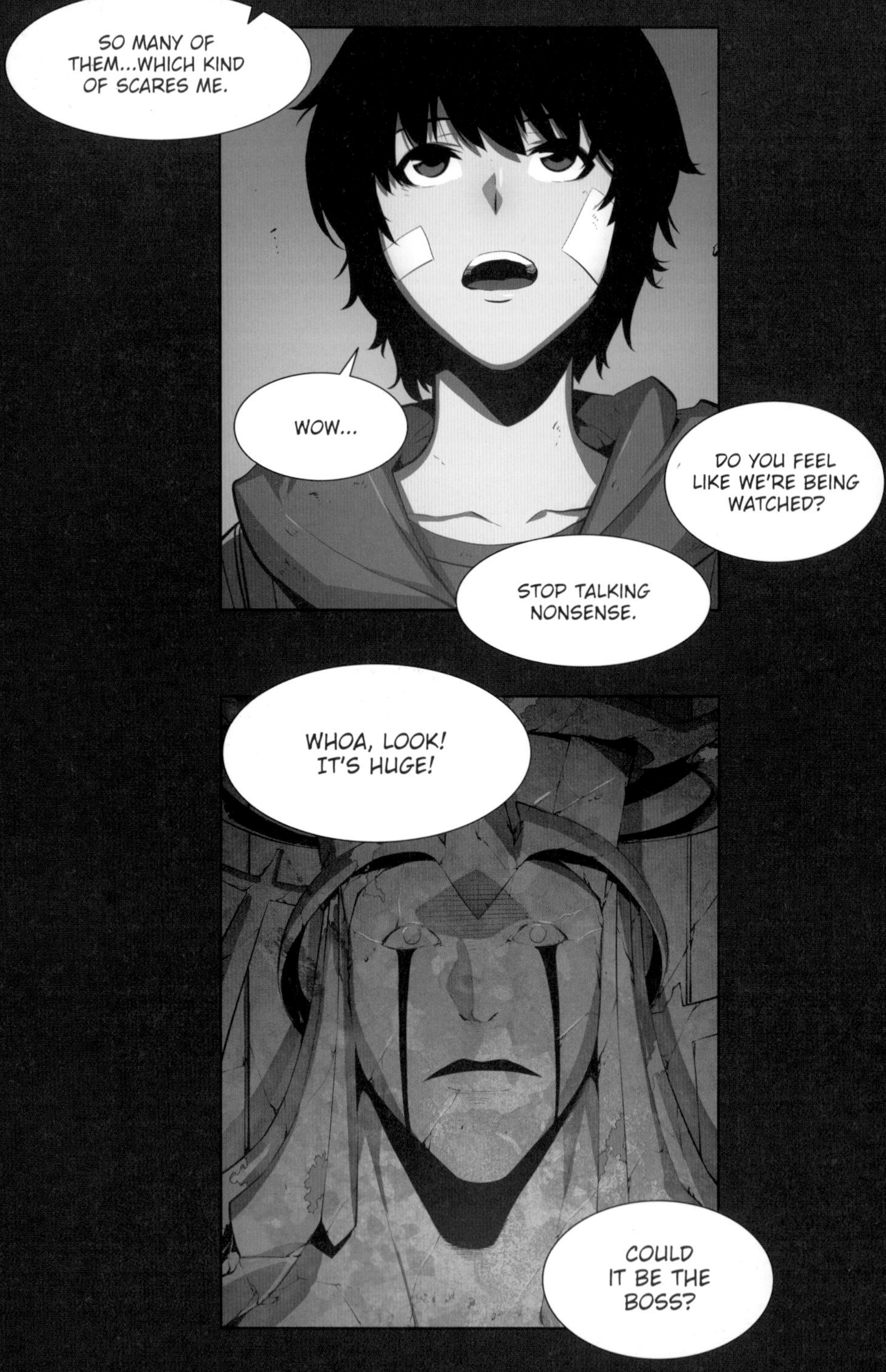
SO MANY OF THEM...WHICH KIND OF SCARES ME.
WOW...
DO YOU FEEL LIKE WE'RE BEING WATCHED?
STOP TALKING NONSENSE.
WHOA, LOOK! IT'S HUGE!
COULD IT BE THE BOSS?

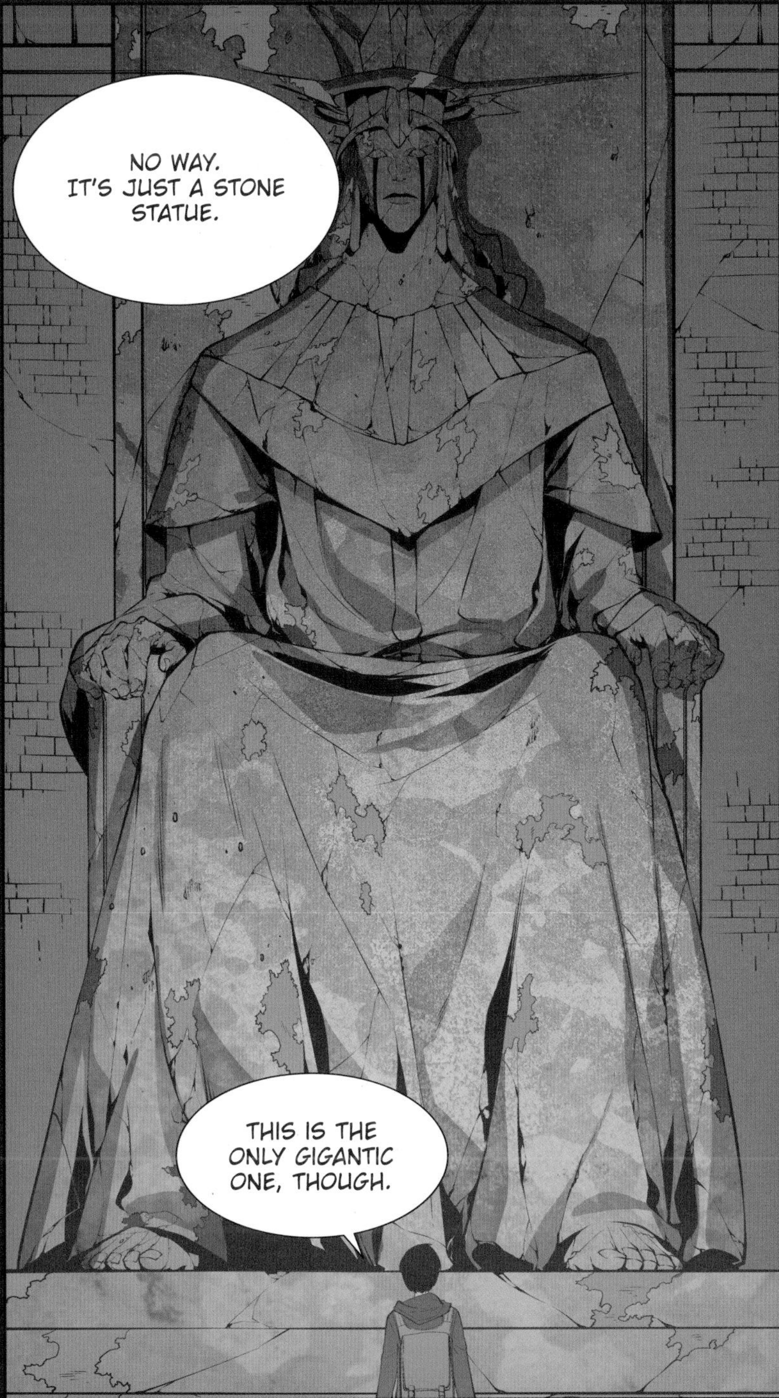
NO WAY. IT'S JUST A STONE STATUE.
THIS IS THE ONLY GIGANTIC ONE, THOUGH.

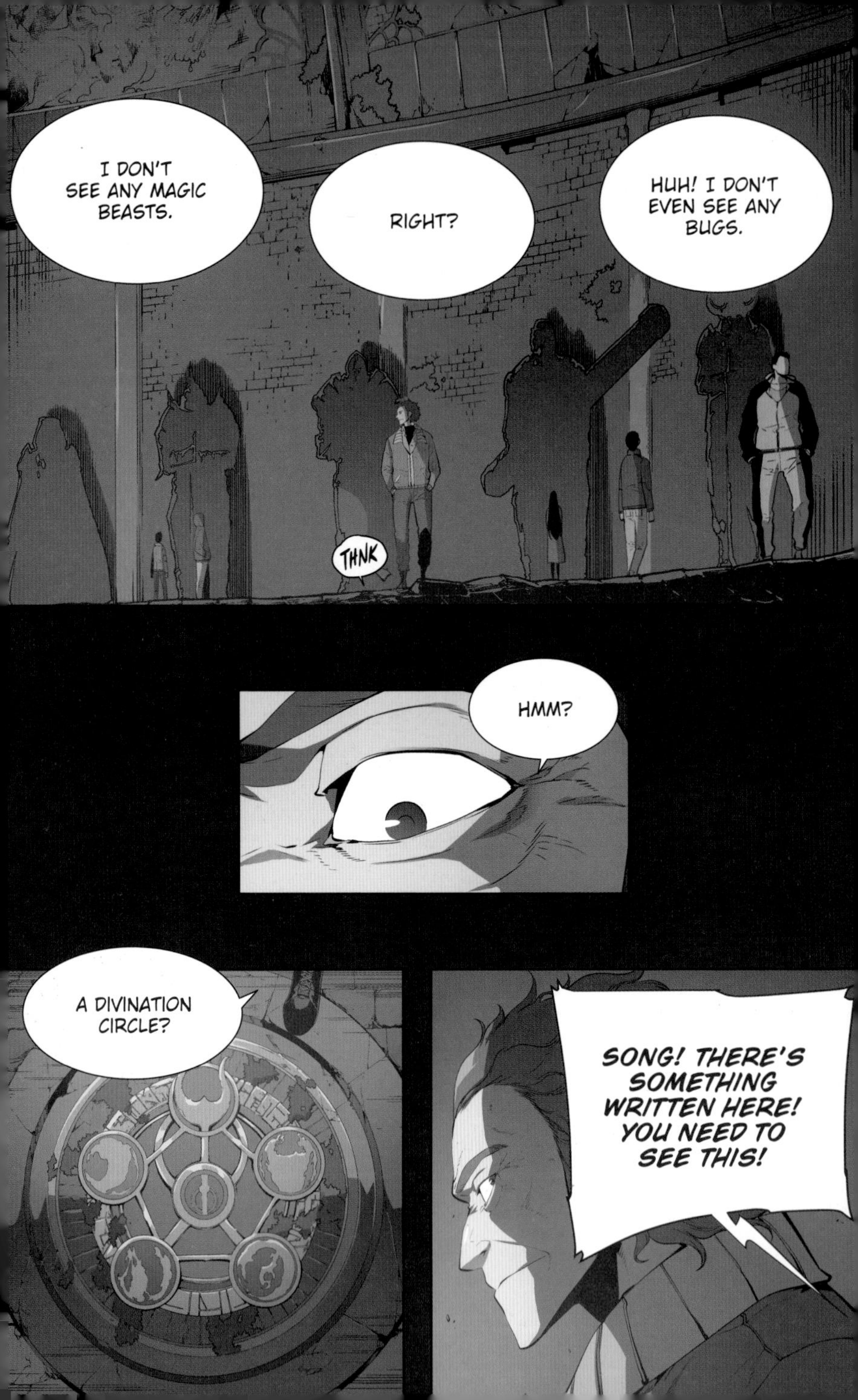

I DON'T SEE ANY MAGIC BEASTS.
RIGHT?
HUH! I DON'T EVEN SEE ANY BUGS.
THNK
HMM?
A DIVINATION CIRCLE?
SONG! THERE'S SOMETHING WRITTEN HERE! YOU NEED TO SEE THIS!

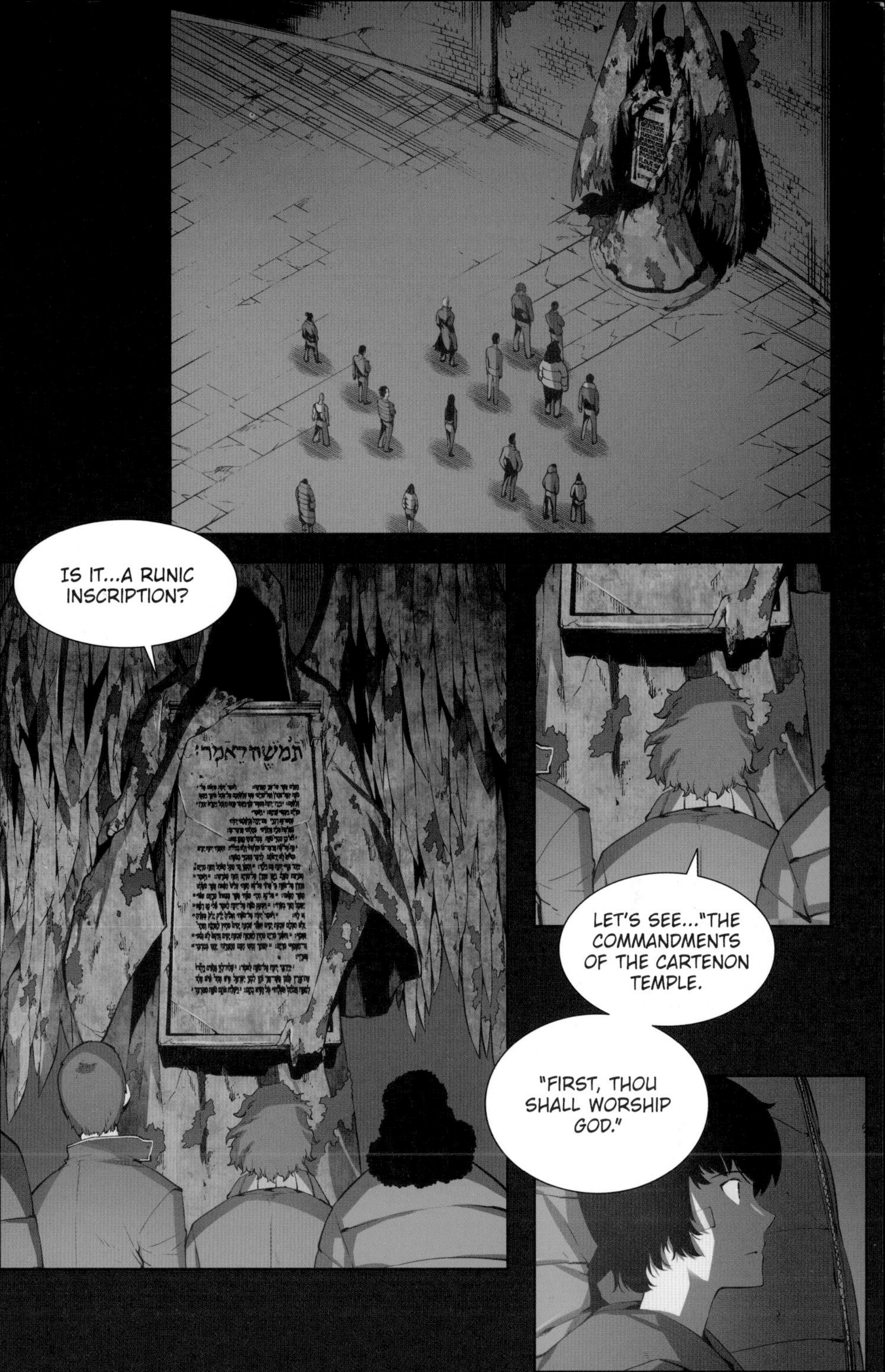
IS IT...A RUNIC INSCRIPTION?
LET'S SEE..."THE COMMANDMENTS OF THE CARTENON TEMPLE.
"FIRST, THOU SHALL WORSHIP GOD."

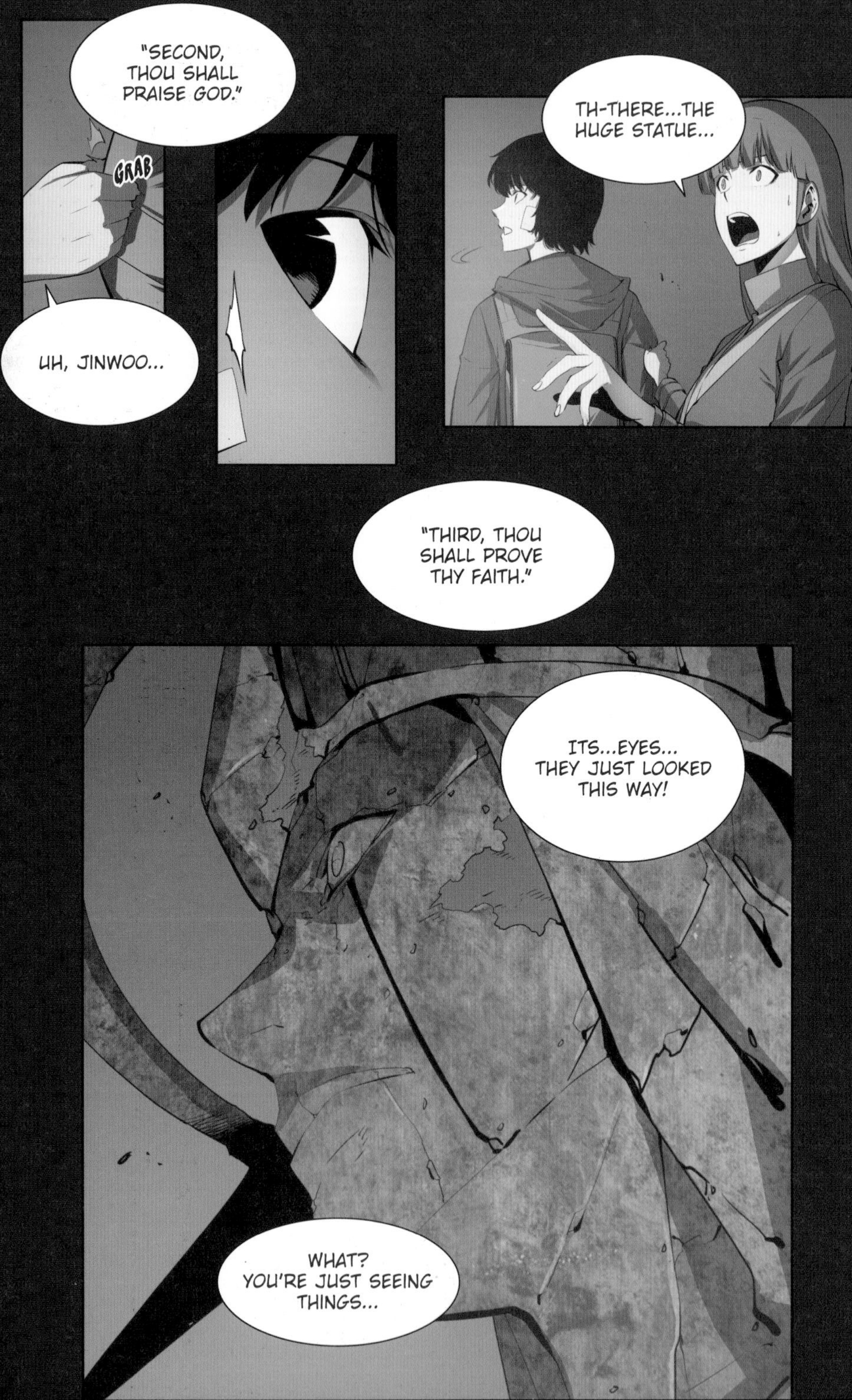
"SECOND, THOU SHALL PRAISE GOD."
GRAB
UH, JINWOO...
TH-THERE...THE HUGE STATUE...
"THIRD, THOU SHALL PROVE THY FAITH."
ITS...EYES... THEY JUST LOOKED THIS WAY!
WHAT? YOU'RE JUST SEEING THINGS...

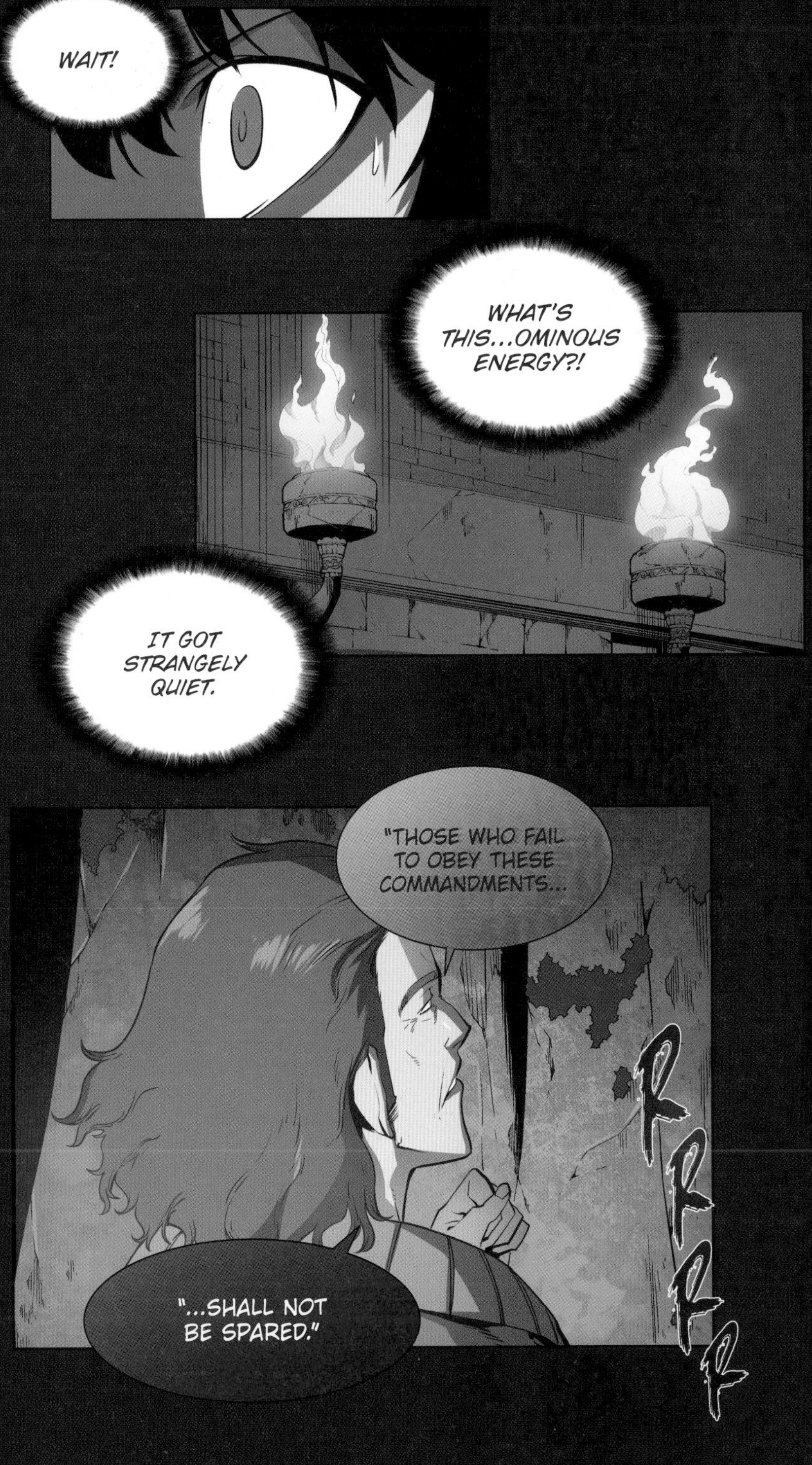
WAIT!
WHAT'S THIS...OMINOUS ENERGY?!
IT GOT STRANGELY QUIET.
"THOSE WHO FAIL TO OBEY THESE COMMANDMENTS...
"...SHALL NOT BE SPARED."
RRRR

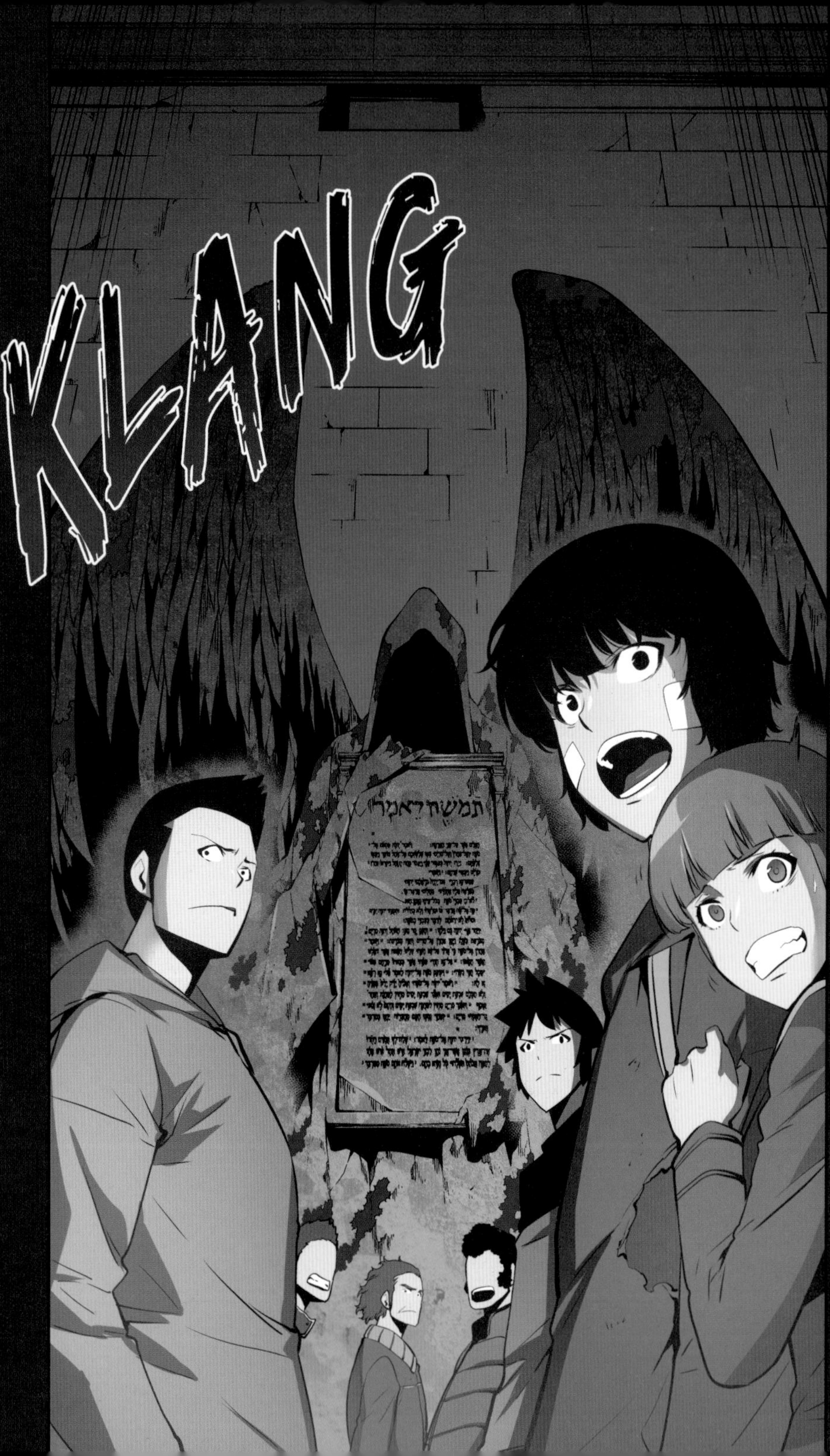
KLANG

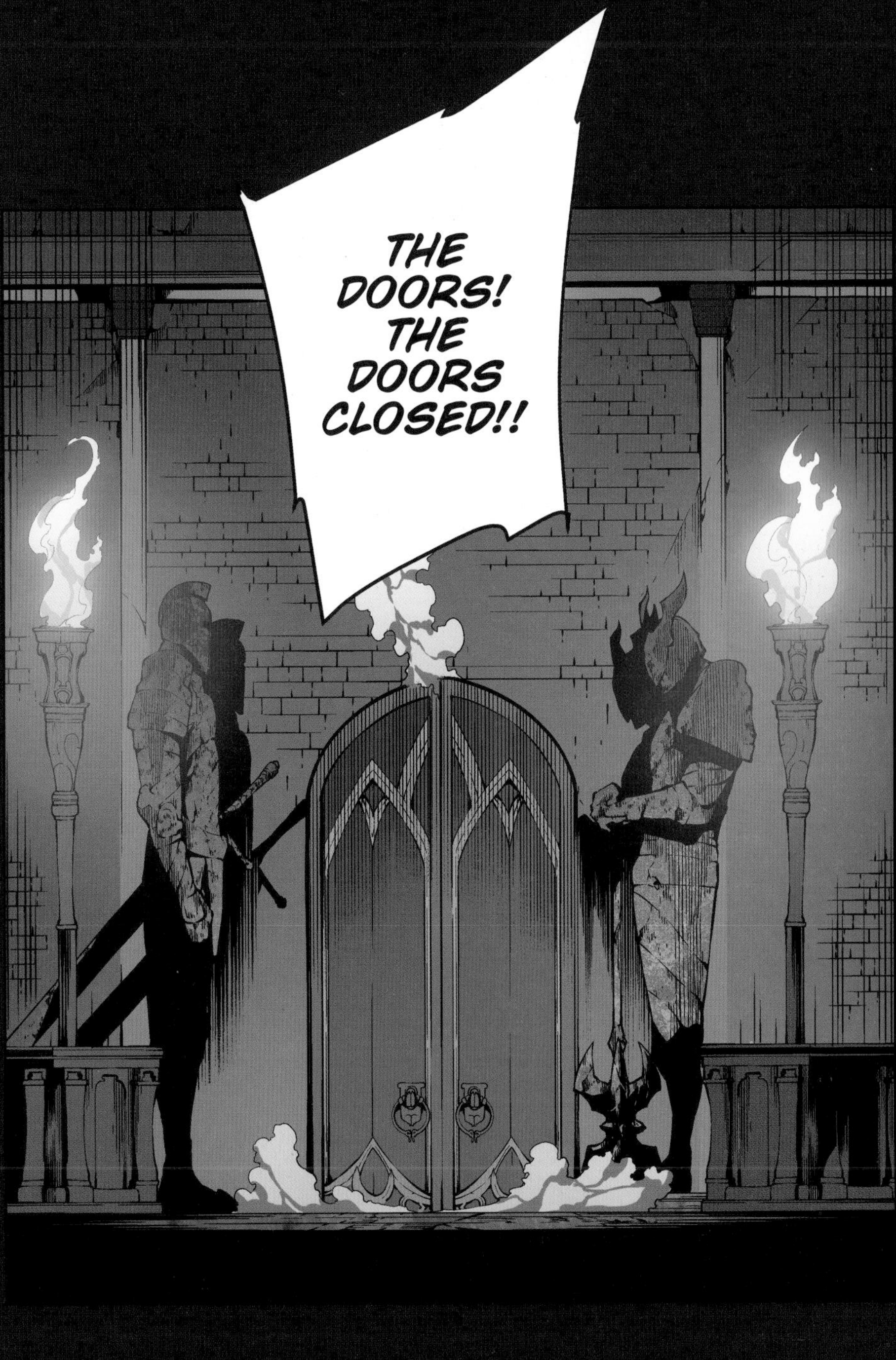
THE DOORS! THE DOORS CLOSED!!

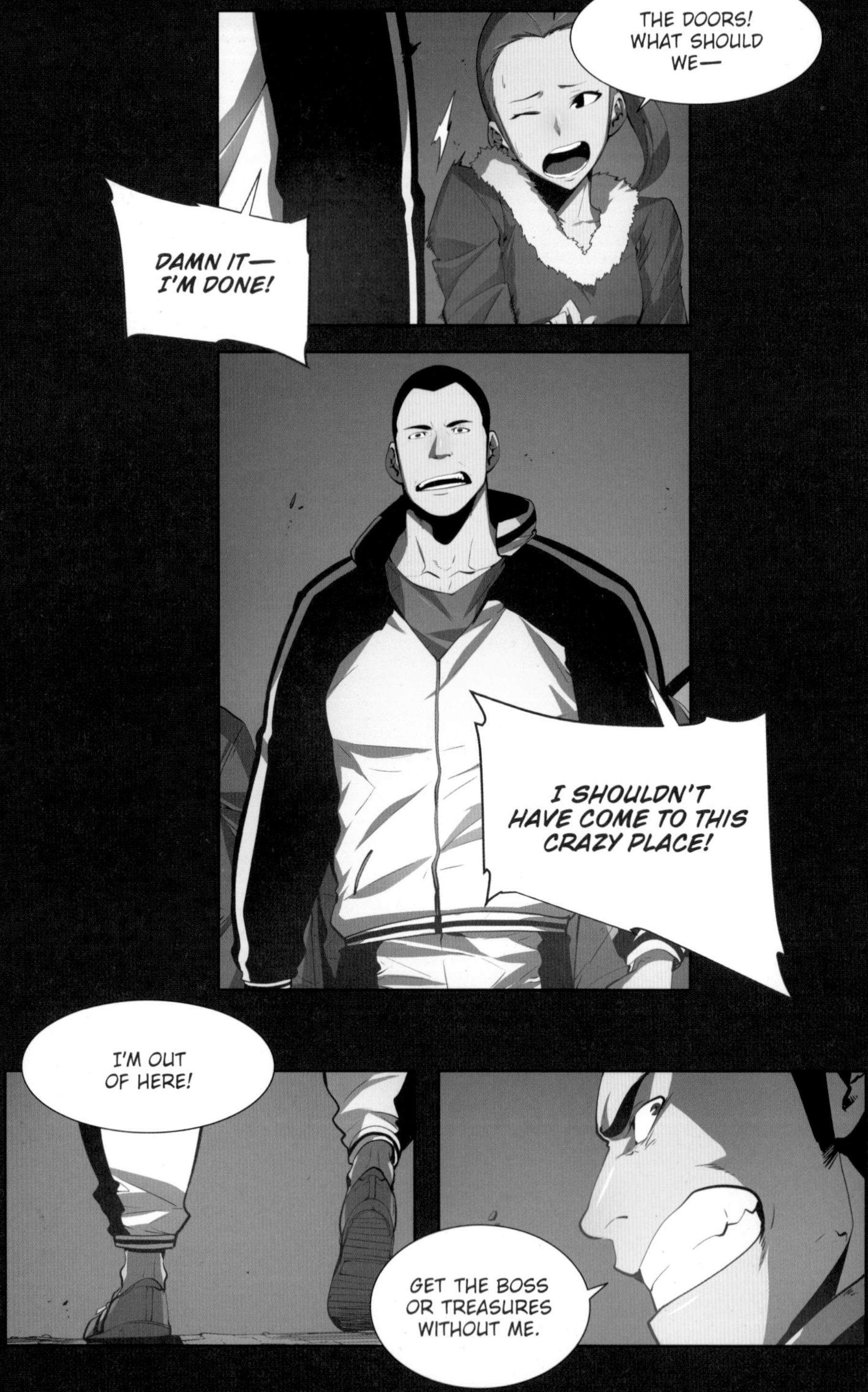

THE DOORS! WHAT SHOULD WE—
DAMN IT— I'M DONE!
I SHOULDN'T HAVE COME TO THIS CRAZY PLACE!
I'M OUT OF HERE!
GET THE BOSS OR TREASURES WITHOUT ME.

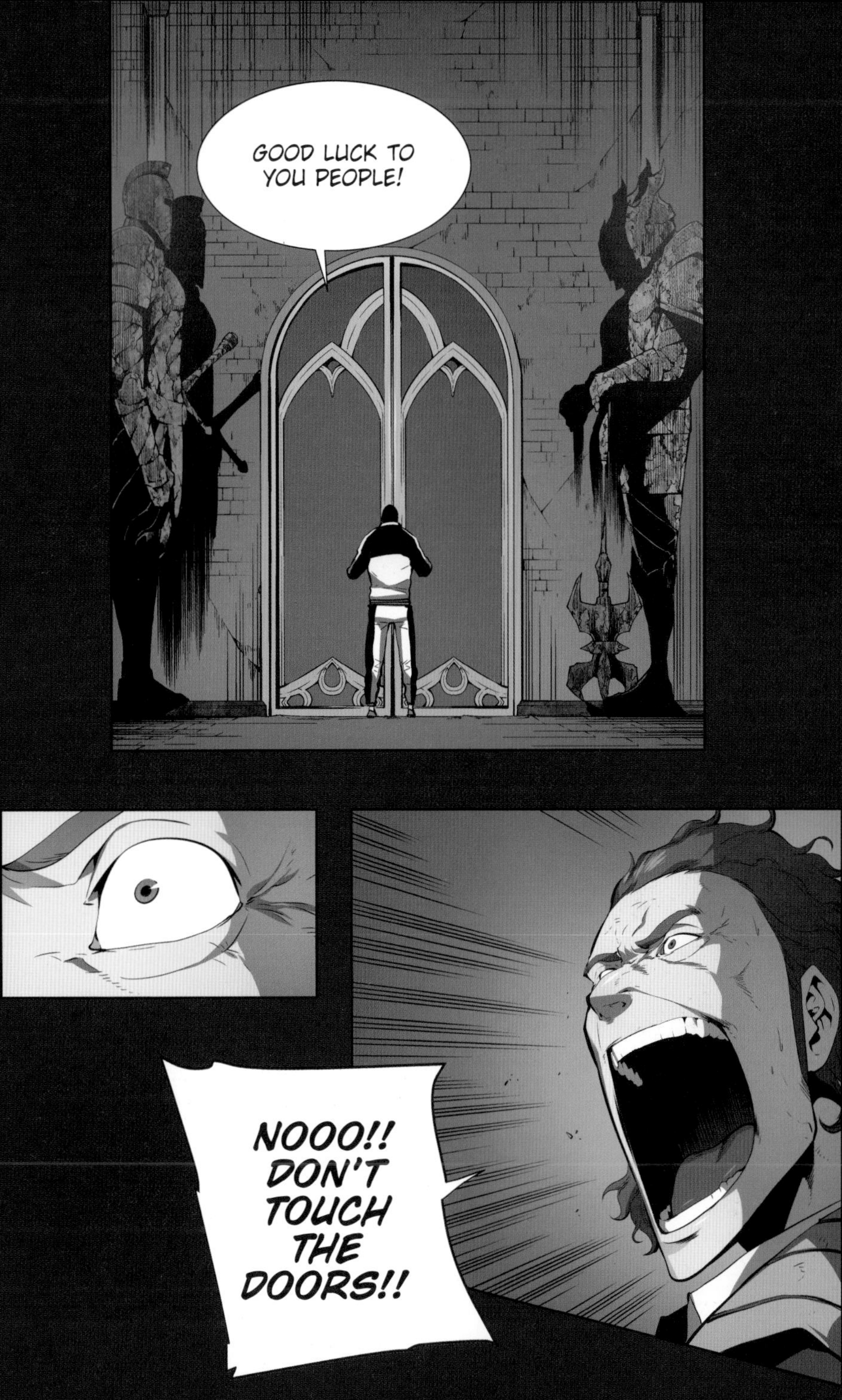
GOOD LUCK TO YOU PEOPLE!
NOOO!! DON'T TOUCH THE DOORS!!

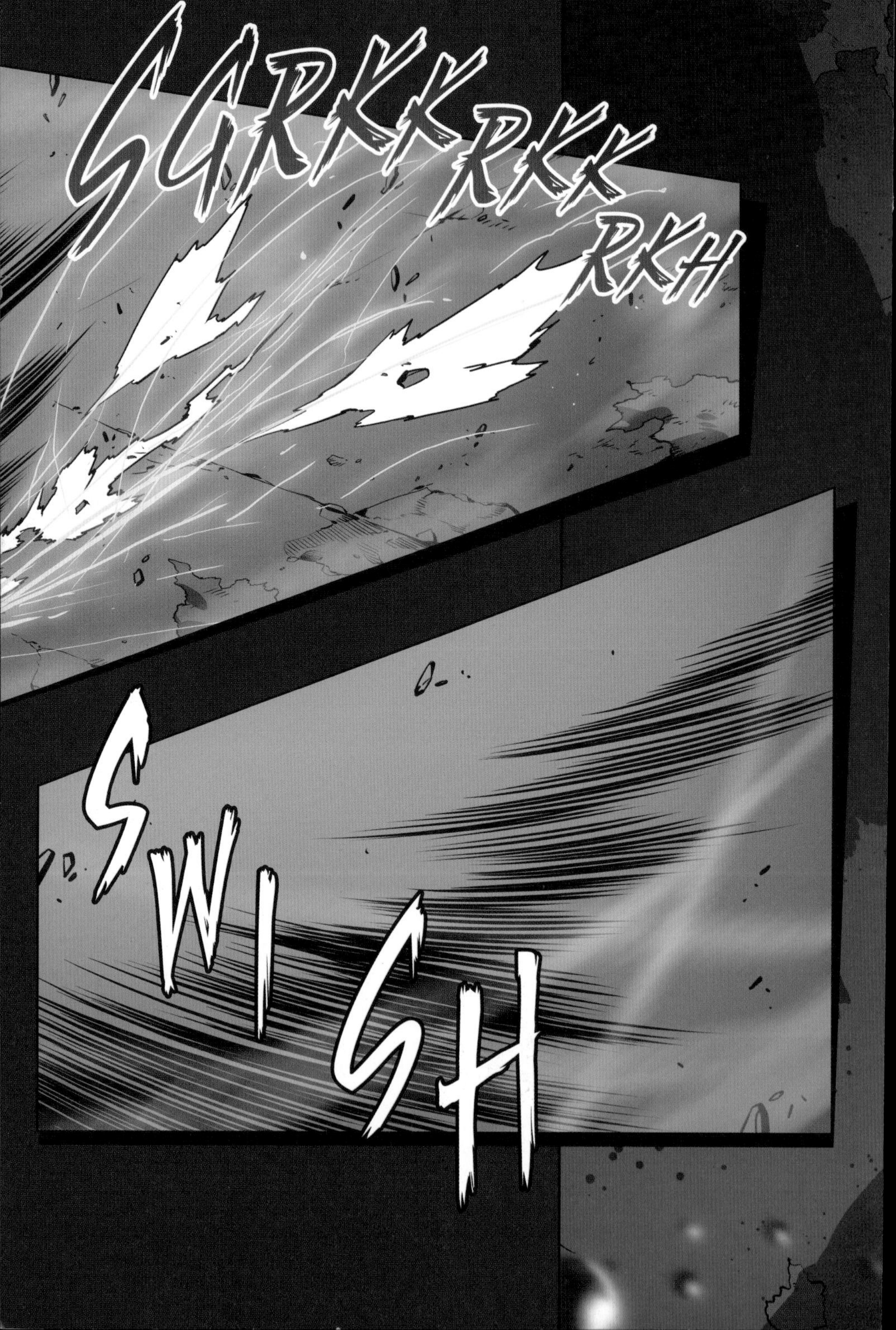
SGRKKRKKRKH
SWISH

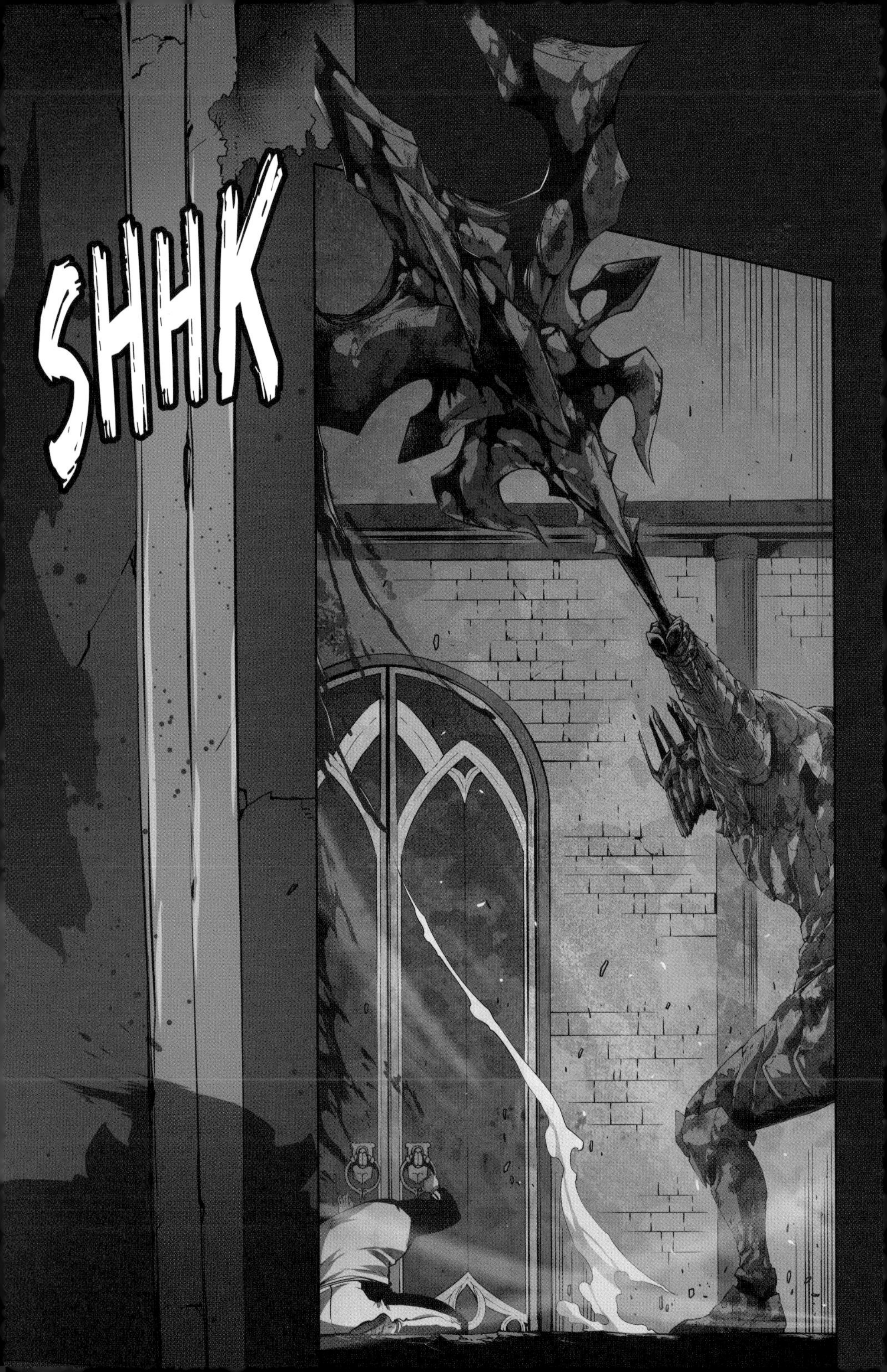
SHHK

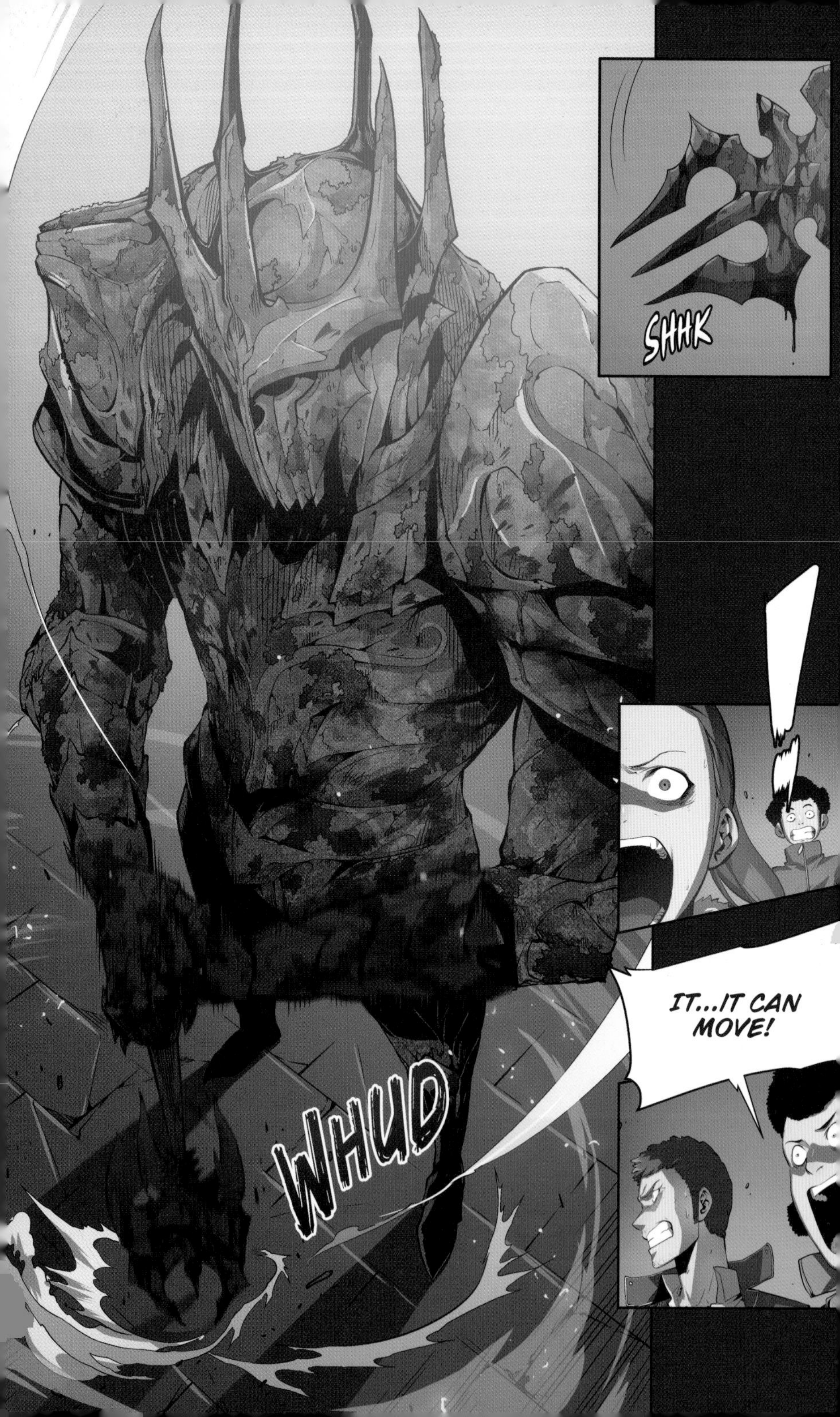
SHHK
!
IT...IT CAN MOVE!
WHUD

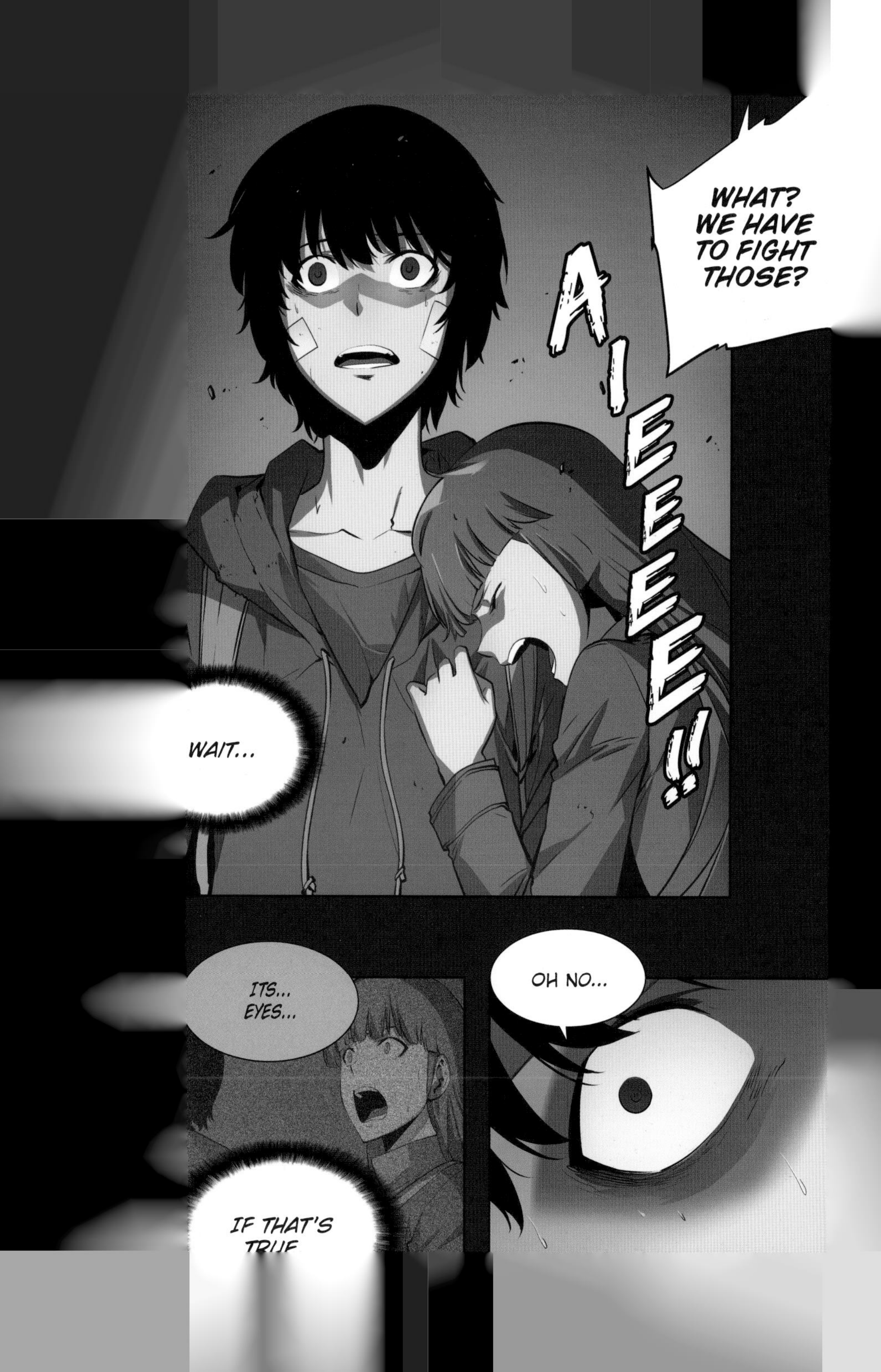
WHAT? WE HAVE TO FIGHT THOSE?
AIEEEEE!!
WAIT...
ITS... EYES...
IF THAT'S
OH NO...

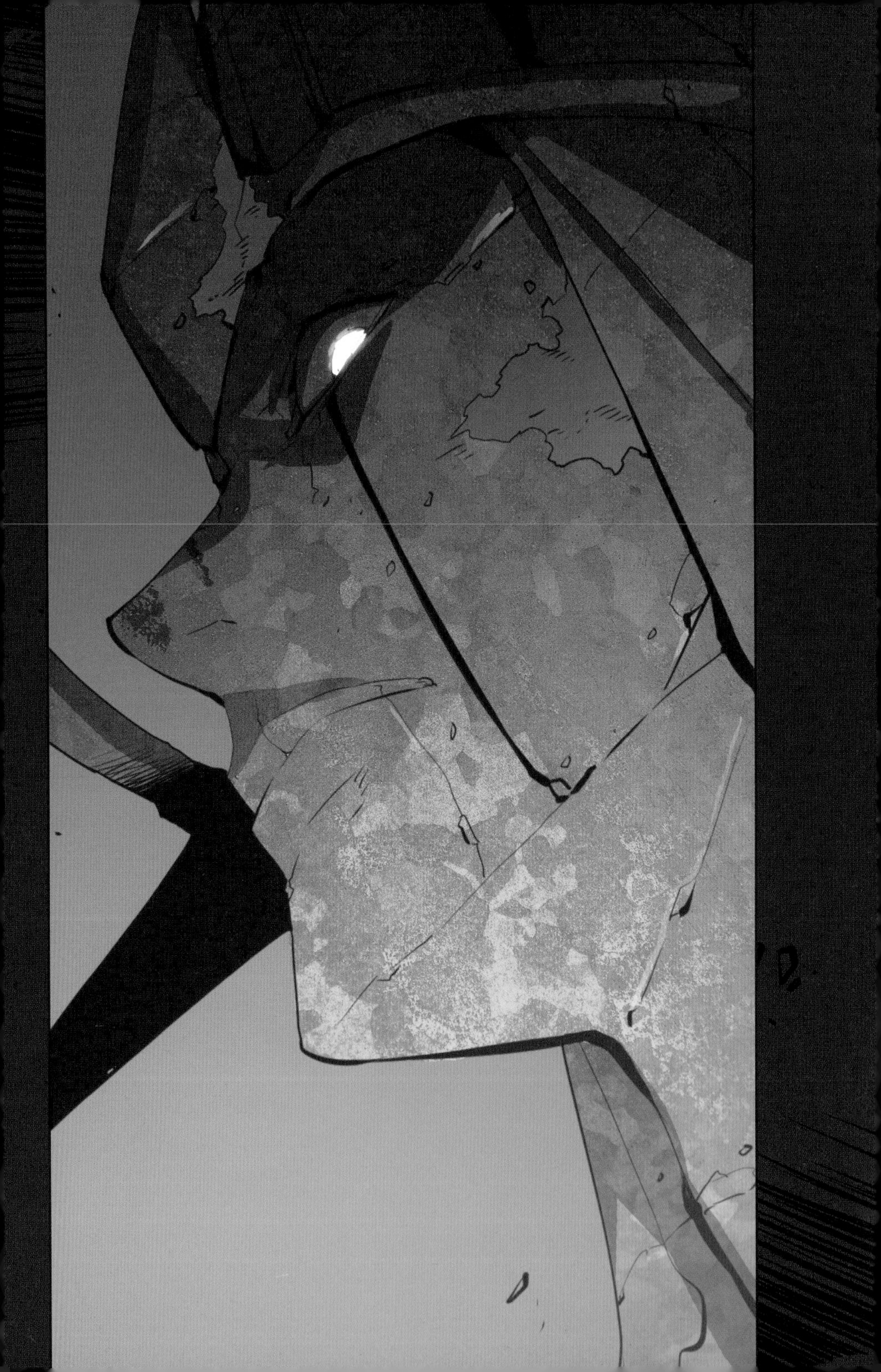

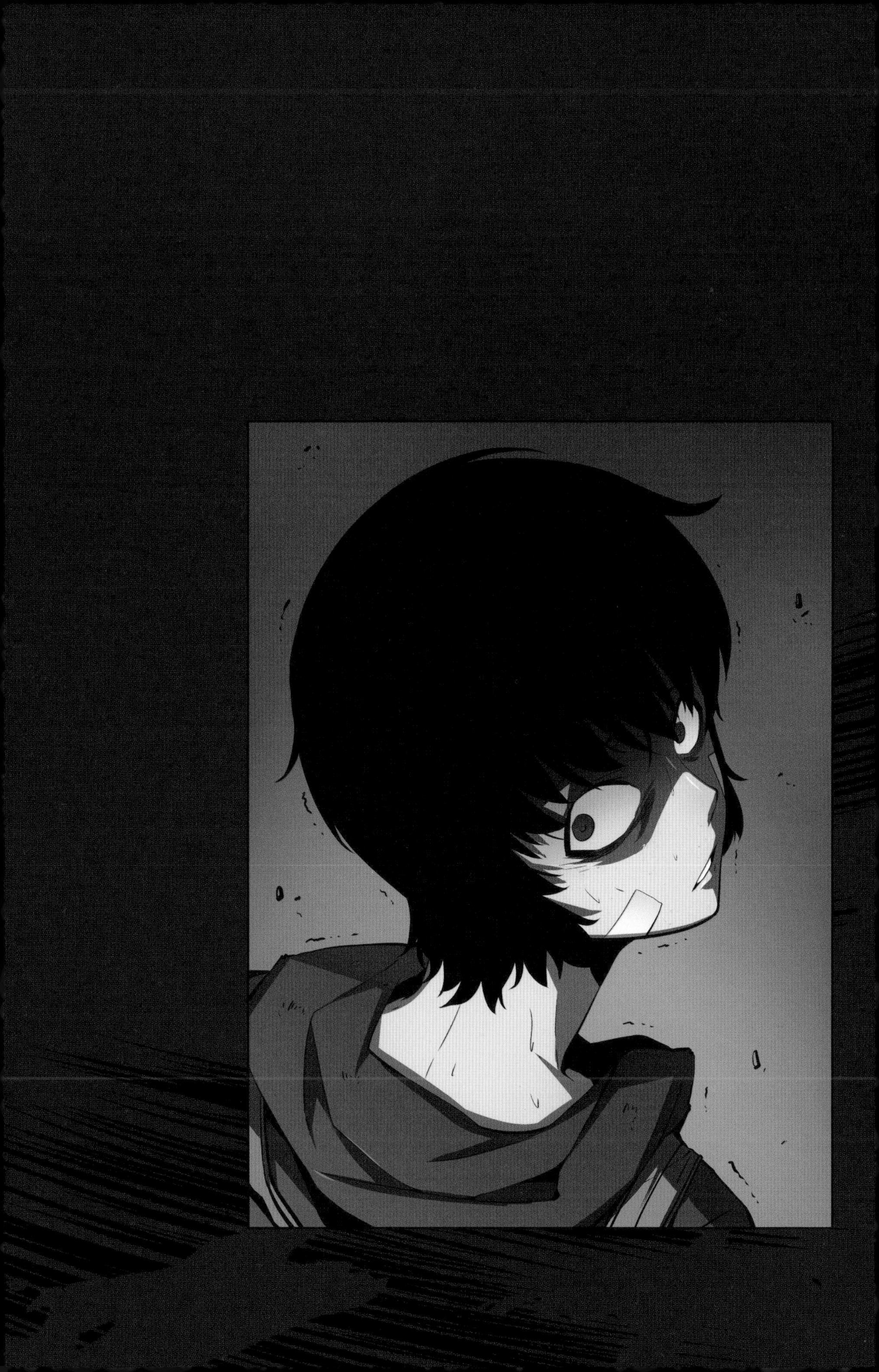

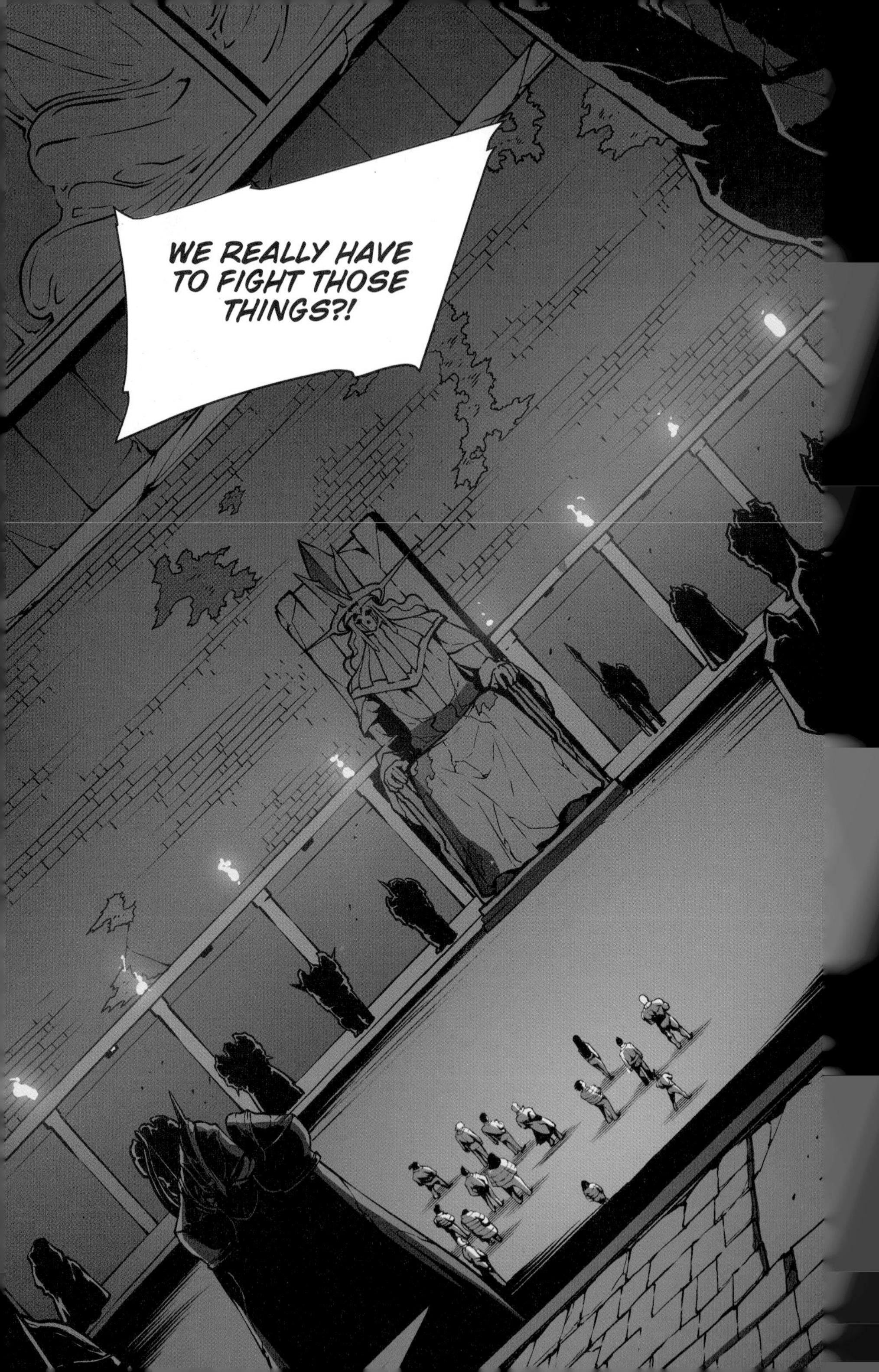
WE REALLY HAVE TO FIGHT THOSE THINGS?!

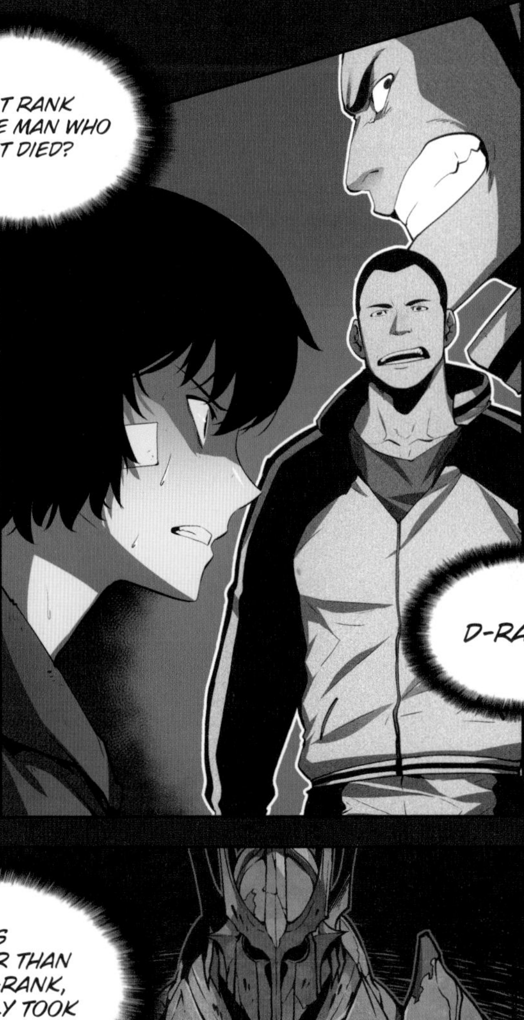
WHAT RANK WAS THE MAN WHO JUST DIED?
D-RANK?
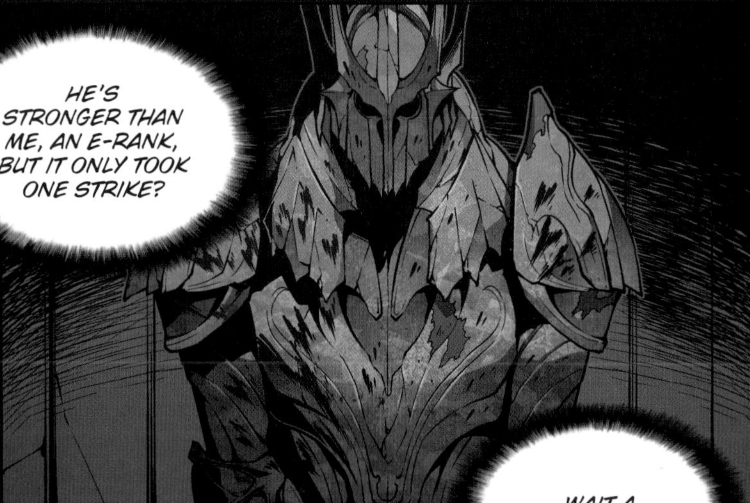
HE'S STRONGER THAN ME, AN E-RANK, BUT IT ONLY TOOK ONE STRIKE?
WAIT A MINUTE...

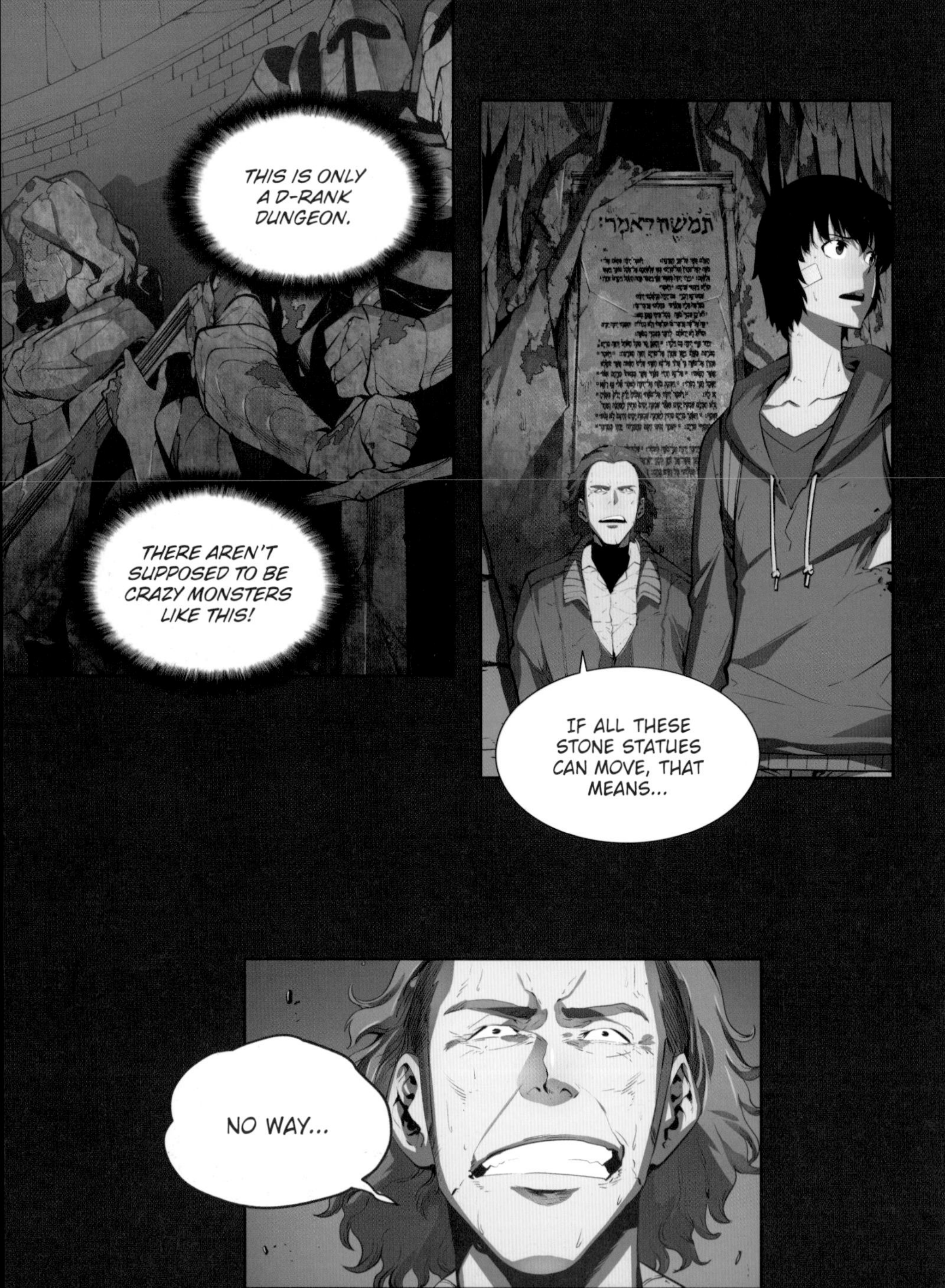
THIS IS ONLY A D-RANK DUNGEON.
THERE AREN'T SUPPOSED TO BE CRAZY MONSTERS LIKE THIS!
IF ALL THESE STONE STATUES CAN MOVE, THAT MEANS...
NO WAY...

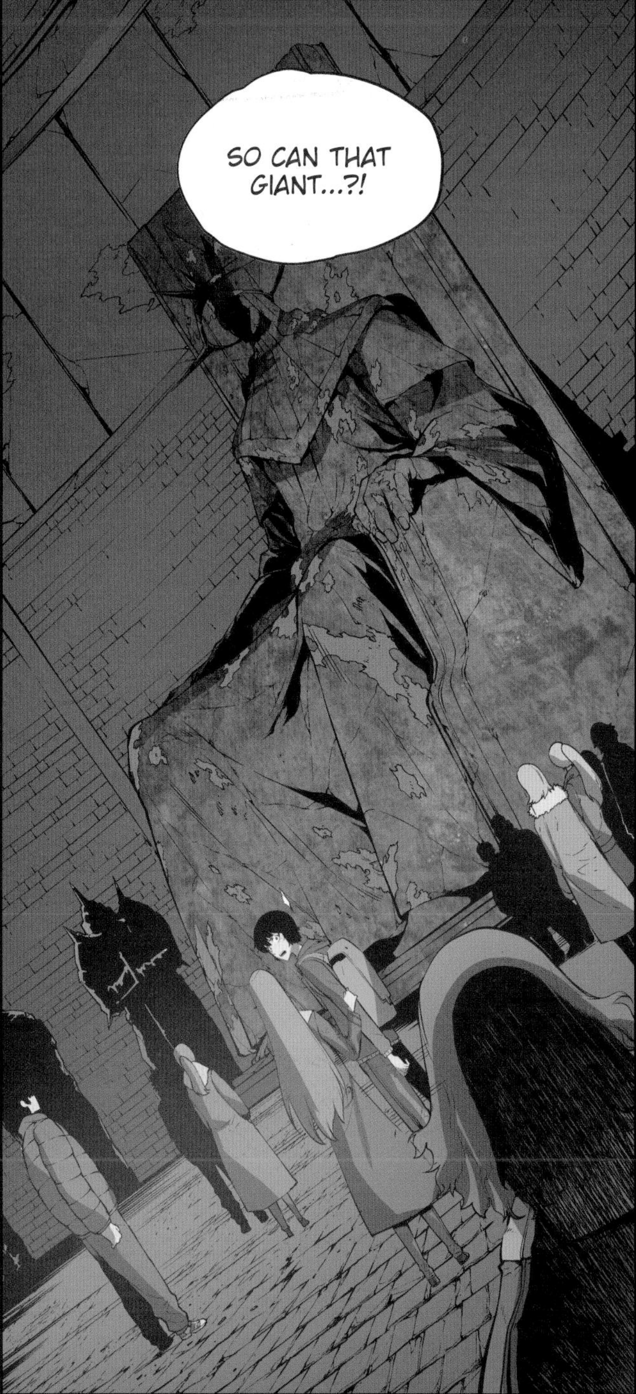
SO CAN THAT GIANT...?!

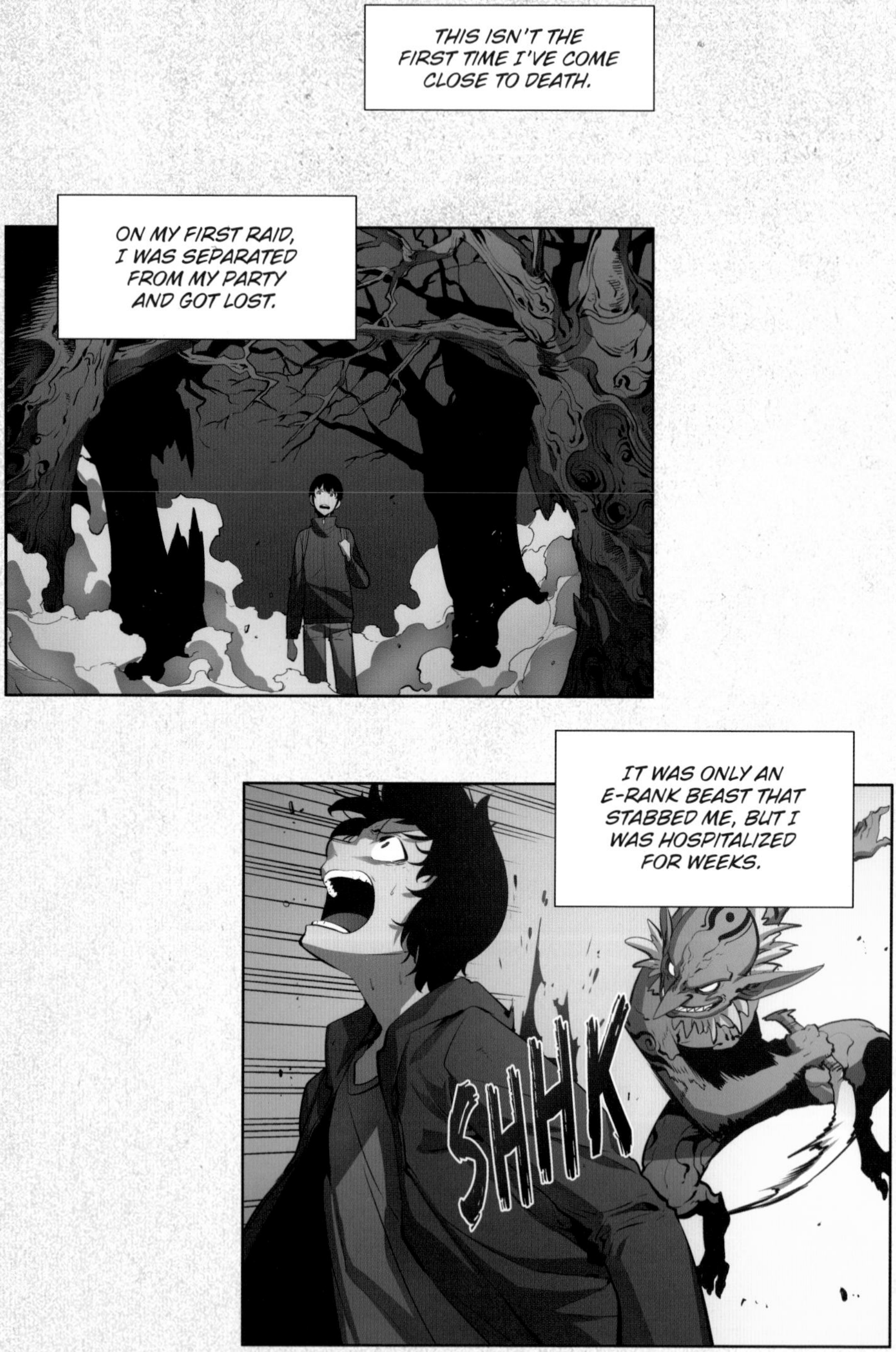
THIS ISN'T THE FIRST TIME I'VE COME CLOSE TO DEATH.
ON MY FIRST RAID, I WAS SEPARATED FROM MY PARTY AND GOT LOST.
IT WAS ONLY AN E-RANK BEAST THAT STABBED ME, BUT I WAS HOSPITALIZED FOR WEEKS.
SHHK

ONCE, I WAS STUCK IN A MAZE AND RAN OUT OF FOOD.

MY LIFE IS IN DANGER EVEN IN LOW-RANK DUNGEONS.

OTHER HUNTERS SELL ESSENCE STONES AND USE THE MONEY TO UPGRADE THEIR WEAPONS...

...SO THAT THEY CAN DEFEAT STRONGER MAGIC BEASTS AND EARN HIGHER FEES.

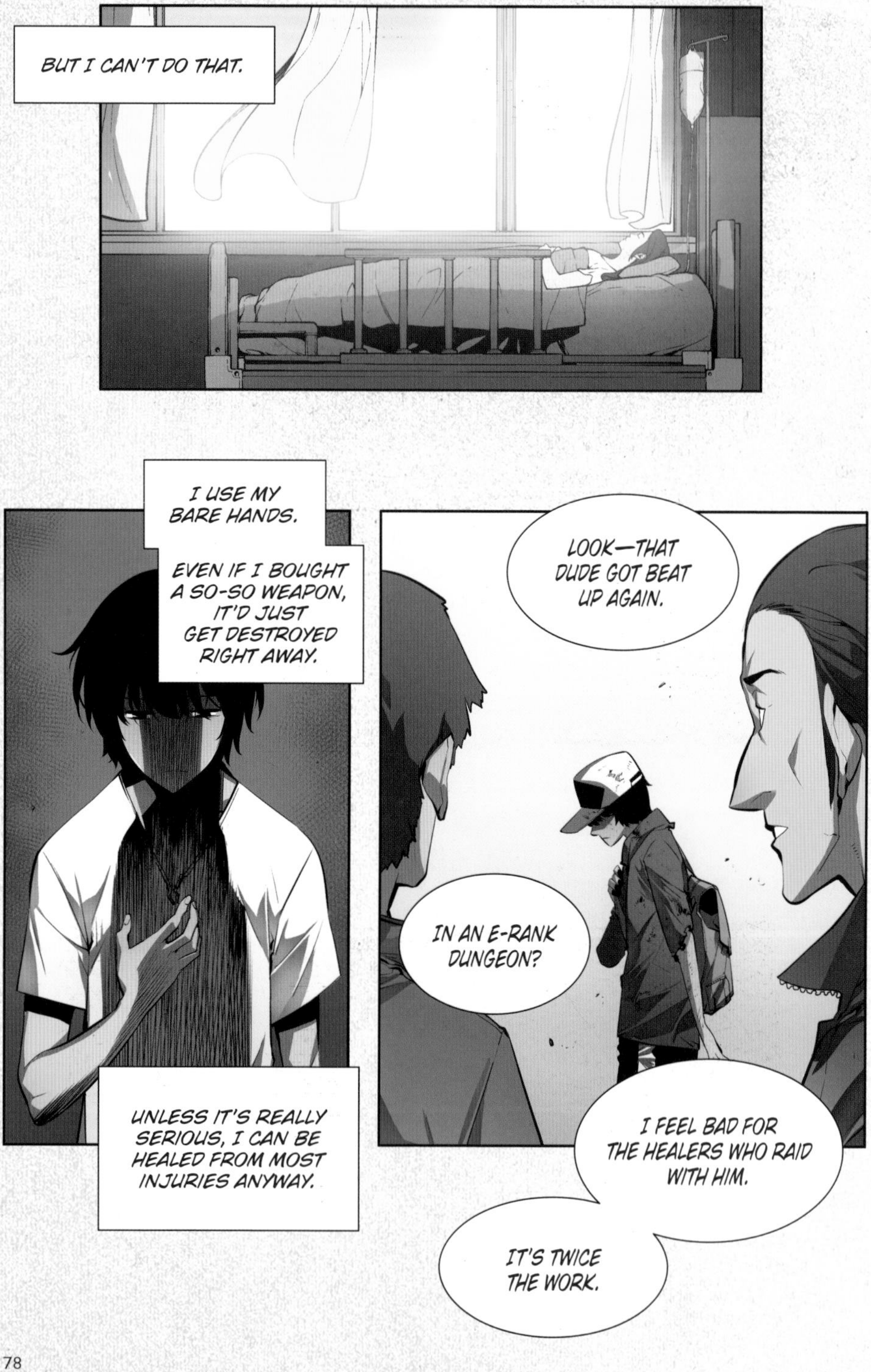
BUT I CAN'T DO THAT.
I USE MY BARE HANDS.
EVEN IF I BOUGHT A SO-SO WEAPON, IT'D JUST GET DESTROYED RIGHT AWAY.
UNLESS IT'S REALLY SERIOUS, I CAN BE HEALED FROM MOST INJURIES ANYWAY.
LOOK—THAT DUDE GOT BEAT UP AGAIN.
IN AN E-RANK DUNGEON?
I FEEL BAD FOR THE HEALERS WHO RAID WITH HIM.
IT'S TWICE THE WORK.

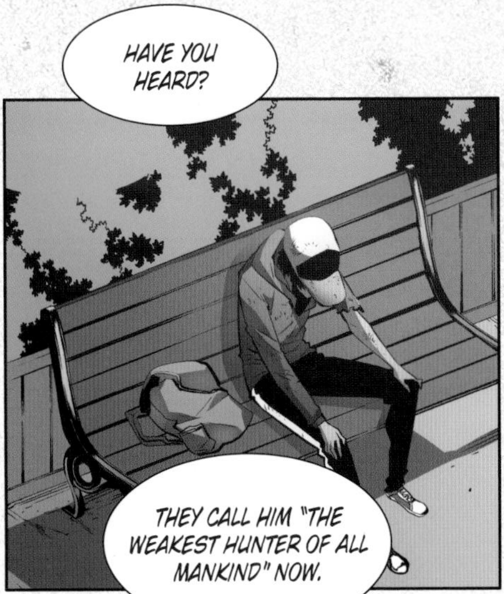
HAVE YOU HEARD?
THEY CALL HIM "THE WEAKEST HUNTER OF ALL MANKIND" NOW.

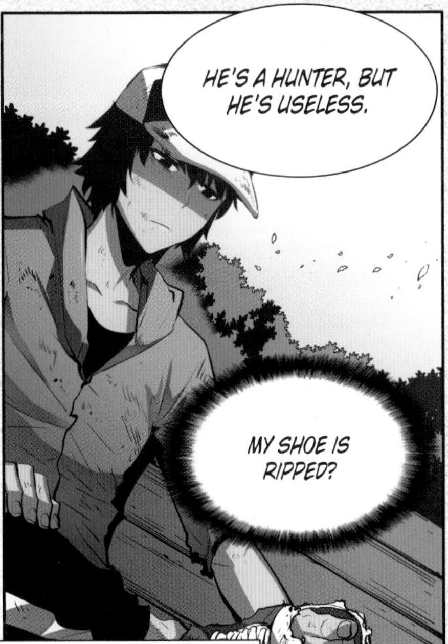
HE'S A HUNTER, BUT HE'S USELESS.
MY SHOE IS RIPPED?

AMID ALL THE MOCKERY, I CONTINUED TO GET BEATEN UP EVERY DAY...

...DOING POORLY AT A DANGEROUS JOB, AND PUTTING MY LIFE ON THE LINE.

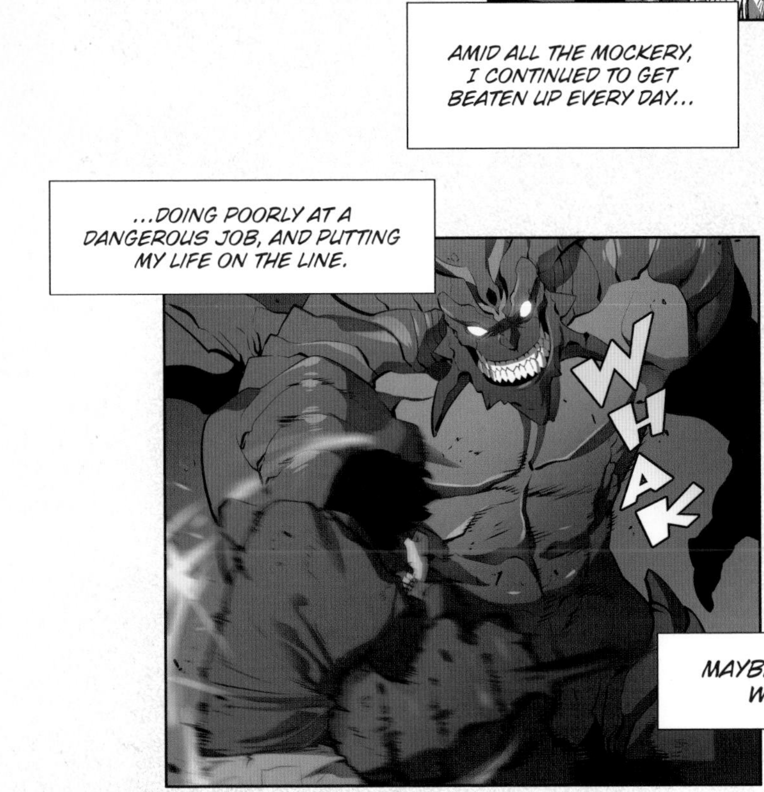
WHAK

MAYBE THAT'S WHY...

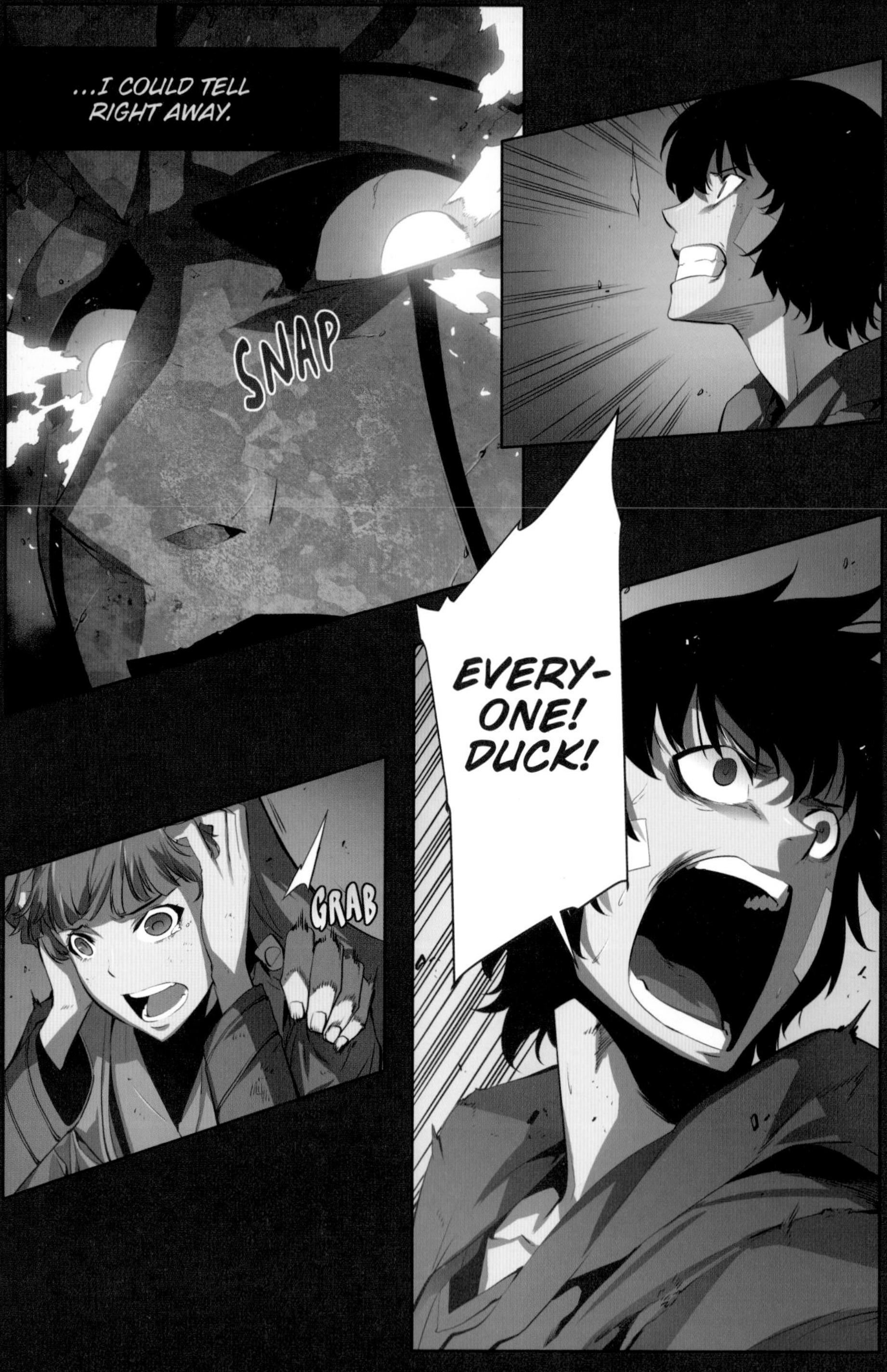
...I COULD TELL RIGHT AWAY.
SNAP
EVERY-ONE! DUCK!
GRAB

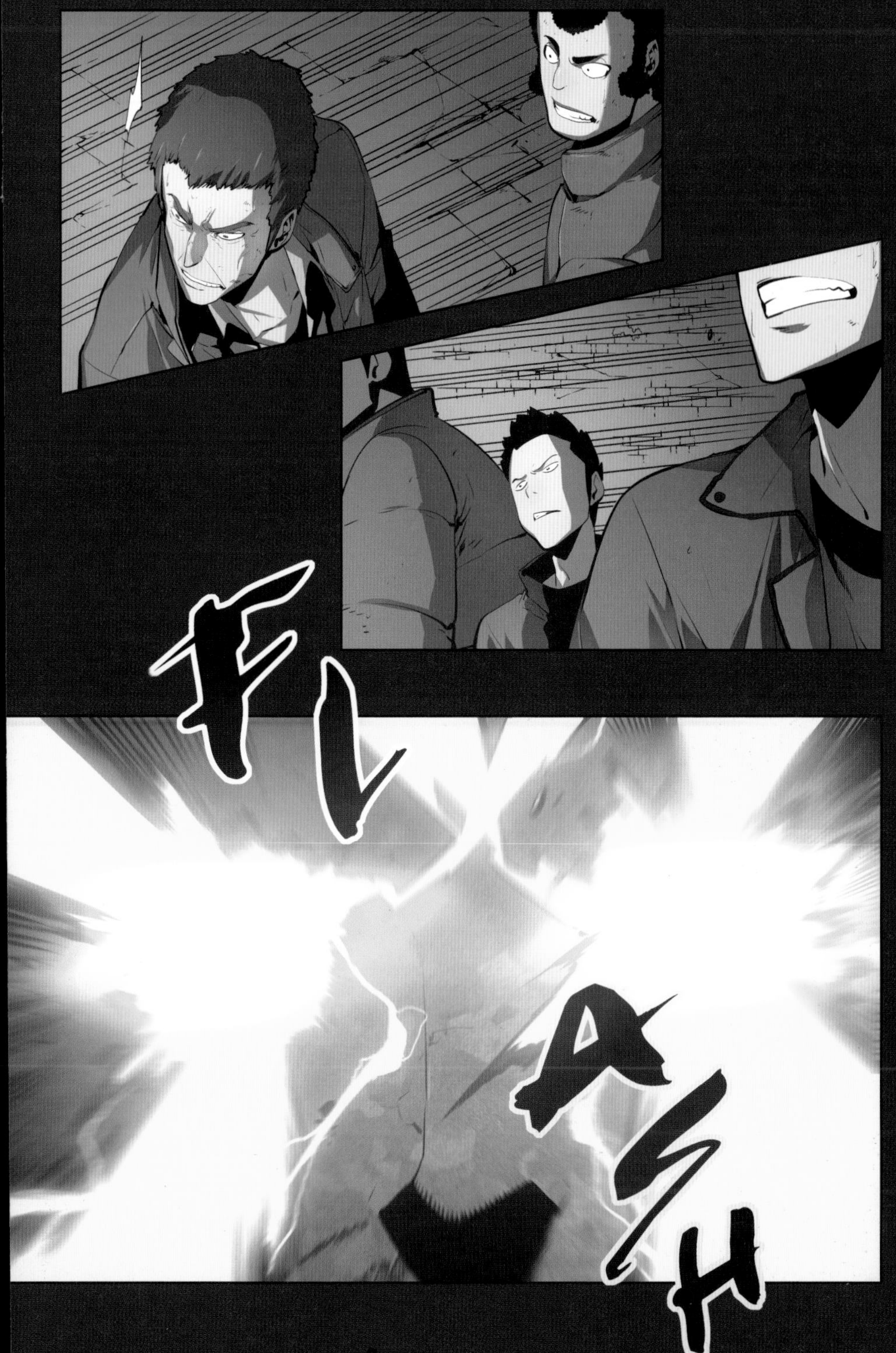
FLASH

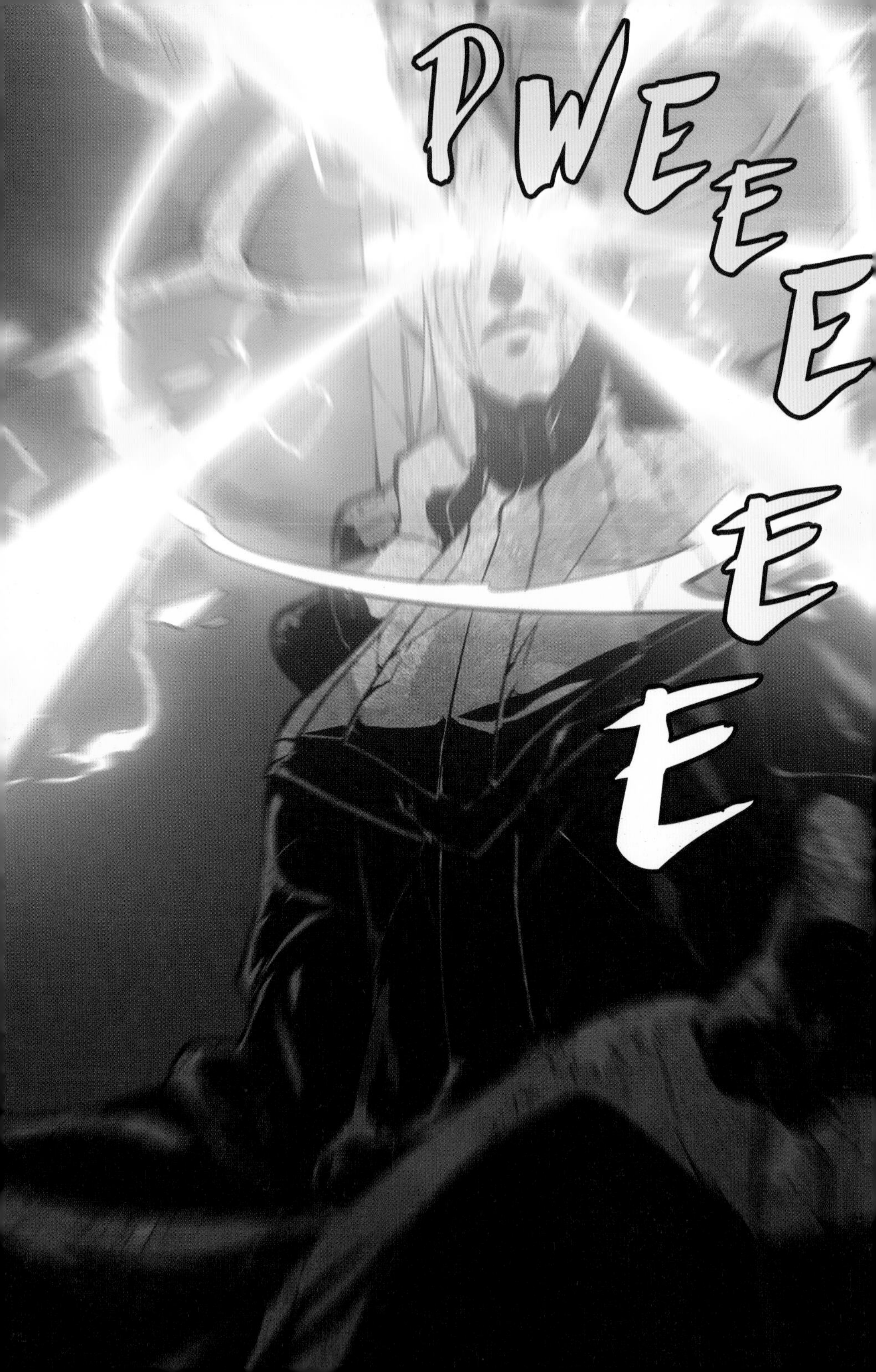
PWEEEEEE

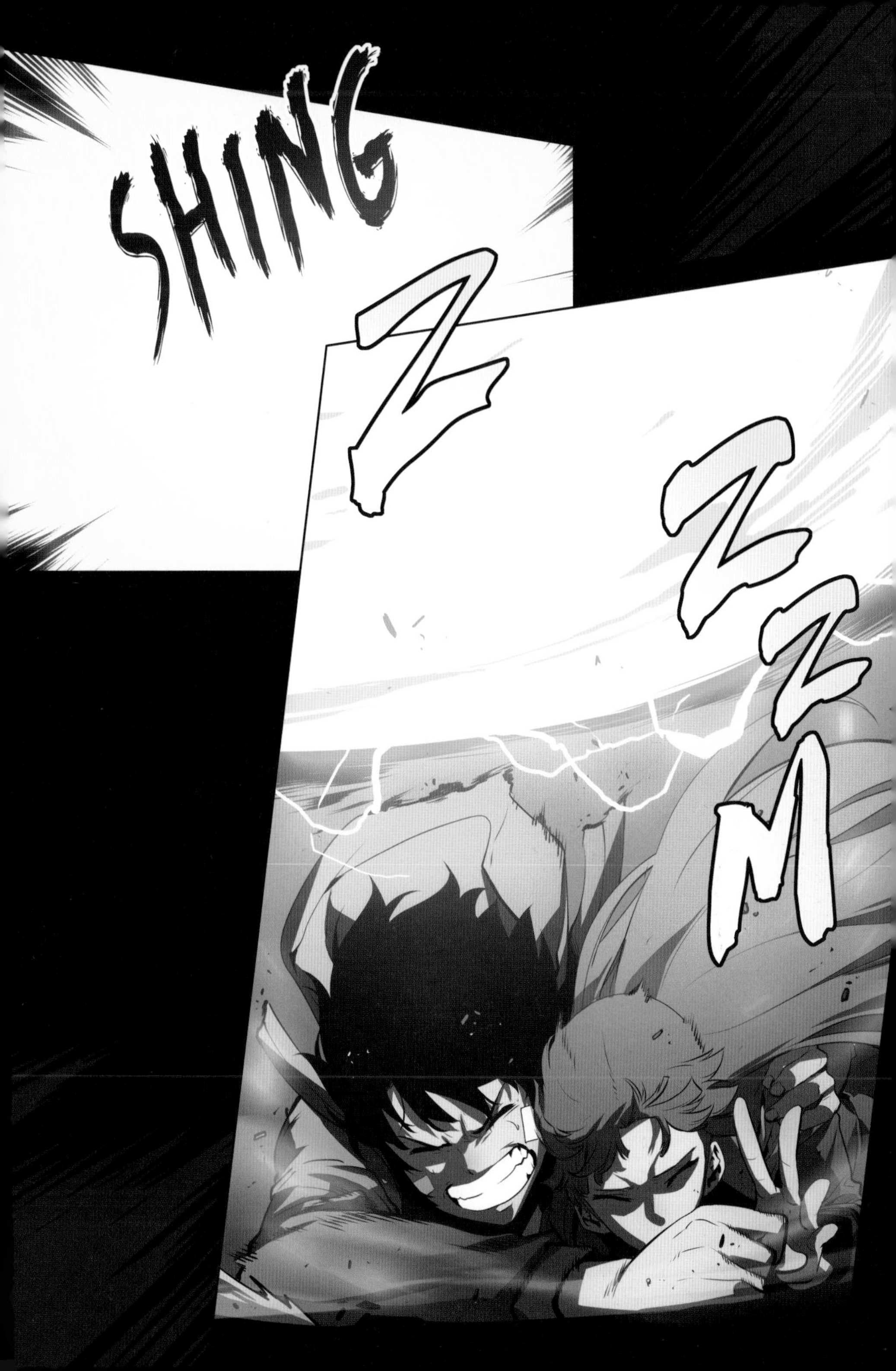
SHING
ZZZM

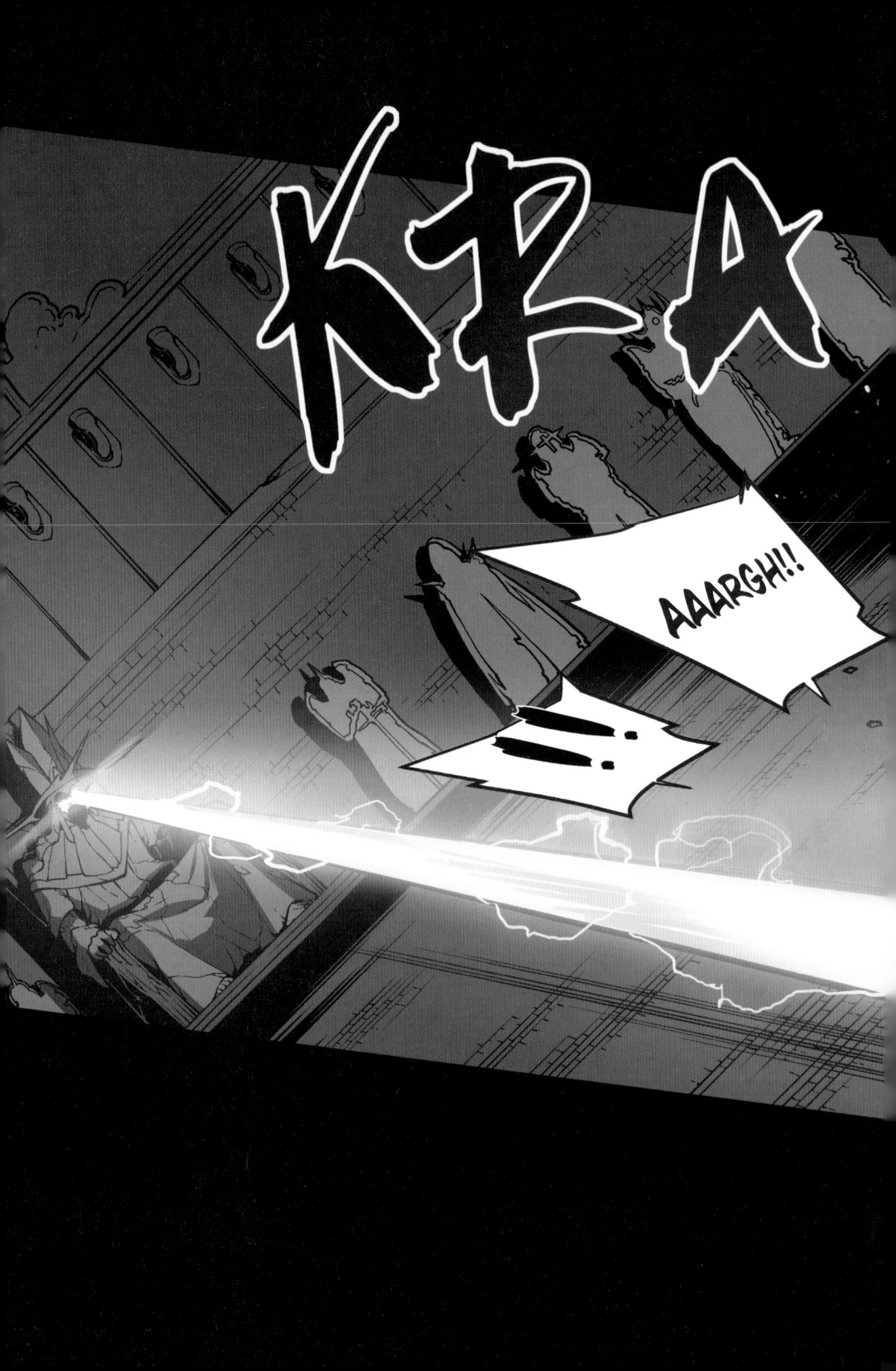
KRA
AAARGH!!
!!

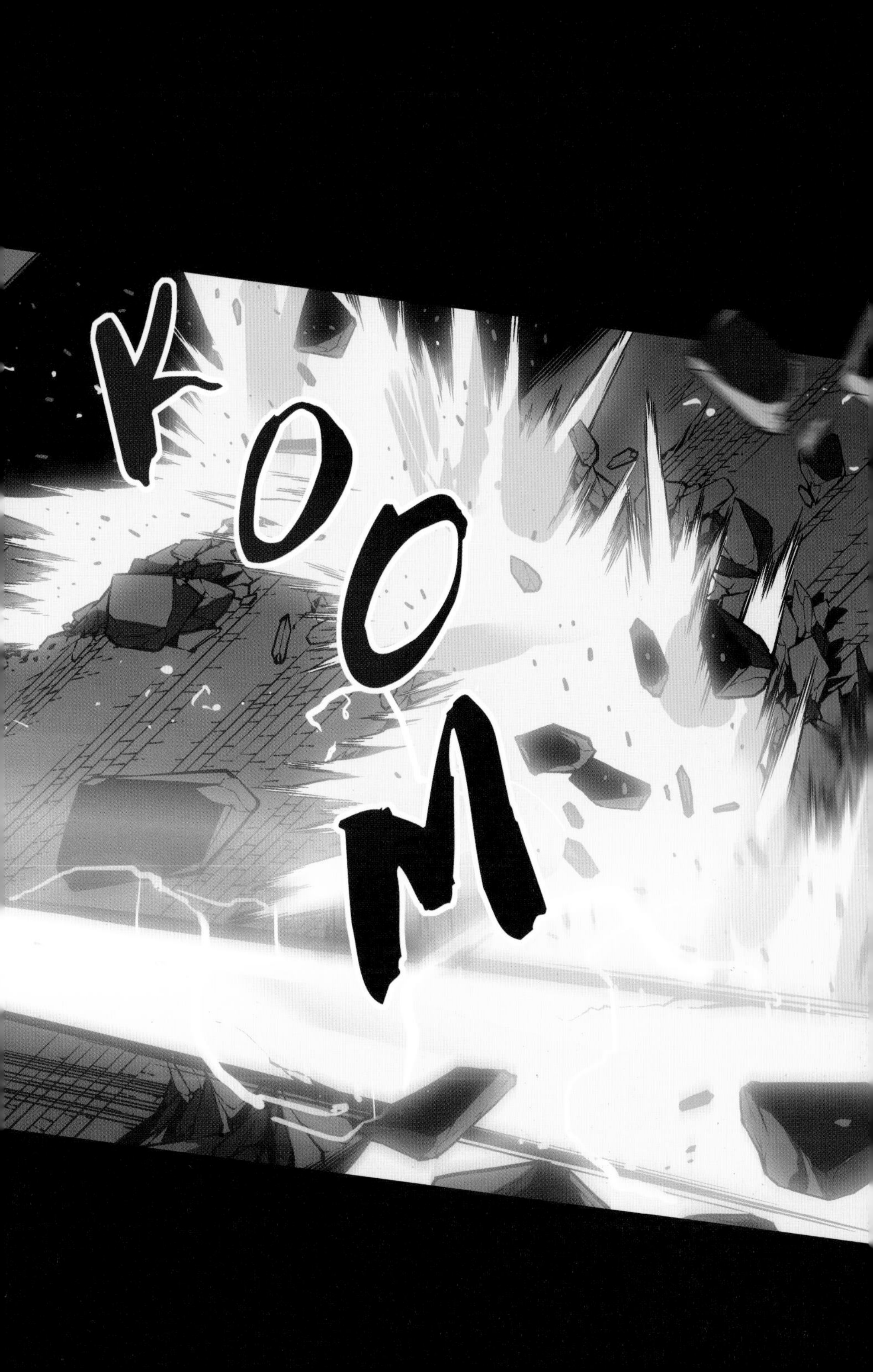
KOOM

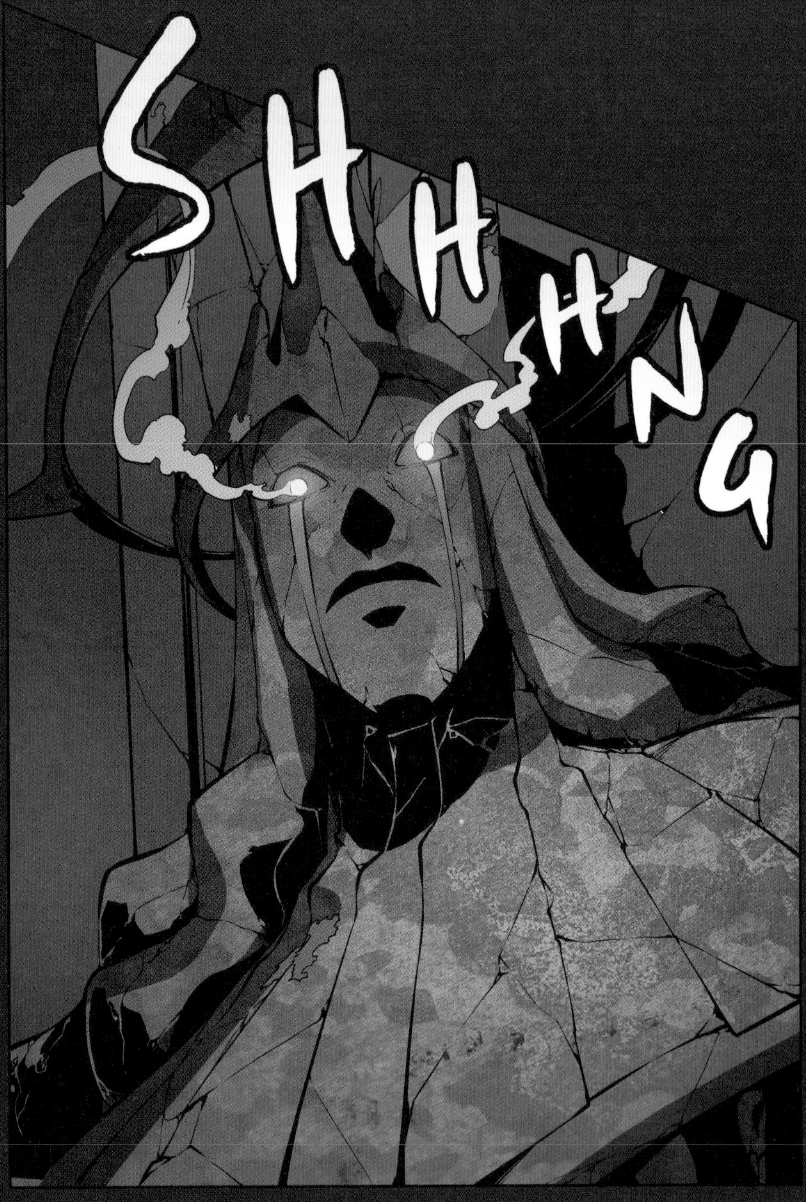
SHHHNG

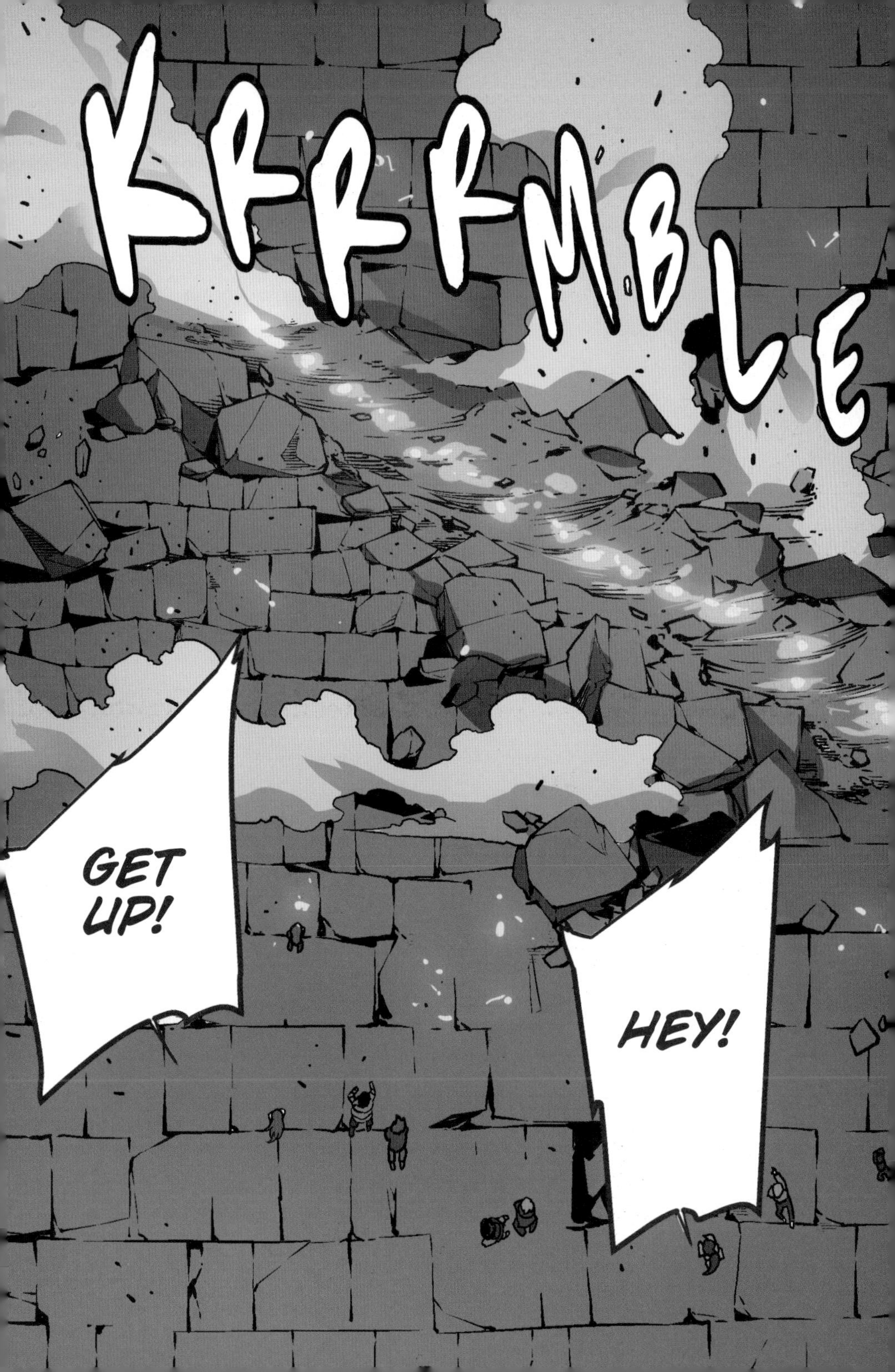
KRRRMBLE
GET UP!
HEY!

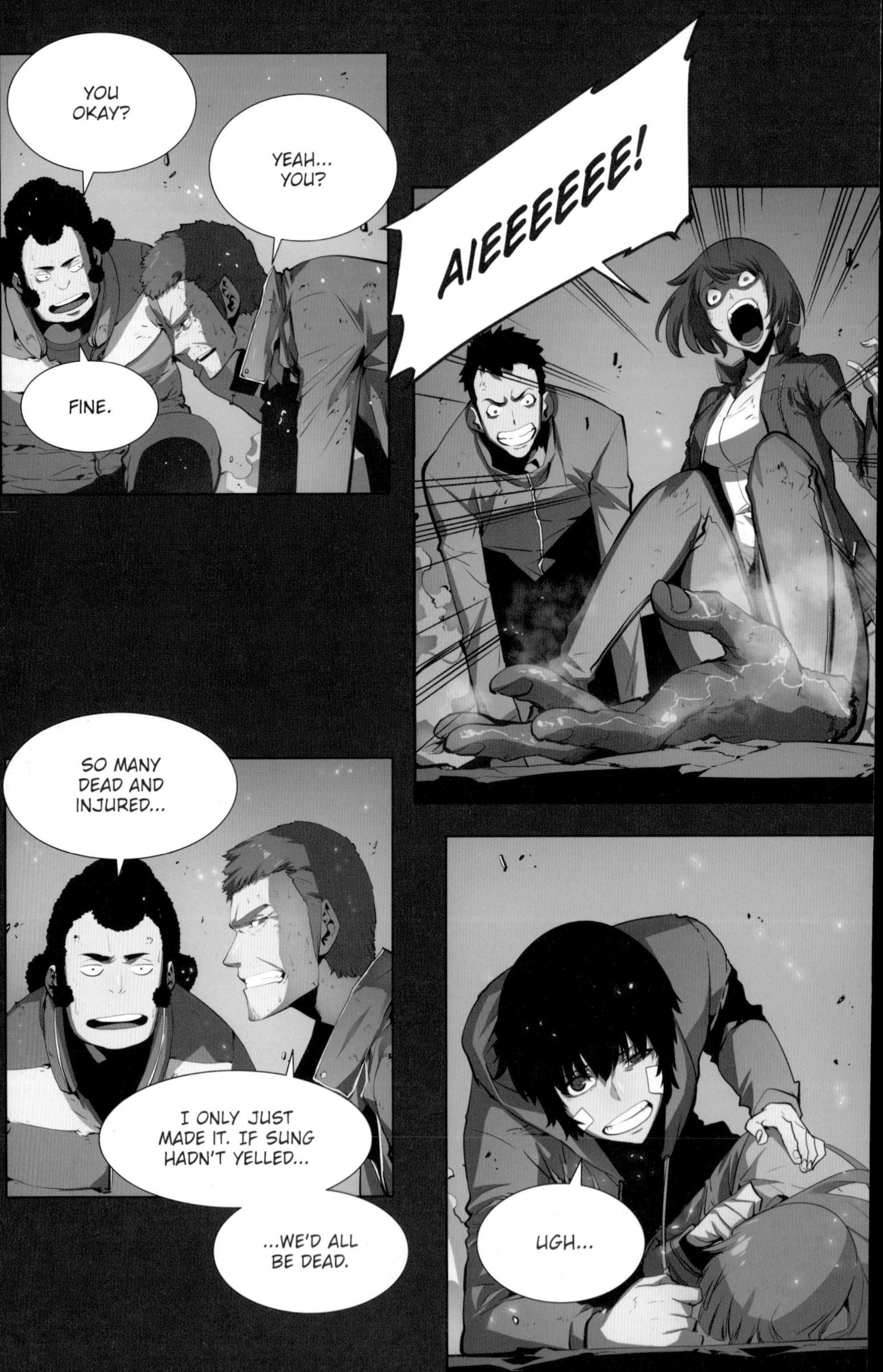
YOU OKAY?
YEAH... YOU?
FINE.
AIEEEEEEE!
SO MANY DEAD AND INJURED...
I ONLY JUST MADE IT. IF SUNG HADN'T YELLED...
...WE'D ALL BE DEAD.
UGH...

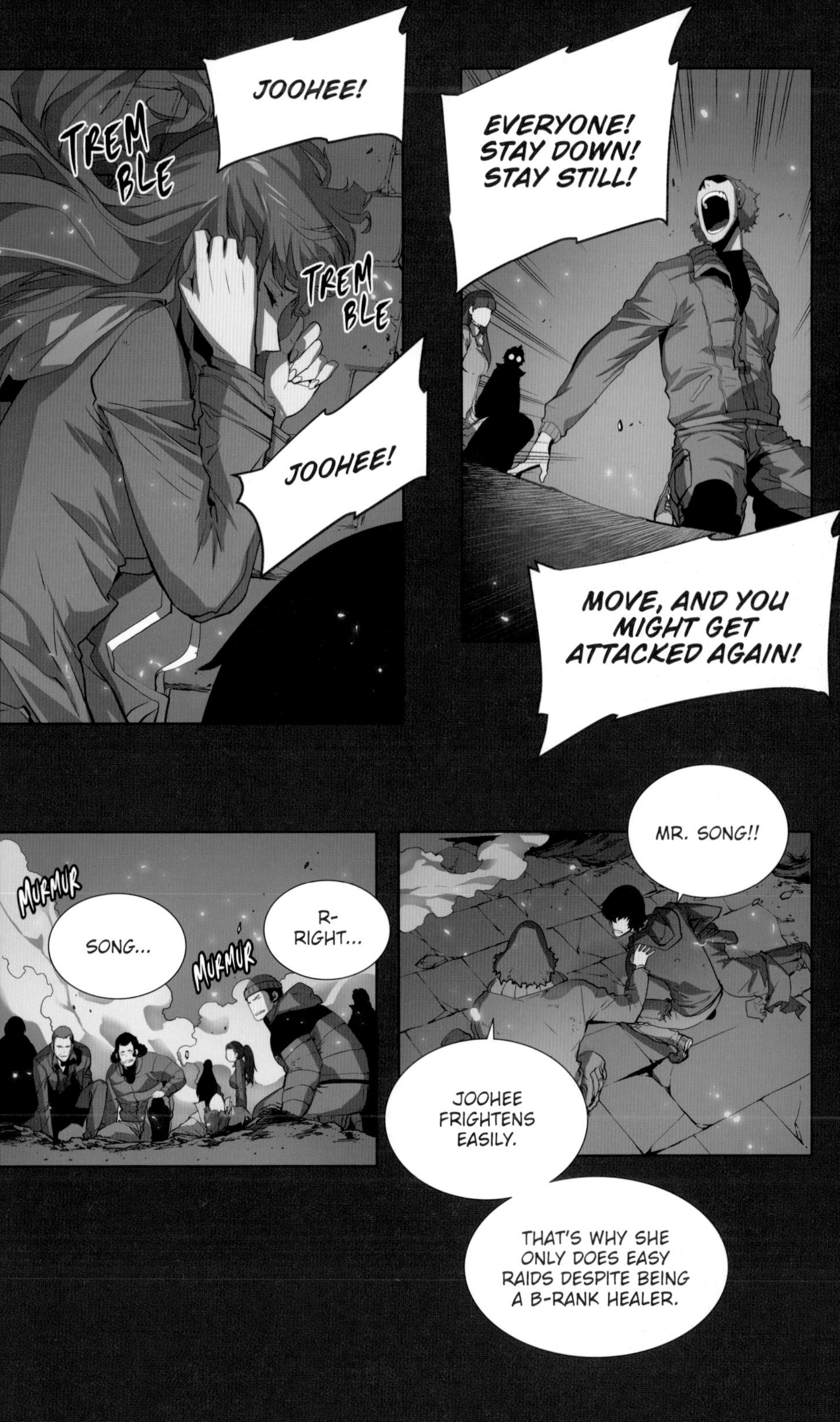
JOOHEE!
TREMBLE
TREMBLE
JOOHEE!
EVERYONE! STAY DOWN! STAY STILL!
MOVE, AND YOU MIGHT GET ATTACKED AGAIN!
MURMUR
SONG...
MURMUR
R- RIGHT...
MR. SONG!!
JOOHEE FRIGHTENS EASILY.
THAT'S WHY SHE ONLY DOES EASY RAIDS DESPITE BEING A B-RANK HEALER.

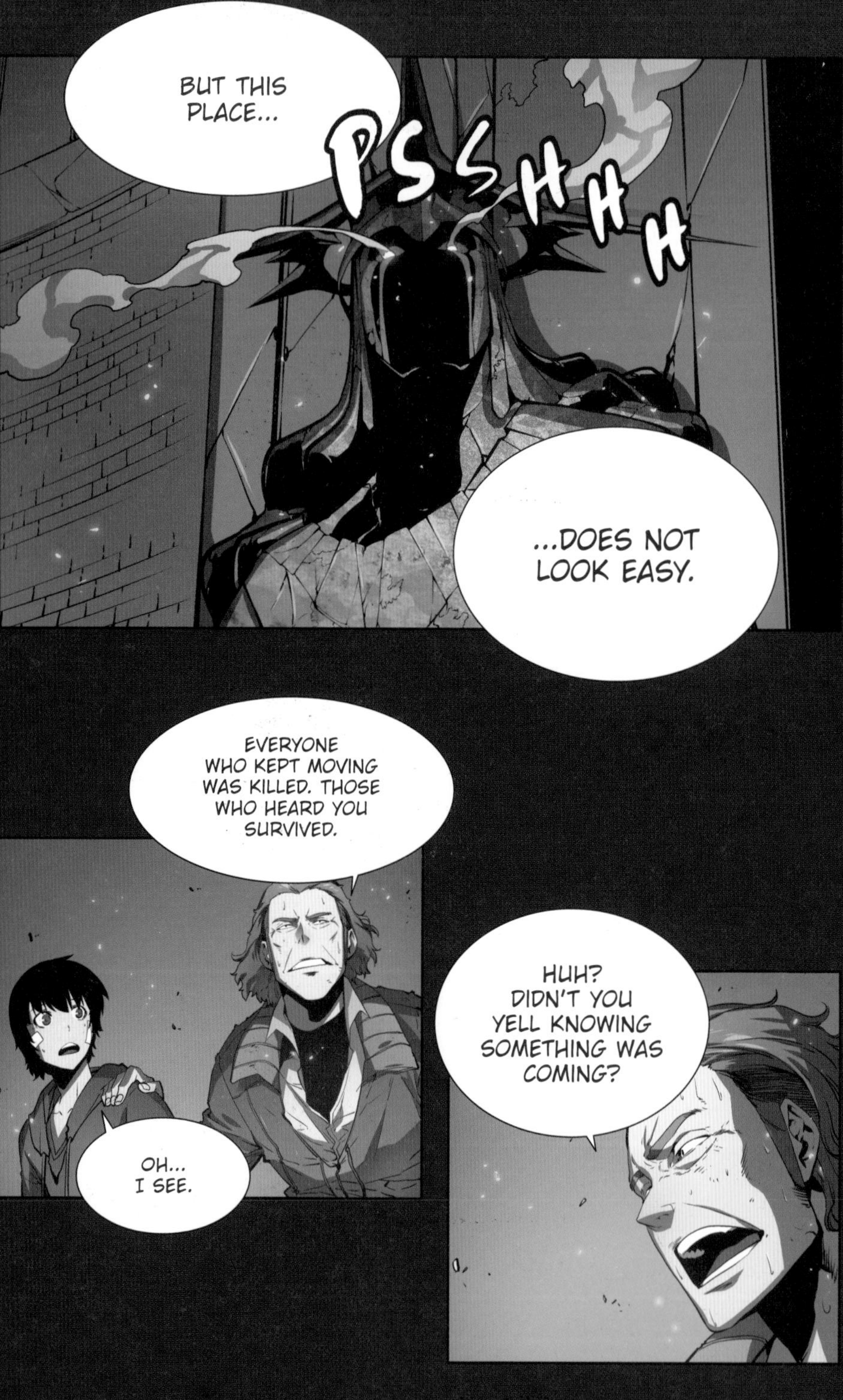
BUT THIS PLACE...
PSSHHH
...DOES NOT LOOK EASY.
EVERYONE WHO KEPT MOVING WAS KILLED. THOSE WHO HEARD YOU SURVIVED.
OH... I SEE.
HUH? DIDN'T YOU YELL KNOWING SOMETHING WAS COMING?

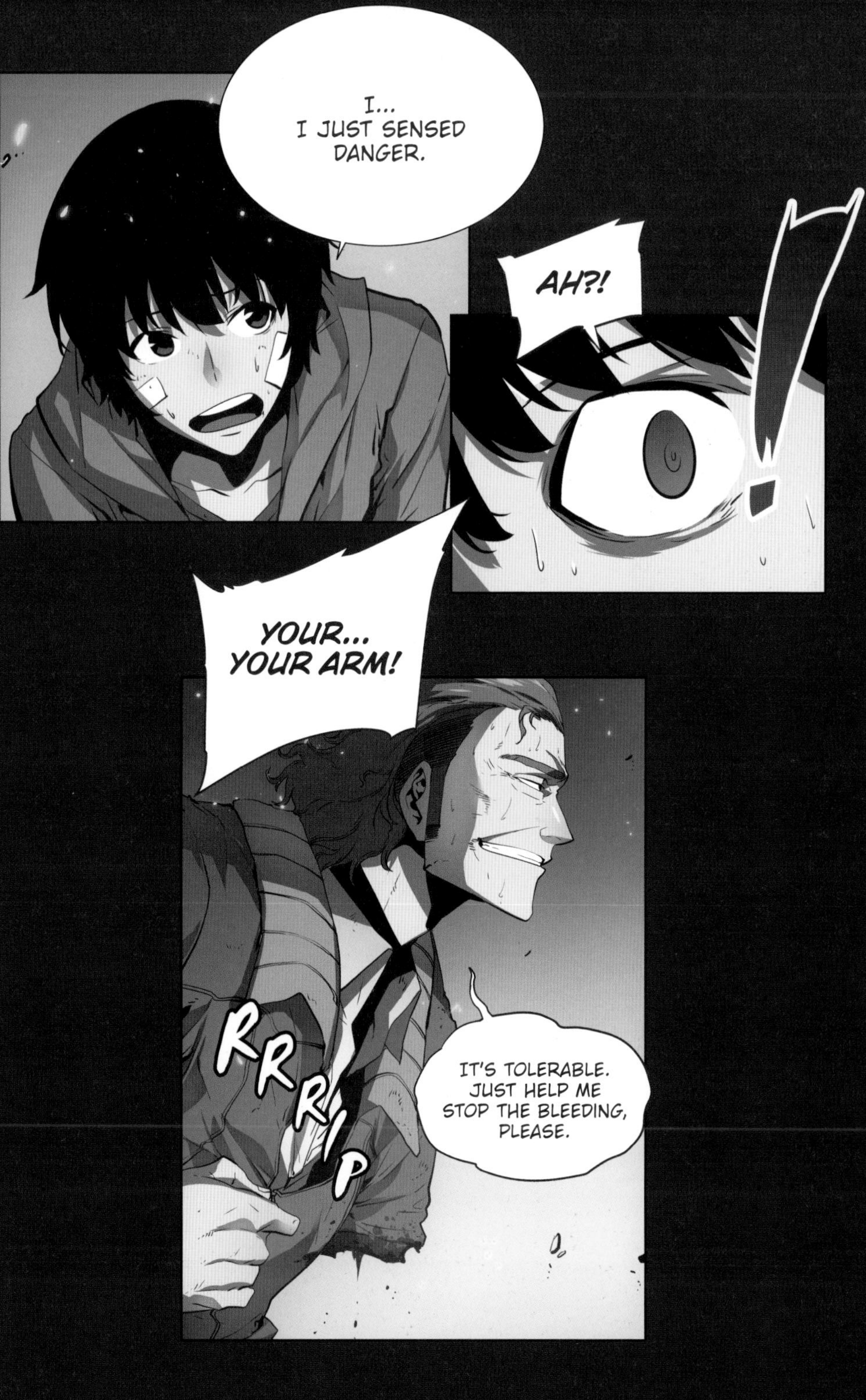
I... I JUST SENSED DANGER.
AH?!
YOUR... YOUR ARM!
RRRIP
IT'S TOLERABLE. JUST HELP ME STOP THE BLEEDING, PLEASE.

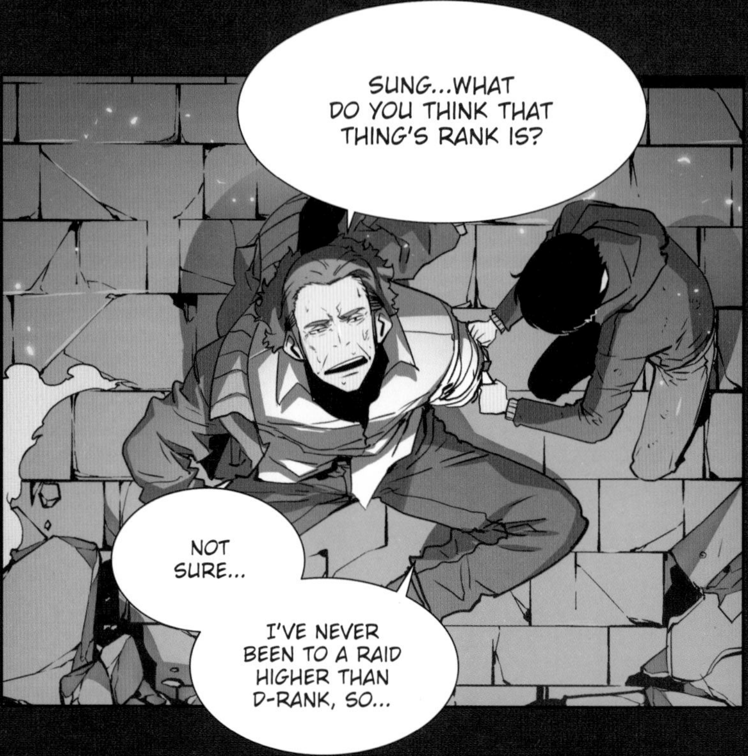
SUNG...WHAT DO YOU THINK THAT THING'S RANK IS?
NOT SURE...
I'VE NEVER BEEN TO A RAID HIGHER THAN D-RANK, SO...
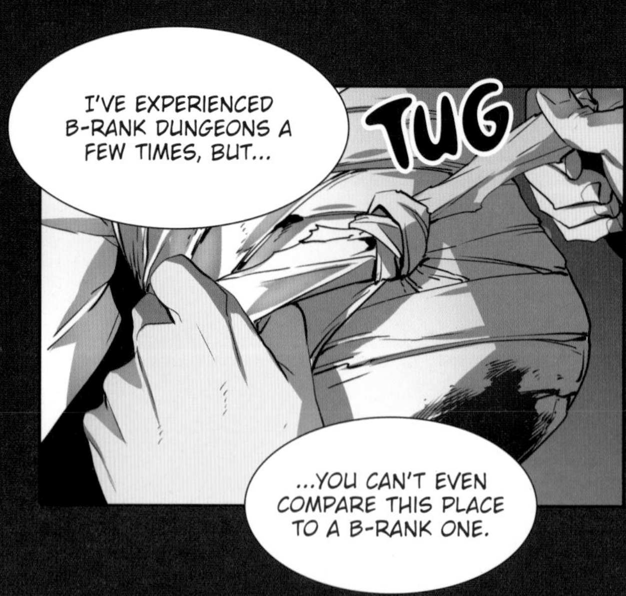
I'VE EXPERIENCED B-RANK DUNGEONS A FEW TIMES, BUT...
TUG
...YOU CAN'T EVEN COMPARE THIS PLACE TO A B-RANK ONE.

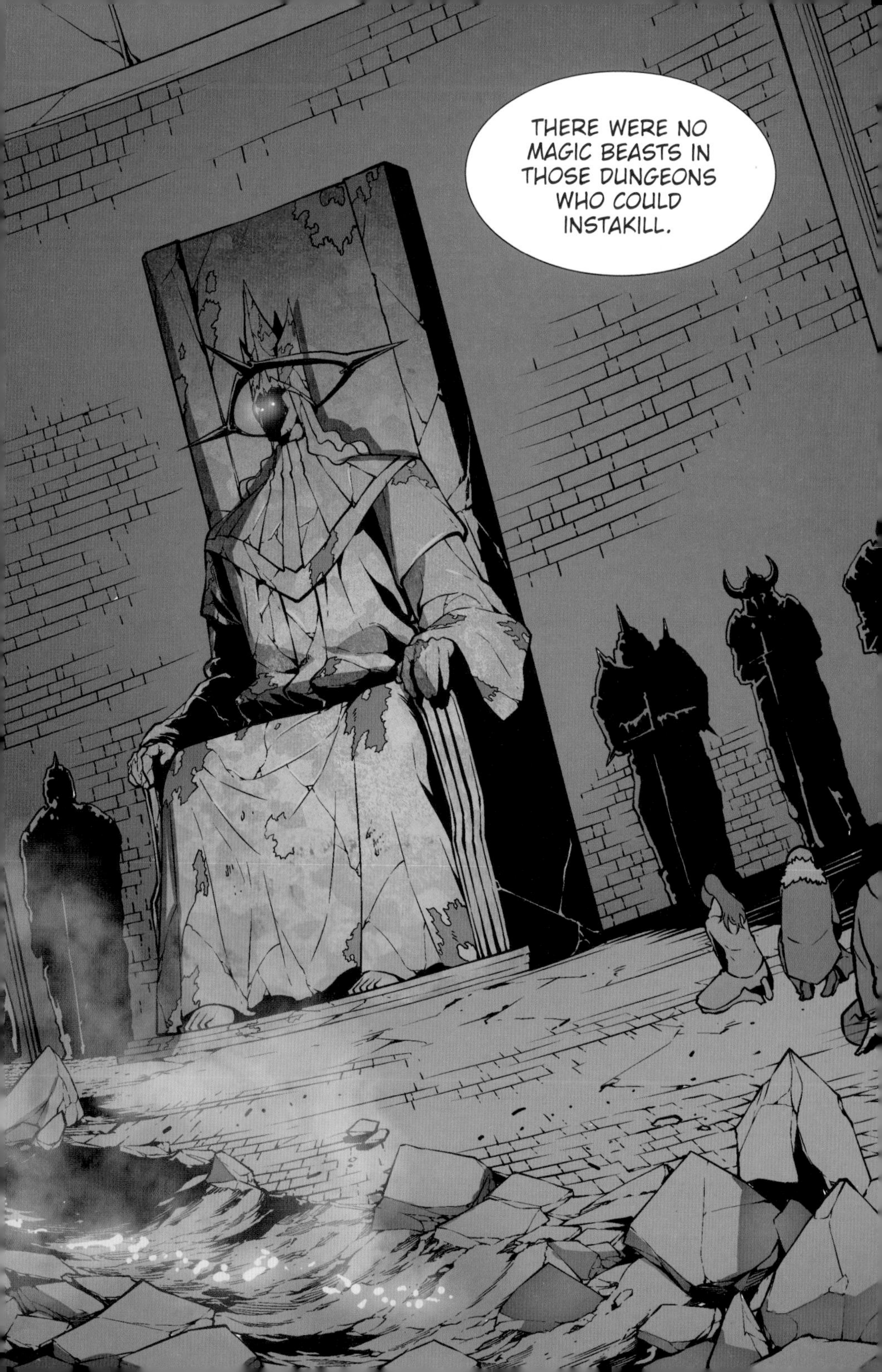
THERE WERE NO MAGIC BEASTS IN THOSE DUNGEONS WHO COULD INSTAKILL.

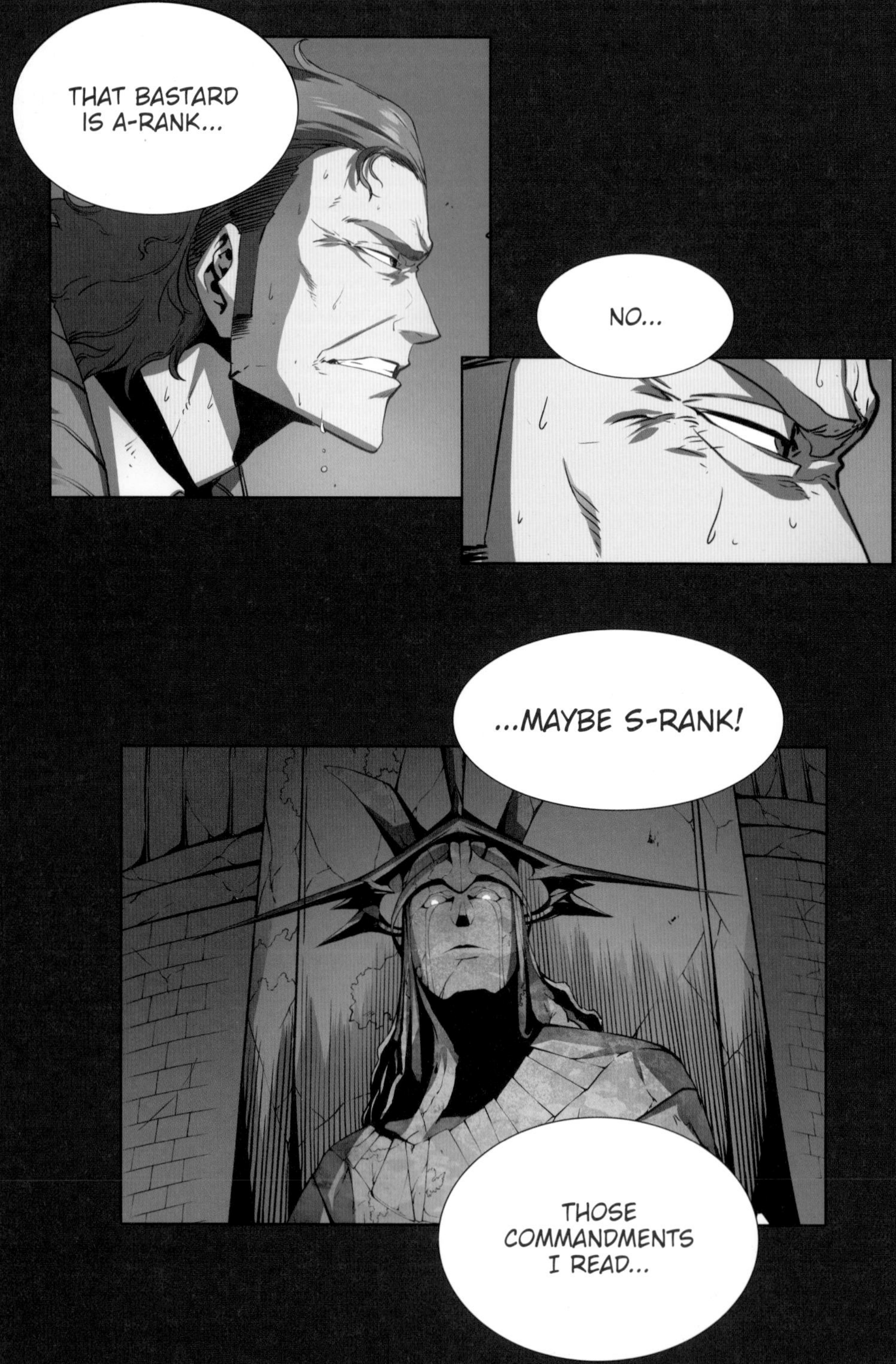
THAT BASTARD IS A-RANK...
NO...
...MAYBE S-RANK!
THOSE COMMANDMENTS I READ...

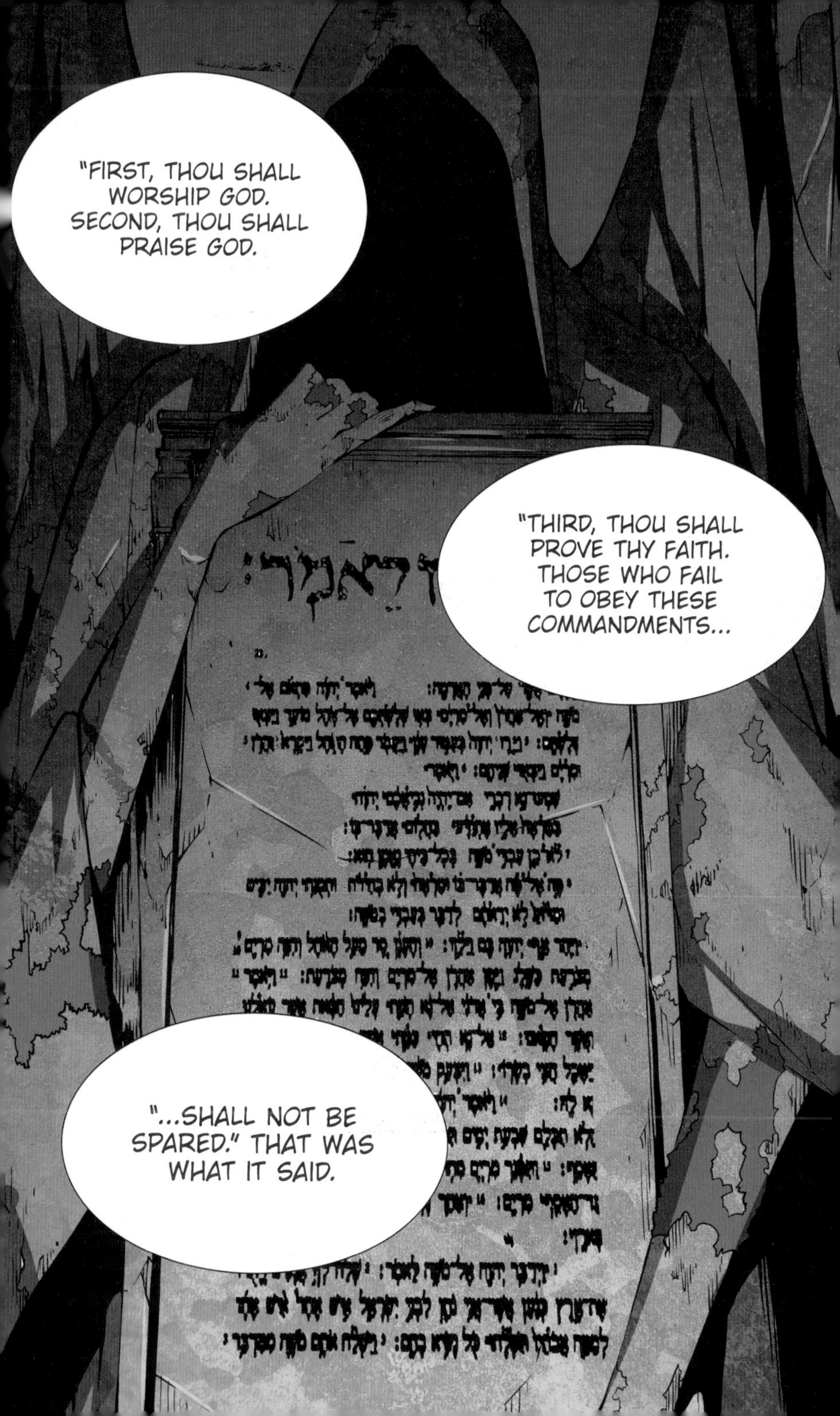
"FIRST, THOU SHALL WORSHIP GOD. SECOND, THOU SHALL PRAISE GOD.
"THIRD, THOU SHALL PROVE THY FAITH. THOSE WHO FAIL TO OBEY THESE COMMANDMENTS...
"...SHALL NOT BE SPARED." THAT WAS WHAT IT SAID.

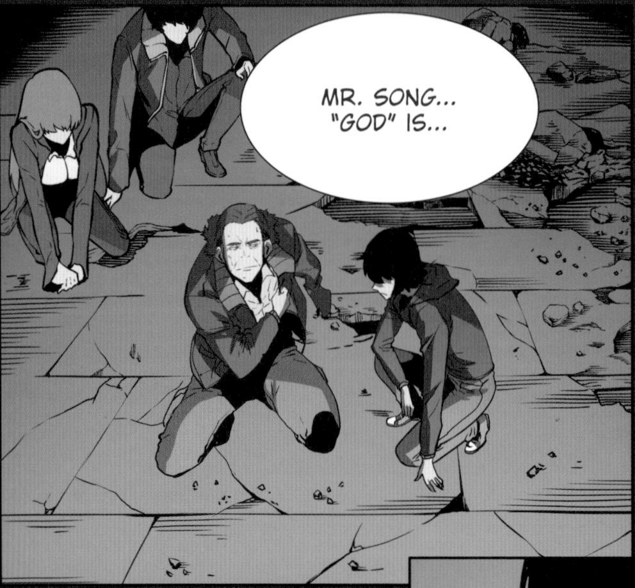
MR. SONG...
"GOD" IS...
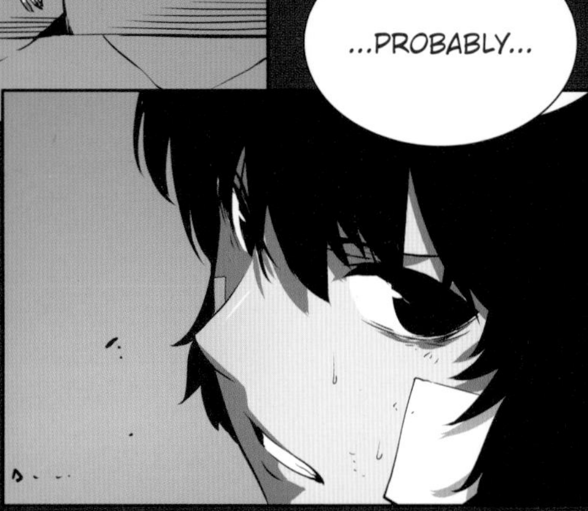
...PROBABLY...
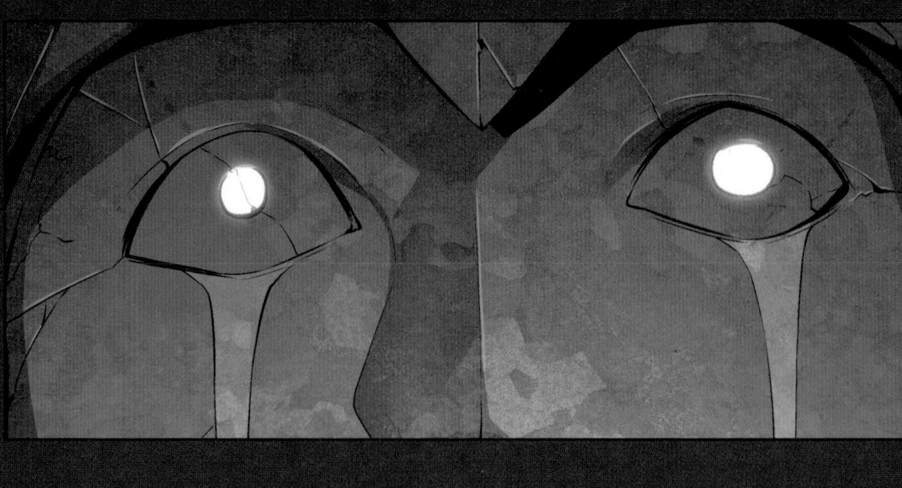

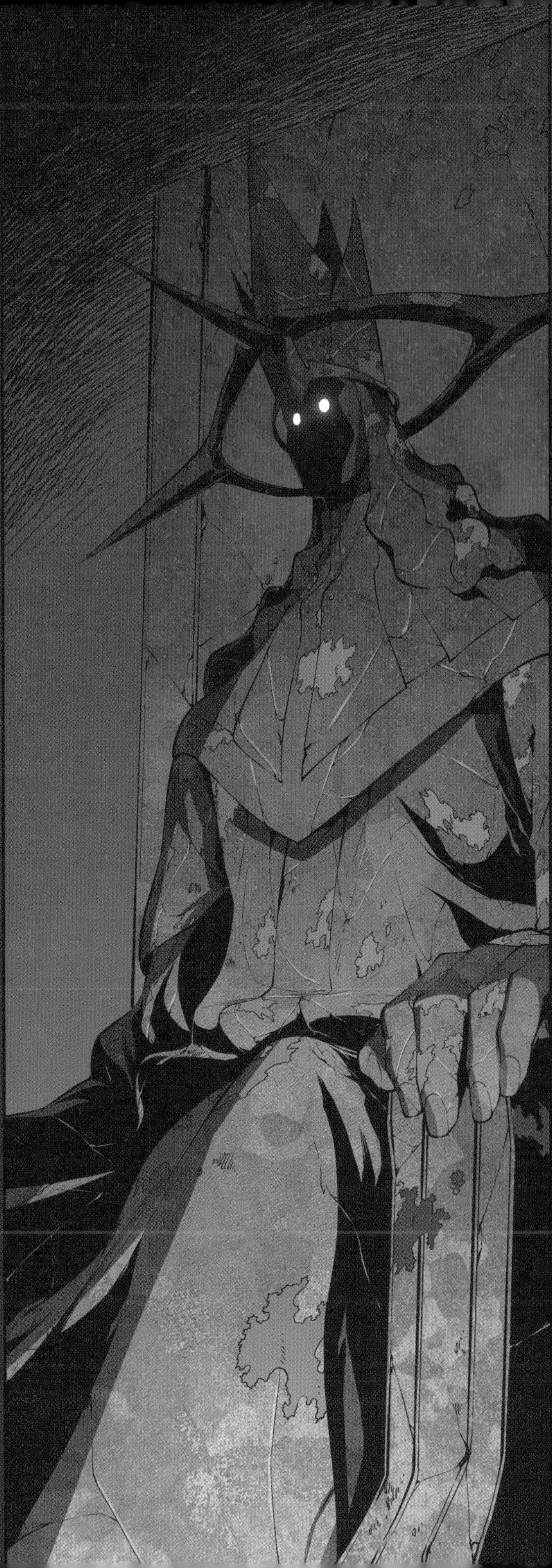

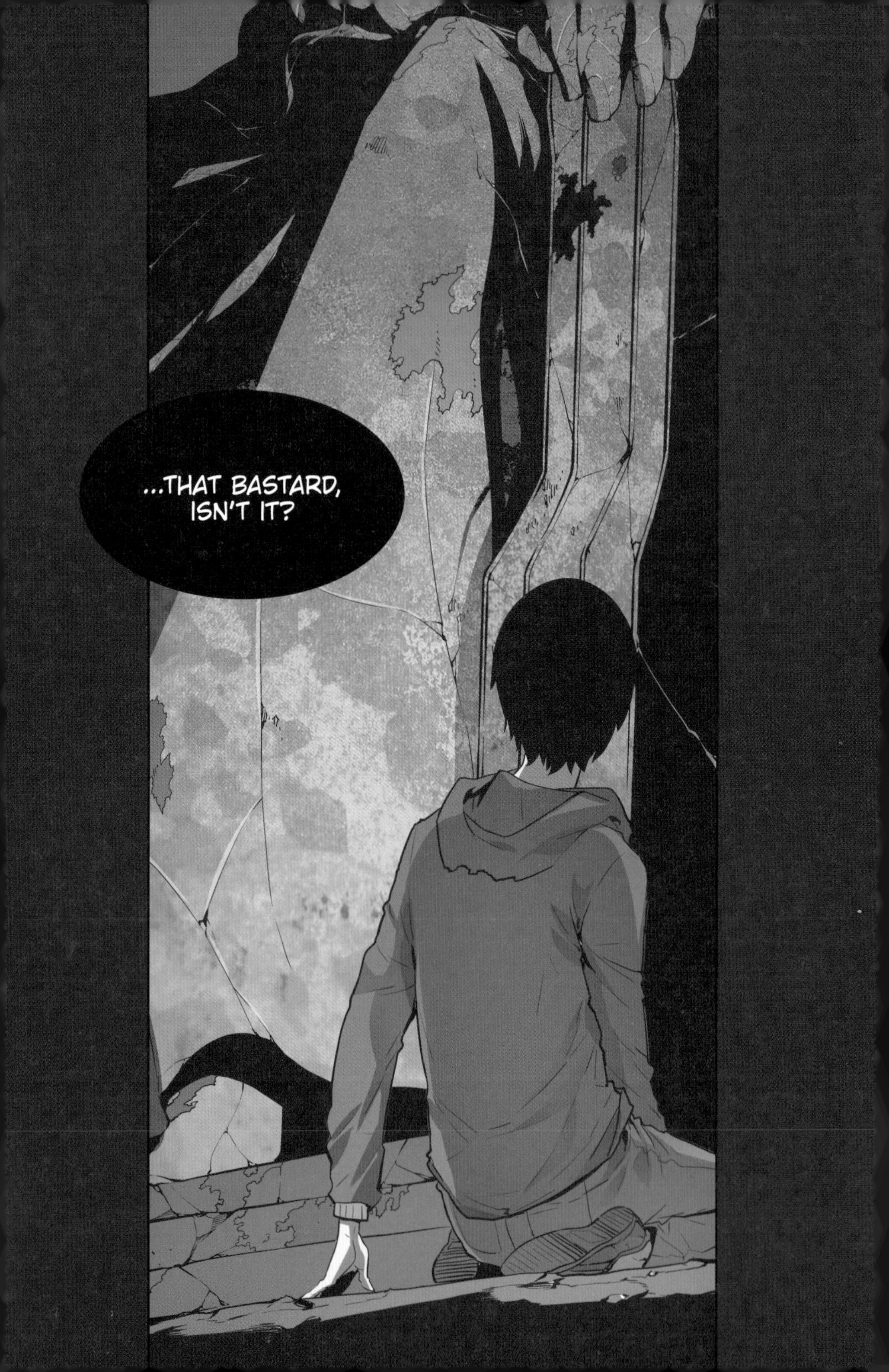
...THAT BASTARD, ISN'T IT?

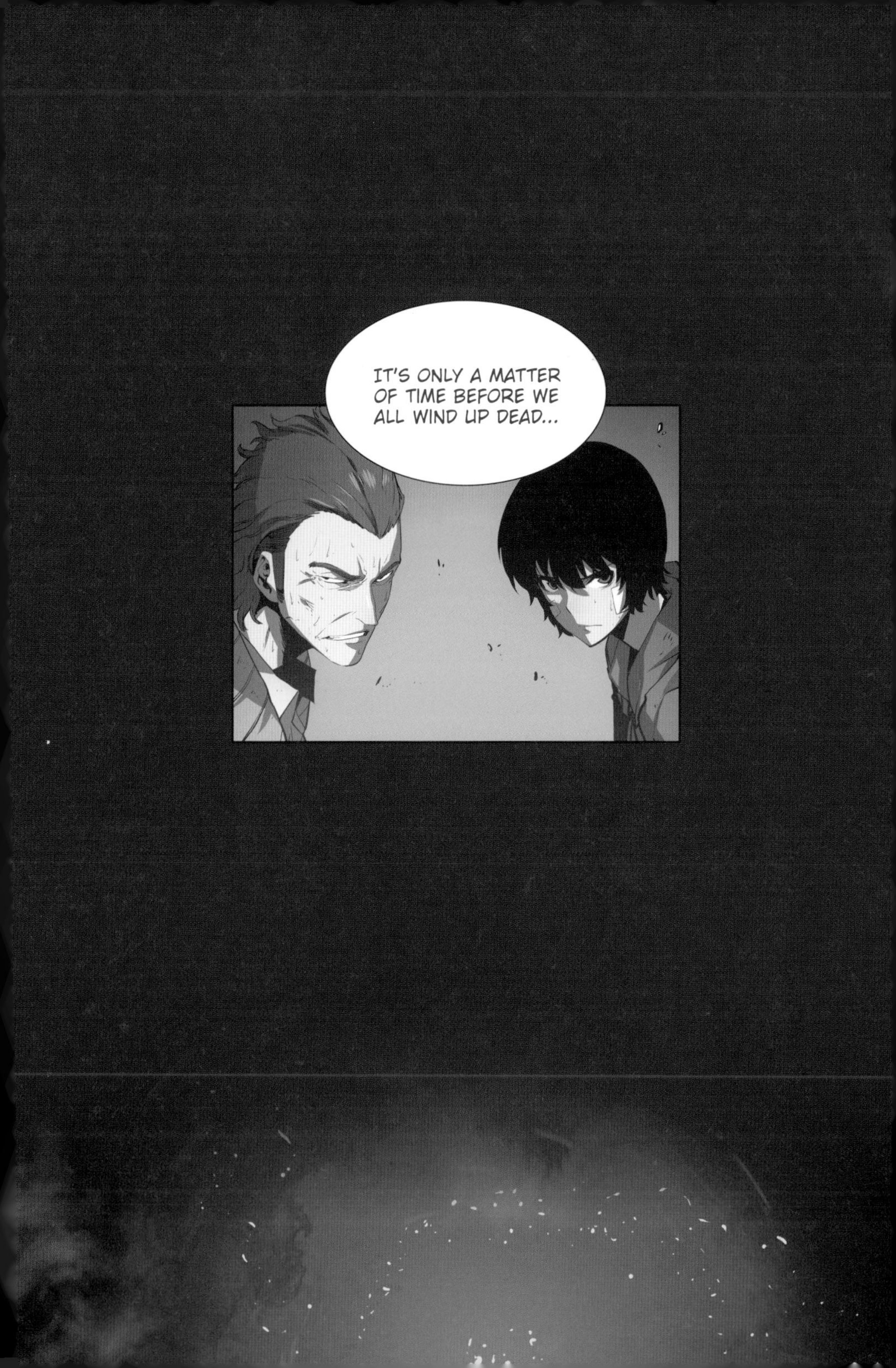
IT'S ONLY A MATTER OF TIME BEFORE WE ALL WIND UP DEAD...

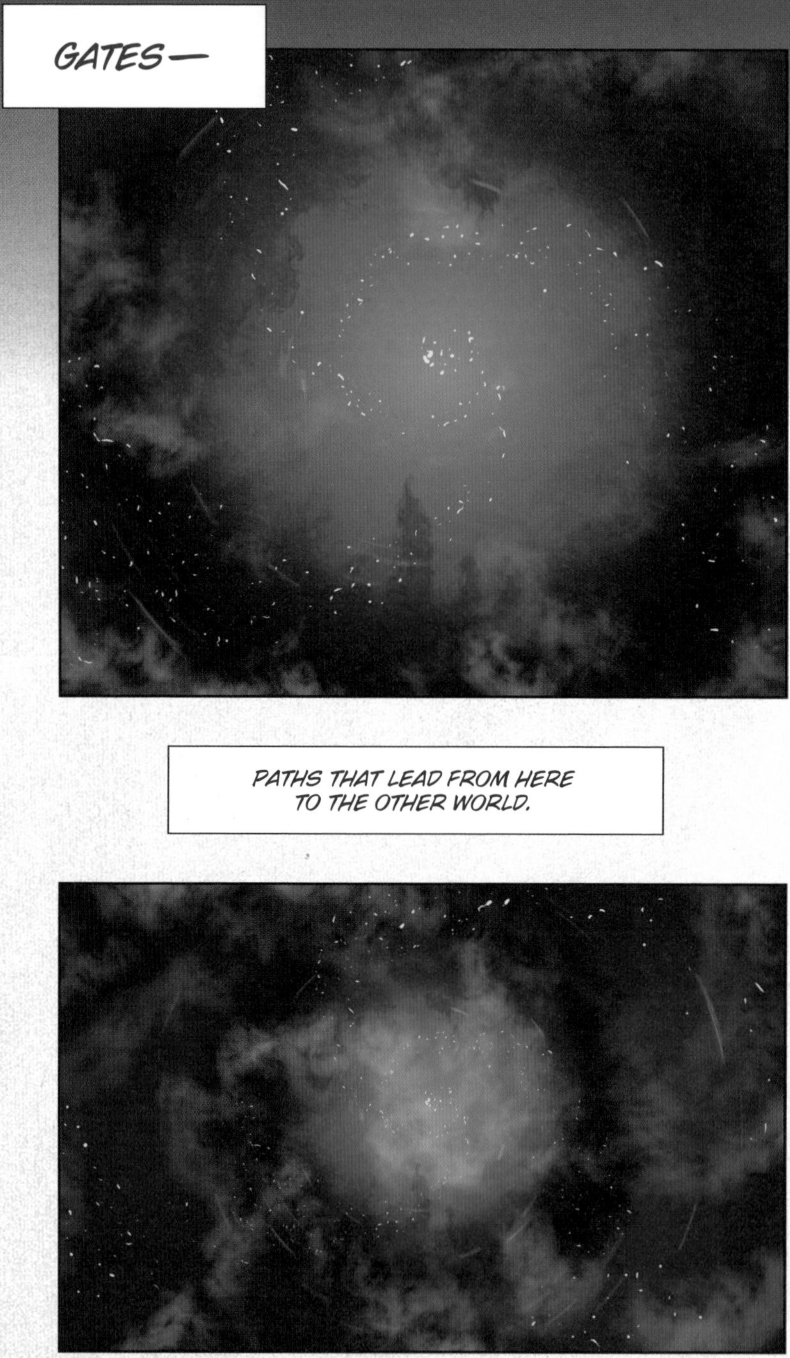
GATES—
PATHS THAT LEAD FROM HERE TO THE OTHER WORLD.

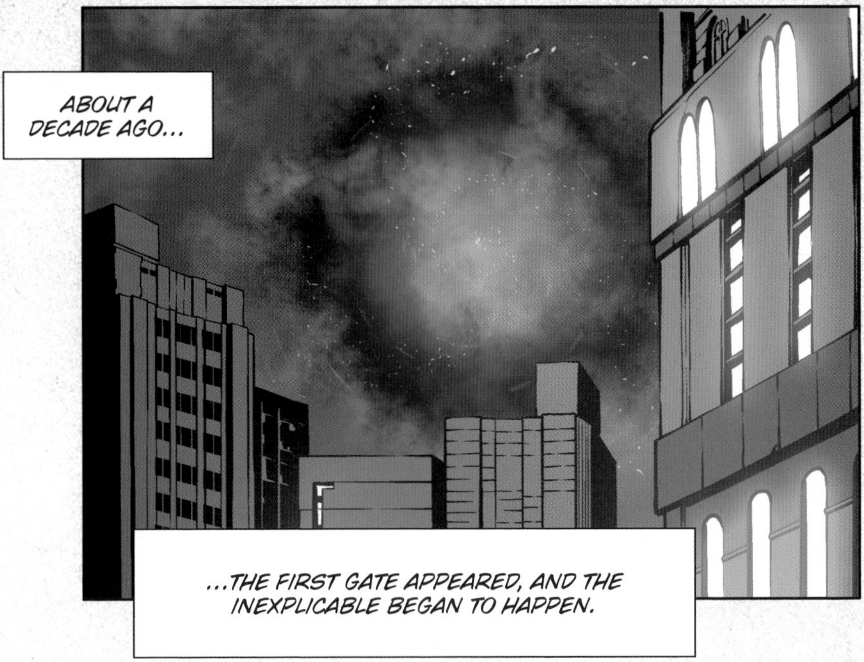
ABOUT A DECADE AGO...
...THE FIRST GATE APPEARED, AND THE INEXPLICABLE BEGAN TO HAPPEN.

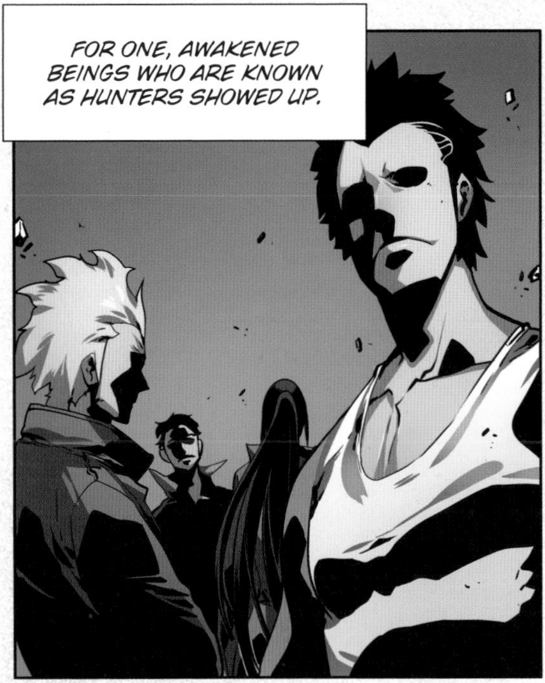
FOR ONE, AWAKENED BEINGS WHO ARE KNOWN AS HUNTERS SHOWED UP.

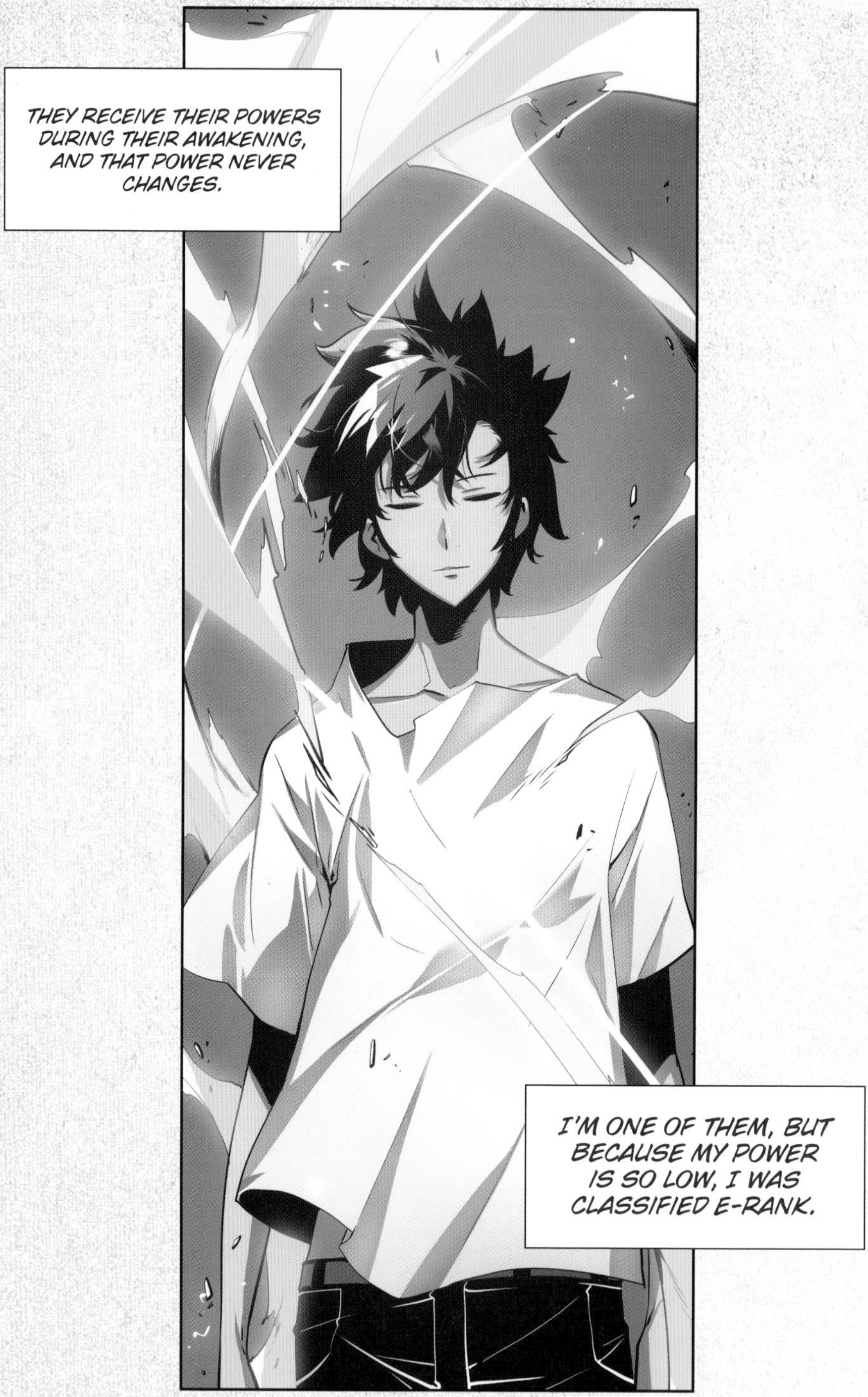
THEY RECEIVE THEIR POWERS DURING THEIR AWAKENING, AND THAT POWER NEVER CHANGES.
I'M ONE OF THEM, BUT BECAUSE MY POWER IS SO LOW, I WAS CLASSIFIED E-RANK.

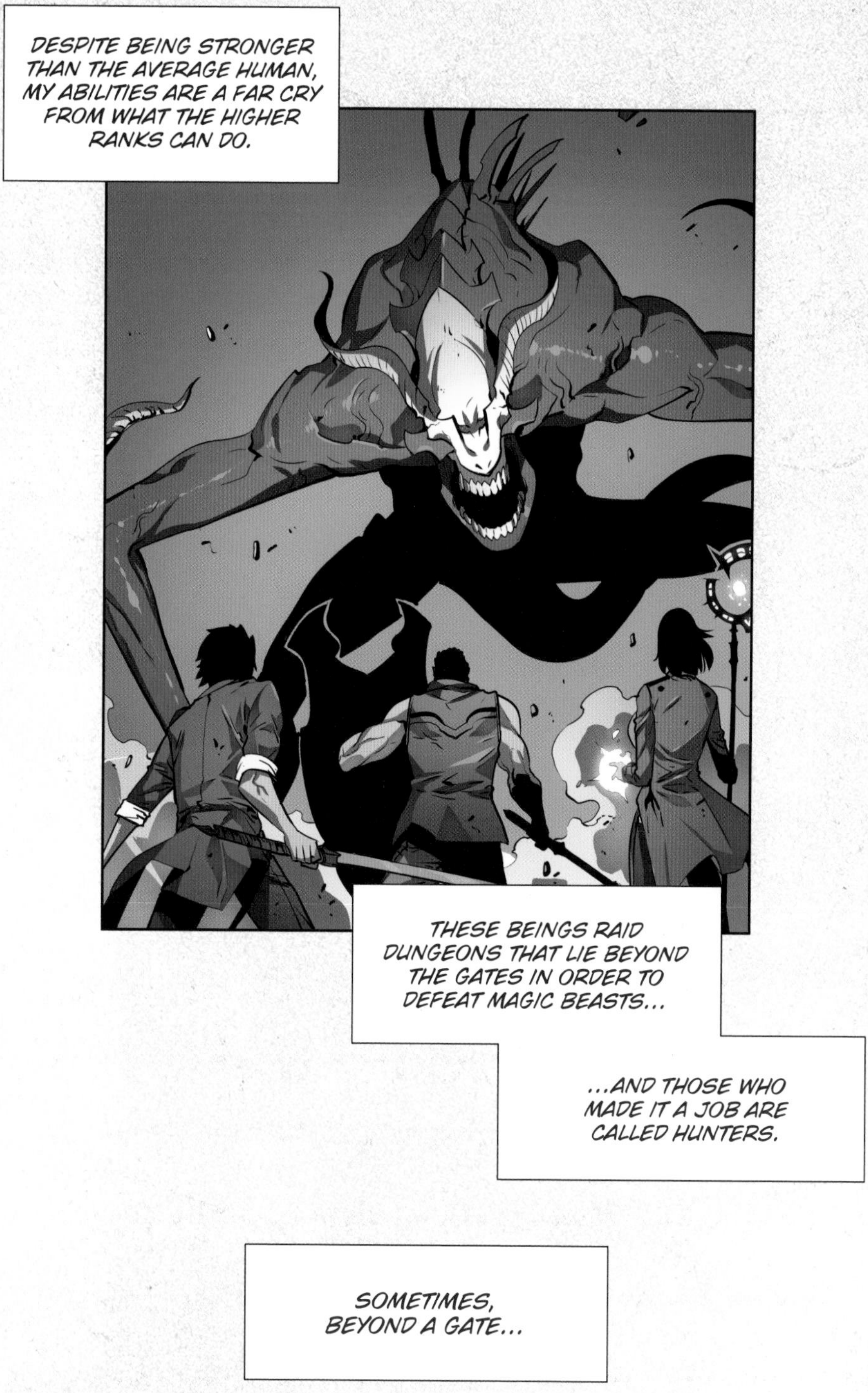
DESPITE BEING STRONGER THAN THE AVERAGE HUMAN, MY ABILITIES ARE A FAR CRY FROM WHAT THE HIGHER RANKS CAN DO.
THESE BEINGS RAID DUNGEONS THAT LIE BEYOND THE GATES IN ORDER TO DEFEAT MAGIC BEASTS...
...AND THOSE WHO MADE IT A JOB ARE CALLED HUNTERS.
SOMETIMES, BEYOND A GATE...

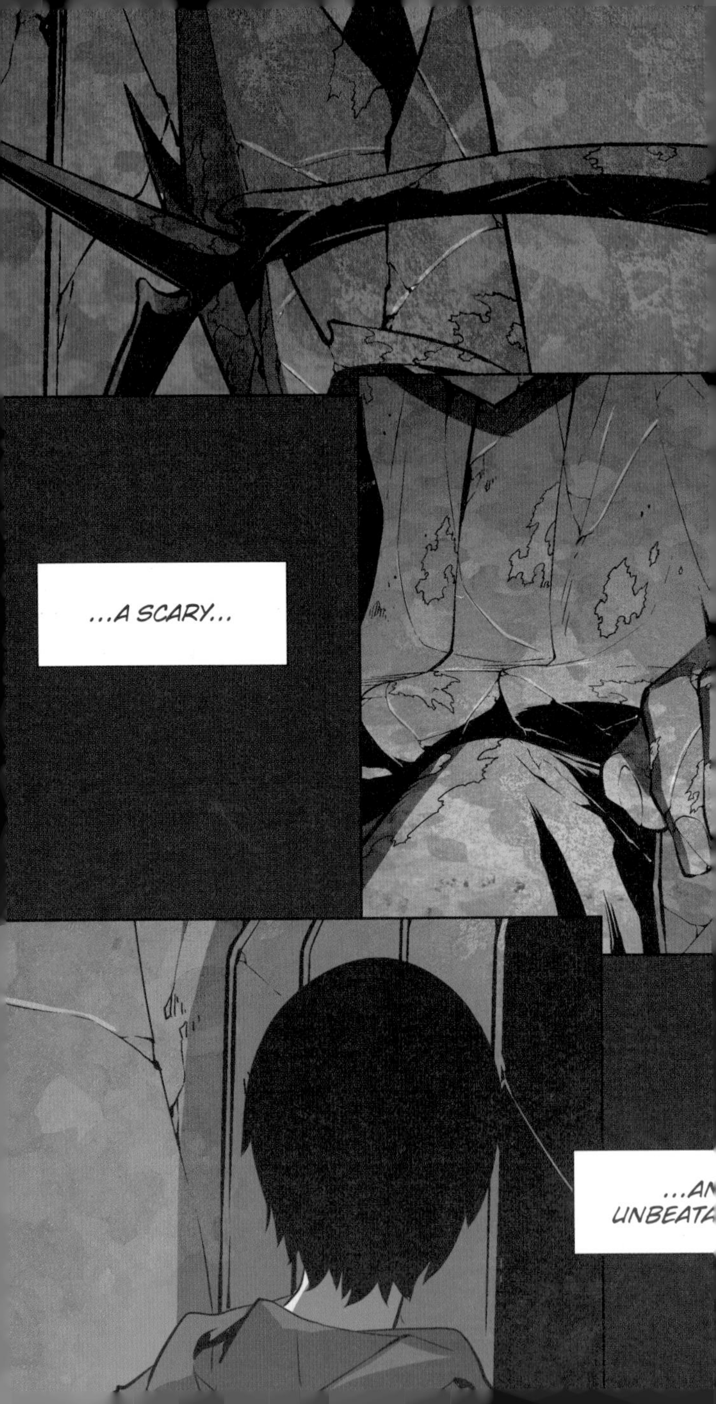
...A SCARY...
...AN
UNBEATA

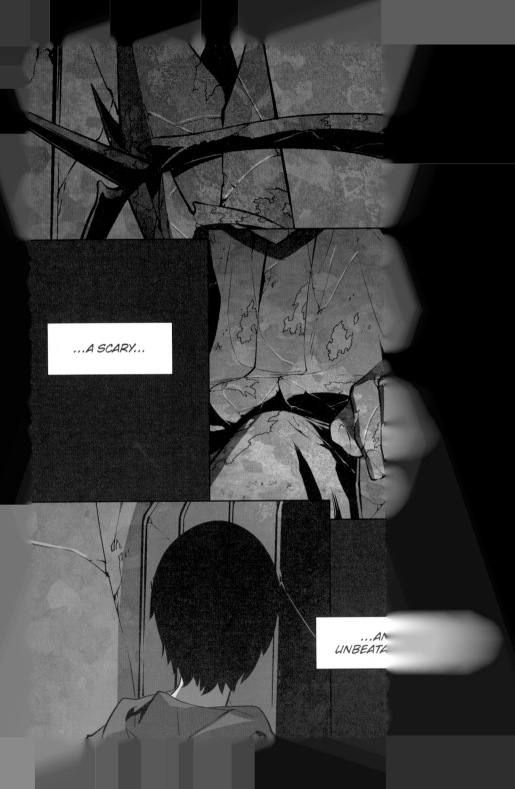

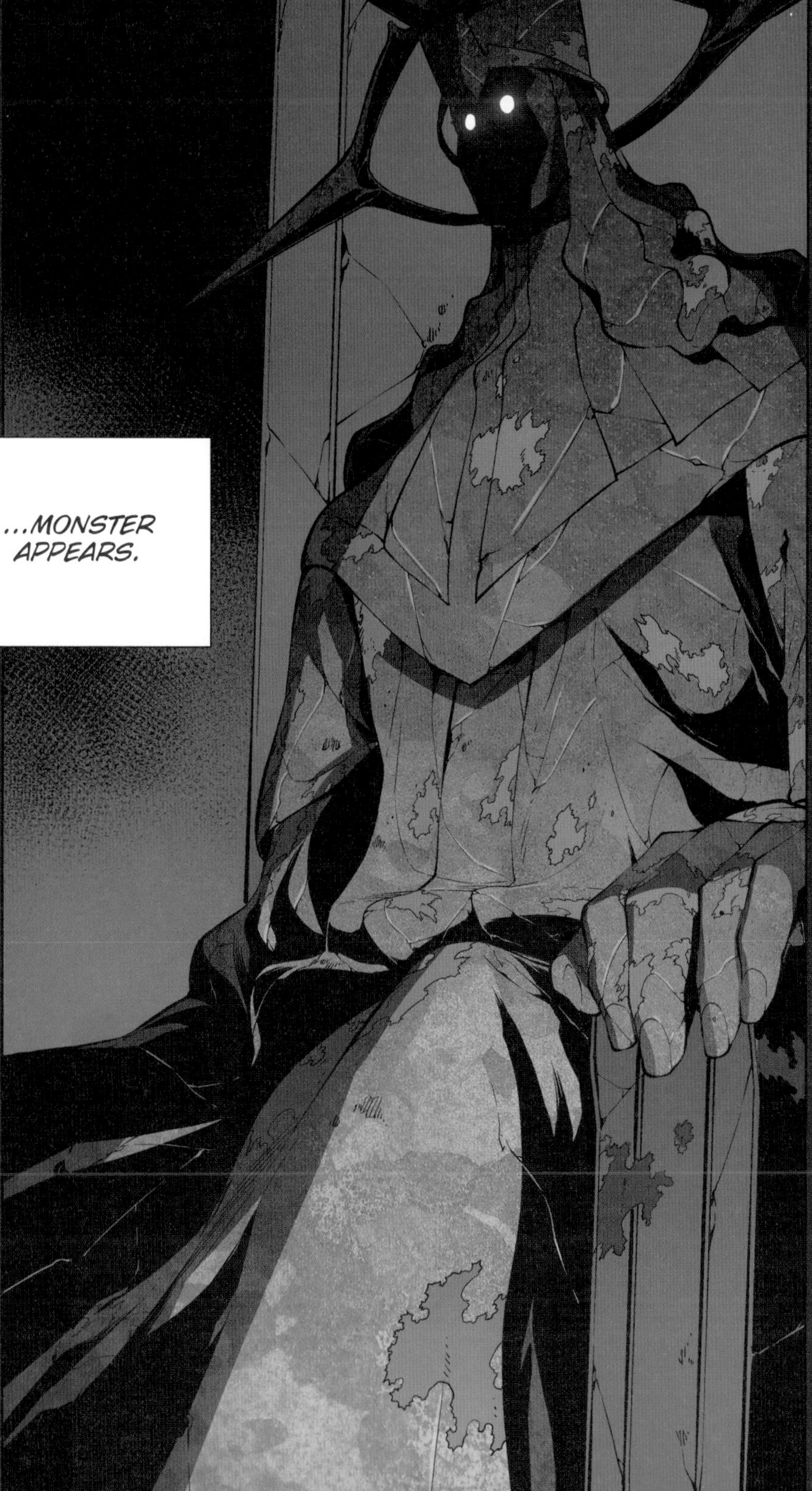
...MONSTER APPEARS.

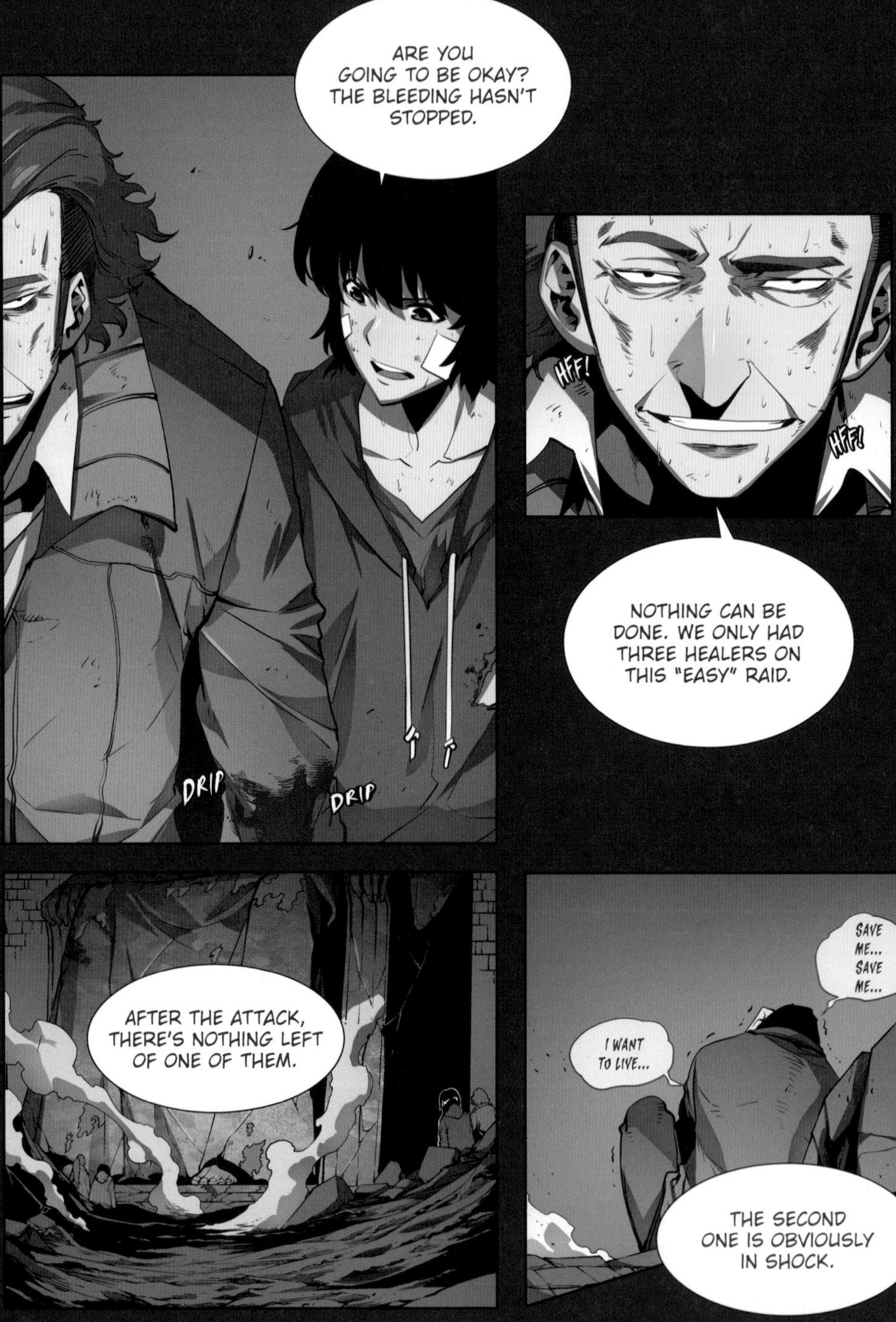
ARE YOU GOING TO BE OKAY? THE BLEEDING HASN'T STOPPED.
DRIP
DRIP
HFF!
HFF!
NOTHING CAN BE DONE. WE ONLY HAD THREE HEALERS ON THIS "EASY" RAID.
AFTER THE ATTACK, THERE'S NOTHING LEFT OF ONE OF THEM.
SAVE ME... SAVE ME...
I WANT TO LIVE...
THE SECOND ONE IS OBVIOUSLY IN SHOCK.

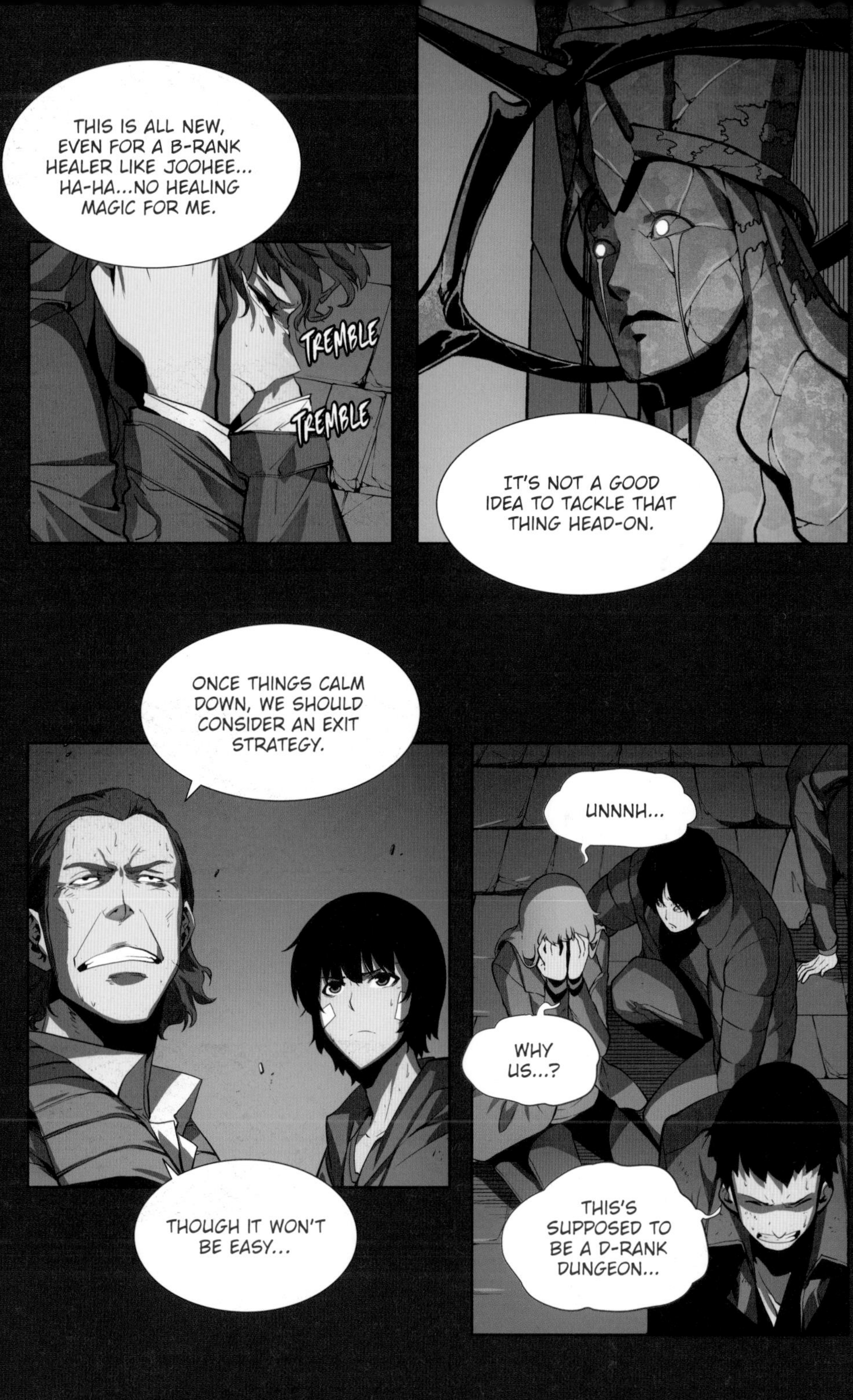

THIS IS ALL NEW, EVEN FOR A B-RANK HEALER LIKE JOOHEE... HA-HA...NO HEALING MAGIC FOR ME.
TREMBLE
TREMBLE
IT'S NOT A GOOD IDEA TO TACKLE THAT THING HEAD-ON.
ONCE THINGS CALM DOWN, WE SHOULD CONSIDER AN EXIT STRATEGY.
THOUGH IT WON'T BE EASY...
UNNNH...
WHY US...?
THIS'S SUPPOSED TO BE A D-RANK DUNGEON...

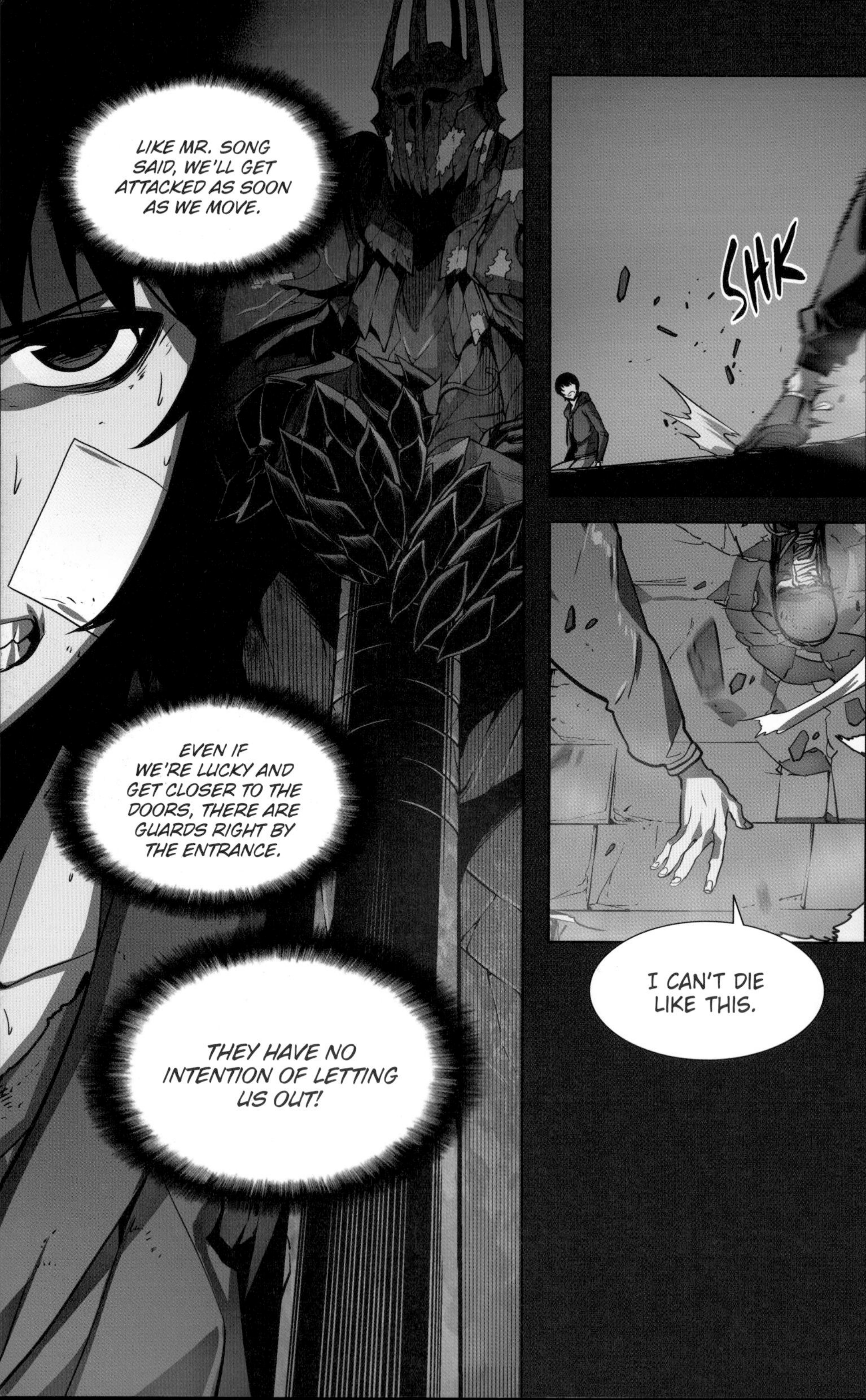
LIKE MR. SONG SAID, WE'LL GET ATTACKED AS SOON AS WE MOVE.
EVEN IF WE'RE LUCKY AND GET CLOSER TO THE DOORS, THERE ARE GUARDS RIGHT BY THE ENTRANCE.
THEY HAVE NO INTENTION OF LETTING US OUT!
SHK
I CAN'T DIE LIKE THIS.

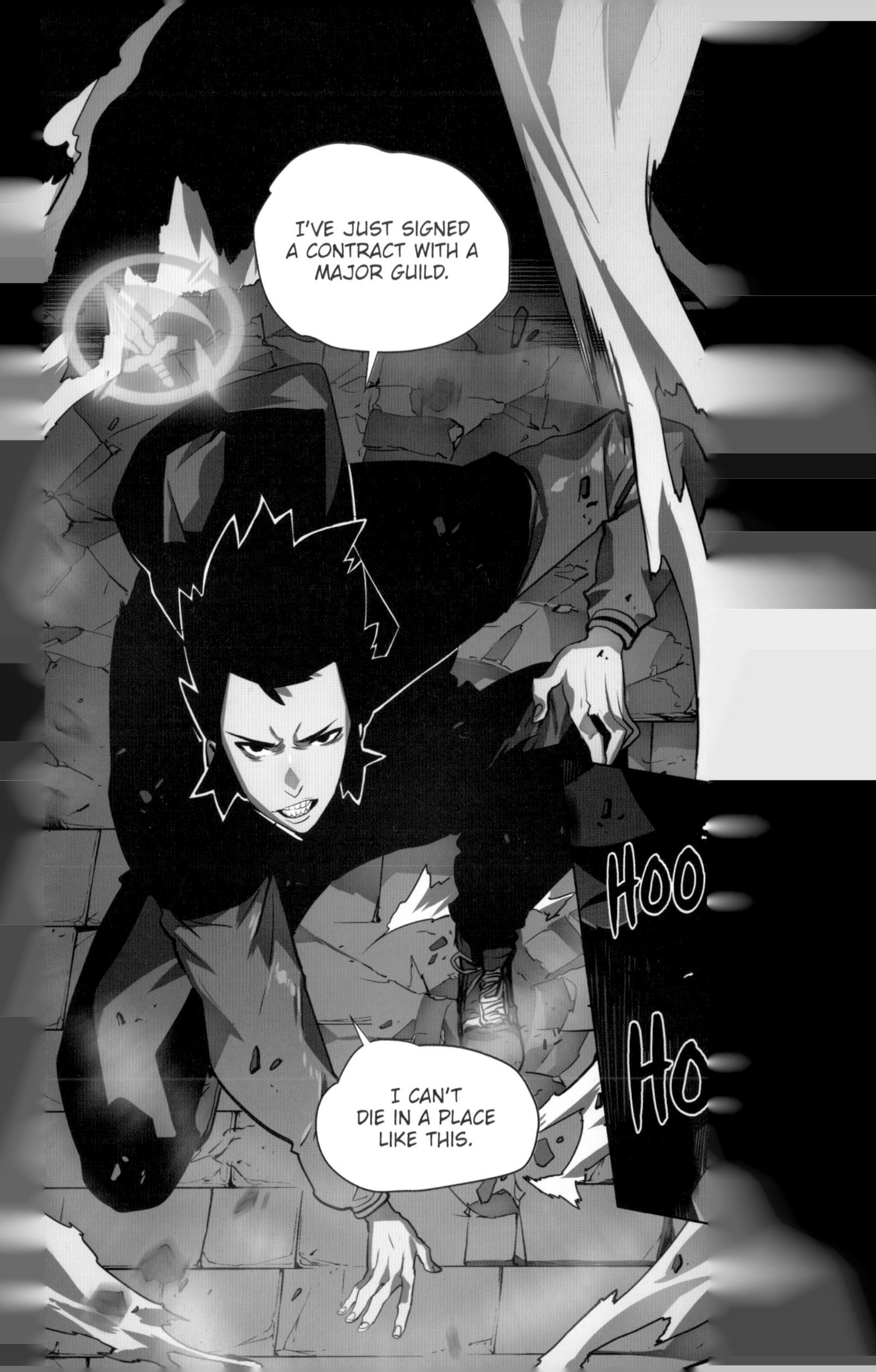
I'VE JUST SIGNED A CONTRACT WITH A MAJOR GUILD.
HOO
HO
I CAN'T DIE IN A PLACE LIKE THIS.

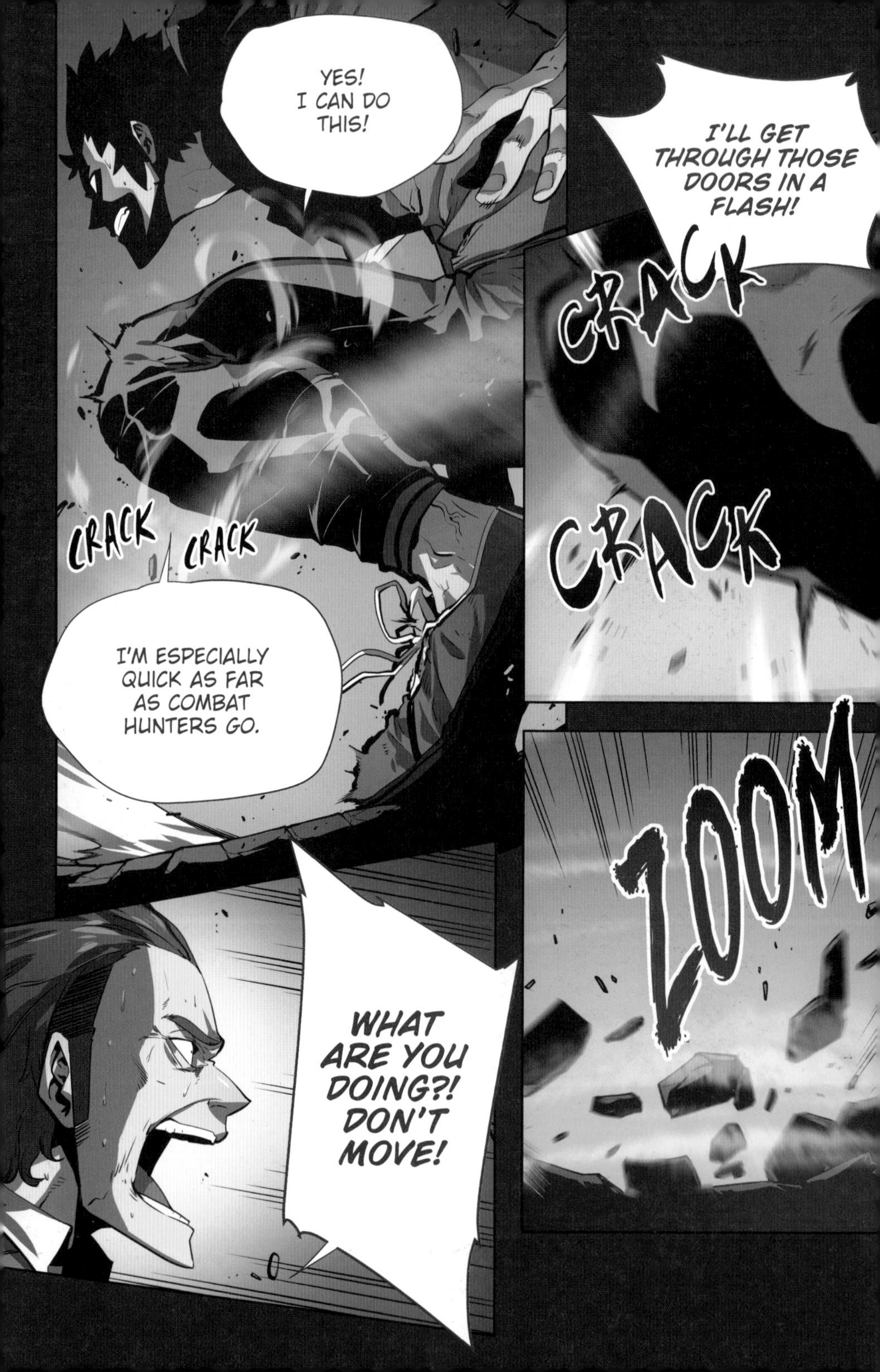
YES! I CAN DO THIS!
CRACK
CRACK
I'M ESPECIALLY QUICK AS FAR AS COMBAT HUNTERS GO.
I'LL GET THROUGH THOSE DOORS IN A FLASH!
CRACK
CRACK
ZOOM
WHAT ARE YOU DOING?! DON'T MOVE!

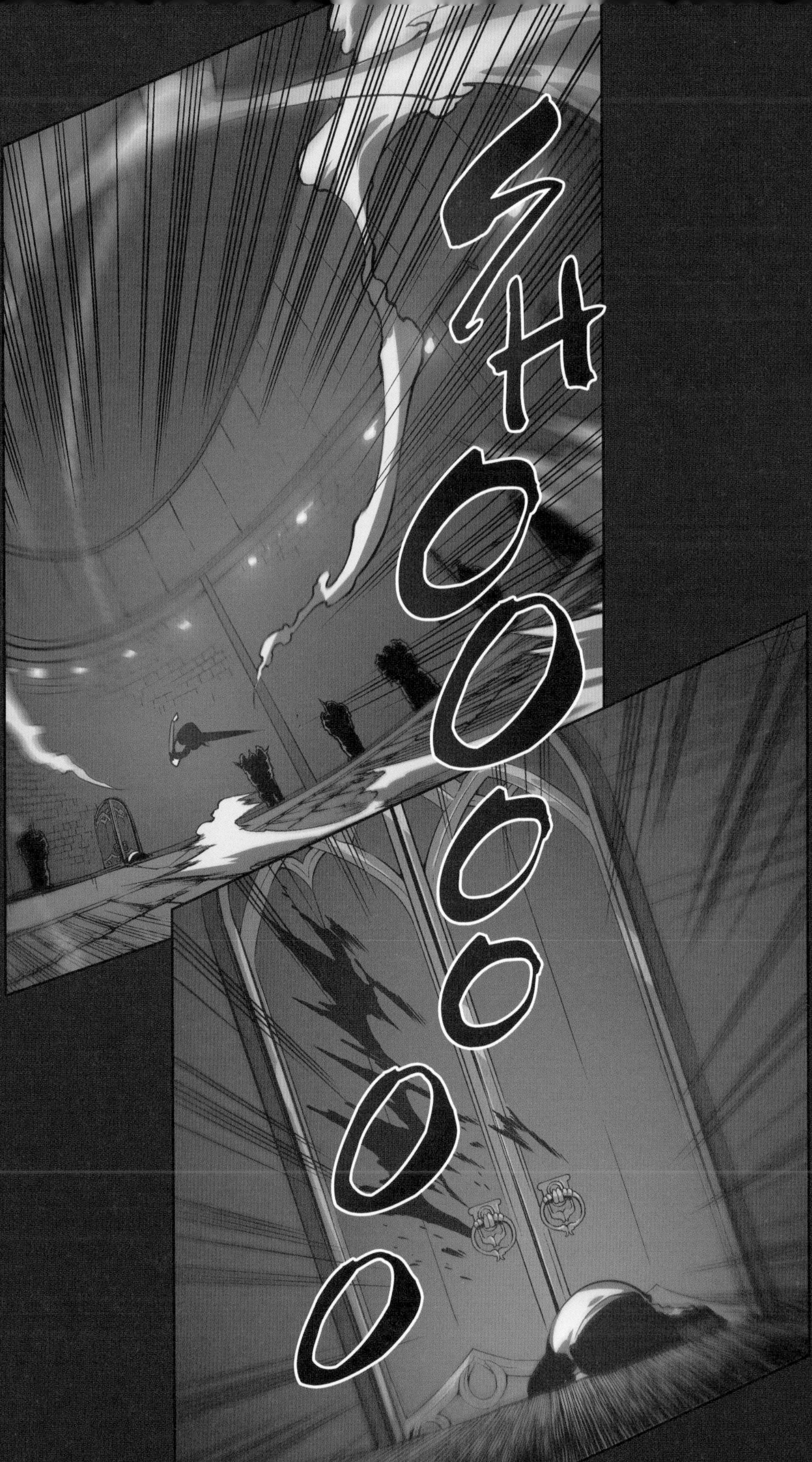
SHOOOOOO

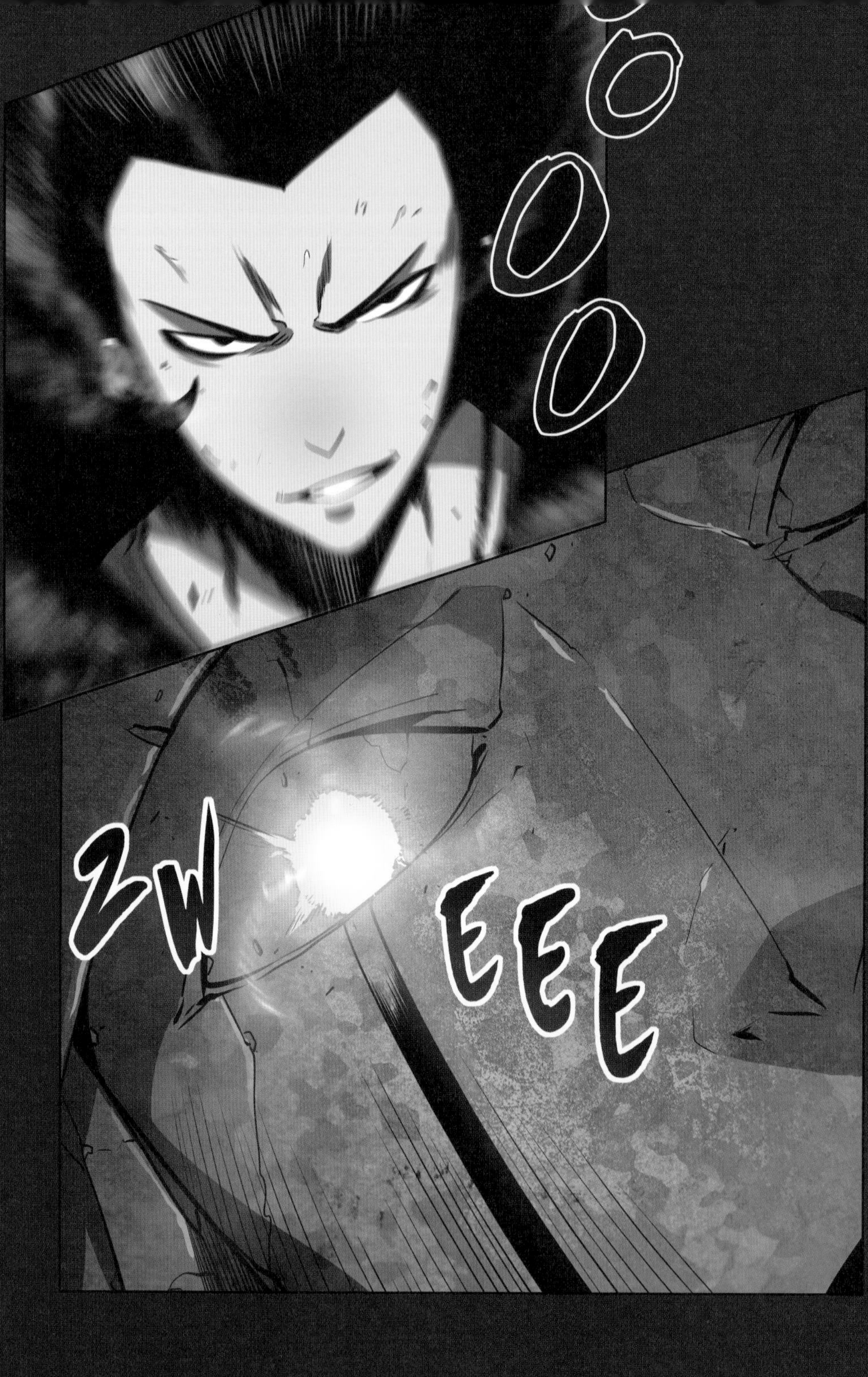
OOOO
ZWEEE

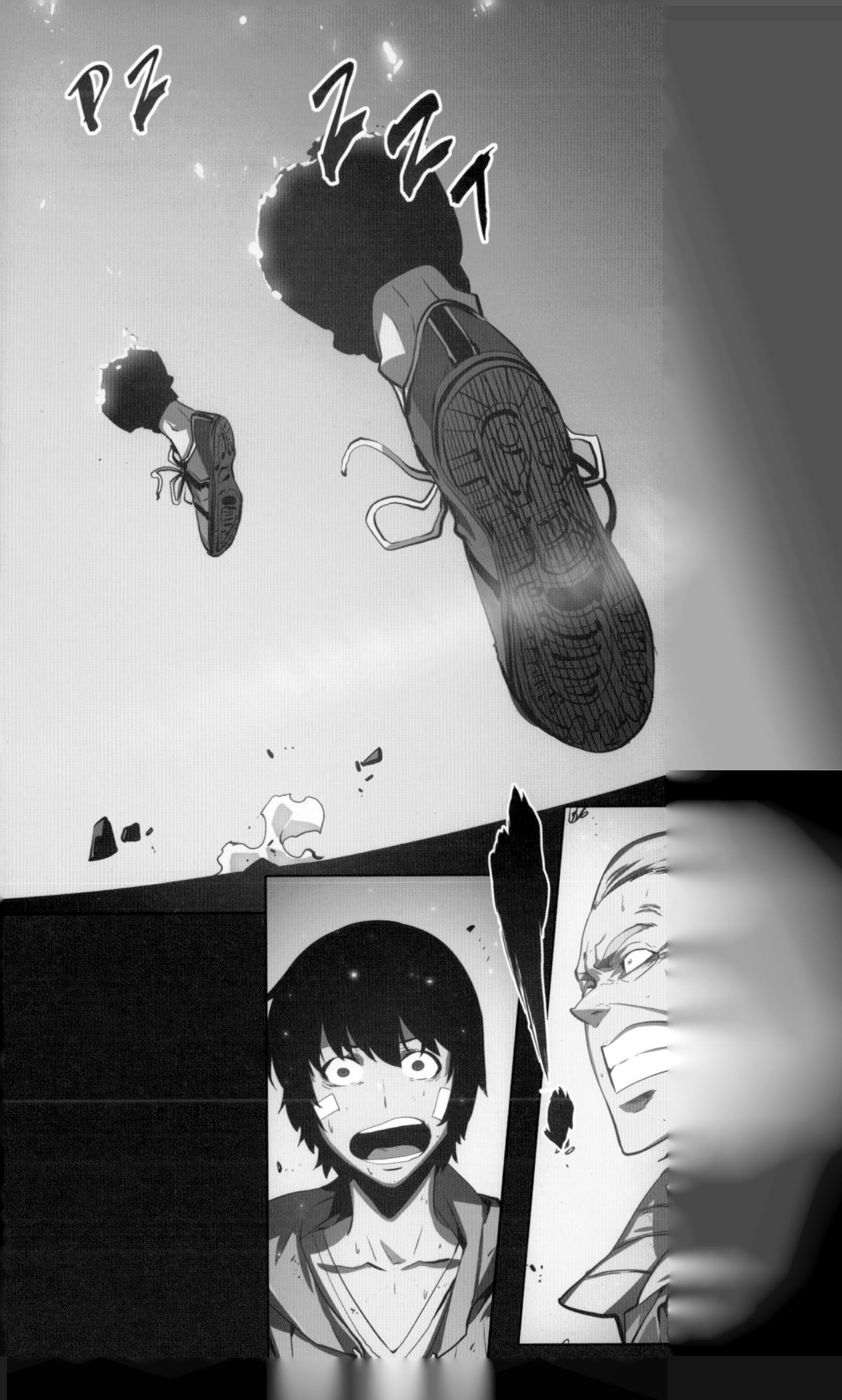
PZ
ZZZT

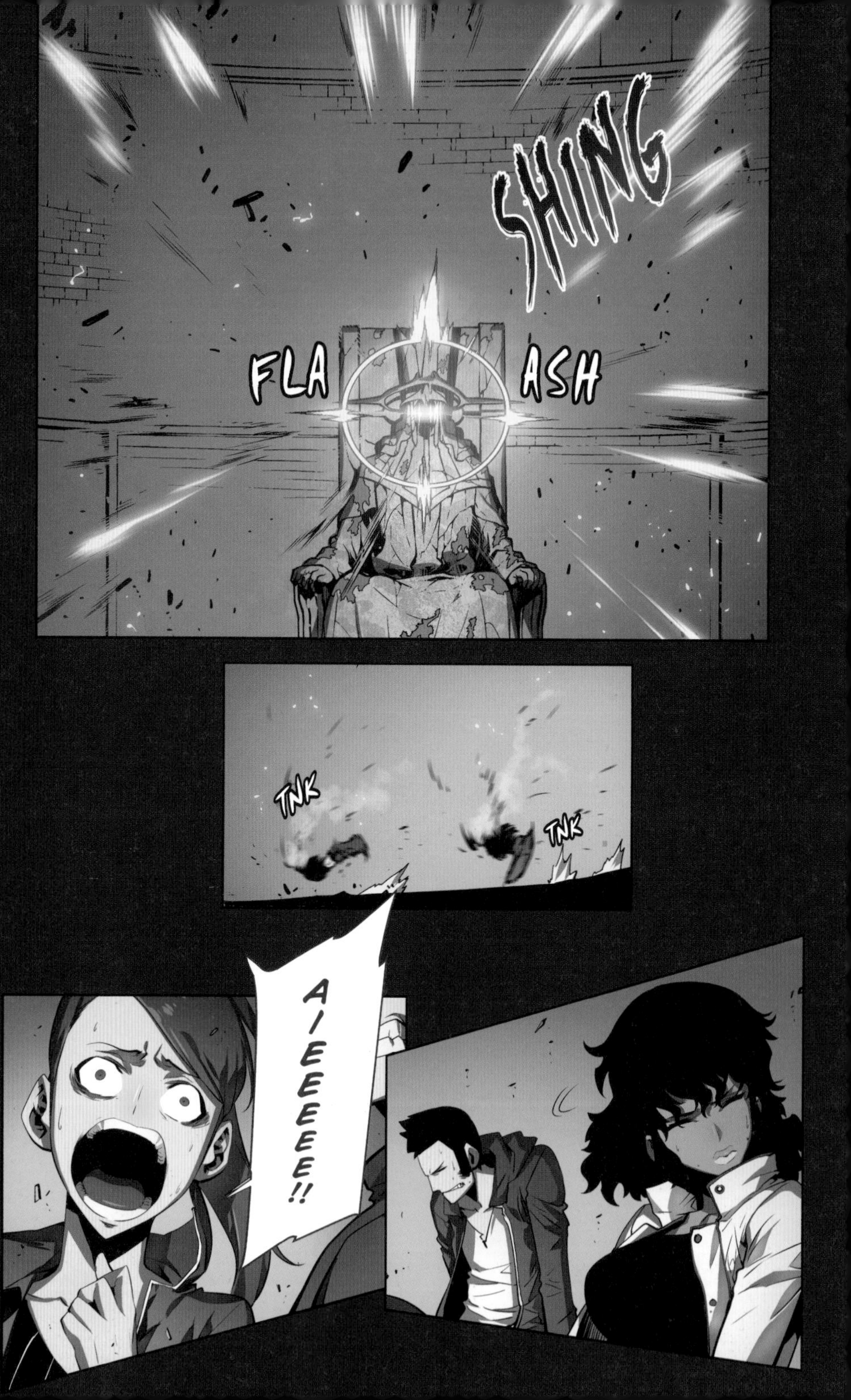
SHING
FLA ASH
TNK
TNK
AIEEEEEE!!

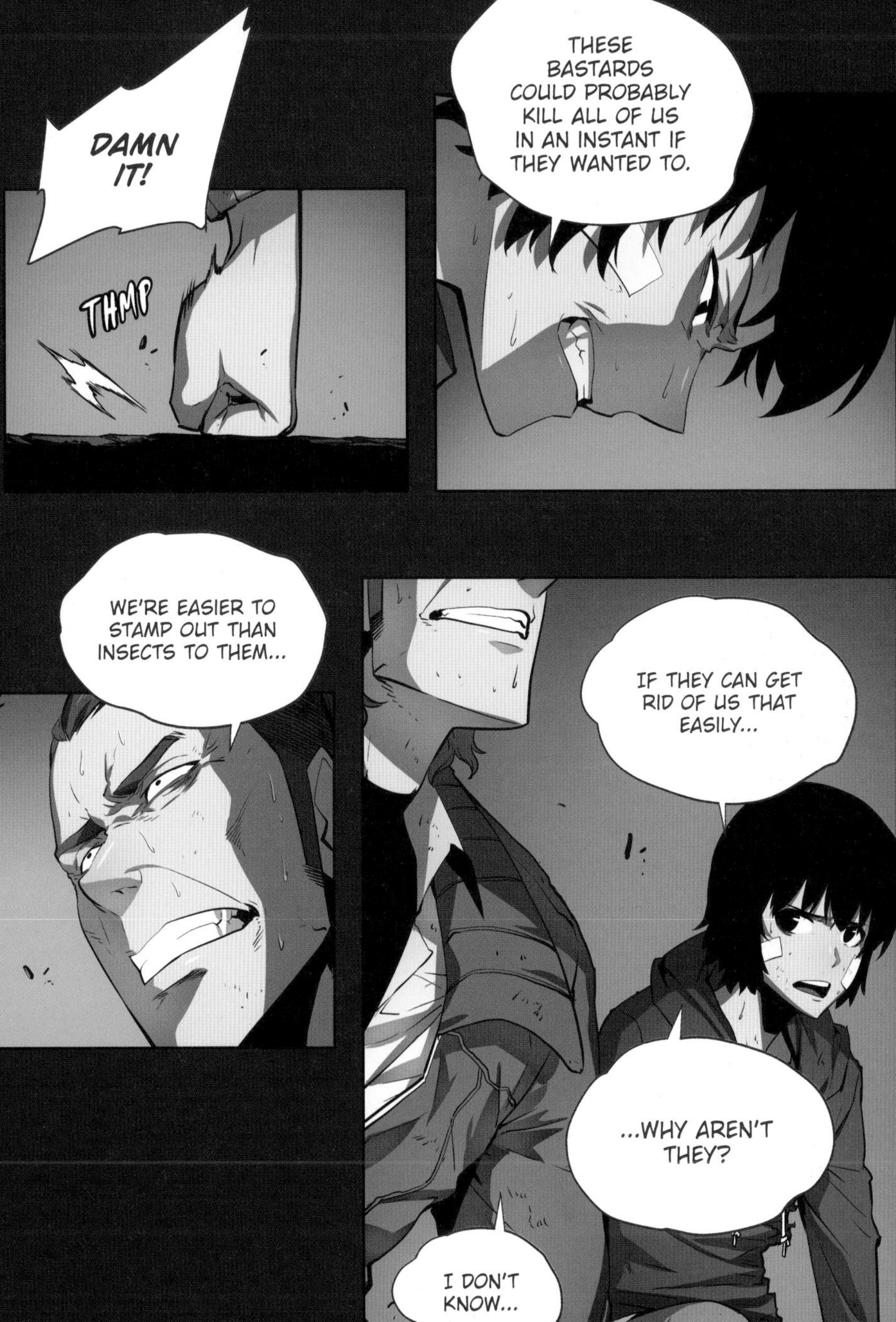
DAMN IT!
THMP
THESE BASTARDS COULD PROBABLY KILL ALL OF US IN AN INSTANT IF THEY WANTED TO.
WE'RE EASIER TO STAMP OUT THAN INSECTS TO THEM...
IF THEY CAN GET RID OF US THAT EASILY...
...WHY AREN'T THEY?
I DON'T KNOW...

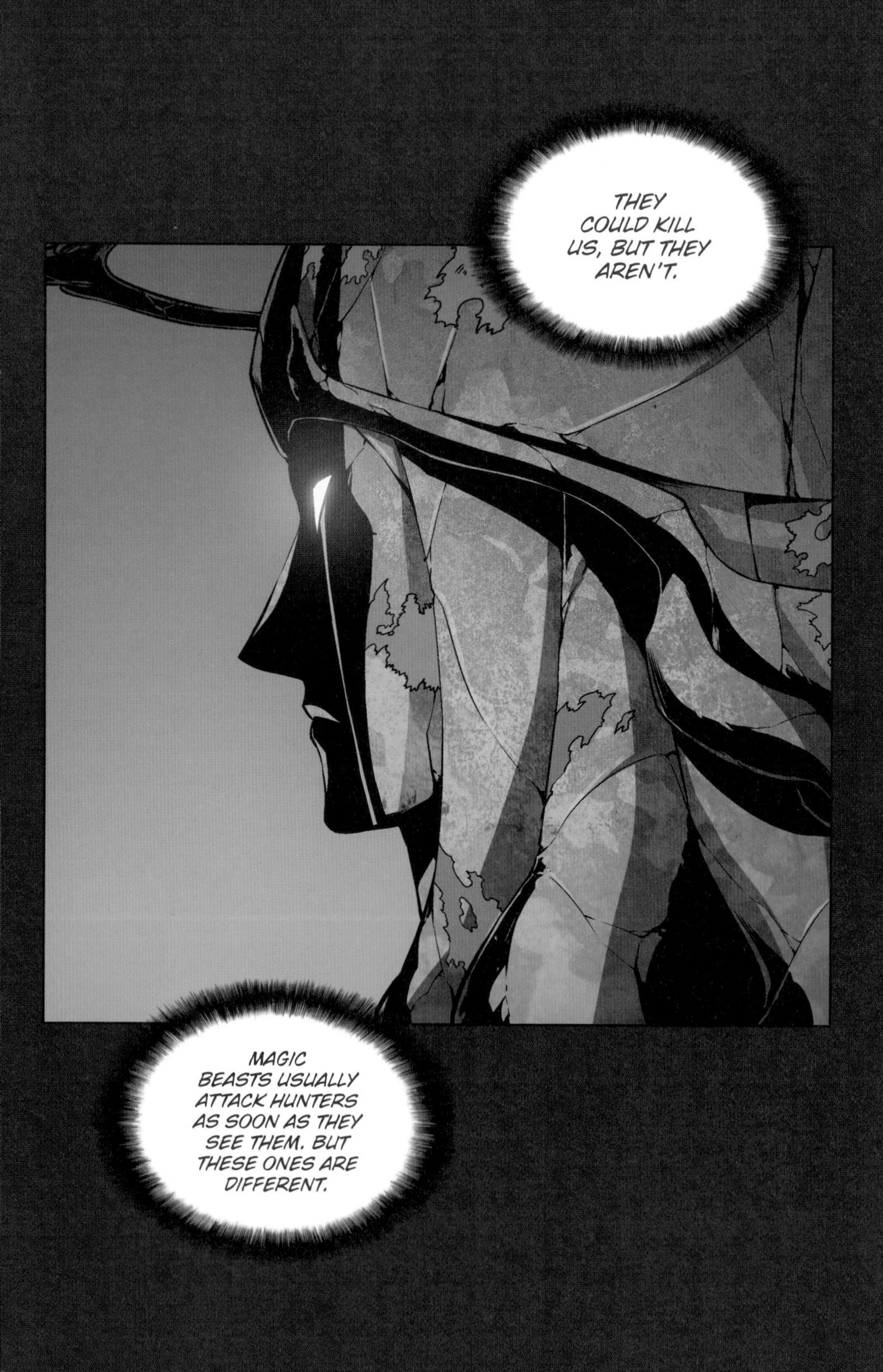
THEY COULD KILL US, BUT THEY AREN'T.
MAGIC BEASTS USUALLY ATTACK HUNTERS AS SOON AS THEY SEE THEM. BUT THESE ONES ARE DIFFERENT.

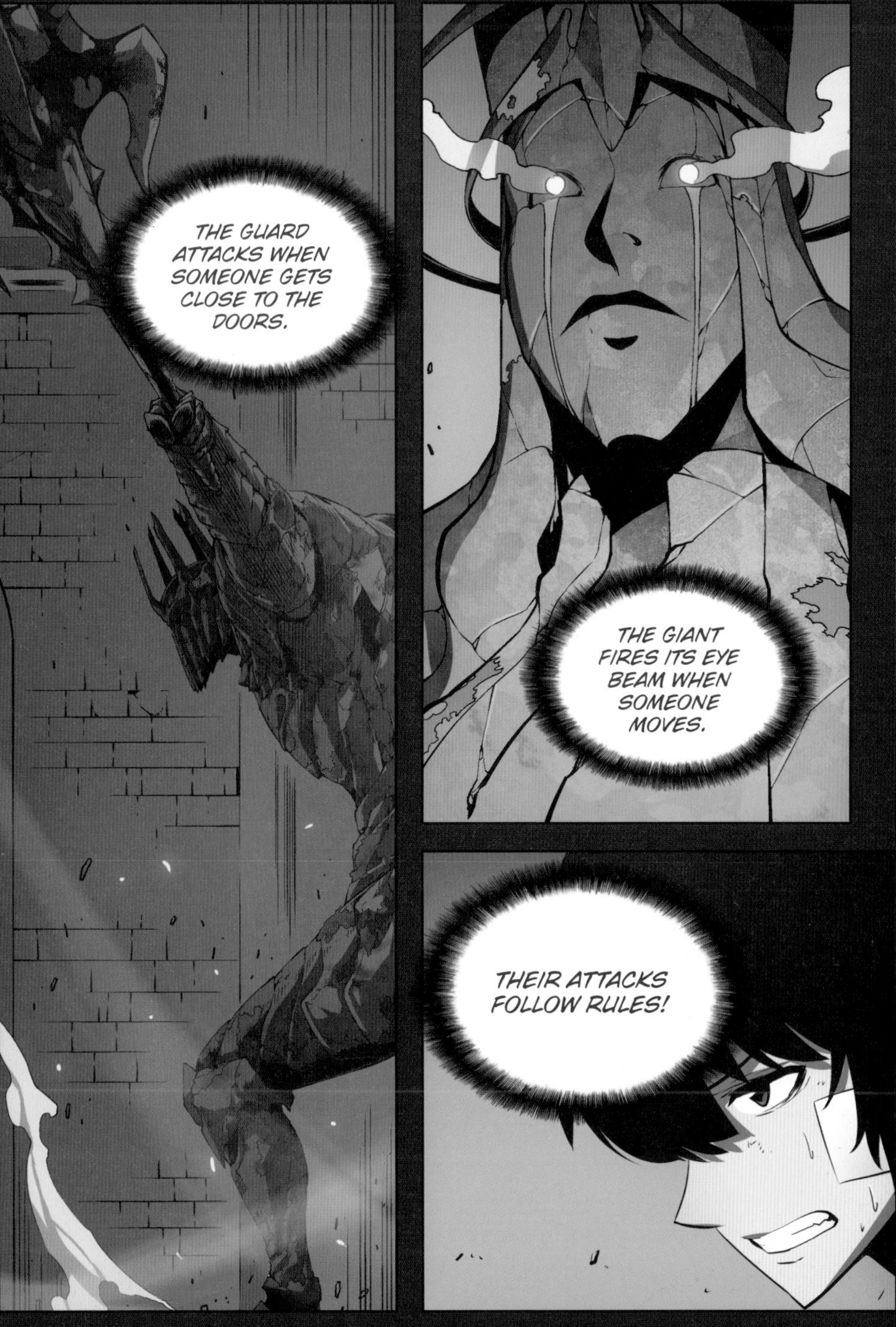
THE GUARD ATTACKS WHEN SOMEONE GETS CLOSE TO THE DOORS.
THE GIANT FIRES ITS EYE BEAM WHEN SOMEONE MOVES.
THEIR ATTACKS FOLLOW RULES!

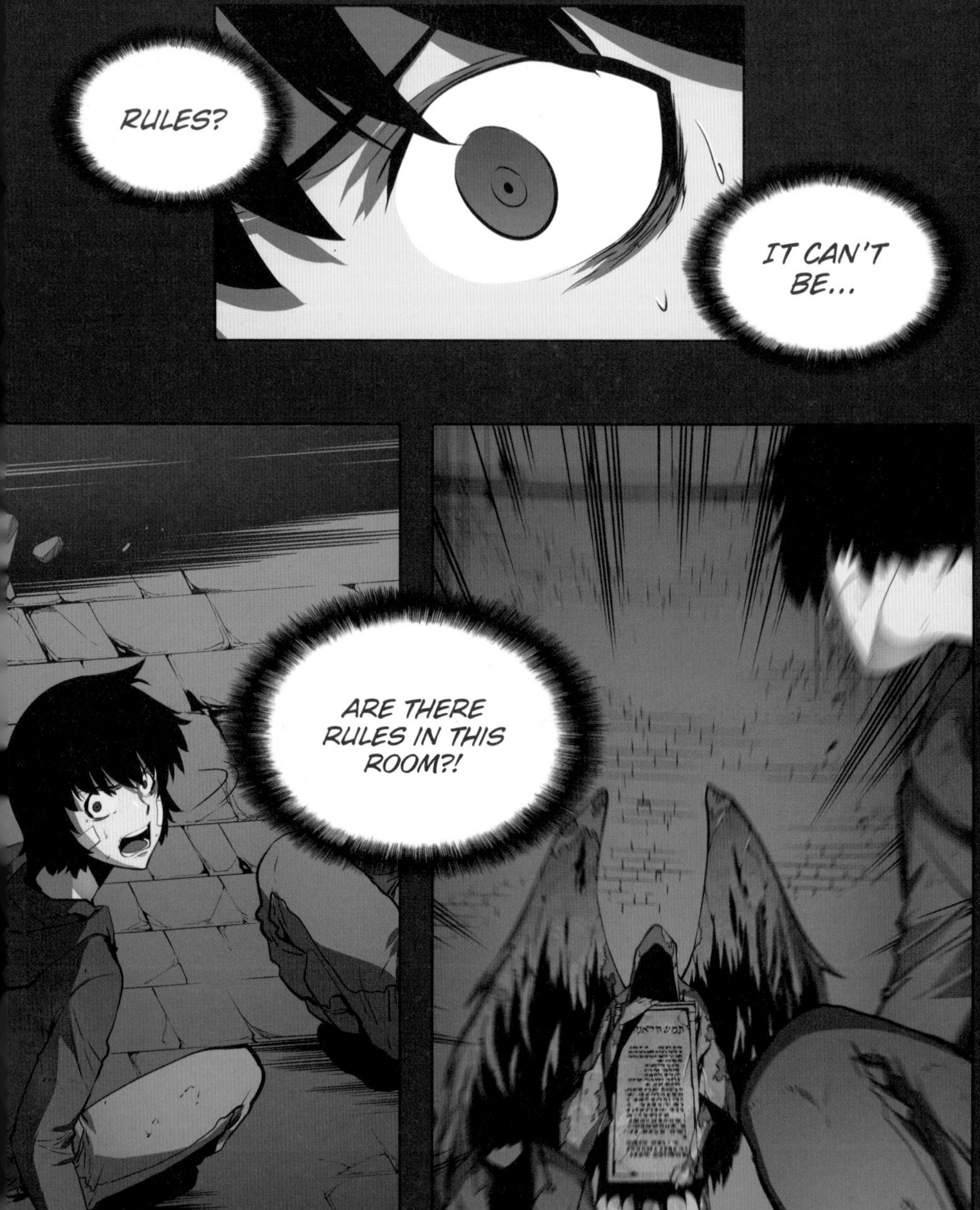
RULES?
IT CAN'T BE...
ARE THERE RULES IN THIS ROOM?!

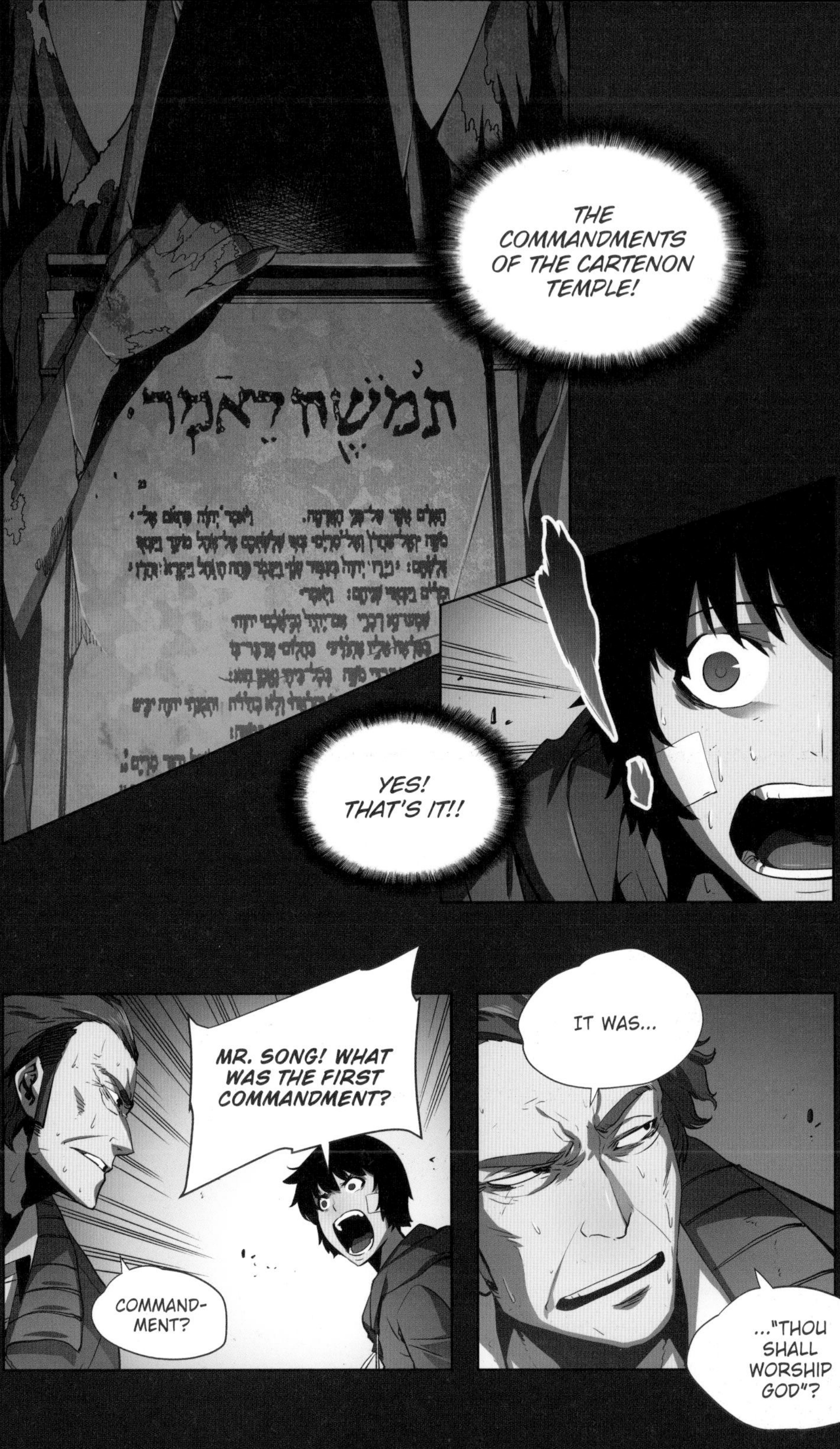
THE COMMANDMENTS OF THE CARTENON TEMPLE!
YES! THAT'S IT!!
MR. SONG! WHAT WAS THE FIRST COMMANDMENT?
COMMAND-MENT?
IT WAS...
..."THOU SHALL WORSHIP GOD"?

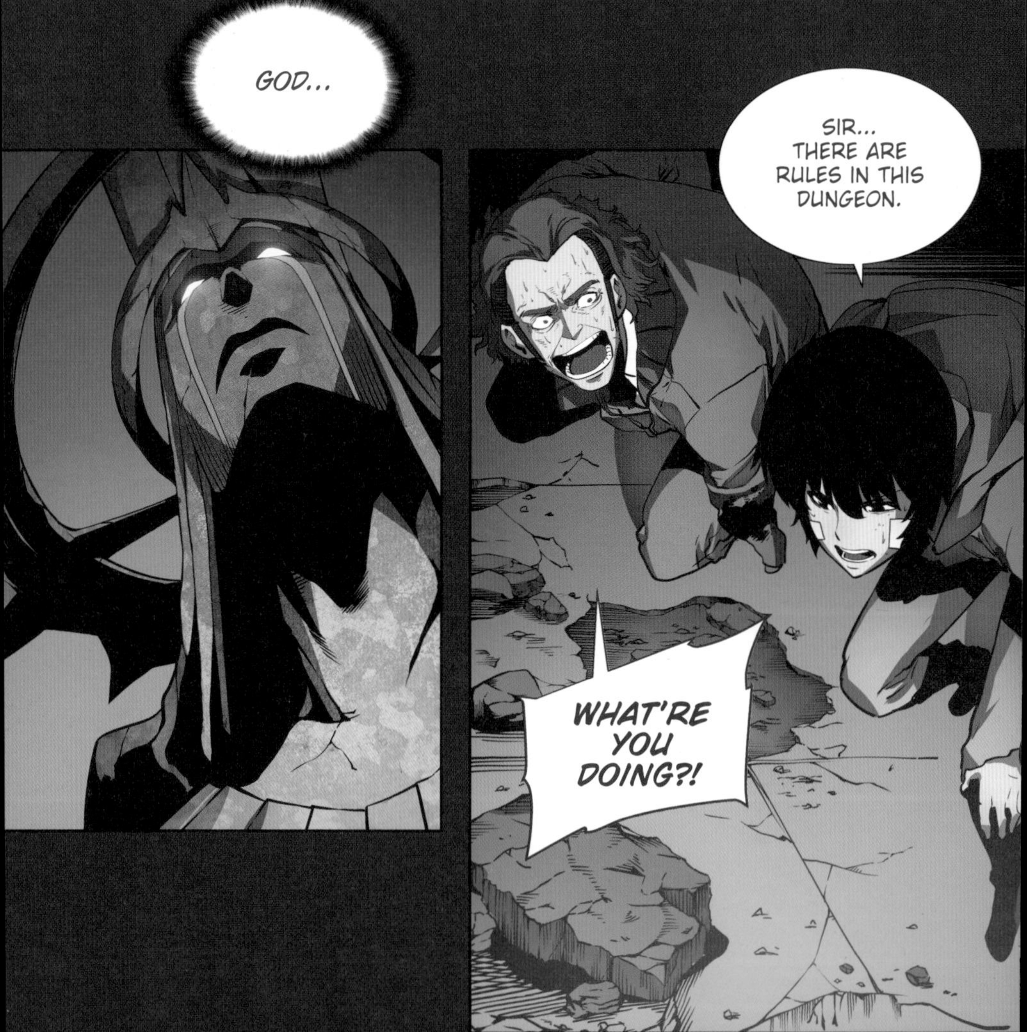
GOD...
SIR... THERE ARE RULES IN THIS DUNGEON.
WHAT'RE YOU DOING?!

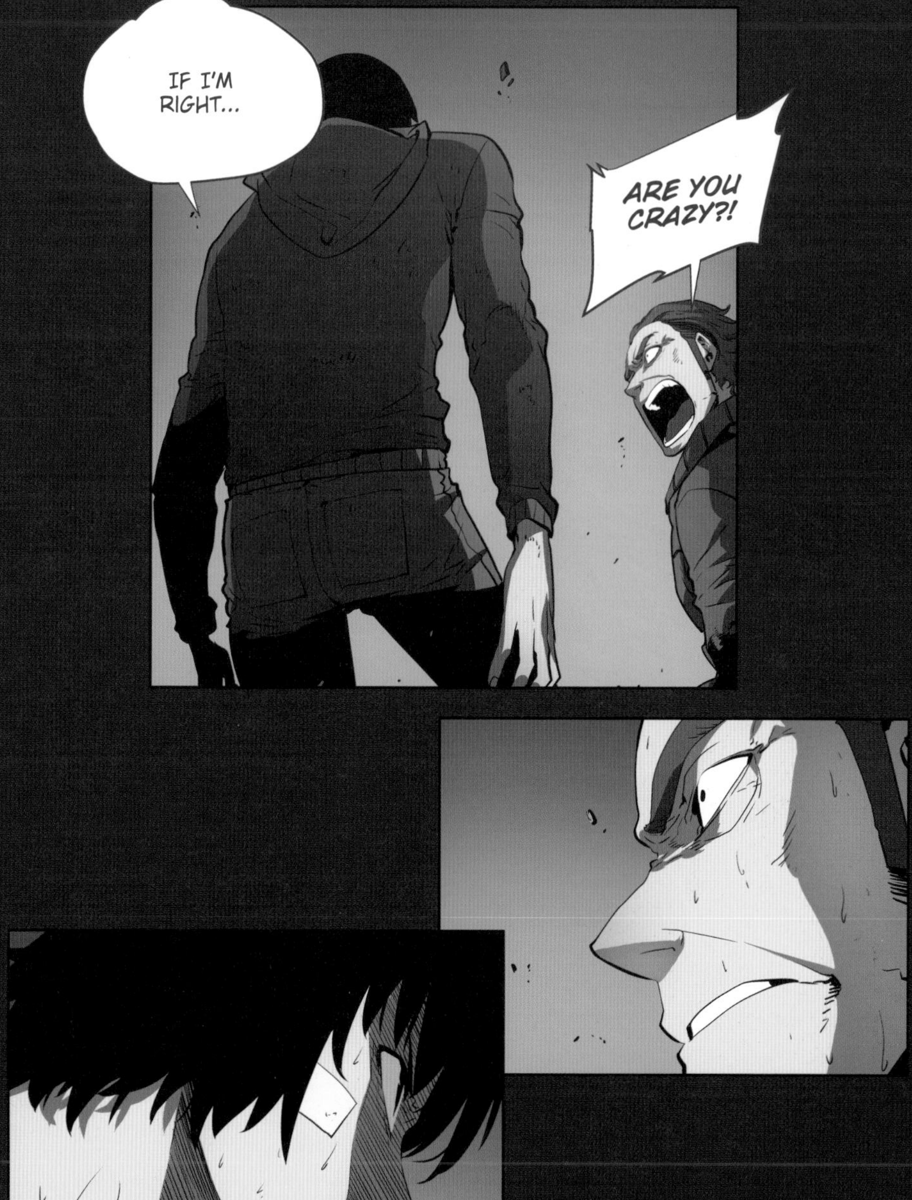
IF I'M RIGHT...
ARE YOU CRAZY?!

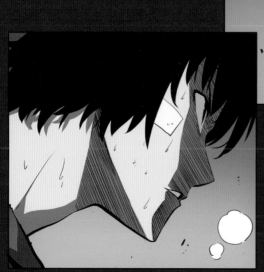

THAT'S THE LOOK OF A FIGHTER.

...THAT STATUE ISN'T ATTACKING ANYTHING THAT MOVES!

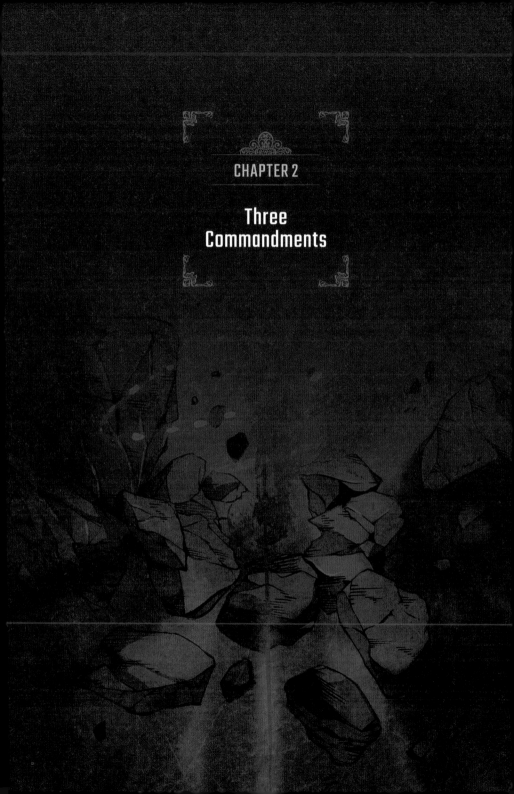

CHAPTER 2

Three
Commandments

Solo Leveling

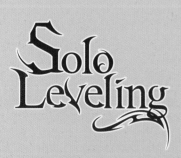

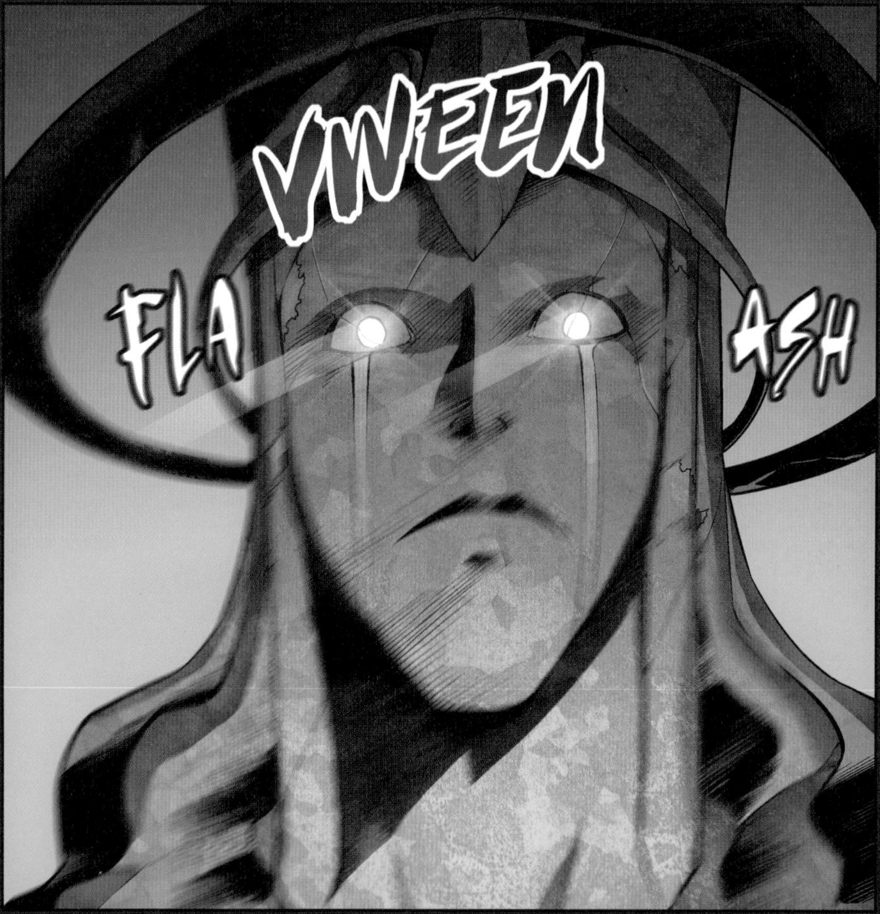
VWEEN
FLA
ASH

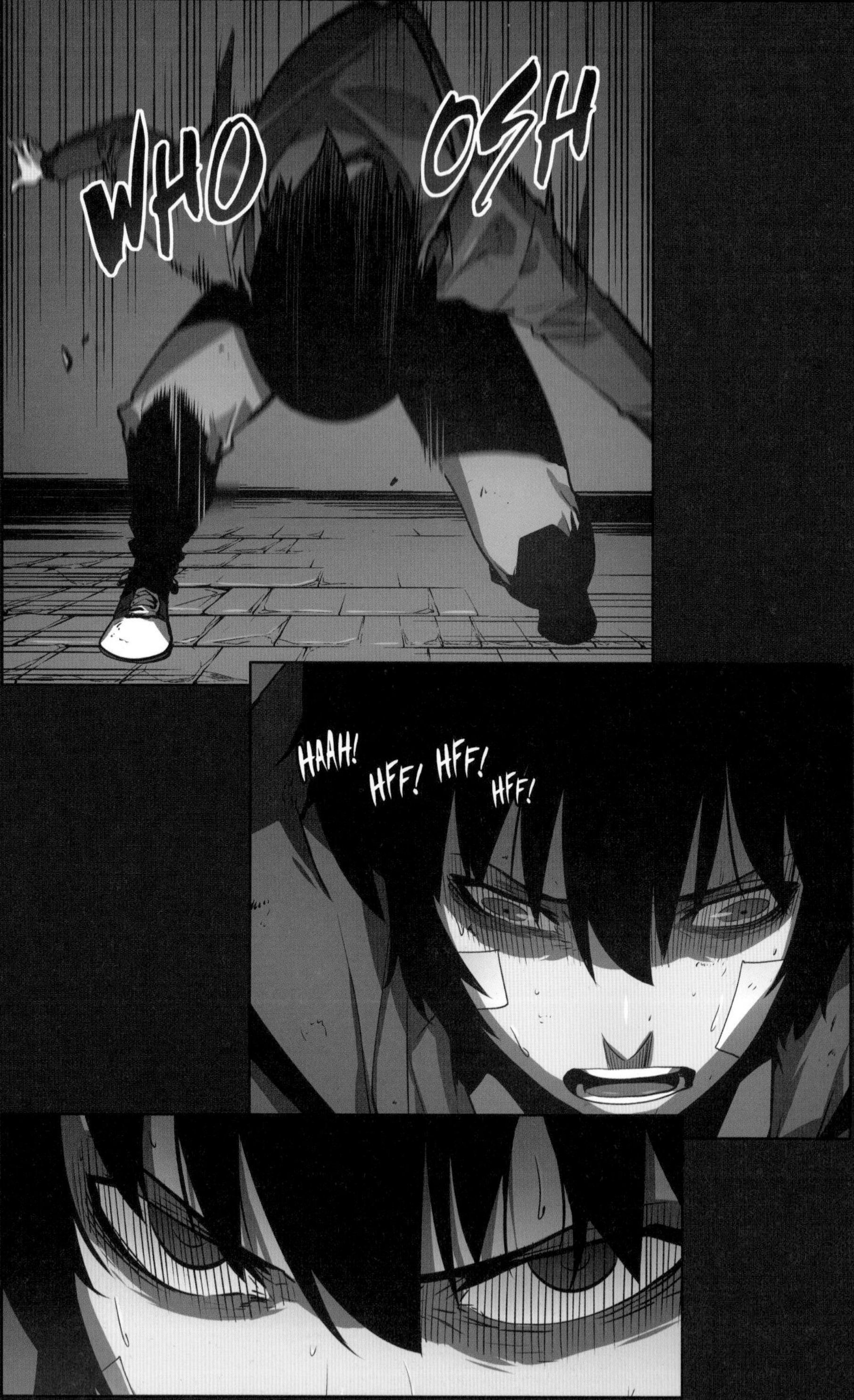
WHO OSH
HAAH!
HFF! HFF!
HFF!

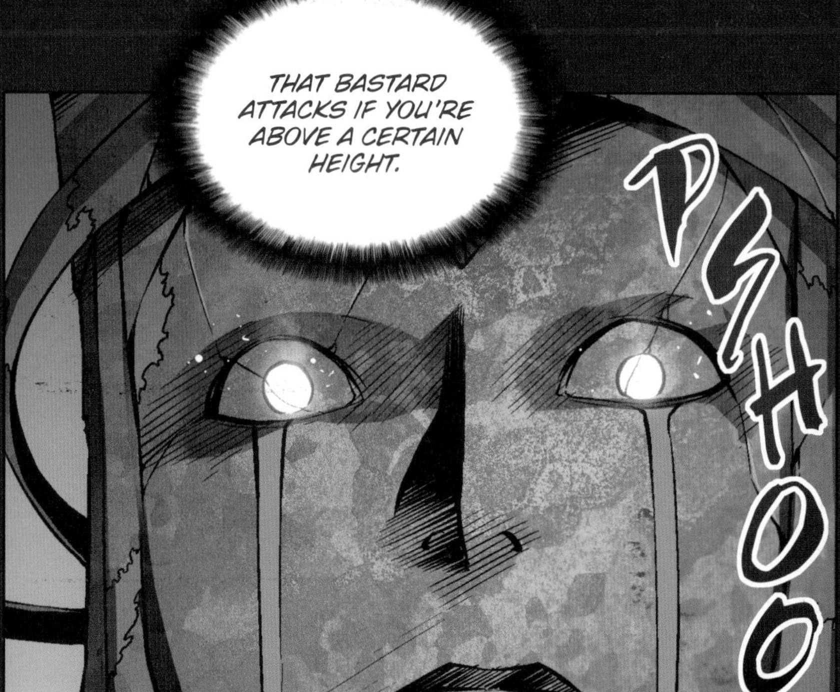
THAT BASTARD ATTACKS IF YOU'RE ABOVE A CERTAIN HEIGHT.
PSHOOOO
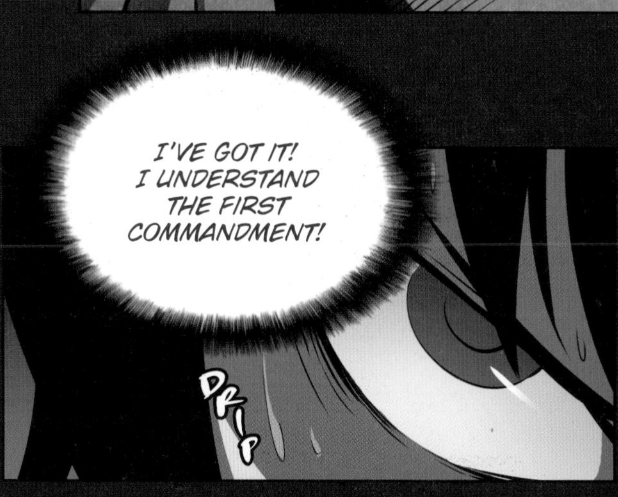
I'VE GOT IT! I UNDERSTAND THE FIRST COMMANDMENT!
DRIP

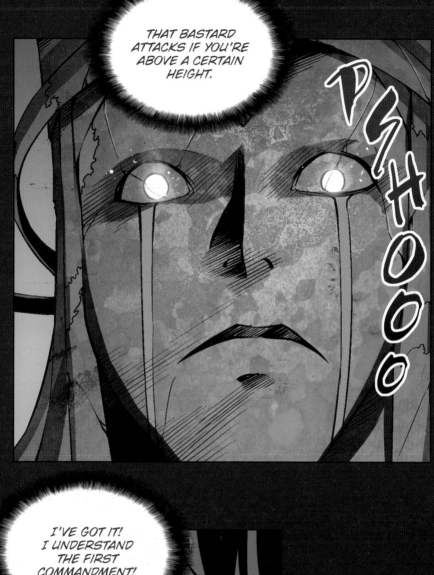

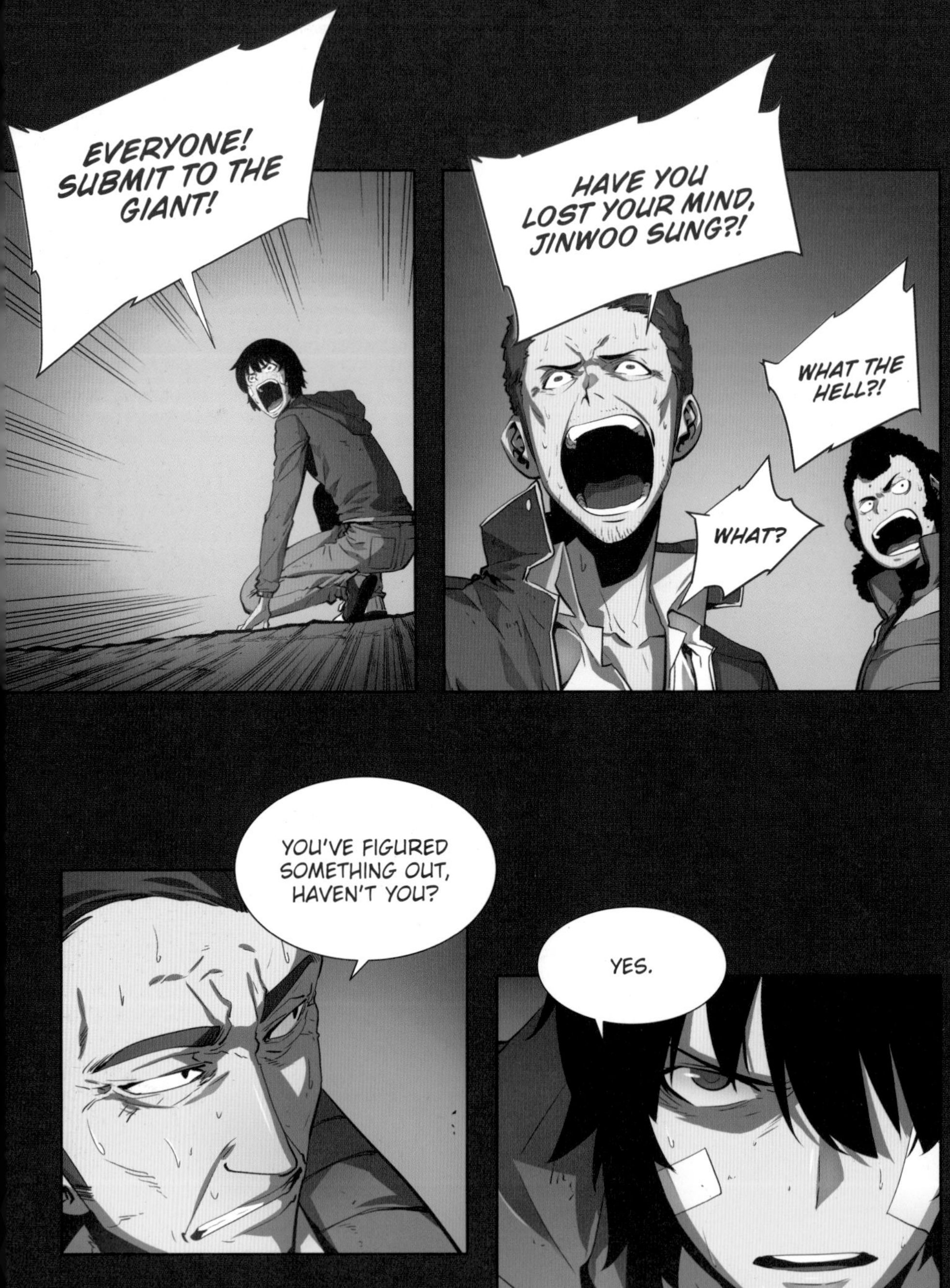
EVERYONE! SUBMIT TO THE GIANT!
HAVE YOU LOST YOUR MIND, JINWOO SUNG?!
WHAT THE HELL?!
WHAT?
YOU'VE FIGURED SOMETHING OUT, HAVEN'T YOU?
YES.

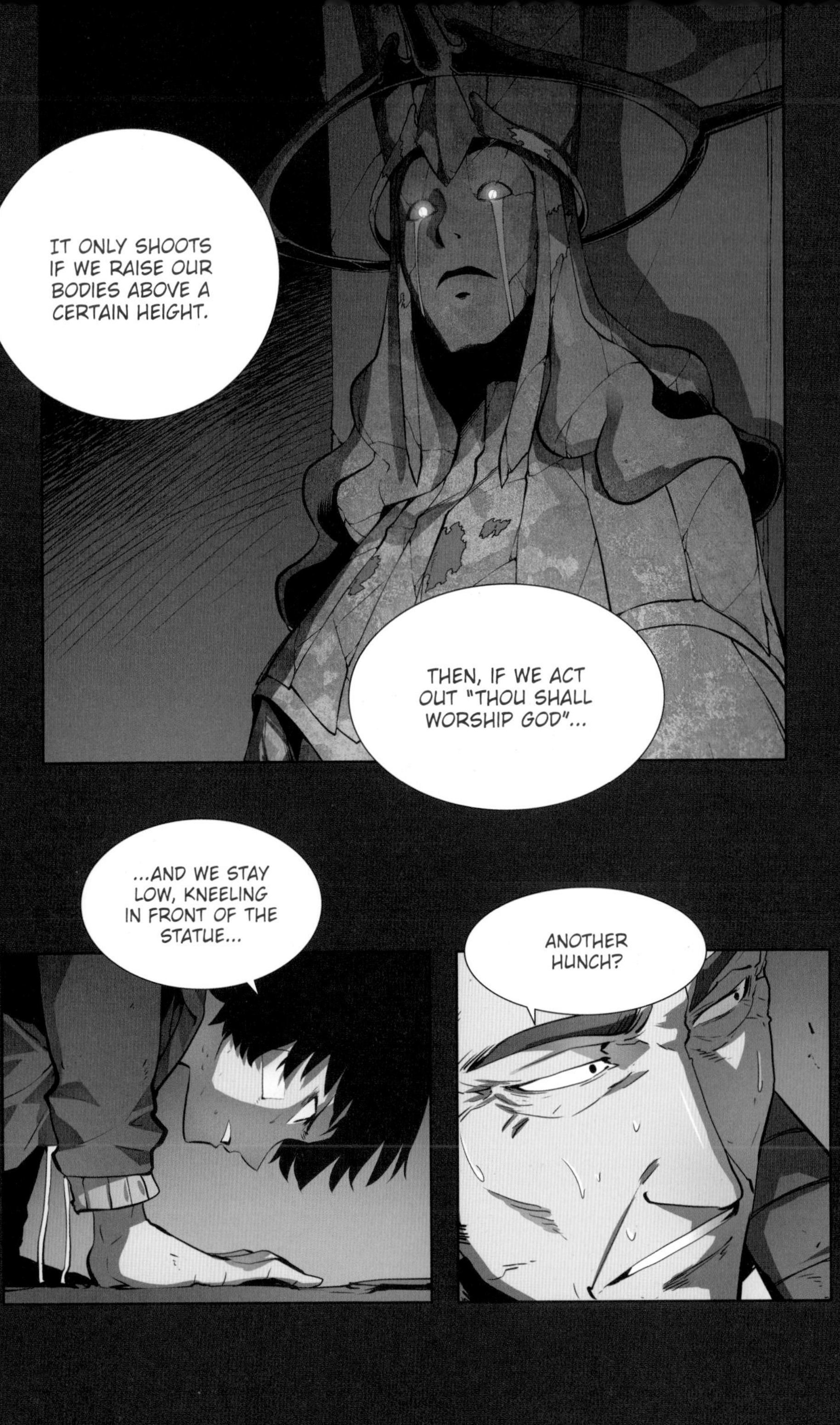

IT ONLY SHOOTS IF WE RAISE OUR BODIES ABOVE A CERTAIN HEIGHT.
THEN, IF WE ACT OUT "THOU SHALL WORSHIP GOD"...
...AND WE STAY LOW, KNEELING IN FRONT OF THE STATUE...
ANOTHER HUNCH?

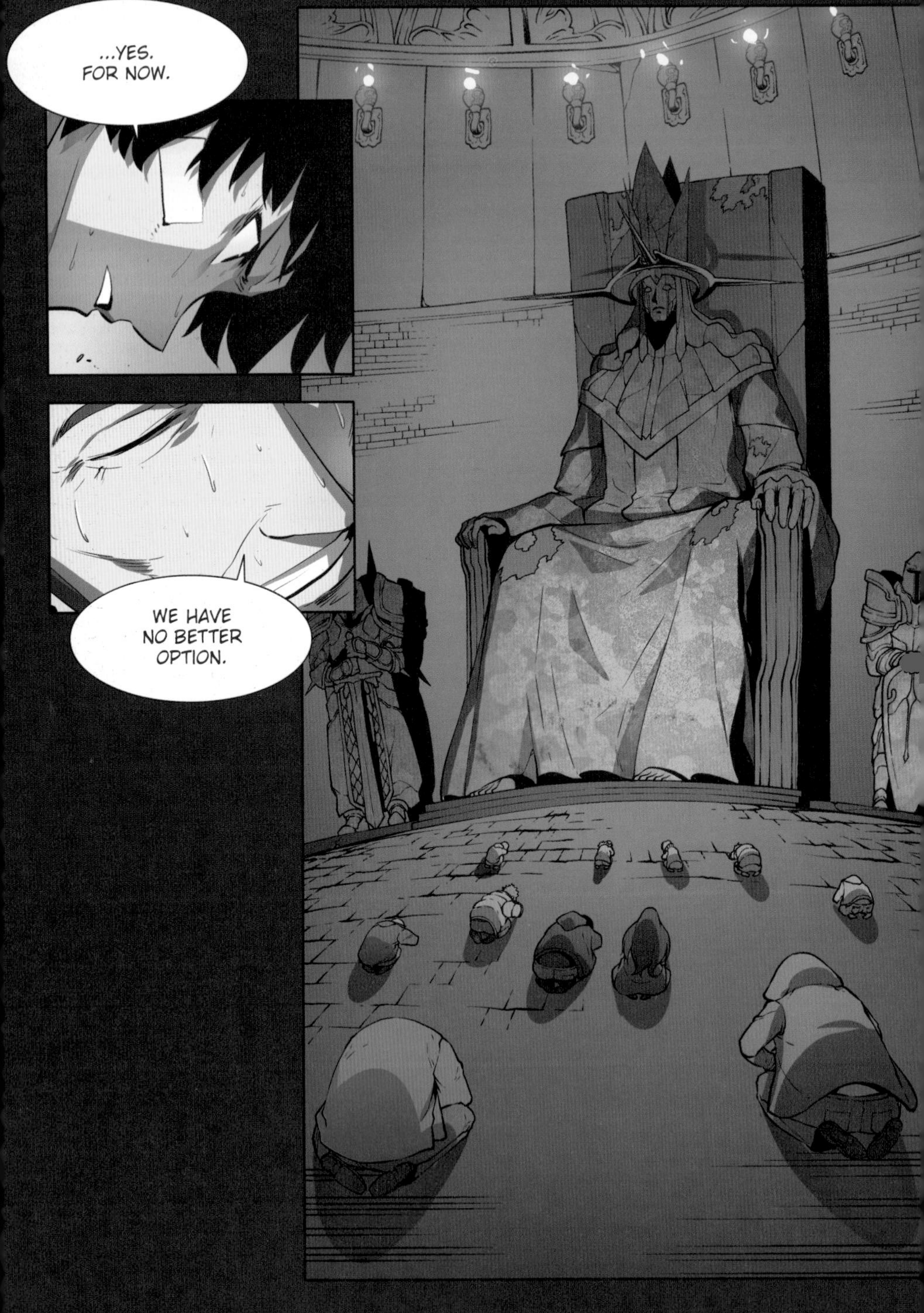
...YES.
FOR NOW.
WE HAVE
NO BETTER
OPTION.

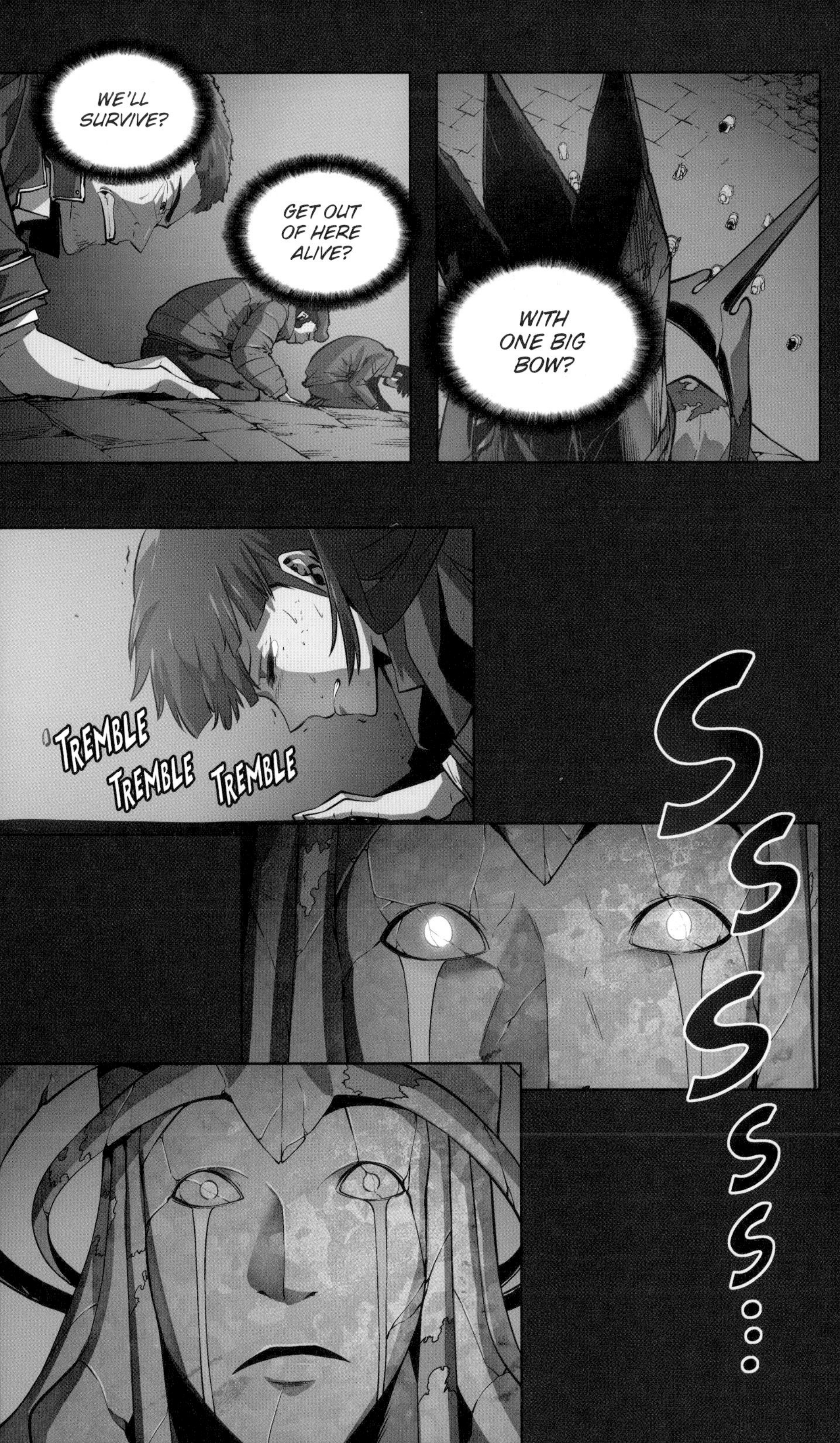
WE'LL SURVIVE?
GET OUT OF HERE ALIVE?
WITH ONE BIG BOW?
TREMBLE TREMBLE TREMBLE
SSSSS...

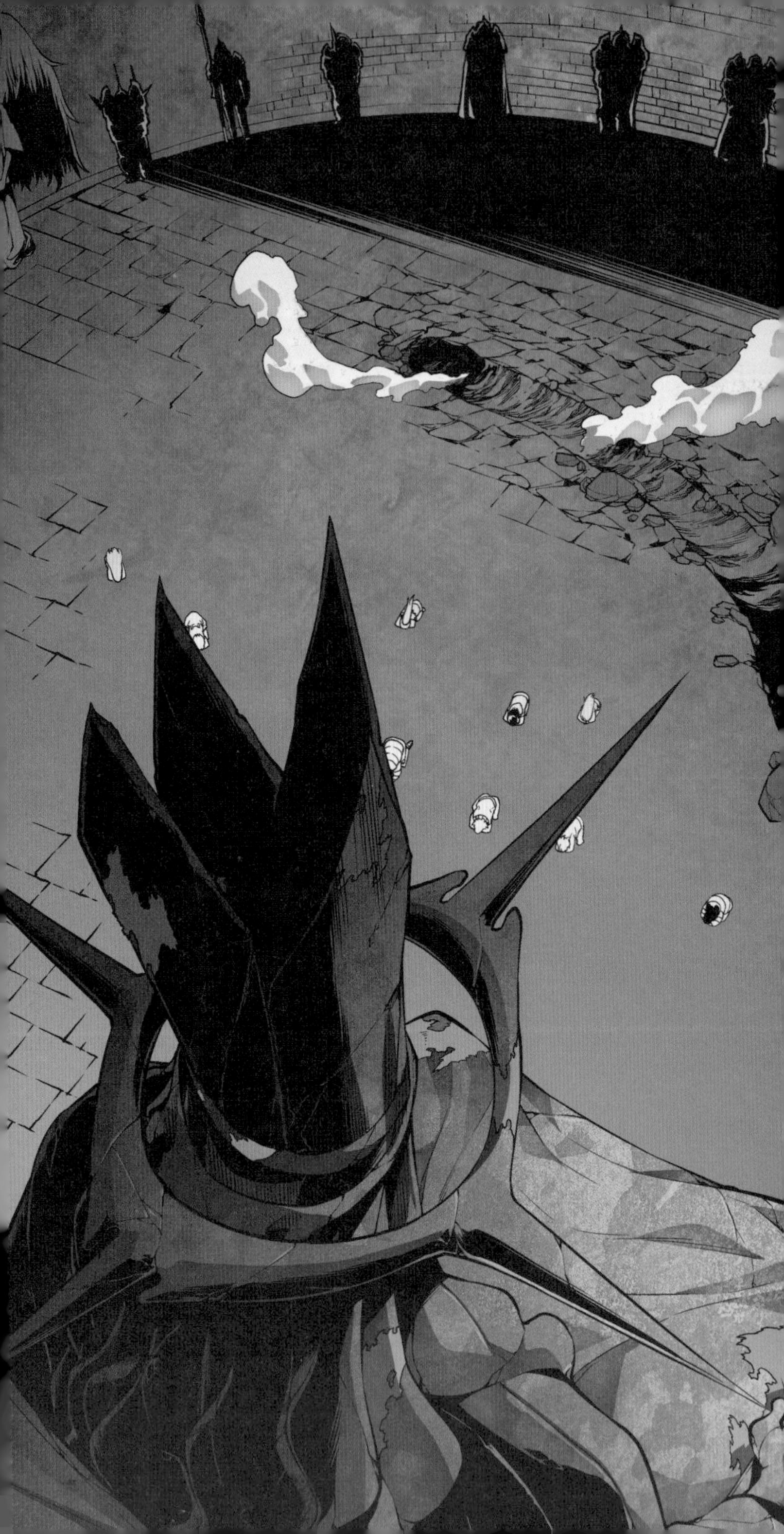

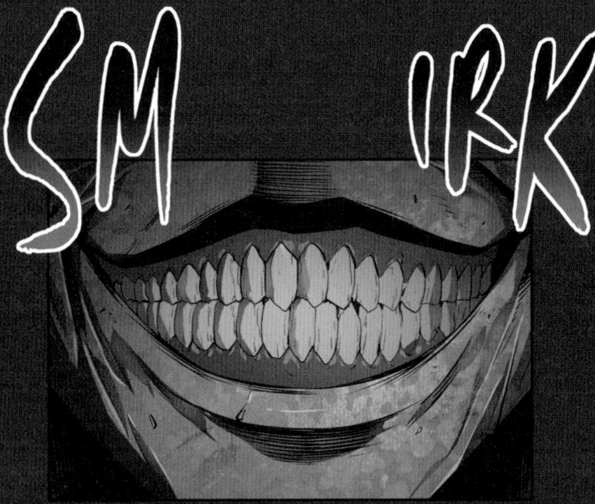
SMIRK

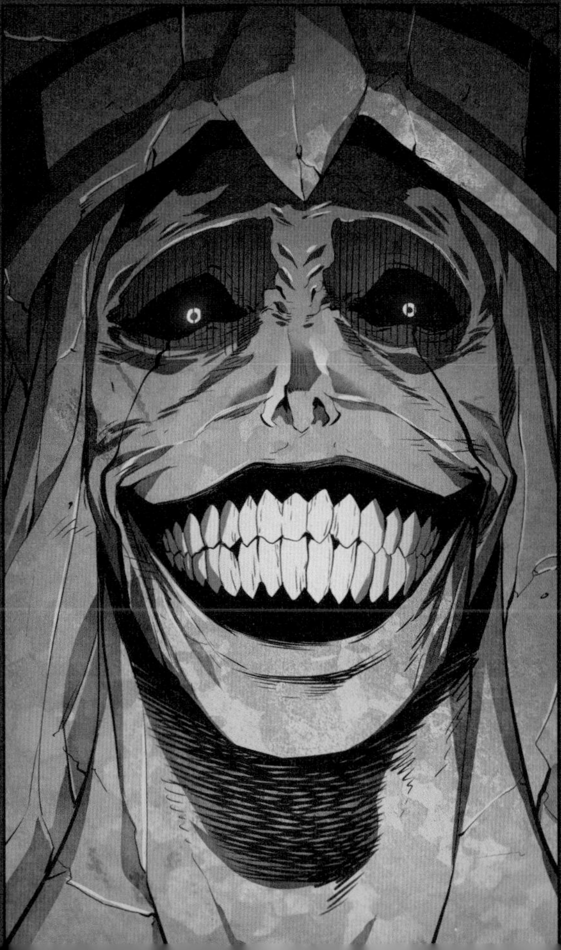

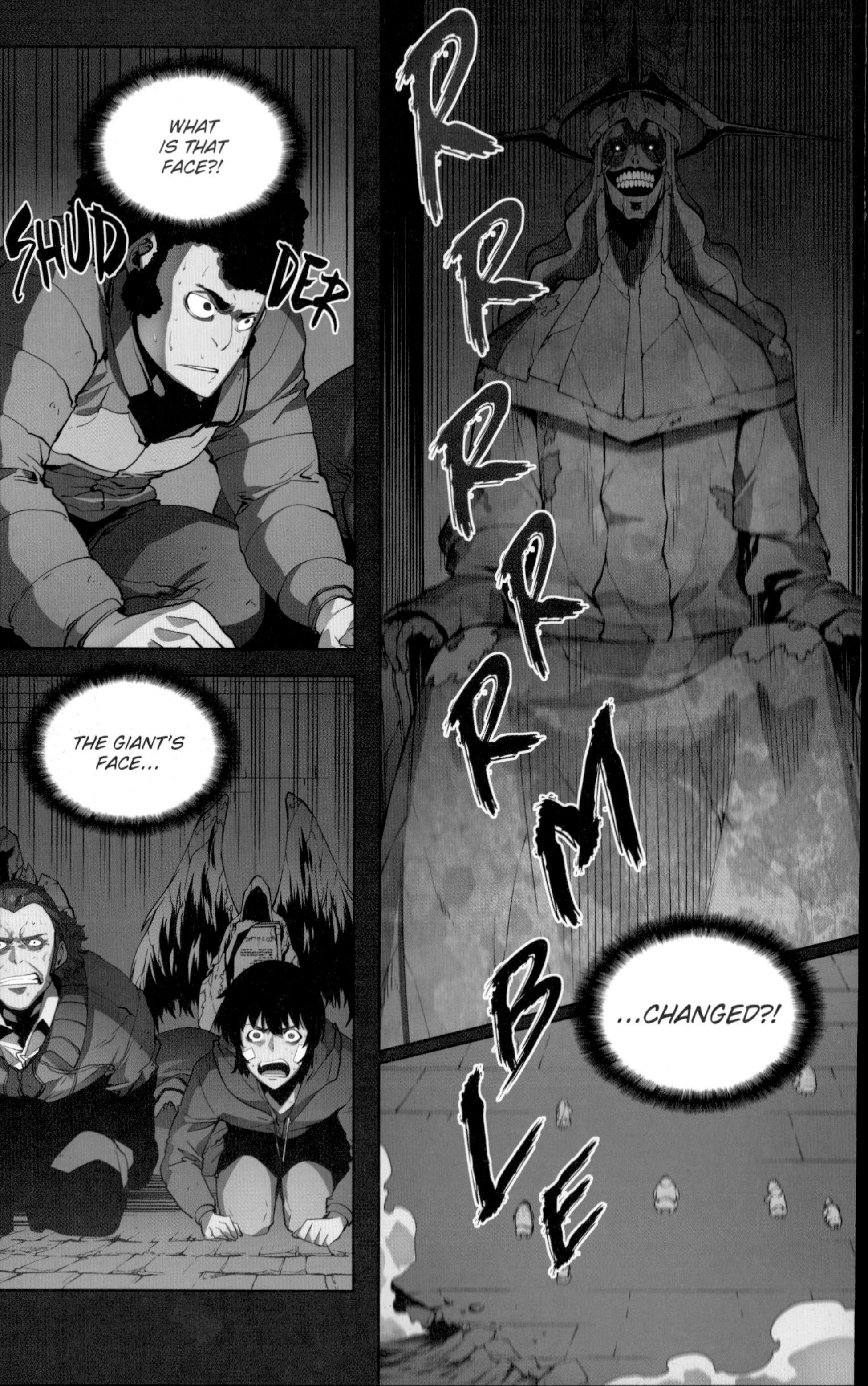
WHAT IS THAT FACE?!
SHUDDER
THE GIANT'S FACE...
RRRRRMBLE
...CHANGED?!

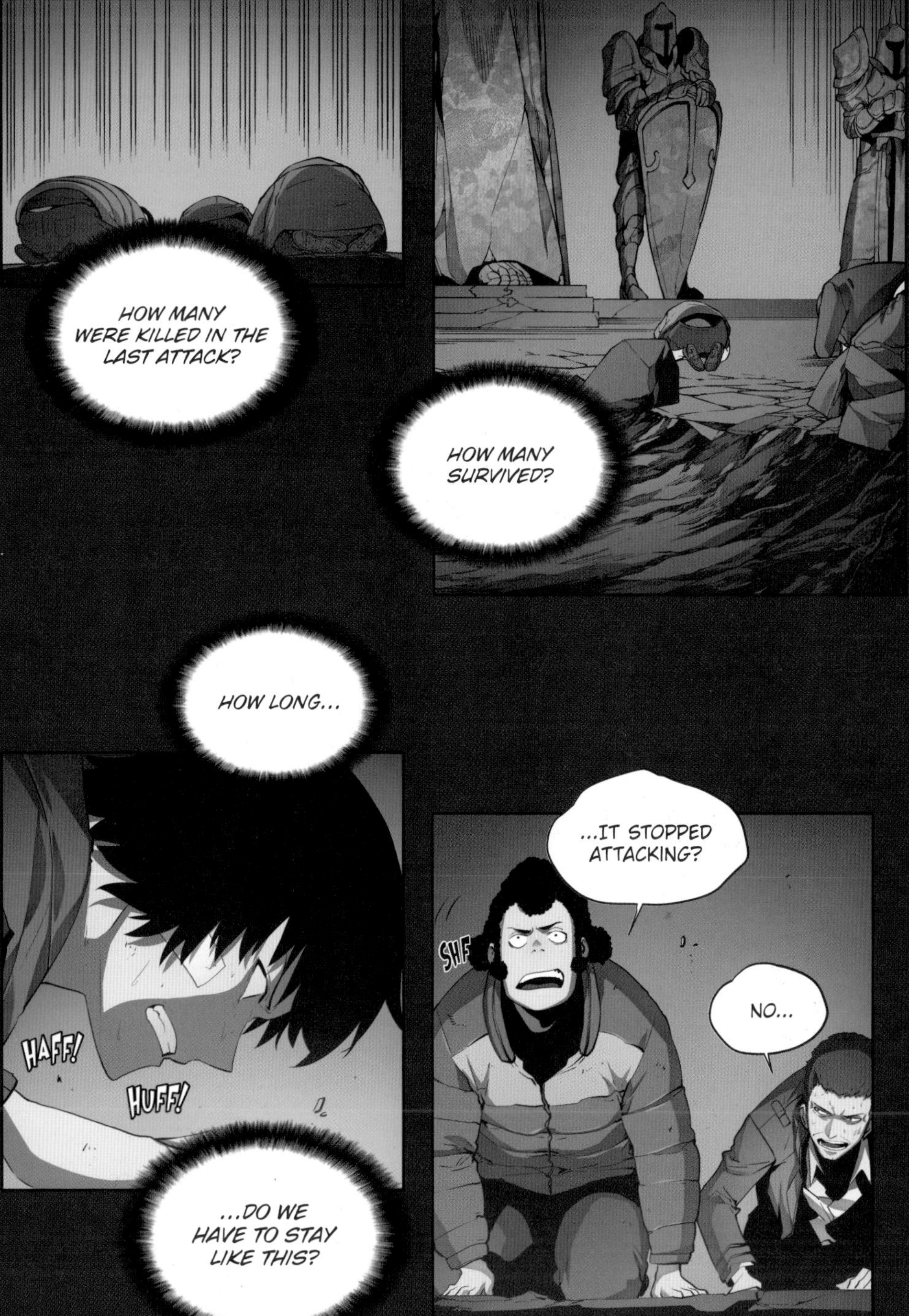
HOW MANY WERE KILLED IN THE LAST ATTACK?
HOW MANY SURVIVED?
HOW LONG...
HAFF!
HUFF!
...DO WE HAVE TO STAY LIKE THIS?
...IT STOPPED ATTACKING?
SHF
NO...

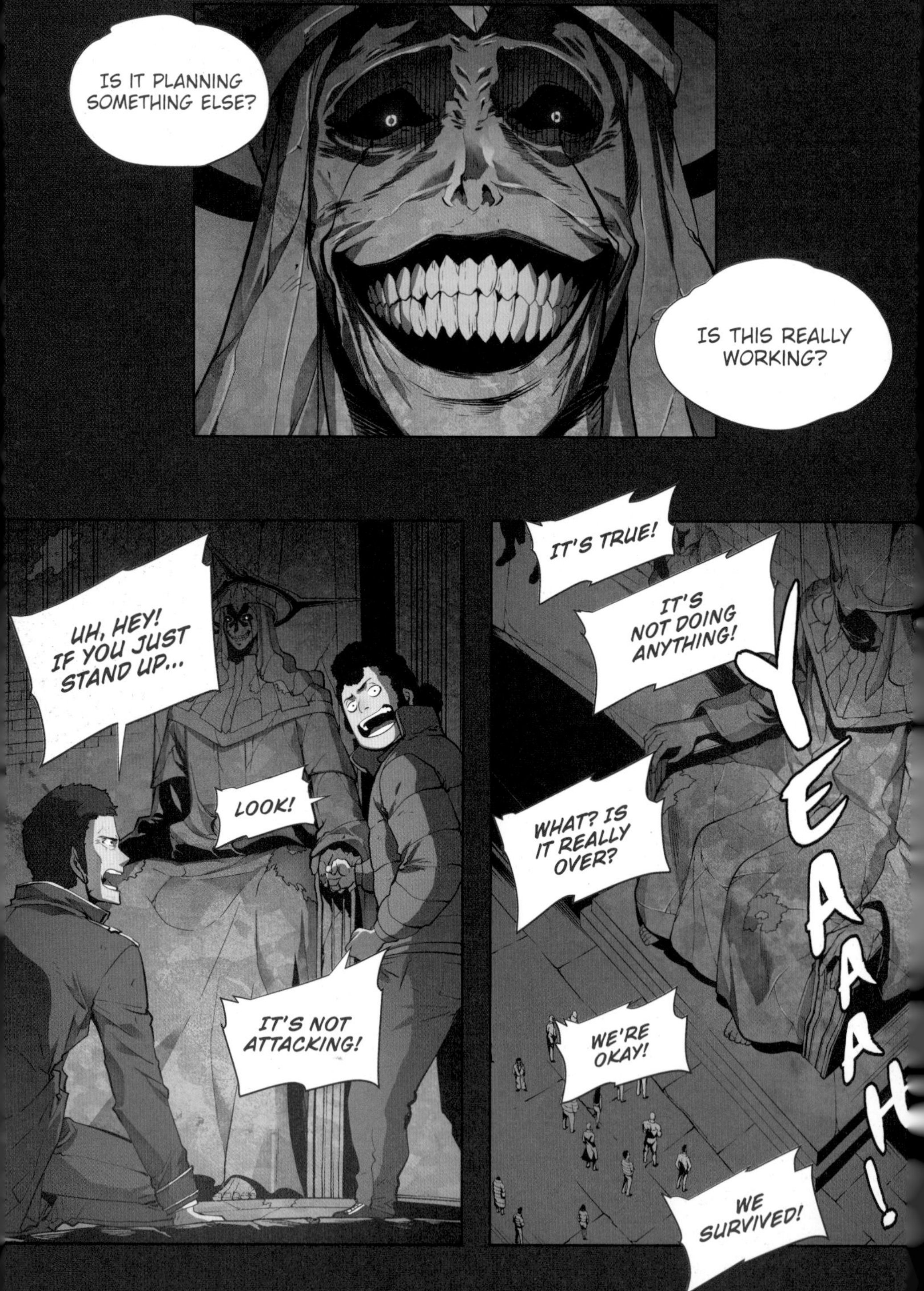
IS IT PLANNING SOMETHING ELSE?
IS THIS REALLY WORKING?
UH, HEY! IF YOU JUST STAND UP...
LOOK!
IT'S NOT ATTACKING!
IT'S TRUE!
IT'S NOT DOING ANYTHING!
WHAT? IS IT REALLY OVER?
WE'RE OKAY!
YEAAAAH!
WE SURVIVED!

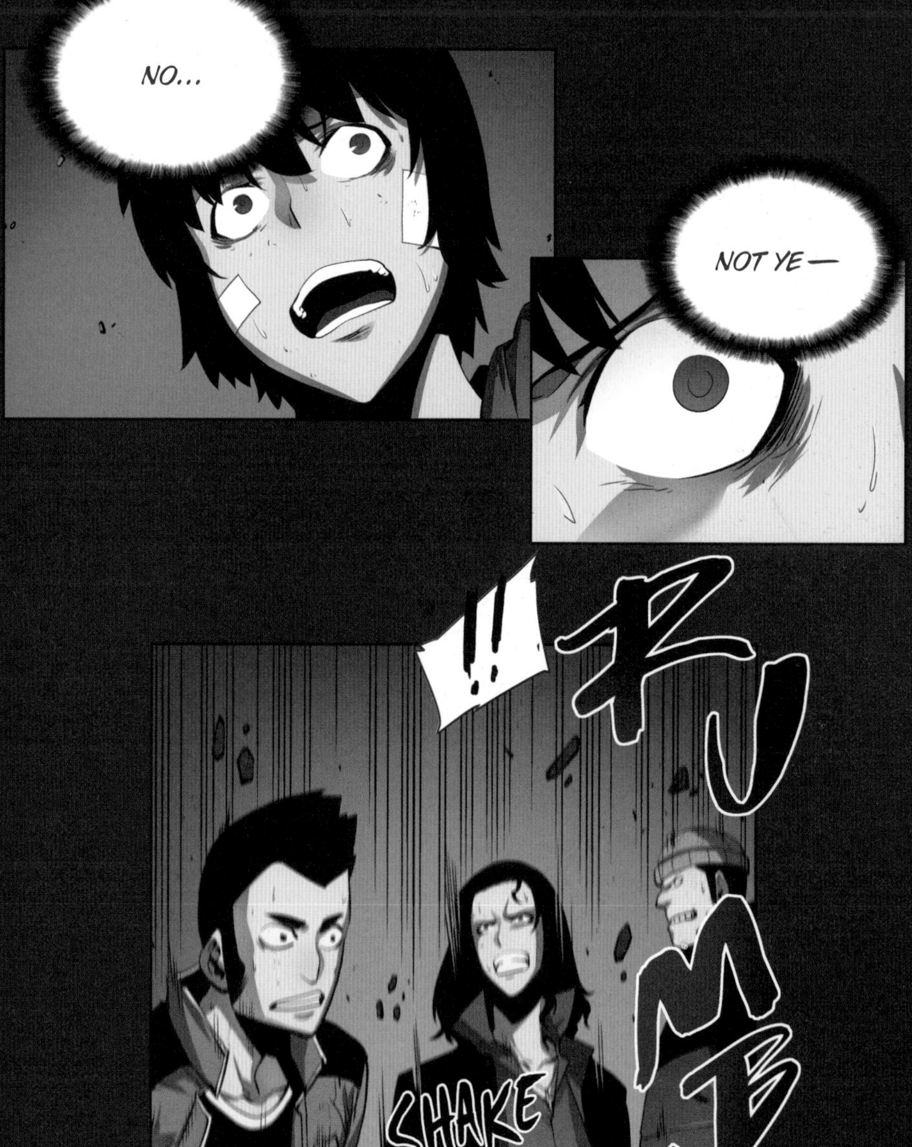
NO...
NOT YE—
!!
RUMBLE
SHAKE

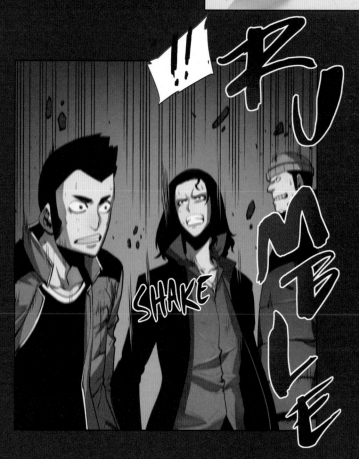

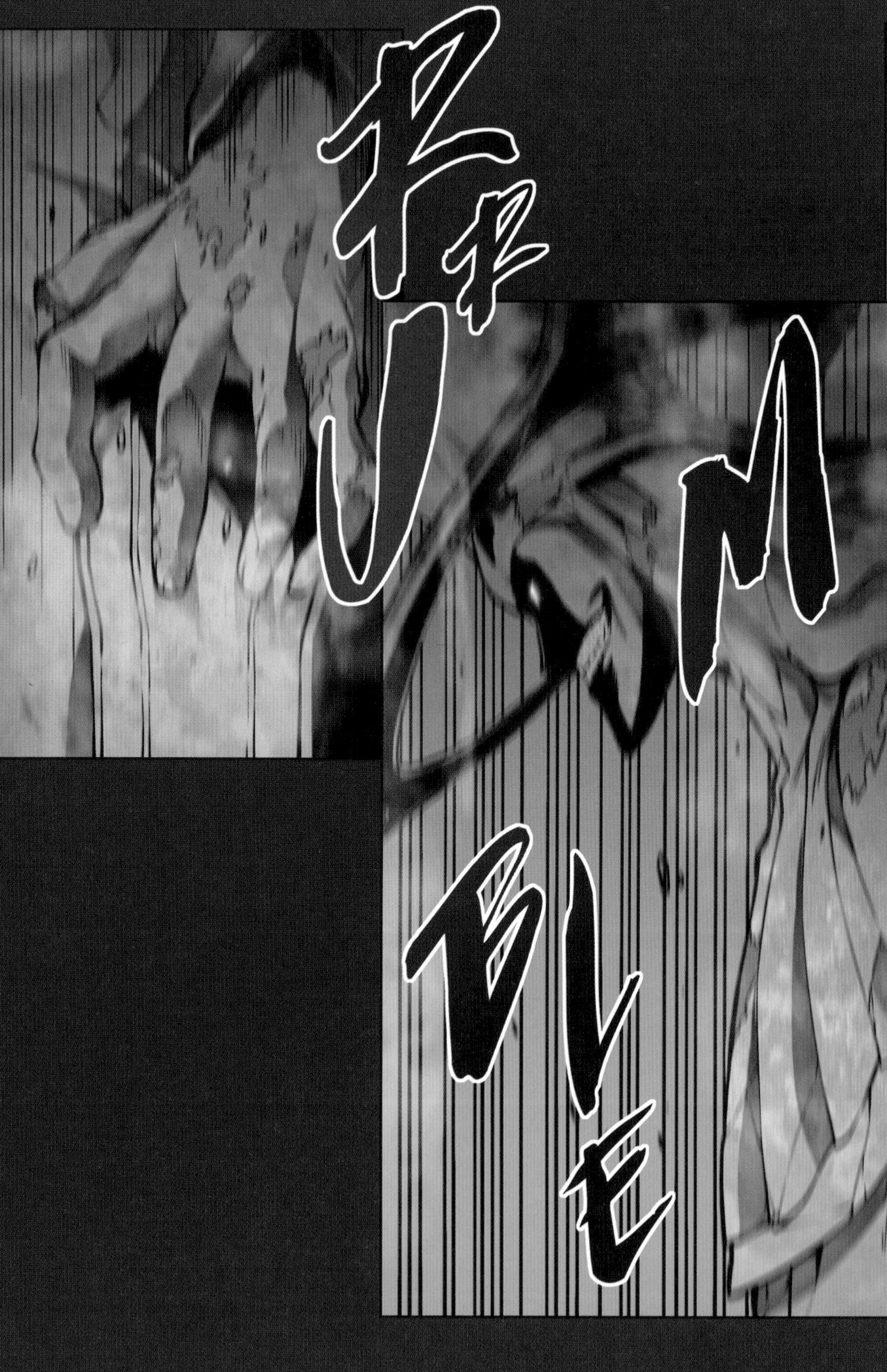
RRUMBLE

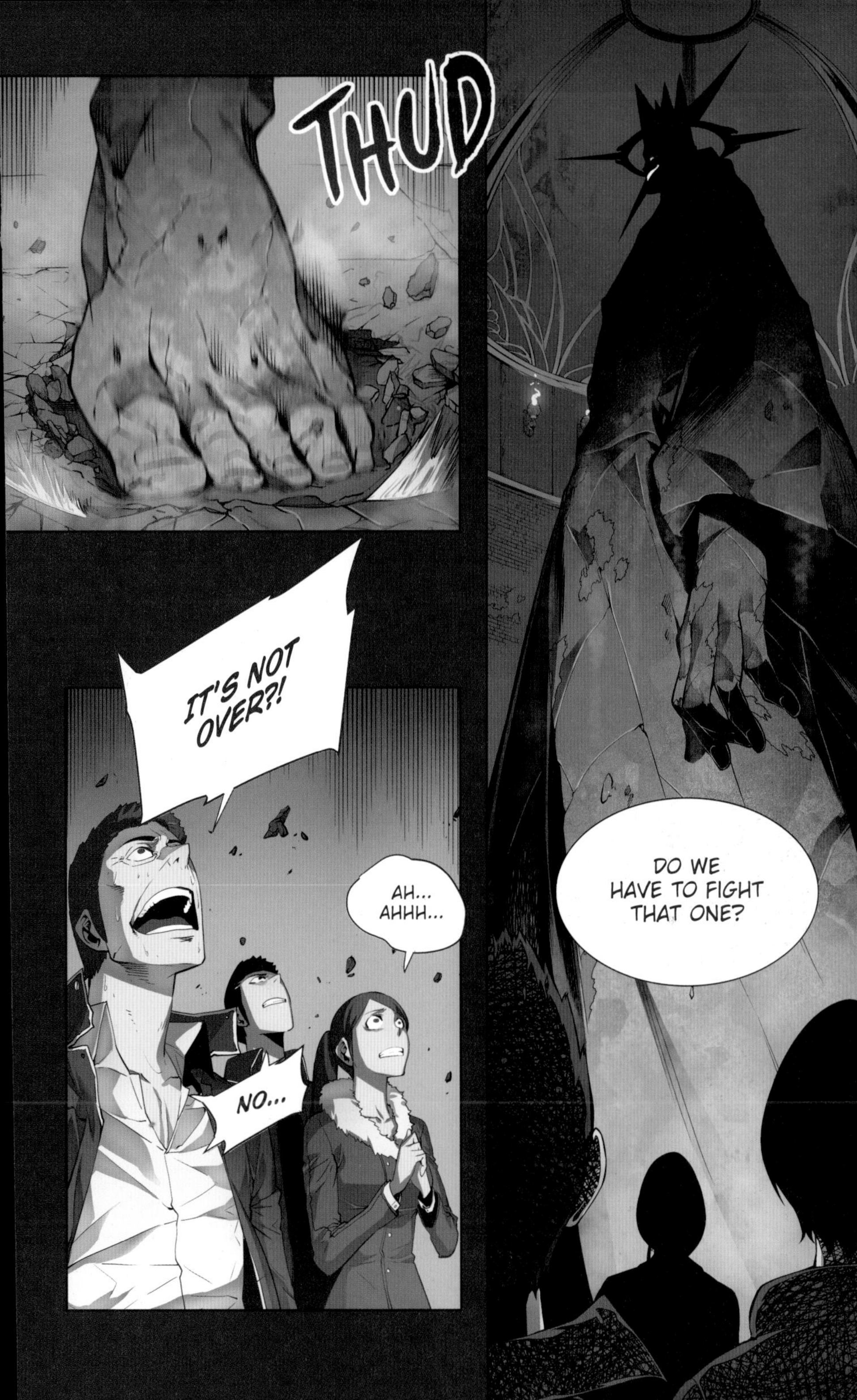
THUD
IT'S NOT OVER?!
AH... AHHH...
NO...
DO WE HAVE TO FIGHT THAT ONE?

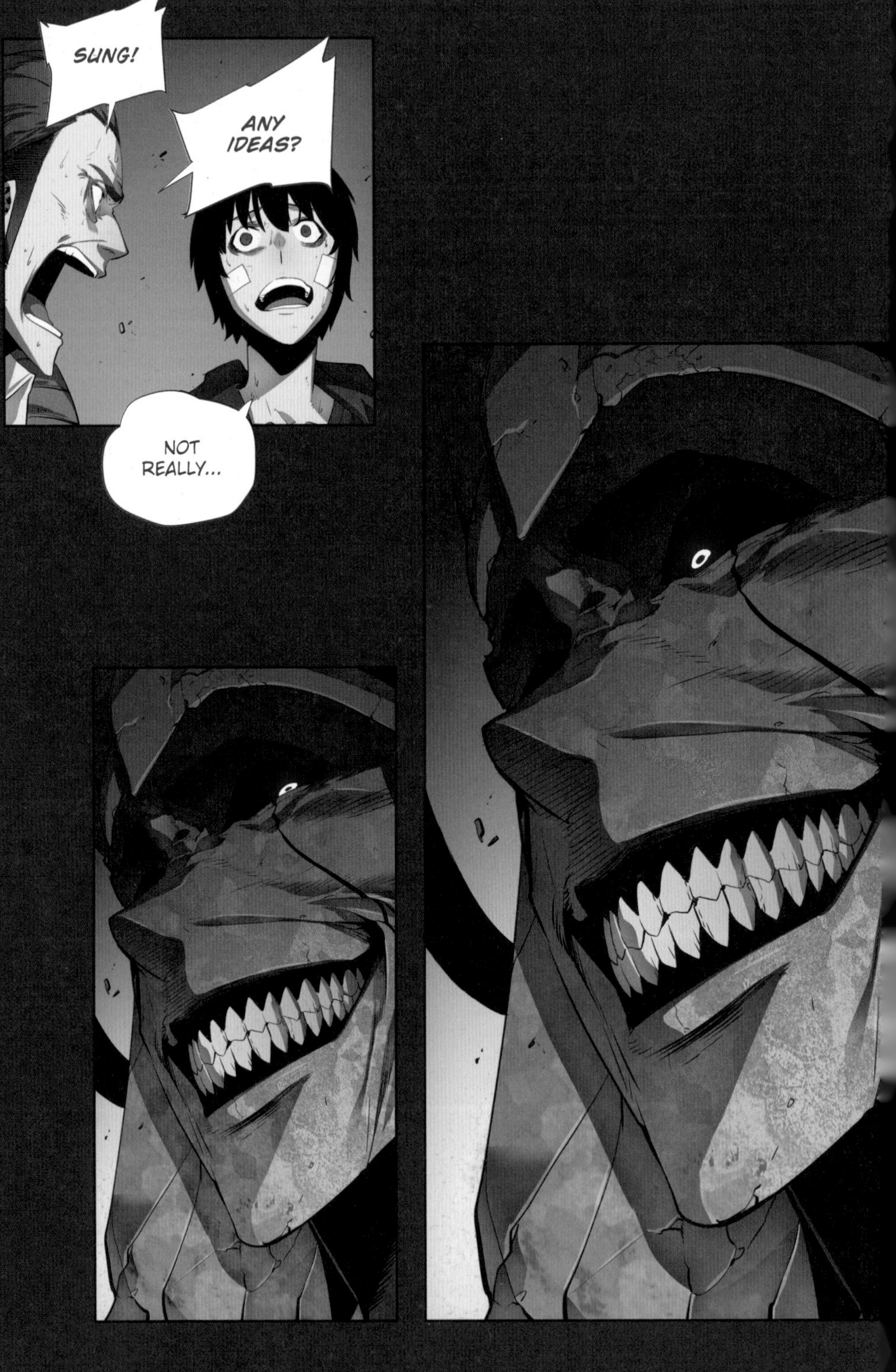
SUNG!
ANY IDEAS?
NOT REALLY...

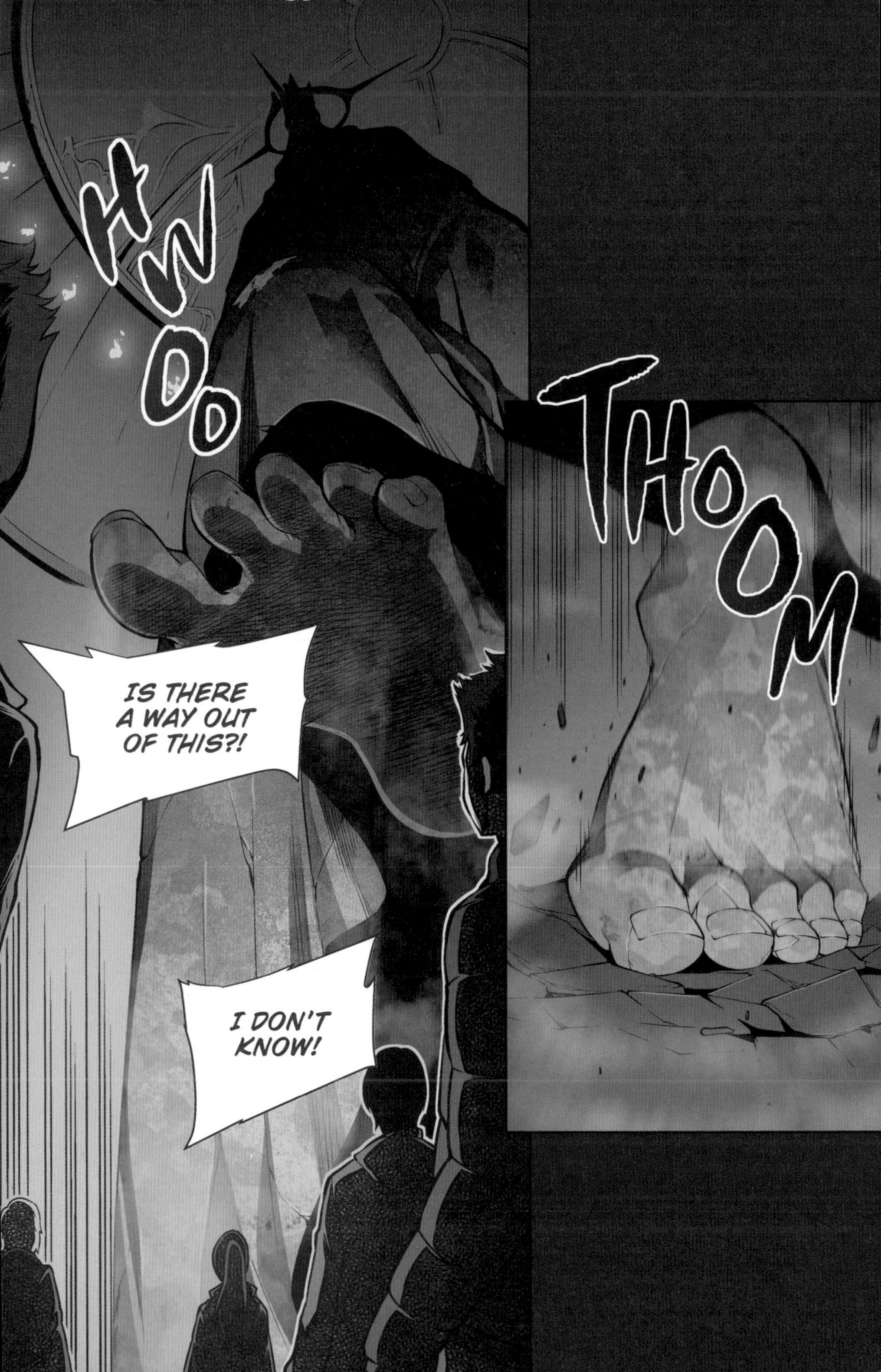
HWOO
IS THERE A WAY OUT OF THIS?!
I DON'T KNOW!
THOOM

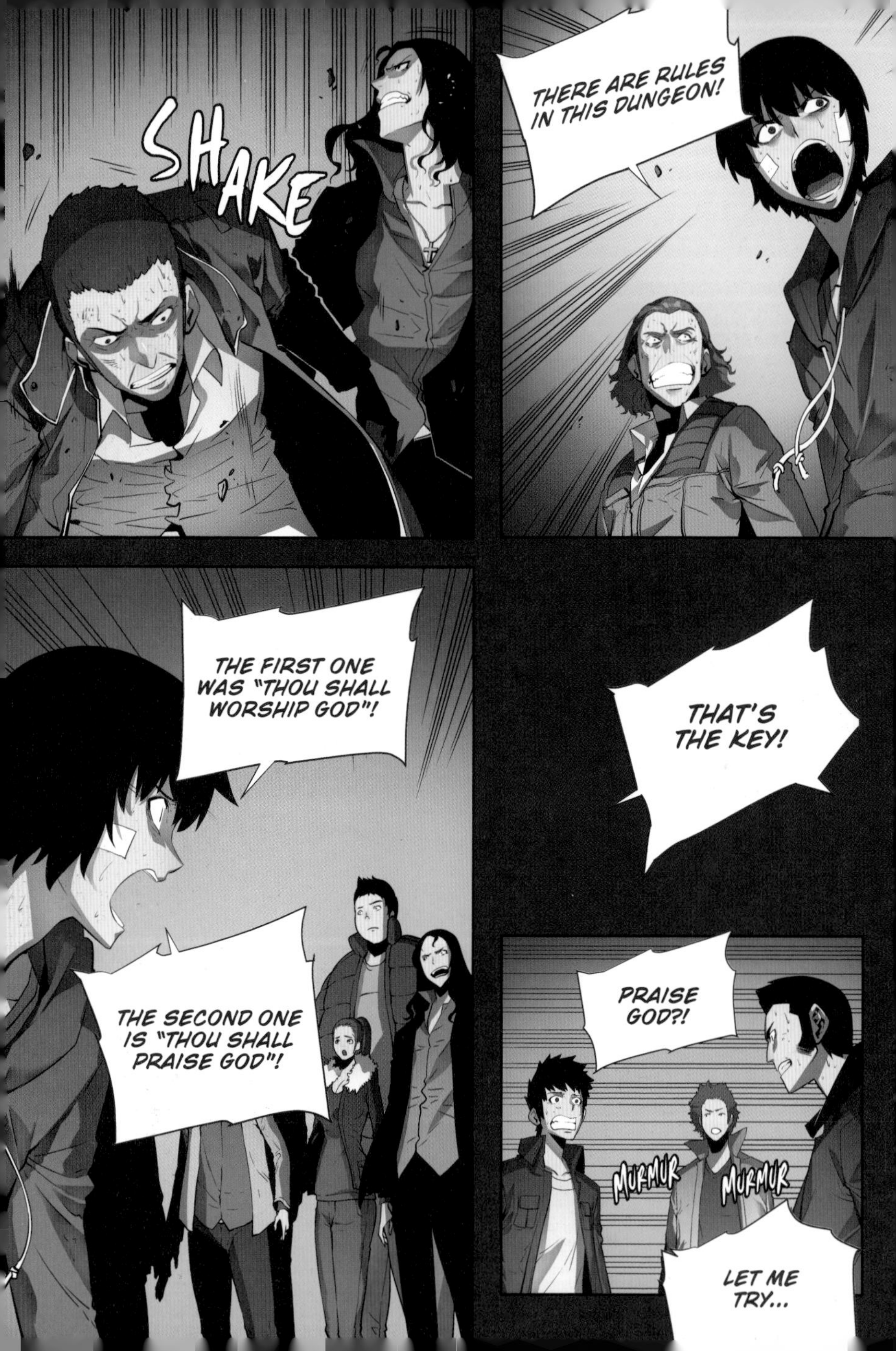
SHAKE
THERE ARE RULES IN THIS DUNGEON!
THE FIRST ONE WAS "THOU SHALL WORSHIP GOD"!
THE SECOND ONE IS "THOU SHALL PRAISE GOD"!
THAT'S THE KEY!
PRAISE GOD?!
MURMUR
MURMUR
LET ME TRY...

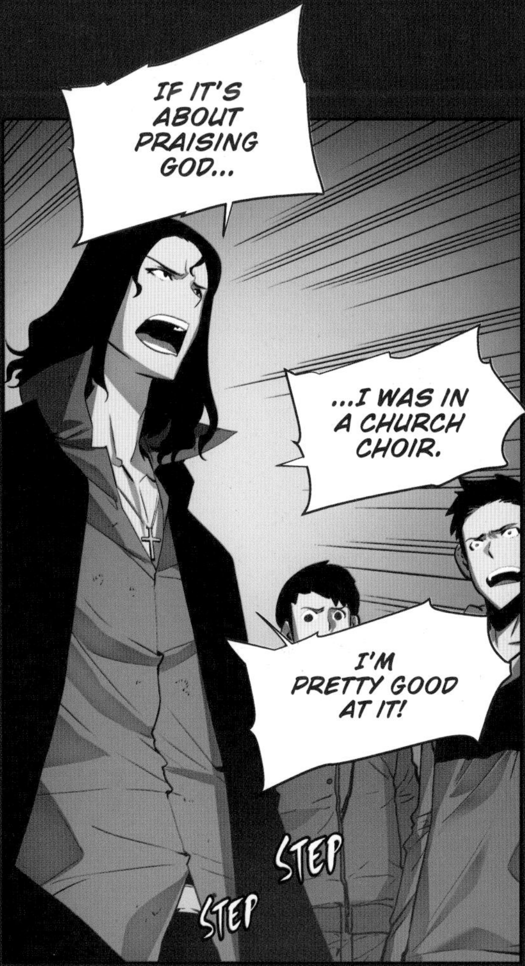
IF IT'S ABOUT PRAISING GOD...
...I WAS IN A CHURCH CHOIR.
I'M PRETTY GOOD AT IT!
STEP
STEP
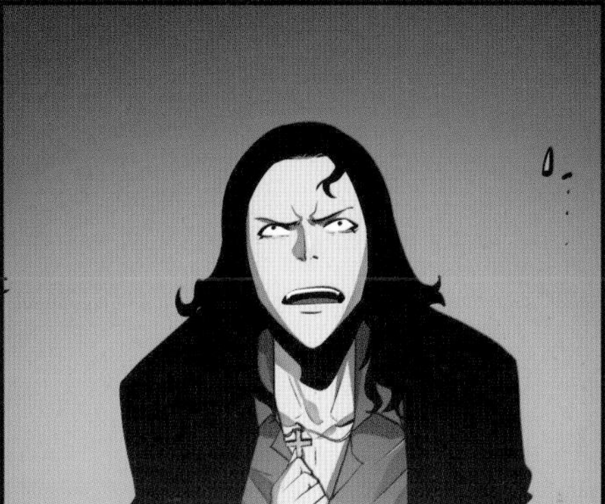
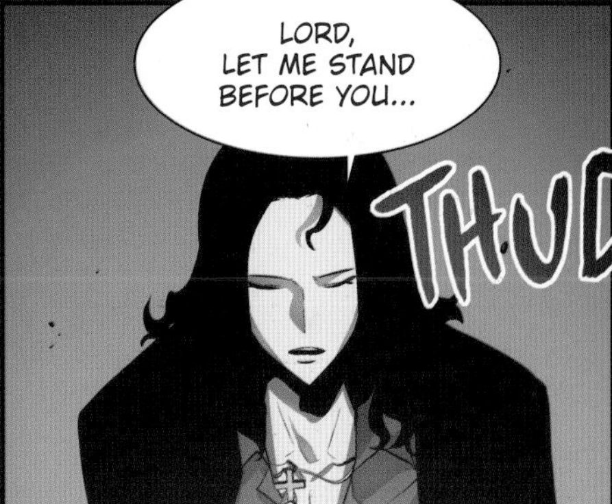
LORD, LET ME STAND BEFORE YOU...
THUD

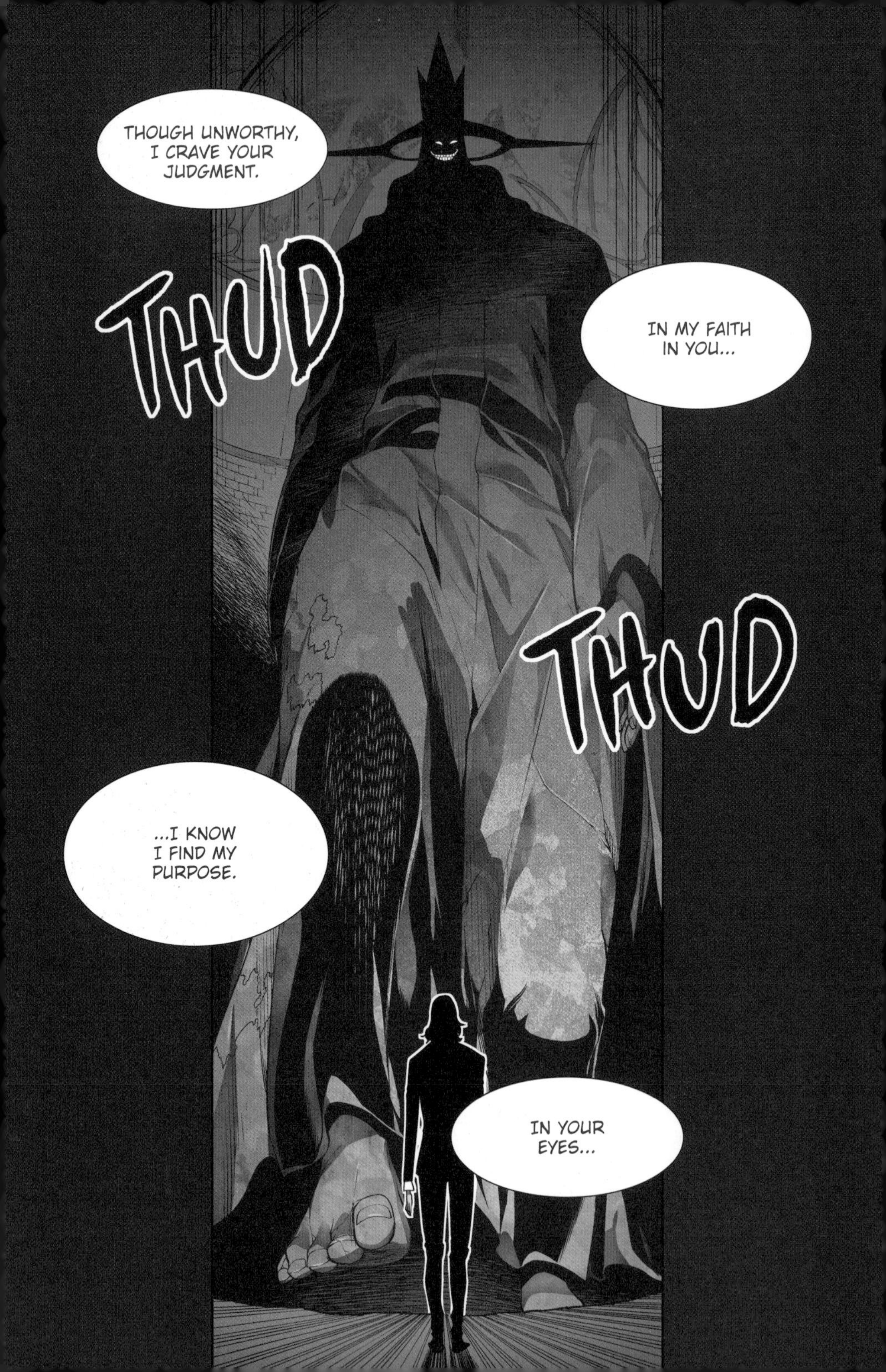
THOUGH UNWORTHY, I CRAVE YOUR JUDGMENT.
THUD
IN MY FAITH IN YOU...
THUD
...I KNOW I FIND MY PURPOSE.
IN YOUR EYES...

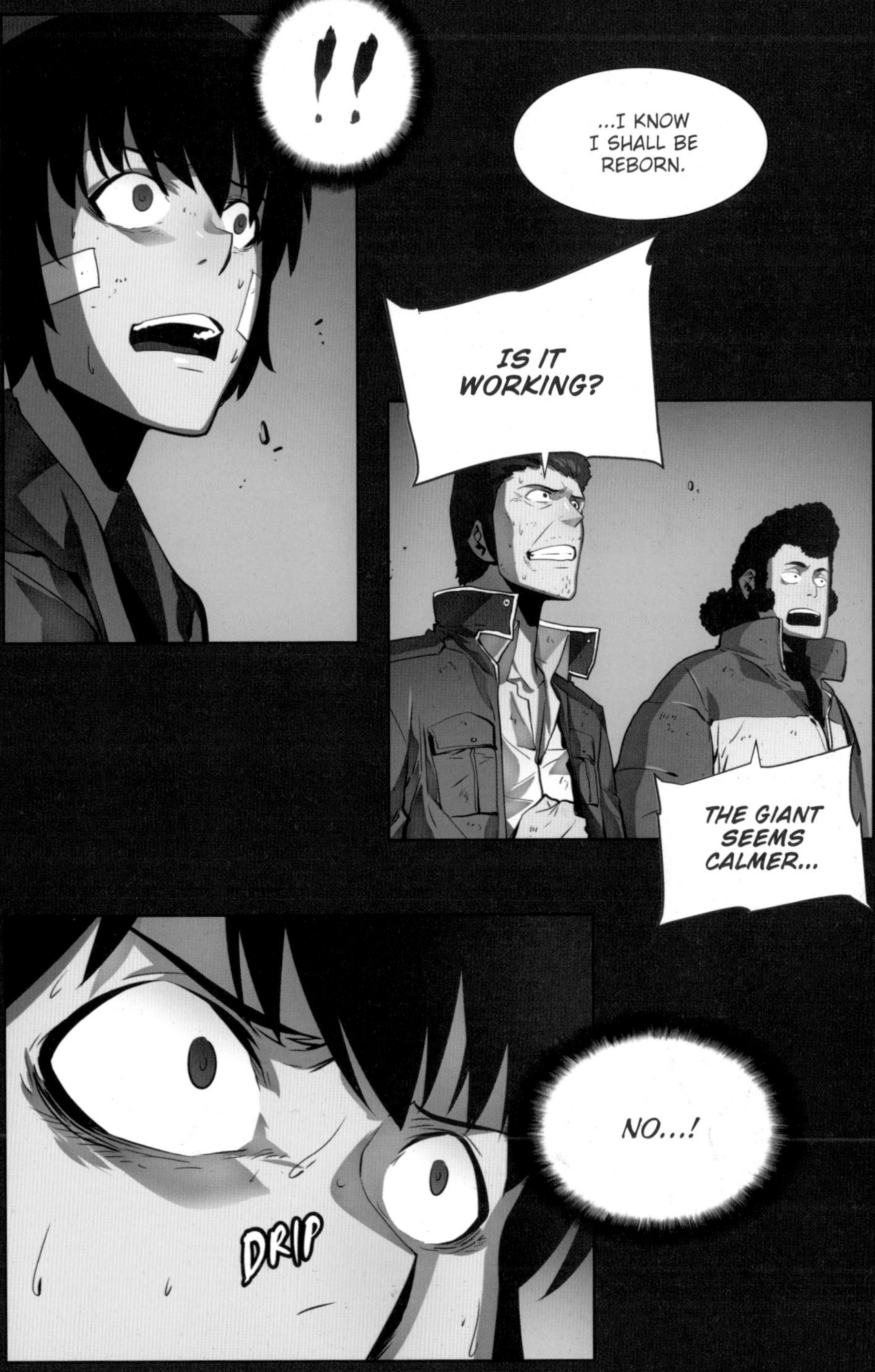
!!
...I KNOW I SHALL BE REBORN.
IS IT WORKING?
THE GIANT SEEMS CALMER...
NO...!
DRIP

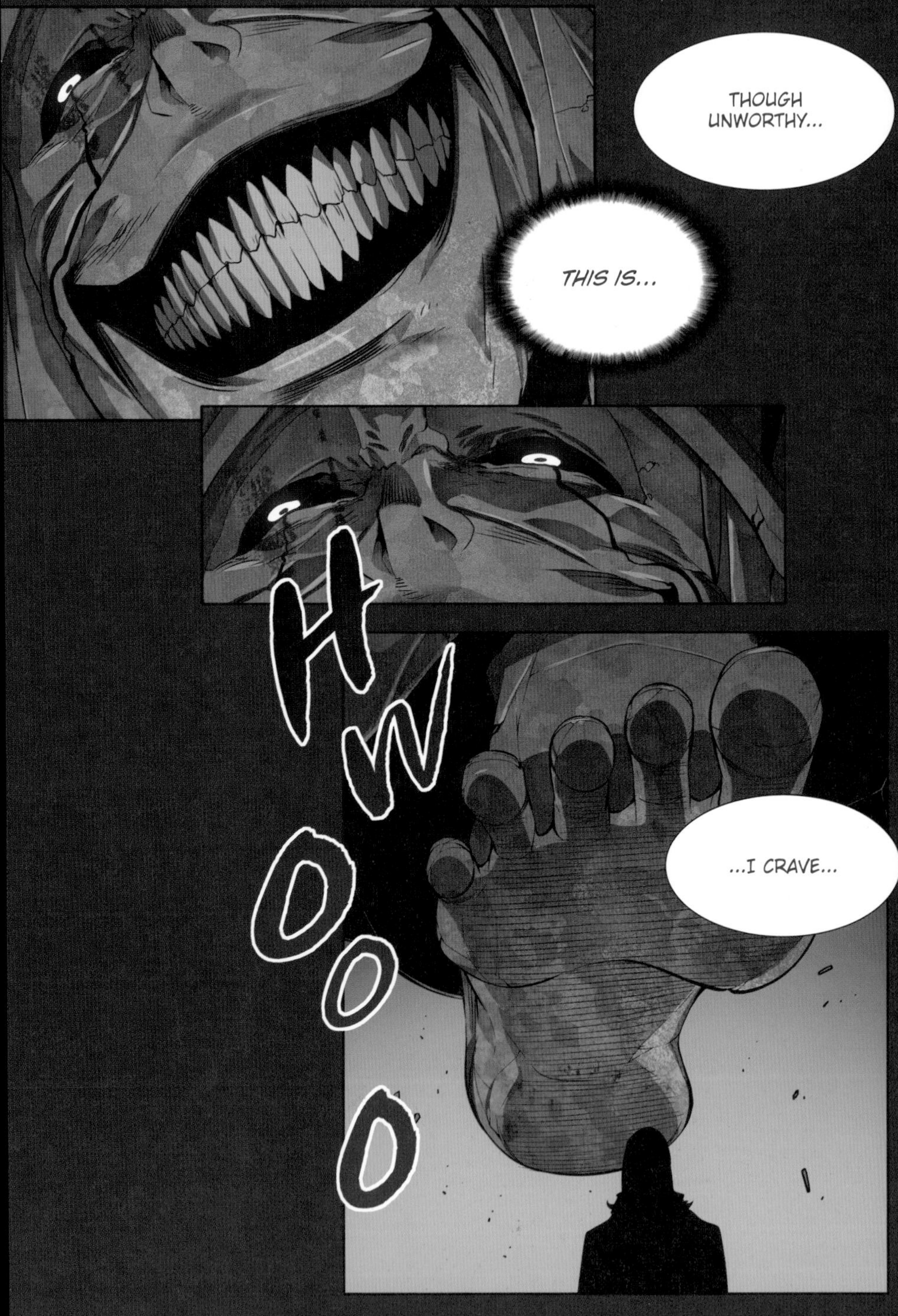
THOUGH UNWORTHY...
THIS IS...
HWOOO
...I CRAVE...

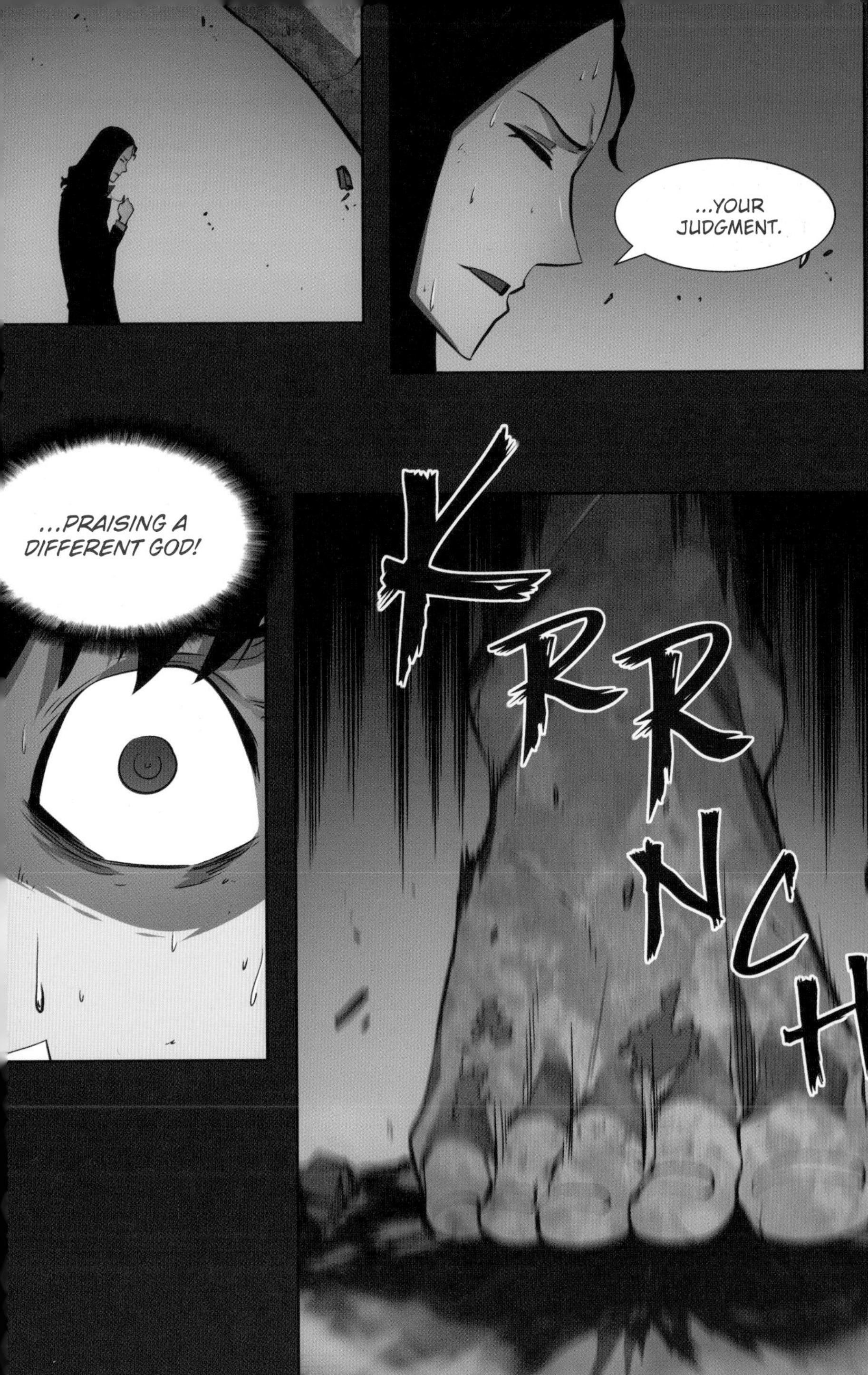
...YOUR JUDGMENT.
...PRAISING A DIFFERENT GOD!
KRRNCH

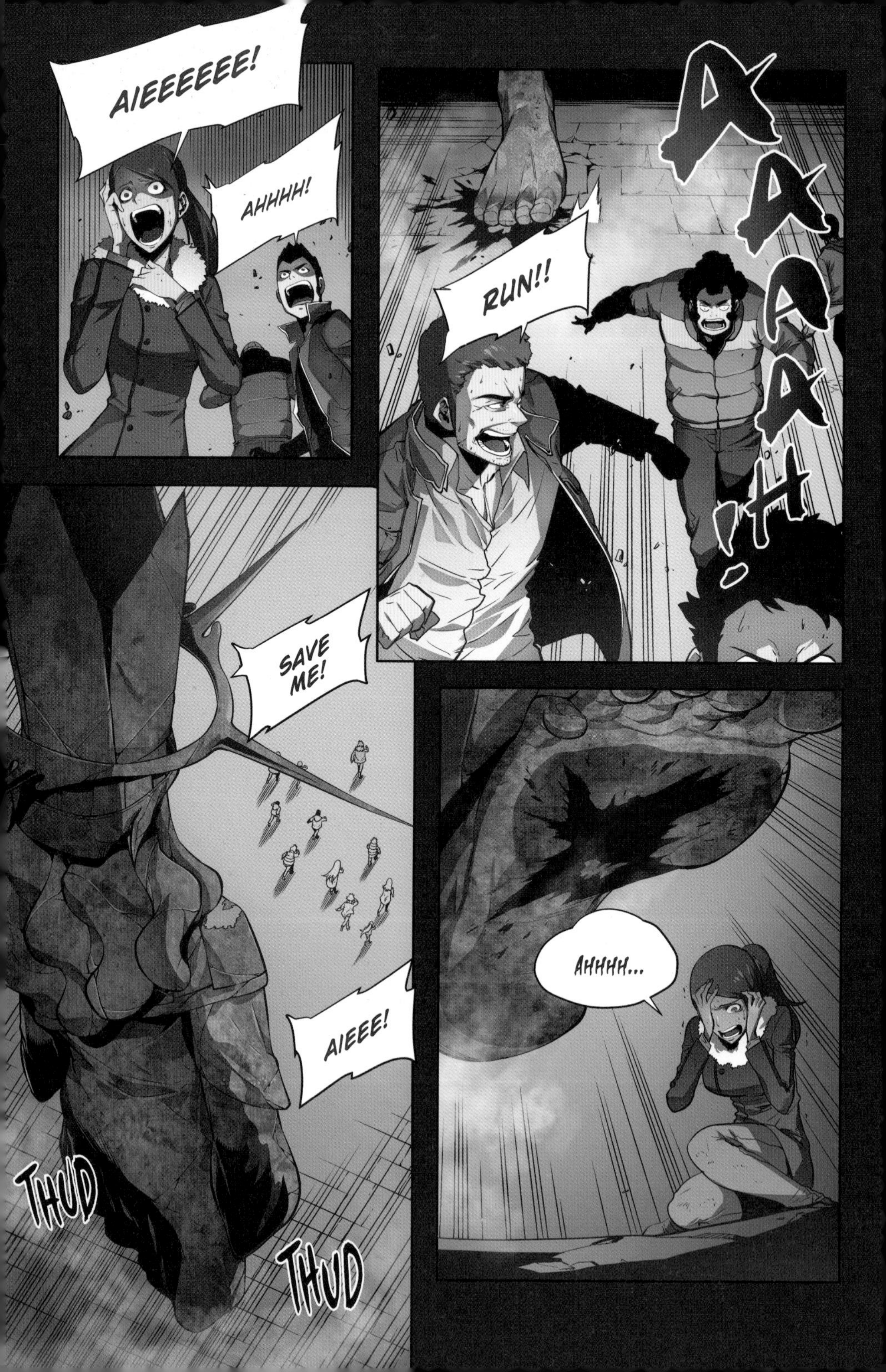
AIEEEEEE!
AHHHH!
RUN!!
AAAAH!
SAVE ME!
AIEEE!
THUD
THUD
AHHHH...

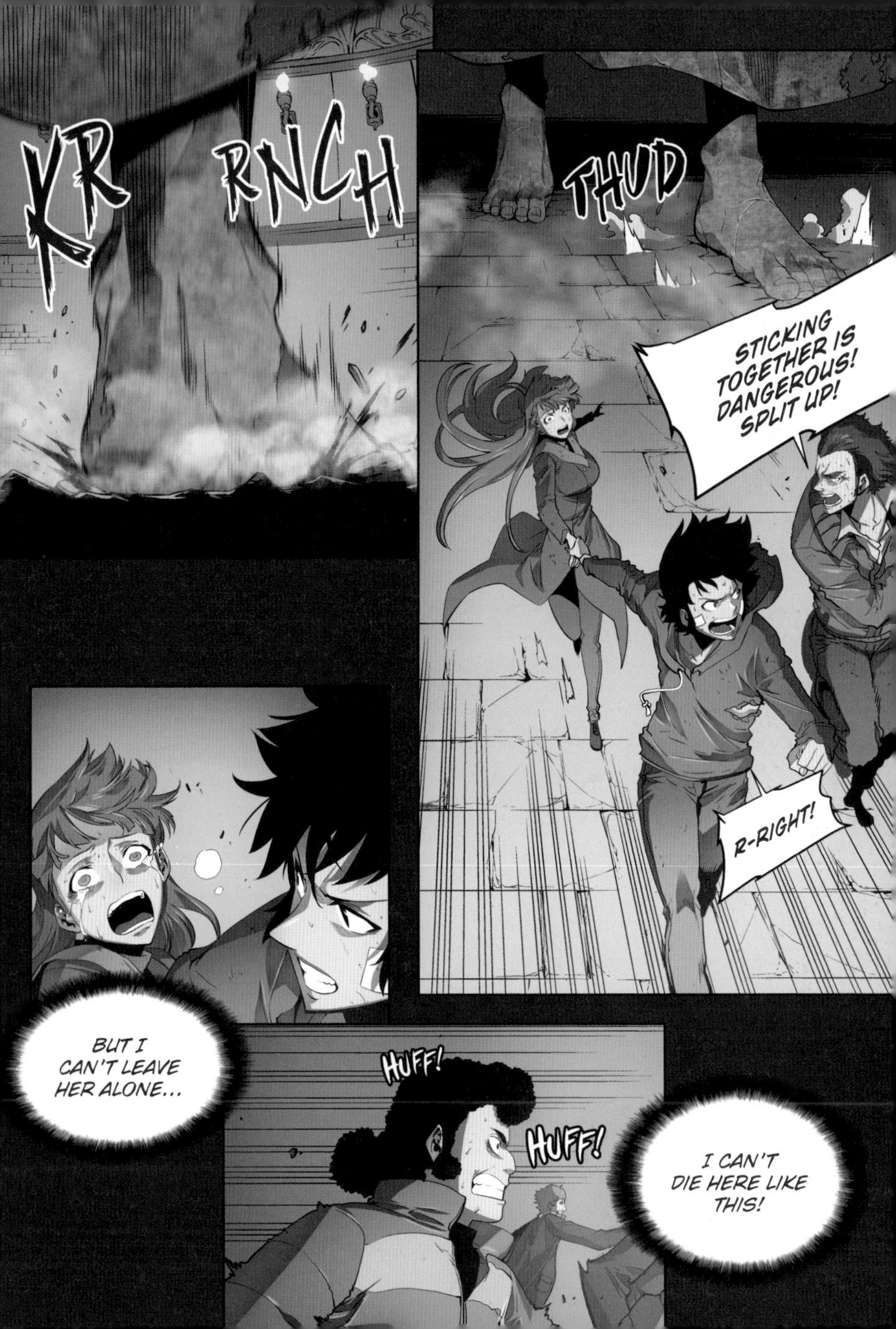
KR RNCH
THUD
STICKING TOGETHER IS DANGEROUS! SPLIT UP!
R-RIGHT!
BUT I CAN'T LEAVE HER ALONE...
HUFF!
HUFF!
I CAN'T DIE HERE LIKE THIS!

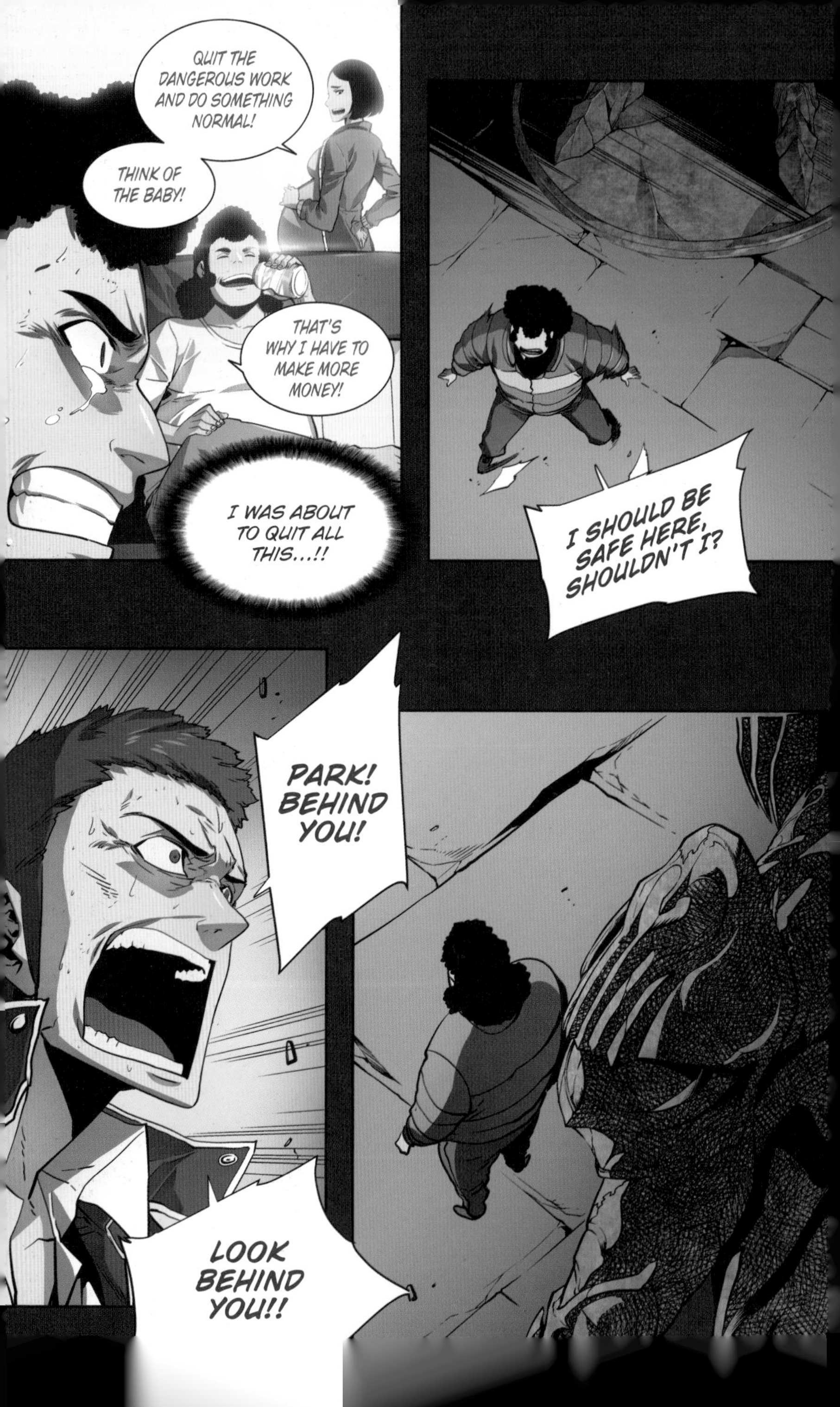
QUIT THE DANGEROUS WORK AND DO SOMETHING NORMAL!
THINK OF THE BABY!
THAT'S WHY I HAVE TO MAKE MORE MONEY!
I WAS ABOUT TO QUIT ALL THIS...!!
I SHOULD BE SAFE HERE, SHOULDN'T I?
PARK! BEHIND YOU!
LOOK BEHIND YOU!!

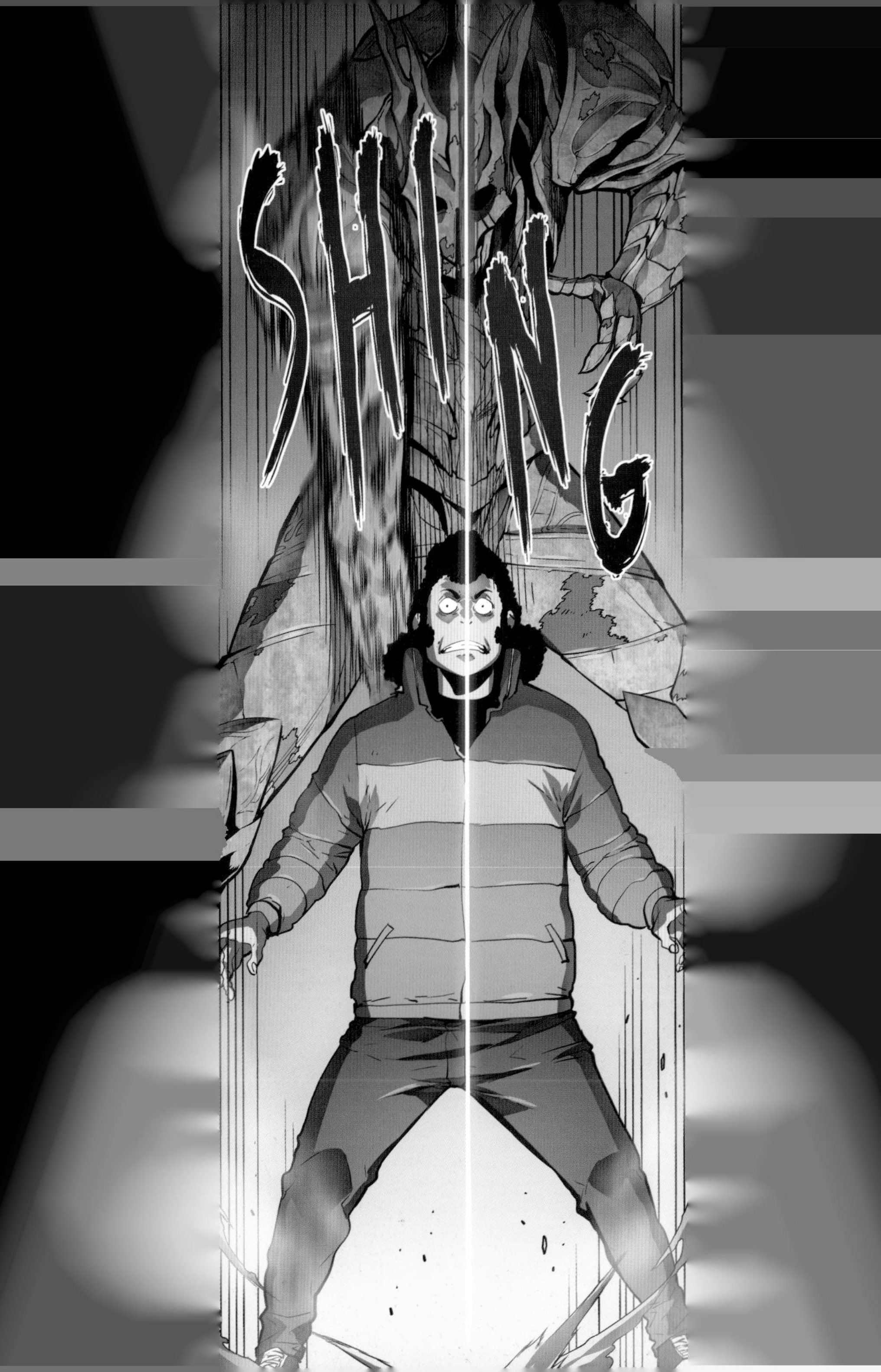
SHIING

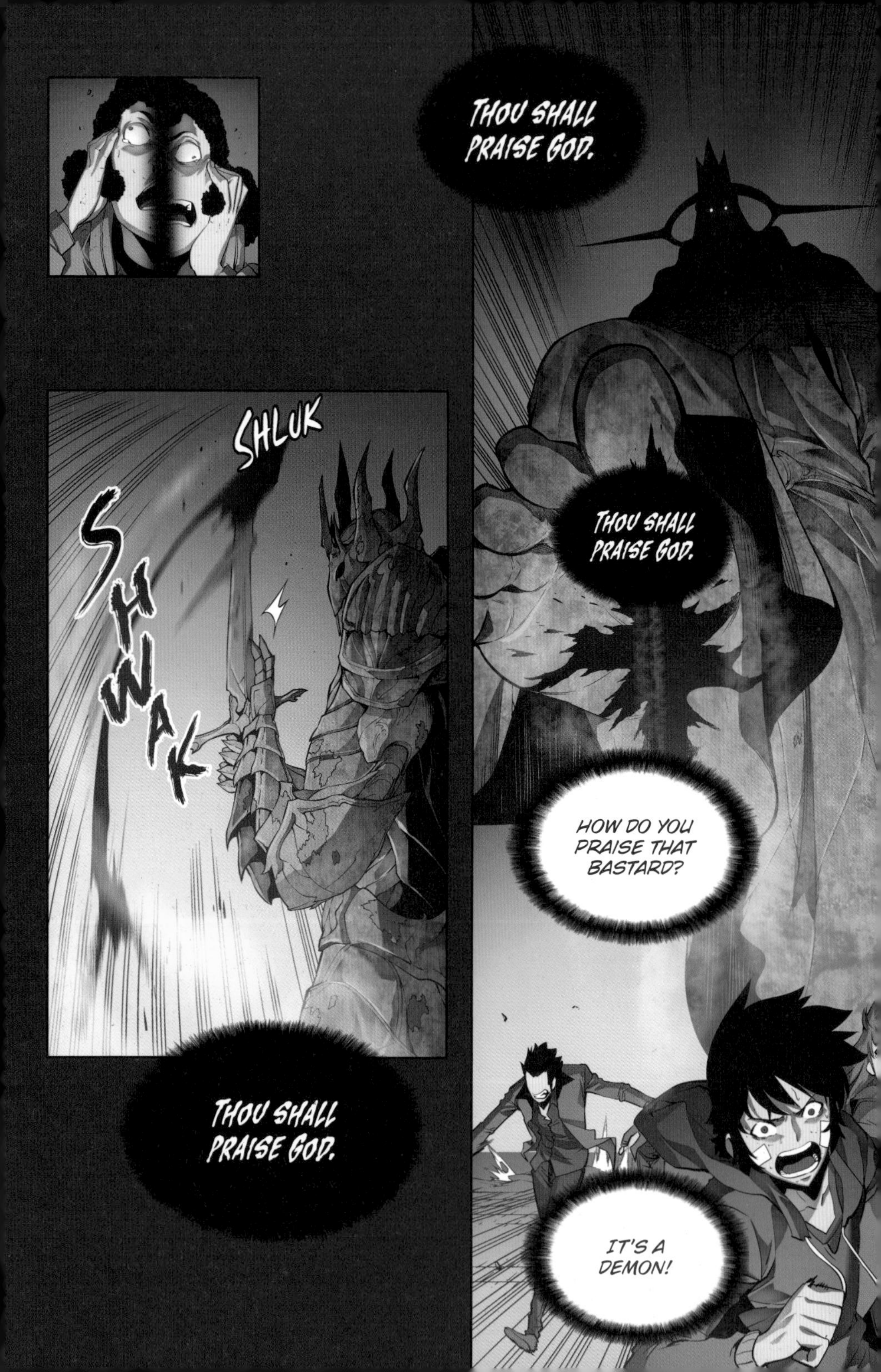
SHLUK
SHWAK
THOU SHALL PRAISE GOD.
THOU SHALL PRAISE GOD.
THOU SHALL PRAISE GOD.
HOW DO YOU PRAISE THAT BASTARD?
IT'S A DEMON!

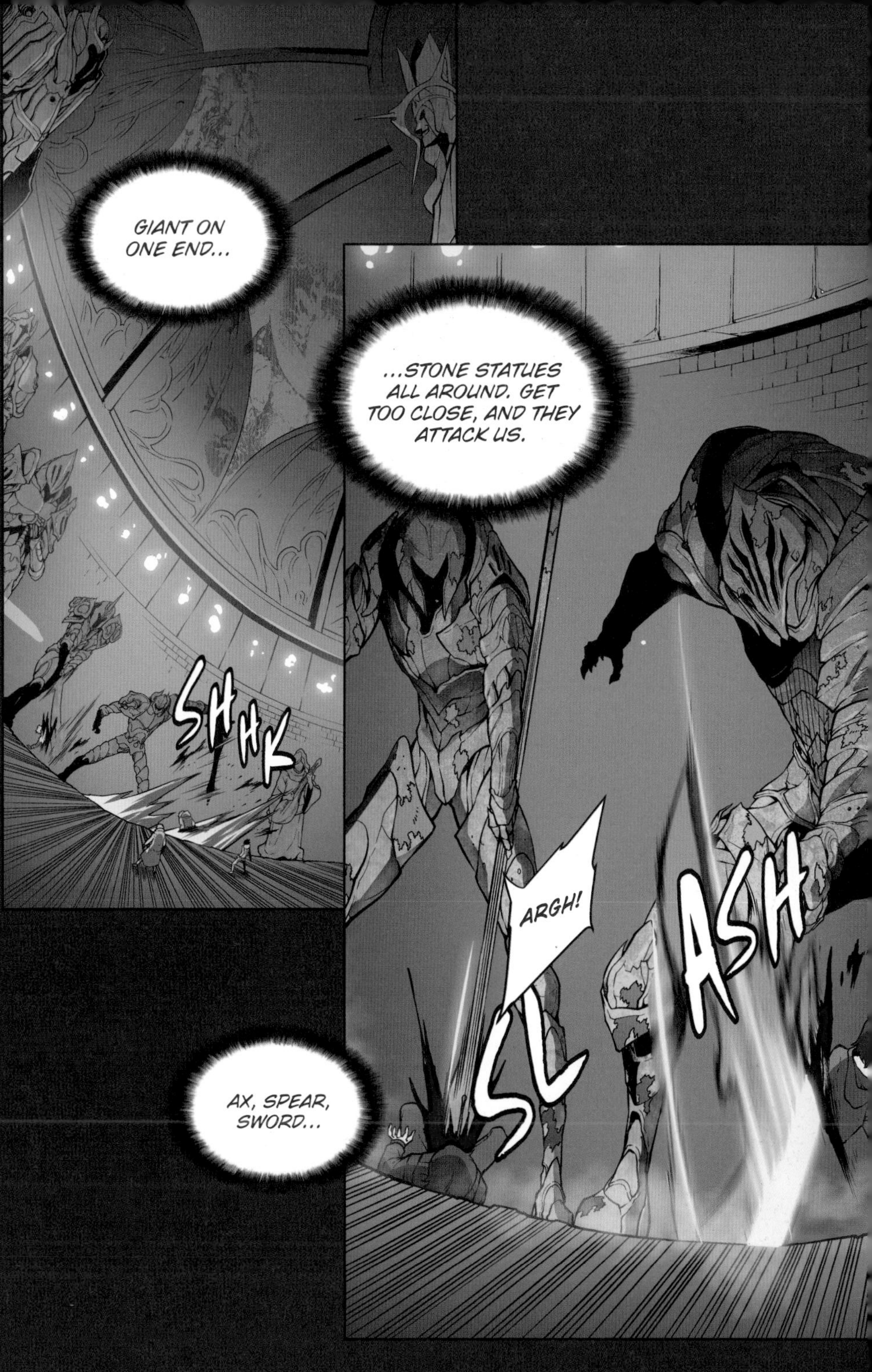
GIANT ON ONE END...
SHHK
...STONE STATUES ALL AROUND. GET TOO CLOSE, AND THEY ATTACK US.
ARGH!
SLASH
AX, SPEAR, SWORD...

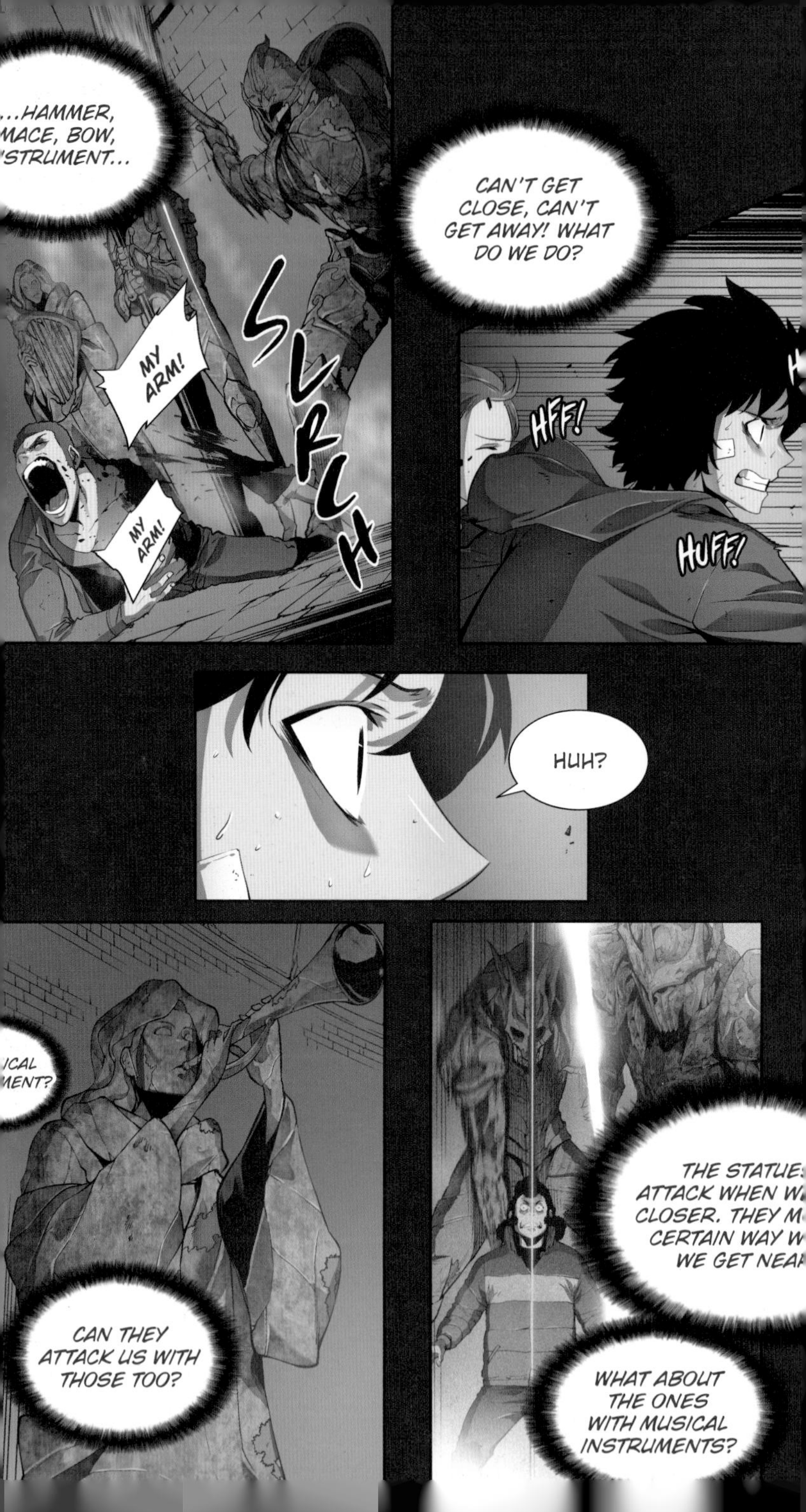
…HAMMER, MACE, BOW, STRUMENT…
MY ARM!
SLRCH
MY ARM!
CAN'T GET CLOSE, CAN'T GET AWAY! WHAT DO WE DO?
HFF!
HUFF!
HUH?
ICAL MENT?
CAN THEY ATTACK US WITH THOSE TOO?
THE STATUE ATTACK WHEN W CLOSER. THEY M CERTAIN WAY W WE GET NEA
WHAT ABOUT THE ONES WITH MUSICAL INSTRUMENTS?

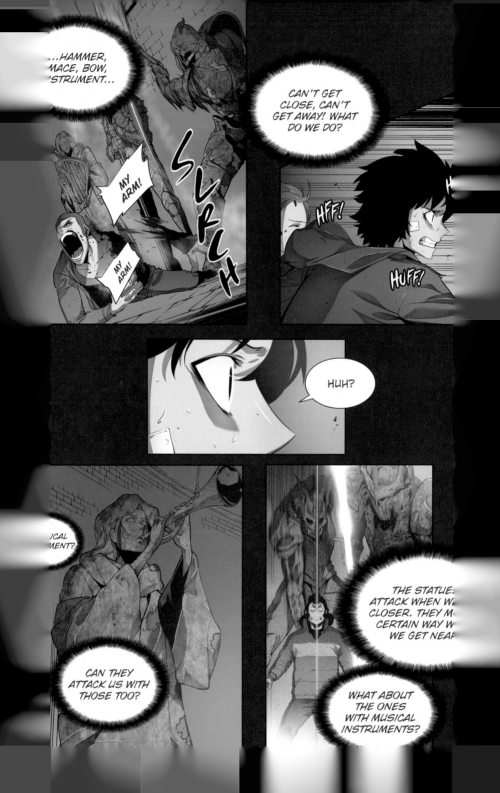

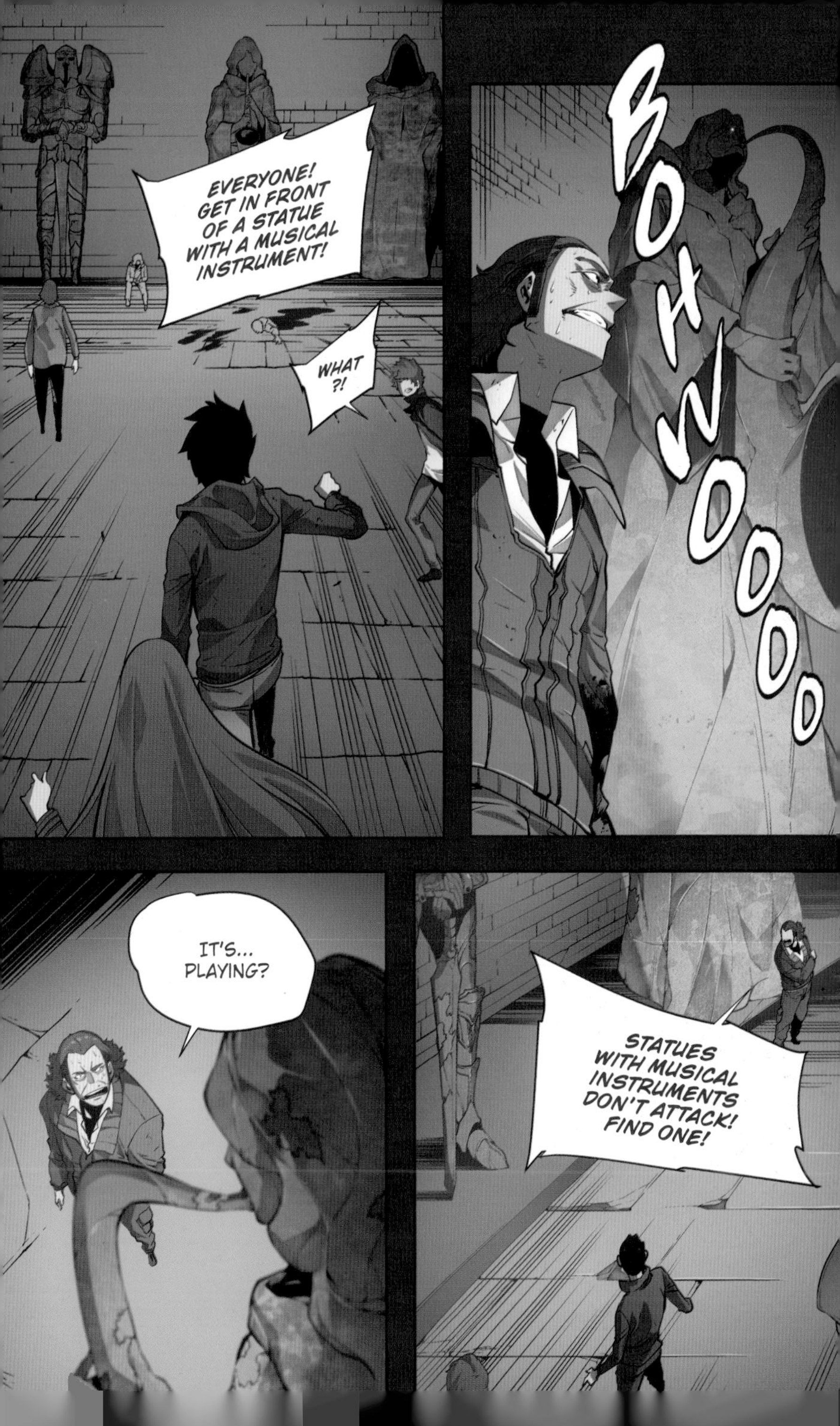
EVERYONE! GET IN FRONT OF A STATUE WITH A MUSICAL INSTRUMENT!
WHAT ?!
BOHWOOOOOO
IT'S... PLAYING?
STATUES WITH MUSICAL INSTRUMENTS DON'T ATTACK! FIND ONE!

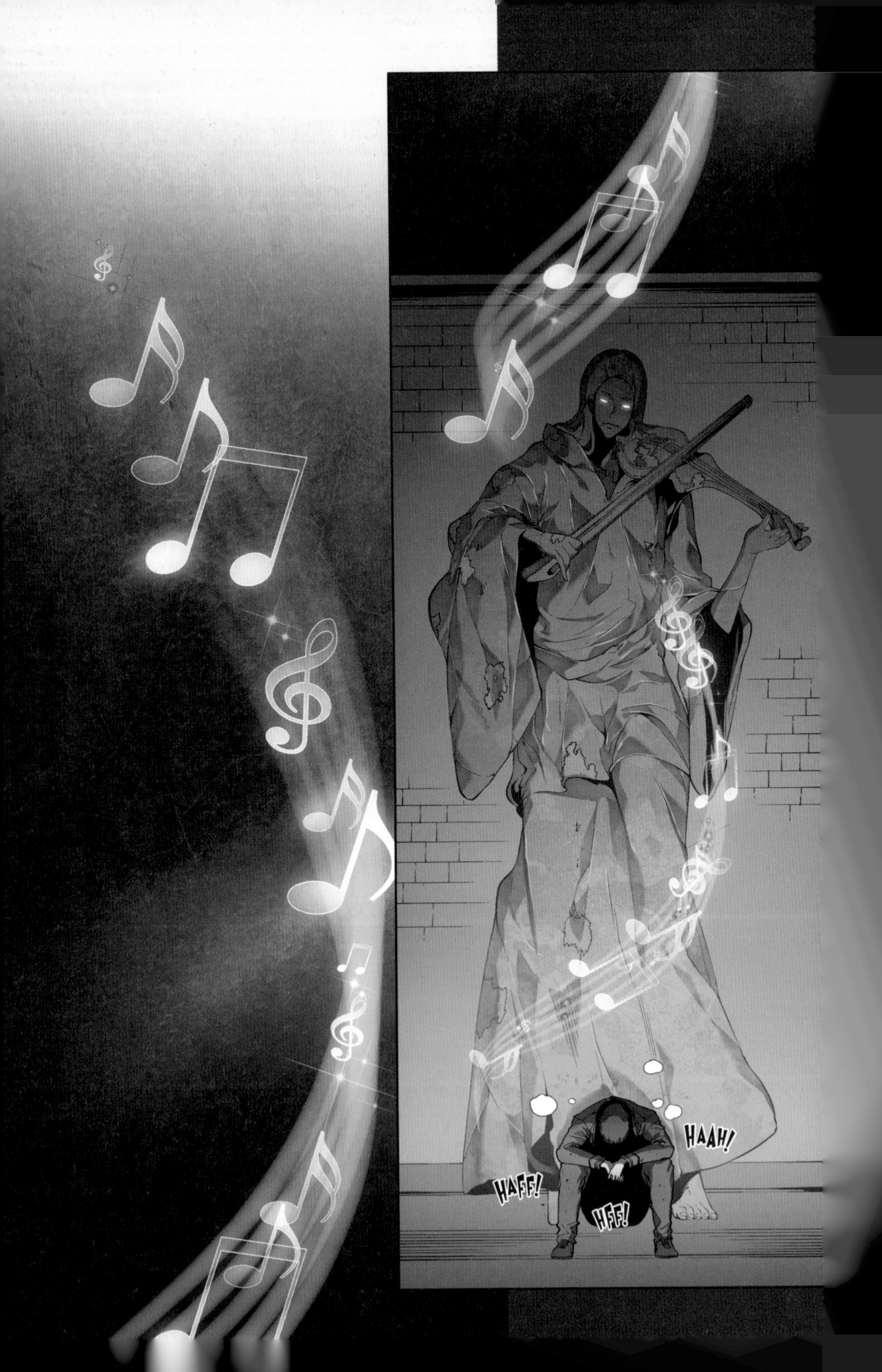
HAAH!
HAFF!
HFF!

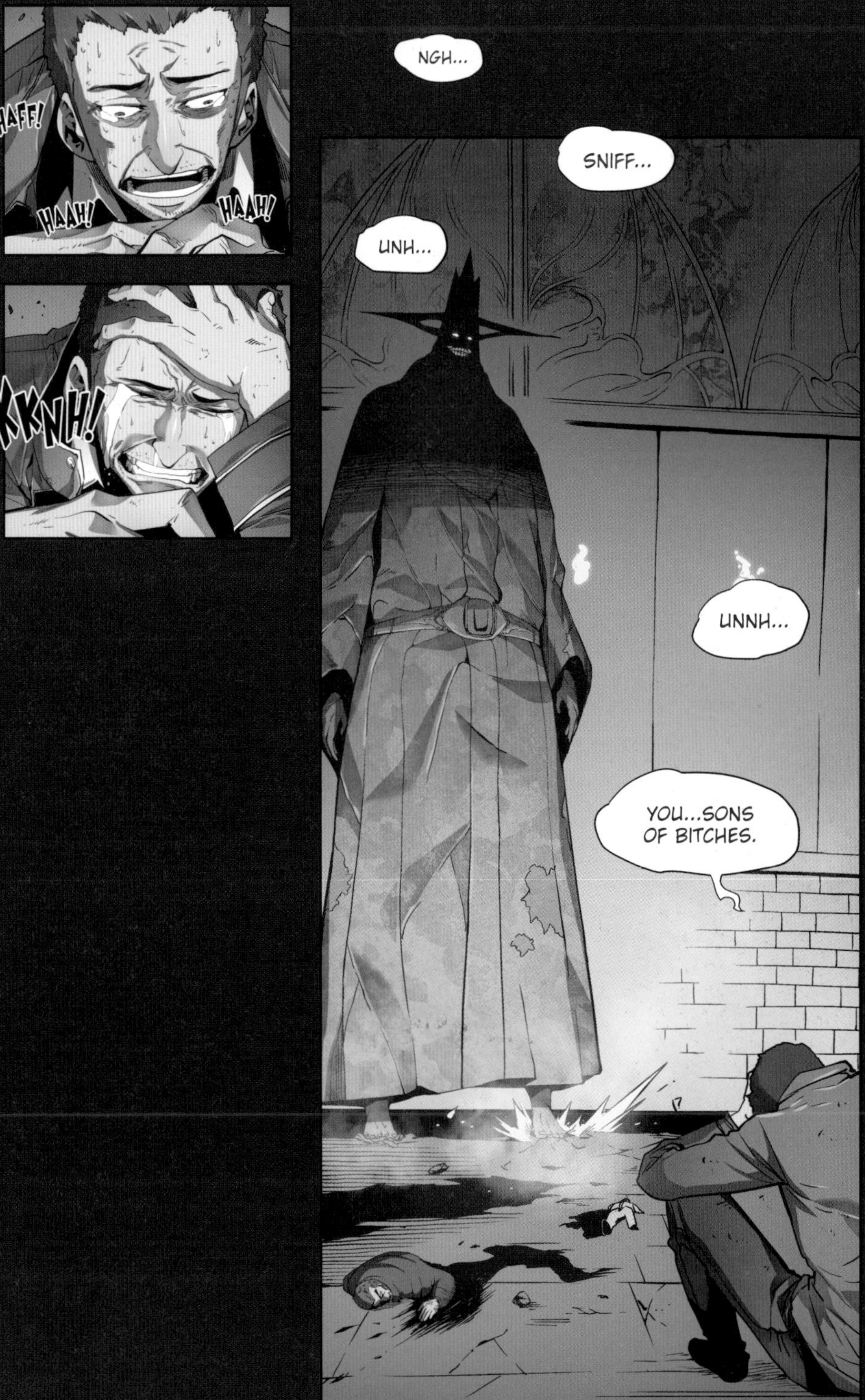
HAFF!
HAAH!
HAAH!
KKNH!
NGH...
SNIFF...
UNH...
UNNH...
YOU...SONS OF BITCHES.

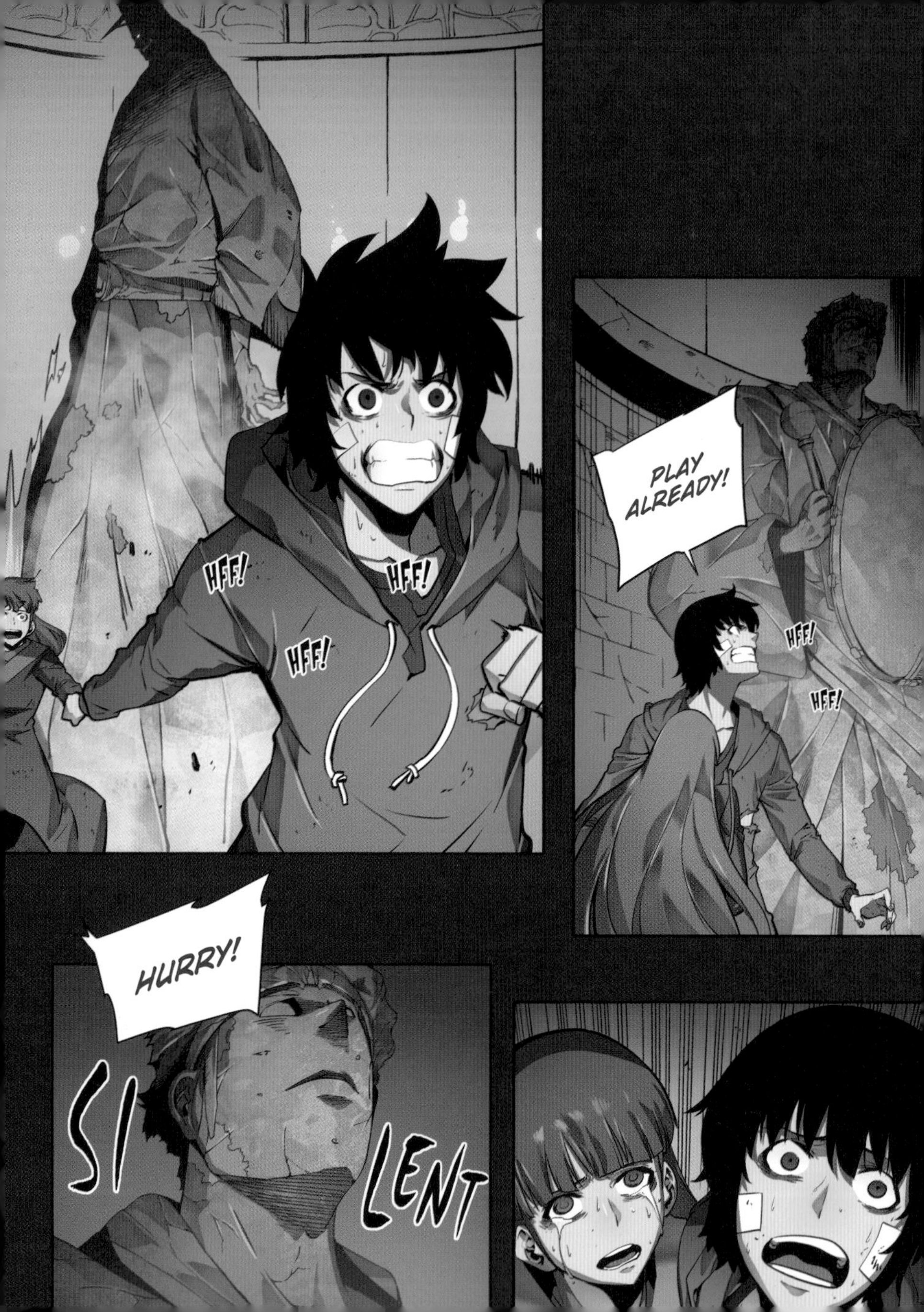
HFF!
HFF!
HFF!
PLAY ALREADY!
HFF!
HFF!
HURRY!
SI LENT

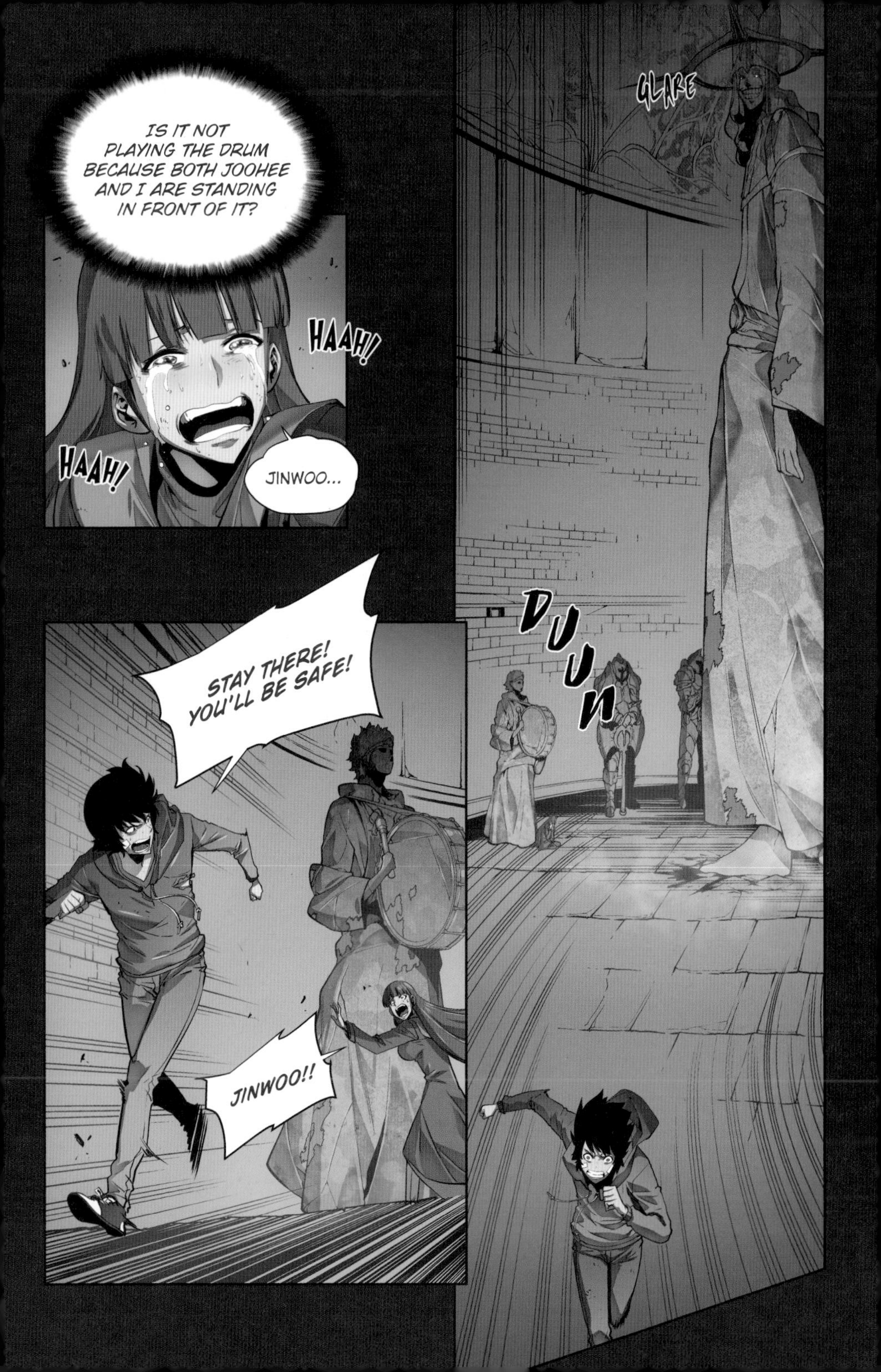
GLARE
IS IT NOT PLAYING THE DRUM BECAUSE BOTH JOOHEE AND I ARE STANDING IN FRONT OF IT?
HAAH!
HAAH!
JINWOO...
DUUN
STAY THERE! YOU'LL BE SAFE!
JINWOO!!

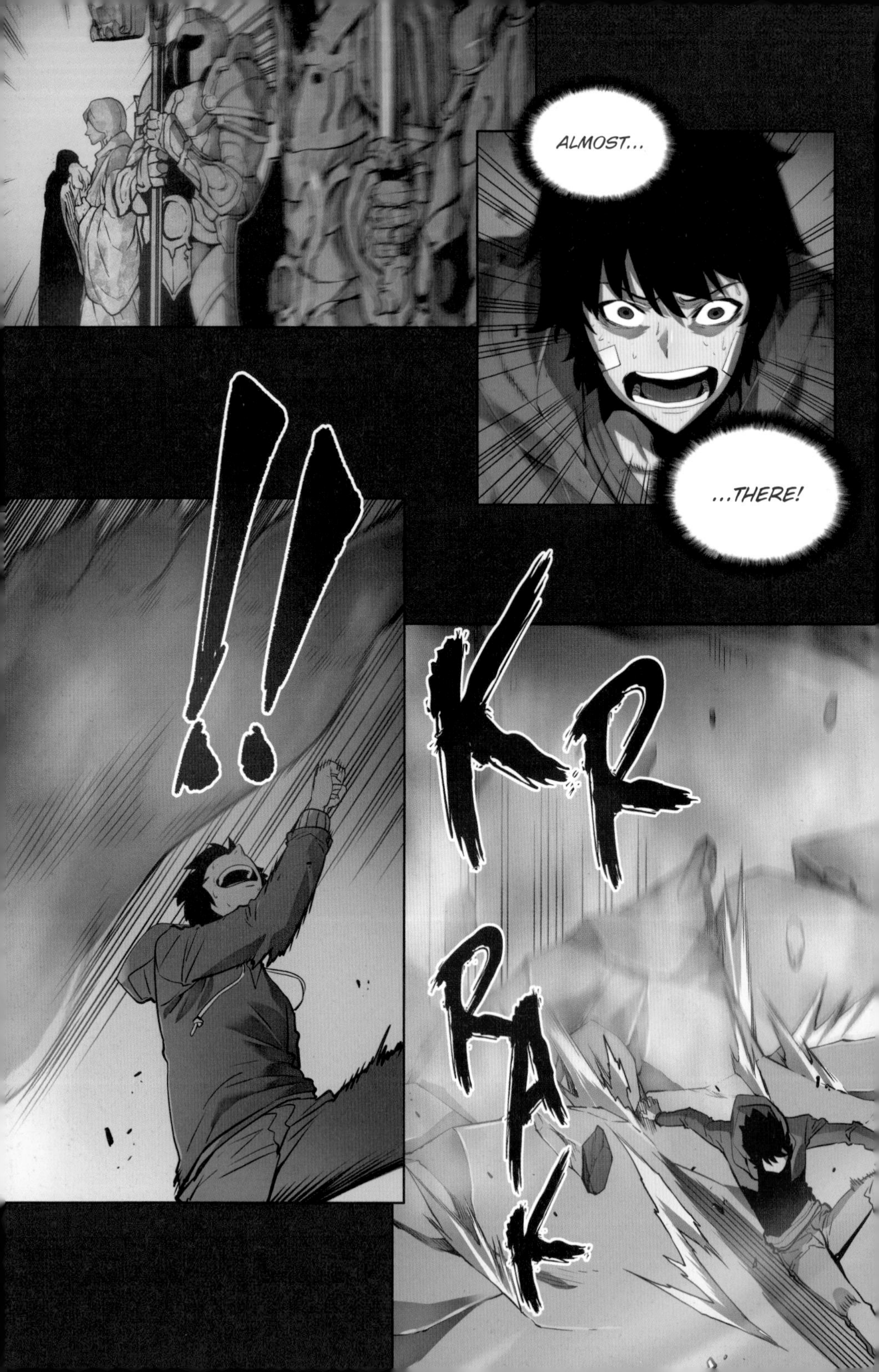
ALMOST...
...THERE!
!!
KRRAK

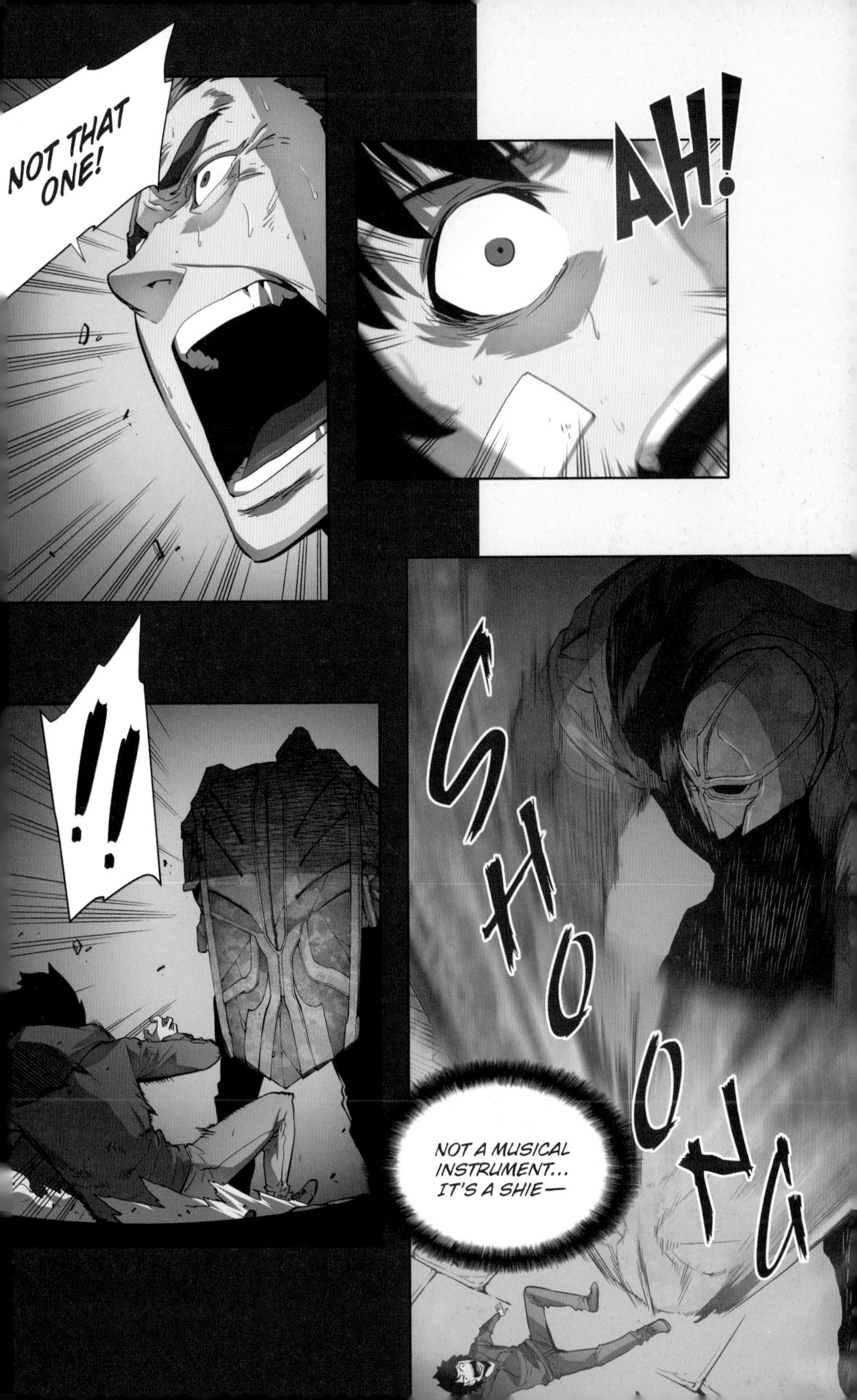
NOT THAT ONE!
AH!
!!
SHOONG
NOT A MUSICAL INSTRUMENT... IT'S A SHIE—

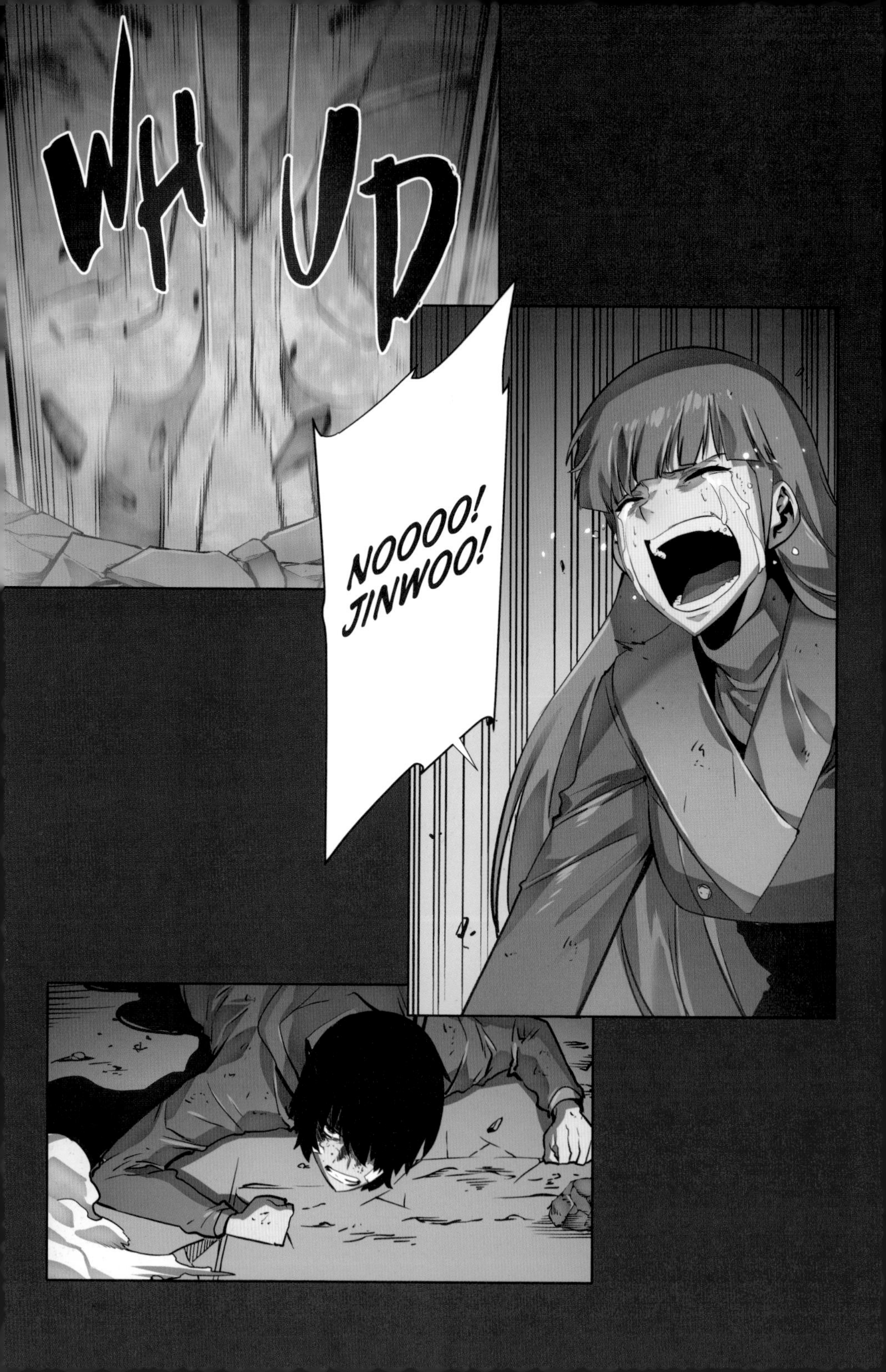
WHUD
NOOOO! JINWOO!

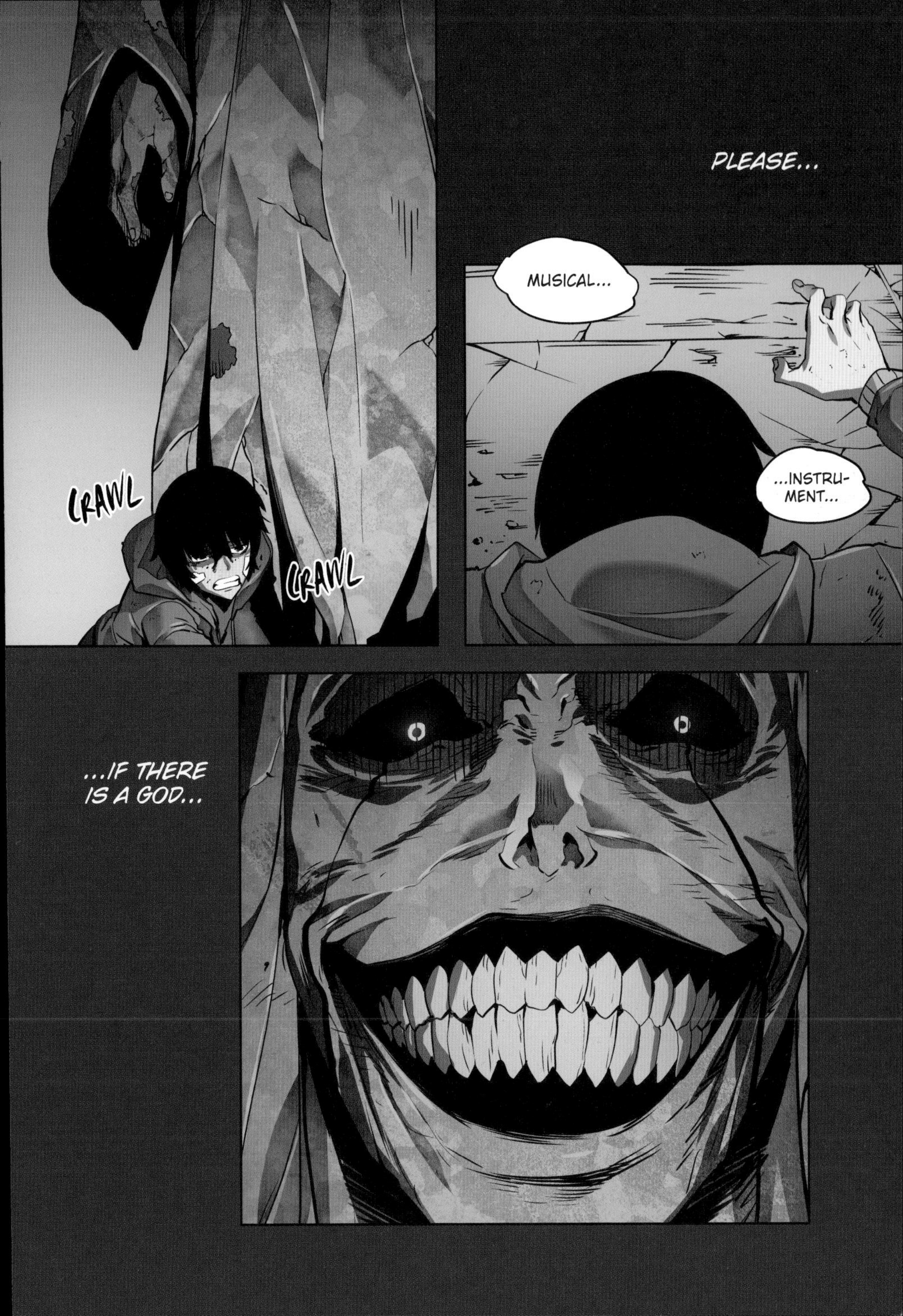
CRAWL
CRAWL
PLEASE...
MUSICAL...
...INSTRU-
MENT...
...IF THERE
IS A GOD...

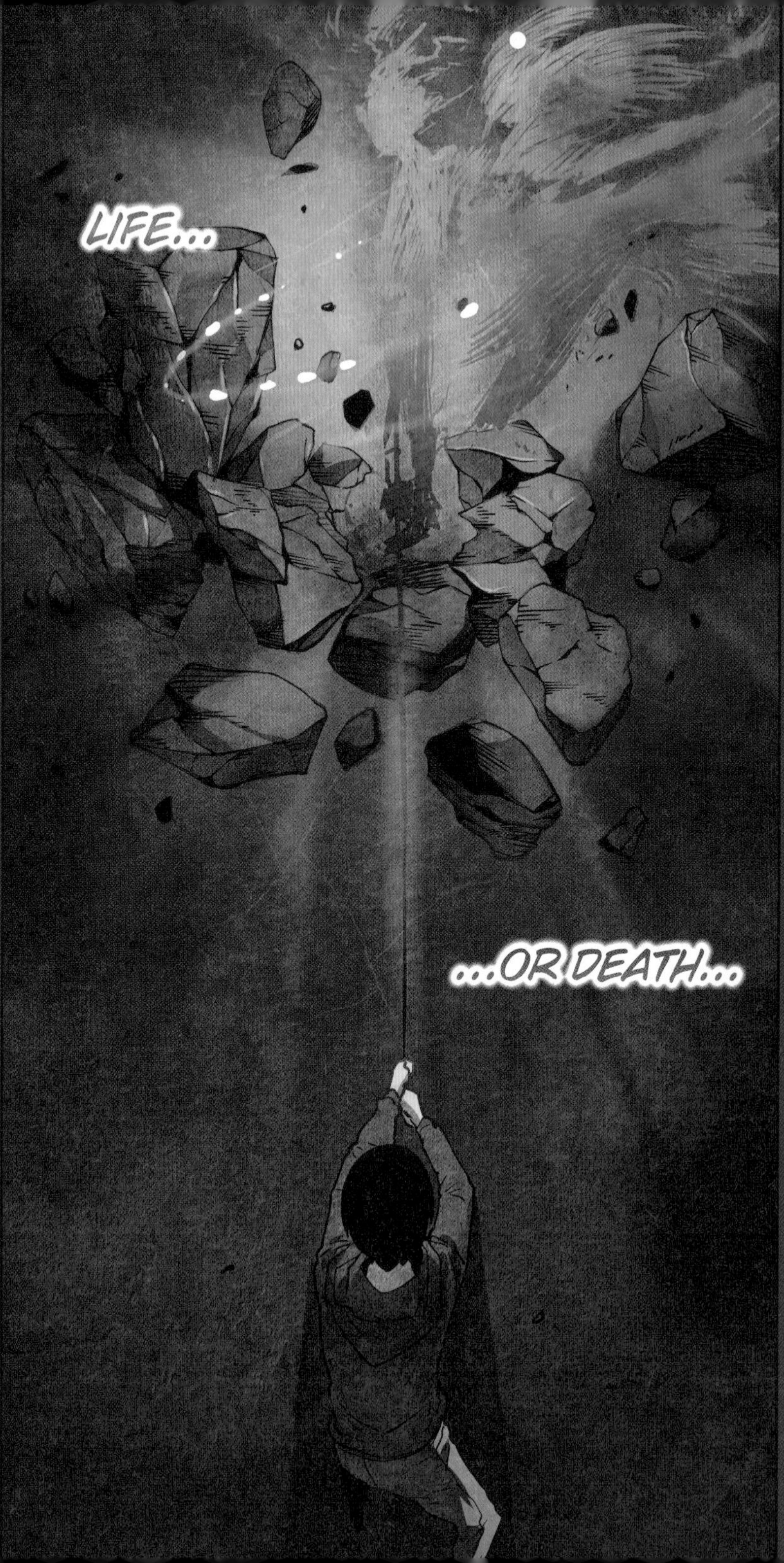
LIFE...
...OR DEATH...

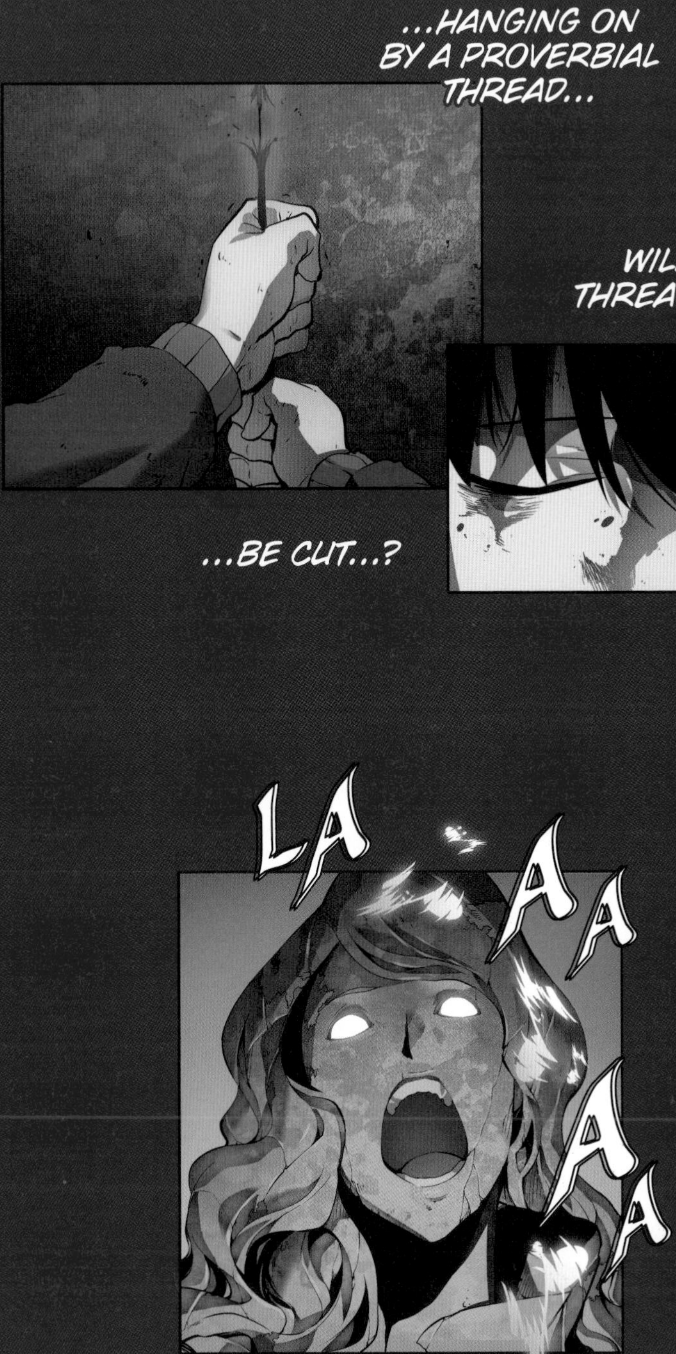
...HANGING ON BY A PROVERBIAL THREAD...
WILL THE THREAD NOW...
...BE CUT...?
LAAAAAA

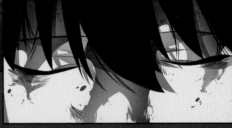

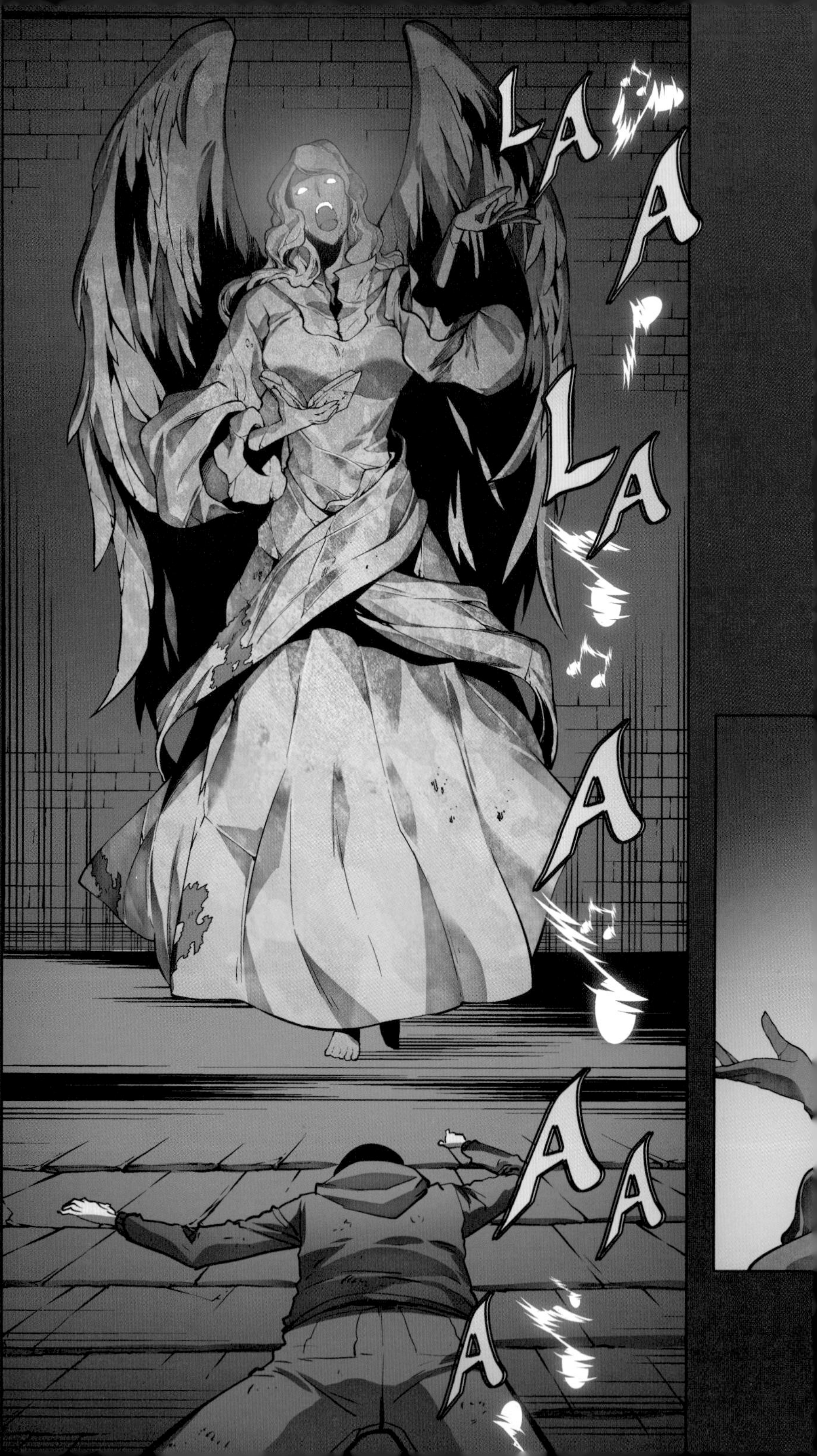
LAA
LAAAAA

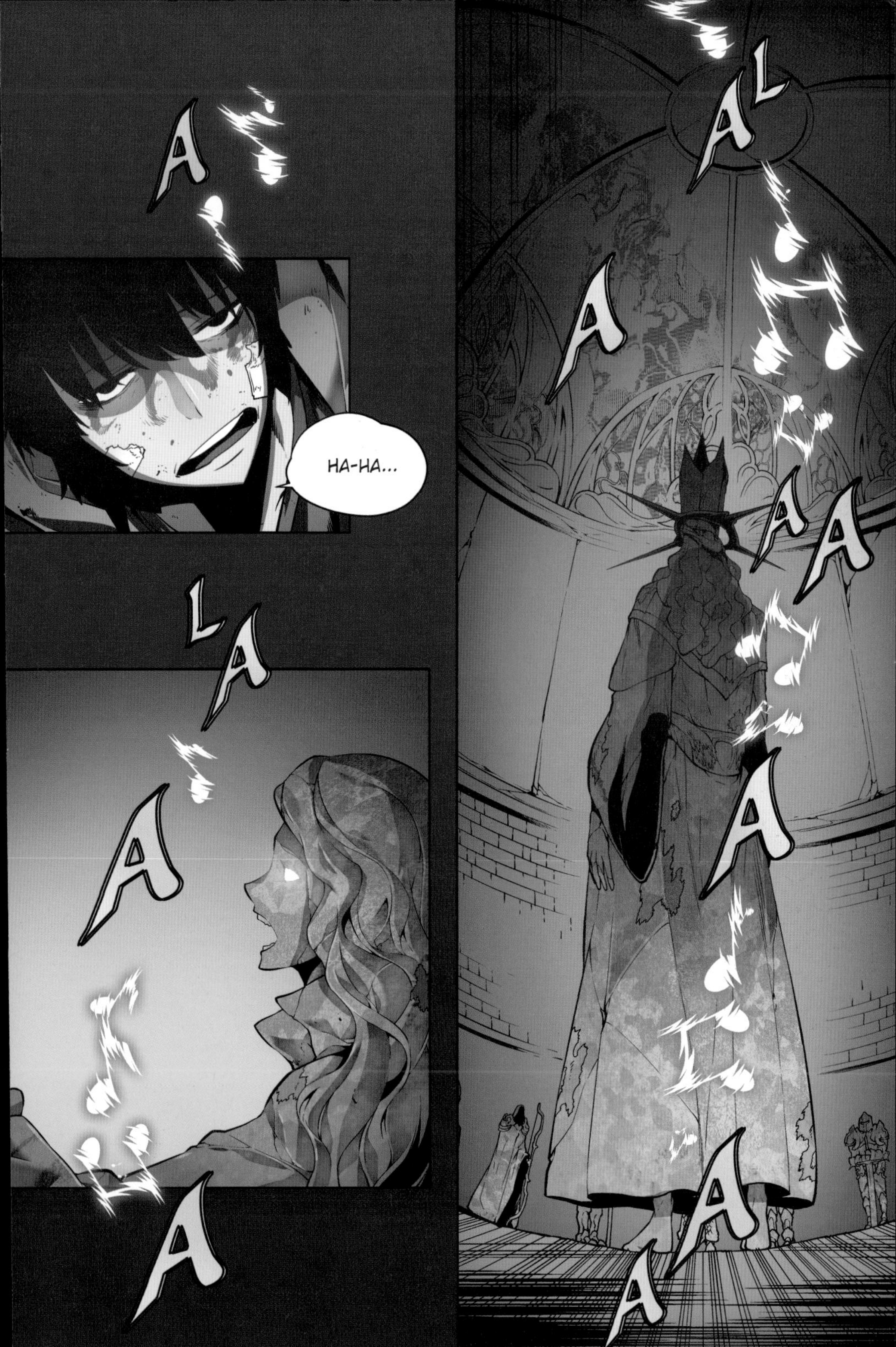
A
HA-HA...
LAAA
LAAAAAAA

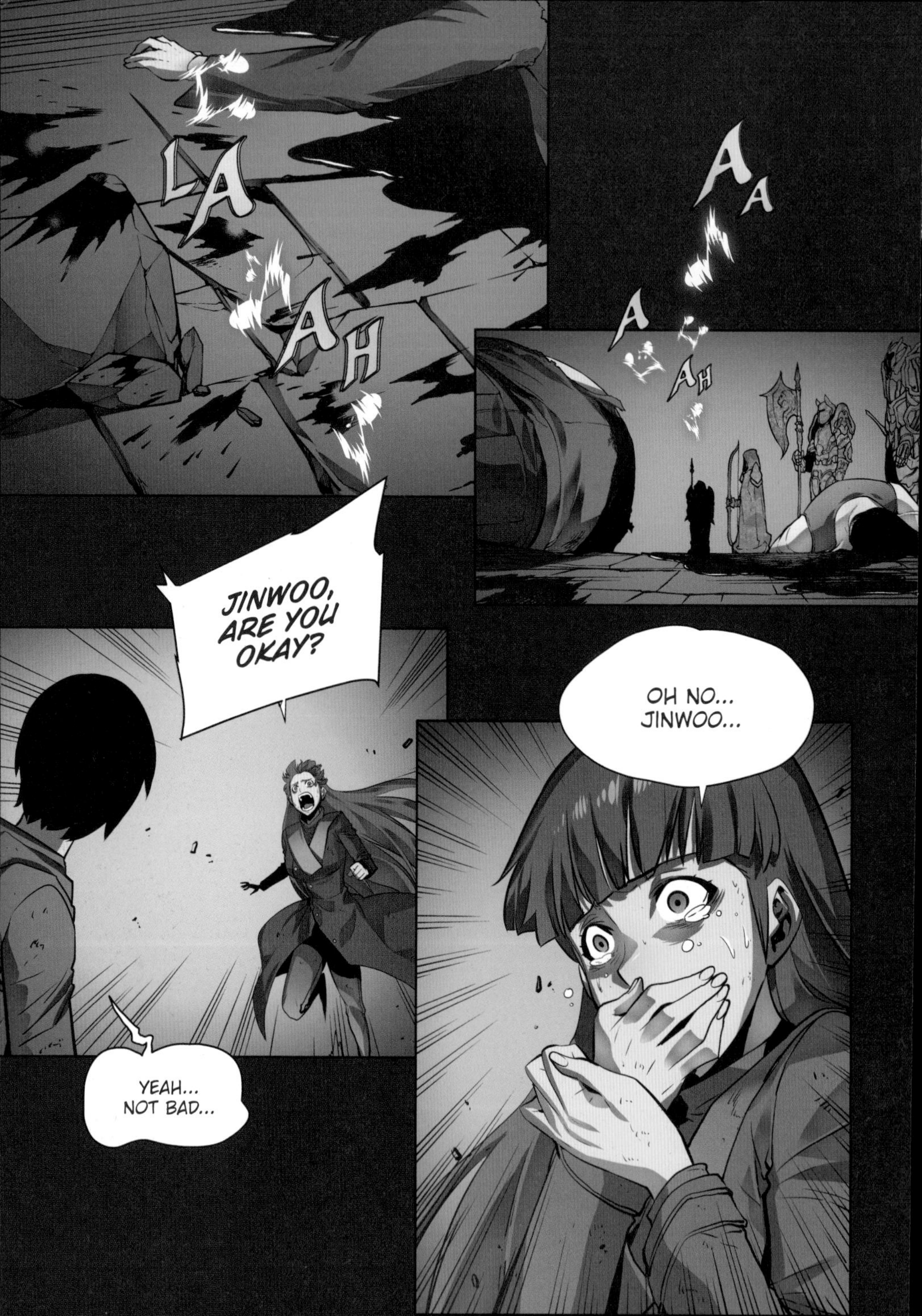
LA AH
AA AA AH
JINWOO, ARE YOU OKAY?
YEAH... NOT BAD...
OH NO... JINWOO...

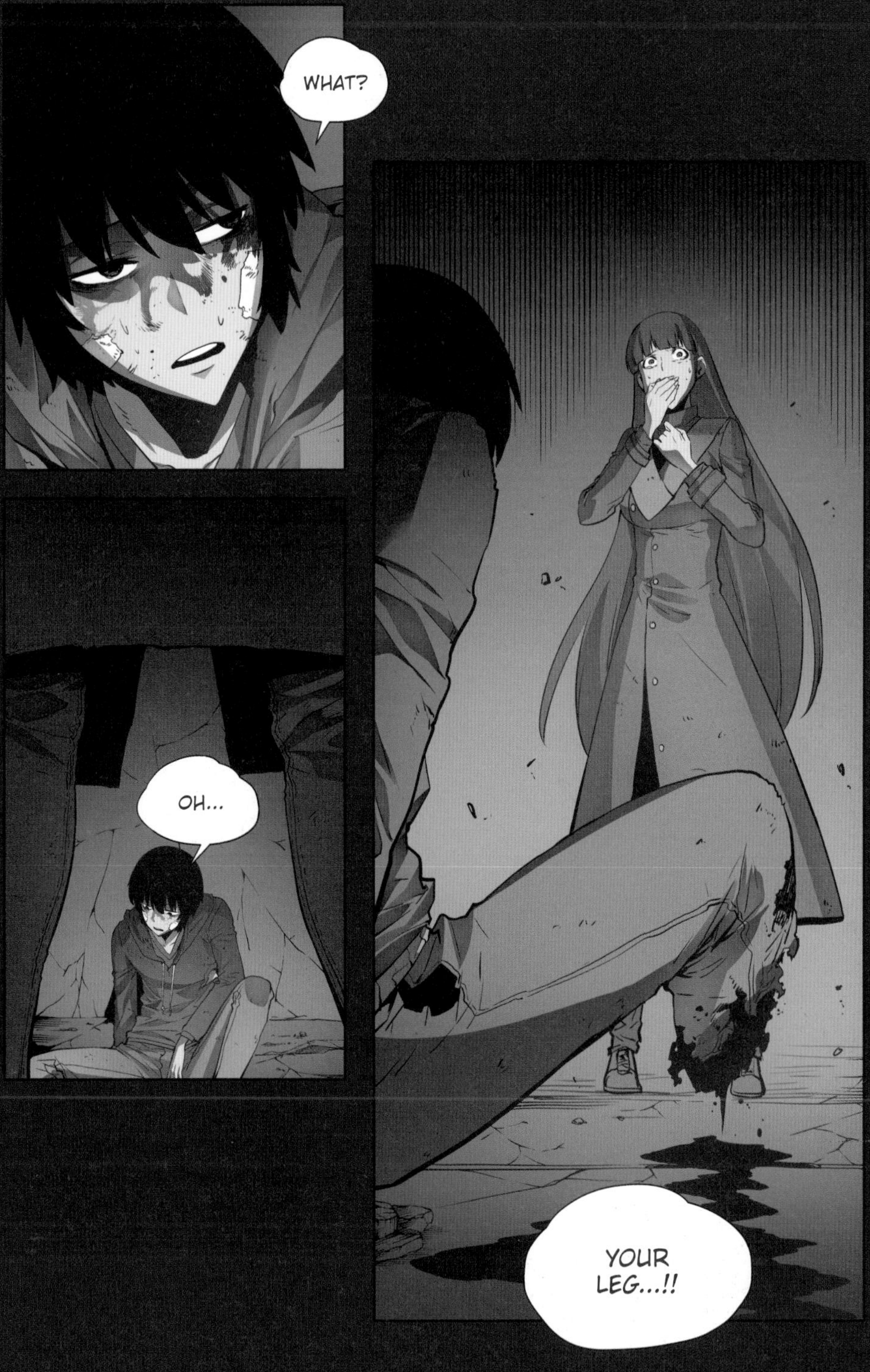
WHAT?
OH...
YOUR LEG...!!

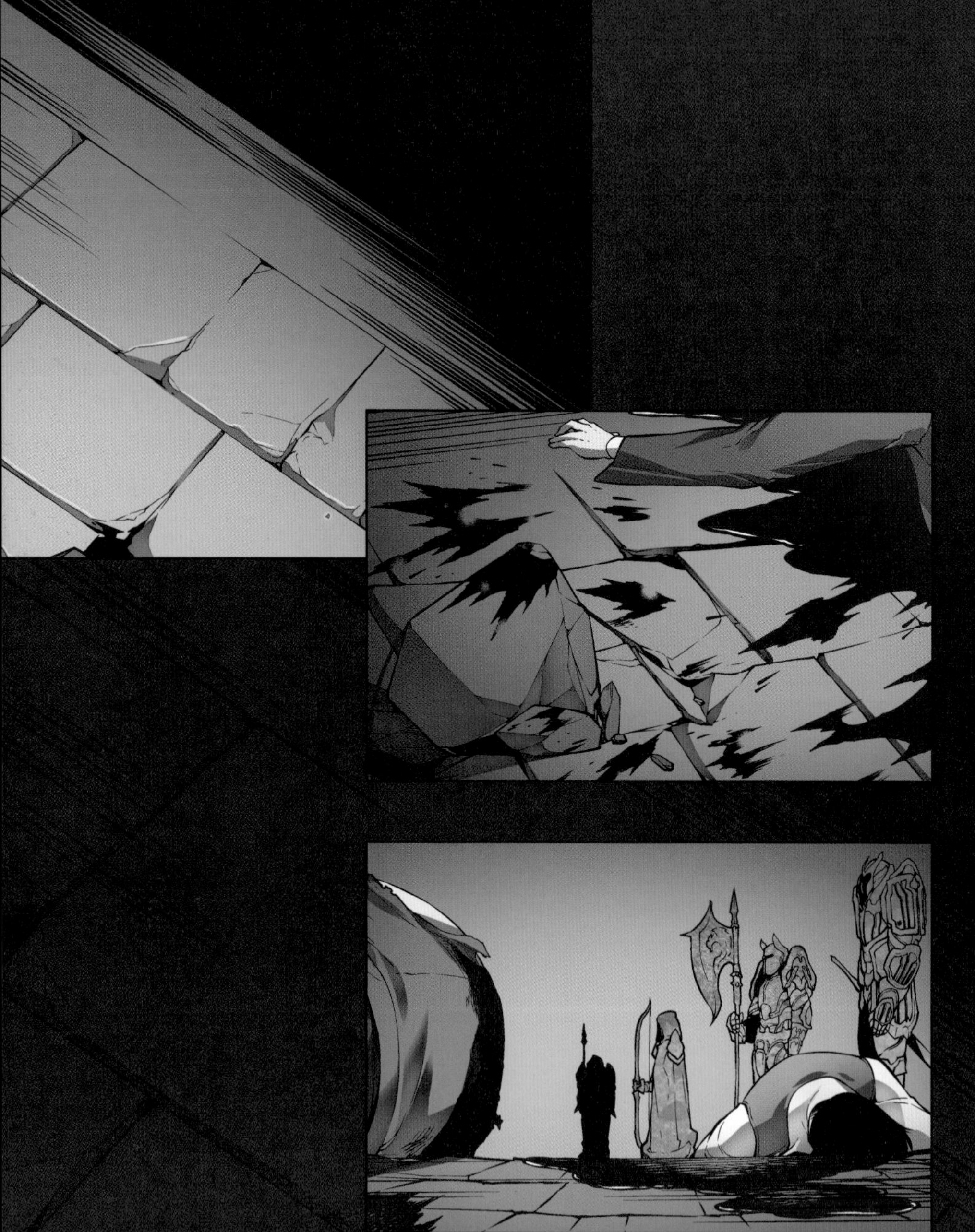

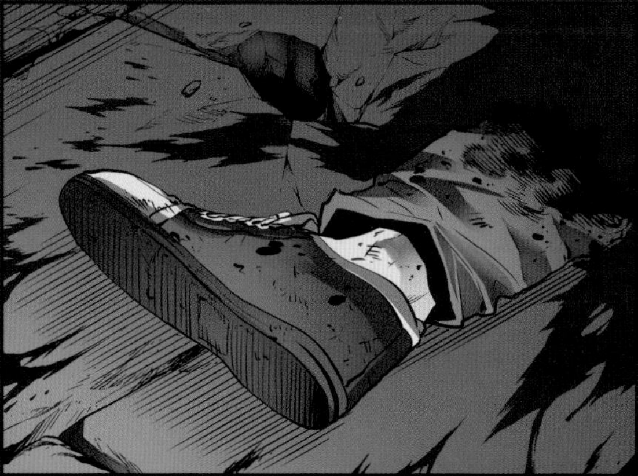
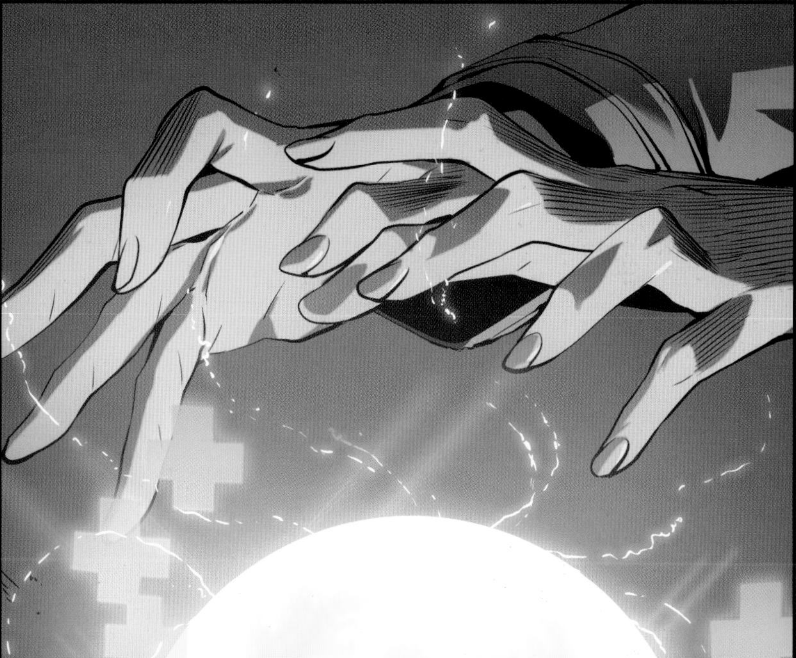

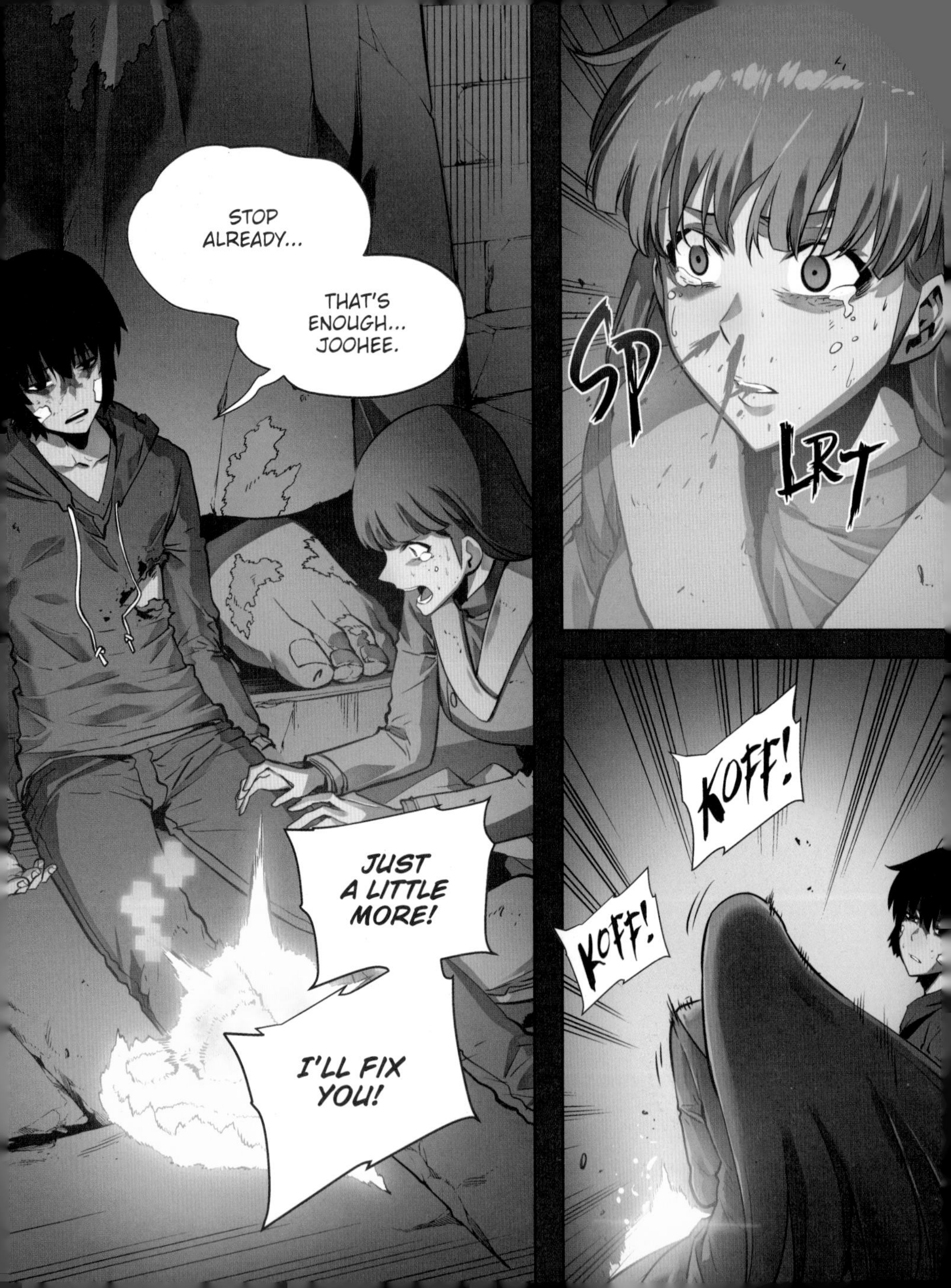
STOP ALREADY...
THAT'S ENOUGH... JOOHEE.
JUST A LITTLE MORE!
I'LL FIX YOU!
SPLRT
KOFF!
KOFF!

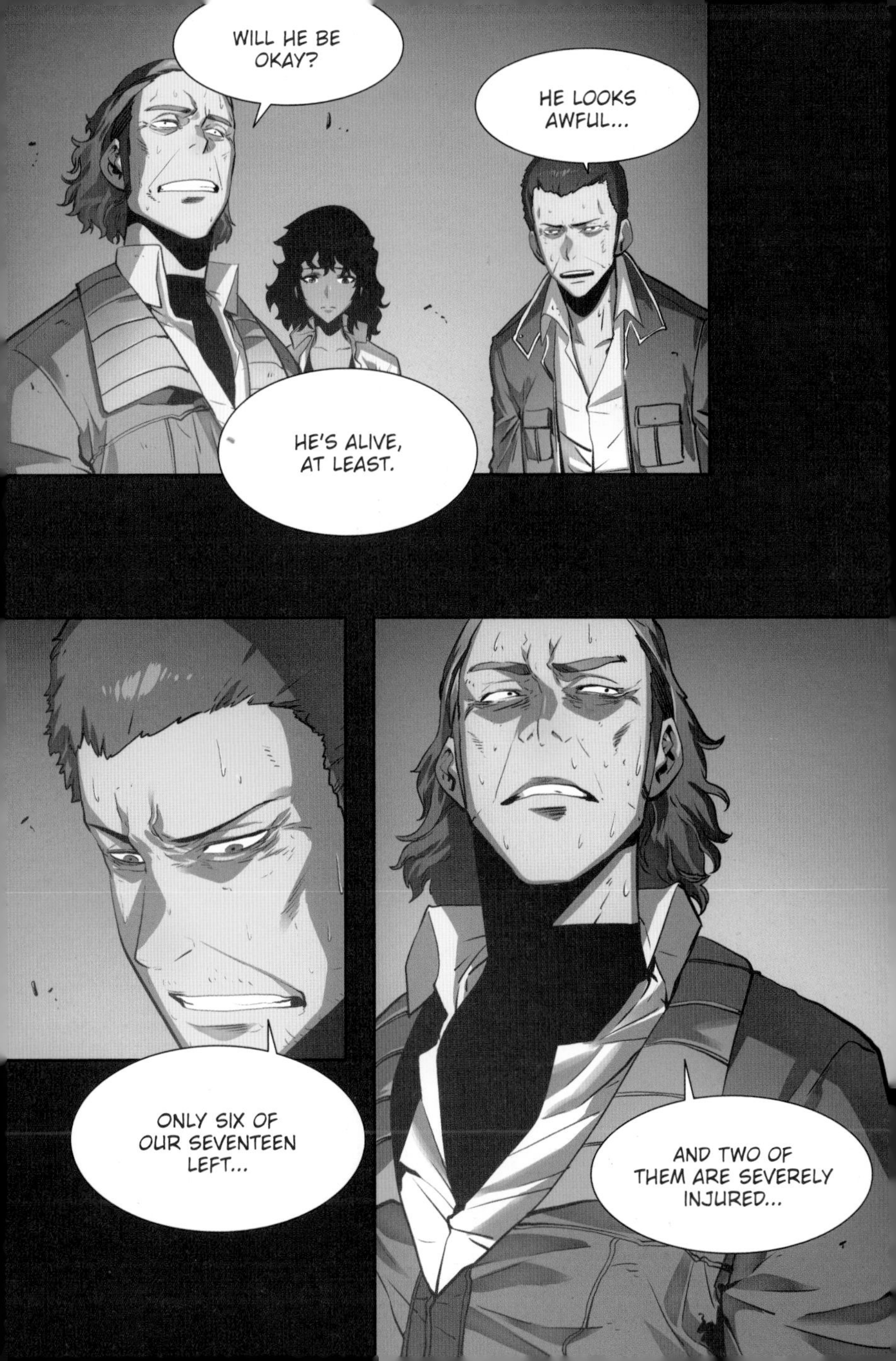
WILL HE BE OKAY?
HE LOOKS AWFUL...
HE'S ALIVE, AT LEAST.
ONLY SIX OF OUR SEVENTEEN LEFT...
AND TWO OF THEM ARE SEVERELY INJURED...

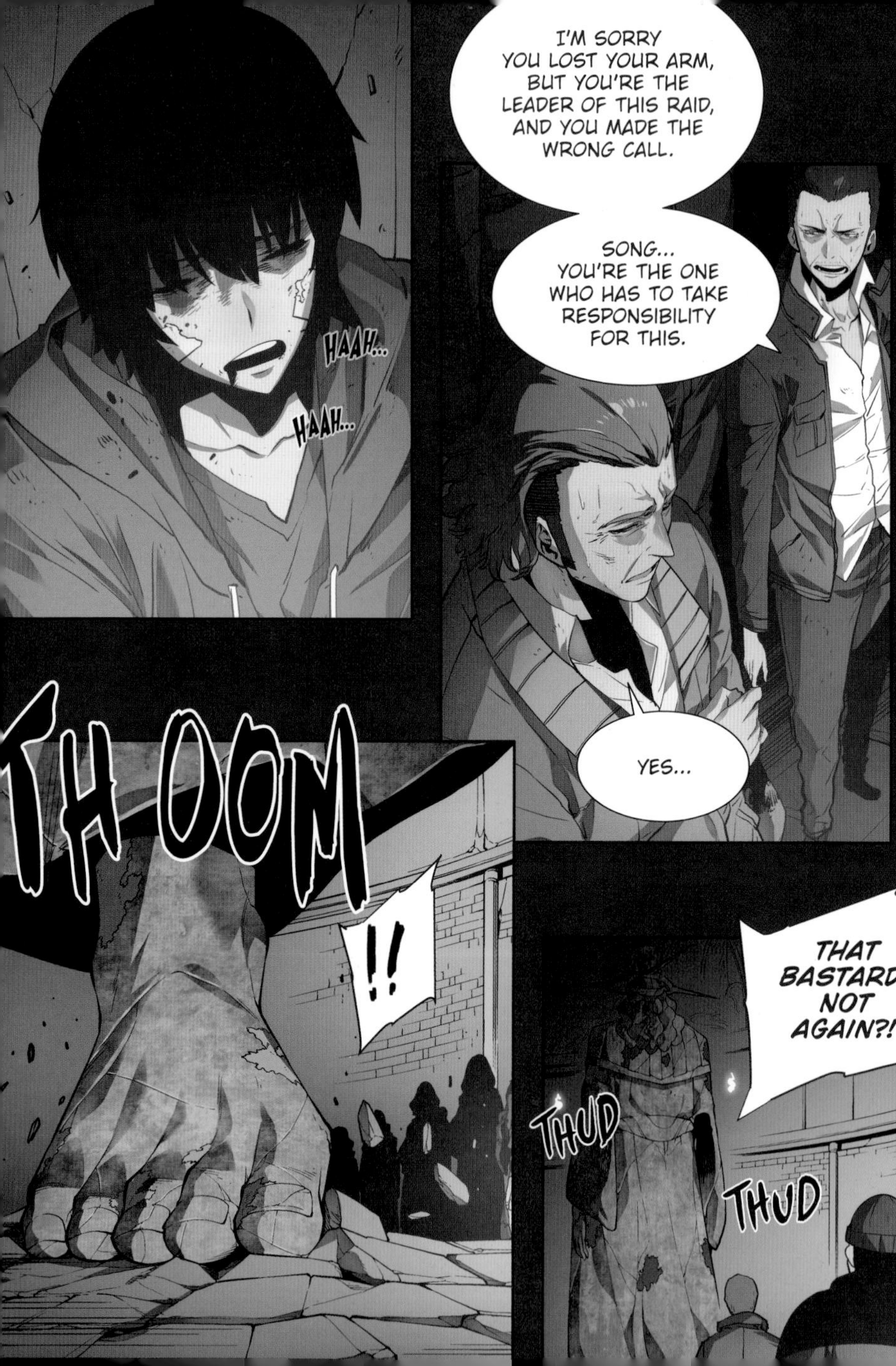
HAAH...
HAAH...
I'M SORRY YOU LOST YOUR ARM, BUT YOU'RE THE LEADER OF THIS RAID, AND YOU MADE THE WRONG CALL.
SONG... YOU'RE THE ONE WHO HAS TO TAKE RESPONSIBILITY FOR THIS.
YES...
THOOM
!!
THAT BASTARD! NOT AGAIN?!
THUD
THUD

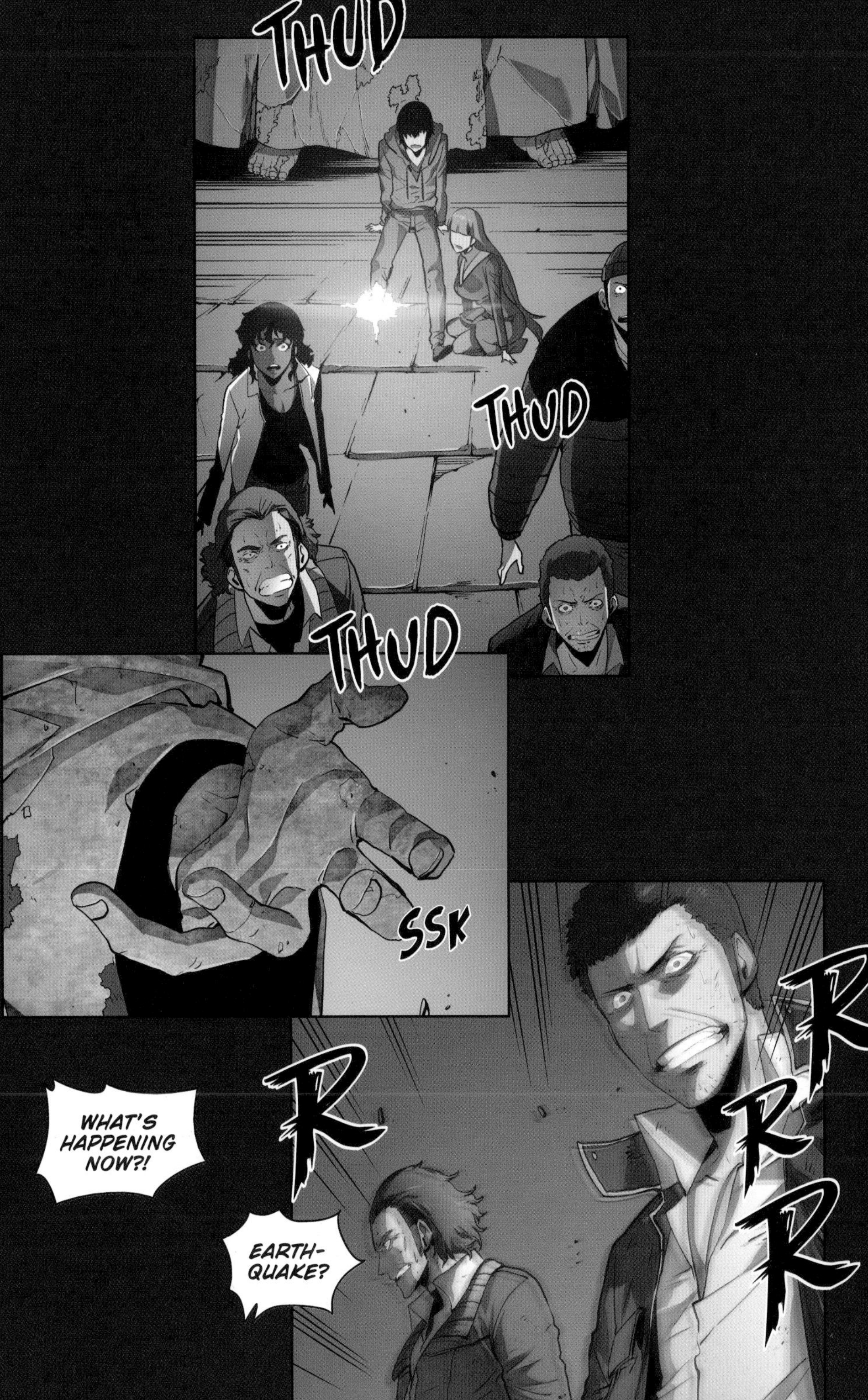
THUD
THUD
THUD
SSK
R
WHAT'S HAPPENING NOW?!
RRR
EARTH-QUAKE?
R

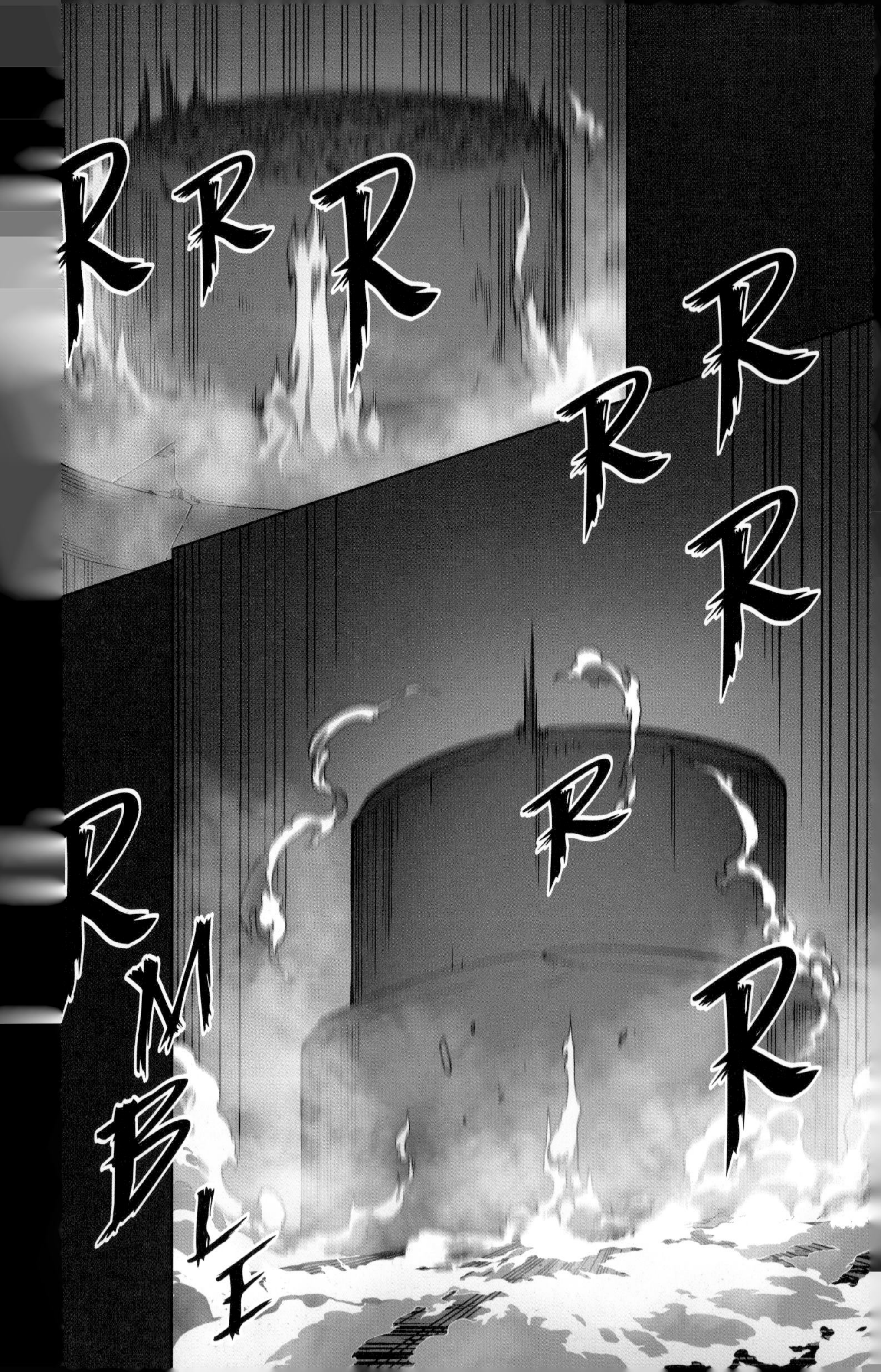
RRRRRRRRRMBLE

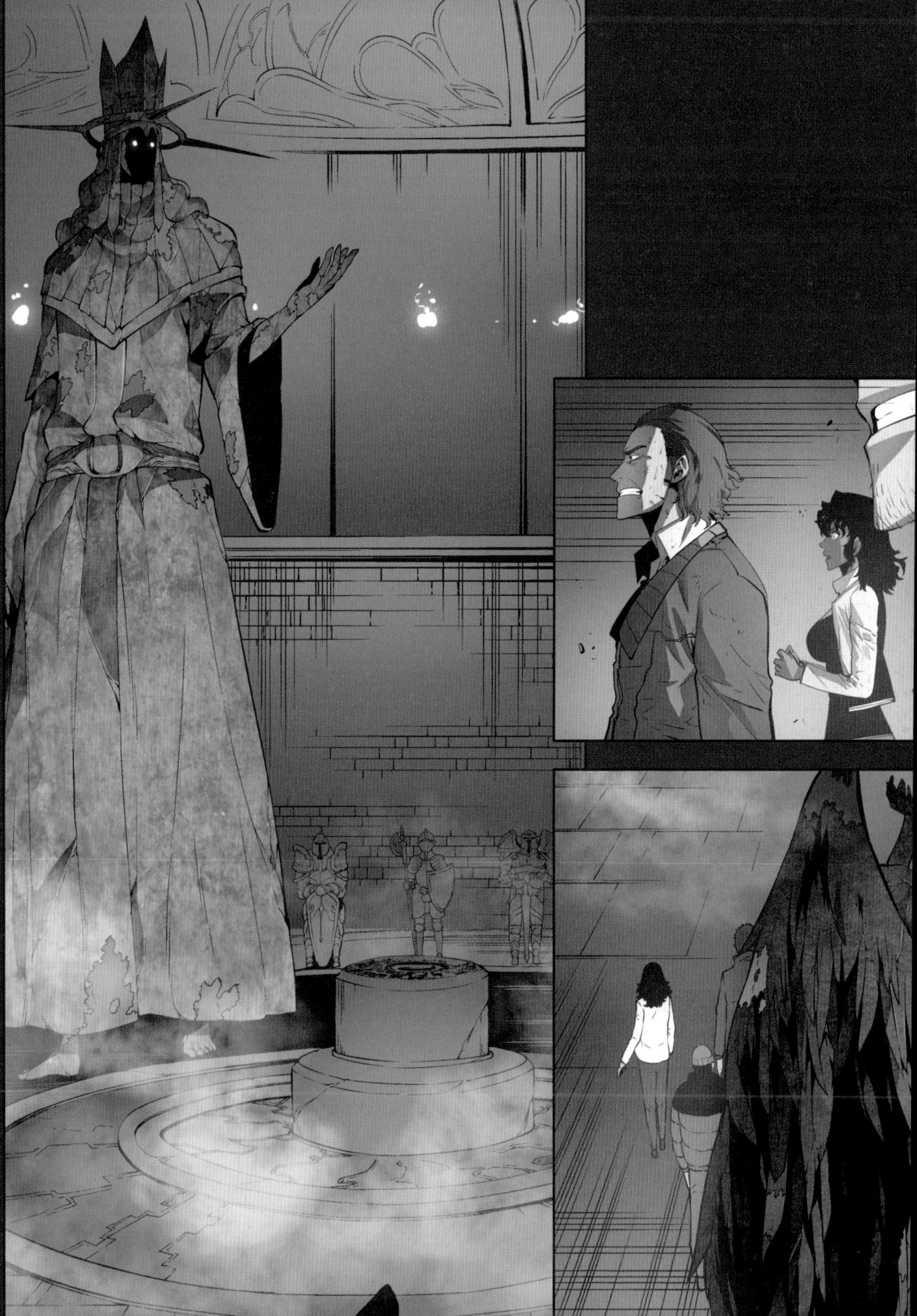

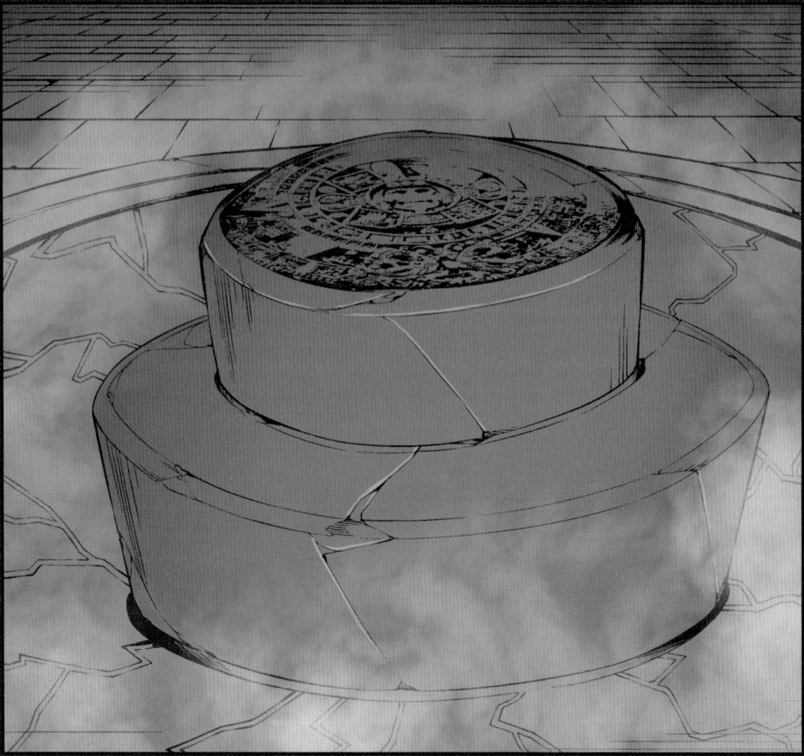
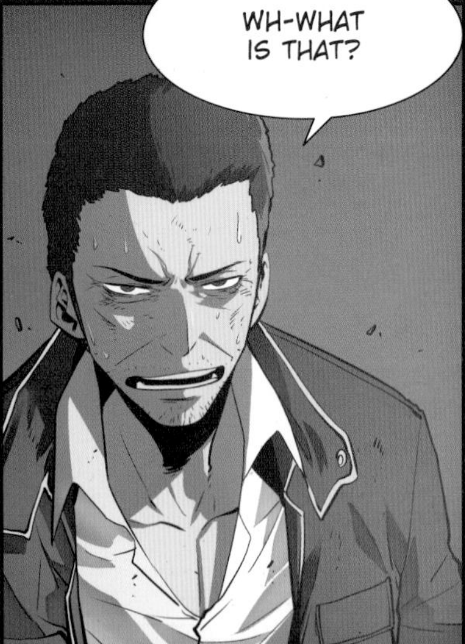
WH-WHAT IS THAT?
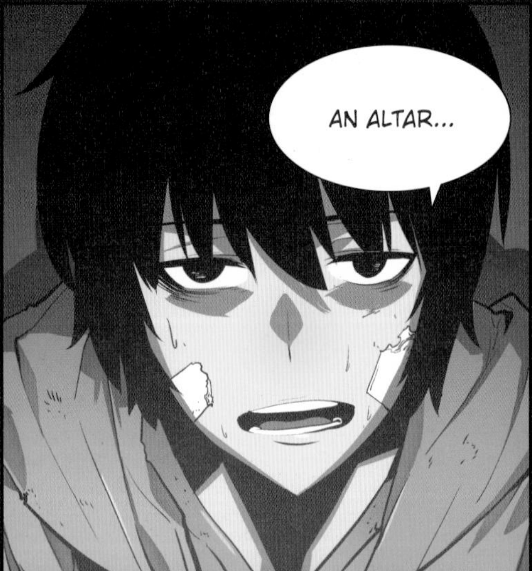
AN ALTAR...

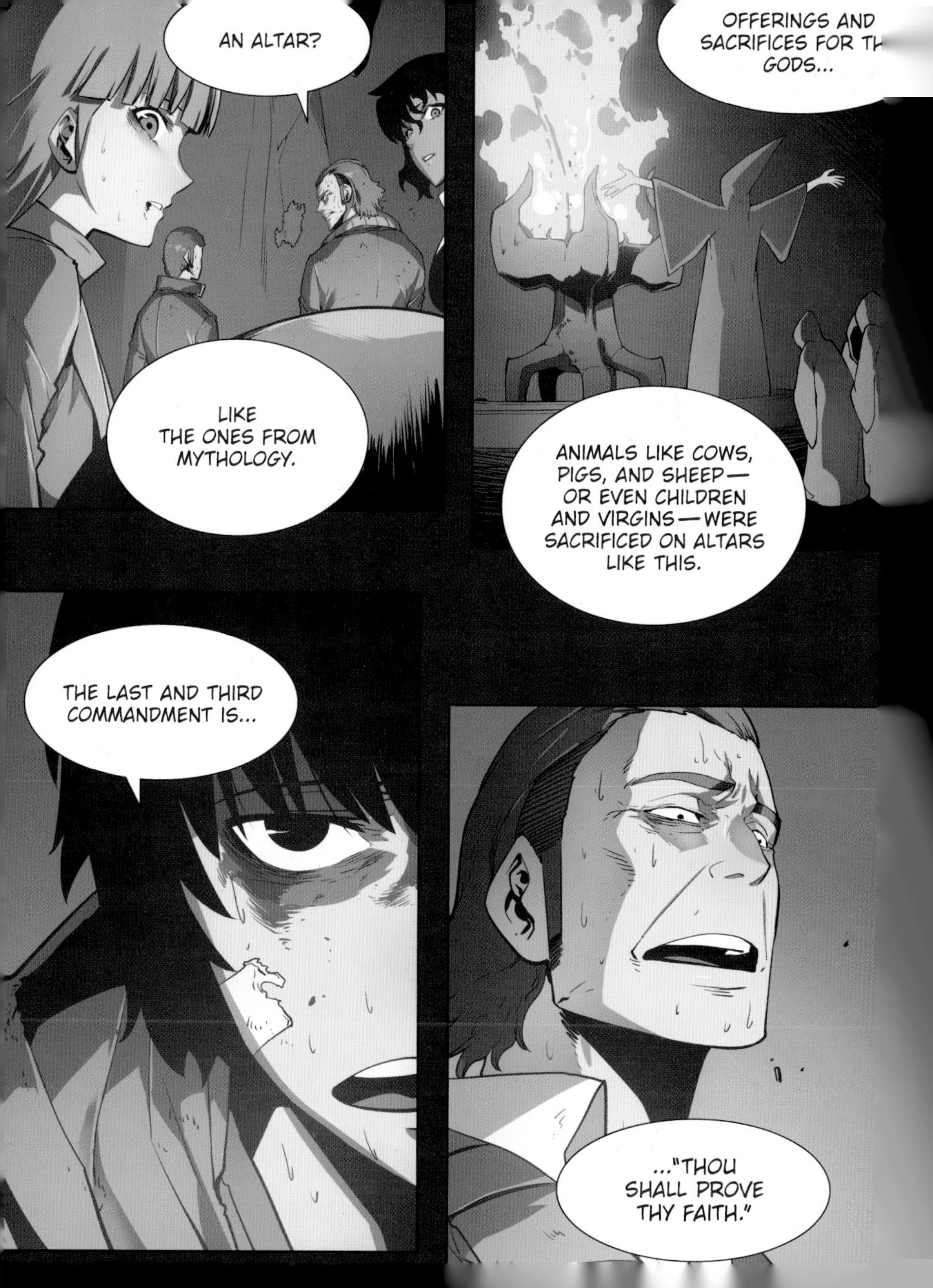
AN ALTAR?
LIKE THE ONES FROM MYTHOLOGY.
OFFERINGS AND SACRIFICES FOR TH GODS...
ANIMALS LIKE COWS, PIGS, AND SHEEP—OR EVEN CHILDREN AND VIRGINS—WERE SACRIFICED ON ALTARS LIKE THIS.
THE LAST AND THIRD COMMANDMENT IS...
..."THOU SHALL PROVE THY FAITH."

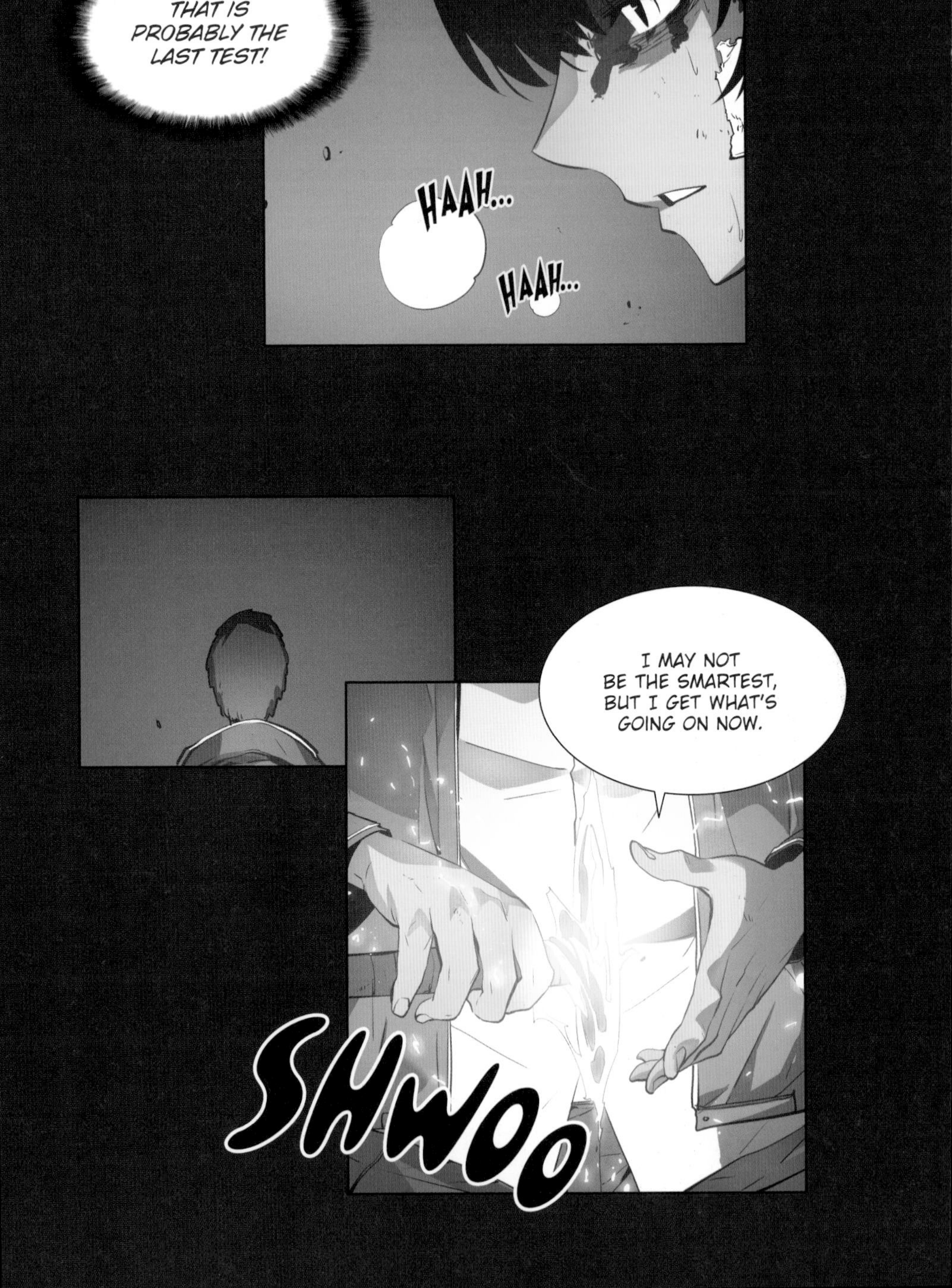
THAT IS PROBABLY THE LAST TEST!
HAAH...
HAAH...
I MAY NOT BE THE SMARTEST, BUT I GET WHAT'S GOING ON NOW.
SHWOO

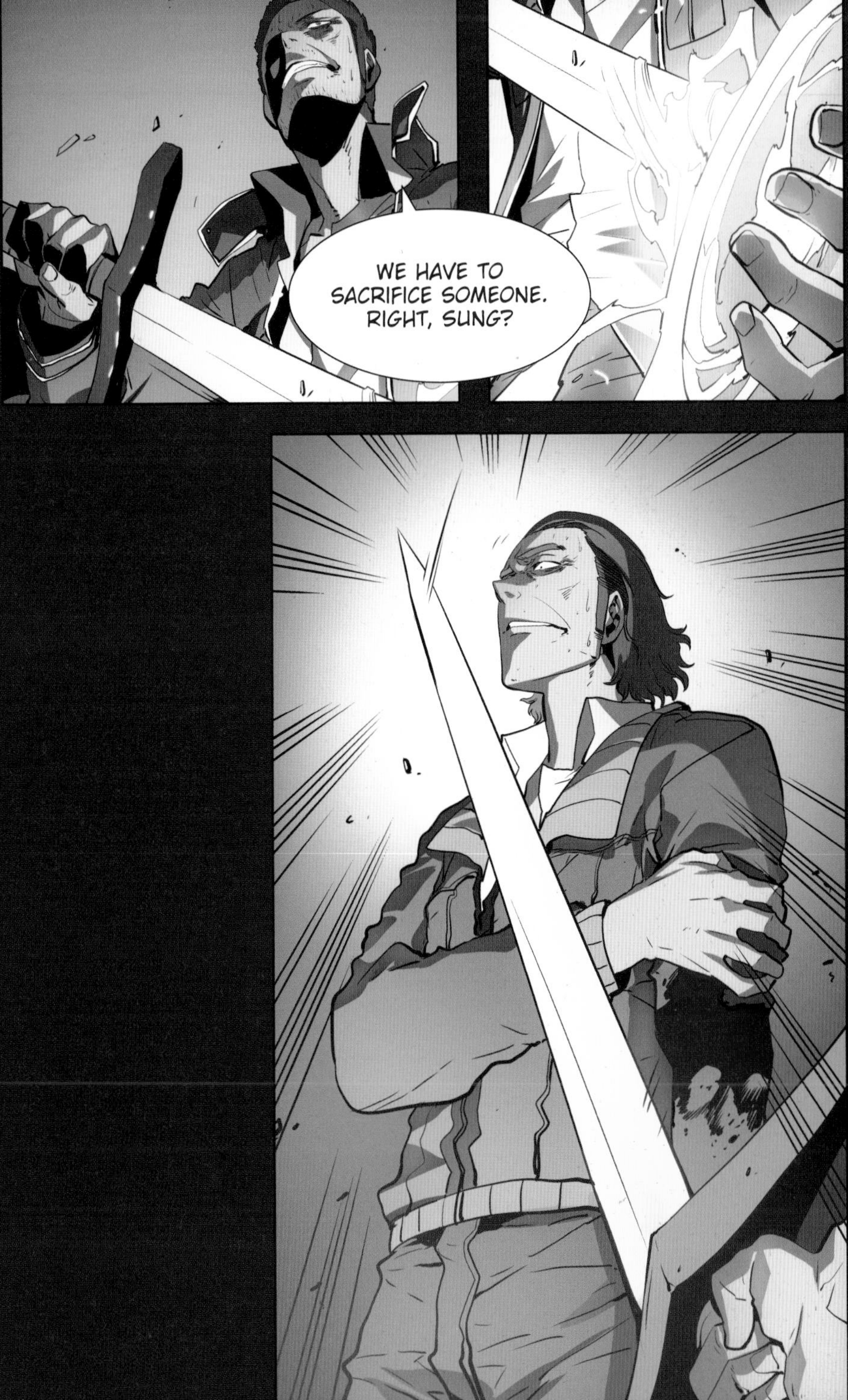
WE HAVE TO SACRIFICE SOMEONE. RIGHT, SUNG?

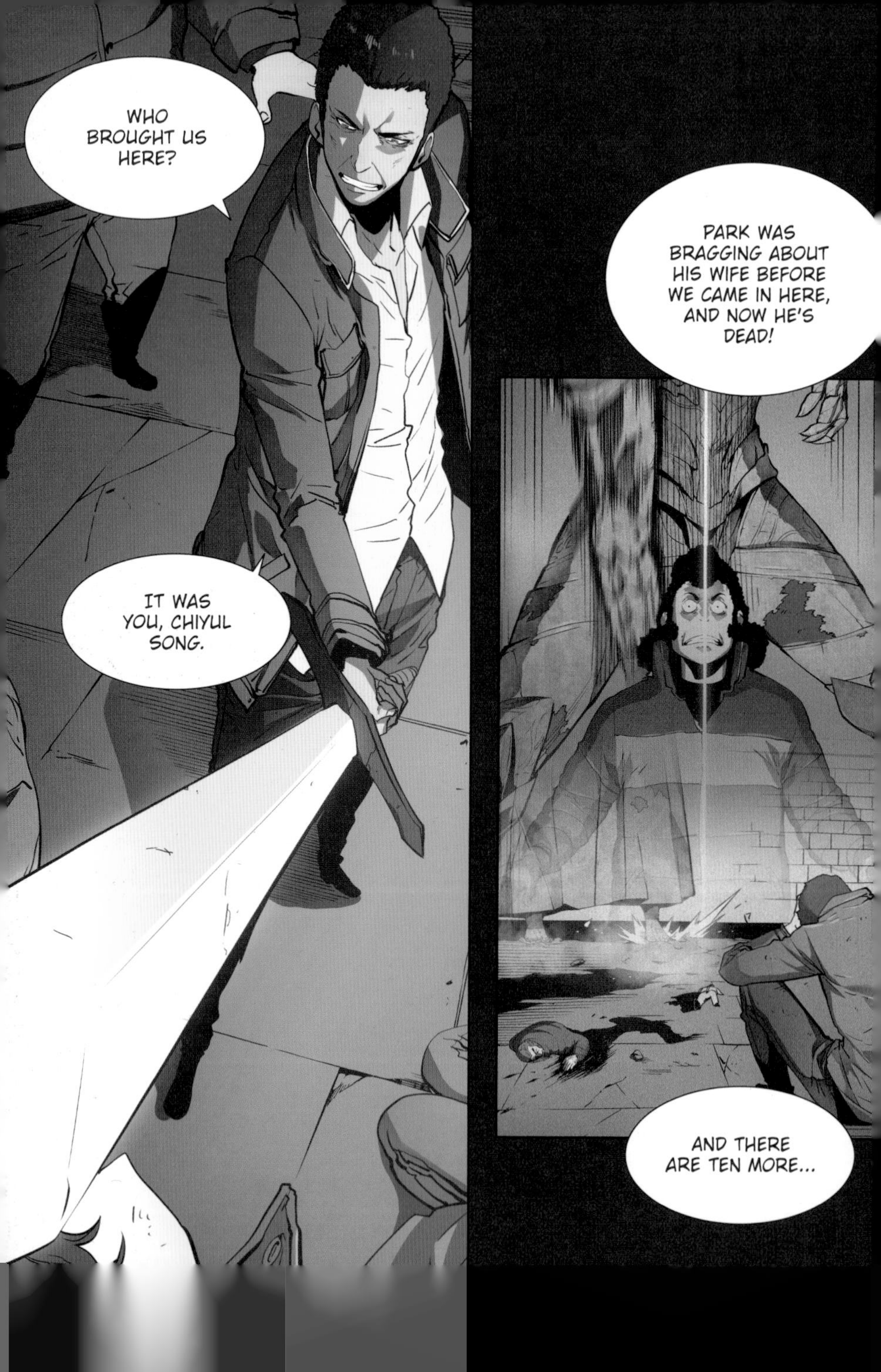
WHO BROUGHT US HERE?
IT WAS YOU, CHIYUL SONG.
PARK WAS BRAGGING ABOUT HIS WIFE BEFORE WE CAME IN HERE, AND NOW HE'S DEAD!
AND THERE ARE TEN MORE...

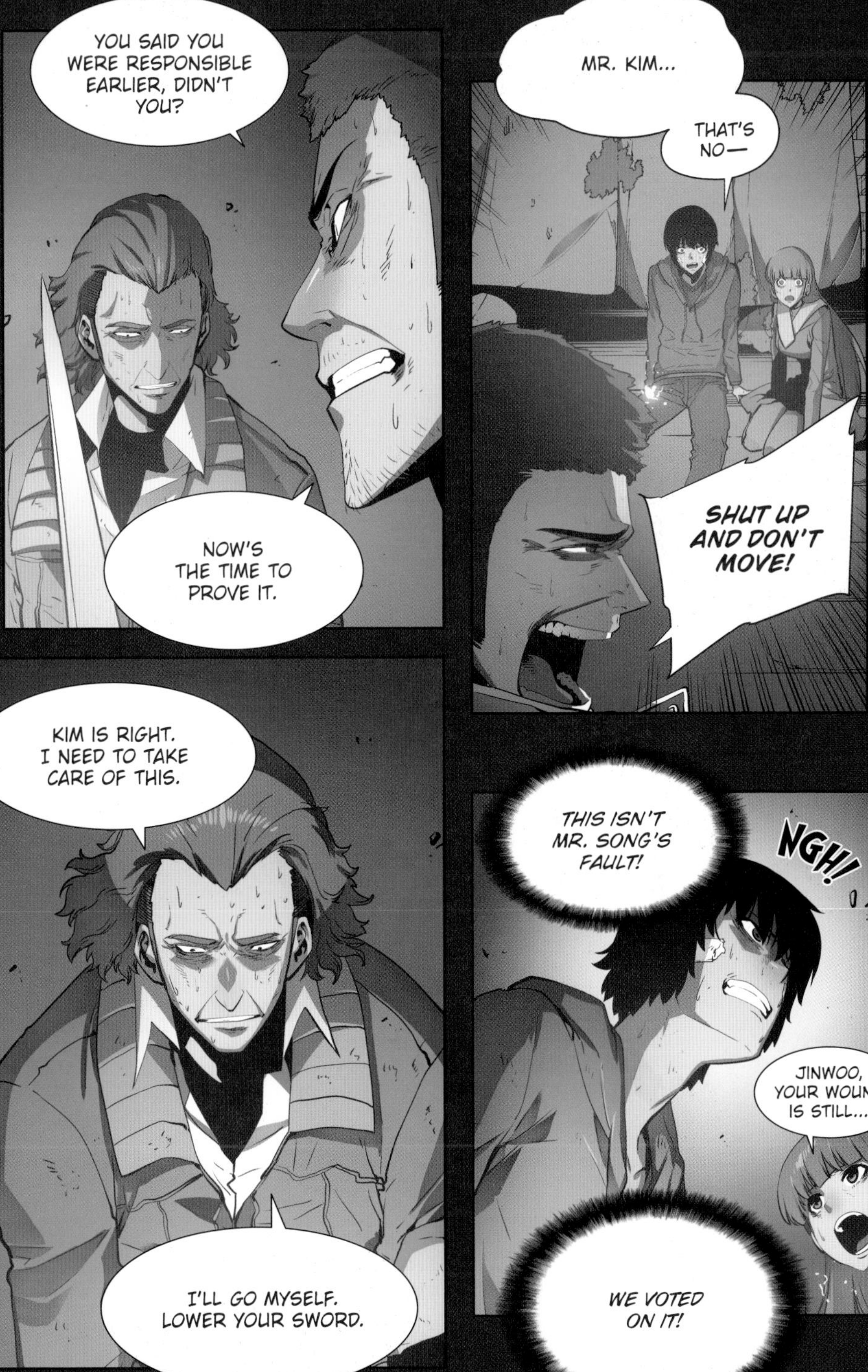
YOU SAID YOU WERE RESPONSIBLE EARLIER, DIDN'T YOU?
NOW'S THE TIME TO PROVE IT.
MR. KIM...
THAT'S NO—
SHUT UP AND DON'T MOVE!
KIM IS RIGHT. I NEED TO TAKE CARE OF THIS.
I'LL GO MYSELF. LOWER YOUR SWORD.
THIS ISN'T MR. SONG'S FAULT!
NGH!
JINWOO, YOUR WOUND IS STILL...
WE VOTED ON IT!

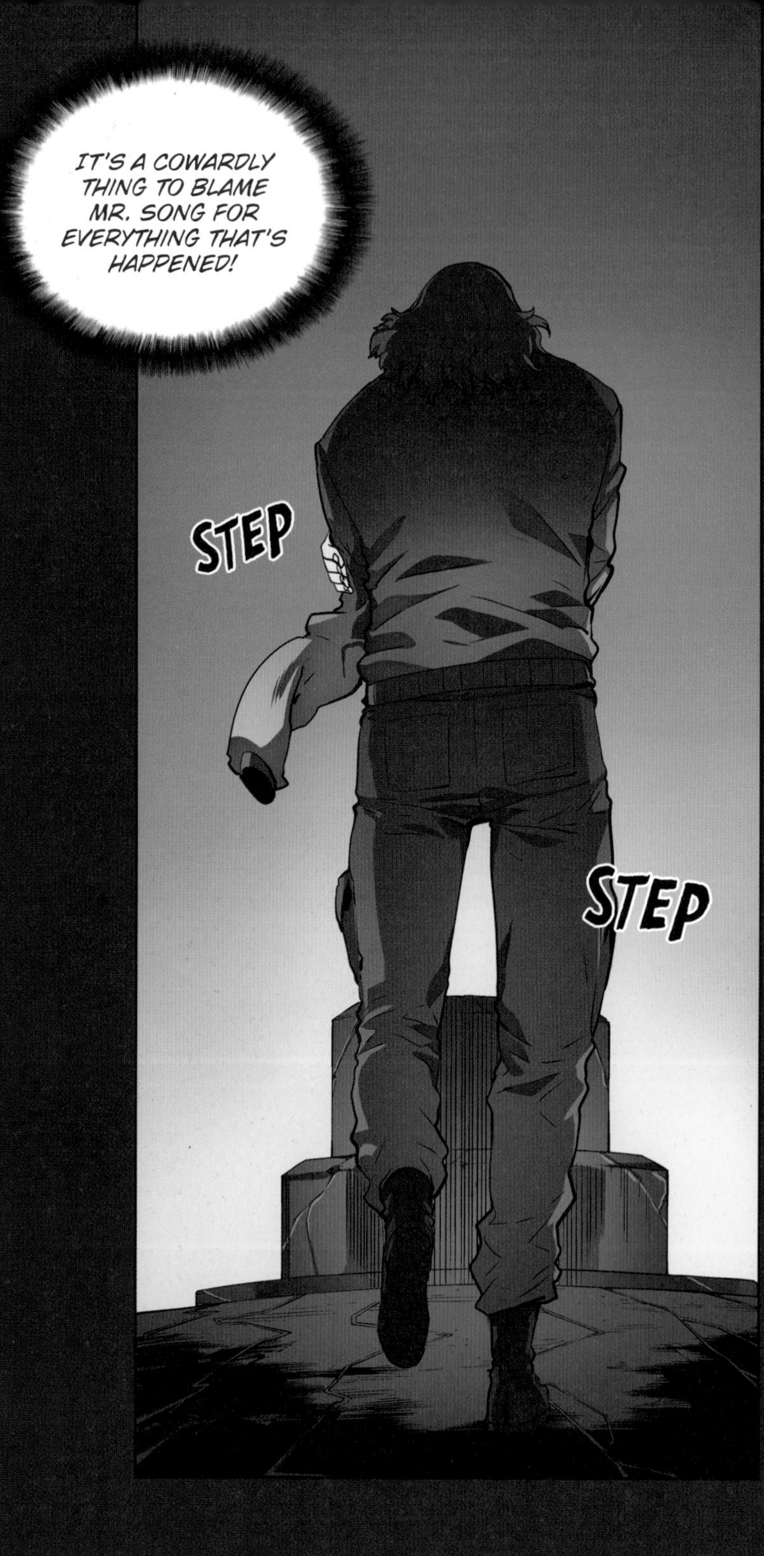
IT'S A COWARDLY THING TO BLAME MR. SONG FOR EVERYTHING THAT'S HAPPENED!
STEP
STEP

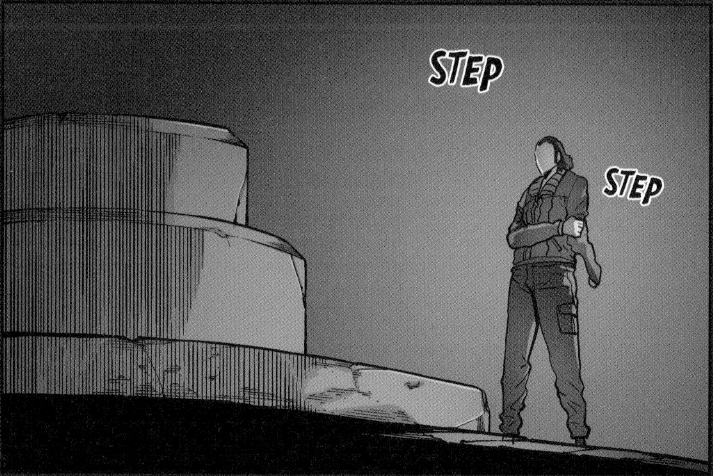
STEP
STEP
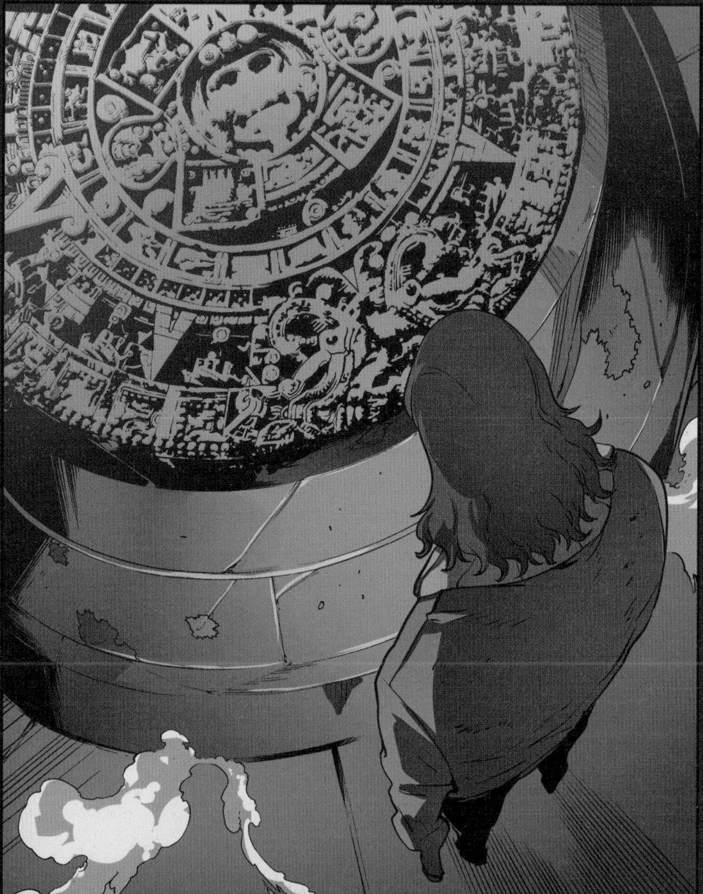

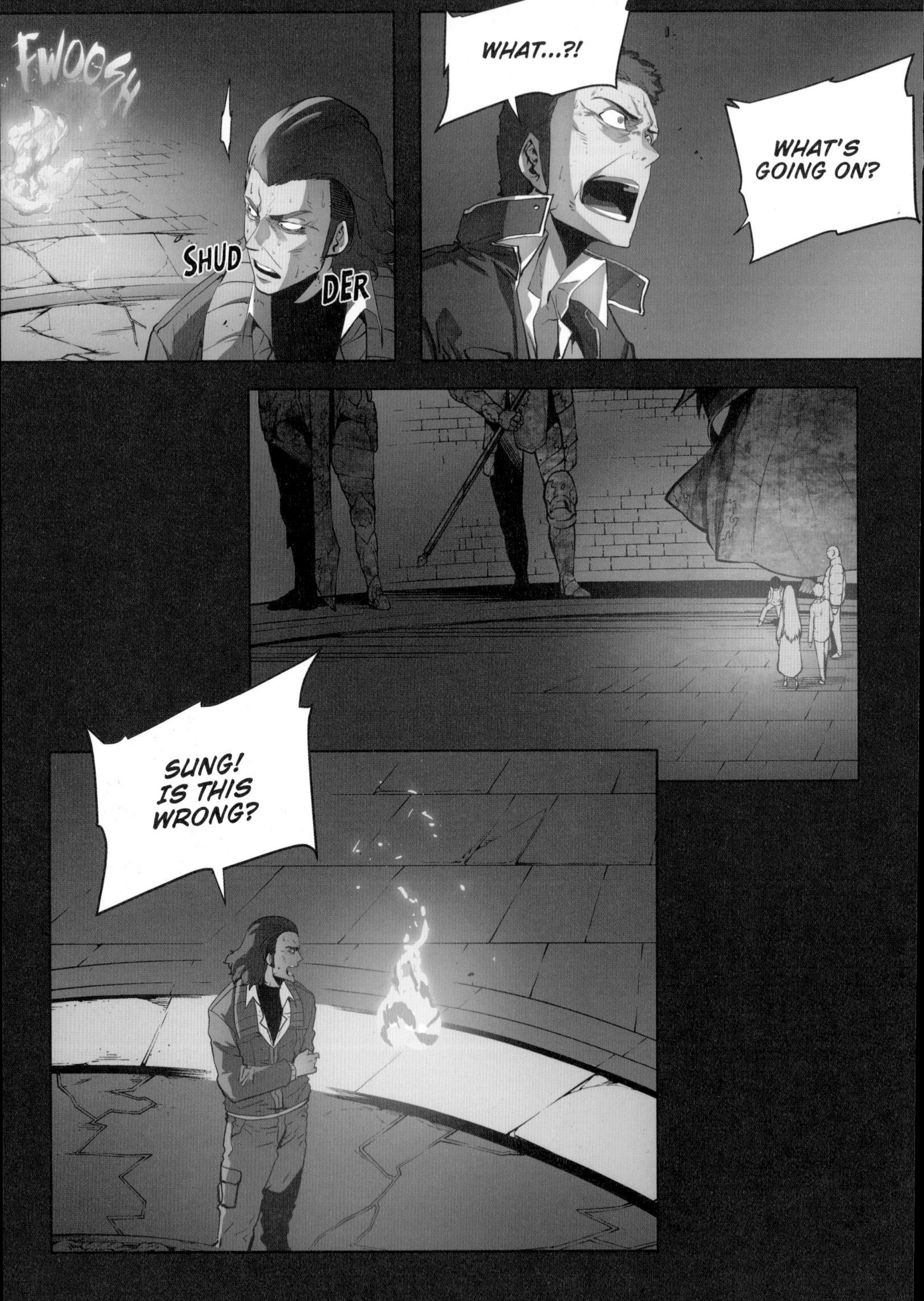
FWOOSH
SHUD
DER
WHAT...?!
WHAT'S GOING ON?
SUNG! IS THIS WRONG?

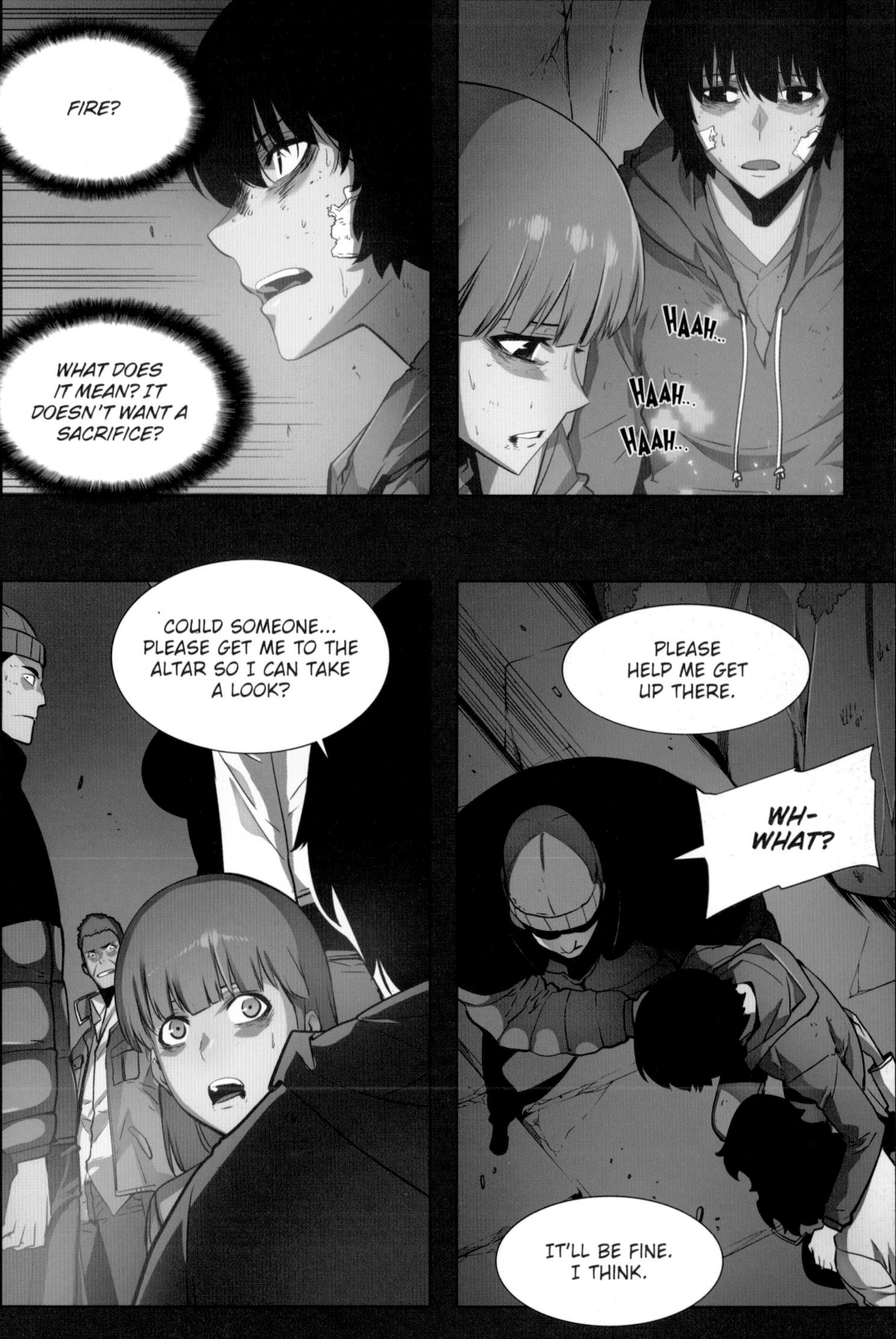
FIRE?
WHAT DOES IT MEAN? IT DOESN'T WANT A SACRIFICE?
HAAH...
HAAH...
HAAH...
COULD SOMEONE... PLEASE GET ME TO THE ALTAR SO I CAN TAKE A LOOK?
PLEASE HELP ME GET UP THERE.
WH-WHAT?
IT'LL BE FINE. I THINK.

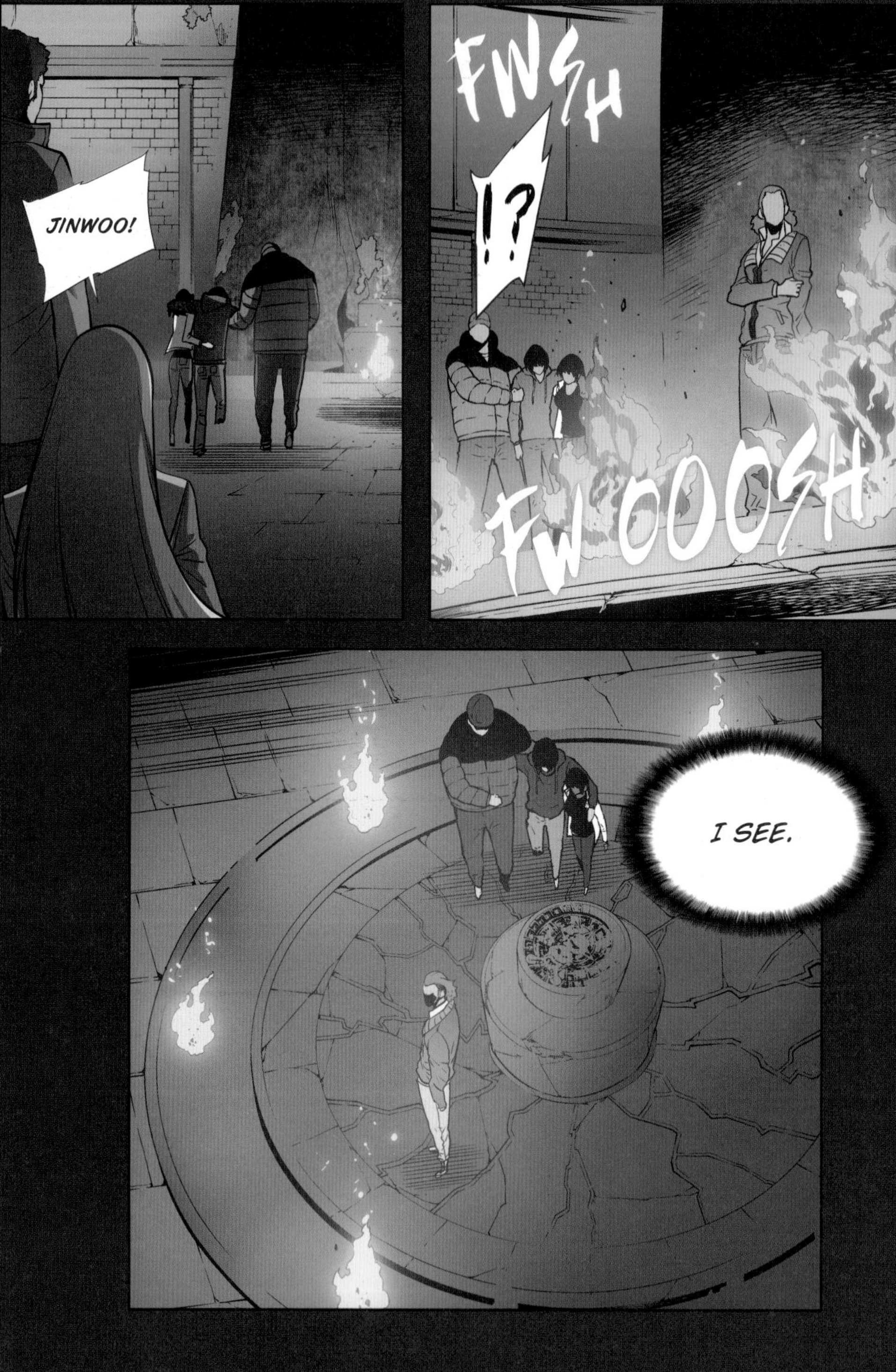
JINWOO!
FWSH
!?
FW OOOSH
I SEE.

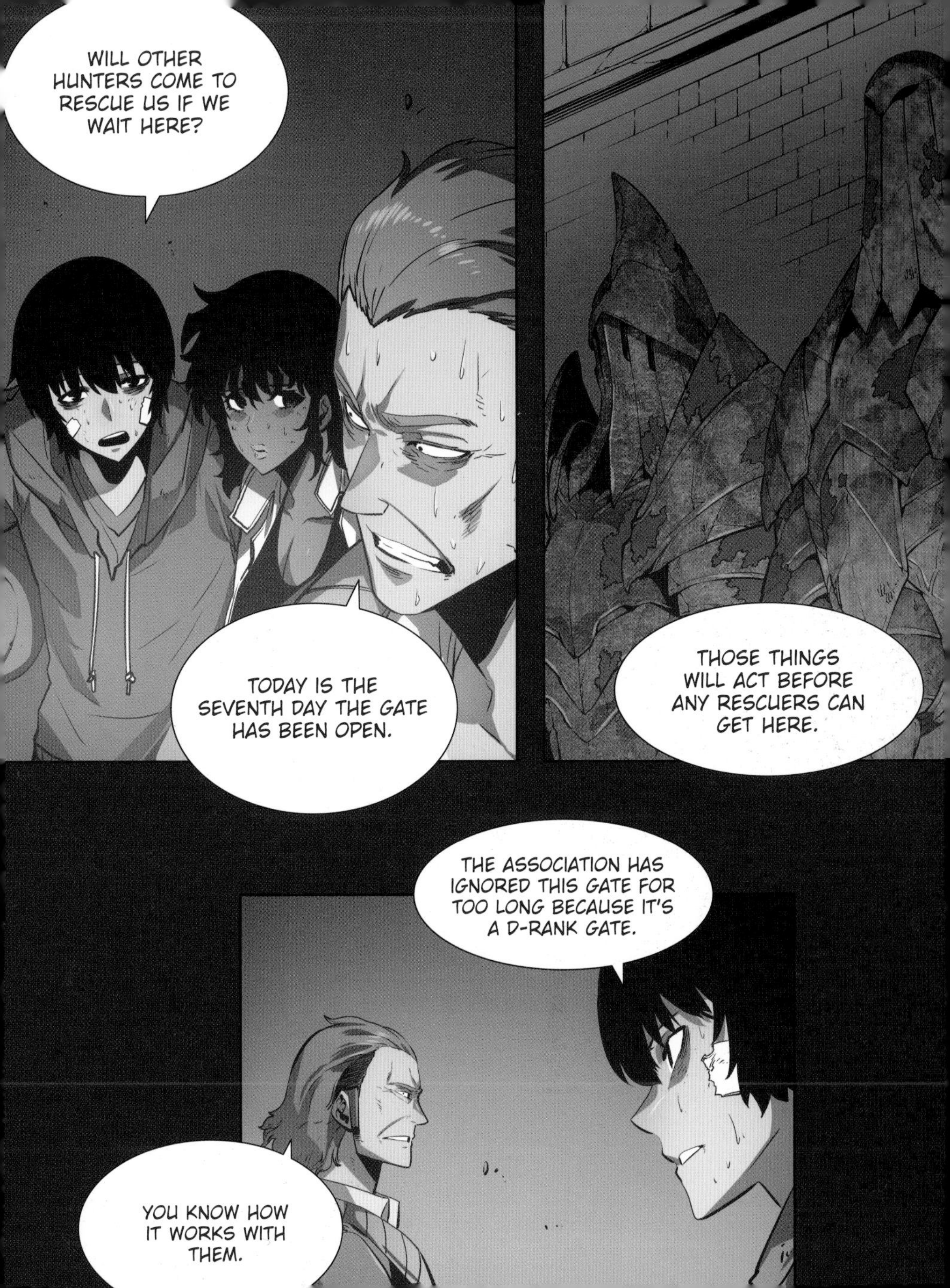
WILL OTHER HUNTERS COME TO RESCUE US IF WE WAIT HERE?
TODAY IS THE SEVENTH DAY THE GATE HAS BEEN OPEN.
THOSE THINGS WILL ACT BEFORE ANY RESCUERS CAN GET HERE.
THE ASSOCIATION HAS IGNORED THIS GATE FOR TOO LONG BECAUSE IT'S A D-RANK GATE.
YOU KNOW HOW IT WORKS WITH THEM.

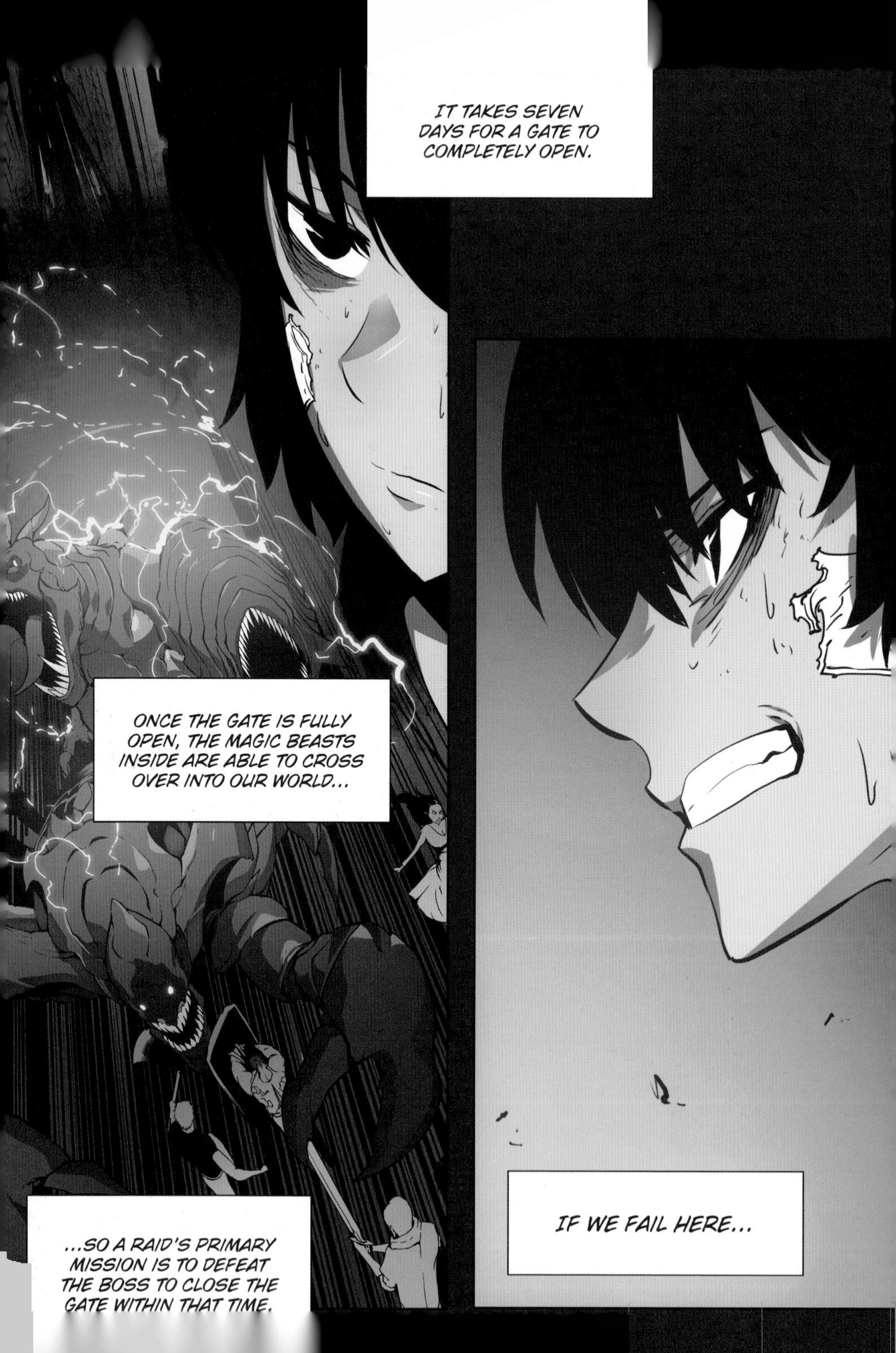
IT TAKES SEVEN DAYS FOR A GATE TO COMPLETELY OPEN.
ONCE THE GATE IS FULLY OPEN, THE MAGIC BEASTS INSIDE ARE ABLE TO CROSS OVER INTO OUR WORLD...
...SO A RAID'S PRIMARY MISSION IS TO DEFEAT THE BOSS TO CLOSE THE GATE WITHIN THAT TIME.
IF WE FAIL HERE...

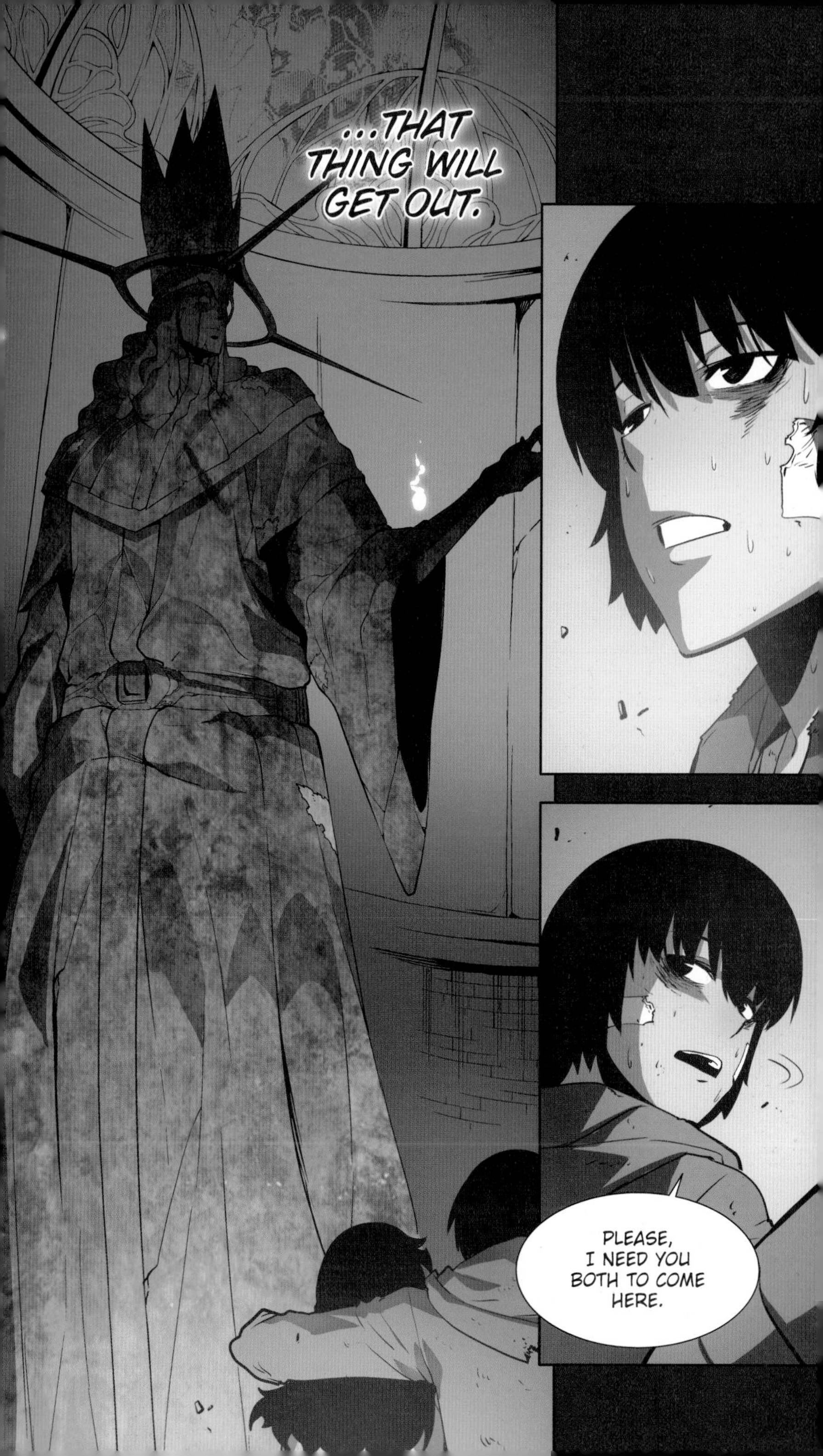
...THAT THING WILL GET OUT.
PLEASE, I NEED YOU BOTH TO COME HERE.

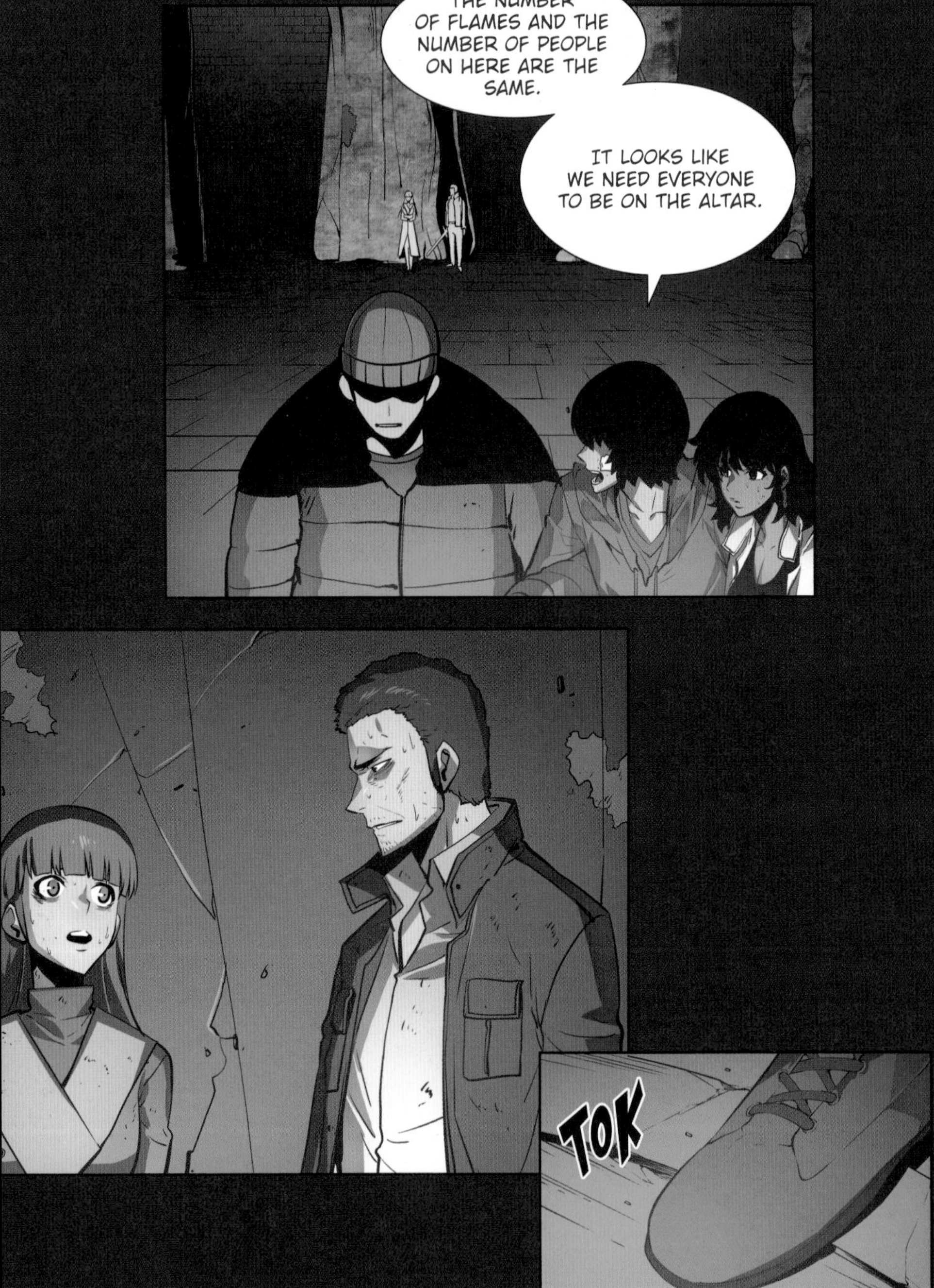
THE NUMBER OF FLAMES AND THE NUMBER OF PEOPLE ON HERE ARE THE SAME.
IT LOOKS LIKE WE NEED EVERYONE TO BE ON THE ALTAR.
TOK

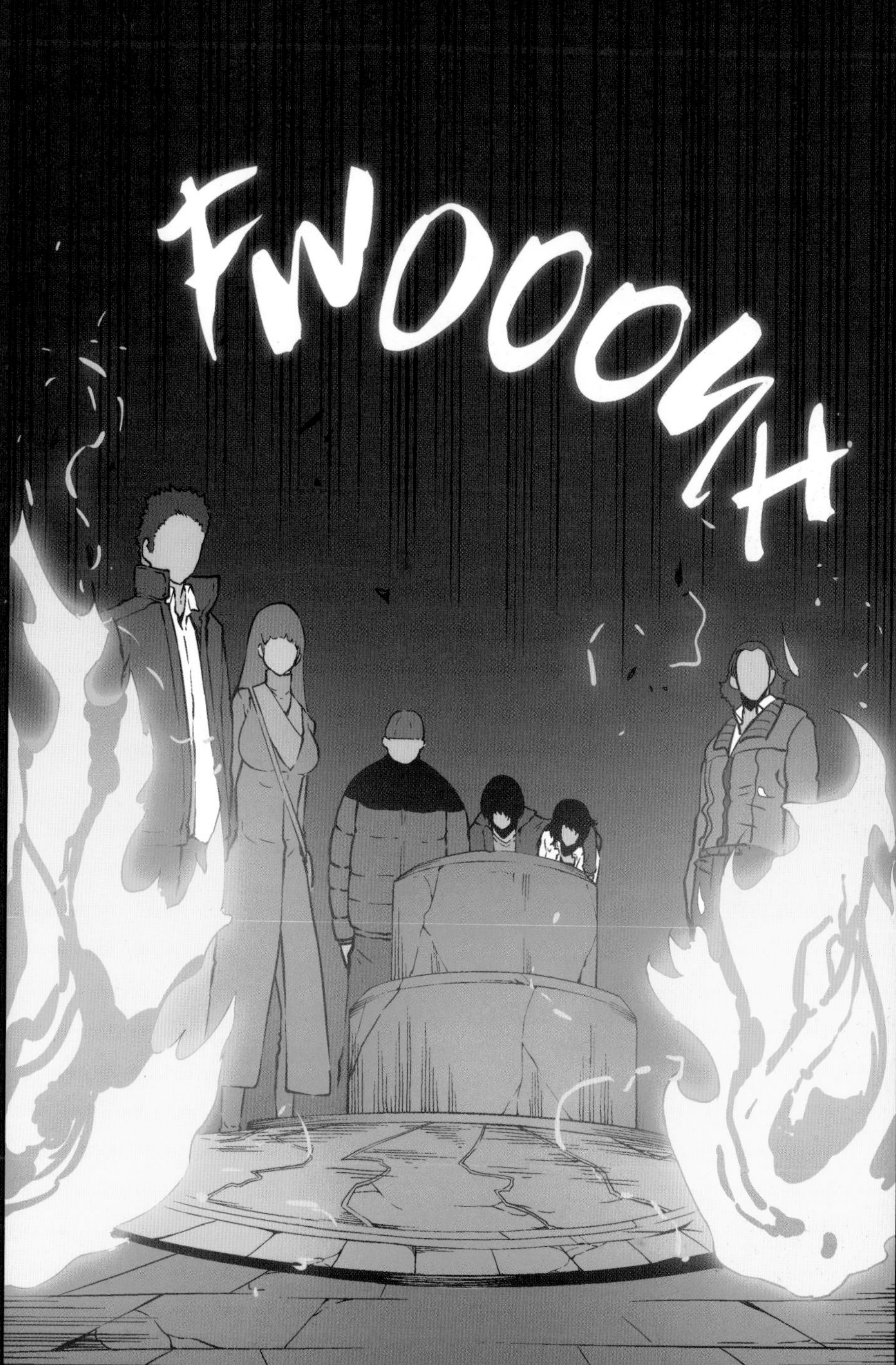
FWOOOSH

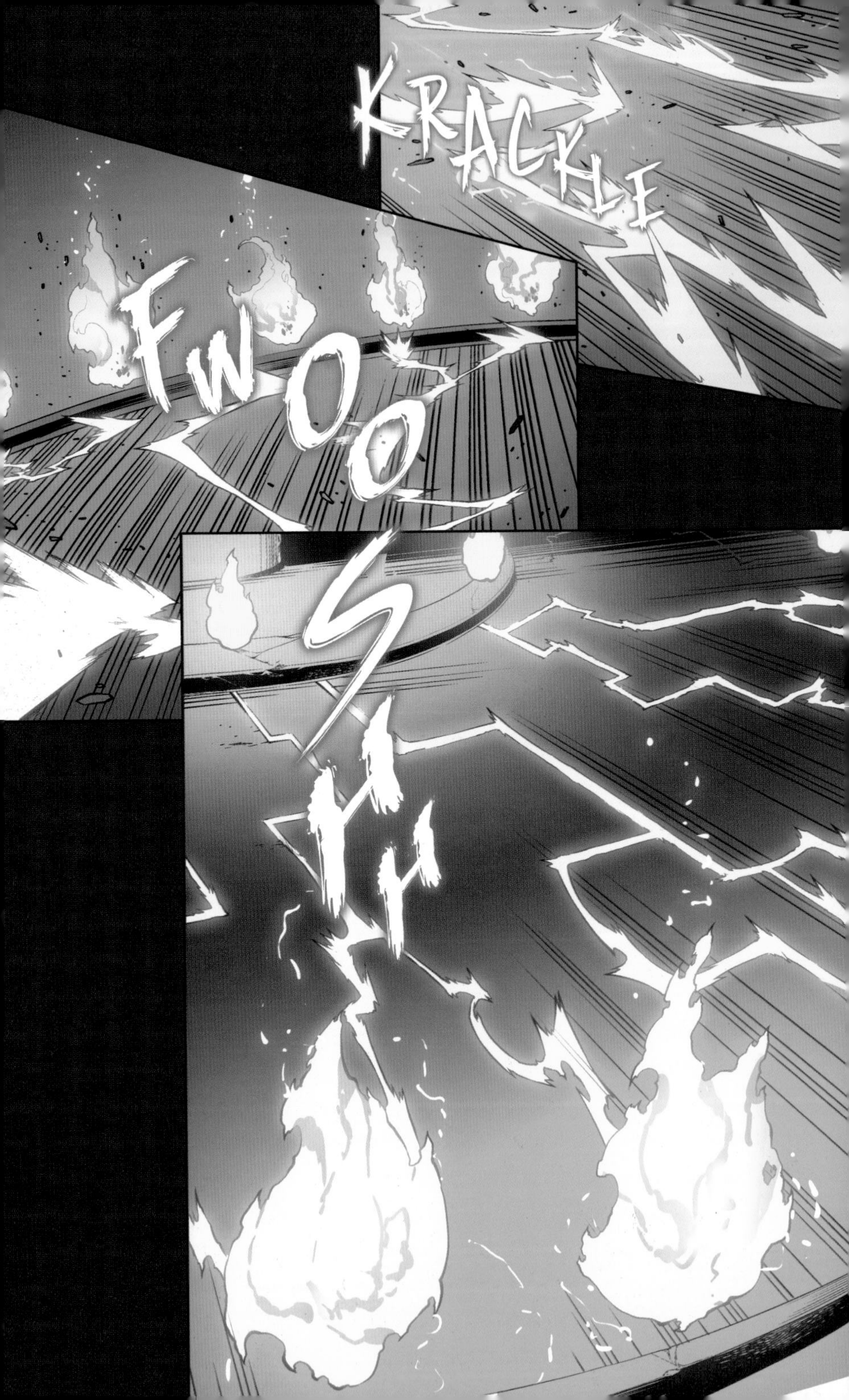
KRACKLE
FWOOSHH

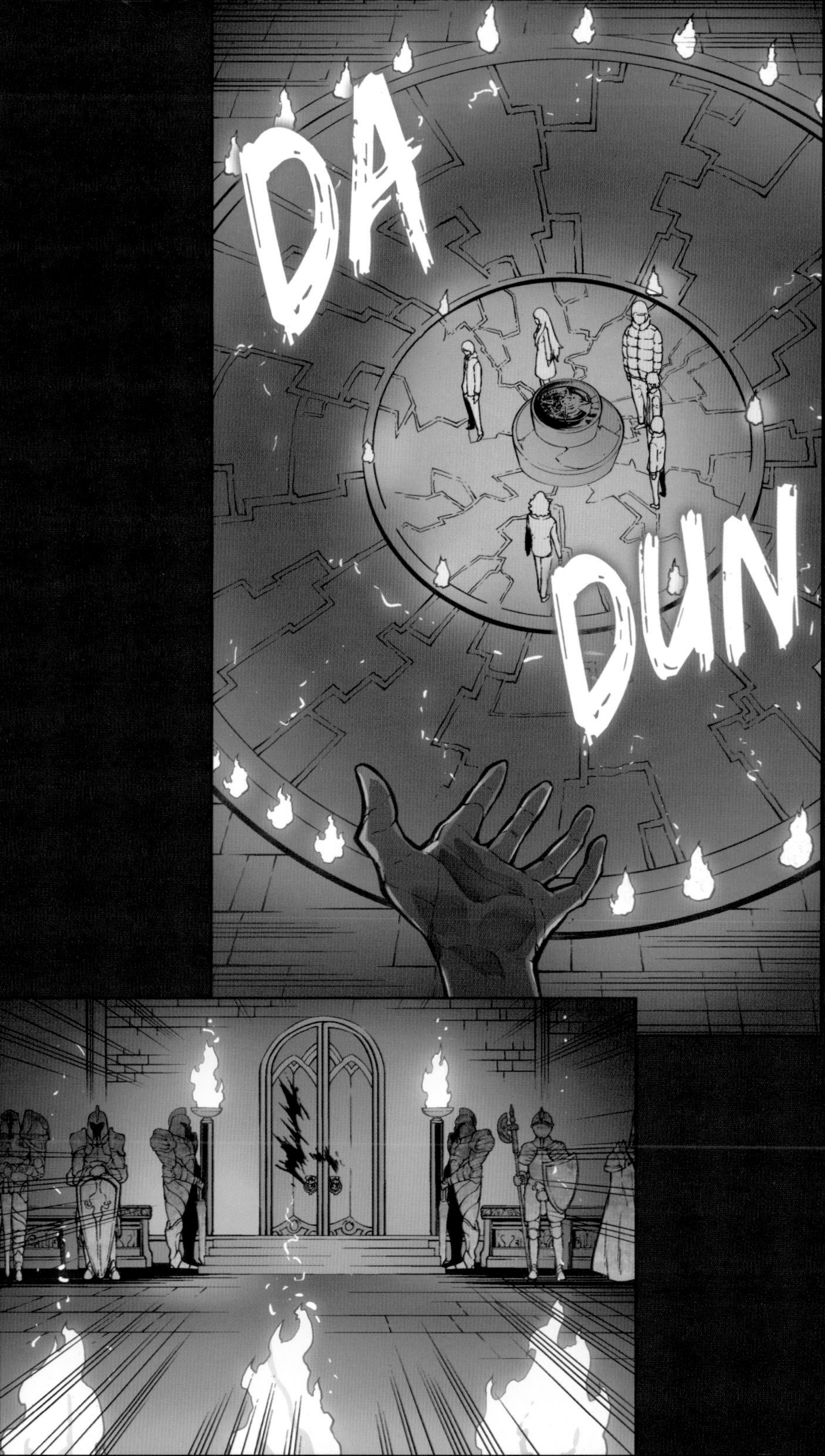
DA
DUN

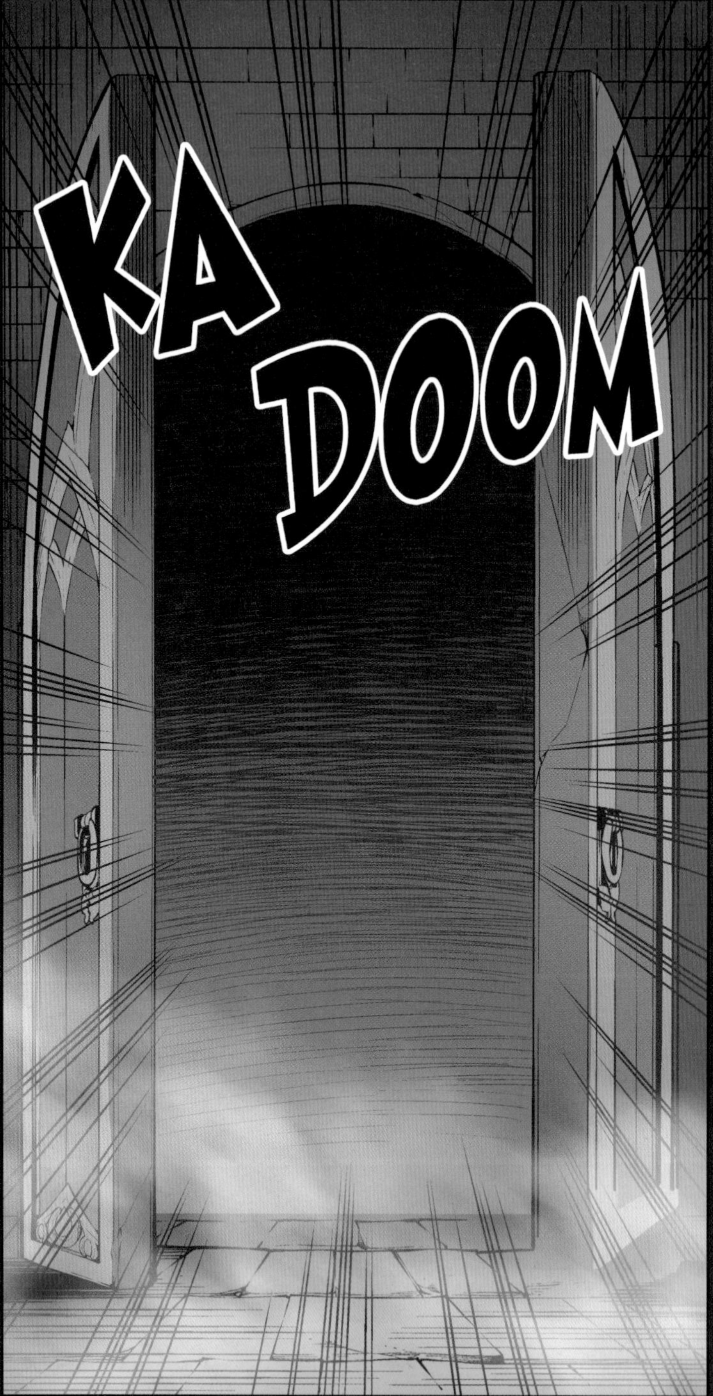
KA DOOM

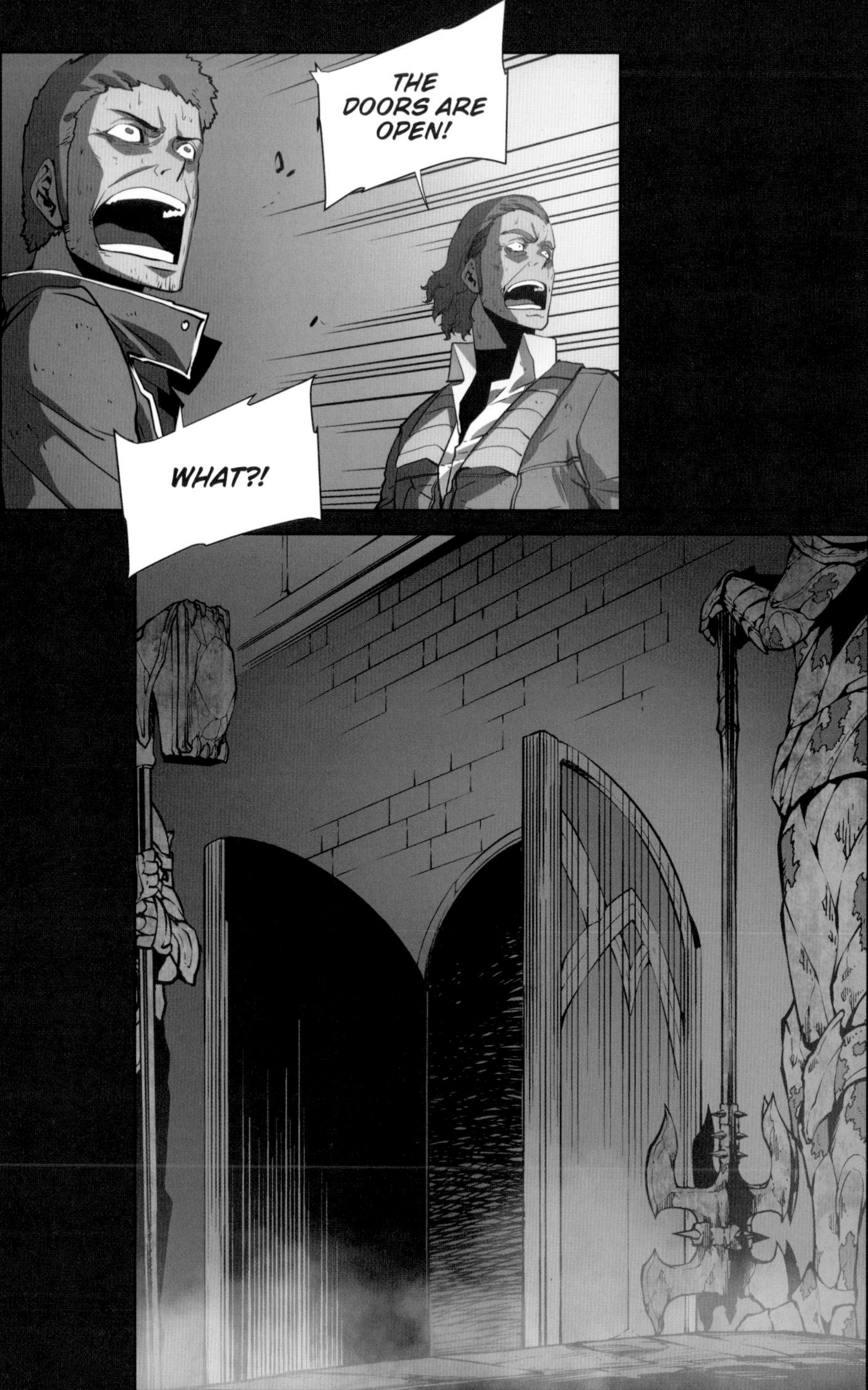
THE DOORS ARE OPEN!
WHAT?!

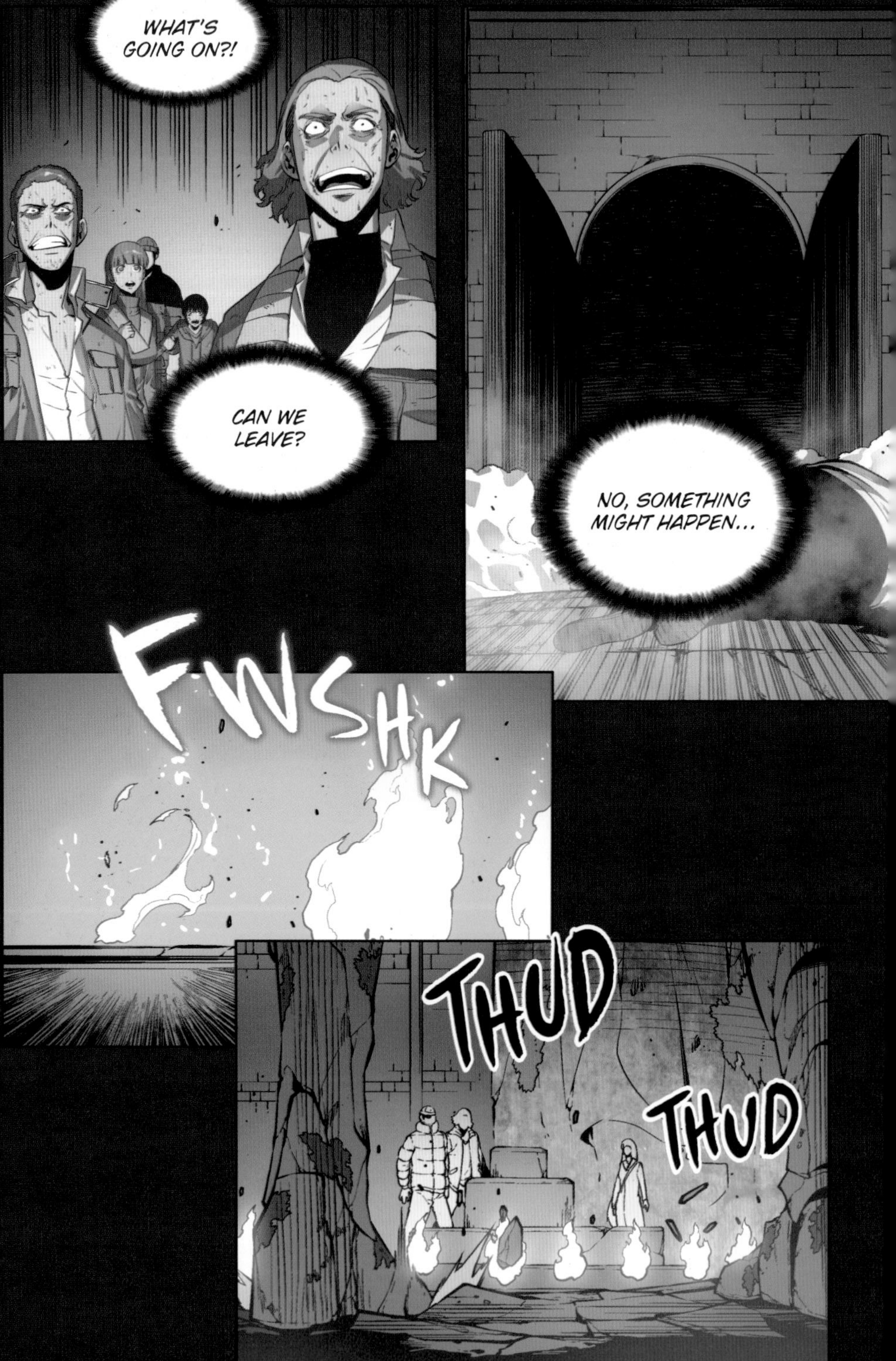
WHAT'S GOING ON?!
CAN WE LEAVE?
NO, SOMETHING MIGHT HAPPEN...
FWSHK
THUD
THUD

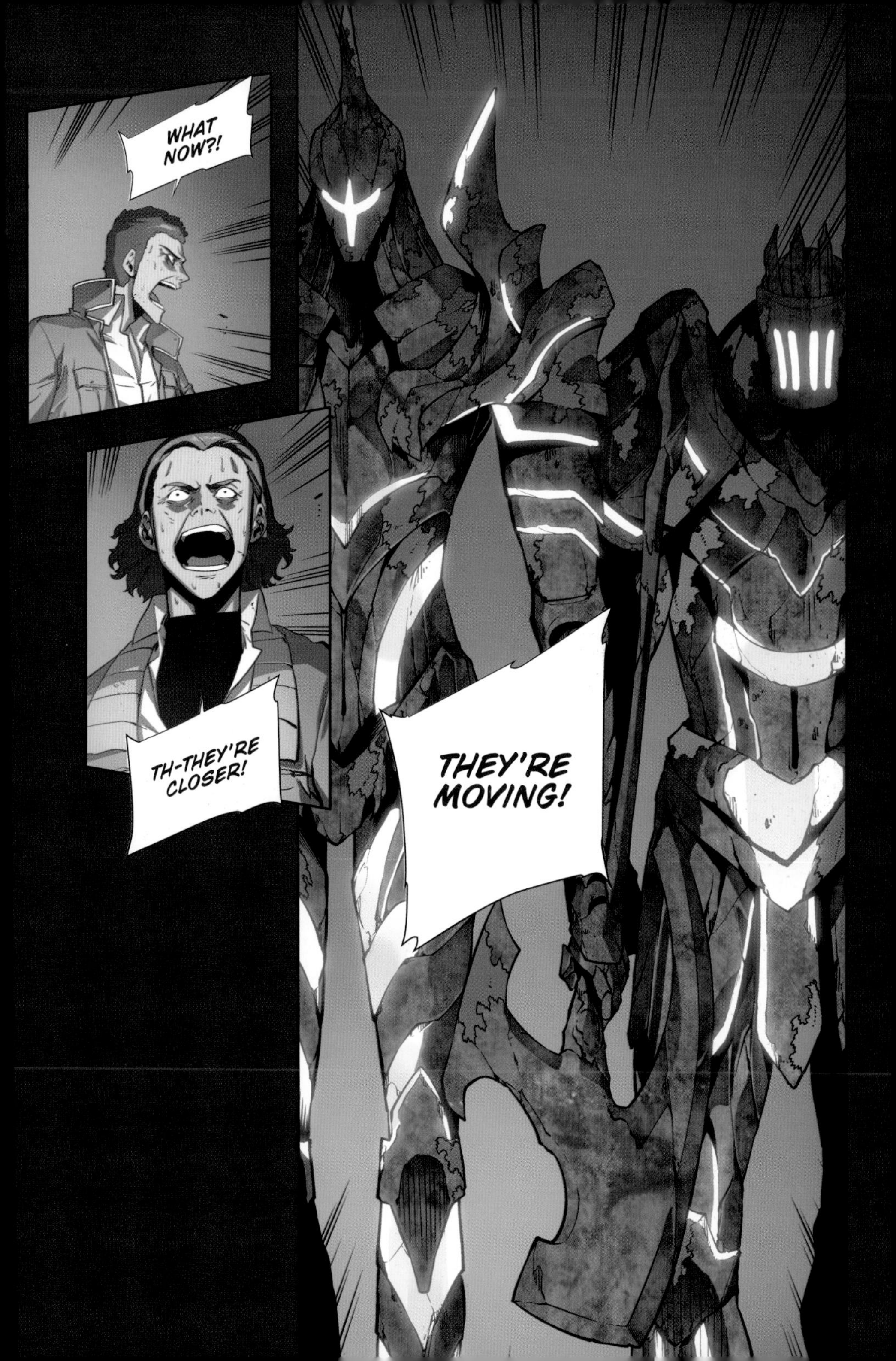
WHAT NOW?!
TH-THEY'RE CLOSER!
THEY'RE MOVING!

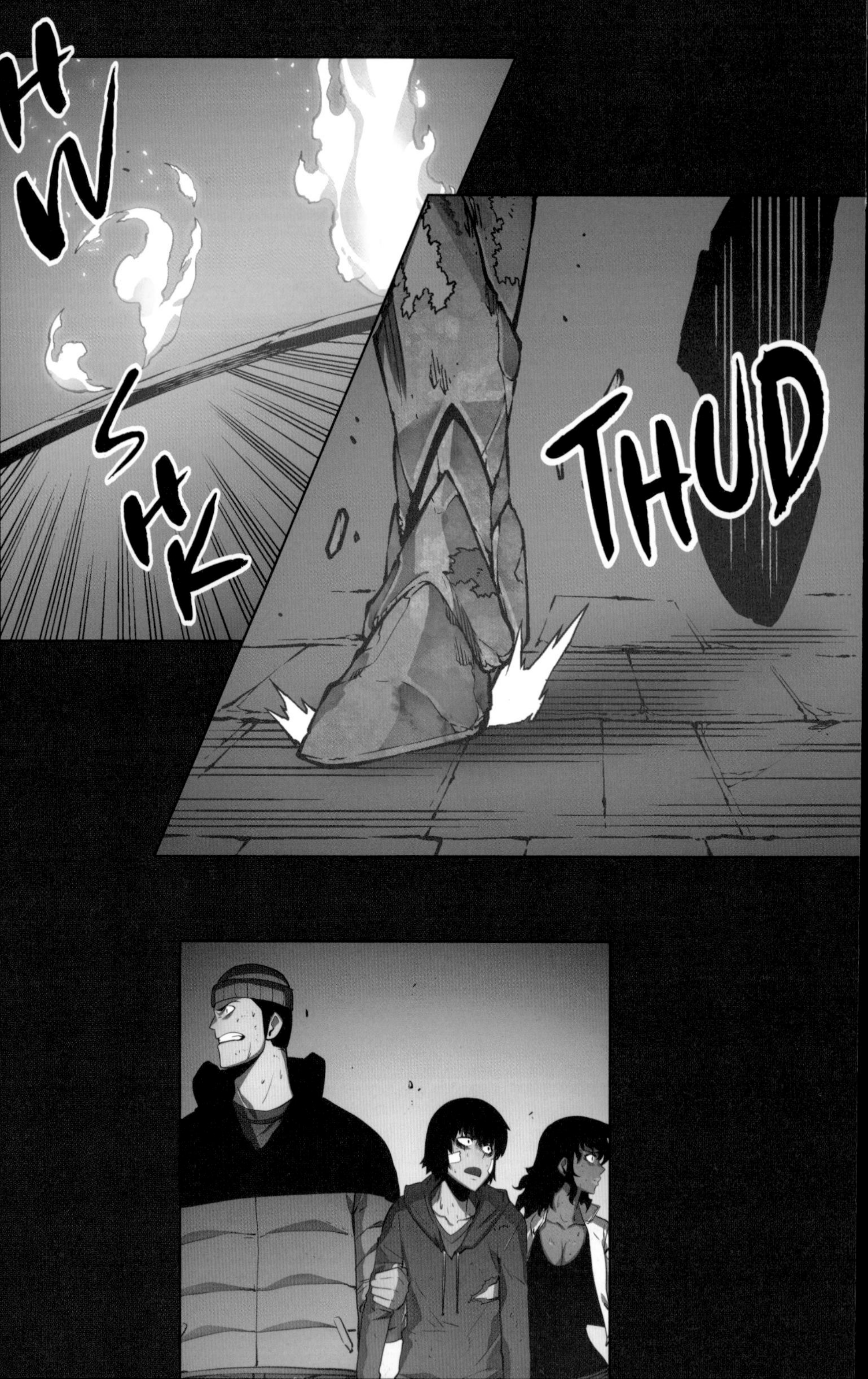
HWSHK
THUD

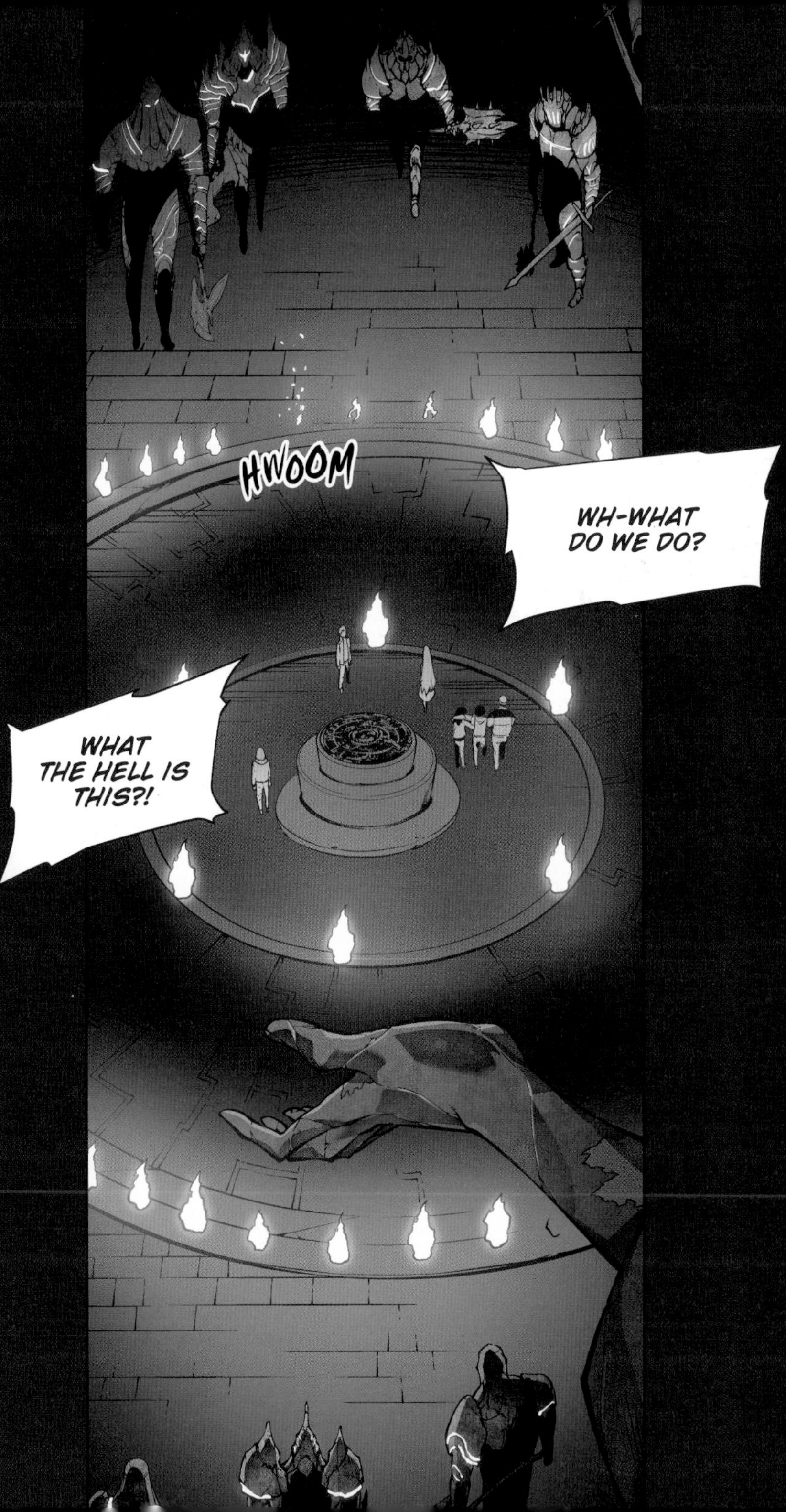
HWOOM
WH-WHAT DO WE DO?
WHAT THE HELL IS THIS?!

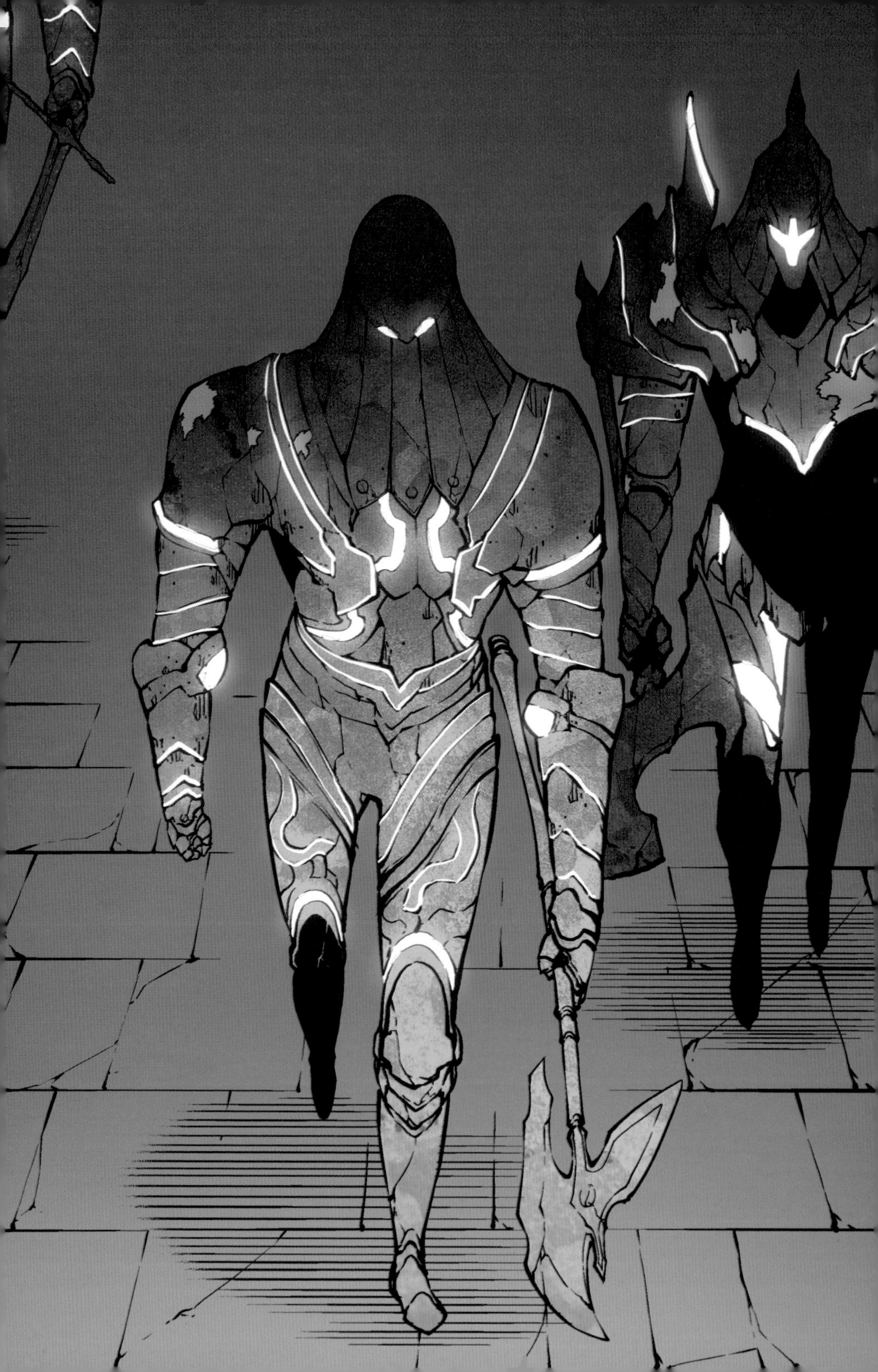

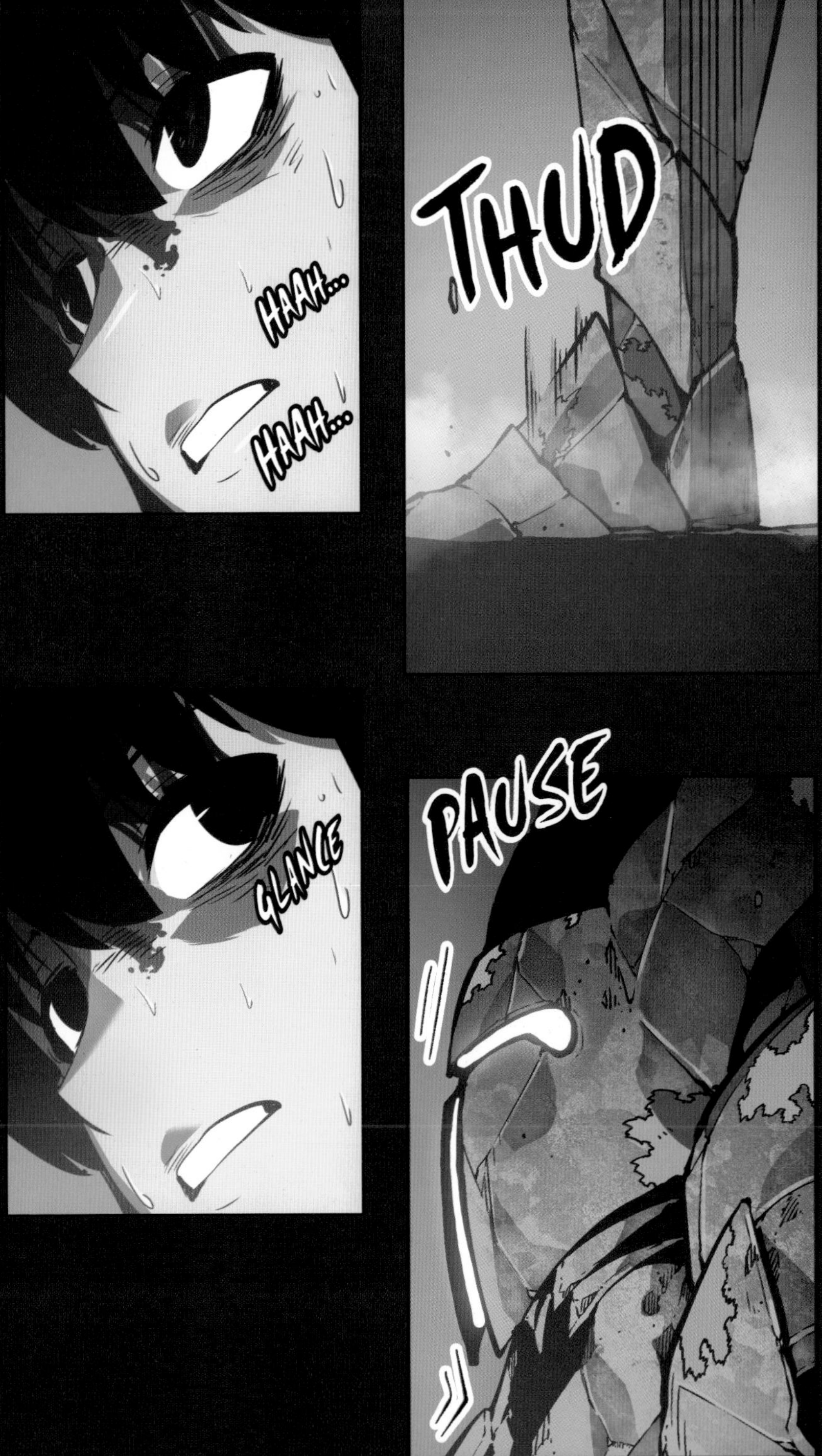
HAAH...
HAAH...
THUD
GLANCE
PAUSE

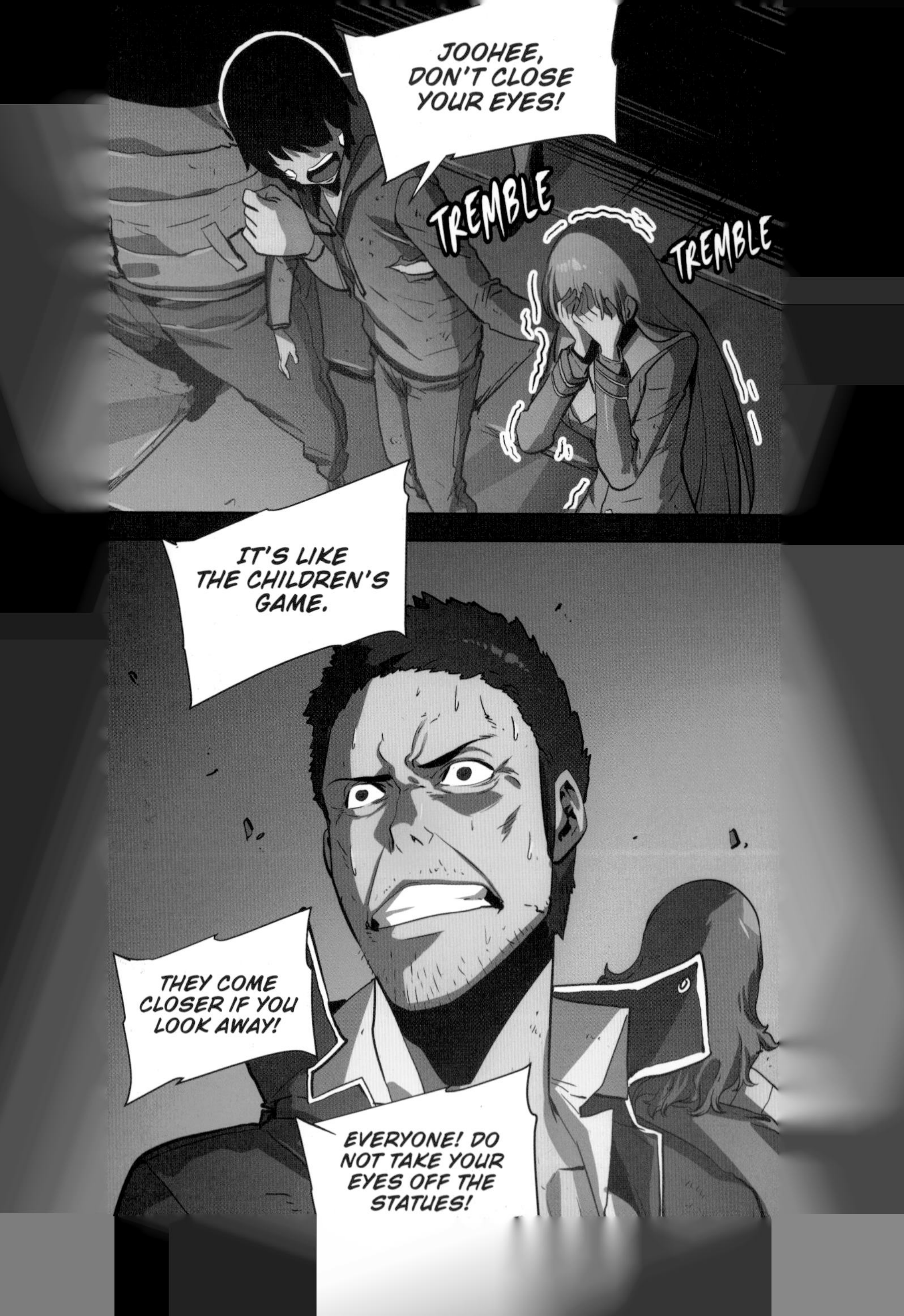
JOOHEE, DON'T CLOSE YOUR EYES!
TREMBLE
TREMBLE
IT'S LIKE THE CHILDREN'S GAME.
THEY COME CLOSER IF YOU LOOK AWAY!
EVERYONE! DO NOT TAKE YOUR EYES OFF THE STATUES!

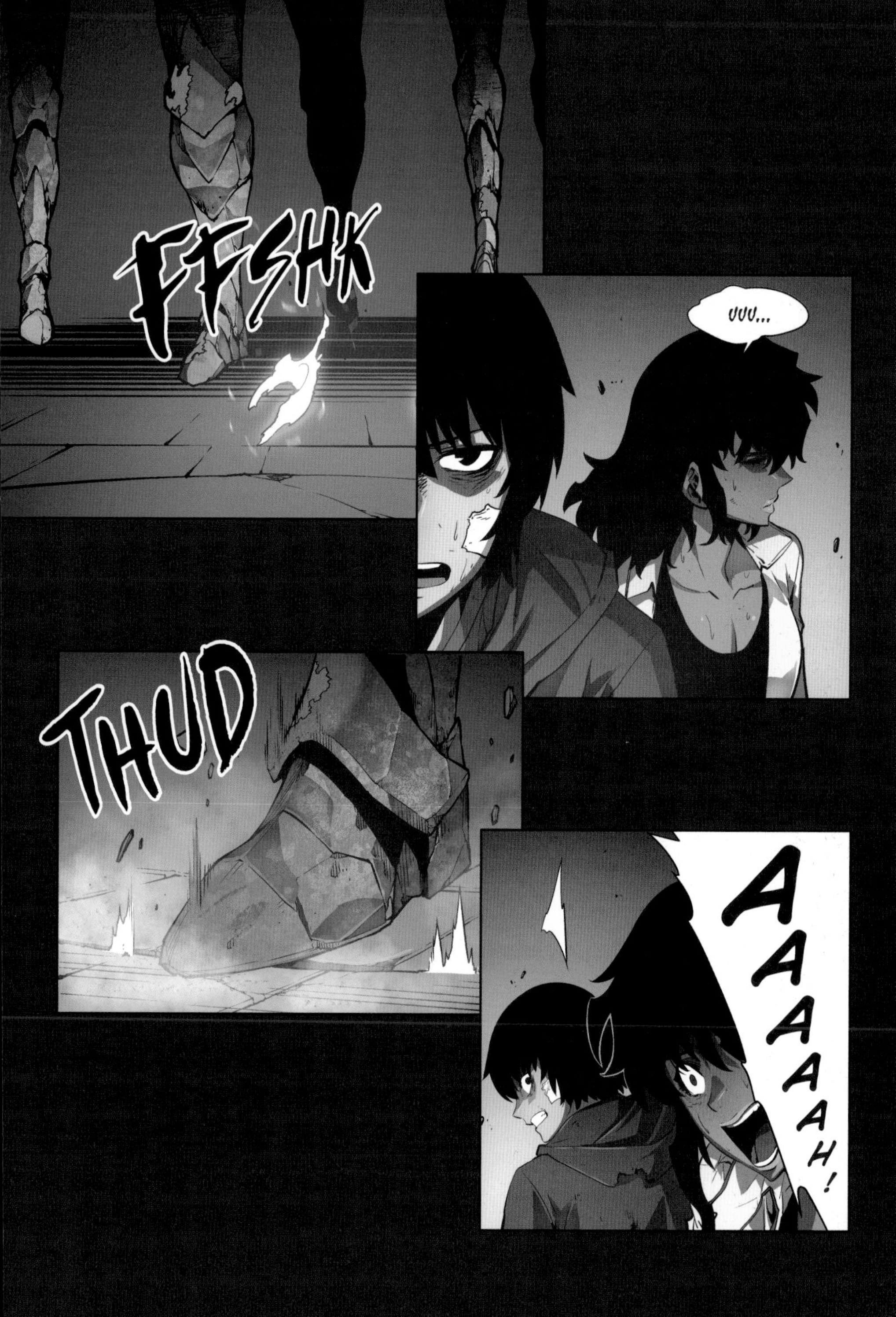
FFSHK
uuu...
THUD
AAAAAAH!

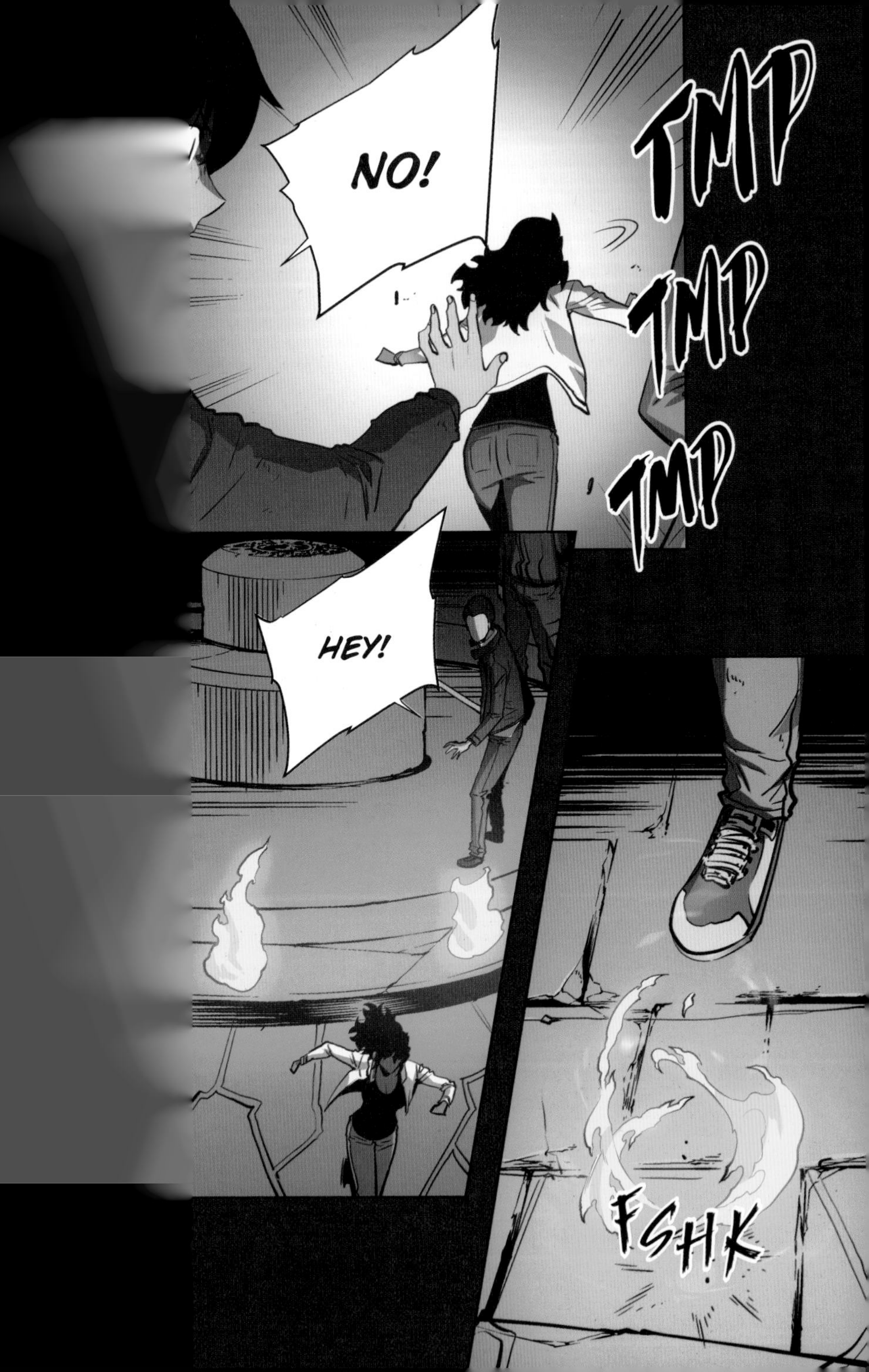
NO!
TMP
TMP
TMP
HEY!
FSHK

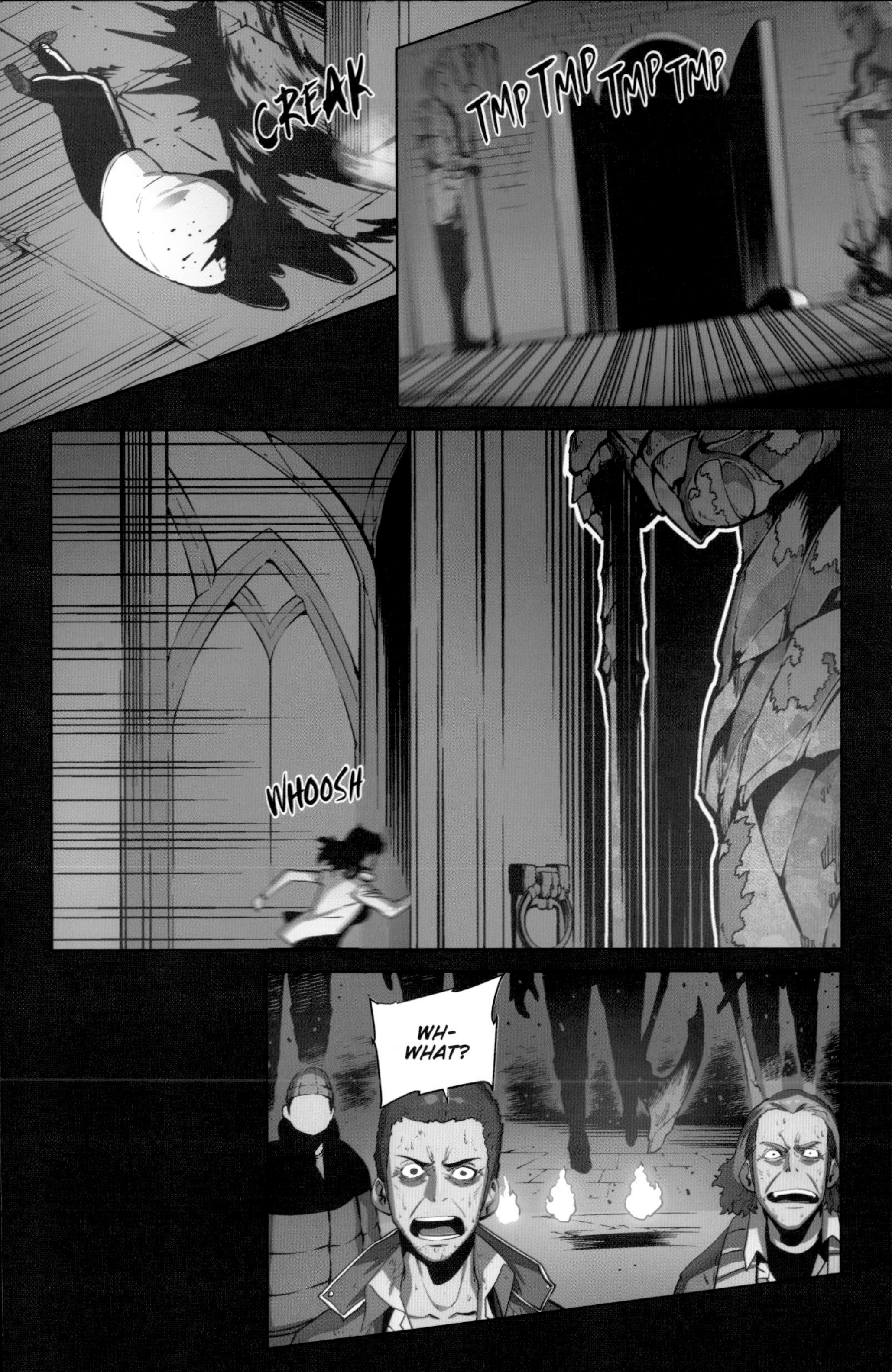
CREAK
TMP TMP TMP TMP
WHOOSH
WH- WHAT?

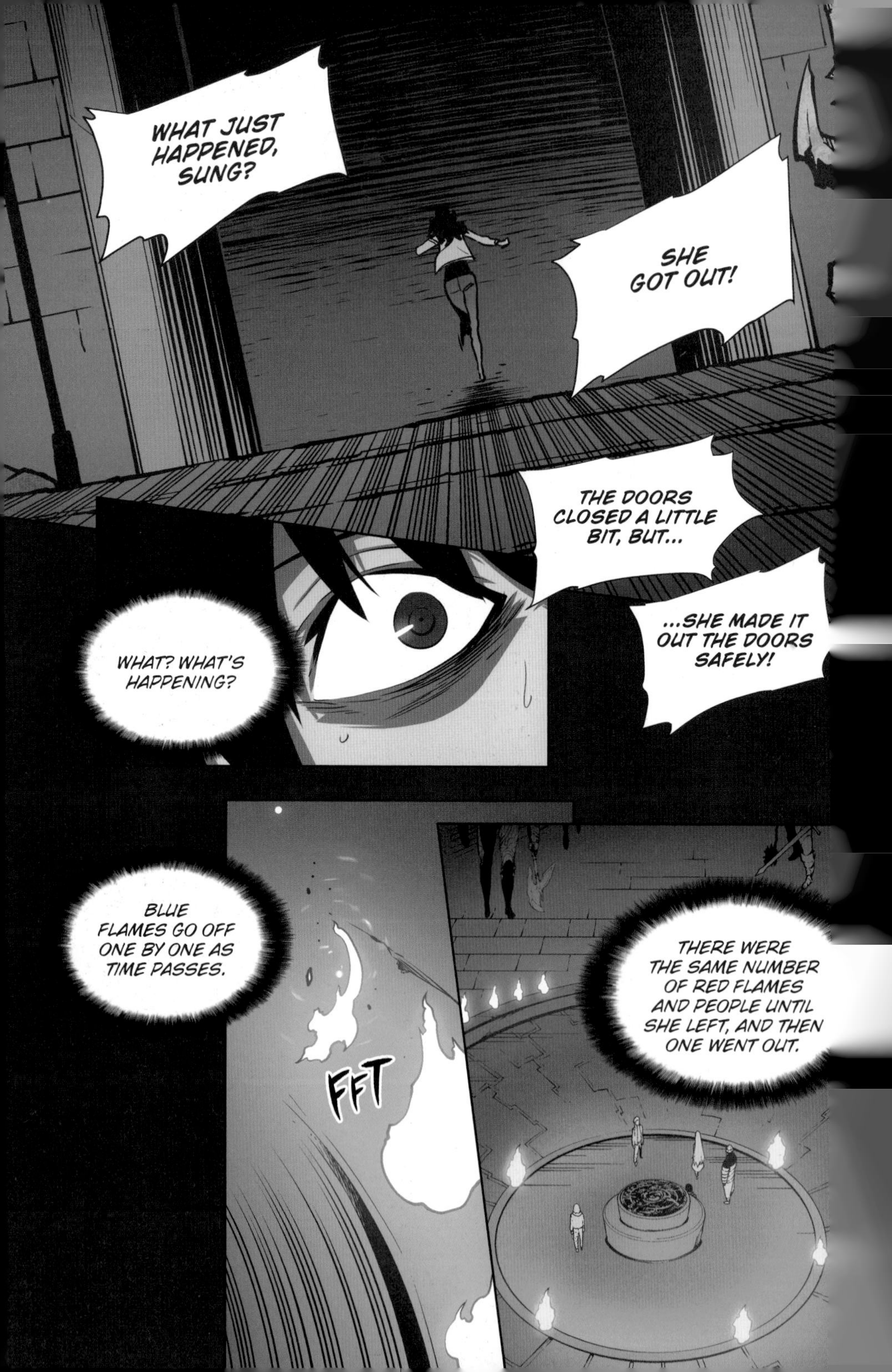
WHAT JUST HAPPENED, SUNG?
SHE GOT OUT!
THE DOORS CLOSED A LITTLE BIT, BUT...
WHAT? WHAT'S HAPPENING?
...SHE MADE IT OUT THE DOORS SAFELY!
BLUE FLAMES GO OFF ONE BY ONE AS TIME PASSES.
FFT
THERE WERE THE SAME NUMBER OF RED FLAMES AND PEOPLE UNTIL SHE LEFT, AND THEN ONE WENT OUT.

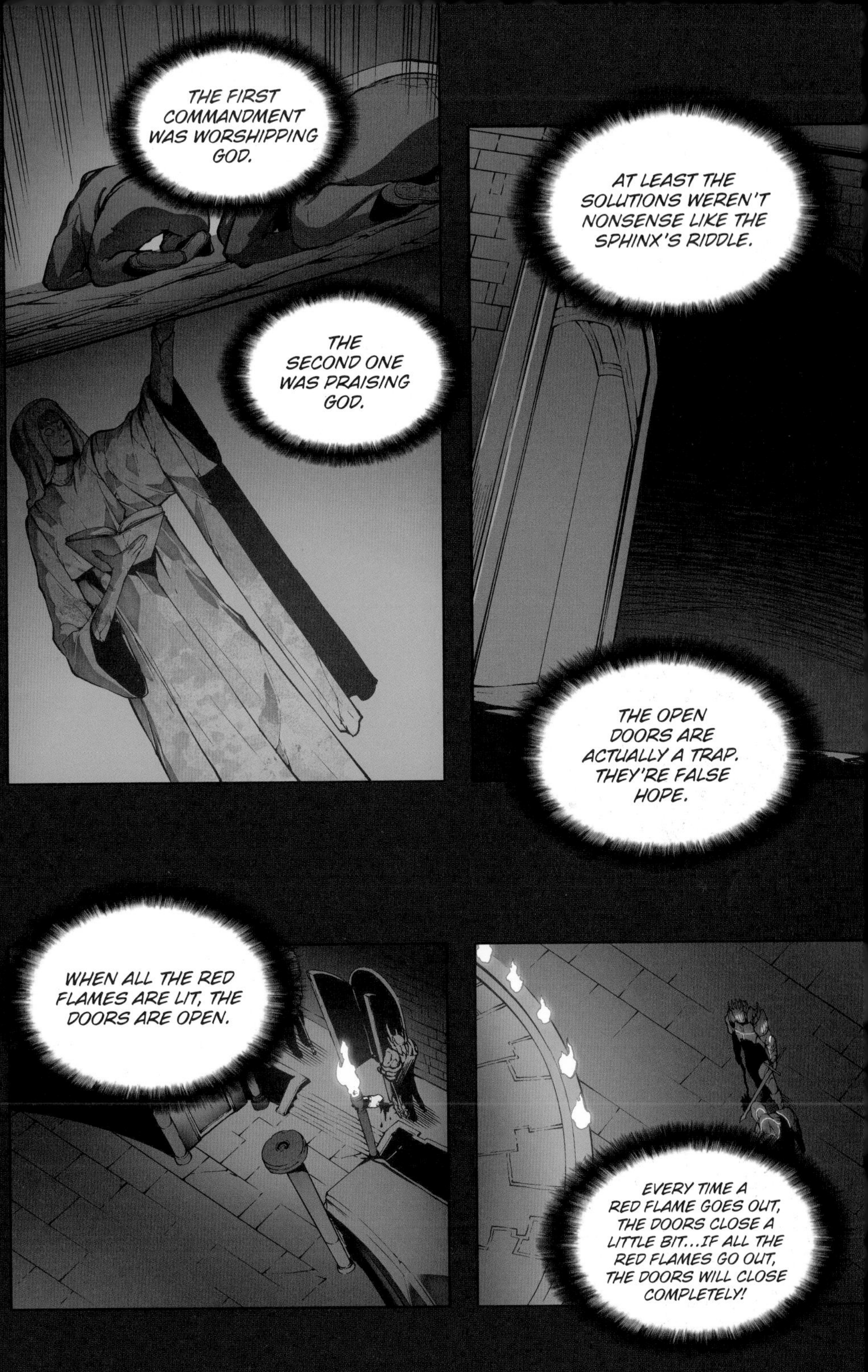
THE FIRST COMMANDMENT WAS WORSHIPPING GOD.
THE SECOND ONE WAS PRAISING GOD.
AT LEAST THE SOLUTIONS WEREN'T NONSENSE LIKE THE SPHINX'S RIDDLE.
THE OPEN DOORS ARE ACTUALLY A TRAP. THEY'RE FALSE HOPE.
WHEN ALL THE RED FLAMES ARE LIT, THE DOORS ARE OPEN.
EVERY TIME A RED FLAME GOES OUT, THE DOORS CLOSE A LITTLE BIT...IF ALL THE RED FLAMES GO OUT, THE DOORS WILL CLOSE COMPLETELY!

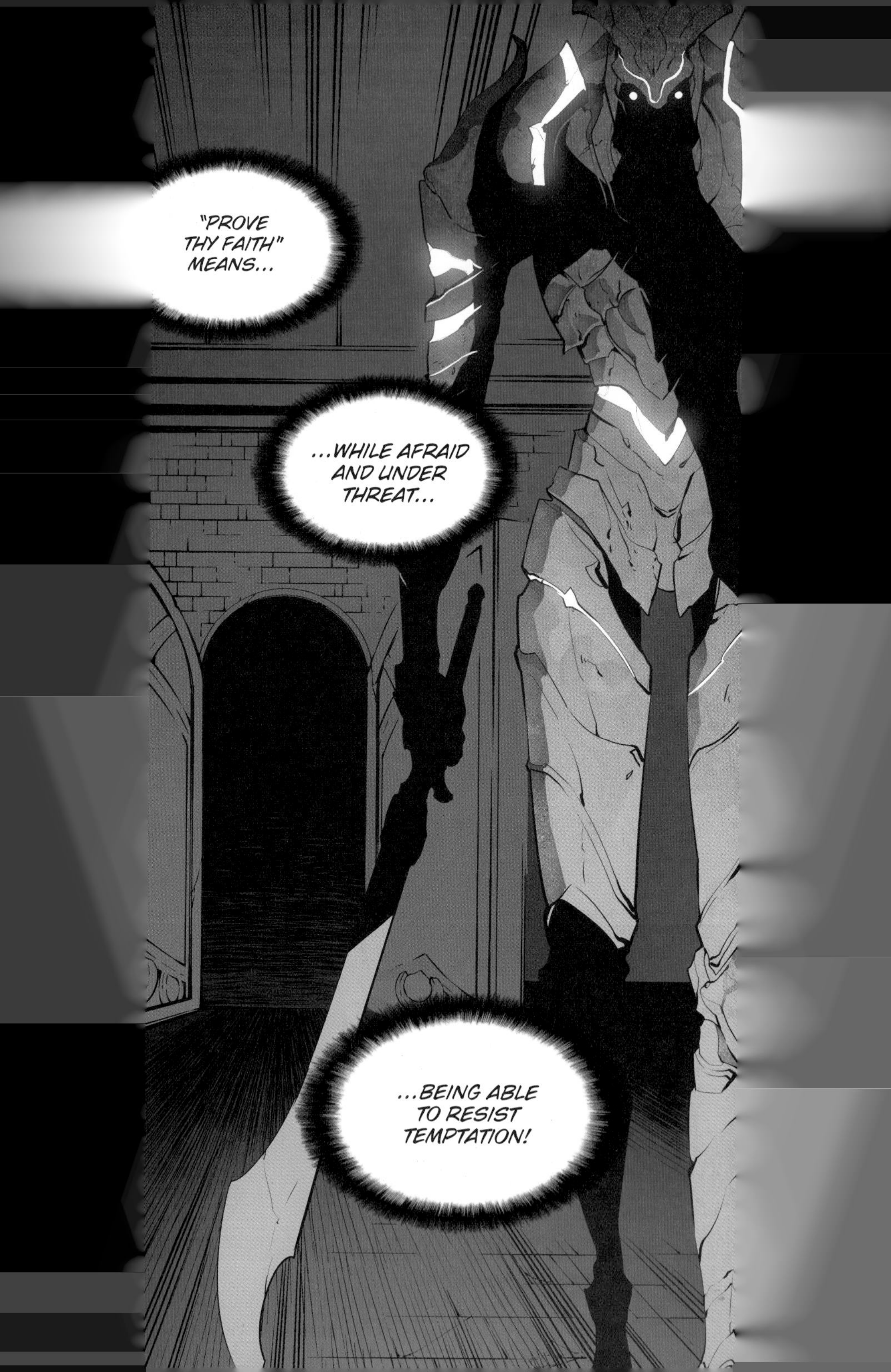
"PROVE THY FAITH" MEANS...
...WHILE AFRAID AND UNDER THREAT...
...BEING ABLE TO RESIST TEMPTATION!

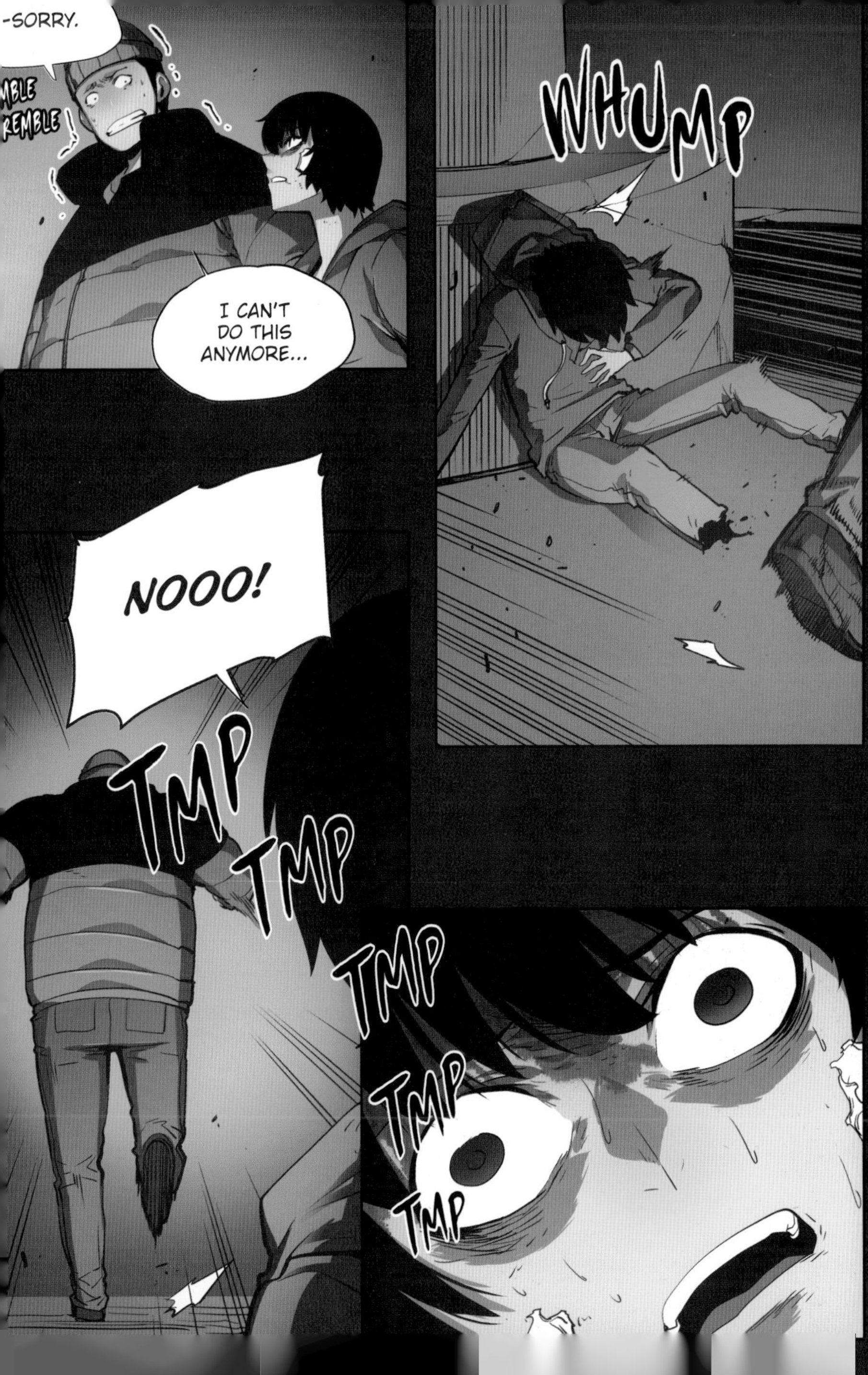
-SORRY.
I CAN'T DO THIS ANYMORE...
WHUMP
NOOO!
TMP
TMP
TMP
TMP
TMP

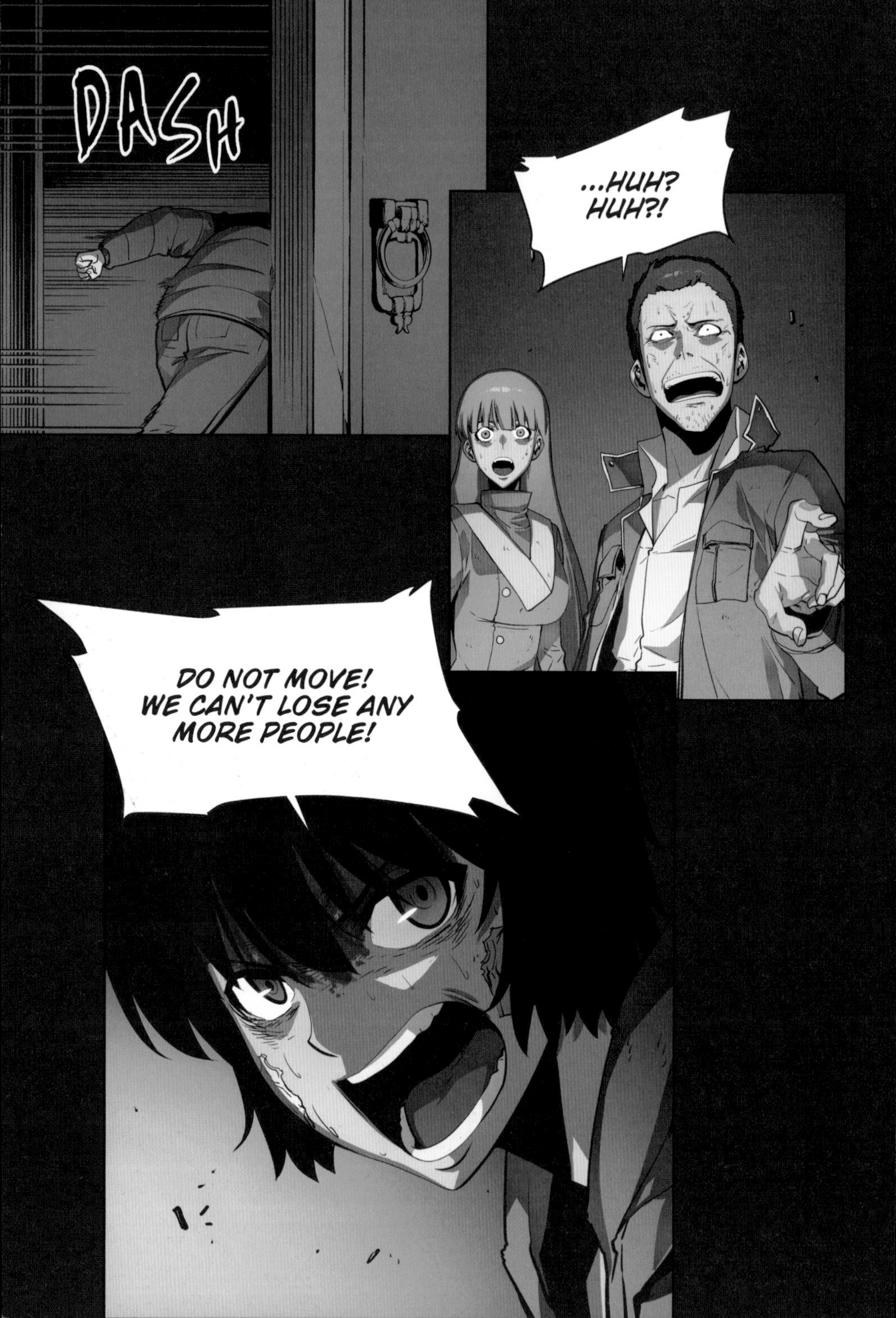
DASH
...HUH? HUH?!
DO NOT MOVE! WE CAN'T LOSE ANY MORE PEOPLE!

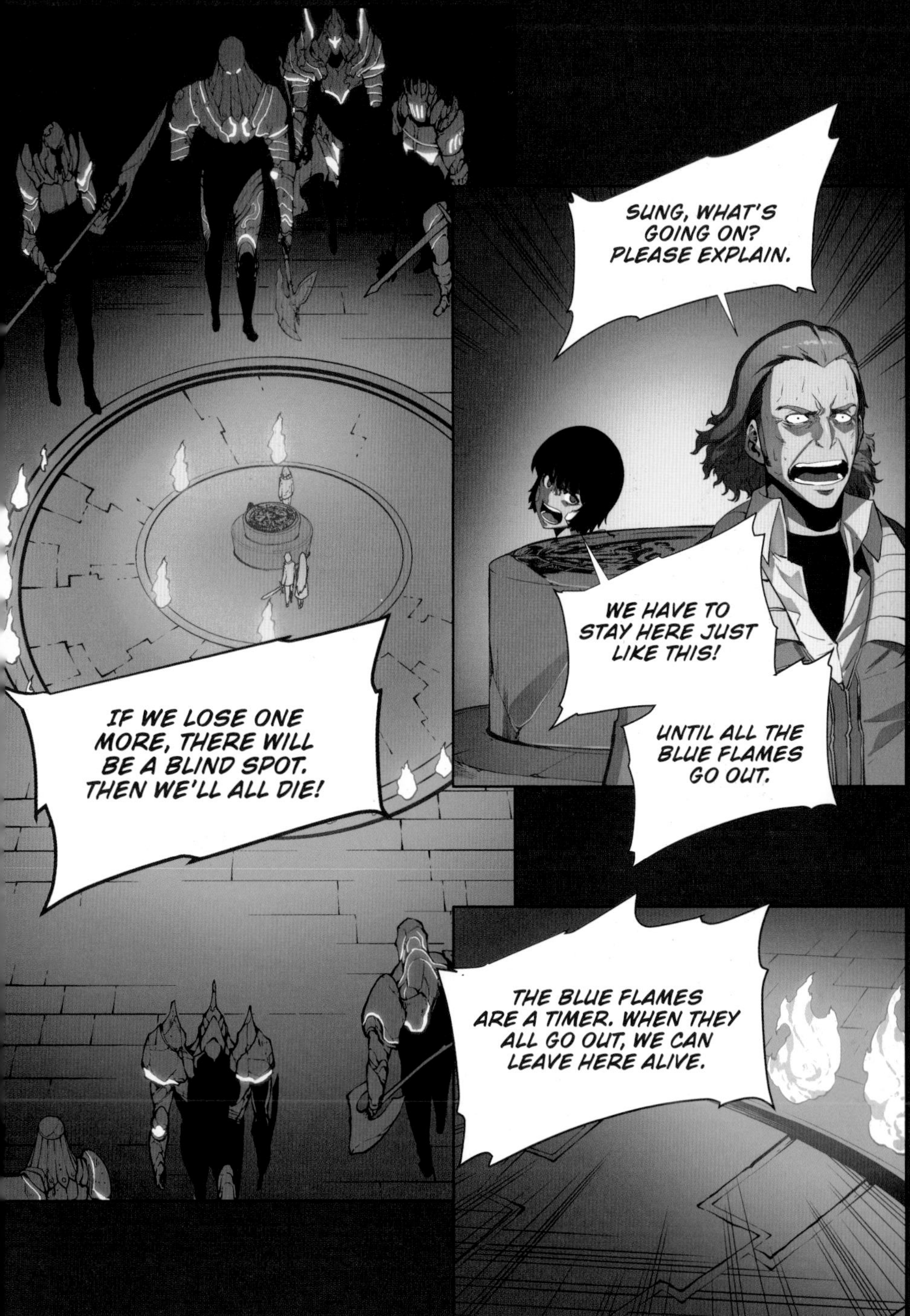
IF WE LOSE ONE MORE, THERE WILL BE A BLIND SPOT. THEN WE'LL ALL DIE!
SUNG, WHAT'S GOING ON? PLEASE EXPLAIN.
WE HAVE TO STAY HERE JUST LIKE THIS!
UNTIL ALL THE BLUE FLAMES GO OUT.
THE BLUE FLAMES ARE A TIMER. WHEN THEY ALL GO OUT, WE CAN LEAVE HERE ALIVE.

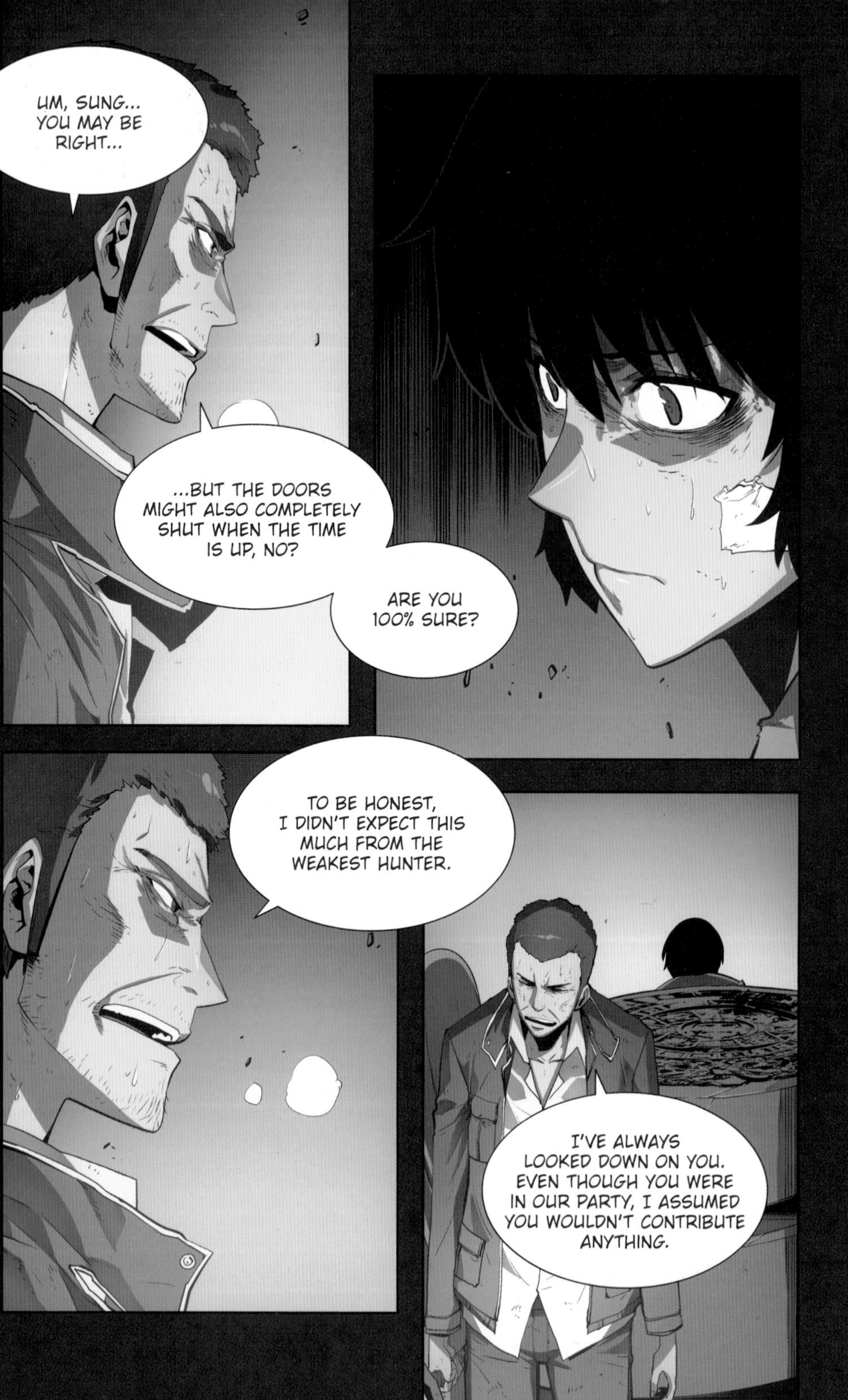
UM, SUNG... YOU MAY BE RIGHT...
...BUT THE DOORS MIGHT ALSO COMPLETELY SHUT WHEN THE TIME IS UP, NO?
ARE YOU 100% SURE?
TO BE HONEST, I DIDN'T EXPECT THIS MUCH FROM THE WEAKEST HUNTER.
I'VE ALWAYS LOOKED DOWN ON YOU. EVEN THOUGH YOU WERE IN OUR PARTY, I ASSUMED YOU WOULDN'T CONTRIBUTE ANYTHING.

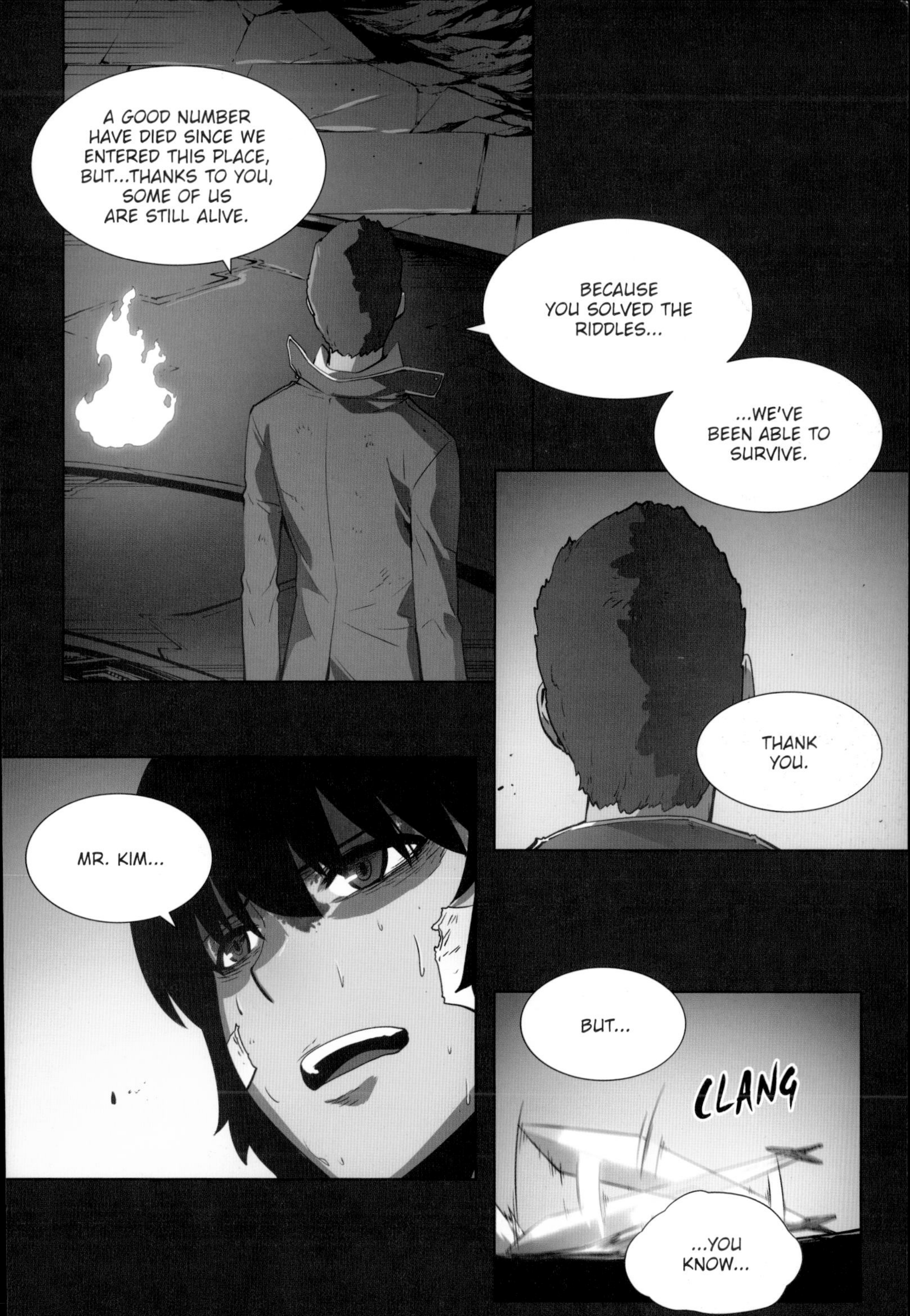
A GOOD NUMBER HAVE DIED SINCE WE ENTERED THIS PLACE, BUT...THANKS TO YOU, SOME OF US ARE STILL ALIVE.
BECAUSE YOU SOLVED THE RIDDLES...
...WE'VE BEEN ABLE TO SURVIVE.
THANK YOU.
MR. KIM...
BUT...
CLANG
...YOU KNOW...

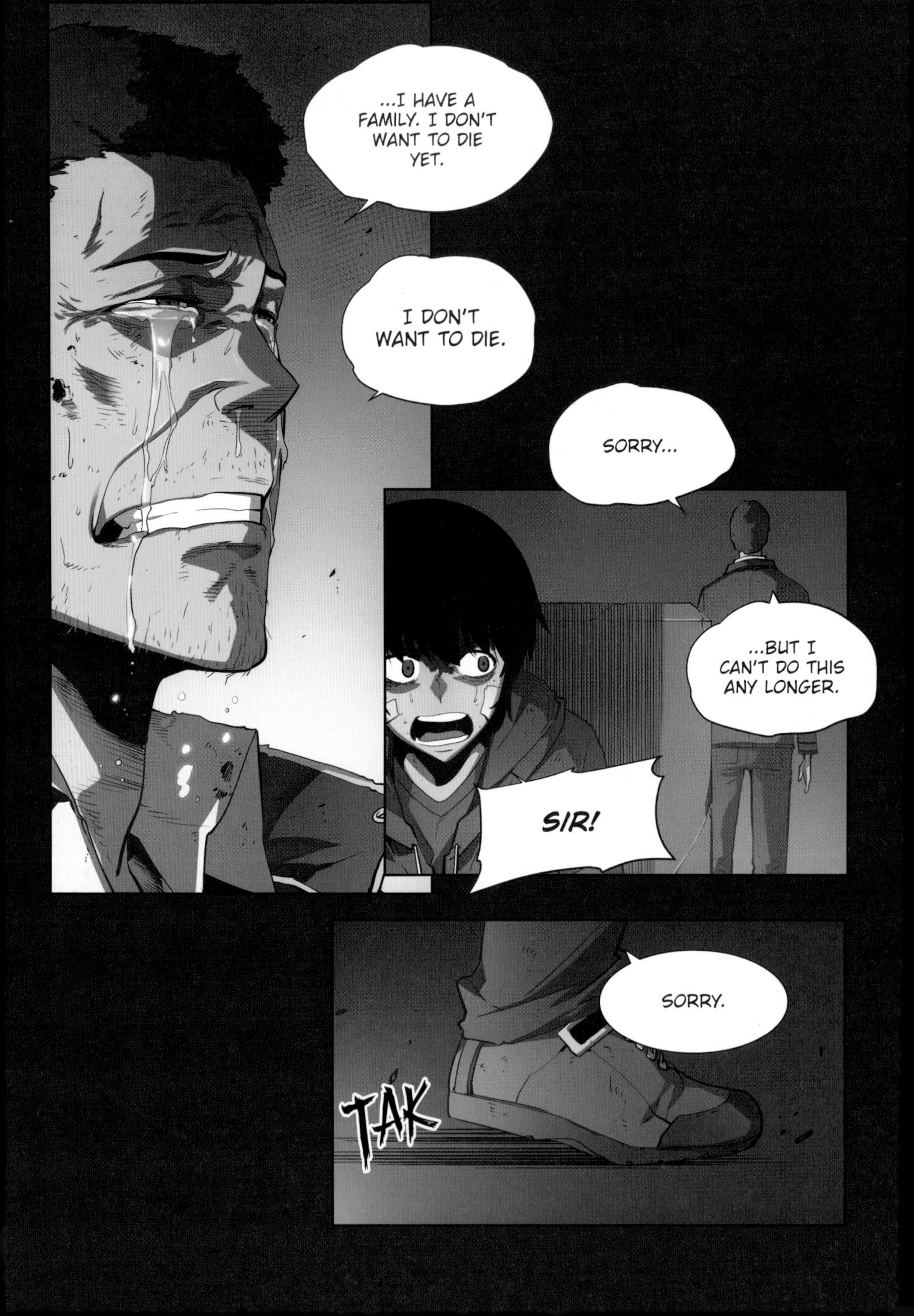
...I HAVE A FAMILY. I DON'T WANT TO DIE YET.
I DON'T WANT TO DIE.
SORRY...
...BUT I CAN'T DO THIS ANY LONGER.
SIR!
SORRY.
TAK

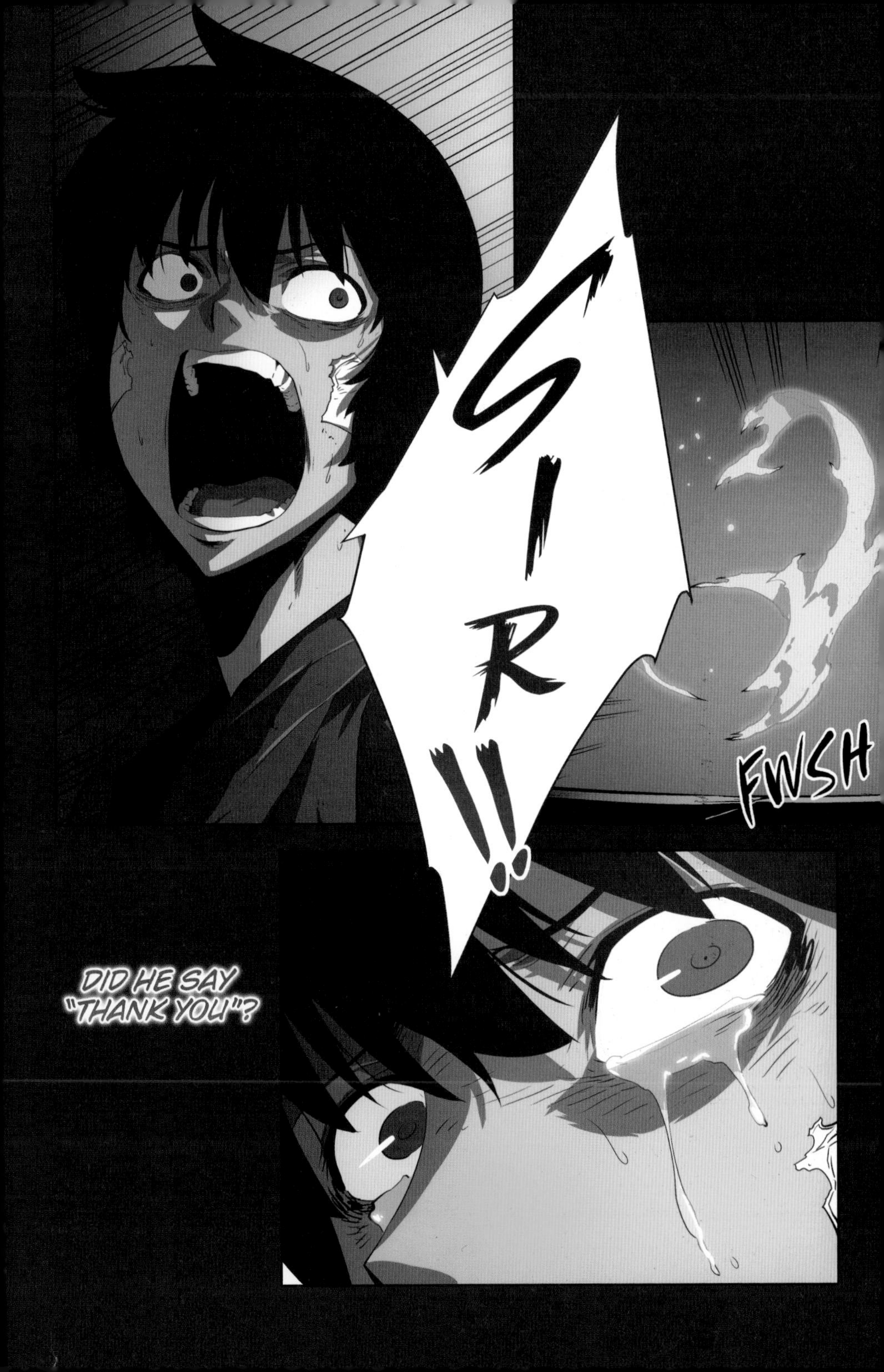
SIR!!
FWSH
DID HE SAY "THANK YOU"?

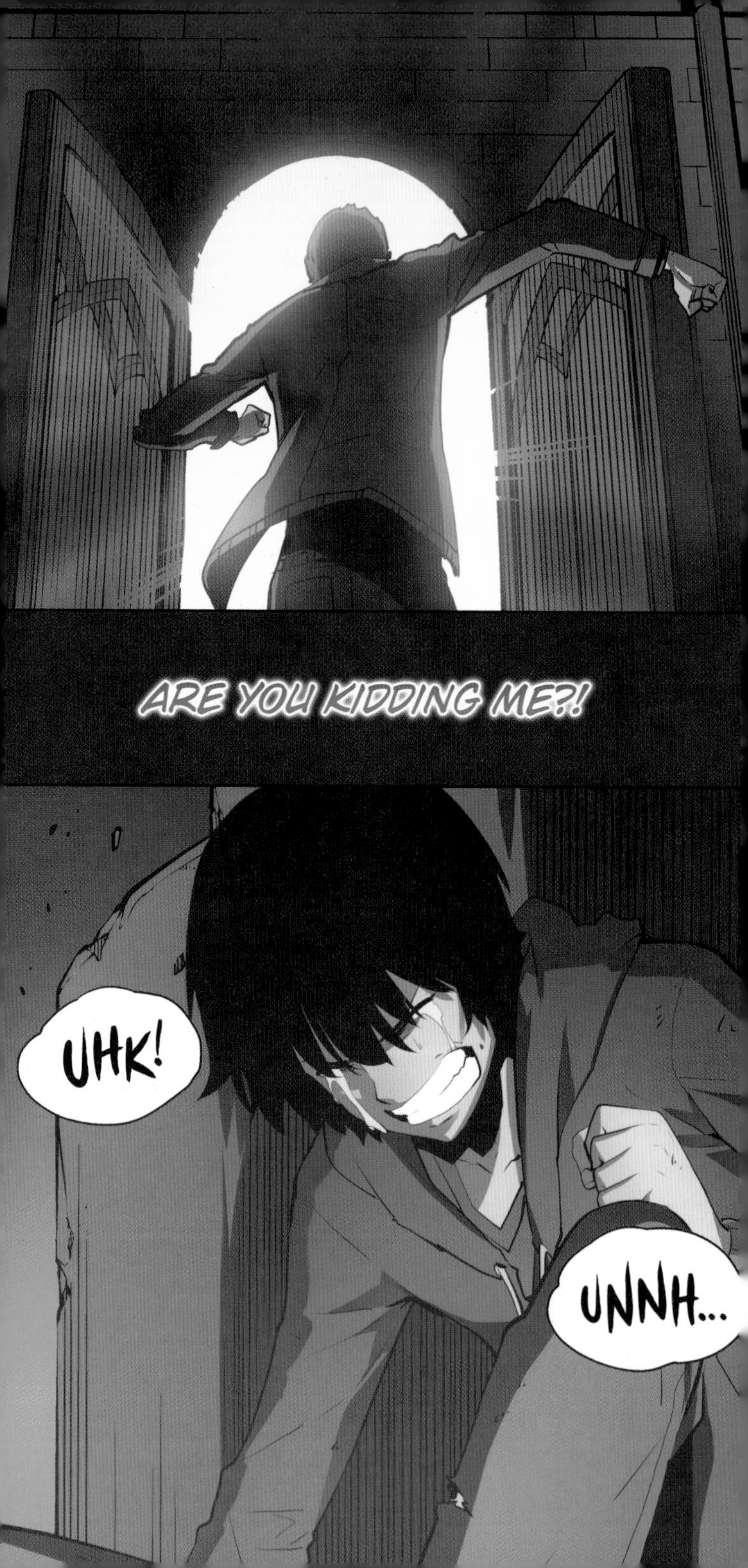
ARE YOU KIDDING ME?!
UHK!
UNNH...

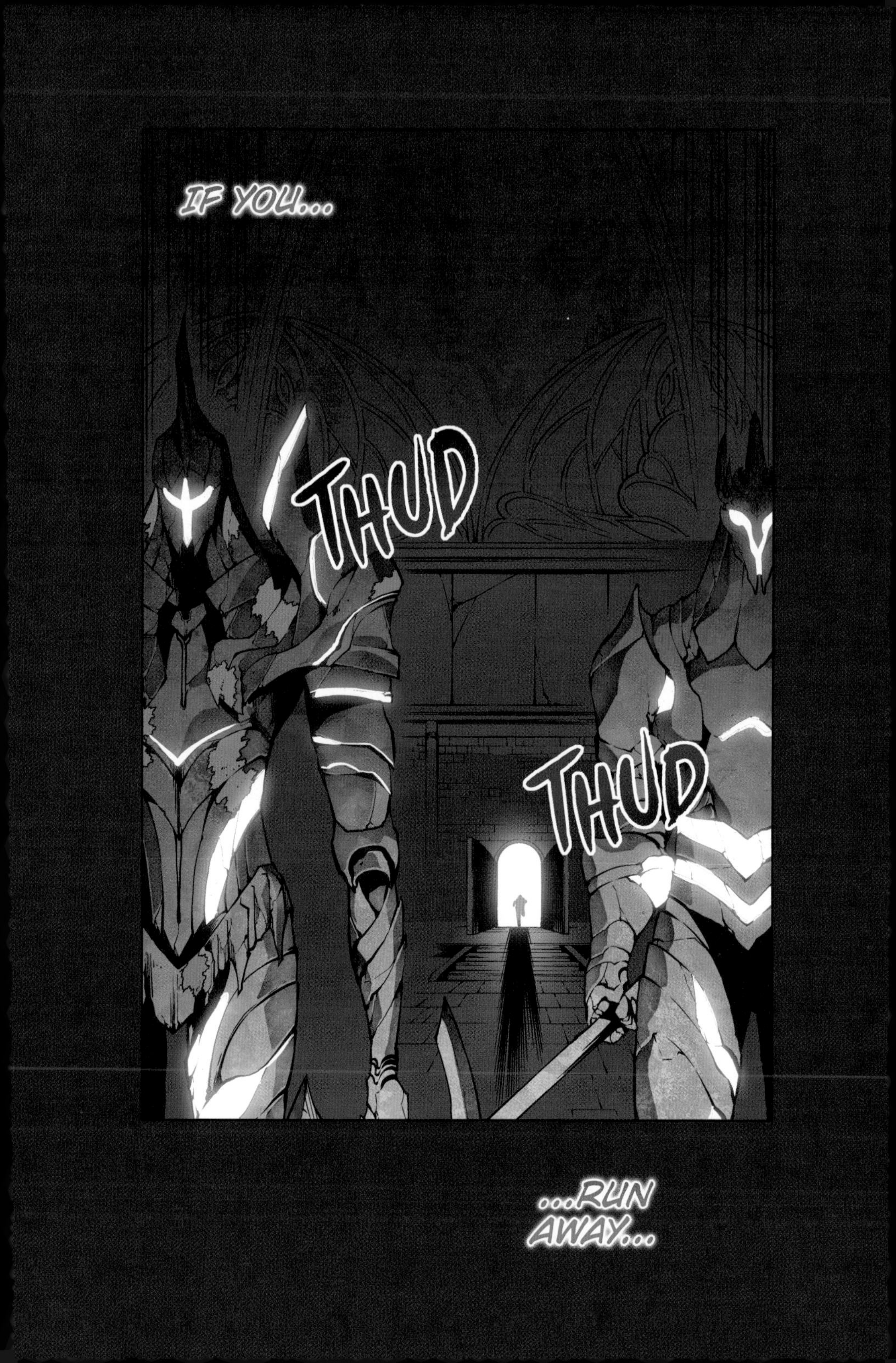
IF YOU...
THUD
THUD
...RUN AWAY...

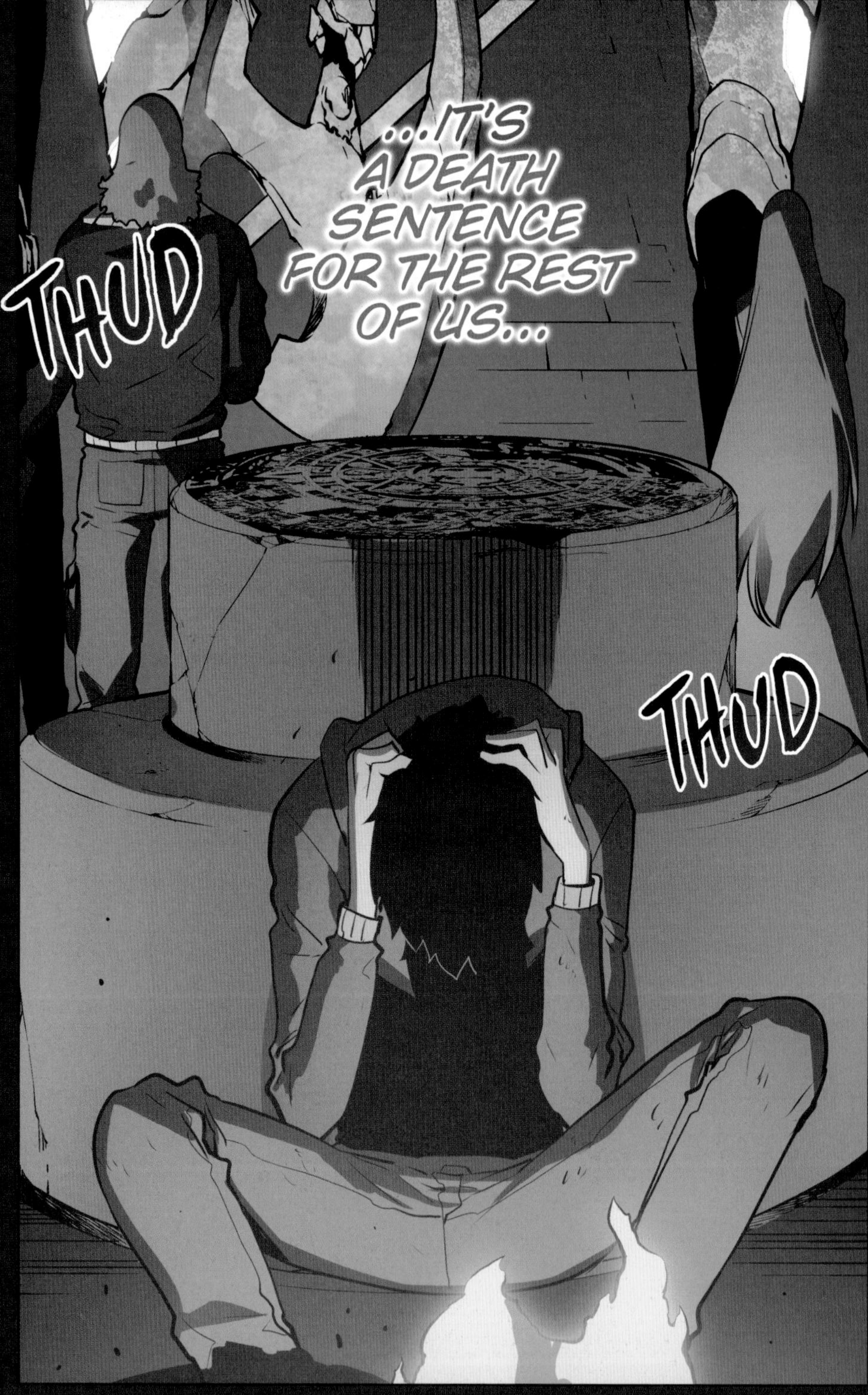

...IT'S A DEATH SENTENCE FOR THE REST OF US...
THUD
THUD

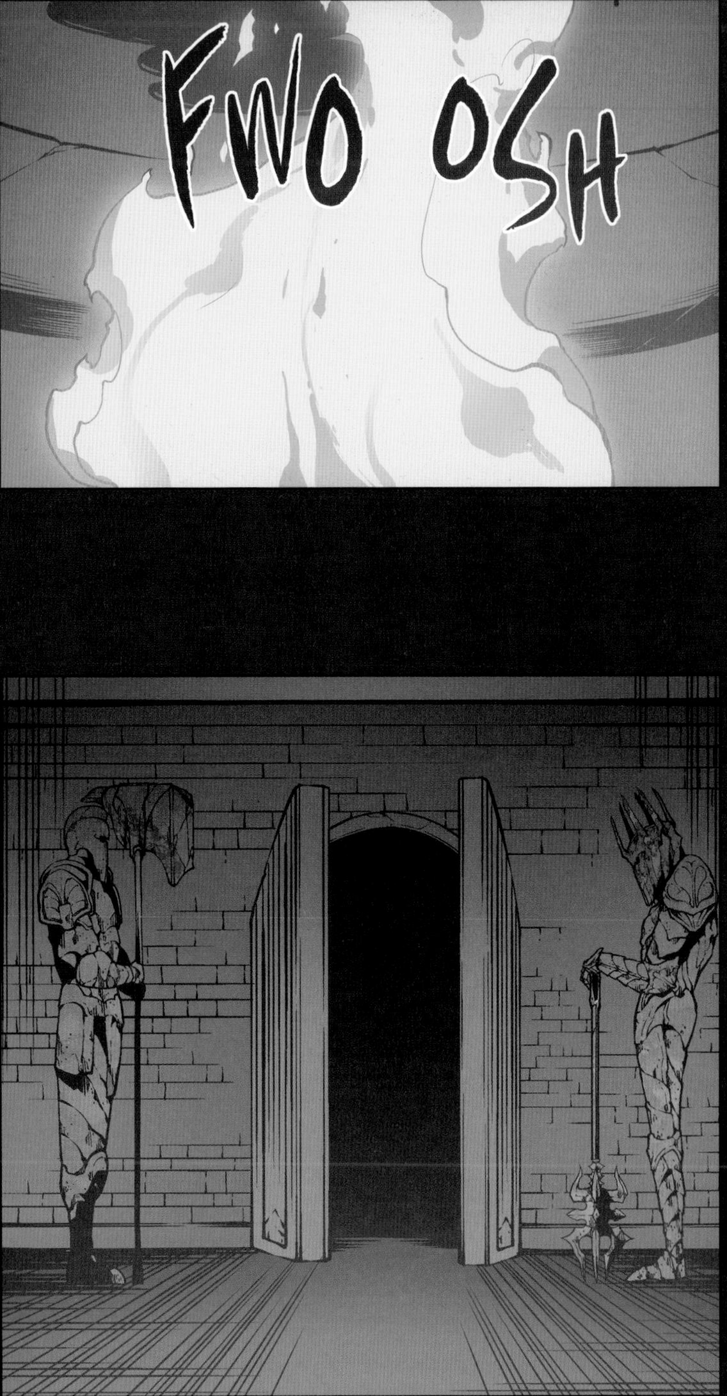
FWOOSH

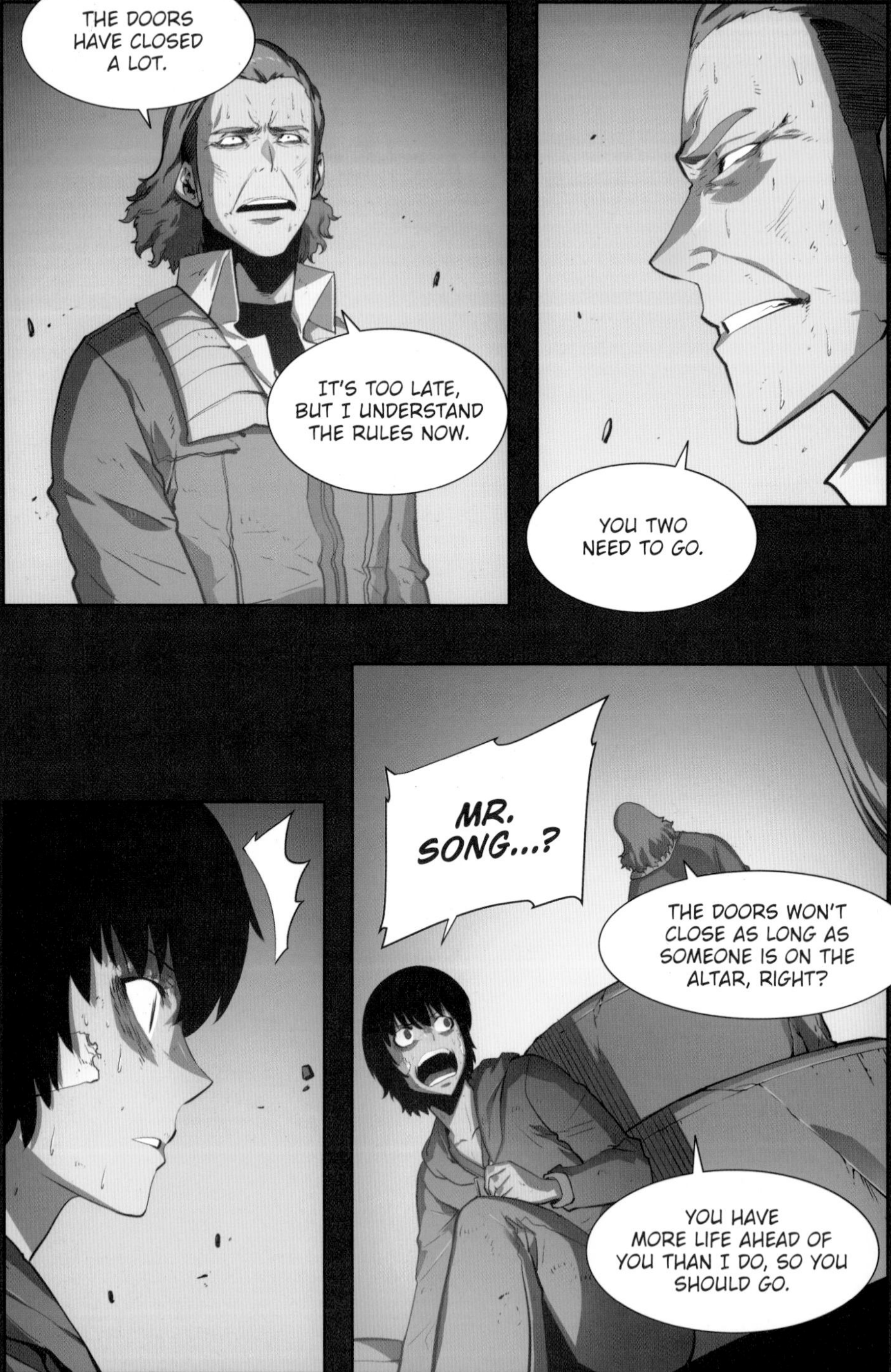
THE DOORS HAVE CLOSED A LOT.
IT'S TOO LATE, BUT I UNDERSTAND THE RULES NOW.
YOU TWO NEED TO GO.
MR. SONG...?
THE DOORS WON'T CLOSE AS LONG AS SOMEONE IS ON THE ALTAR, RIGHT?
YOU HAVE MORE LIFE AHEAD OF YOU THAN I DO, SO YOU SHOULD GO.

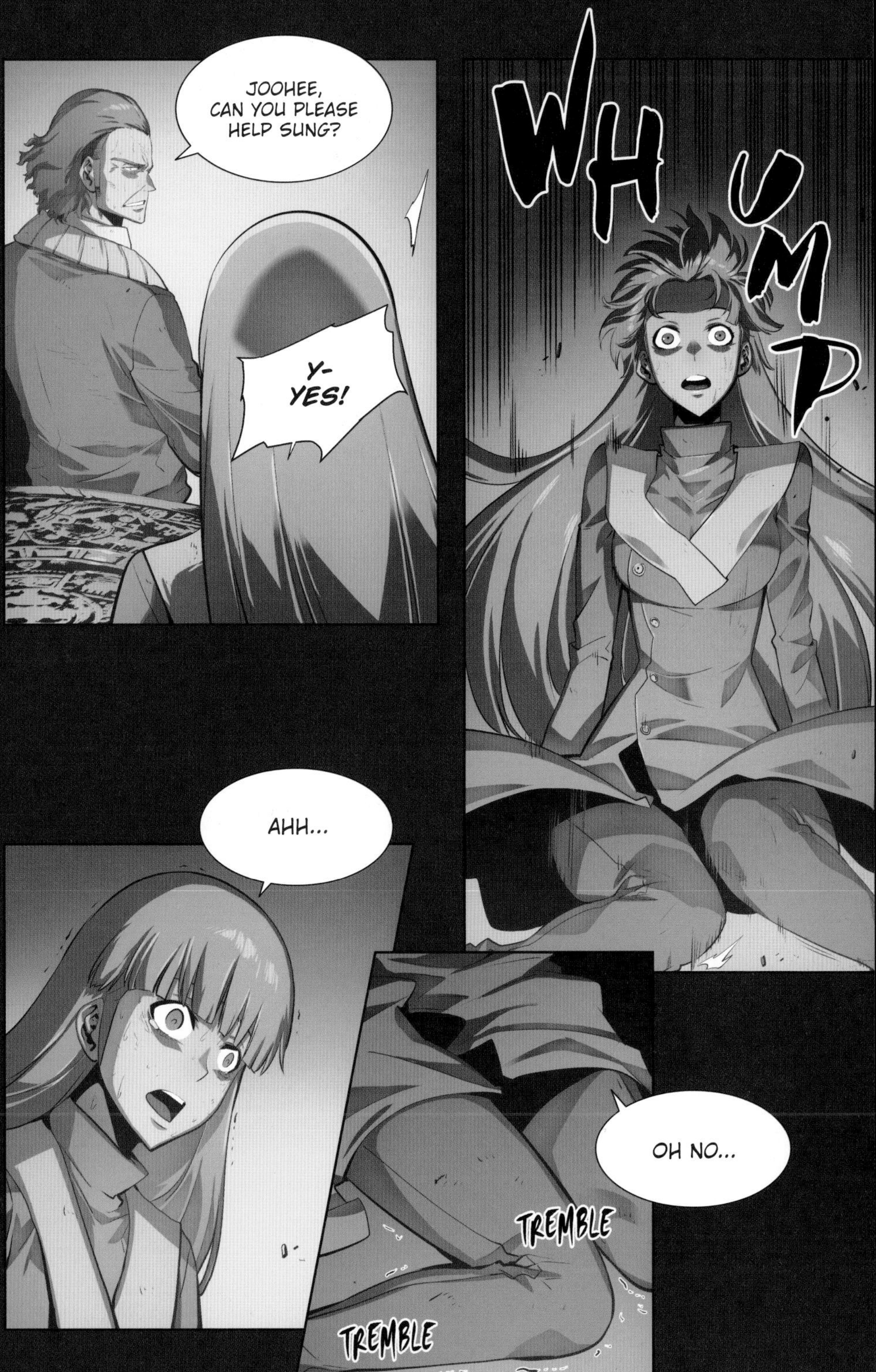
JOOHEE, CAN YOU PLEASE HELP SUNG?
Y- YES!
WHUMP
AHH...
OH NO...
TREMBLE
TREMBLE

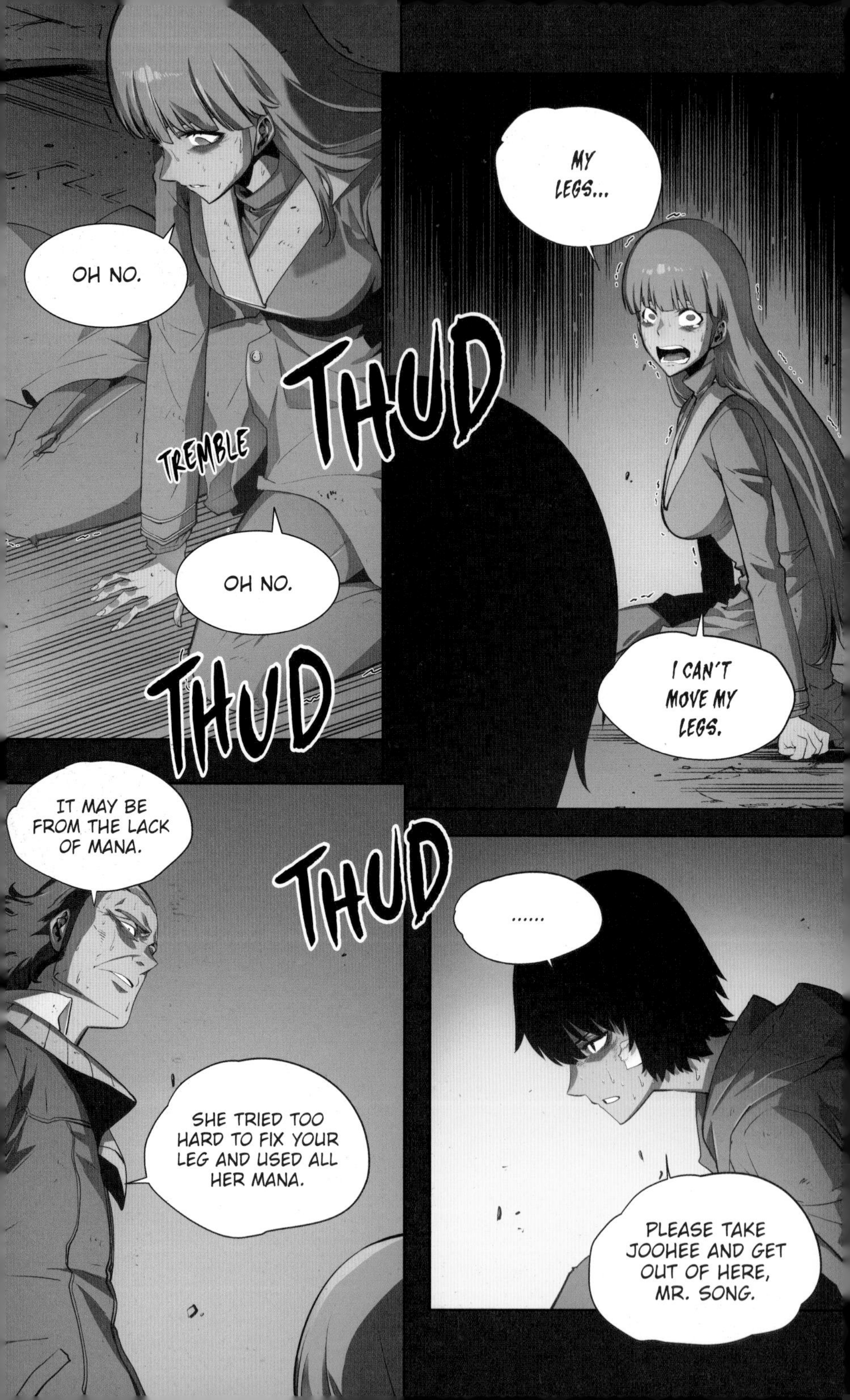
OH NO.
TREMBLE
THUD
OH NO.
THUD
MY LEGS...
I CAN'T MOVE MY LEGS.
IT MAY BE FROM THE LACK OF MANA.
THUD
SHE TRIED TOO HARD TO FIX YOUR LEG AND USED ALL HER MANA.
......
PLEASE TAKE JOOHEE AND GET OUT OF HERE, MR. SONG.

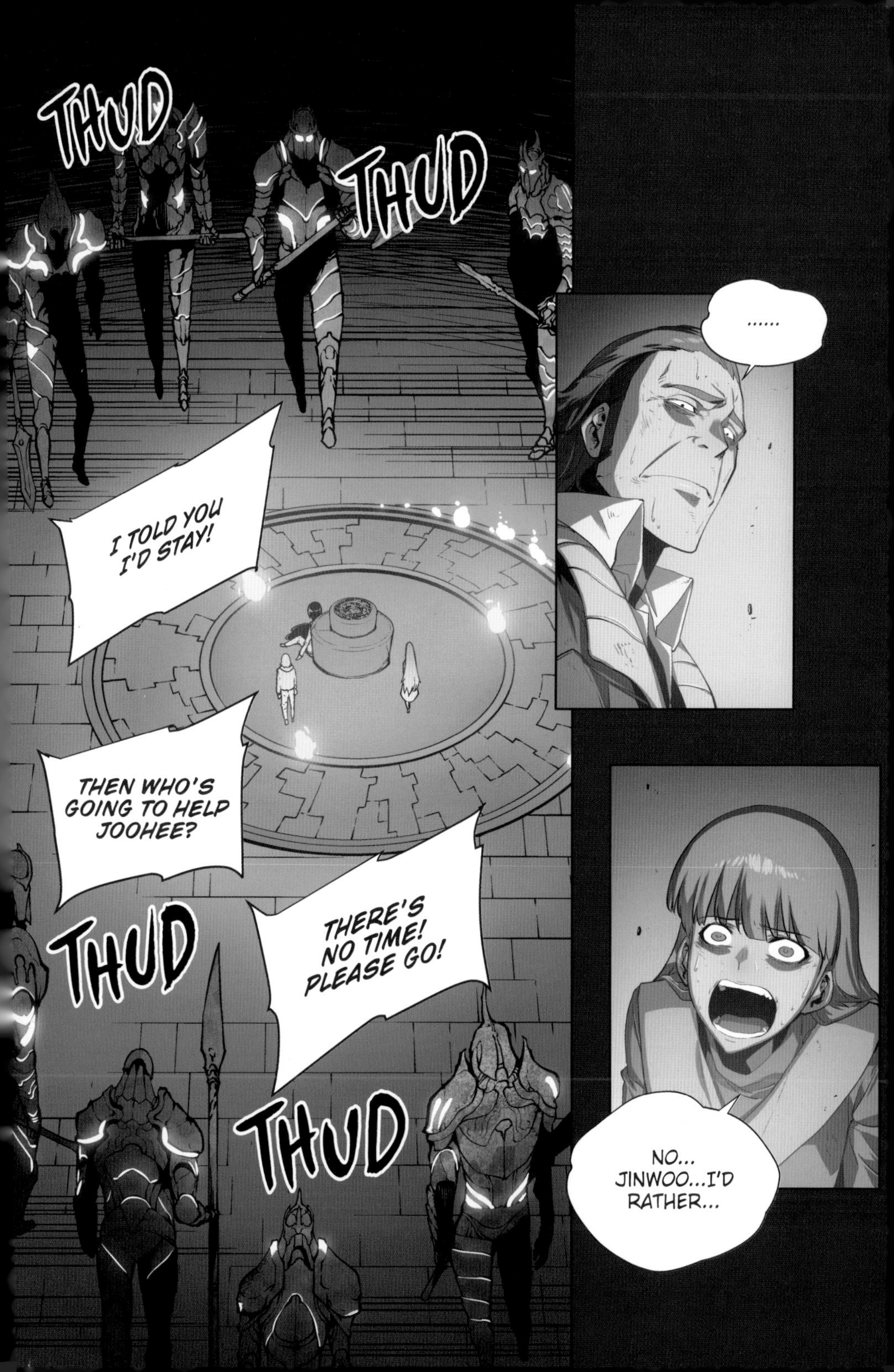
THUD
THUD
I TOLD YOU I'D STAY!
THEN WHO'S GOING TO HELP JOOHEE?
THUD
THERE'S NO TIME! PLEASE GO!
THUD
......
NO... JINWOO...I'D RATHER...

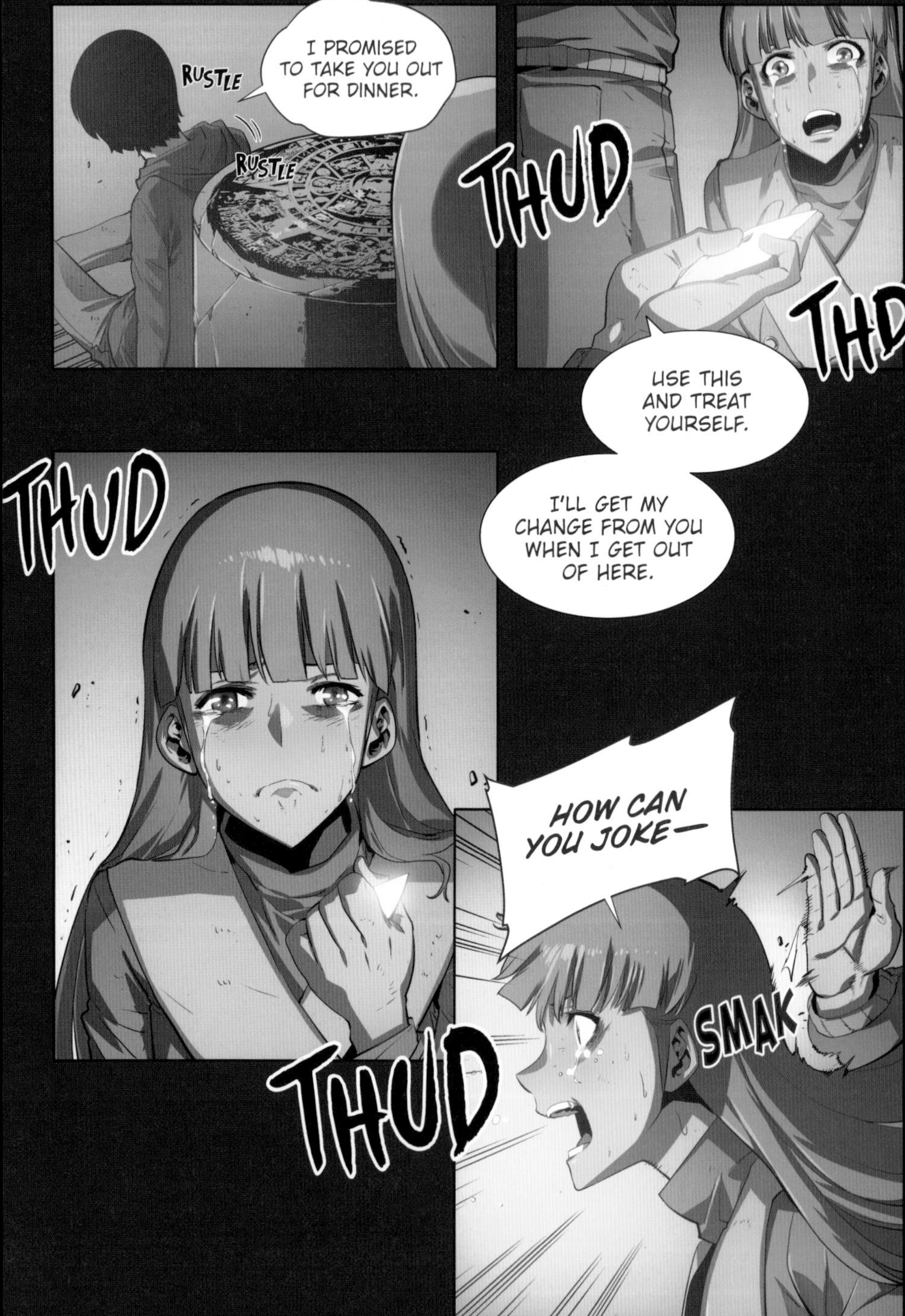
RUSTLE
I PROMISED TO TAKE YOU OUT FOR DINNER.
RUSTLE
THUD
THD
USE THIS AND TREAT YOURSELF.
I'LL GET MY CHANGE FROM YOU WHEN I GET OUT OF HERE.
THUD
HOW CAN YOU JOKE—
SMAK
THUD

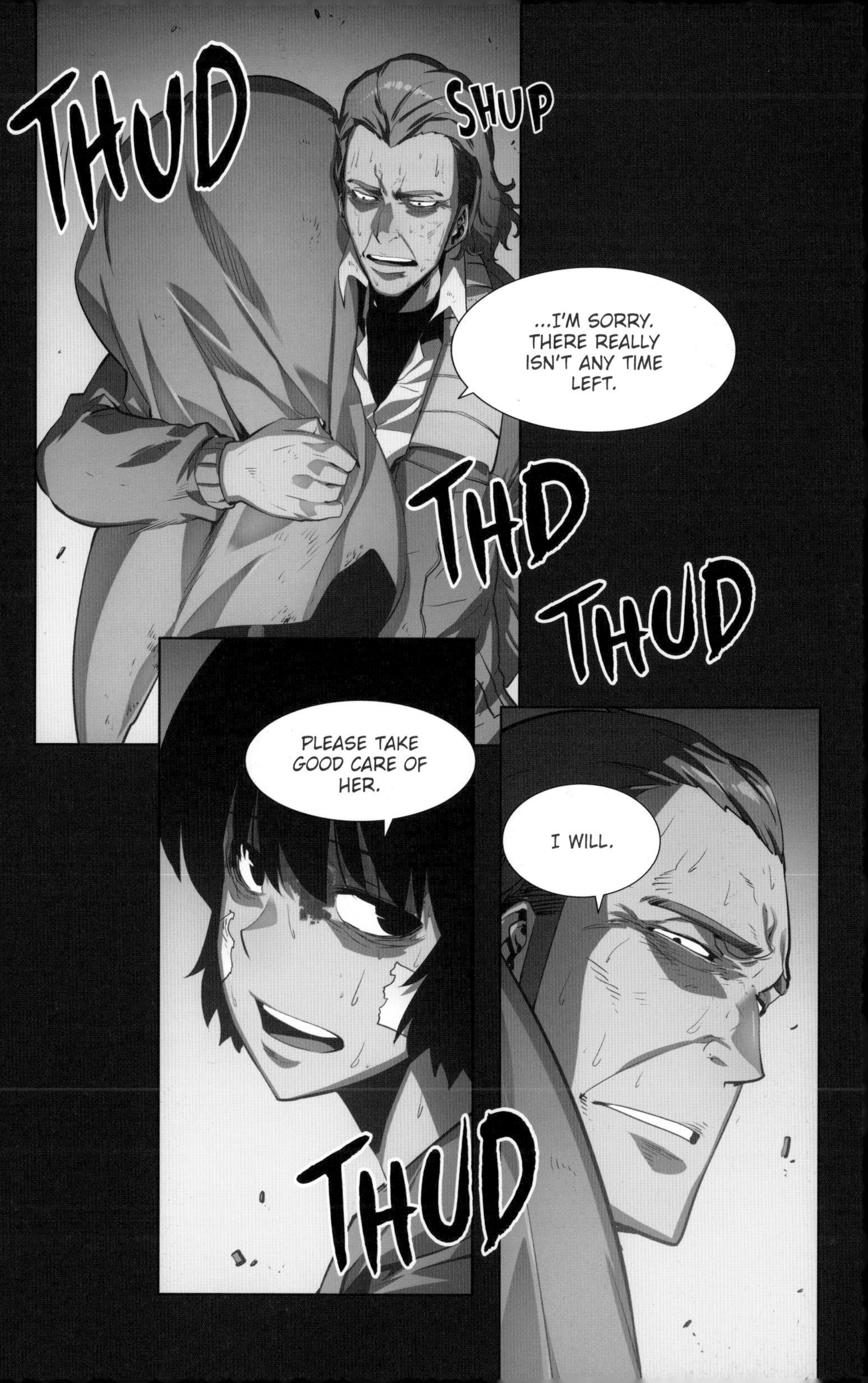
THUD
SHUP
...I'M SORRY. THERE REALLY ISN'T ANY TIME LEFT.
THD
THUD
PLEASE TAKE GOOD CARE OF HER.
I WILL.
THUD

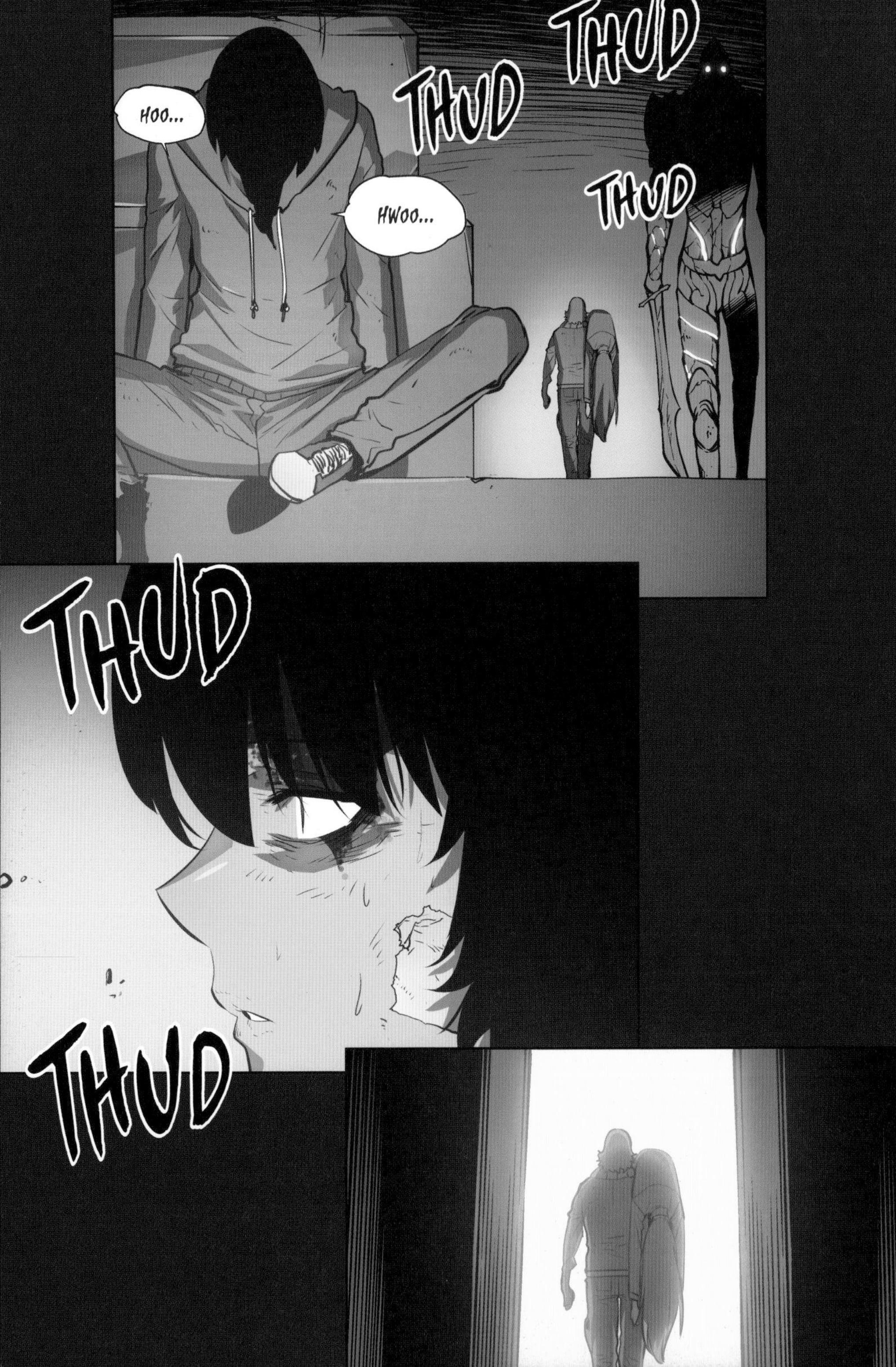
HOO...
HWOO...
THUD
THUD
THUD
THUD
THUD

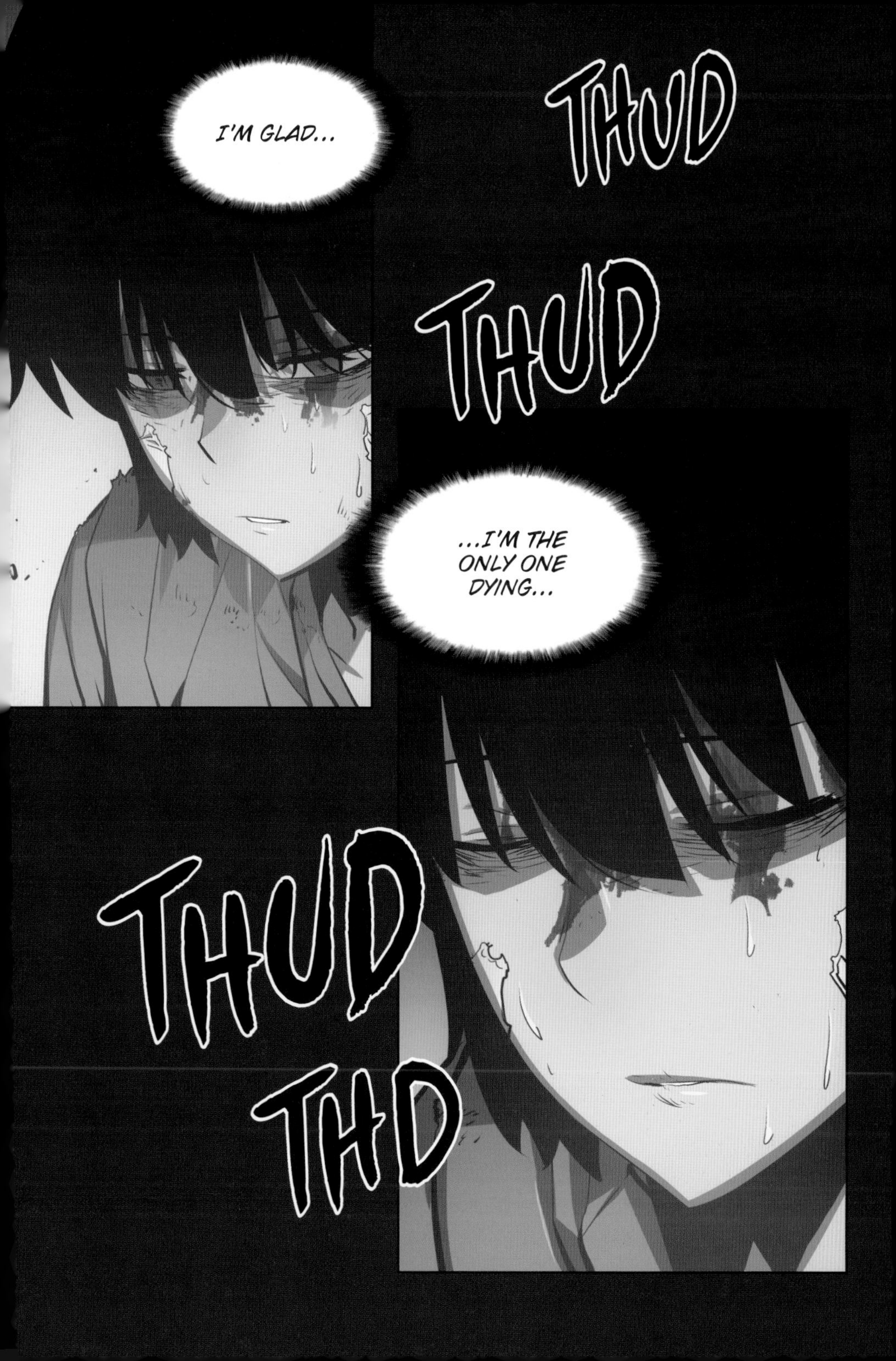
I'M GLAD...
THUD
THUD
...I'M THE ONLY ONE DYING...
THUD
THD

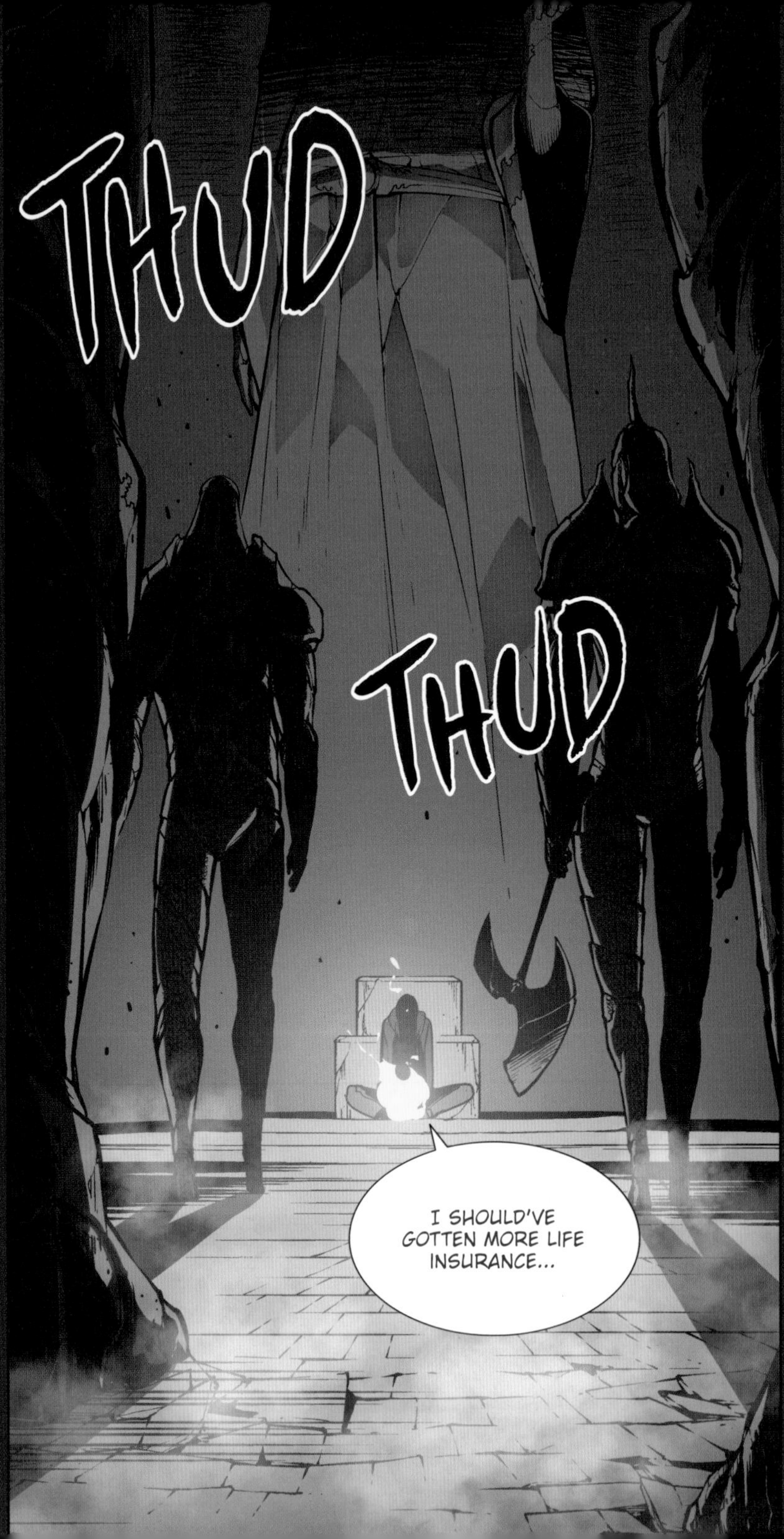
THUD
THUD
I SHOULD'VE GOTTEN MORE LIFE INSURANCE...

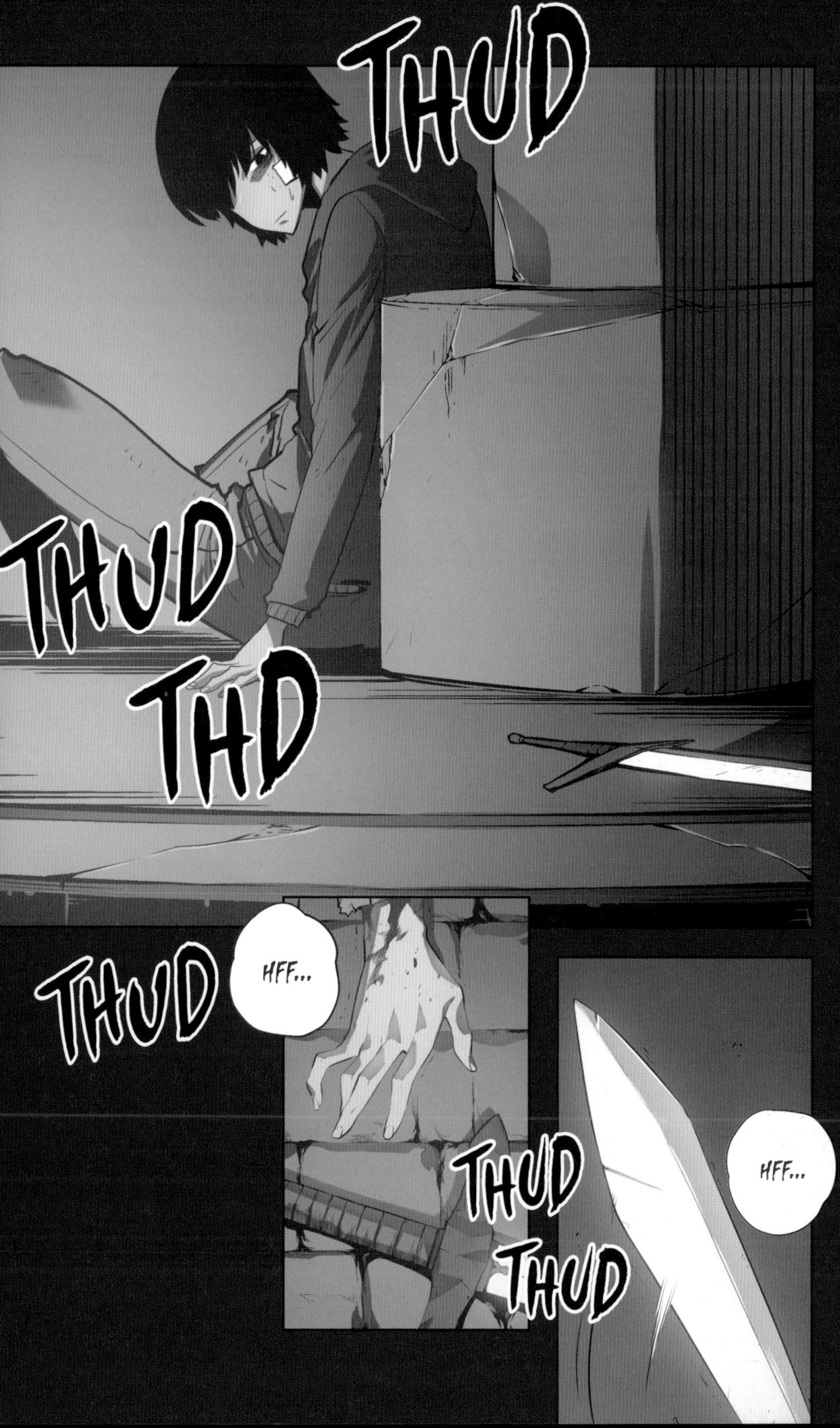
THUD
THUD
THD
THUD
HFF...
THUD
THUD
HFF...

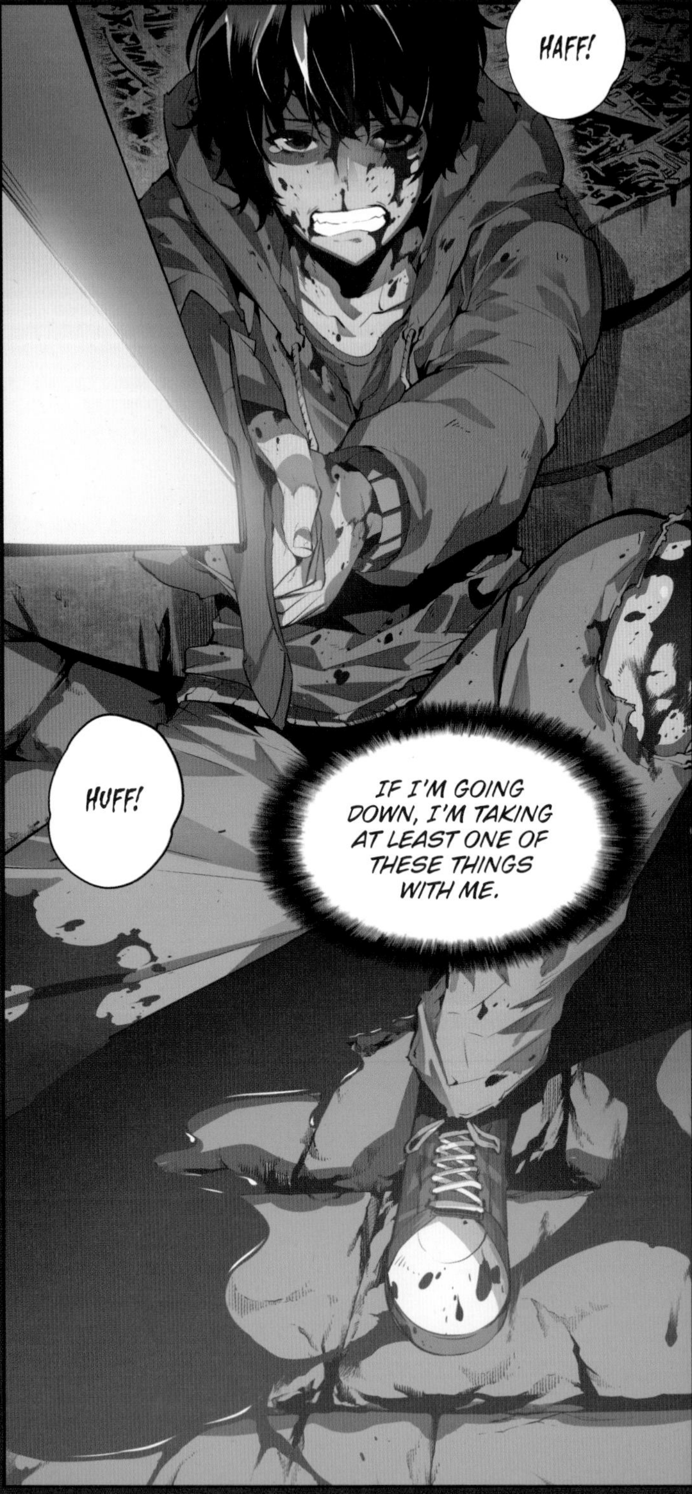
HAFF!
HUFF!
IF I'M GOING DOWN, I'M TAKING AT LEAST ONE OF THESE THINGS WITH ME.

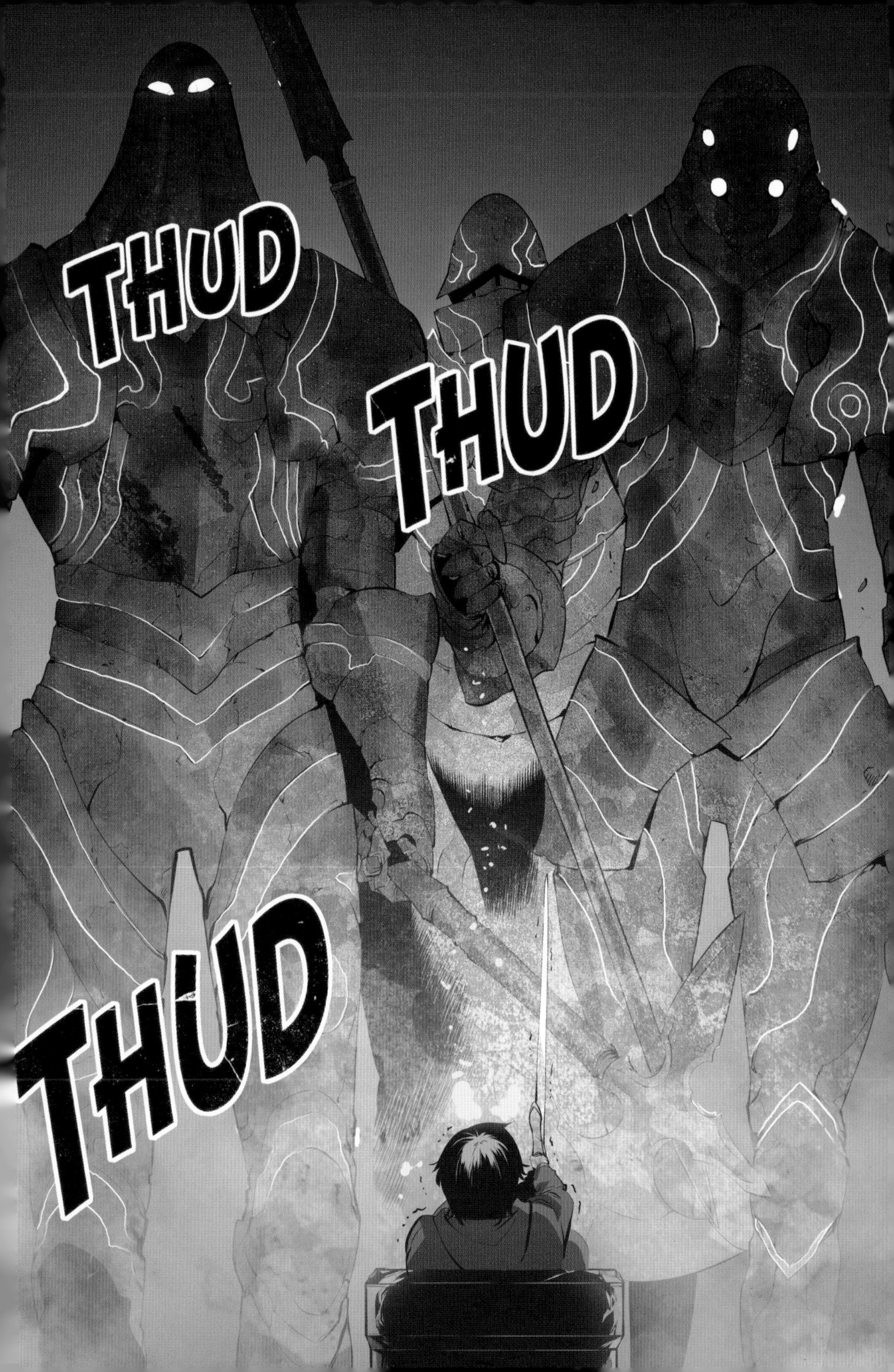
THUD
THUD
THUD

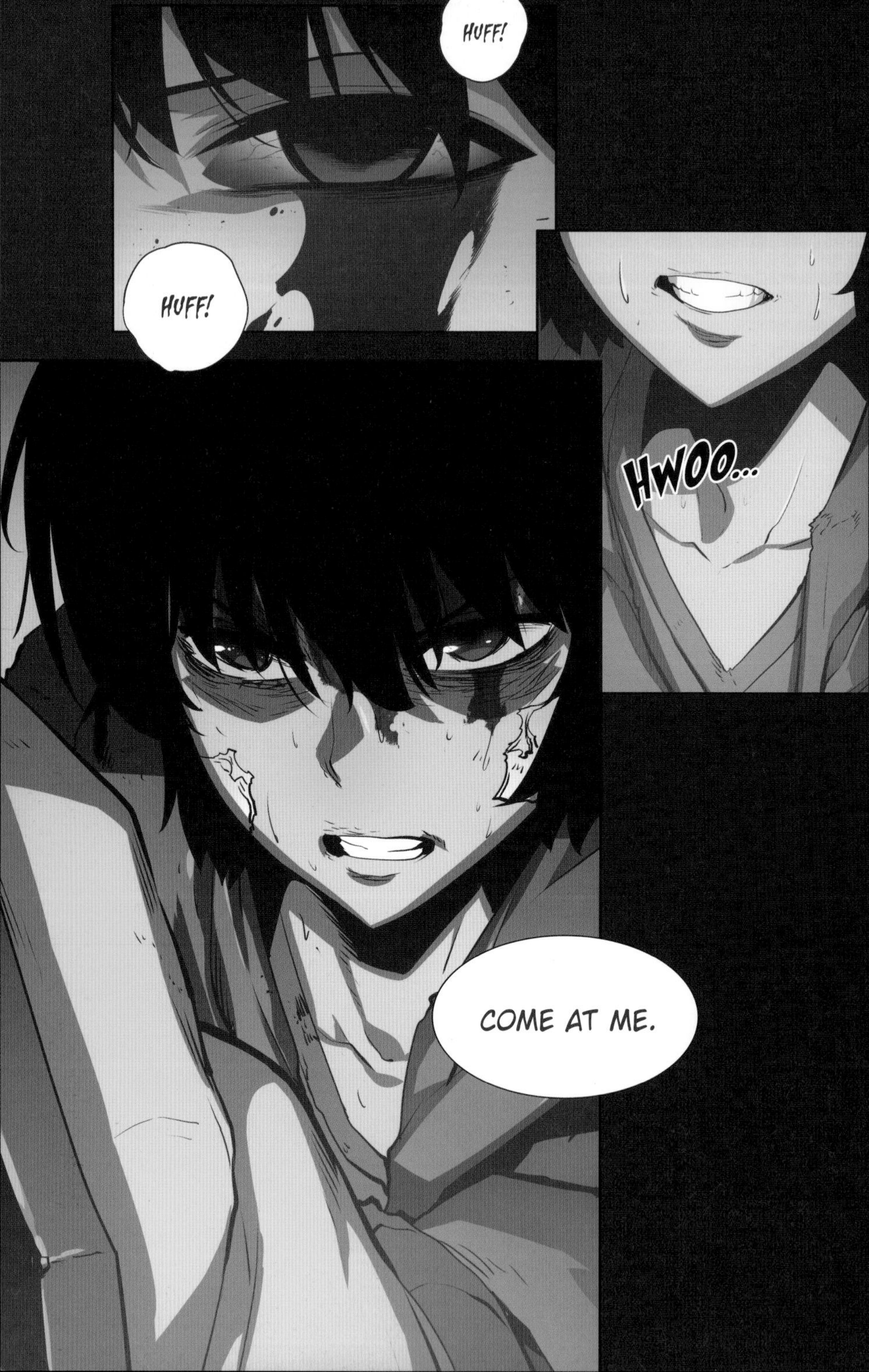
HUFF!
HUFF!
HWOO...
COME AT ME.

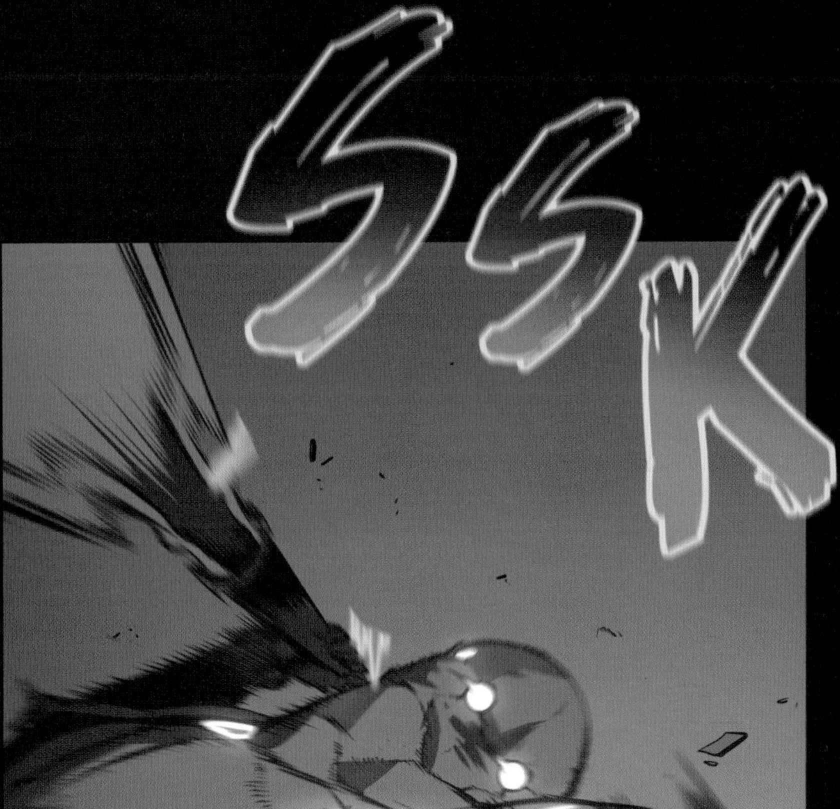
SSK

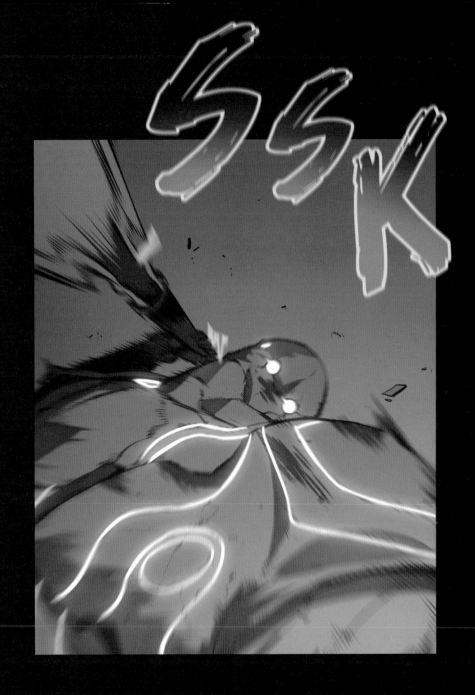

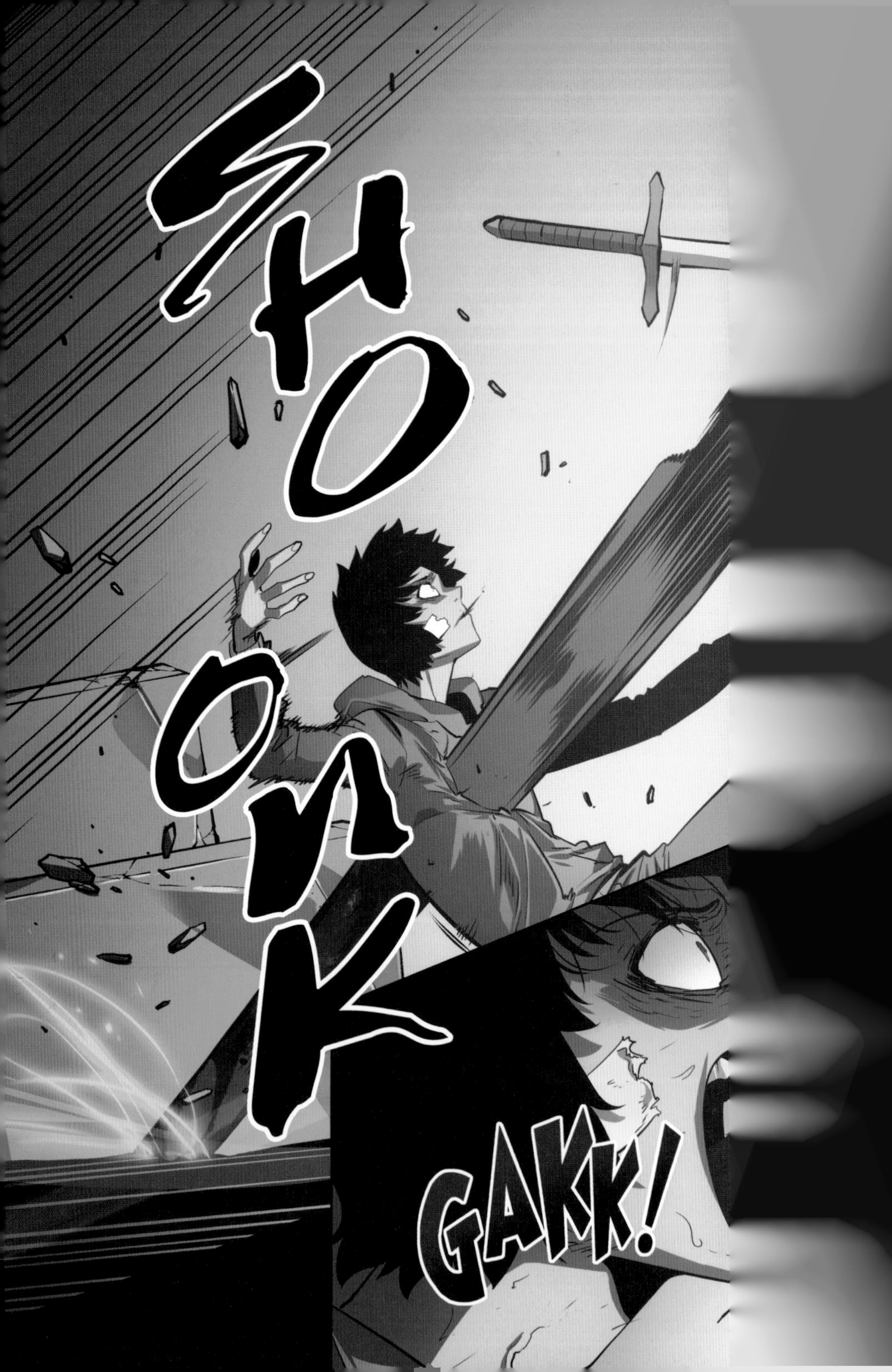
SHOOMK
GAKK!

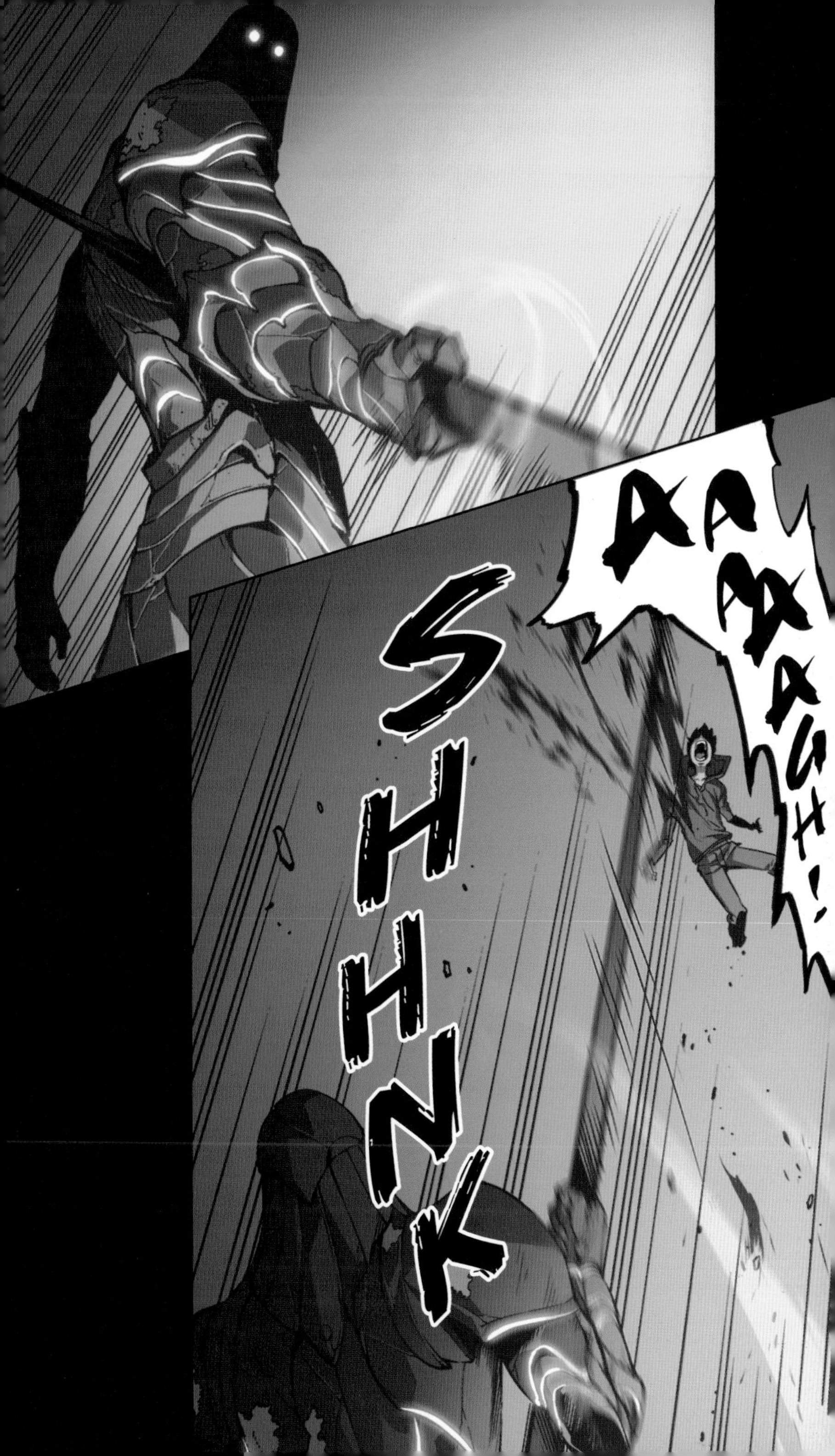
AAAAAUH!
SHHNK

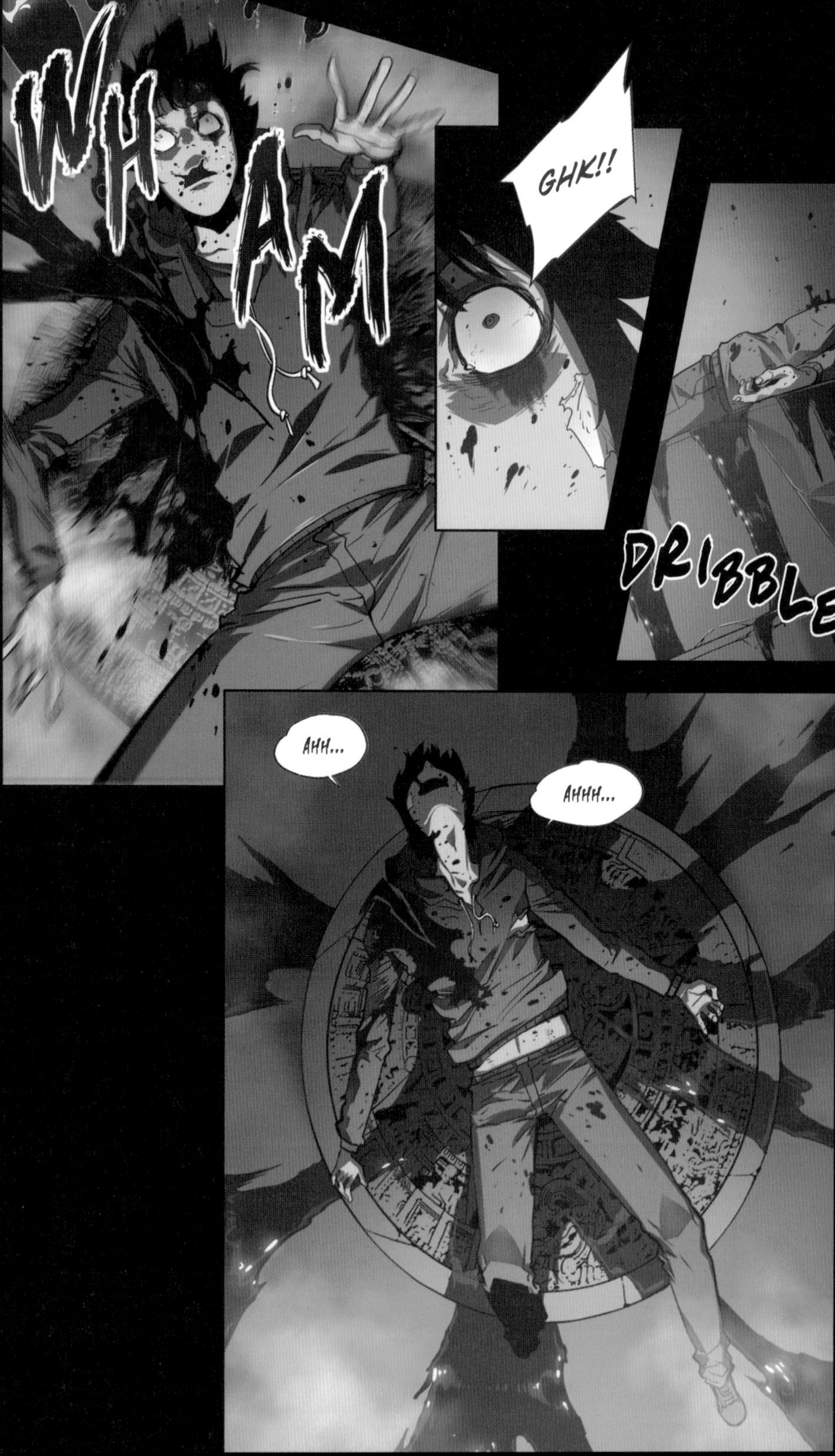
WHAM
GHK!!
DRIBBLE
AHH...
AHHH...

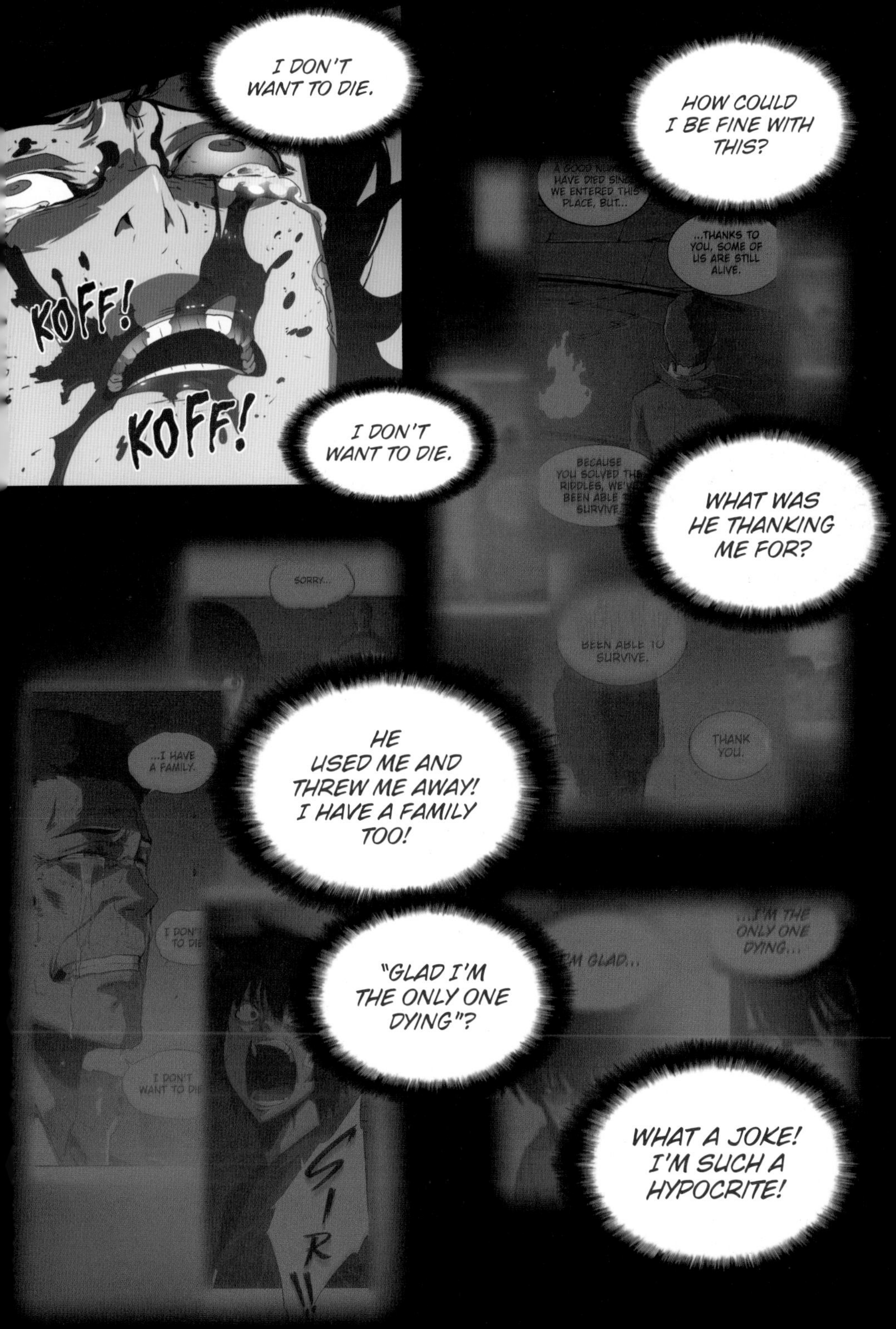
I DON'T WANT TO DIE.
KOFF!
KOFF!
I DON'T WANT TO DIE.
HOW COULD I BE FINE WITH THIS?
...THANKS TO YOU, SOME OF US ARE STILL ALIVE.
WHAT WAS HE THANKING ME FOR?
SORRY...
...I HAVE A FAMILY.
HE USED ME AND THREW ME AWAY! I HAVE A FAMILY TOO!
BEEN ABLE TO SURVIVE.
THANK YOU.
"GLAD I'M THE ONLY ONE DYING"?
...I'M THE ONLY ONE DYING...
SIR!!
WHAT A JOKE! I'M SUCH A HYPOCRITE!

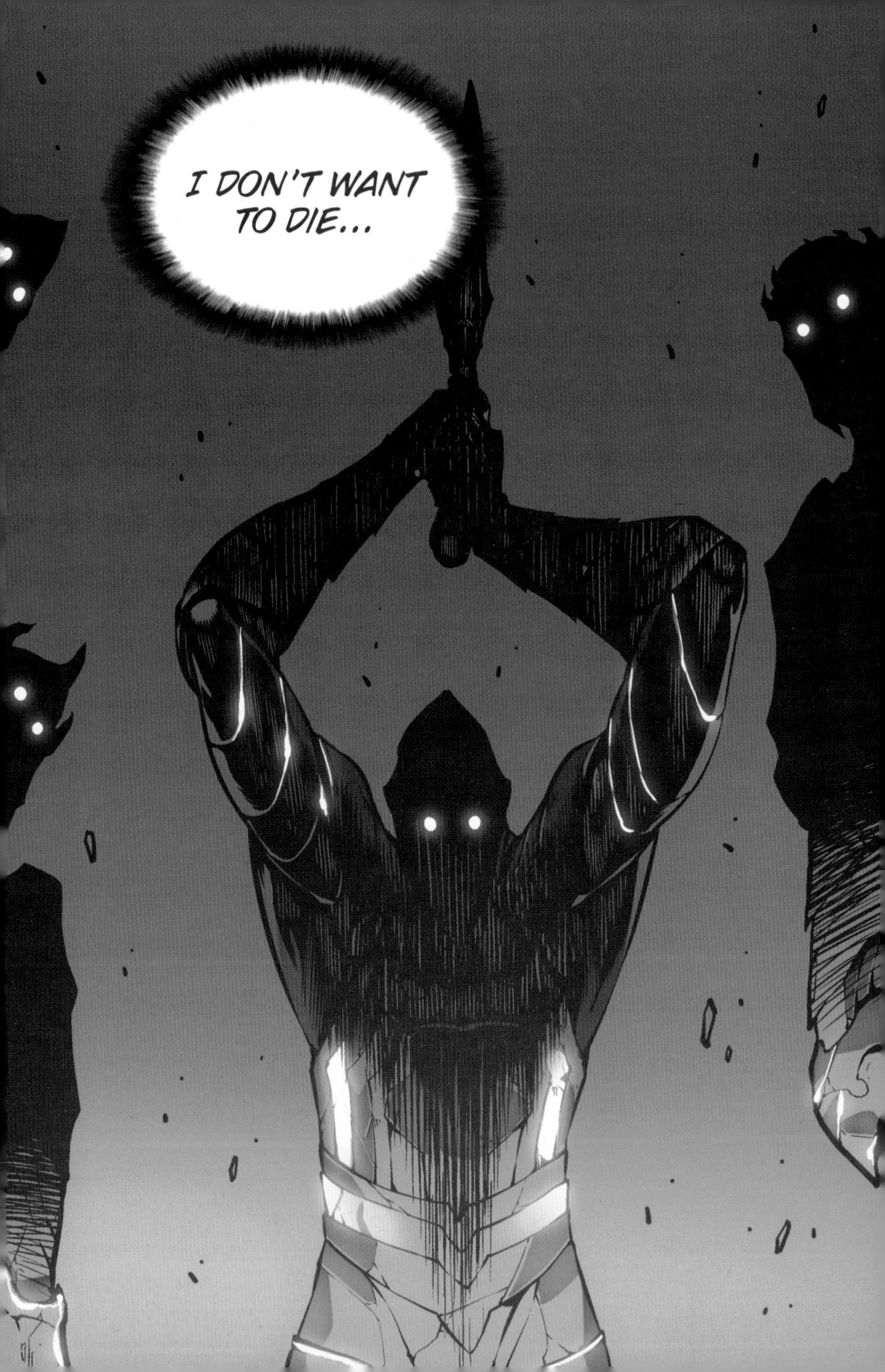
I DON'T WANT TO DIE...

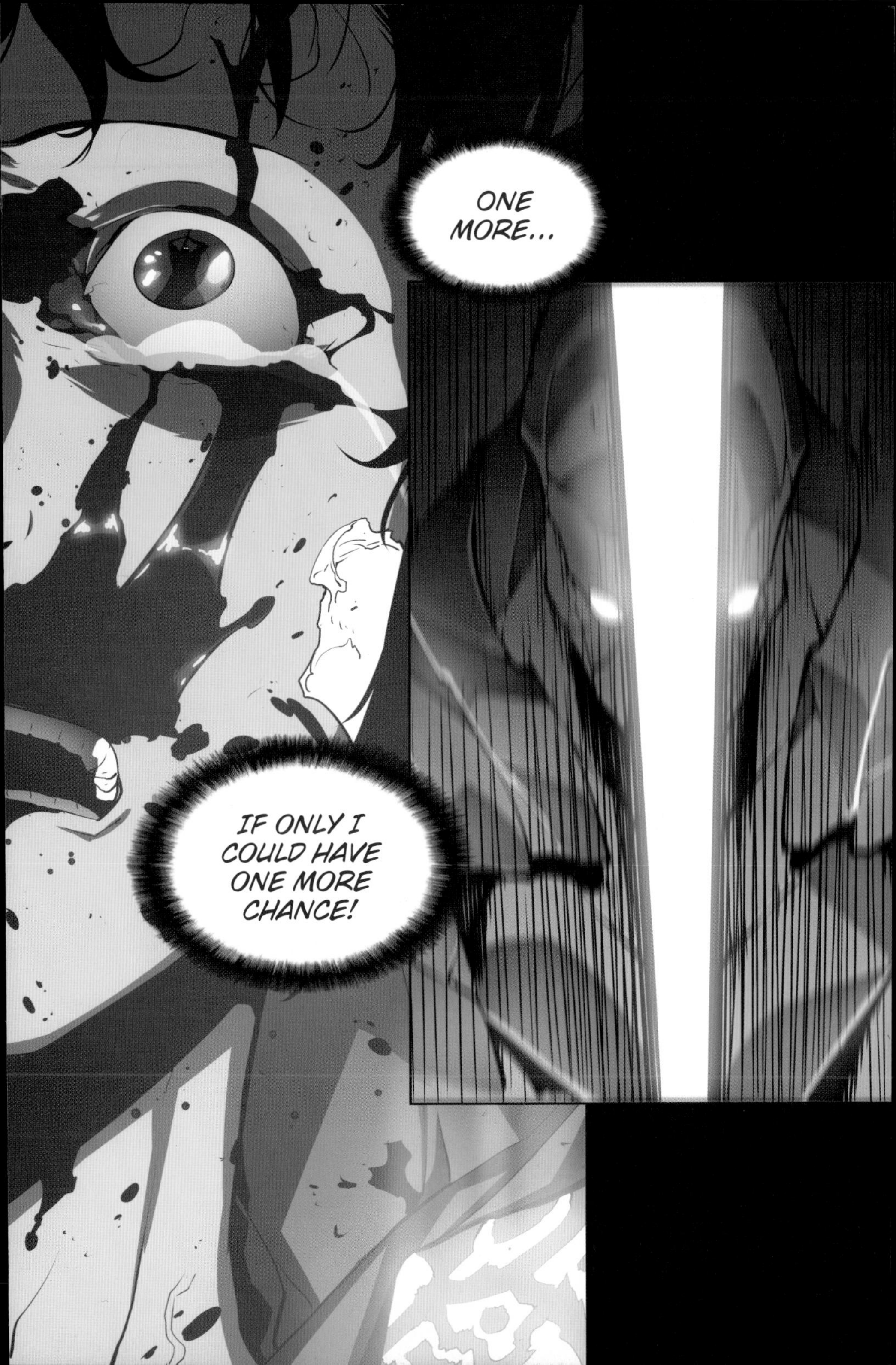
ONE MORE...
IF ONLY I COULD HAVE ONE MORE CHANCE!

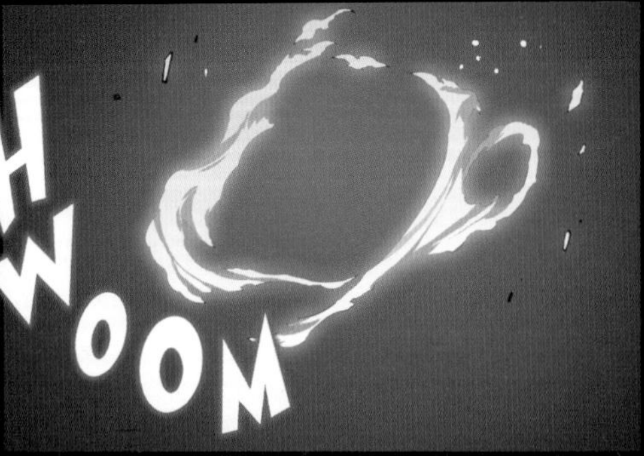
HWOOM

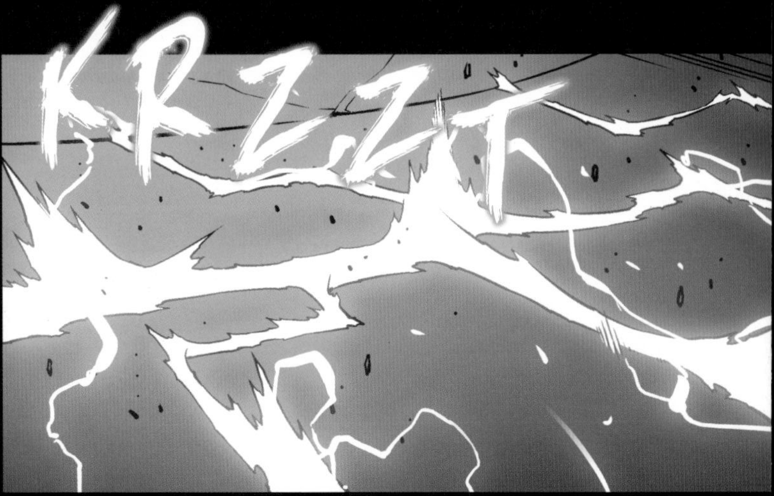
KRZZZT

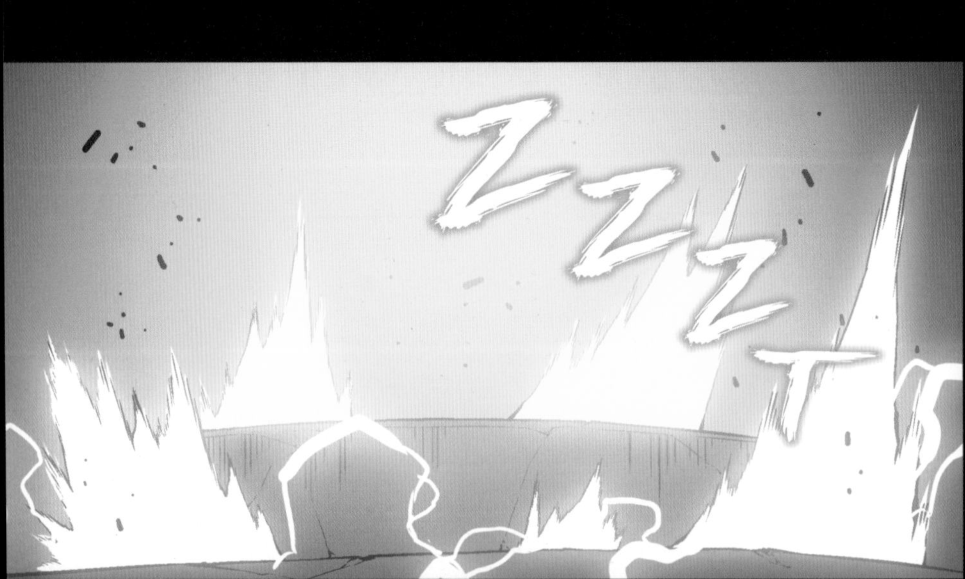
ZZZZT

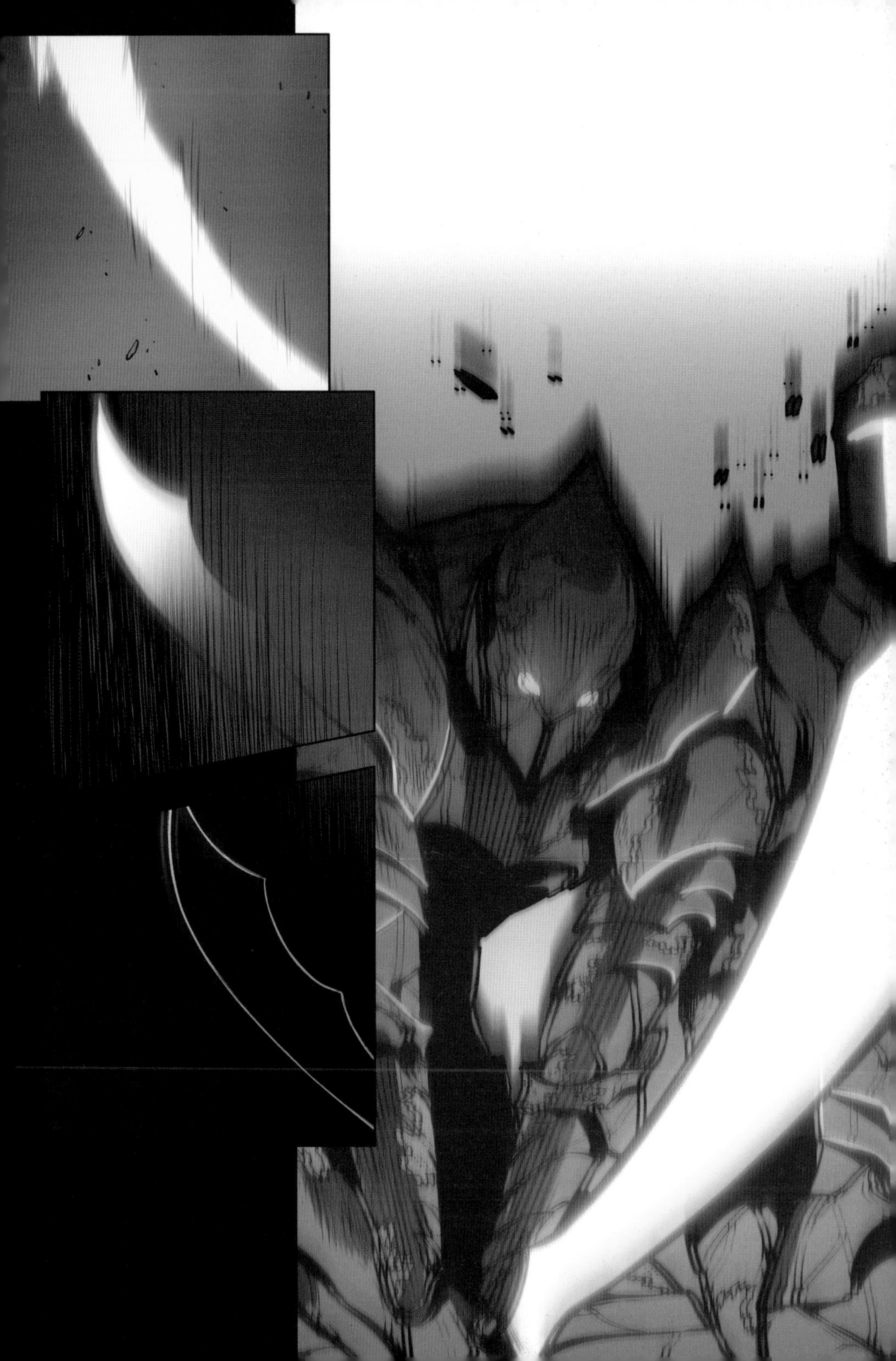

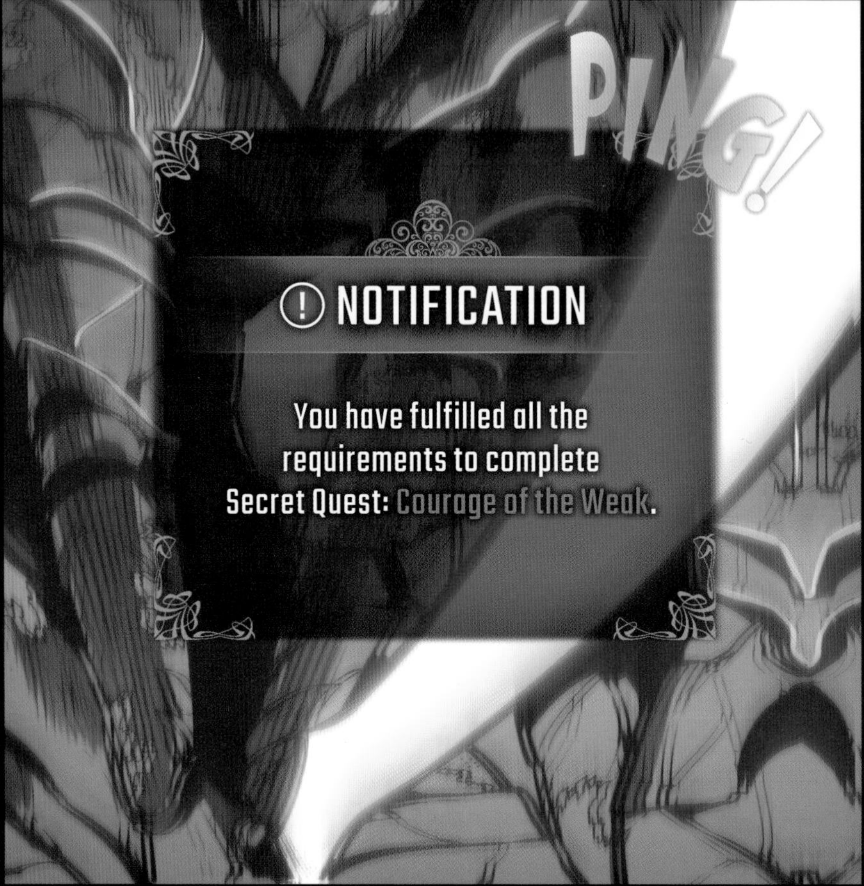
PING!!
NOTIFICATION
You have fulfilled all the requirements to complete Secret Quest: Courage of the Weak.
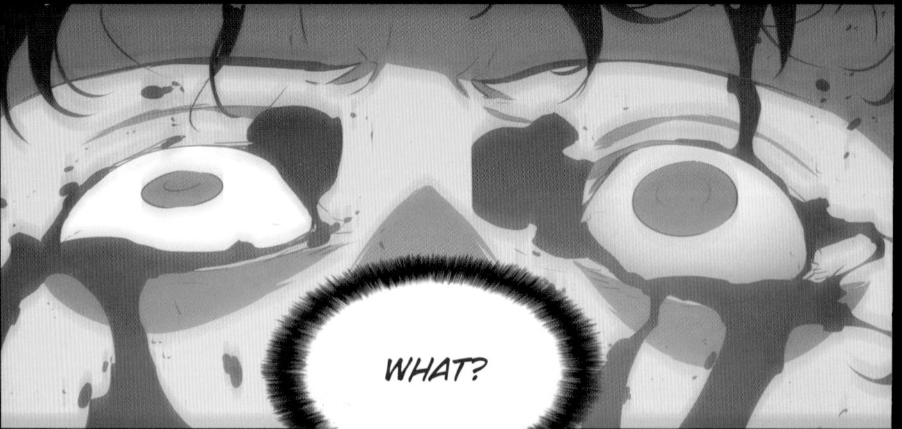
WHAT?

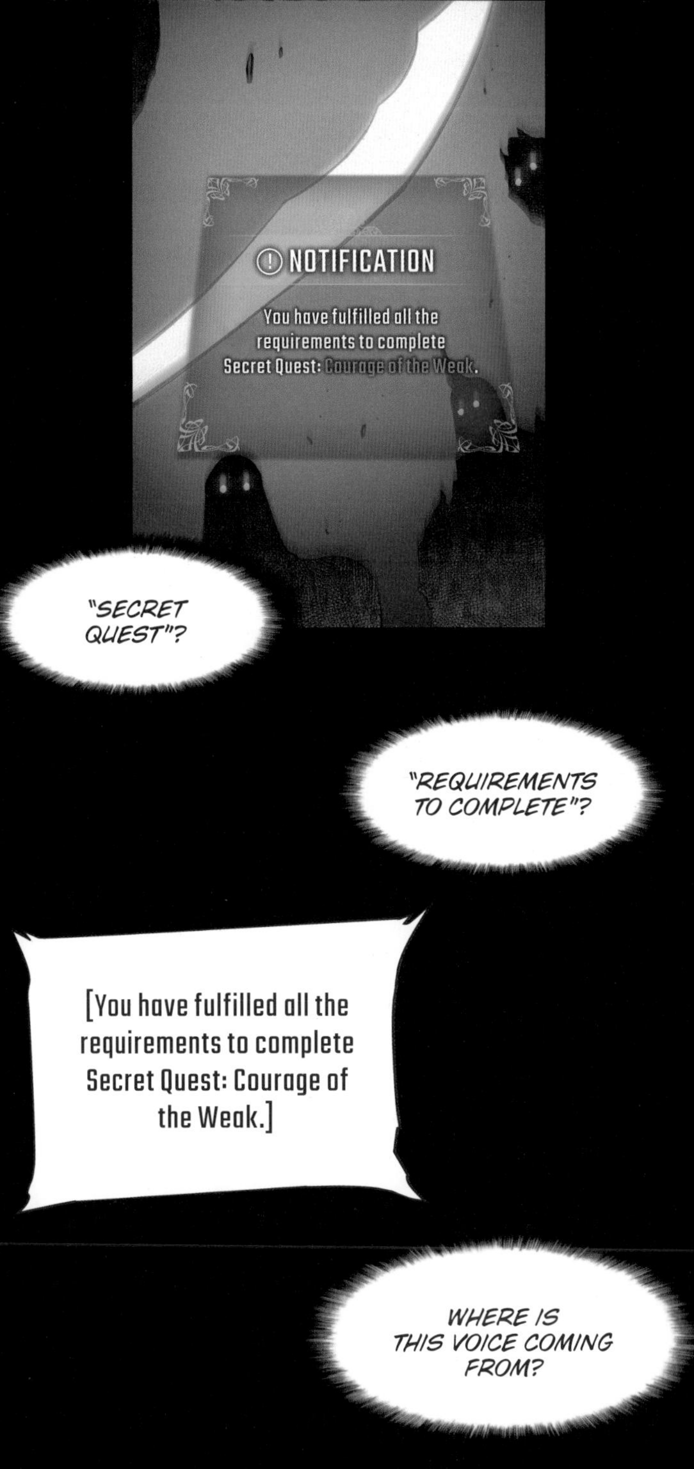
NOTIFICATION
You have fulfilled all the requirements to complete Secret Quest: Courage of the Weak.
"SECRET QUEST"?
"REQUIREMENTS TO COMPLETE"?
[You have fulfilled all the requirements to complete Secret Quest: Courage of the Weak.]
WHERE IS THIS VOICE COMING FROM?

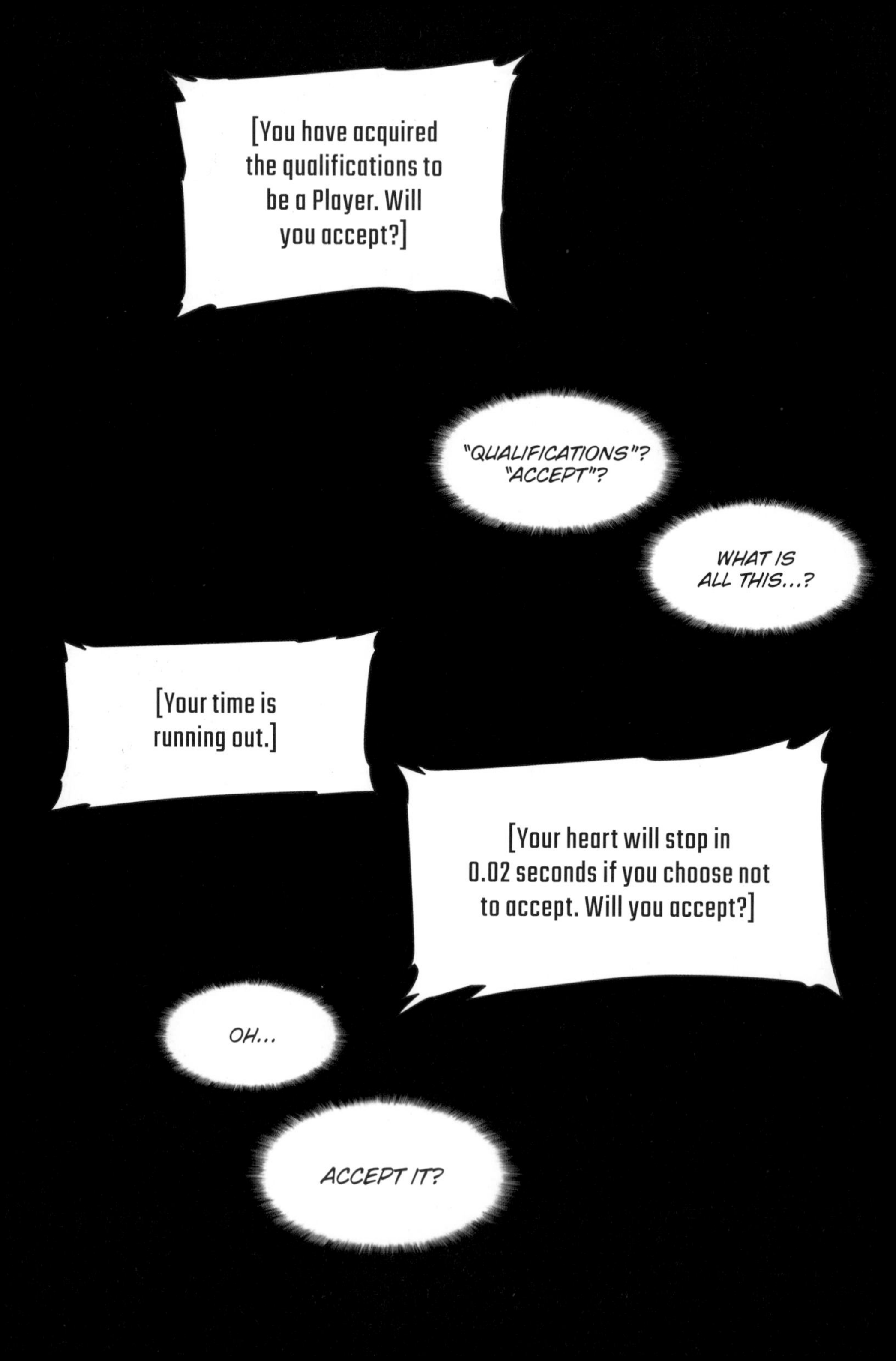
[You have acquired the qualifications to be a Player. Will you accept?]
"QUALIFICATIONS"? "ACCEPT"?
WHAT IS ALL THIS...?
[Your time is running out.]
[Your heart will stop in 0.02 seconds if you choose not to accept. Will you accept?]
OH...
ACCEPT IT?

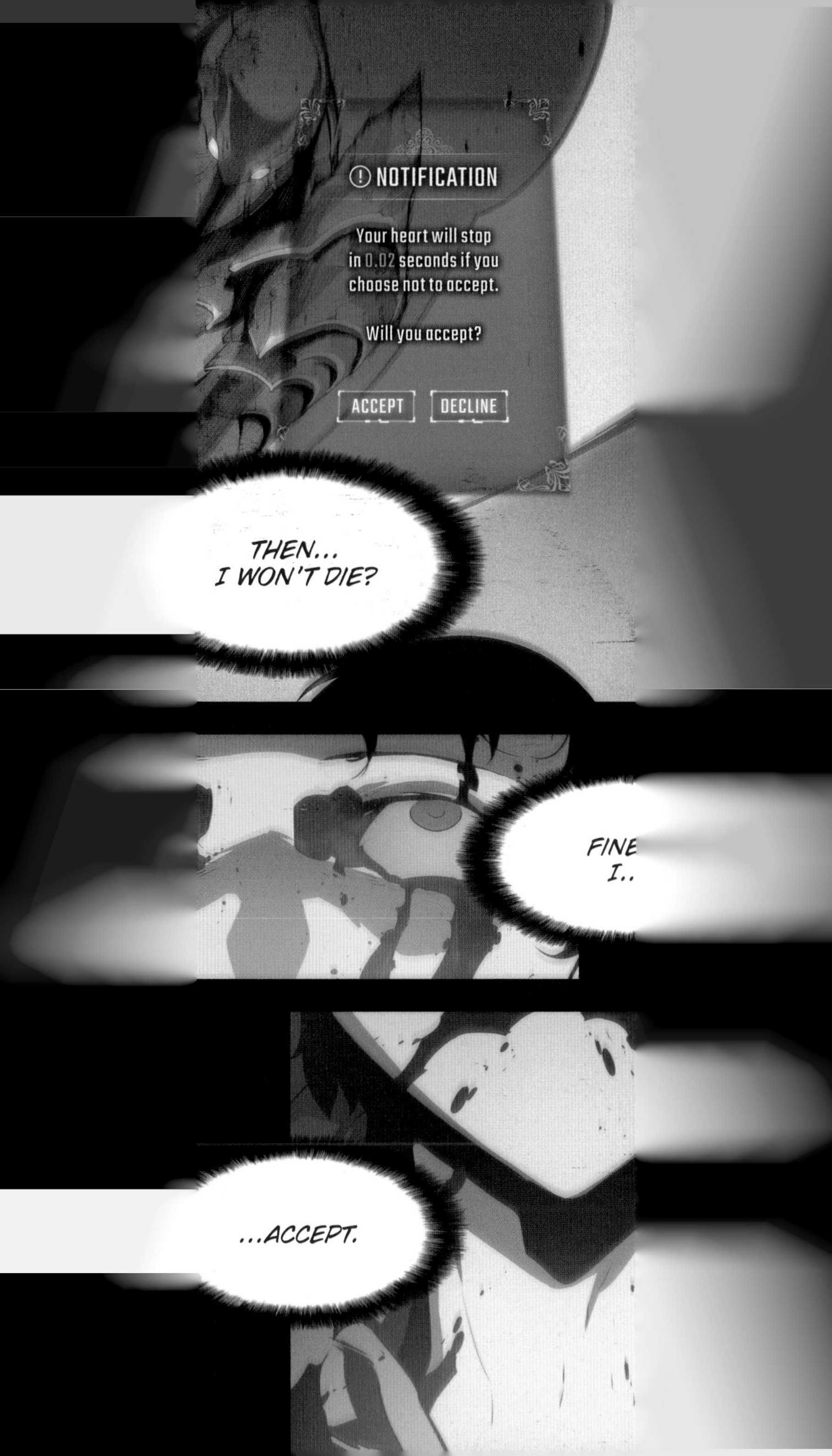
NOTIFICATION
Your heart will stop in 0.02 seconds if you choose not to accept.
Will you accept?
ACCEPT
DECLINE
THEN... I WON'T DIE?
FINE
I..
...ACCEPT.

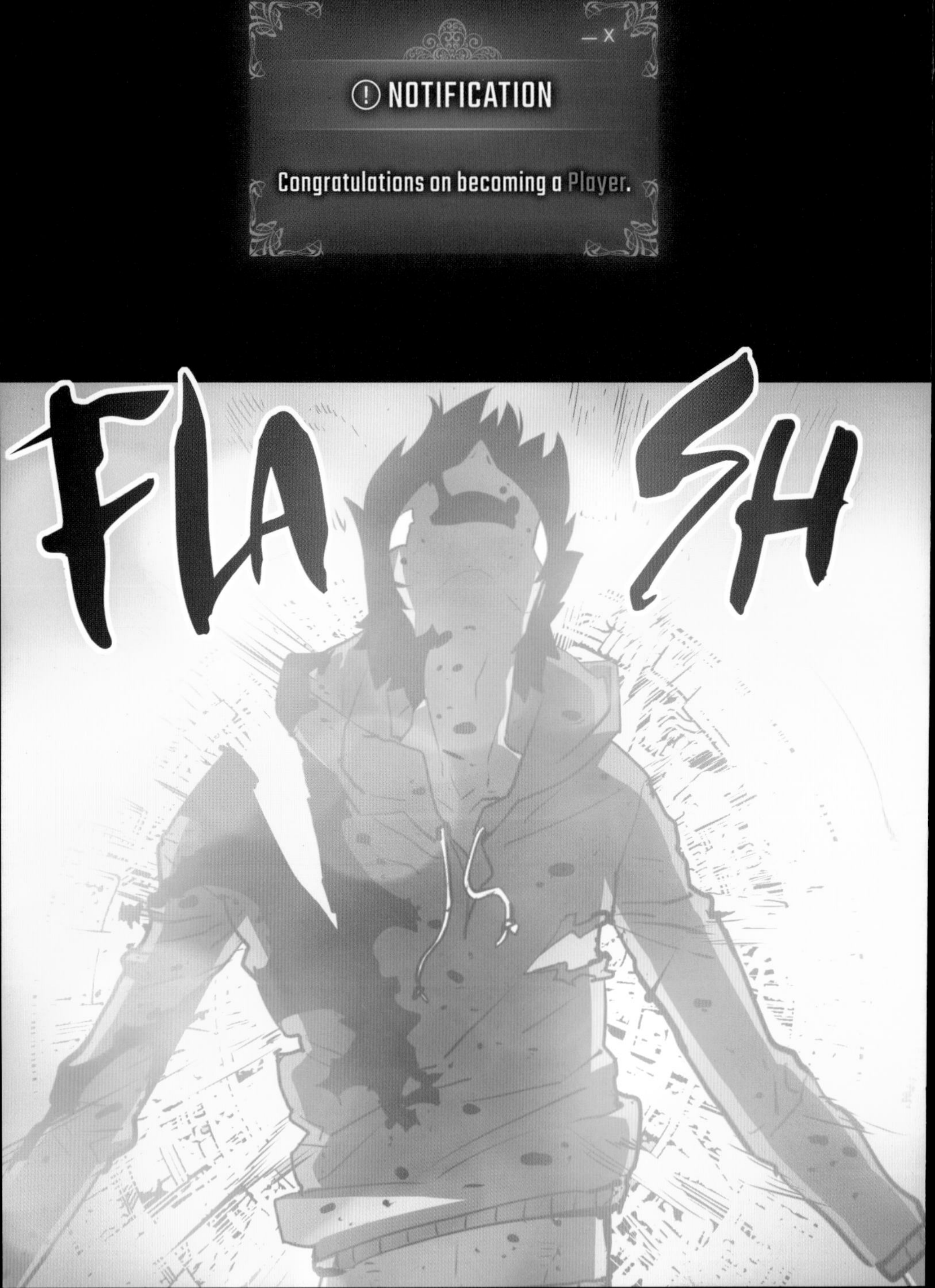
NOTIFICATION
Congratulations on becoming a Player.
FLASH

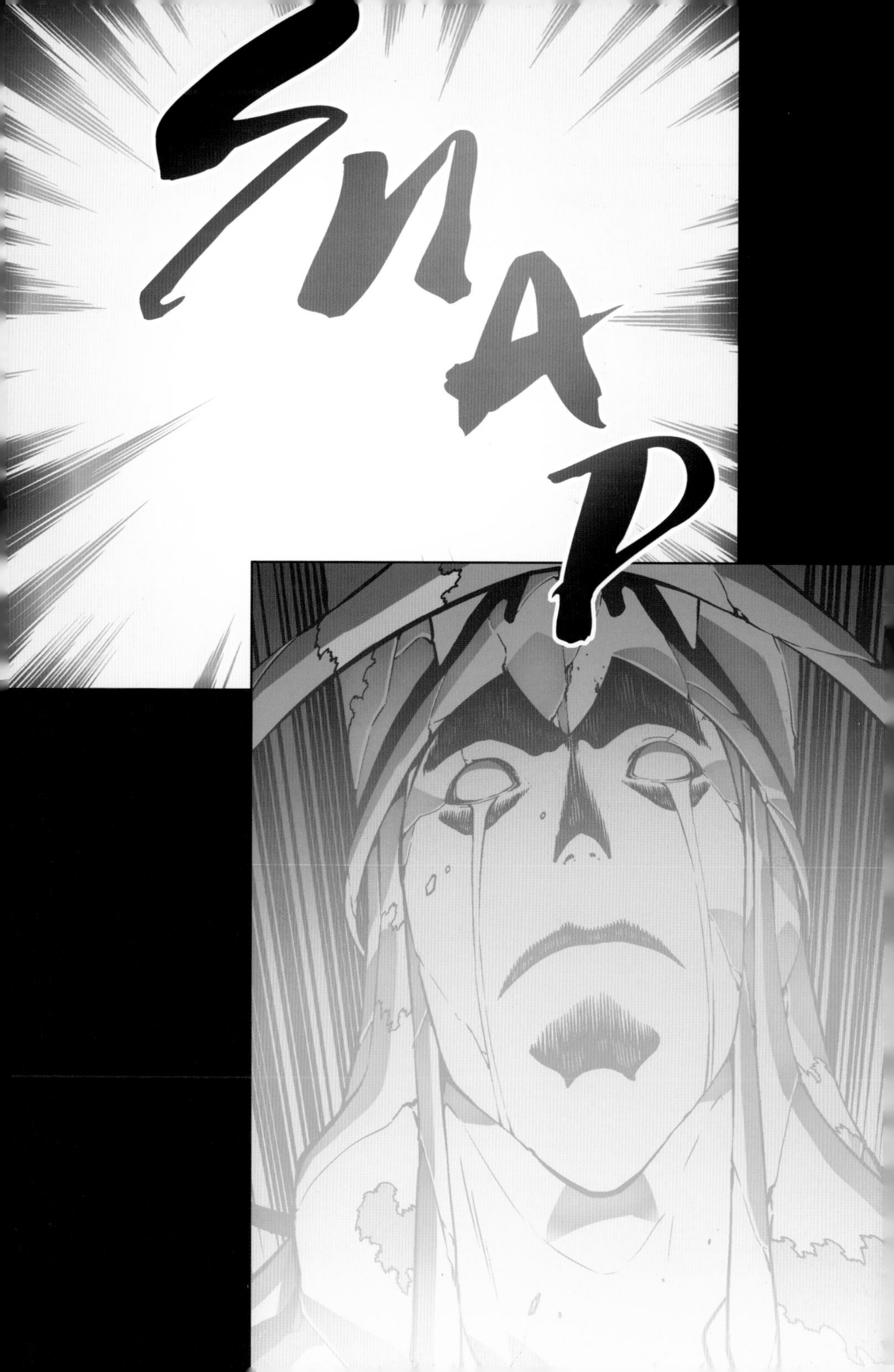
SNAP

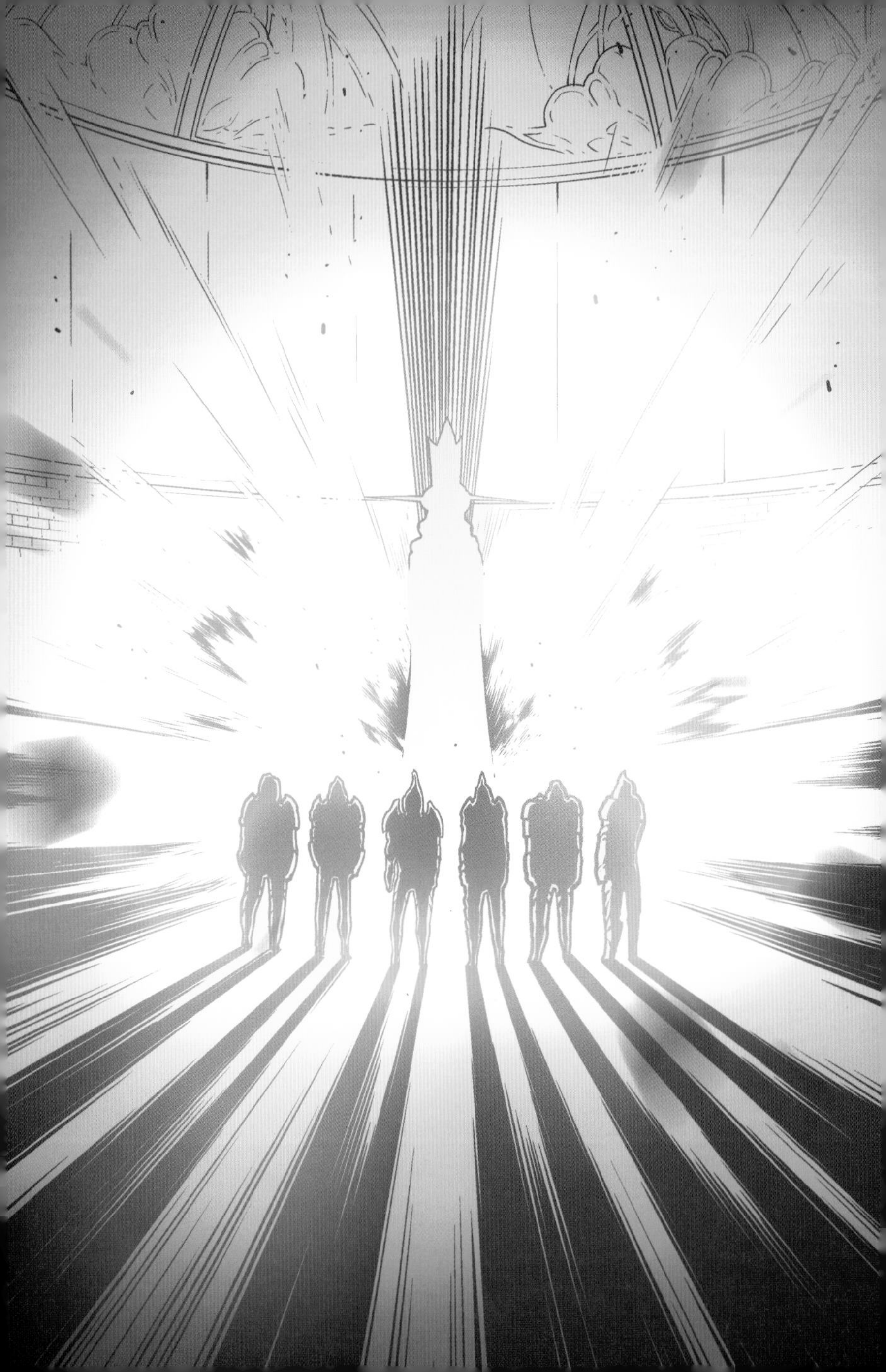

Solo Leveling

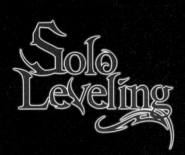

CHAPTER 3

Quest

Solo Leveling

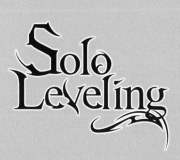

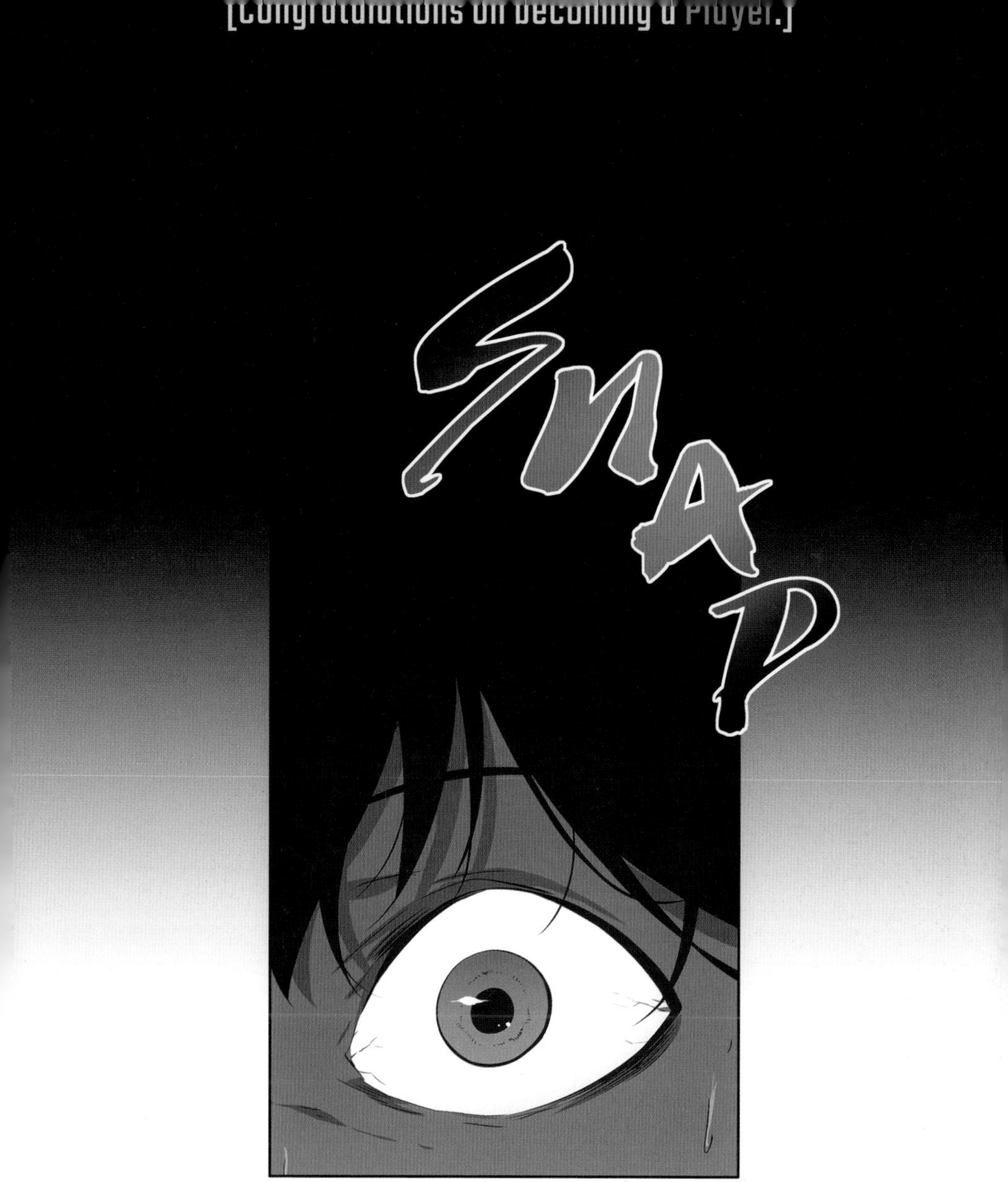
[Congratulations on becoming a Player.]
SNAP

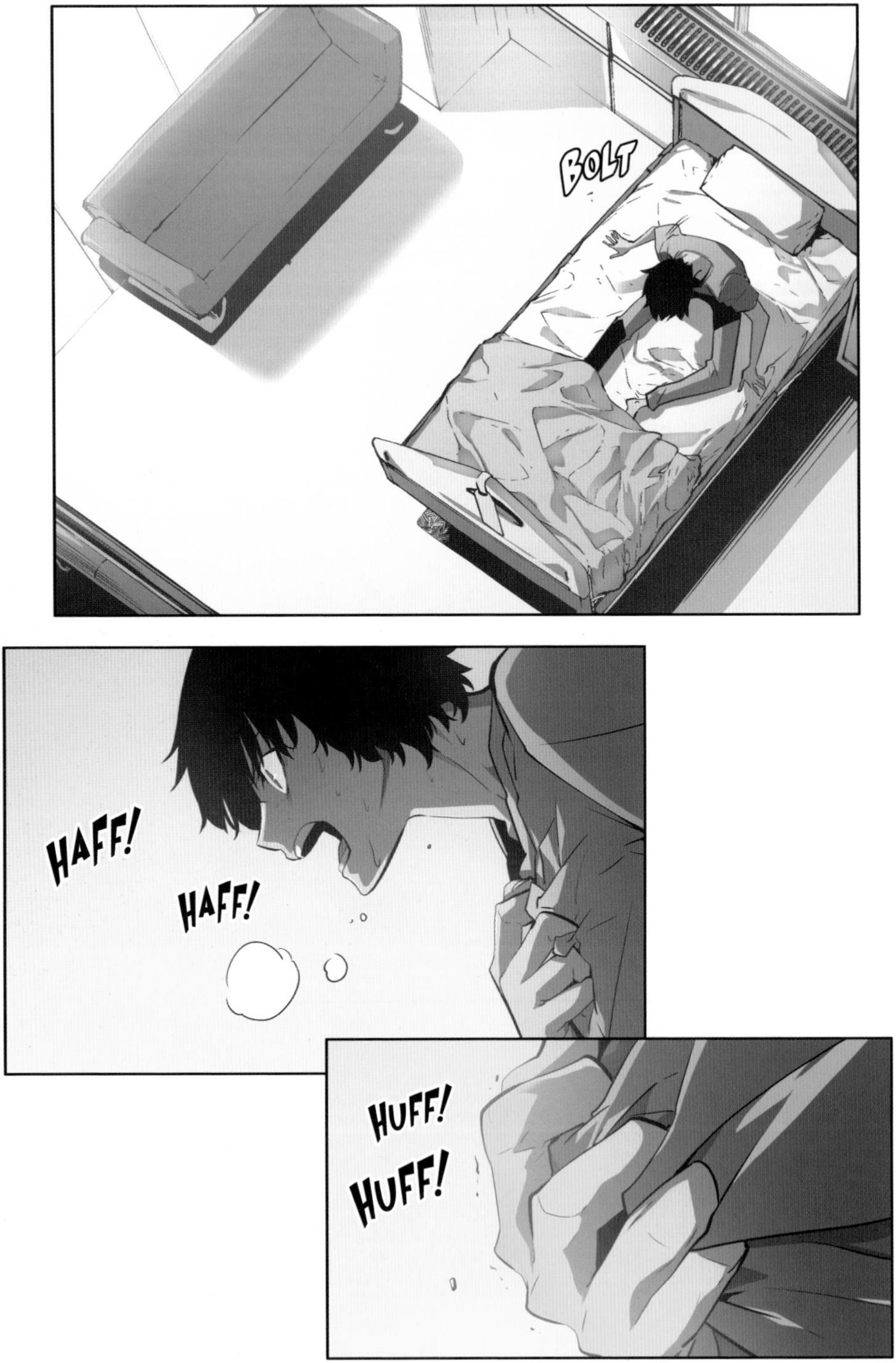
BOLT
HAFF!
HAFF!
HUFF!
HUFF!

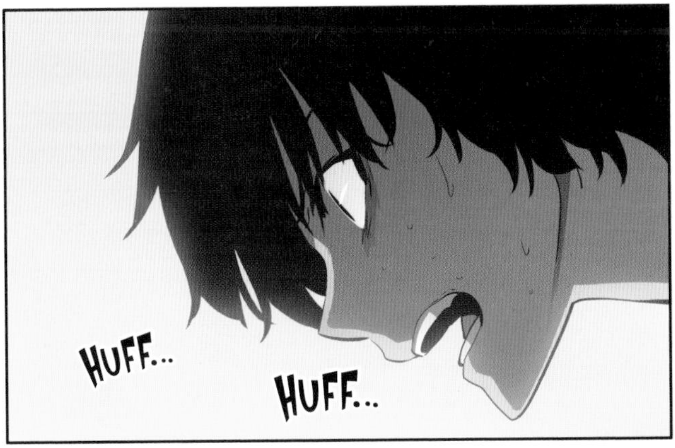
HUFF...
HUFF...

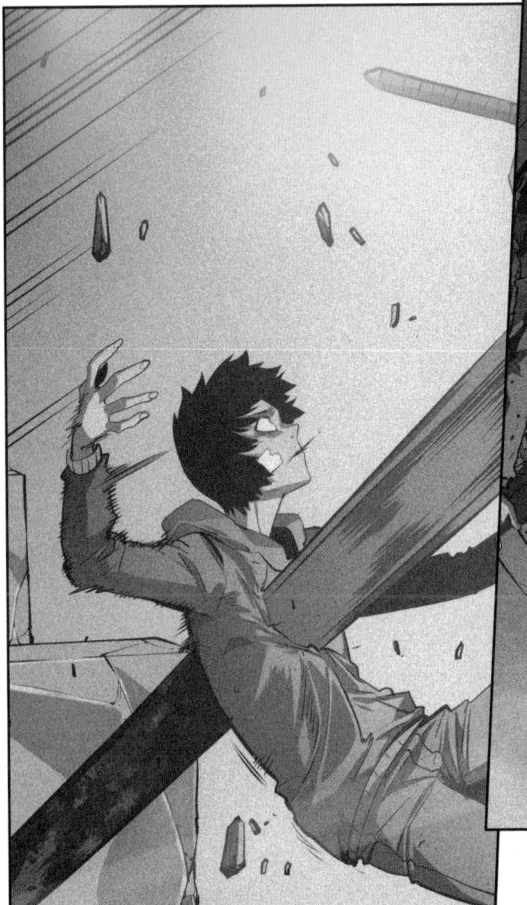

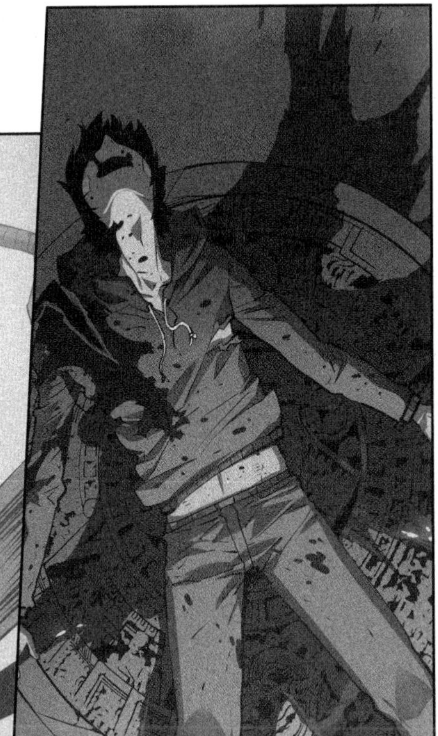

DREAM...?

WAS IT A DREAM?

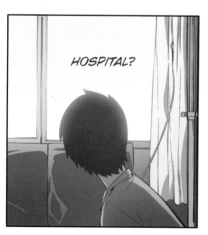

HOSPITAL?

KA-CHAK

YOU'RE AWAKE?

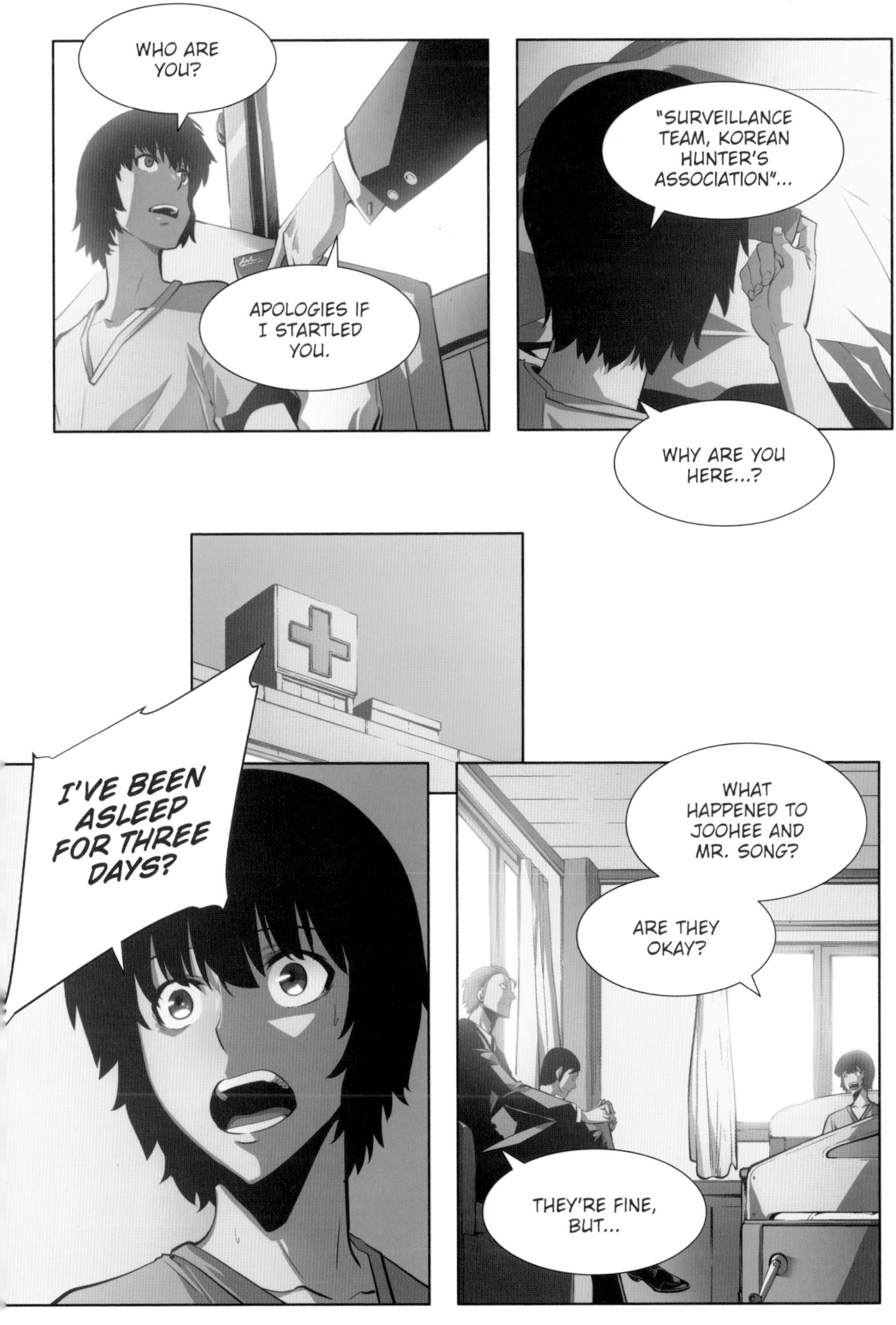
WHO ARE YOU?
APOLOGIES IF I STARTLED YOU.
"SURVEILLANCE TEAM, KOREAN HUNTER'S ASSOCIATION"...
WHY ARE YOU HERE...?
I'VE BEEN ASLEEP FOR THREE DAYS?
WHAT HAPPENED TO JOOHEE AND MR. SONG?
ARE THEY OKAY?
THEY'RE FINE, BUT...

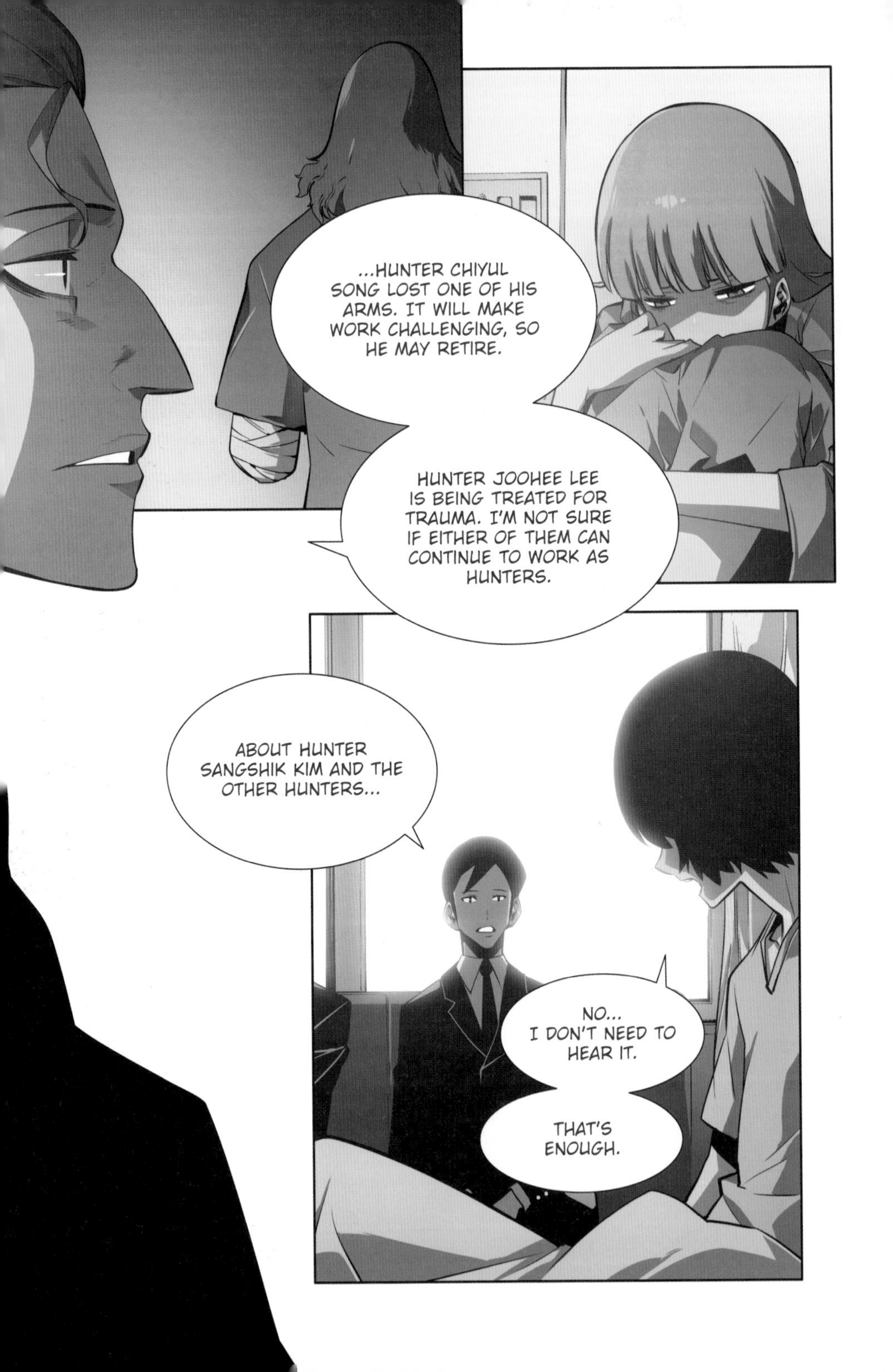
...HUNTER CHIYUL SONG LOST ONE OF HIS ARMS. IT WILL MAKE WORK CHALLENGING, SO HE MAY RETIRE.
HUNTER JOOHEE LEE IS BEING TREATED FOR TRAUMA. I'M NOT SURE IF EITHER OF THEM CAN CONTINUE TO WORK AS HUNTERS.
ABOUT HUNTER SANGSHIK KIM AND THE OTHER HUNTERS...
NO... I DON'T NEED TO HEAR IT.
THAT'S ENOUGH.

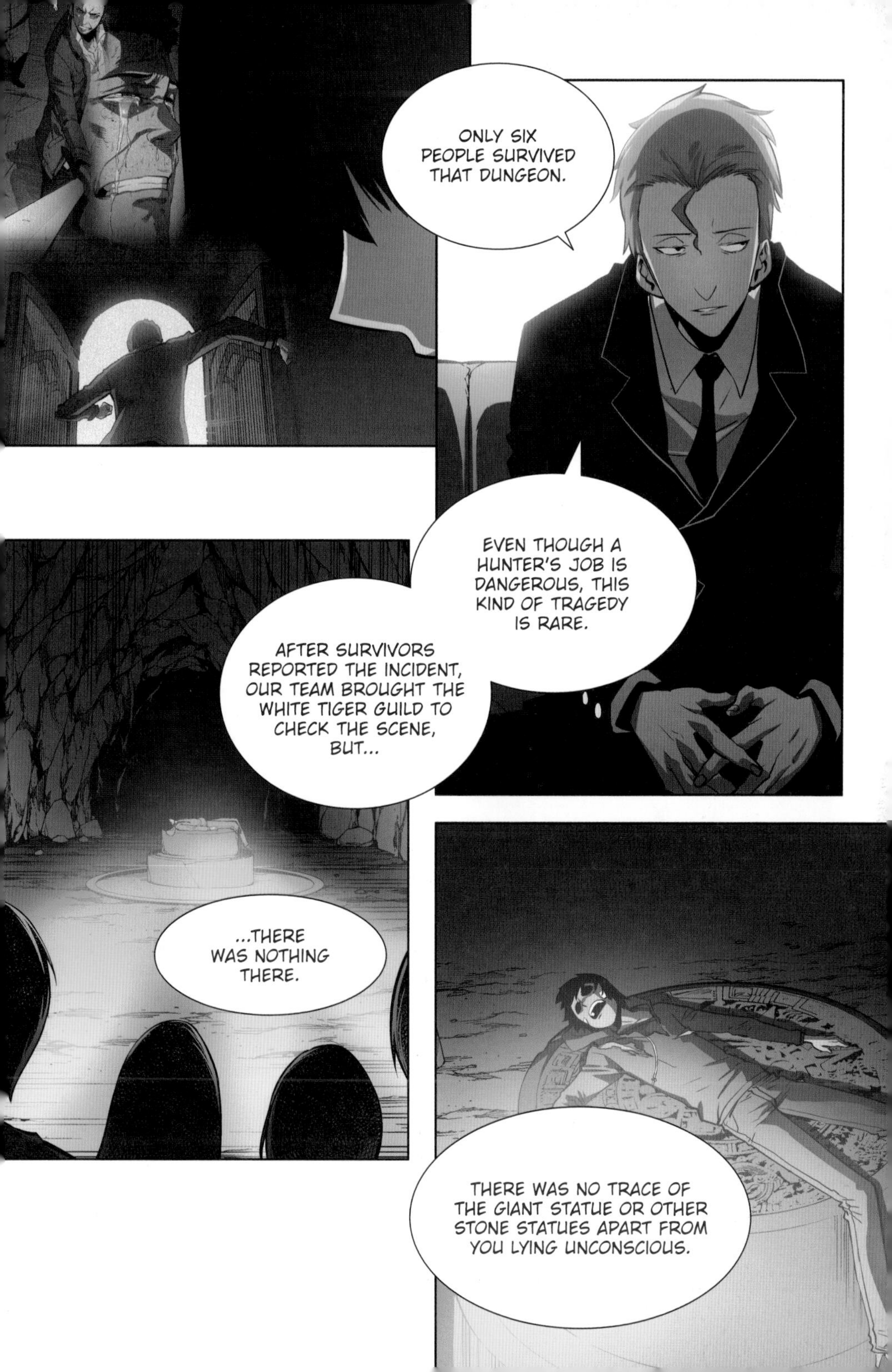
ONLY SIX PEOPLE SURVIVED THAT DUNGEON.
EVEN THOUGH A HUNTER'S JOB IS DANGEROUS, THIS KIND OF TRAGEDY IS RARE.
AFTER SURVIVORS REPORTED THE INCIDENT, OUR TEAM BROUGHT THE WHITE TIGER GUILD TO CHECK THE SCENE, BUT...
...THERE WAS NOTHING THERE.
THERE WAS NO TRACE OF THE GIANT STATUE OR OTHER STONE STATUES APART FROM YOU LYING UNCONSCIOUS.

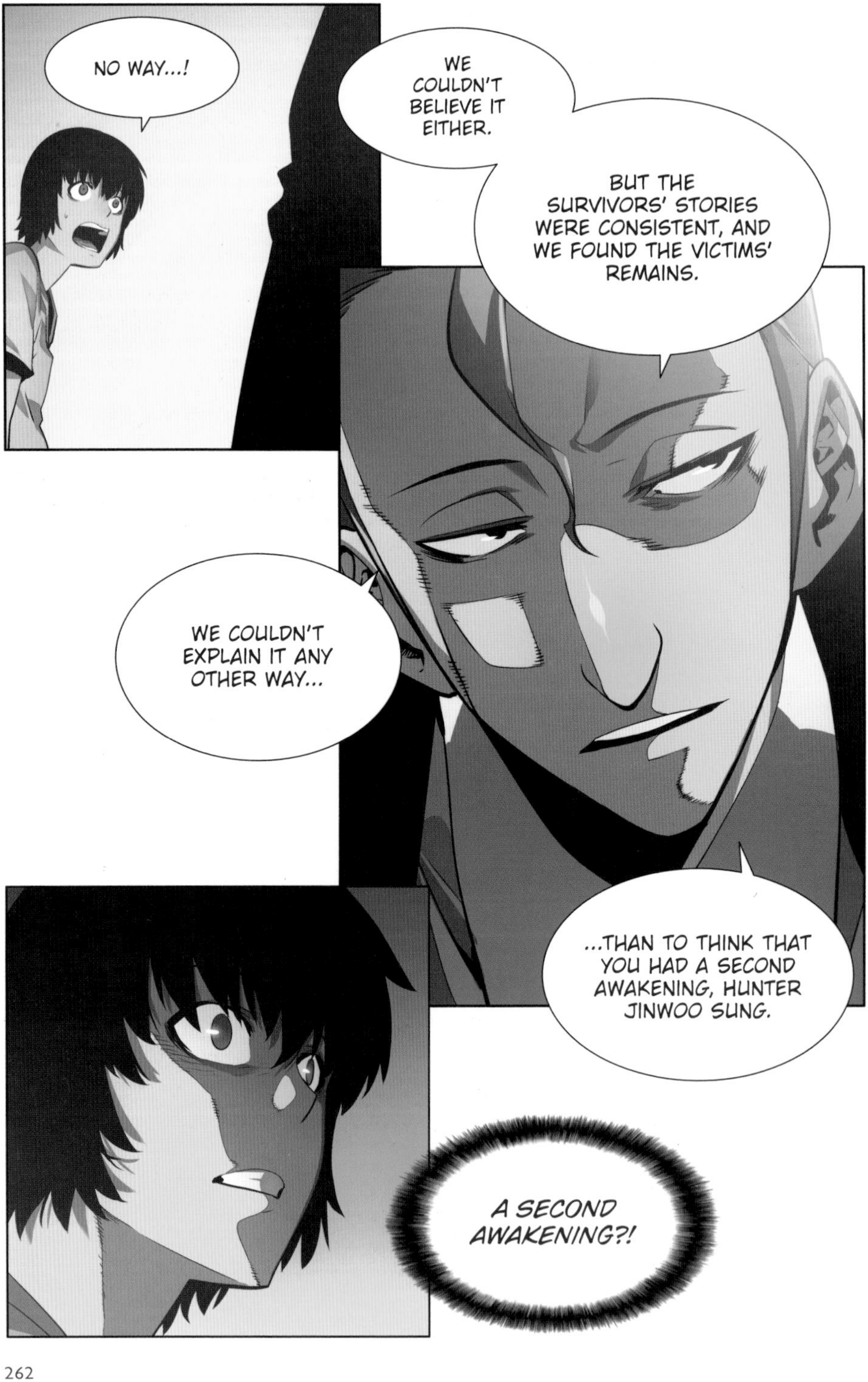
NO WAY...!
WE COULDN'T BELIEVE IT EITHER.
BUT THE SURVIVORS' STORIES WERE CONSISTENT, AND WE FOUND THE VICTIMS' REMAINS.
WE COULDN'T EXPLAIN IT ANY OTHER WAY...
...THAN TO THINK THAT YOU HAD A SECOND AWAKENING, HUNTER JINWOO SUNG.
A SECOND AWAKENING?!

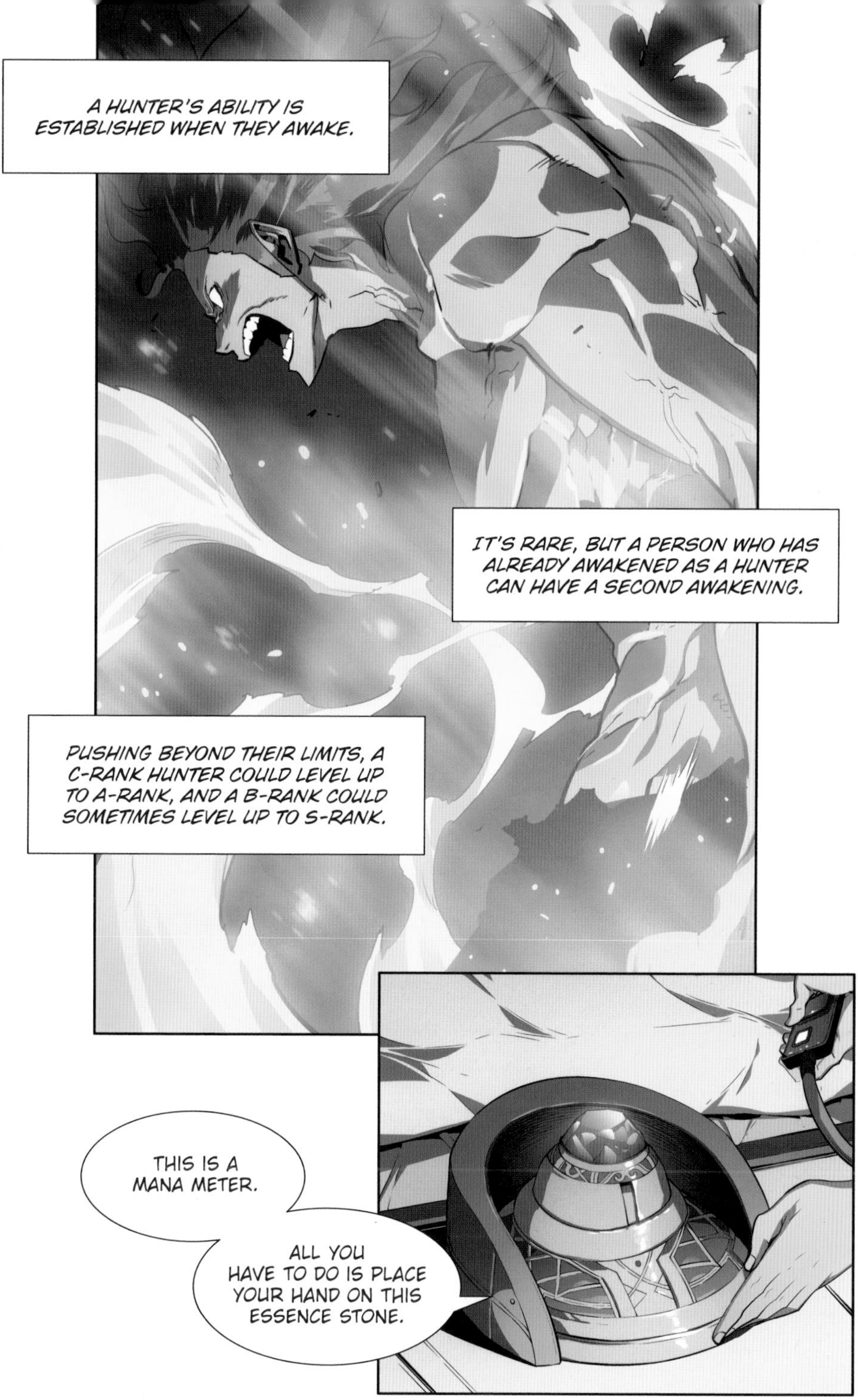
A HUNTER'S ABILITY IS ESTABLISHED WHEN THEY AWAKE.
IT'S RARE, BUT A PERSON WHO HAS ALREADY AWAKENED AS A HUNTER CAN HAVE A SECOND AWAKENING.
PUSHING BEYOND THEIR LIMITS, A C-RANK HUNTER COULD LEVEL UP TO A-RANK, AND A B-RANK COULD SOMETIMES LEVEL UP TO S-RANK.
THIS IS A MANA METER.
ALL YOU HAVE TO DO IS PLACE YOUR HAND ON THIS ESSENCE STONE.

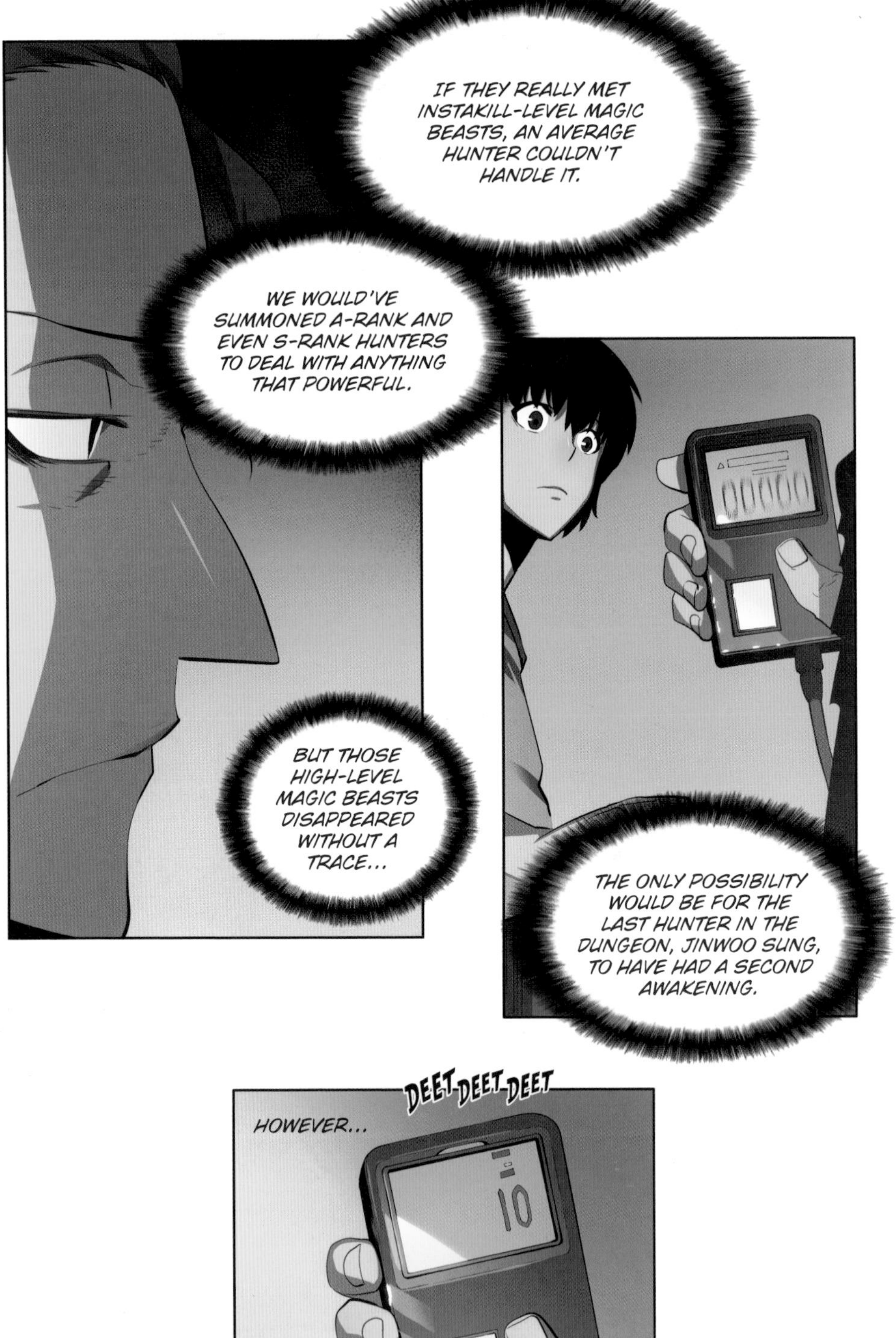
IF THEY REALLY MET INSTAKILL-LEVEL MAGIC BEASTS, AN AVERAGE HUNTER COULDN'T HANDLE IT.
WE WOULD'VE SUMMONED A-RANK AND EVEN S-RANK HUNTERS TO DEAL WITH ANYTHING THAT POWERFUL.
BUT THOSE HIGH-LEVEL MAGIC BEASTS DISAPPEARED WITHOUT A TRACE...
THE ONLY POSSIBILITY WOULD BE FOR THE LAST HUNTER IN THE DUNGEON, JINWOO SUNG, TO HAVE HAD A SECOND AWAKENING.
DEET DEET DEET
HOWEVER...
10

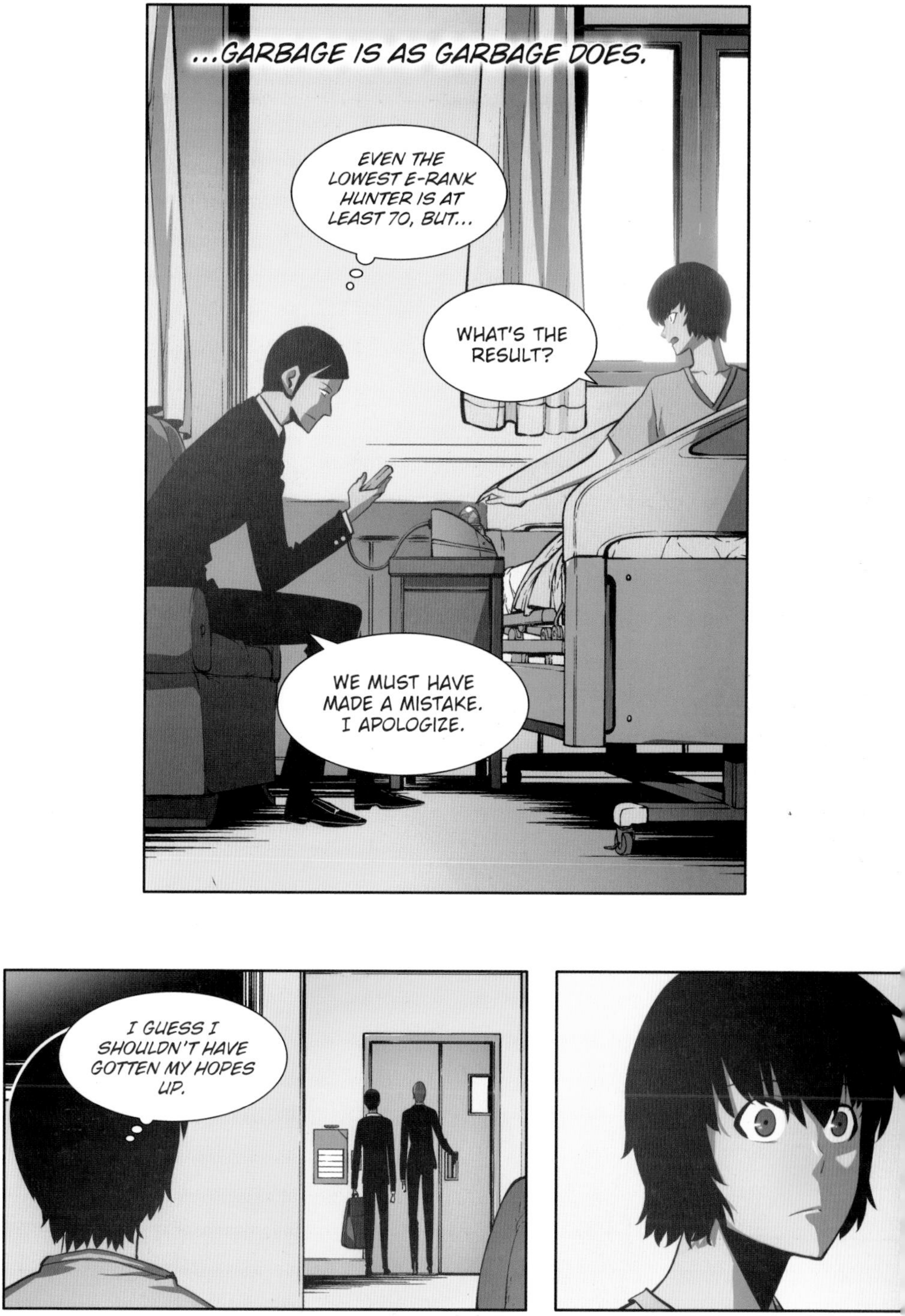
...GARBAGE IS AS GARBAGE DOES.
EVEN THE LOWEST E-RANK HUNTER IS AT LEAST 70, BUT...
WHAT'S THE RESULT?
WE MUST HAVE MADE A MISTAKE. I APOLOGIZE.
I GUESS I SHOULDN'T HAVE GOTTEN MY HOPES UP.

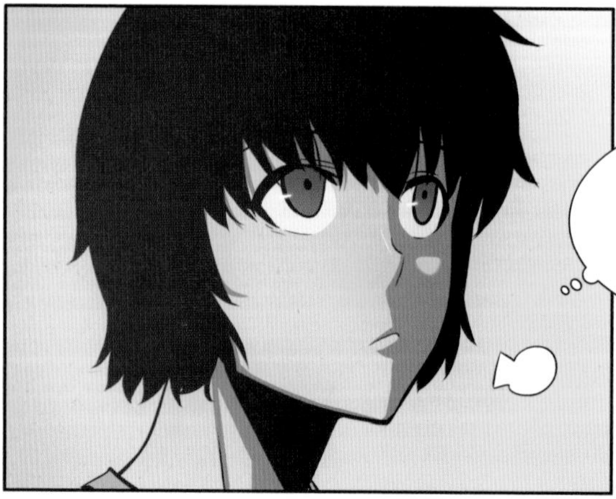
SO...THIS THING DIDN'T BOTHER THEM?

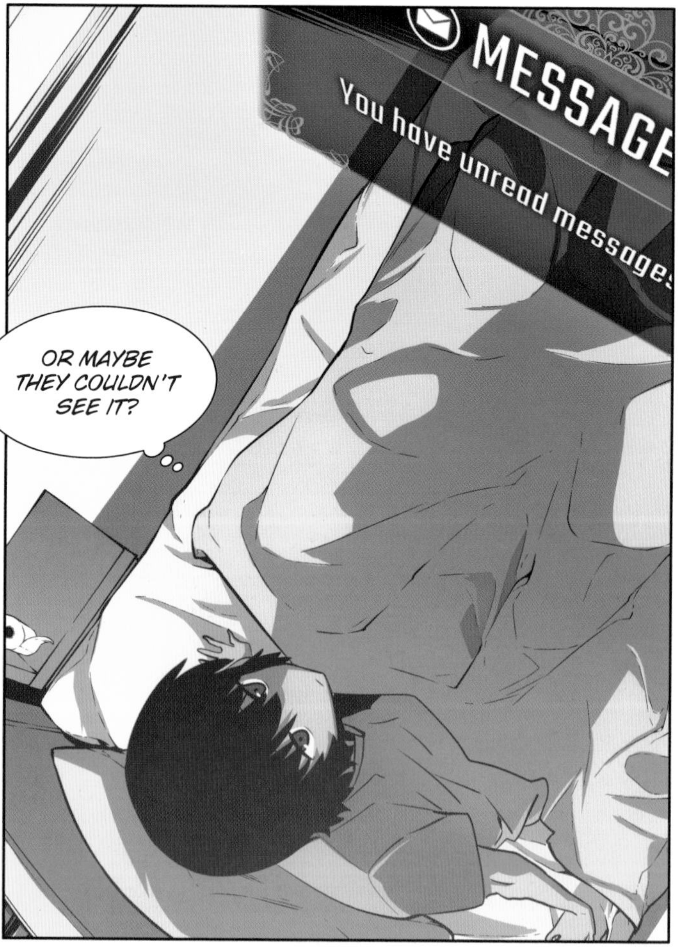
MESSAGE
You have unread messages
OR MAYBE THEY COULDN'T SEE IT?

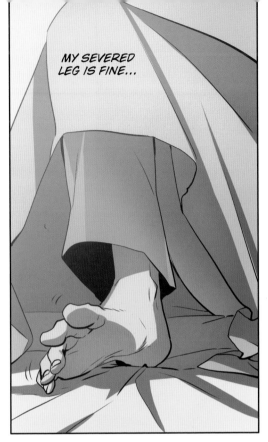

MY SEVERED
LEG IS FINE...

...AND NOT EVEN A SCRATCH
WHERE I WAS STABBED THROUGH
BEFORE I DIED.

WHAT WAS A DREAM...
AND WHAT WAS REAL...?

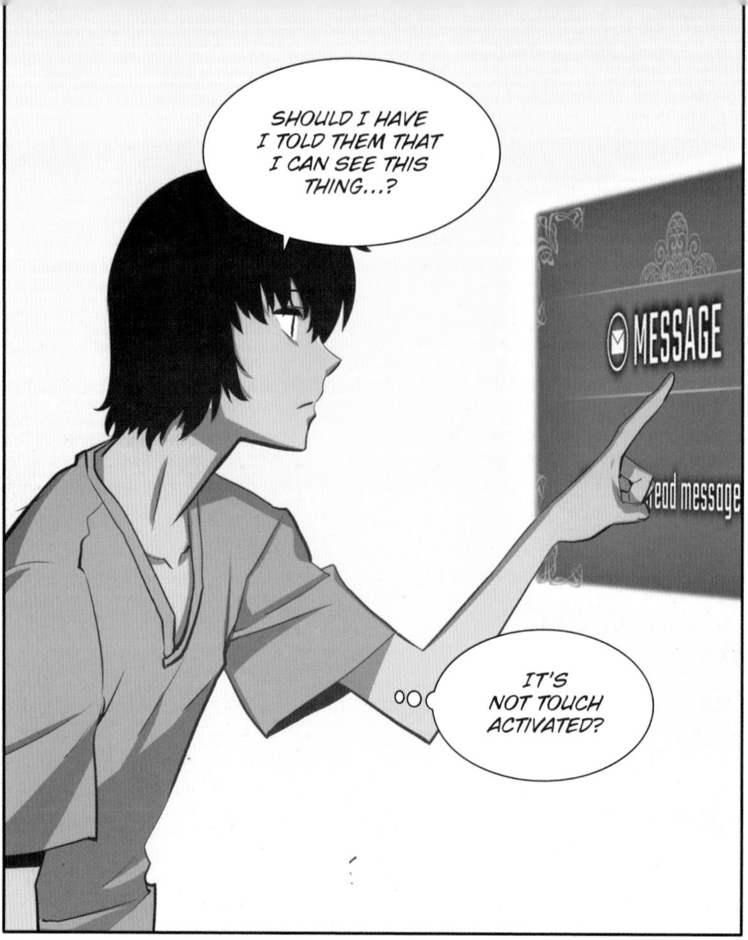
SHOULD I HAVE I TOLD THEM THAT I CAN SEE THIS THING...?
MESSAGE
IT'S NOT TOUCH ACTIVATED?

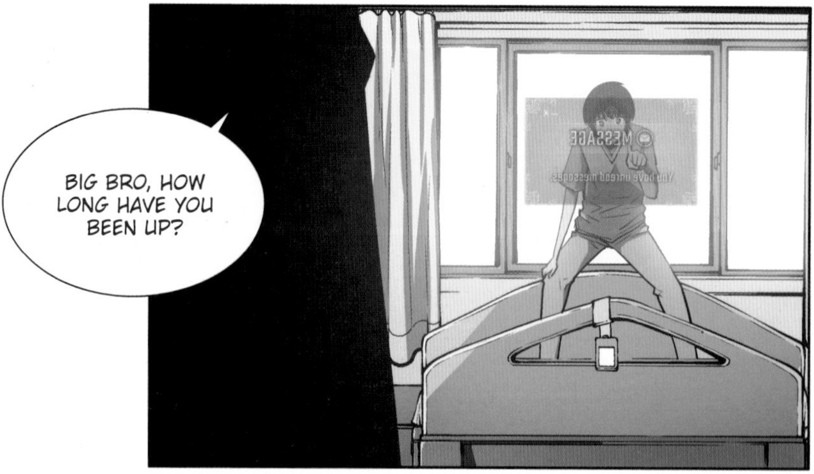
BIG BRO, HOW LONG HAVE YOU BEEN UP?

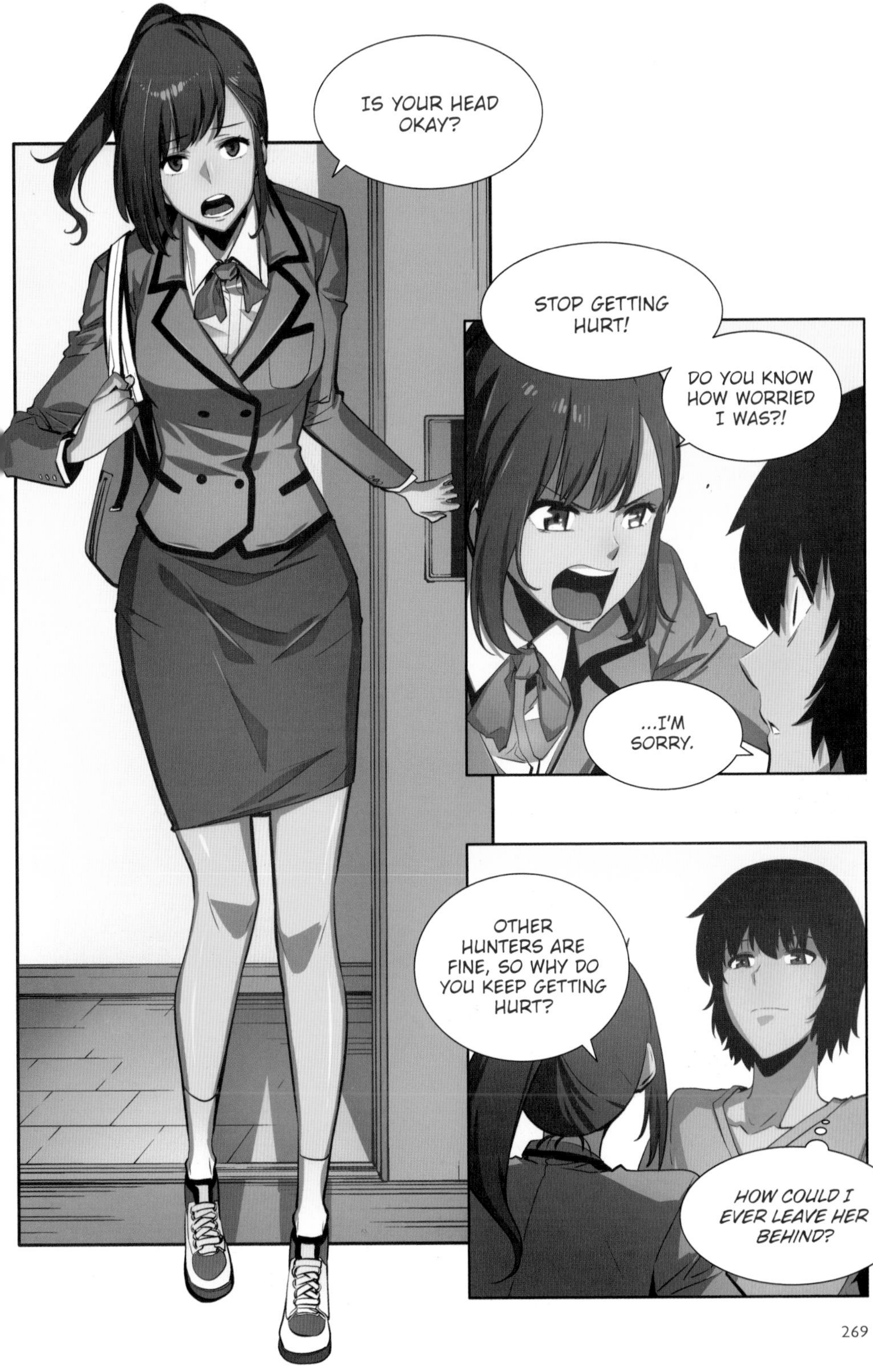
IS YOUR HEAD OKAY?
STOP GETTING HURT!
DO YOU KNOW HOW WORRIED I WAS?!
...I'M SORRY.
OTHER HUNTERS ARE FINE, SO WHY DO YOU KEEP GETTING HURT?
HOW COULD I EVER LEAVE HER BEHIND?

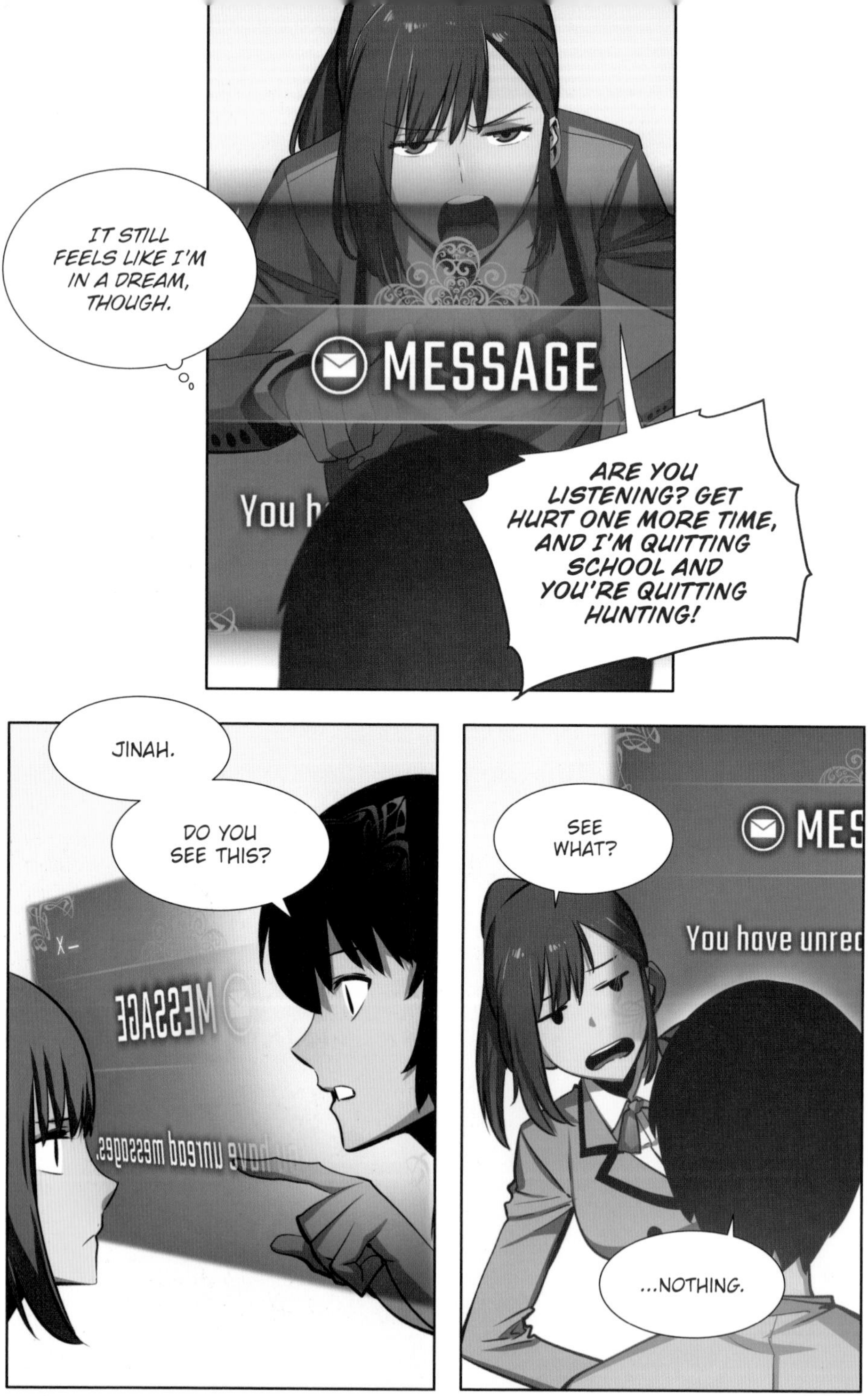
MESSAGE
IT STILL FEELS LIKE I'M IN A DREAM, THOUGH.
ARE YOU LISTENING? GET HURT ONE MORE TIME, AND I'M QUITTING SCHOOL AND YOU'RE QUITTING HUNTING!
JINAH.
DO YOU SEE THIS?
SEE WHAT?
...NOTHING.

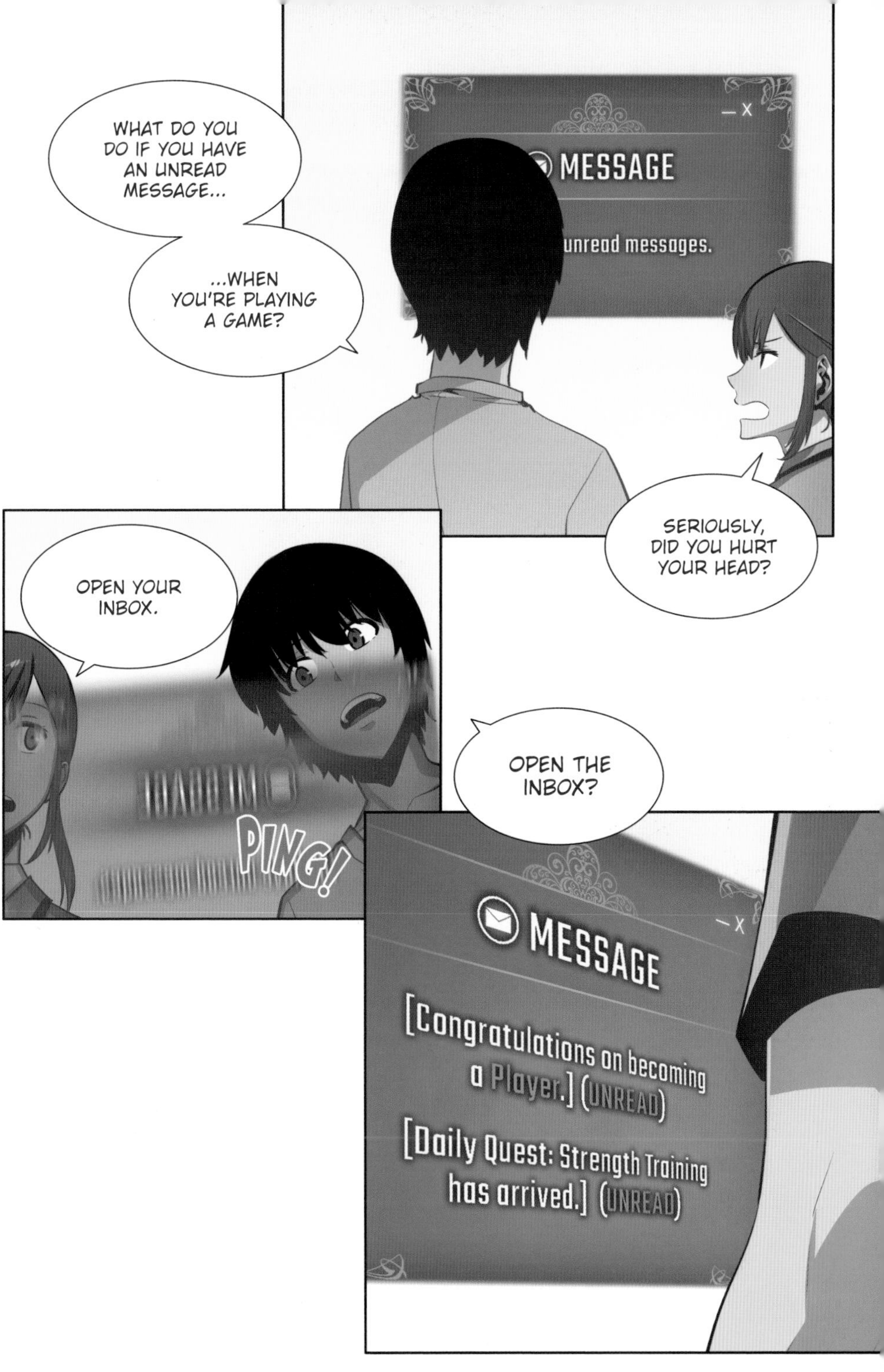
WHAT DO YOU DO IF YOU HAVE AN UNREAD MESSAGE...
...WHEN YOU'RE PLAYING A GAME?
MESSAGE
unread messages.
SERIOUSLY, DID YOU HURT YOUR HEAD?
OPEN YOUR INBOX.
PING!
OPEN THE INBOX?
MESSAGE
[Congratulations on becoming a Player.] (UNREAD)
[Daily Quest: Strength Training has arrived.] (UNREAD)

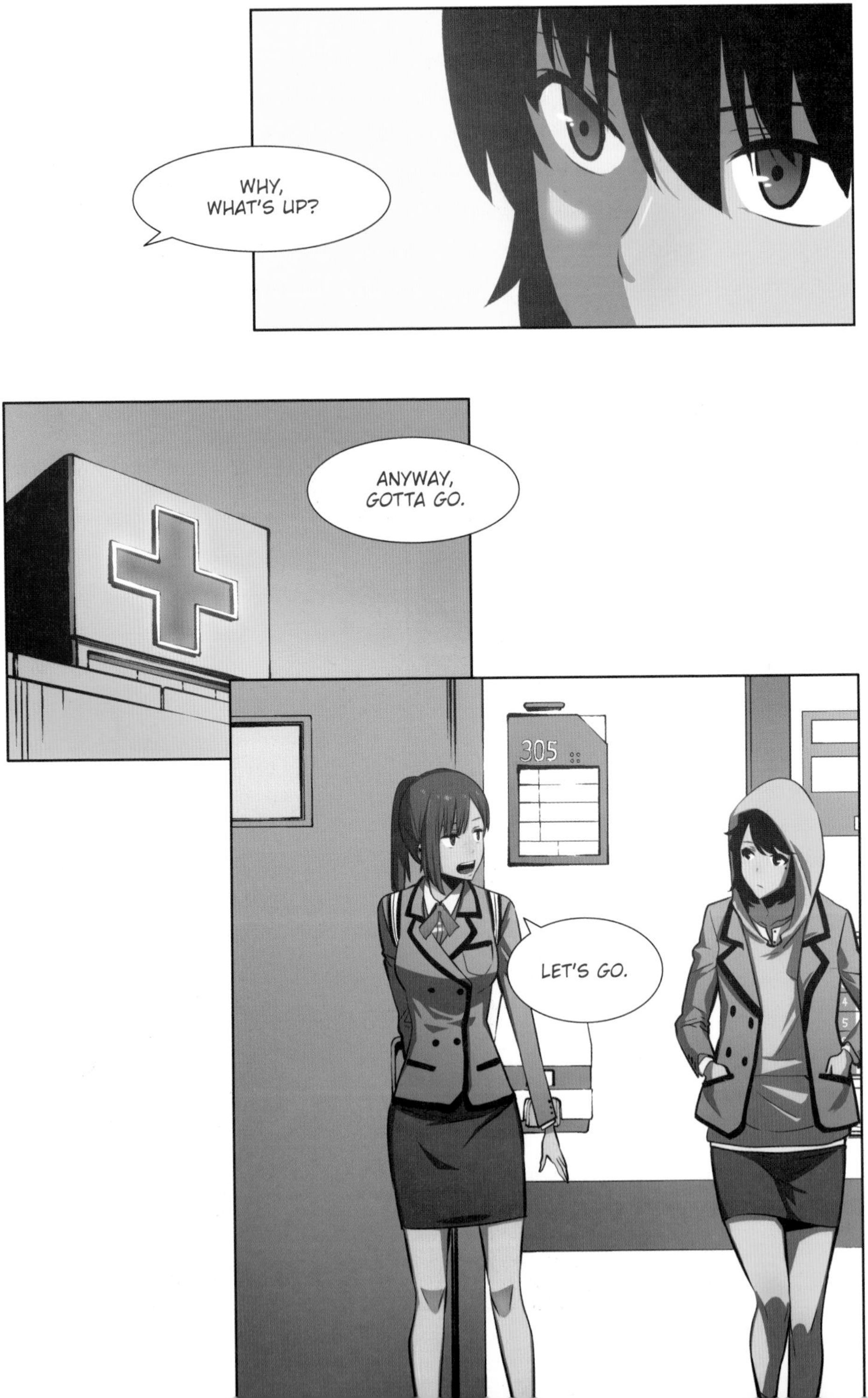
WHY, WHAT'S UP?
ANYWAY, GOTTA GO.
305
LET'S GO.

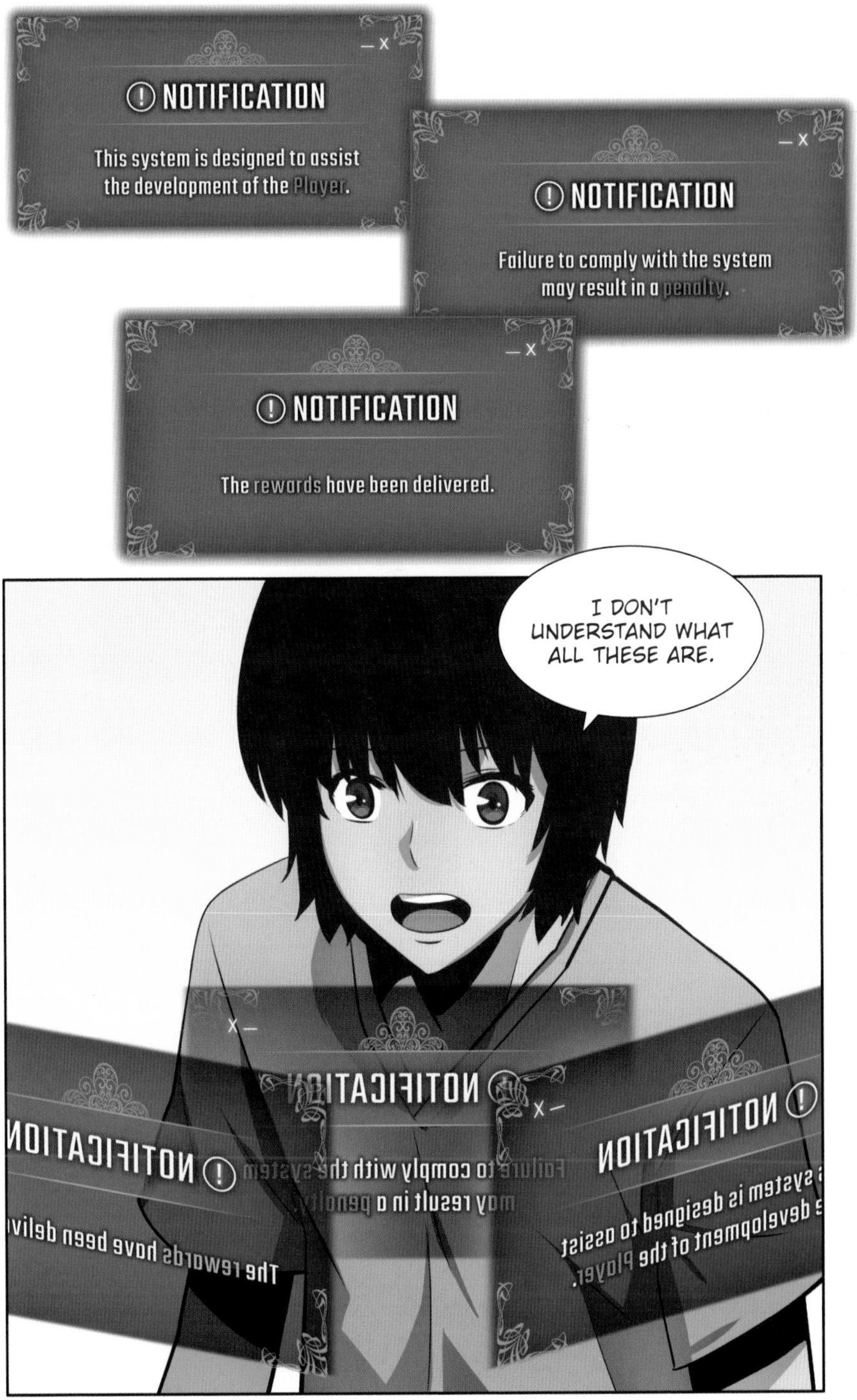
NOTIFICATION
This system is designed to assist the development of the Player.
NOTIFICATION
Failure to comply with the system may result in a penalty.
NOTIFICATION
The rewards have been delivered.
I DON'T UNDERSTAND WHAT ALL THESE ARE.

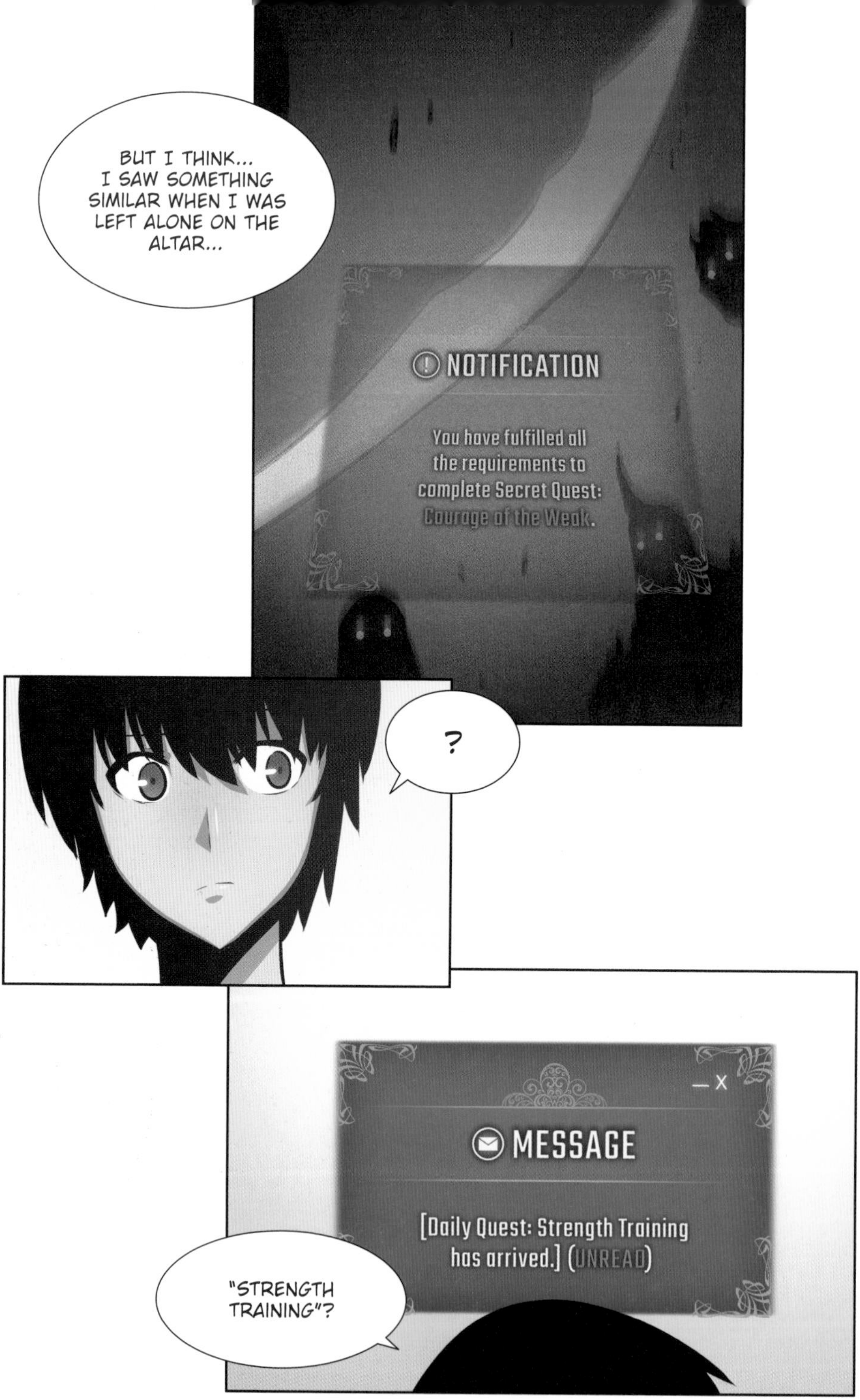
BUT I THINK... I SAW SOMETHING SIMILAR WHEN I WAS LEFT ALONE ON THE ALTAR...
NOTIFICATION
You have fulfilled all the requirements to complete Secret Quest: Courage of the Weak.
?
MESSAGE
[Daily Quest: Strength Training has arrived.] (UNREAD)
"STRENGTH TRAINING"?

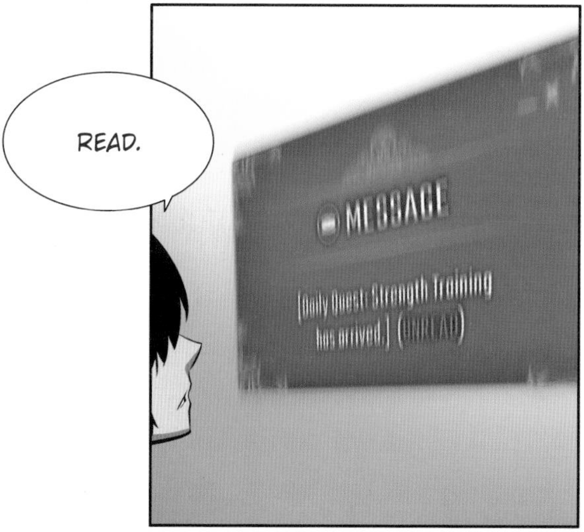
READ.
[Daily Quest: Strength Training has arrived.]

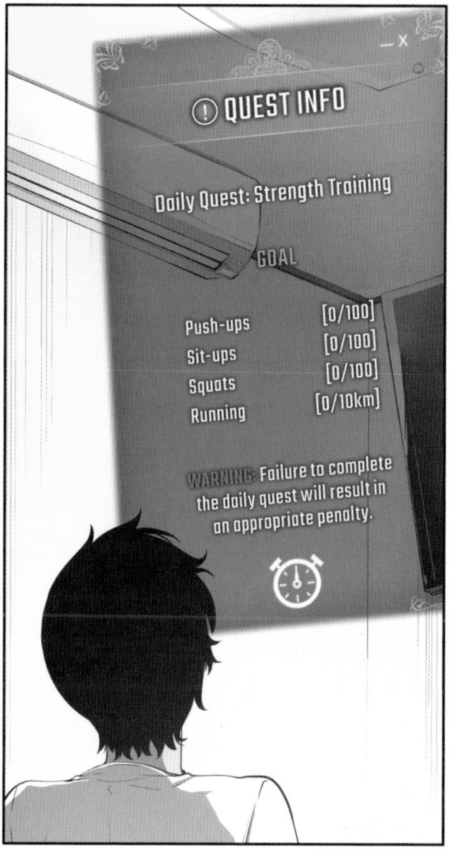
QUEST INFO
Daily Quest: Strength Training
GOAL
Push-ups [0/100]
Sit-ups [0/100]
Squats [0/100]
Running [0/10km]
WARNING: Failure to complete the daily quest will result in an appropriate penalty.

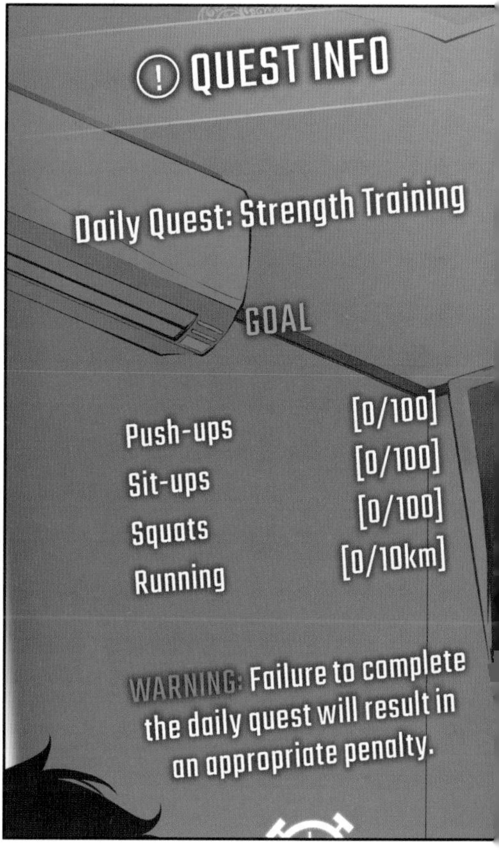
QUEST INFO
Daily Quest: Strength Training
GOAL
Push-ups [0/100]
Sit-ups [0/100]
Squats [0/100]
Running [0/10km]
WARNING: Failure to complete the daily quest will result in an appropriate penalty.

WARNING: Failure to complete the daily quest will result in an appropriate penalty.

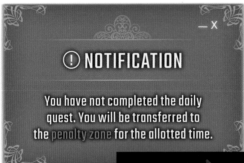

— X

ⓘ NOTIFICATION

You have not completed the daily quest. You will be transferred to the penalty zone for the allotted time.

RRRUMBLE

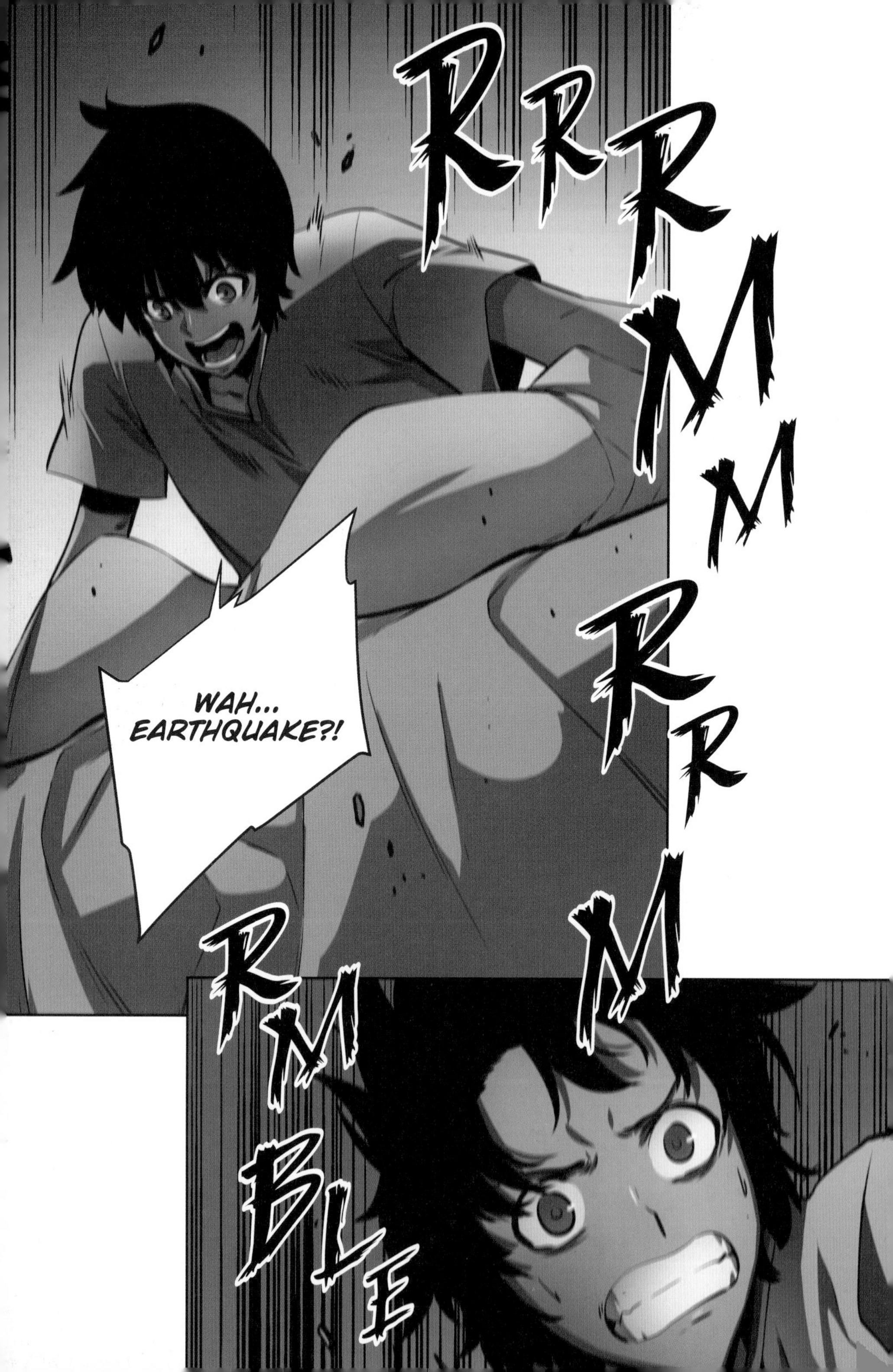
WAH... EARTHQUAKE?!
RRRMMRRMRMBLE

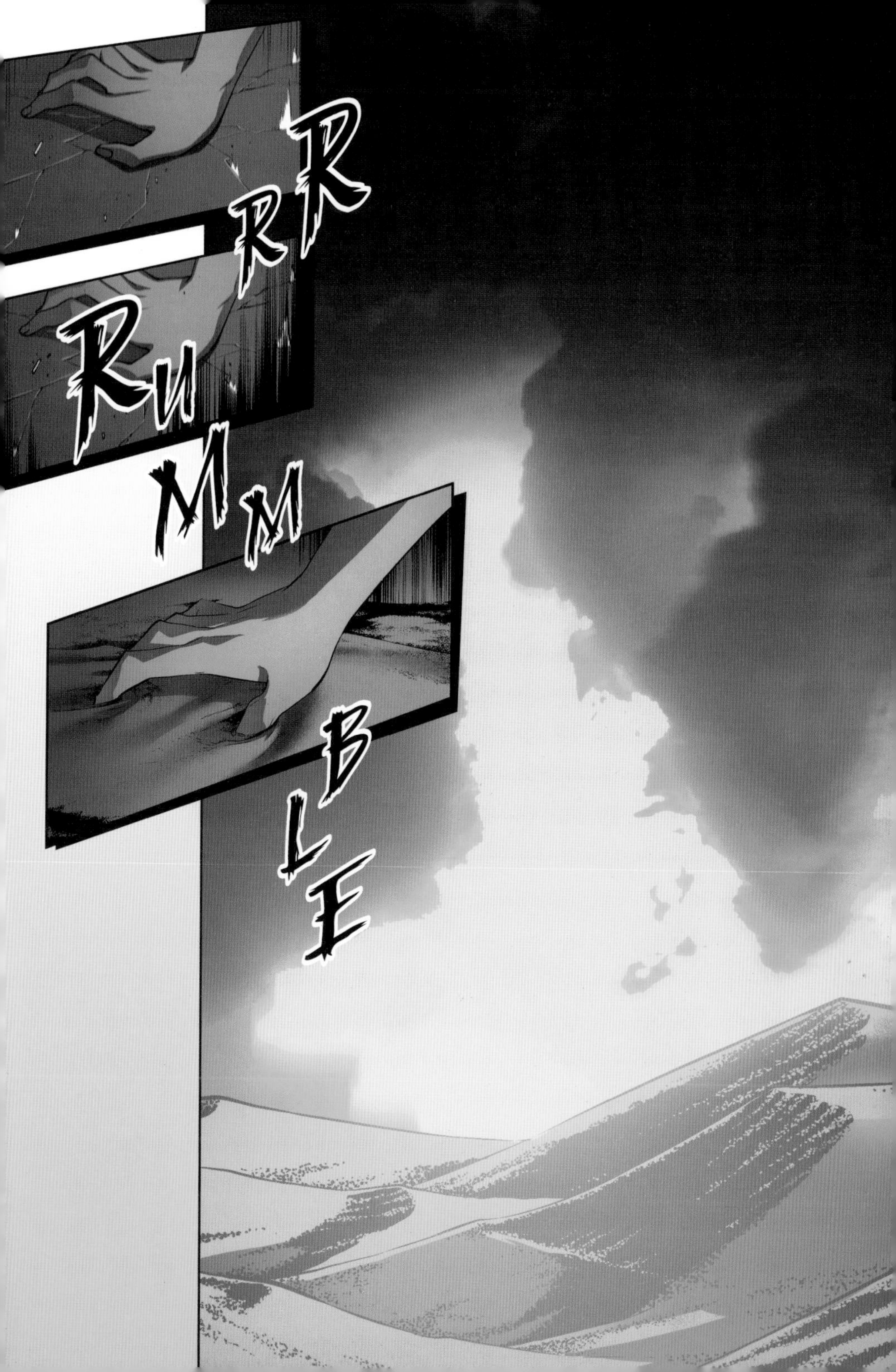
RRRUMMBLE

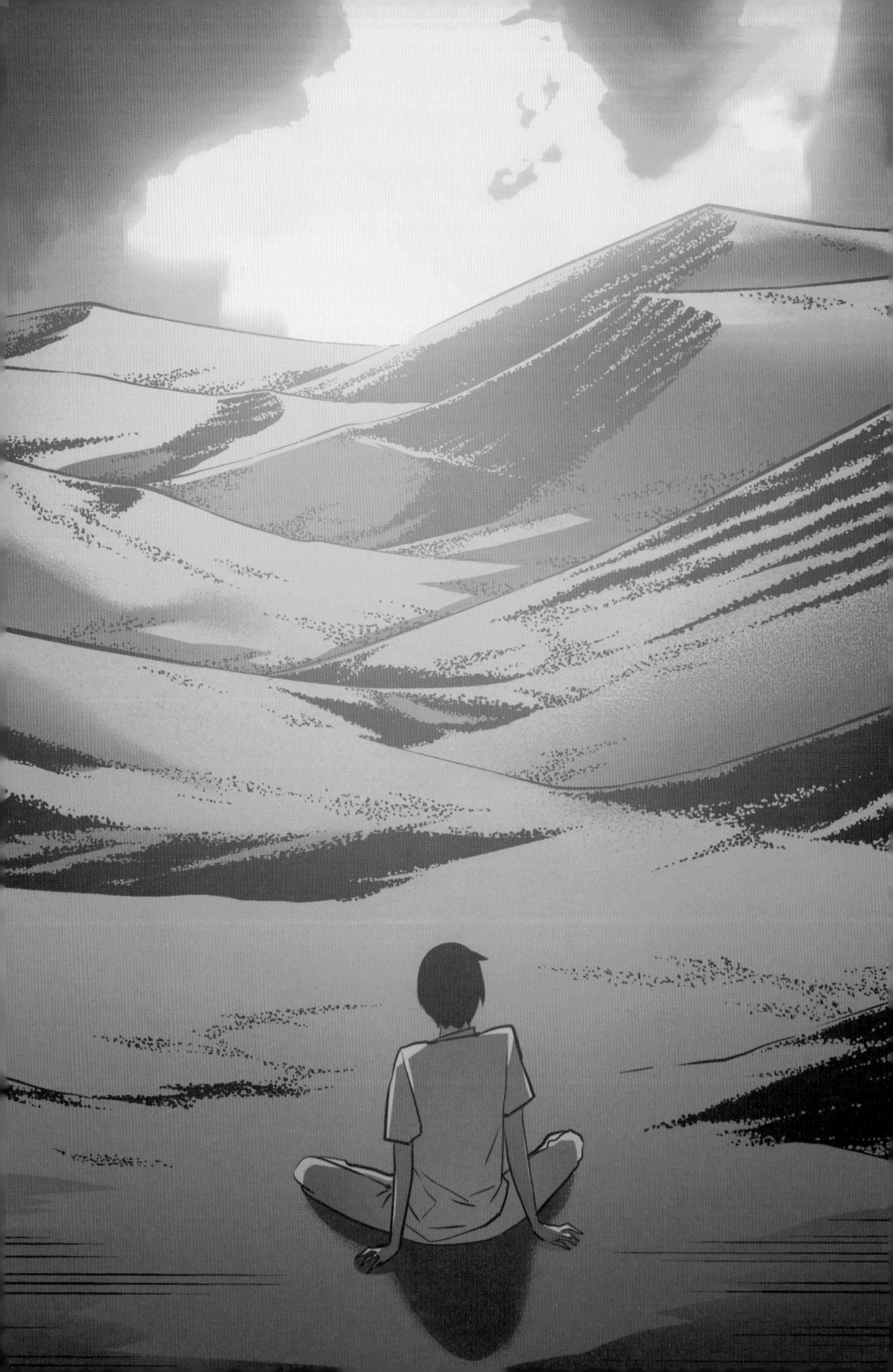

WH-WHAT?
A DESERT...?!

THIS DOESN'T
MAKE SENSE...
AM I DREAMING?

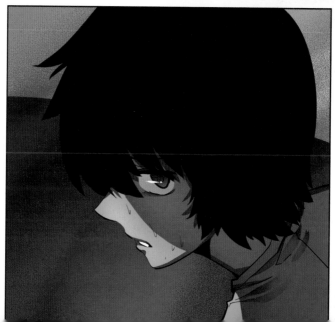

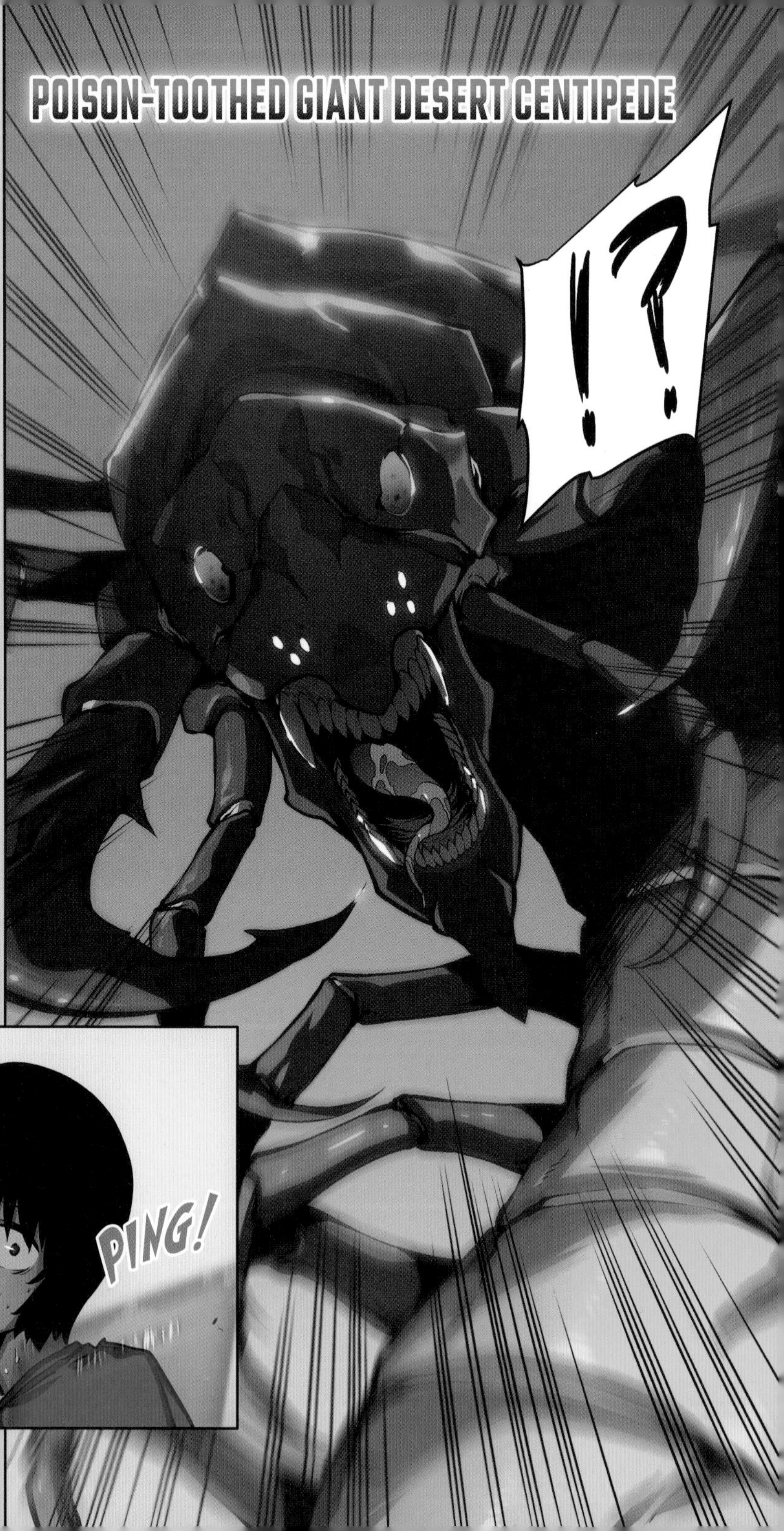
POISON-TOOTHED GIANT DESERT CENTIPEDE
!?
PING!

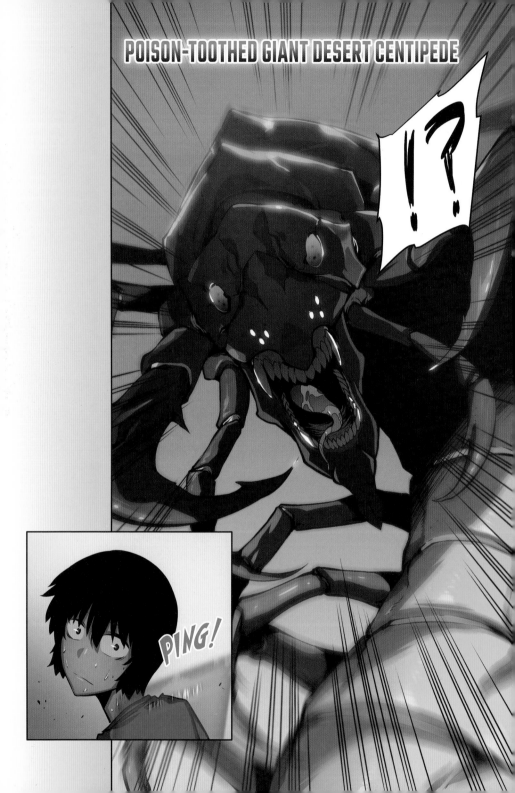

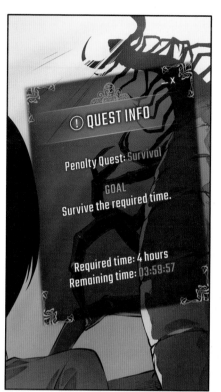

⚠ QUEST INFO

Penalty Quest: Survival

GOAL
Survive the required time.

Required time: 4 hours
Remaining time: 03:59:57

YOU'VE GOTTA
BE KIDDING ME...

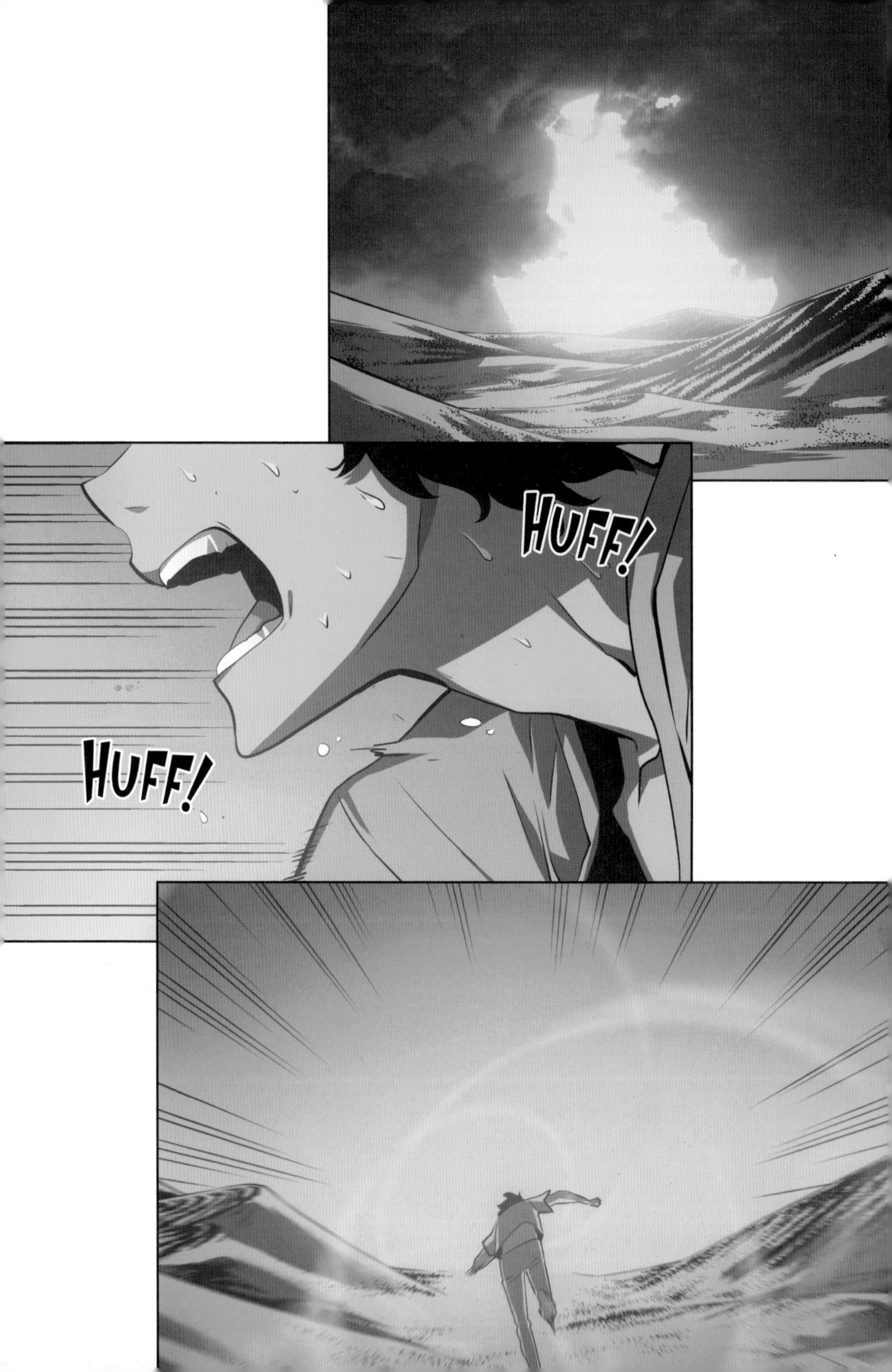
HUFF!
HUFF!

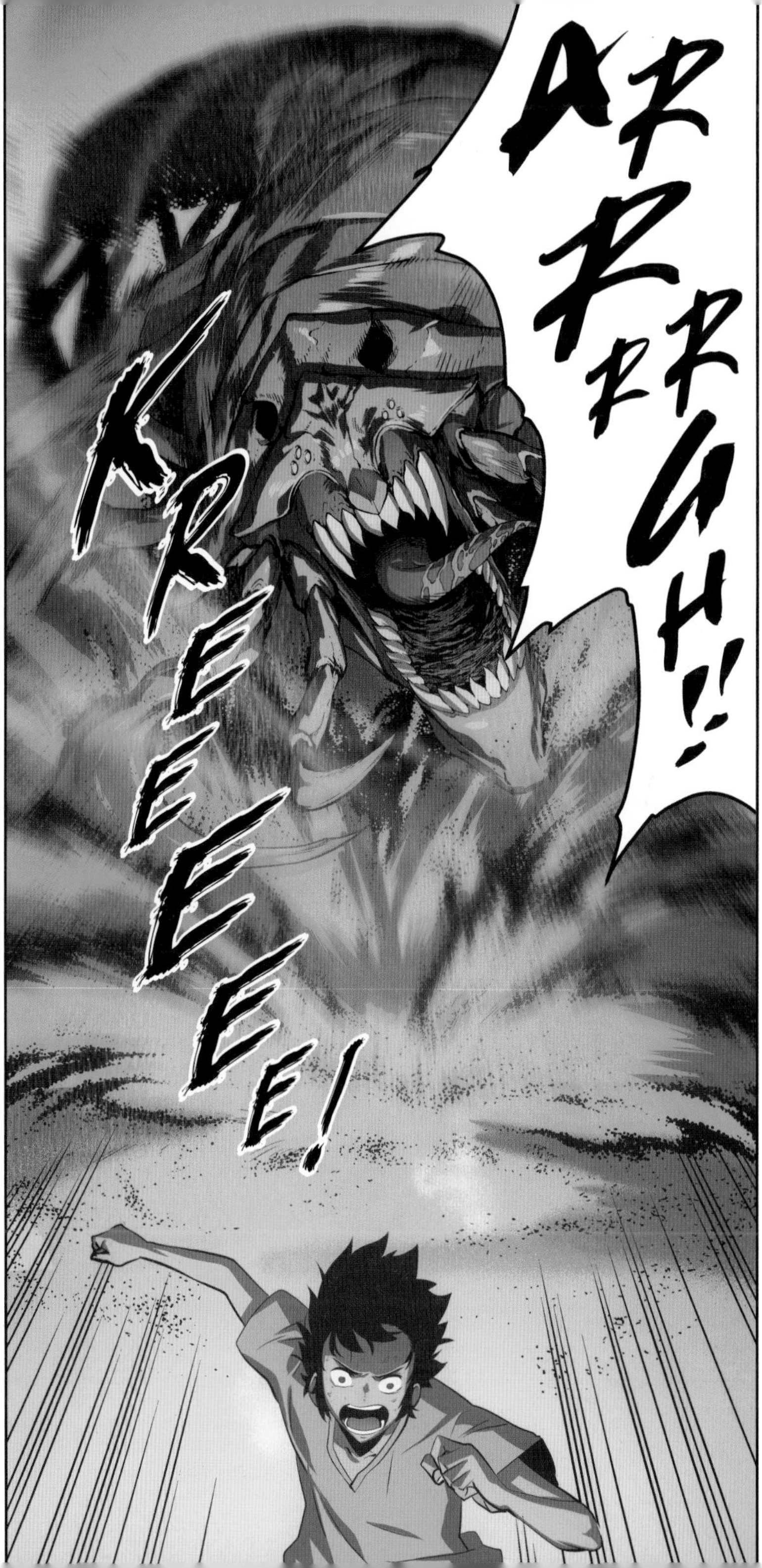
ARRRRRUHH!!
KREEEEEEE!

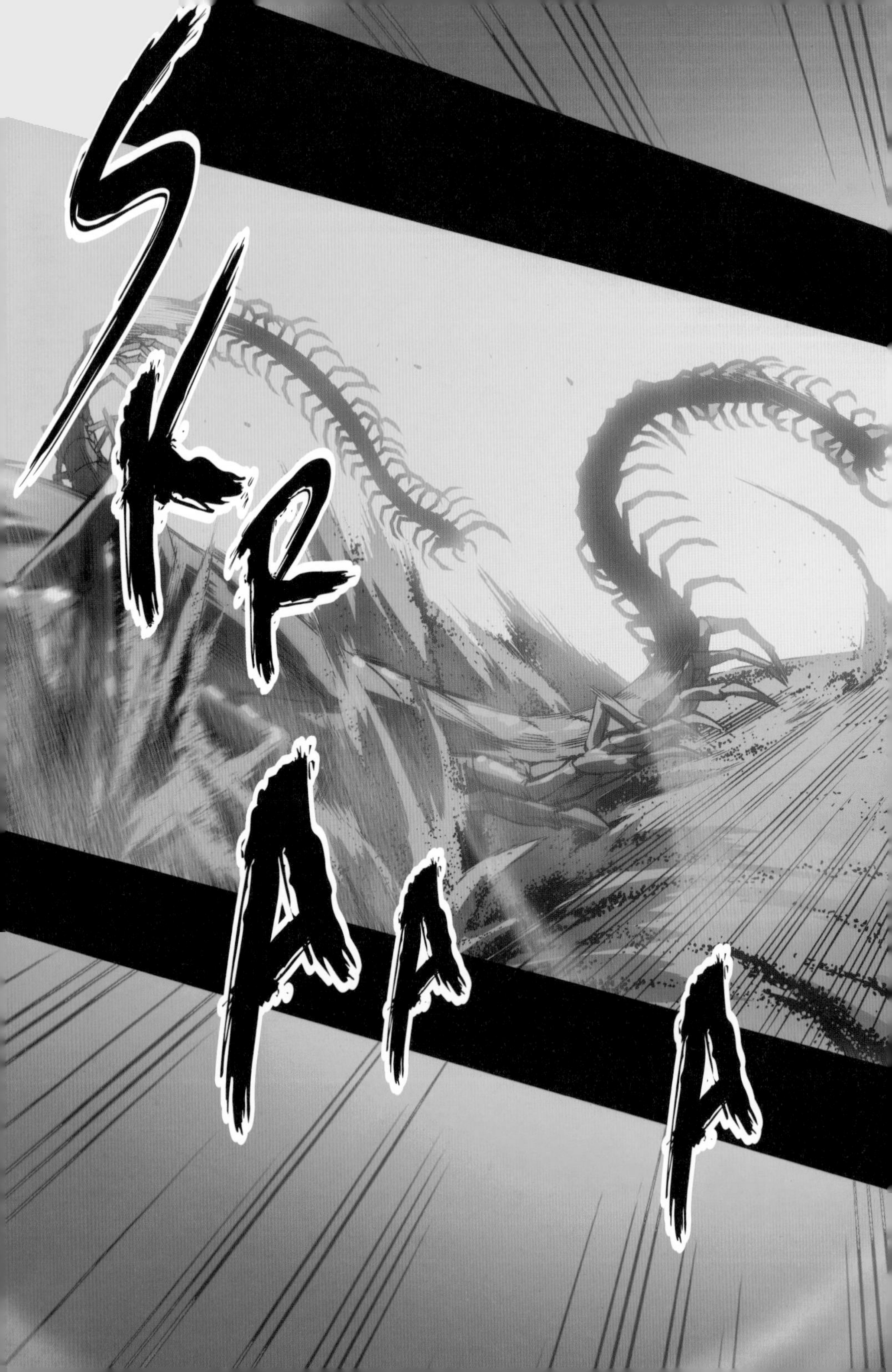
SKRAAA

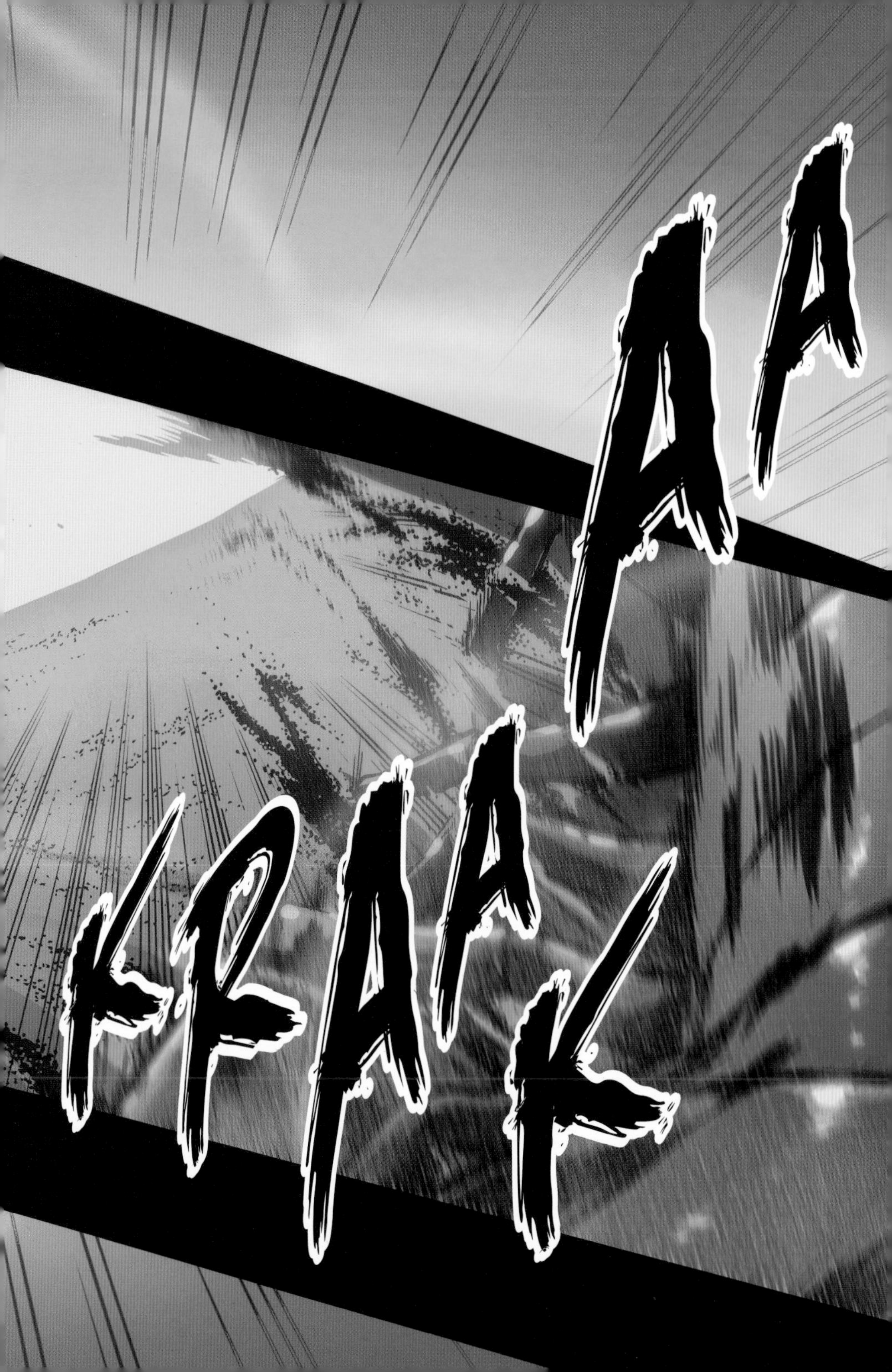
AA
KRAAK

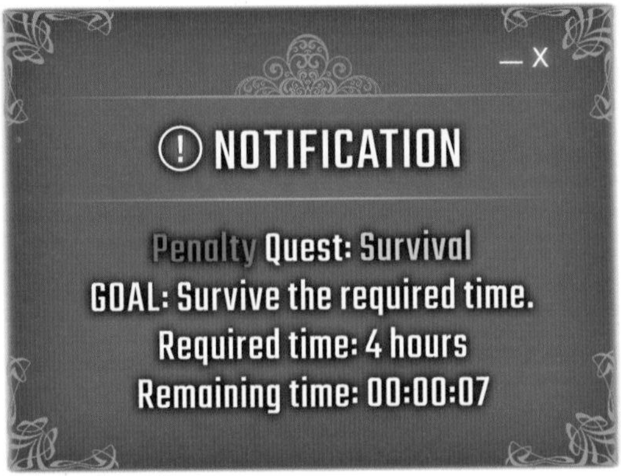

— X
NOTIFICATION
Penalty Quest: Survival
GOAL: Survive the required time.
Required time: 4 hours
Remaining time: 00:00:07

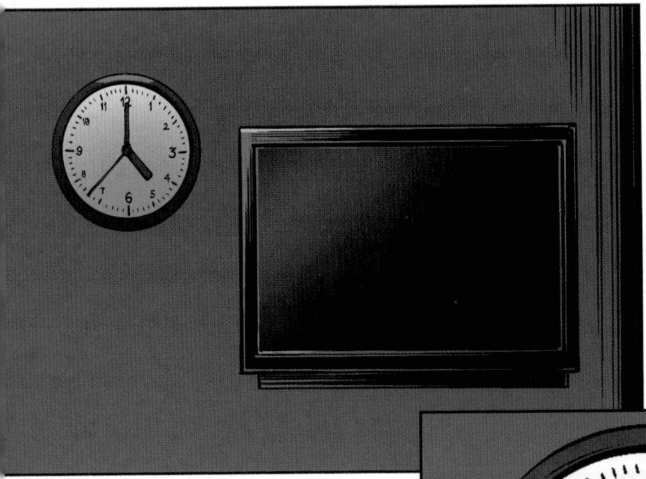

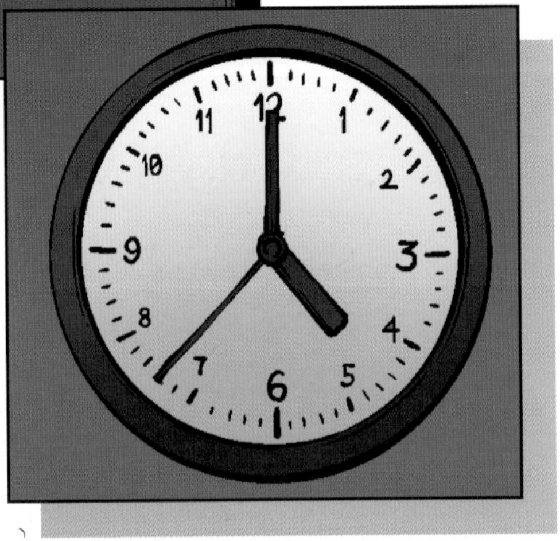

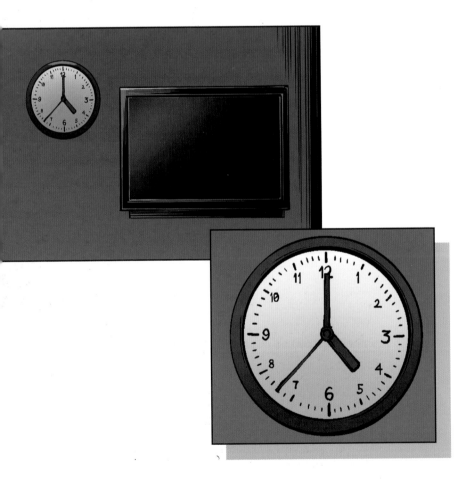

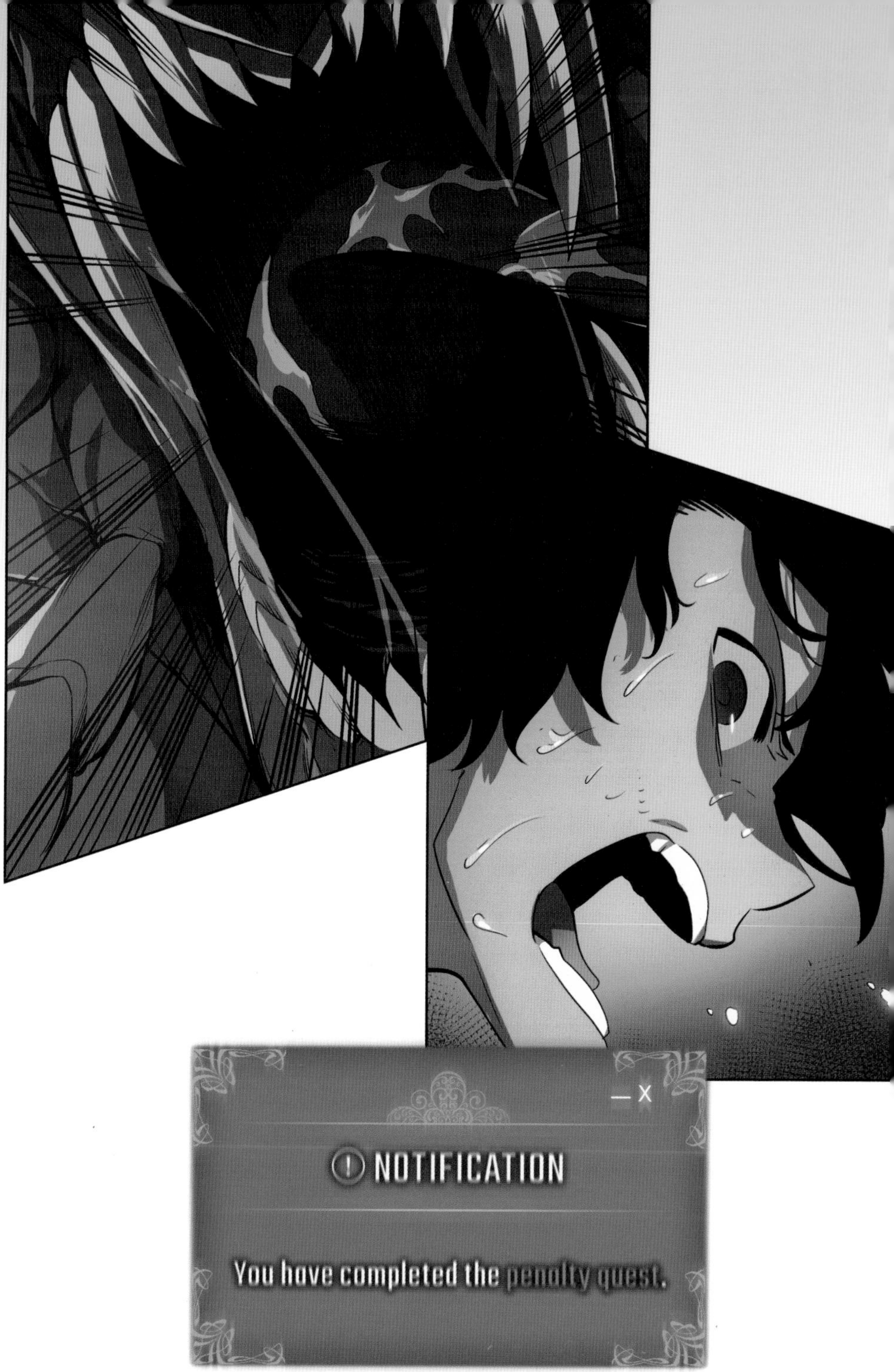
NOTIFICATION
You have completed the penalty quest.

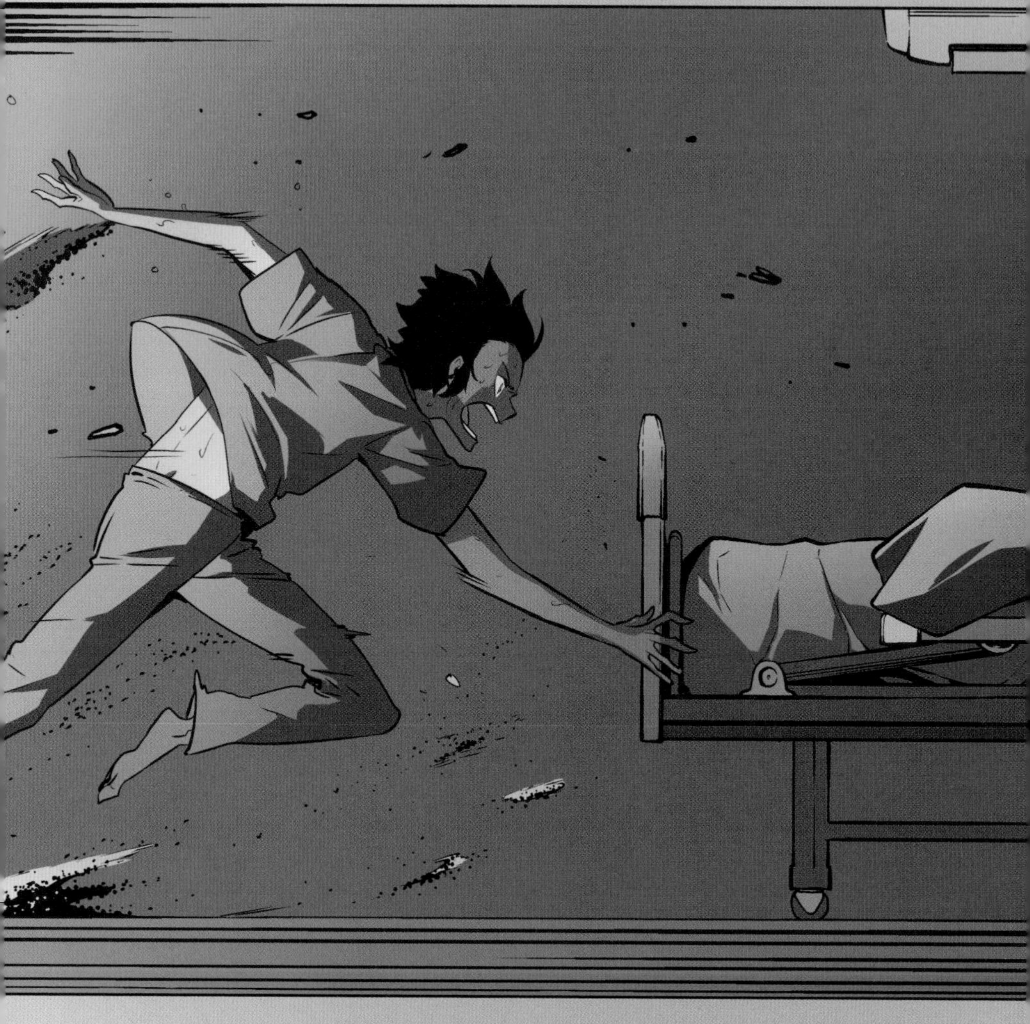

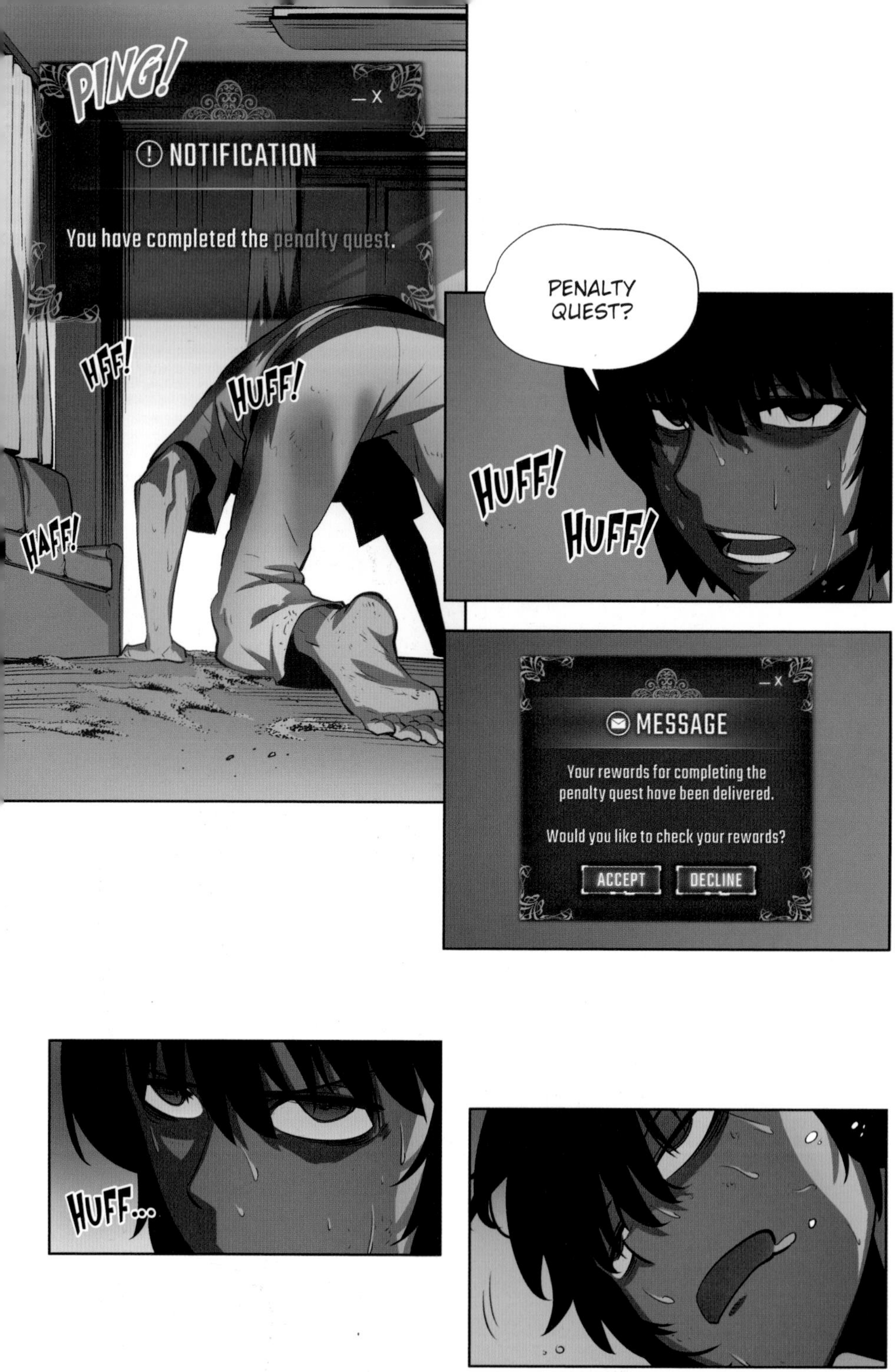

PING!
— X
NOTIFICATION
You have completed the penalty quest.
HFF!
HUFF!
HAFF!
PENALTY QUEST?
HUFF!
HUFF!
— X
MESSAGE
Your rewards for completing the penalty quest have been delivered.
Would you like to check your rewards?
ACCEPT
DECLINE
HUFF...

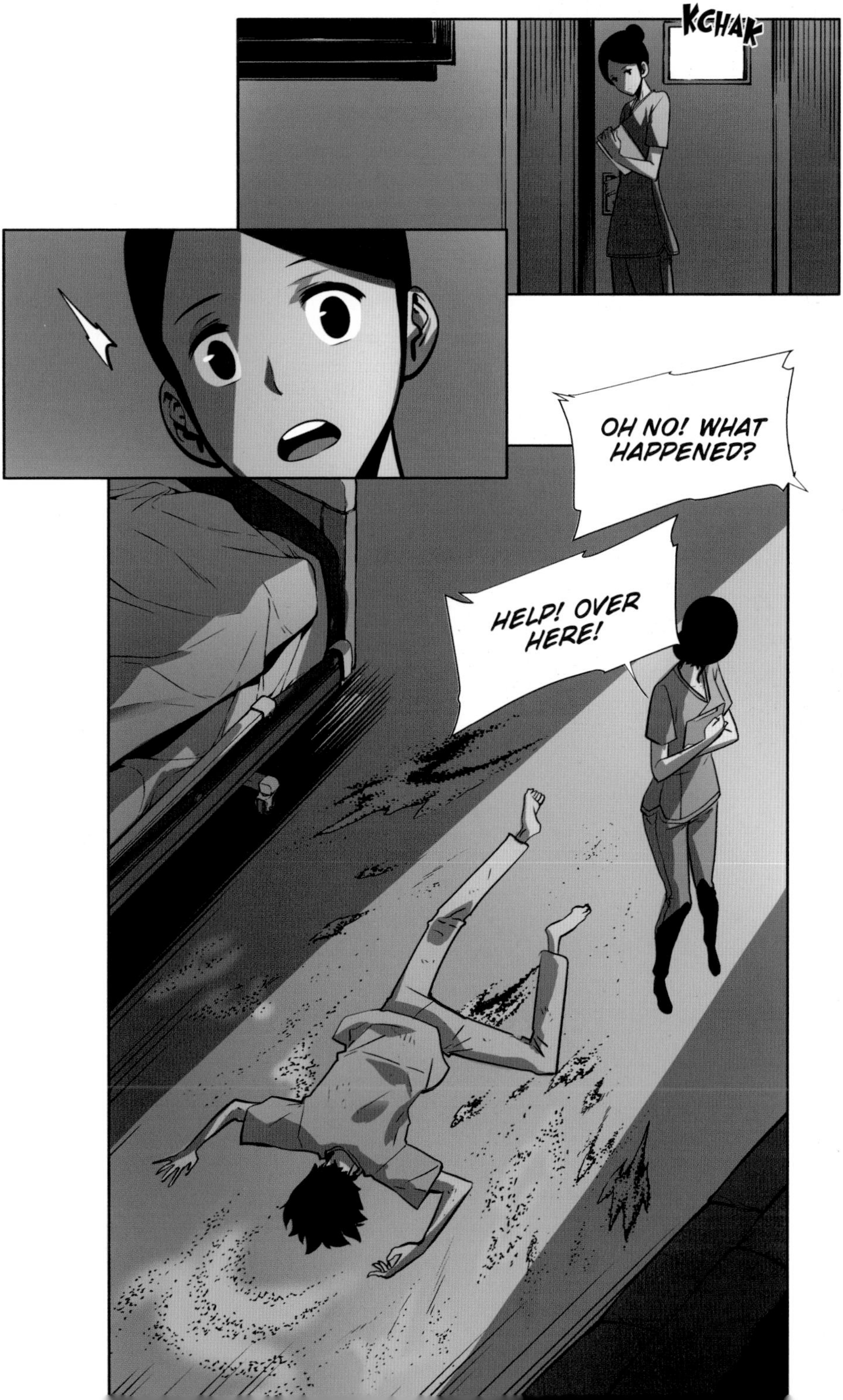
KCHAK
OH NO! WHAT HAPPENED?
HELP! OVER HERE!

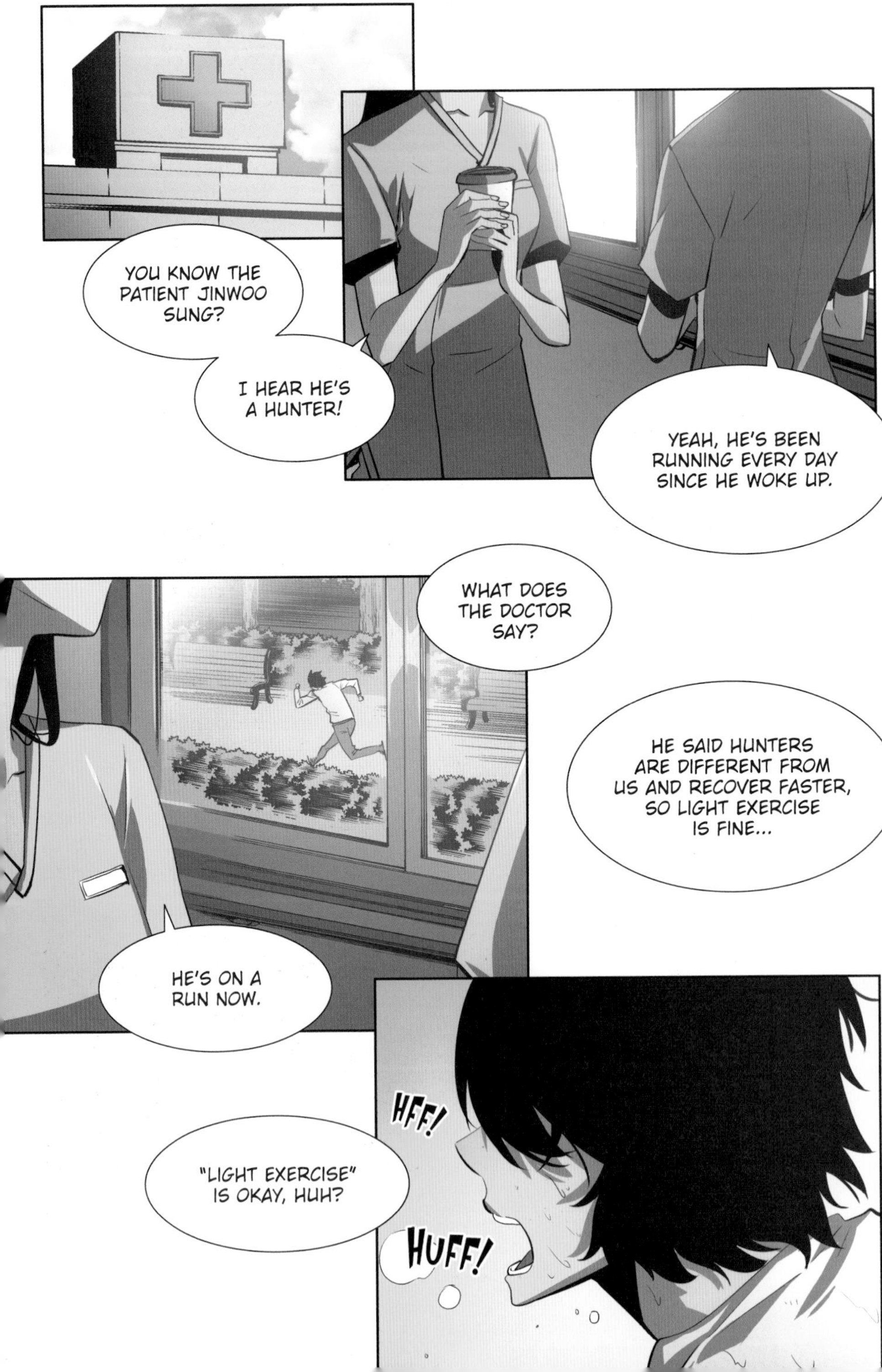
YOU KNOW THE PATIENT JINWOO SUNG?
I HEAR HE'S A HUNTER!
YEAH, HE'S BEEN RUNNING EVERY DAY SINCE HE WOKE UP.
WHAT DOES THE DOCTOR SAY?
HE SAID HUNTERS ARE DIFFERENT FROM US AND RECOVER FASTER, SO LIGHT EXERCISE IS FINE...
HE'S ON A RUN NOW.
HFF!
"LIGHT EXERCISE" IS OKAY, HUH?
HUFF!

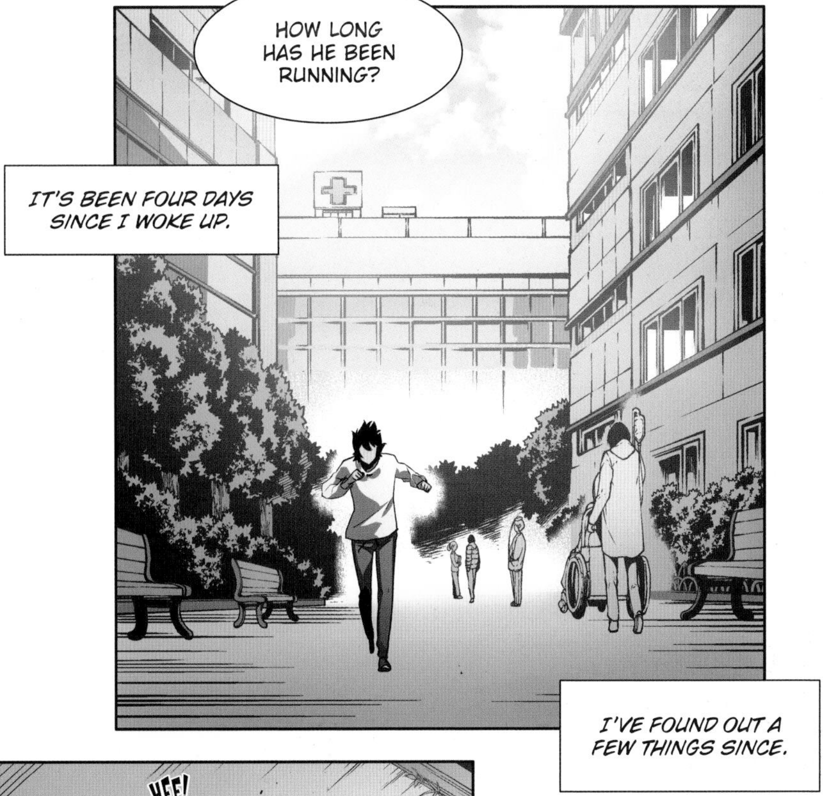
HOW LONG HAS HE BEEN RUNNING?
IT'S BEEN FOUR DAYS SINCE I WOKE UP.
I'VE FOUND OUT A FEW THINGS SINCE.

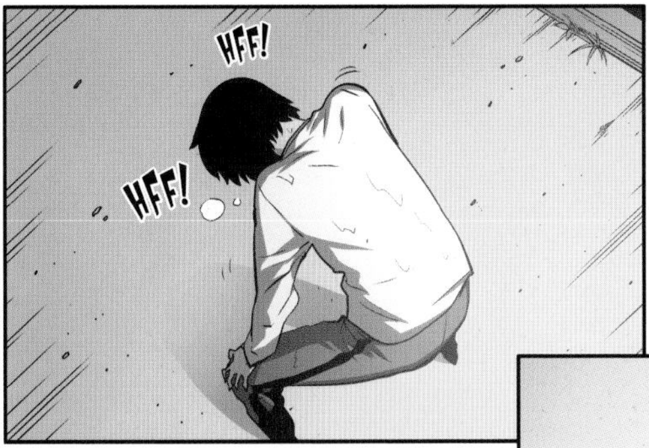
HFF!
HFF!

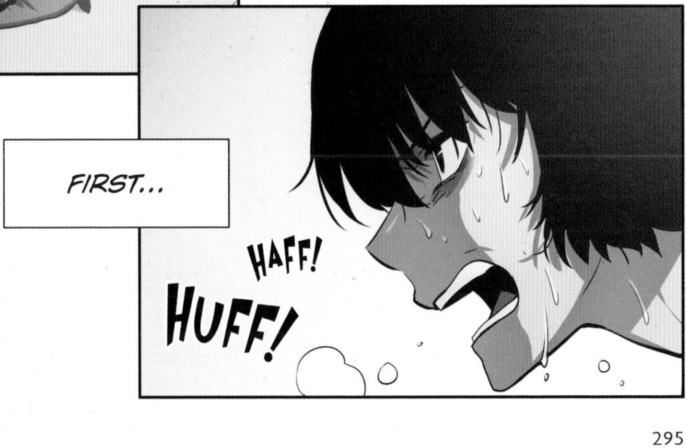
FIRST...
HAFF!
HUFF!

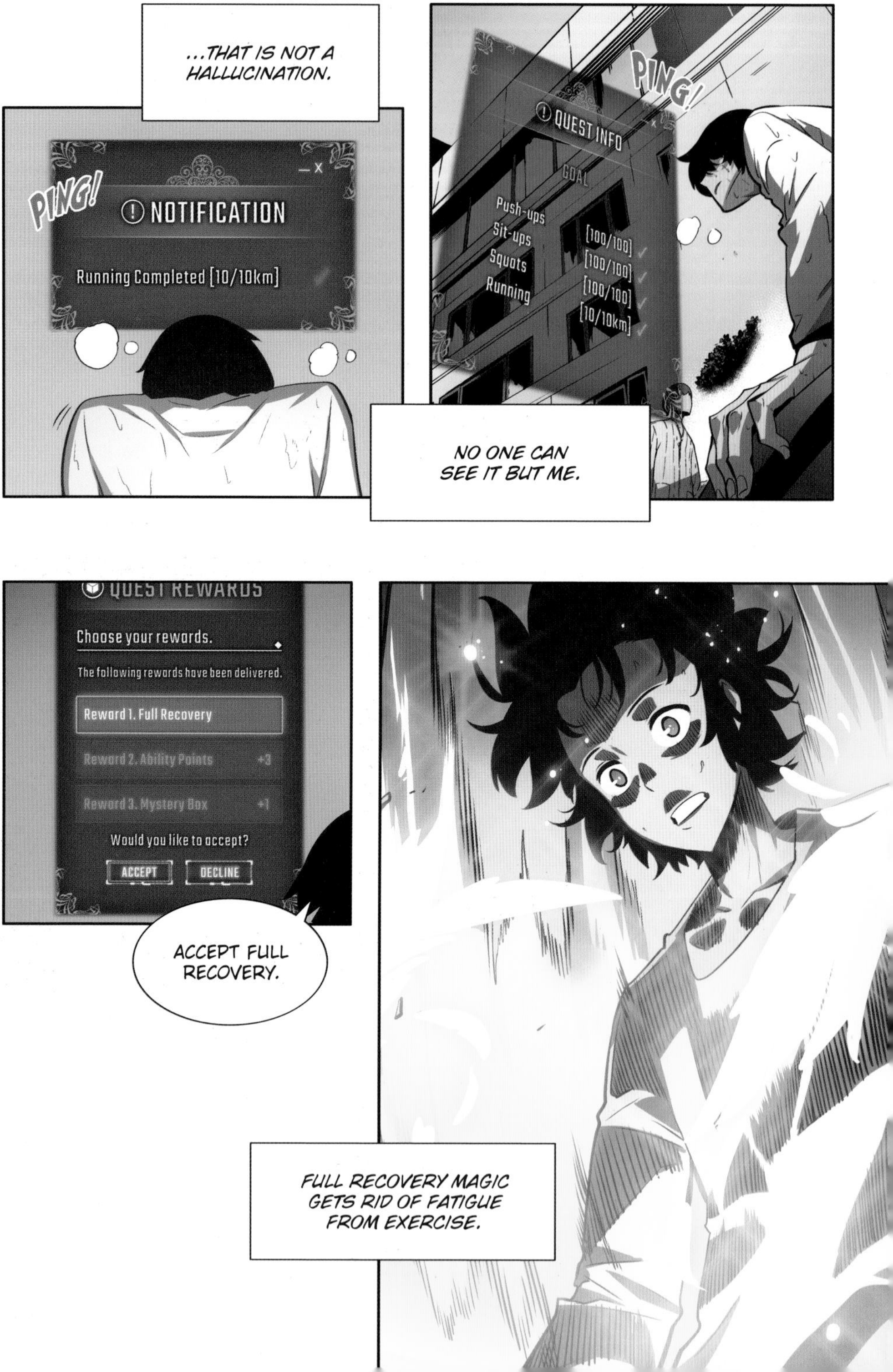
...THAT IS NOT A HALLUCINATION.
PING!
NOTIFICATION
Running Completed [10/10km]
PING!
QUEST INFO
GOAL
Push-ups [100/100]
Sit-ups [100/100]
Squats [100/100]
Running [10/10km]
NO ONE CAN SEE IT BUT ME.
QUEST REWARDS
Choose your rewards.
The following rewards have been delivered.
Reward 1. Full Recovery
Reward 2. Ability Points +3
Reward 3. Mystery Box +1
Would you like to accept?
ACCEPT
DECLINE
ACCEPT FULL RECOVERY.
FULL RECOVERY MAGIC GETS RID OF FATIGUE FROM EXERCISE.

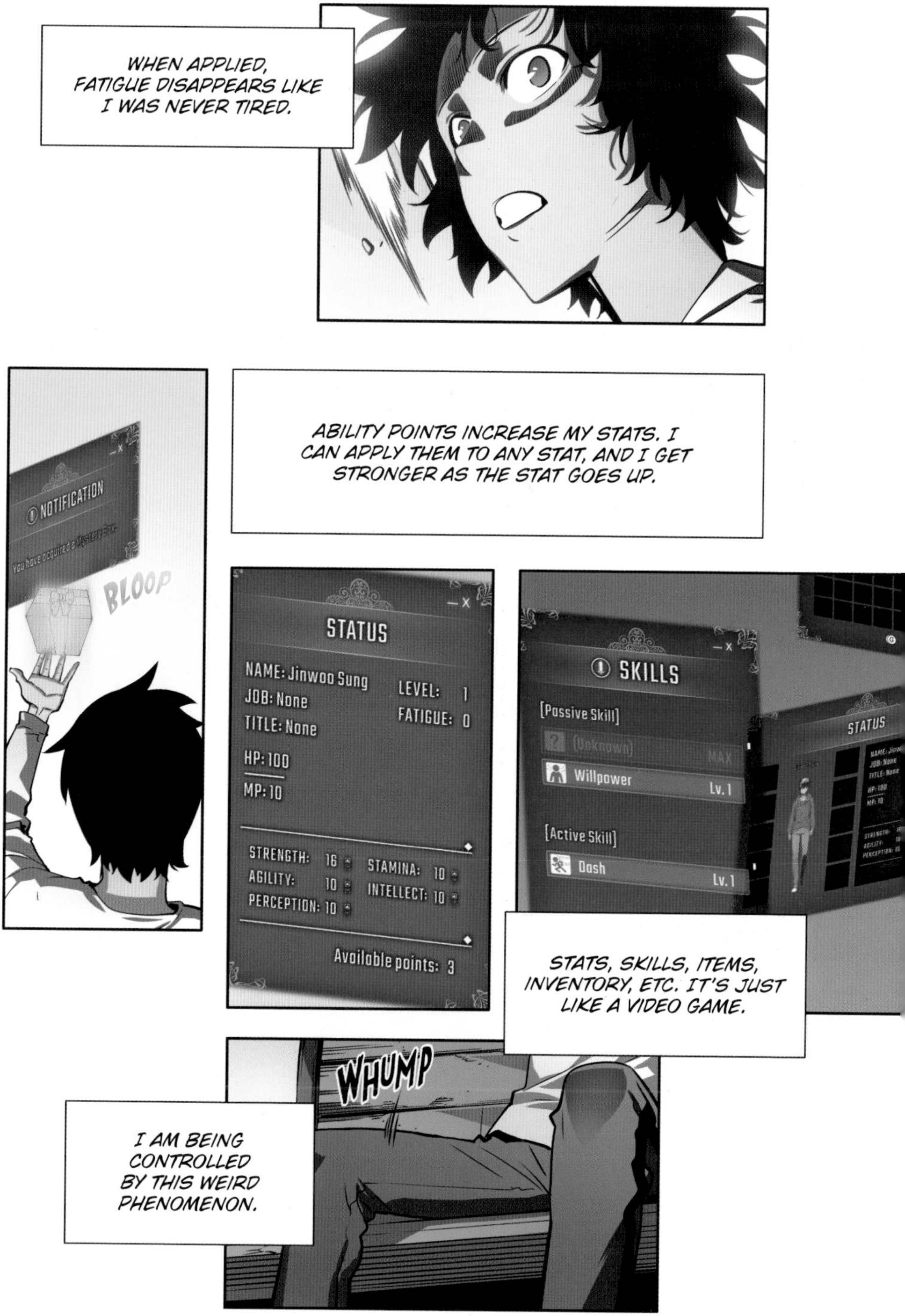
WHEN APPLIED, FATIGUE DISAPPEARS LIKE I WAS NEVER TIRED.
NOTIFICATION
You have acquired a Mystery Box.
BLOOP
ABILITY POINTS INCREASE MY STATS. I CAN APPLY THEM TO ANY STAT, AND I GET STRONGER AS THE STAT GOES UP.
STATUS
NAME: Jinwoo Sung
JOB: None
TITLE: None
LEVEL: 1
FATIGUE: 0
HP: 100
MP: 10
STRENGTH: 16
STAMINA: 10
AGILITY: 10
INTELLECT: 10
PERCEPTION: 10
Available points: 3
SKILLS
[Passive Skill]
(Unknown) MAX
Willpower Lv. 1
[Active Skill]
Dash Lv. 1
STATUS
STATS, SKILLS, ITEMS, INVENTORY, ETC. IT'S JUST LIKE A VIDEO GAME.
WHUMP
I AM BEING CONTROLLED BY THIS WEIRD PHENOMENON.

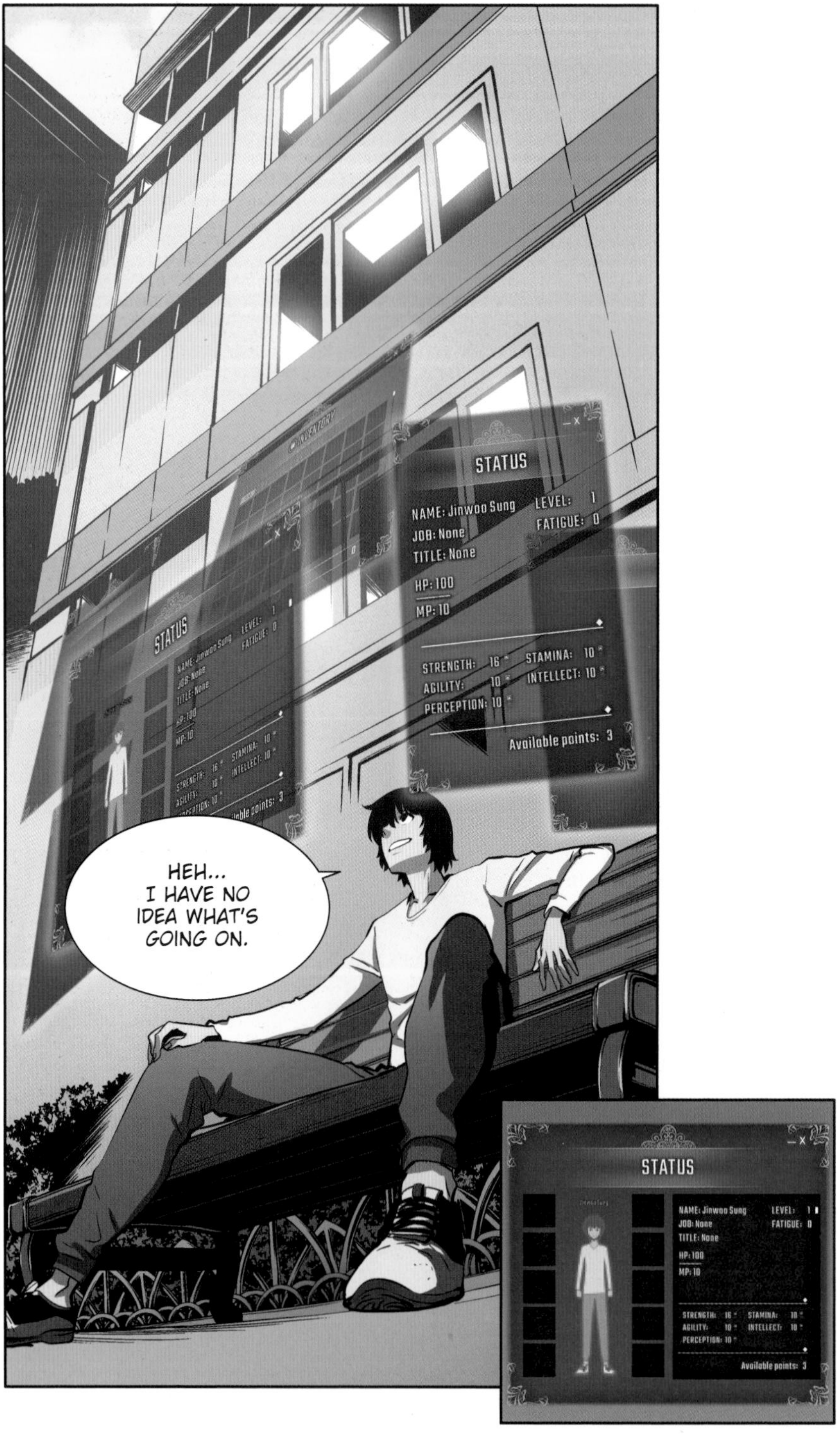
STATUS
NAME: Jinwoo Sung LEVEL: 1
FATIGUE: 0
JOB: None
TITLE: None
HP: 100
MP: 10
STRENGTH: 16 STAMINA: 10
AGILITY: 10 INTELLECT: 10
PERCEPTION: 10
Available points: 3
HEH... I HAVE NO IDEA WHAT'S GOING ON.
STATUS
NAME: Jinwoo Sung LEVEL: 1
JOB: None FATIGUE: 0
TITLE: None
HP: 100
MP: 10
STRENGTH: 16 STAMINA: 10
AGILITY: 10 INTELLECT: 10
PERCEPTION: 10
Available points: 3

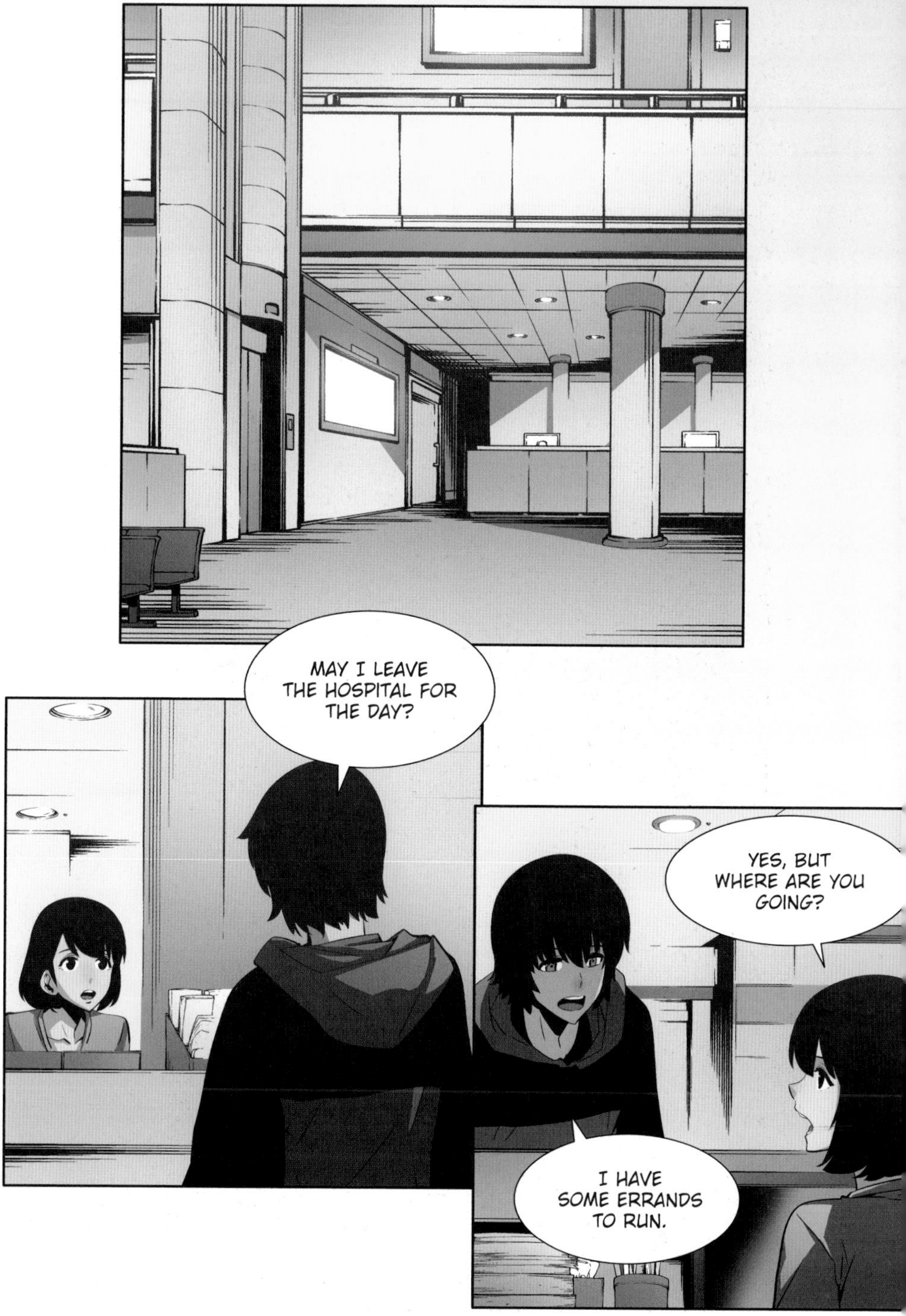
MAY I LEAVE THE HOSPITAL FOR THE DAY?
YES, BUT WHERE ARE YOU GOING?
I HAVE SOME ERRANDS TO RUN.

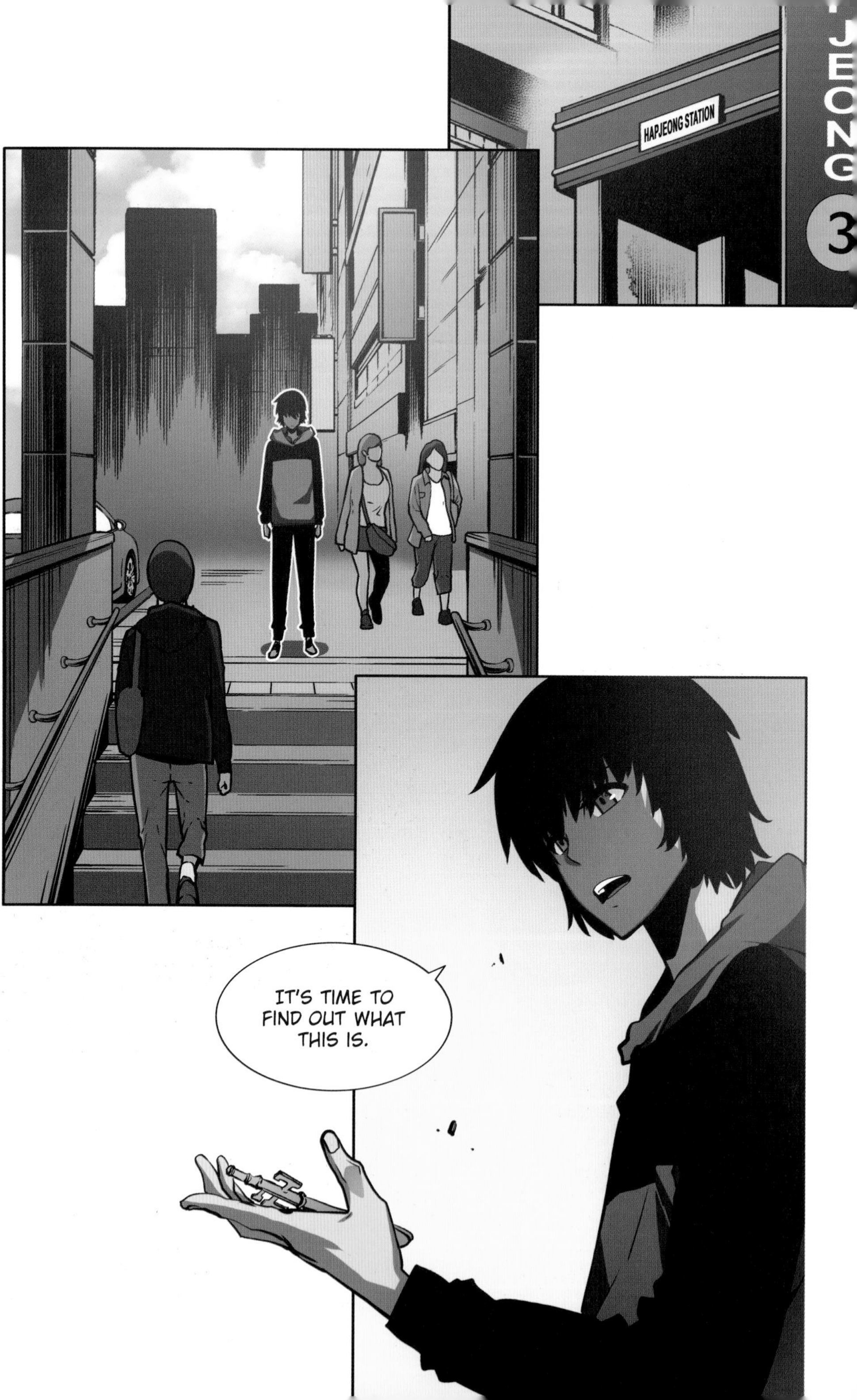
HAPJEONG STATION
IT'S TIME TO FIND OUT WHAT THIS IS.

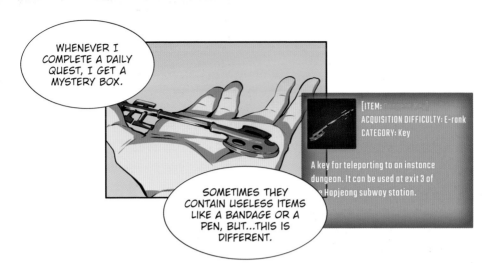

WHENEVER I COMPLETE A DAILY QUEST, I GET A MYSTERY BOX.

[ITEM: Dungeon Key]
ACQUISITION DIFFICULTY: E-rank
CATEGORY: Key

A key for teleporting to an instance dungeon. It can be used at exit 3 of the Hapjeong subway station.

SOMETIMES THEY CONTAIN USELESS ITEMS LIKE A BANDAGE OR A PEN, BUT...THIS IS DIFFERENT.

A KEY FOR "AN INSTANCE DUNGEON."

QUEST, STATS, REWARDS...WHAT IF ALL THIS WEIRD VIDEO GAME STUFF'S PART OF A SECOND AWAKENING?

STATUS

NAME: Jinwoo Sung   FATIGUE:
JOB: None
TITLE: None
HP: 100
MP: 10

STRENGTH: 15   STAMINA: 10
AGILITY: 10   INTELLECT: 10
PERCEPTION: 10

[ITEM: Dungeon
ACQUISITION
CATEGORY: Ke

A key that will take you t
dungeon. It can be used a
the Hapjeong subway stat

A SIGN THE REAWAKENING WILL HAPPEN?

OR PART OF THE PROCESS?

GRIP

IF SO, THIS IS WORTH A SHOT!

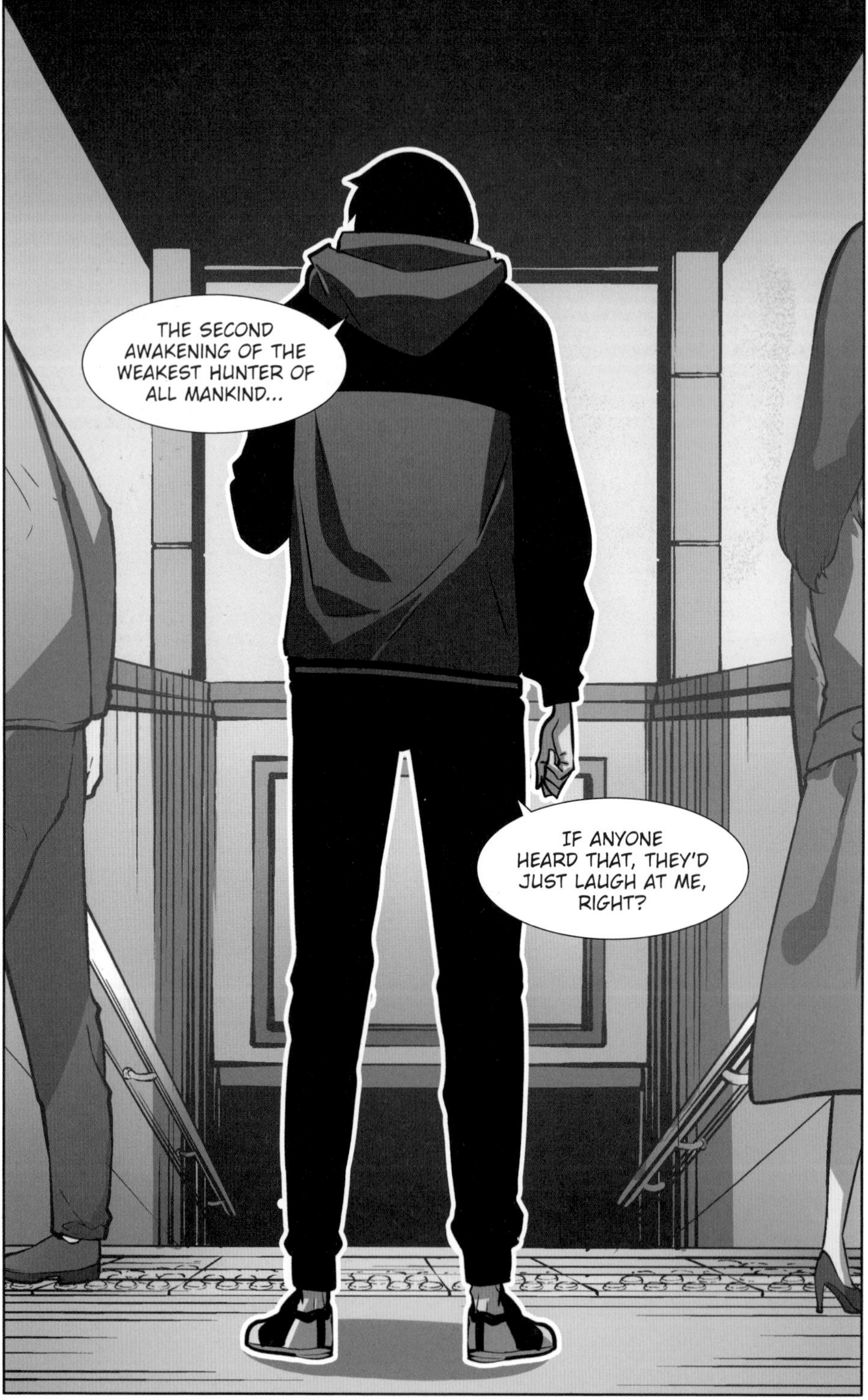
THE SECOND AWAKENING OF THE WEAKEST HUNTER OF ALL MANKIND...
IF ANYONE HEARD THAT, THEY'D JUST LAUGH AT ME, RIGHT?

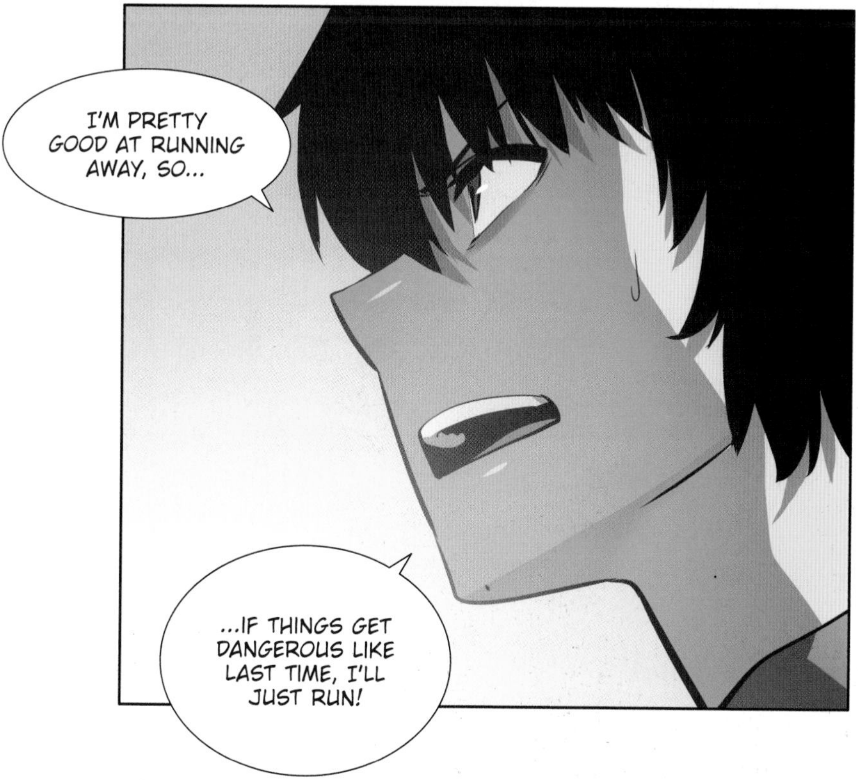
I'M PRETTY GOOD AT RUNNING AWAY, SO...
...IF THINGS GET DANGEROUS LIKE LAST TIME, I'LL JUST RUN!

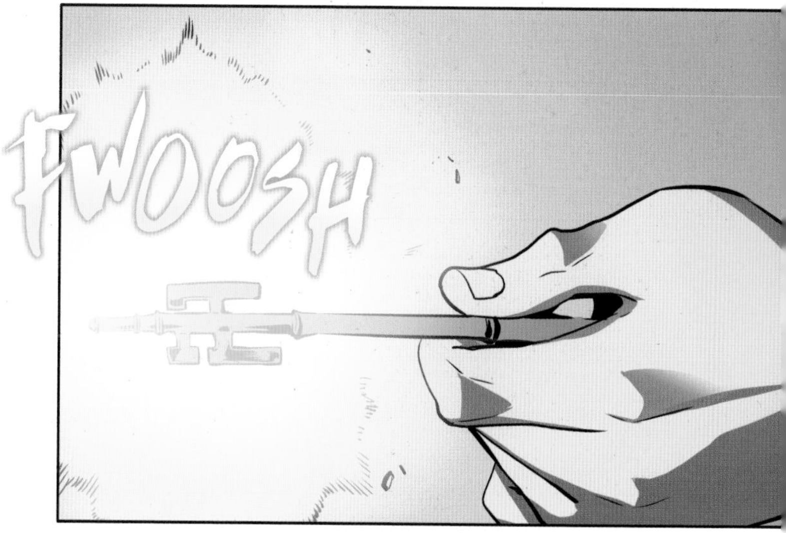
FWOOSH

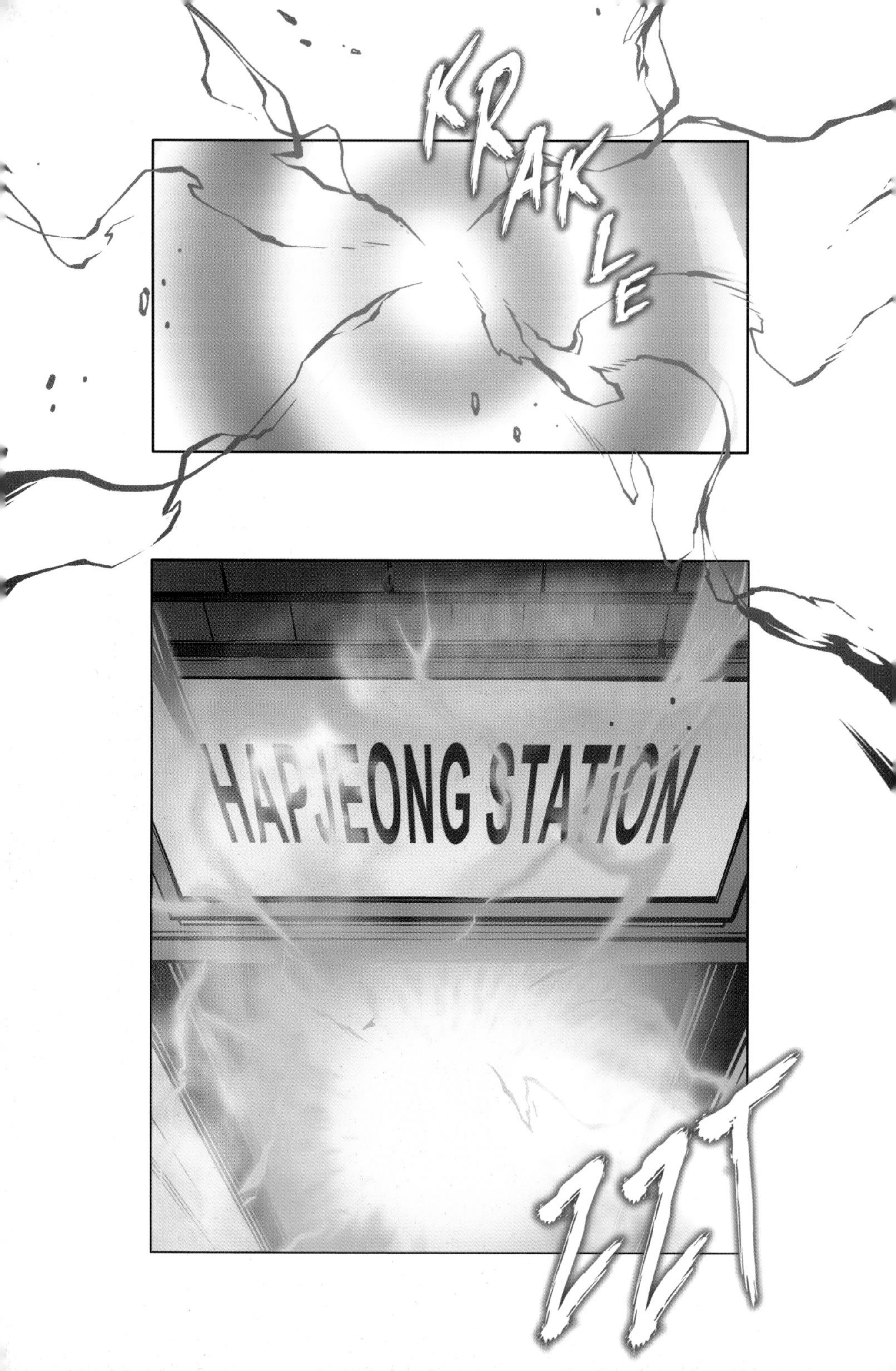
KRAKLE
HAPJEONG STATION
ZZT

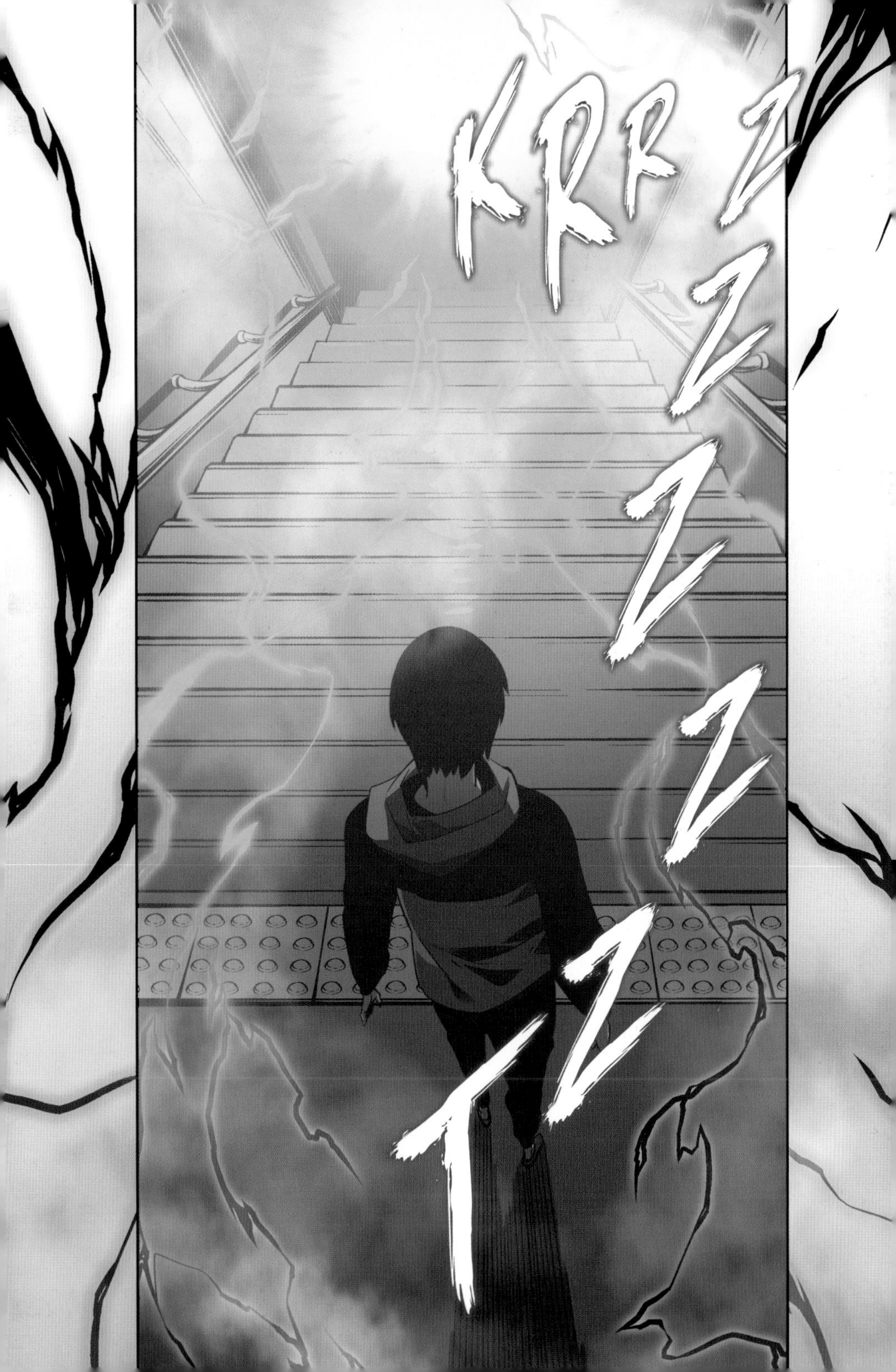
KRRZZZZZT

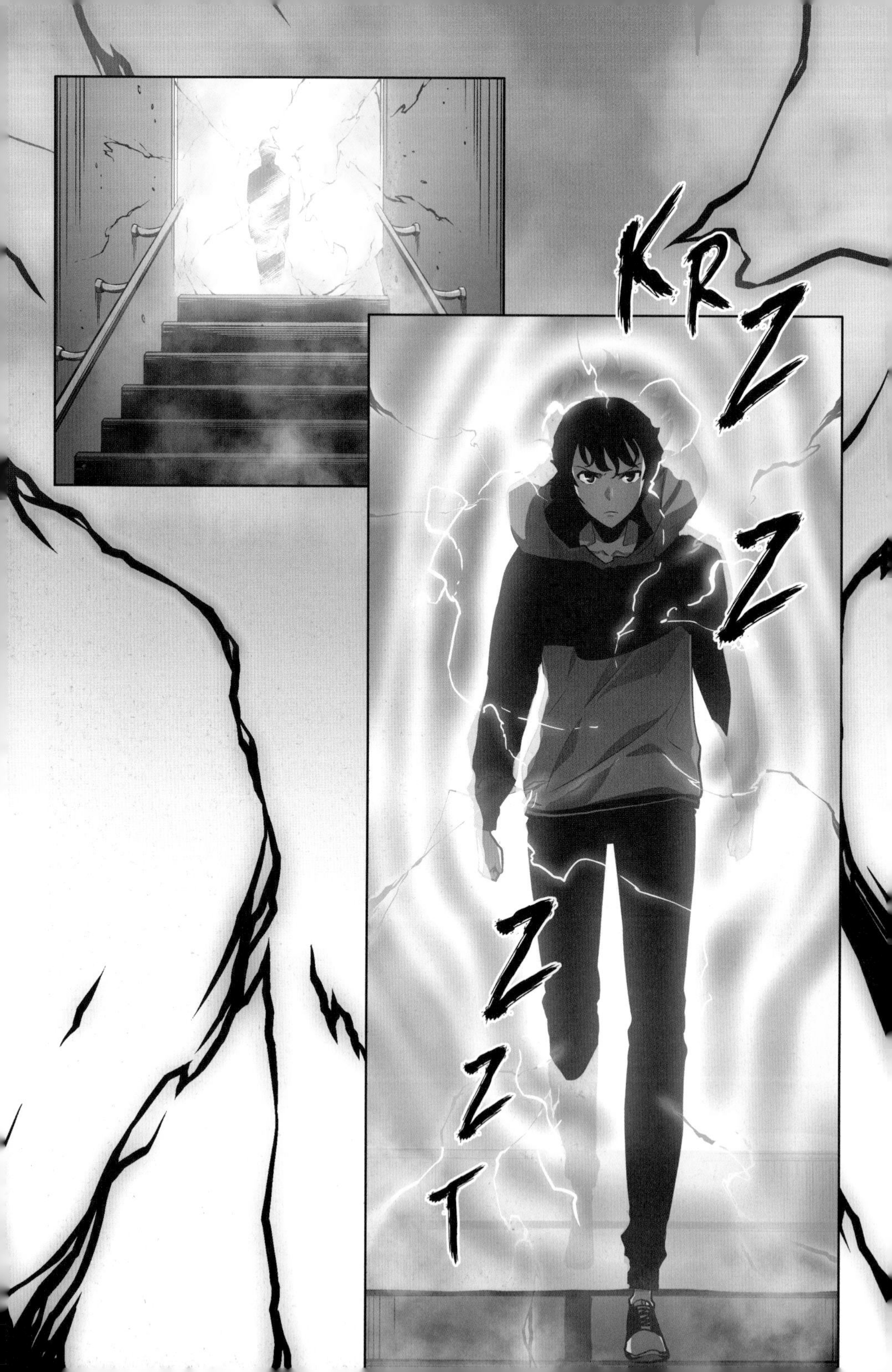
KRZZZZZT

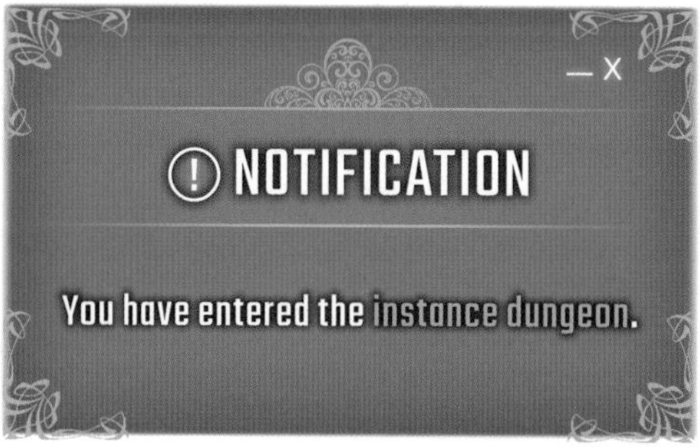
— X
! NOTIFICATION
You have entered the instance dungeon.

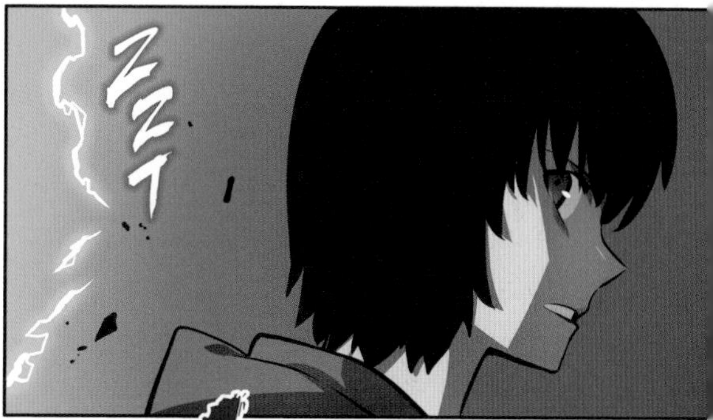
ZZZT

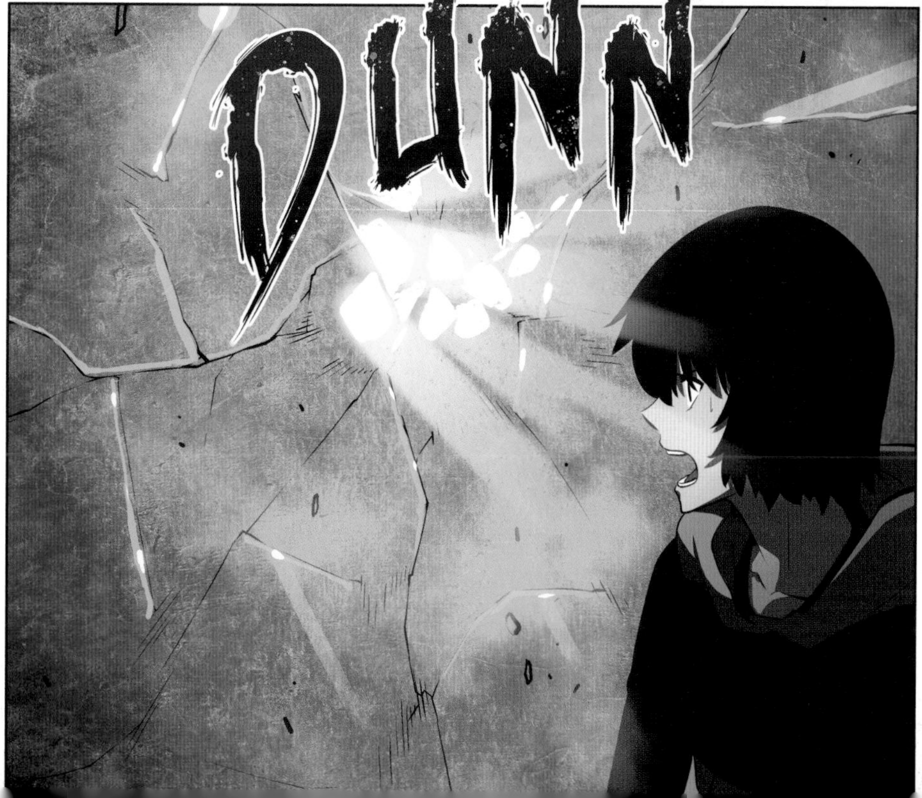
DUNN

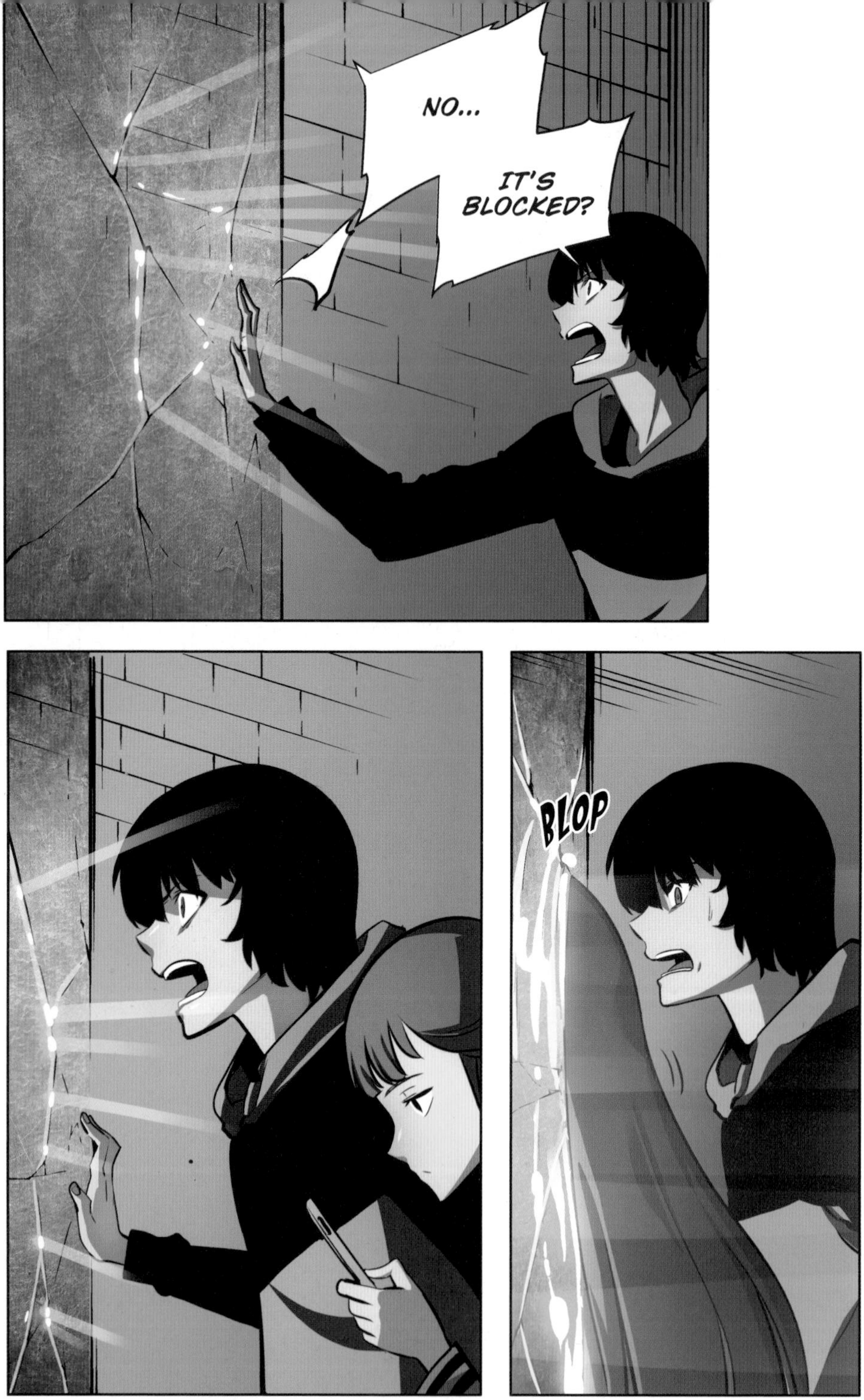
NO...
IT'S BLOCKED?
BLOP

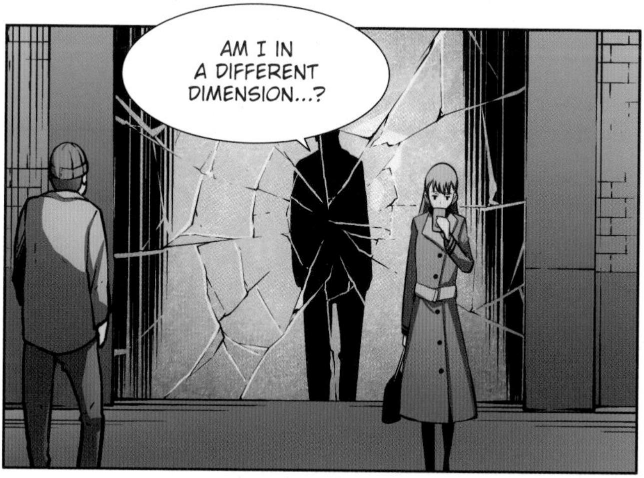
AM I IN A DIFFERENT DIMENSION...?

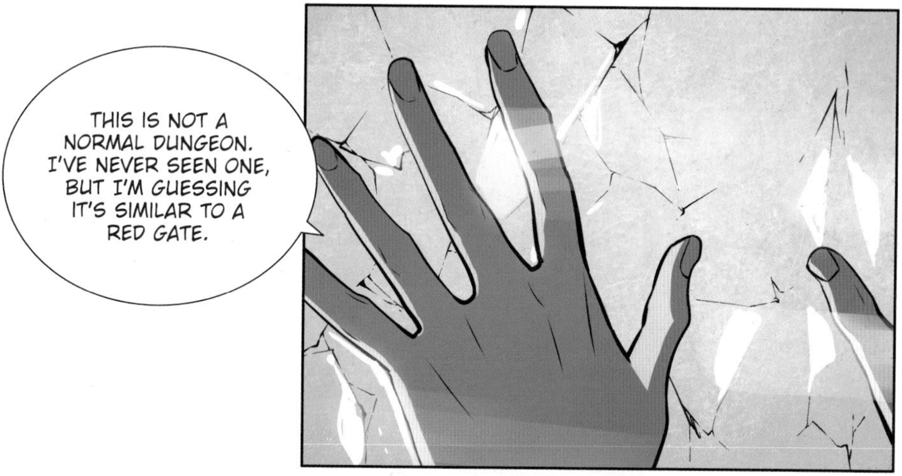
THIS IS NOT A NORMAL DUNGEON. I'VE NEVER SEEN ONE, BUT I'M GUESSING IT'S SIMILAR TO A RED GATE.

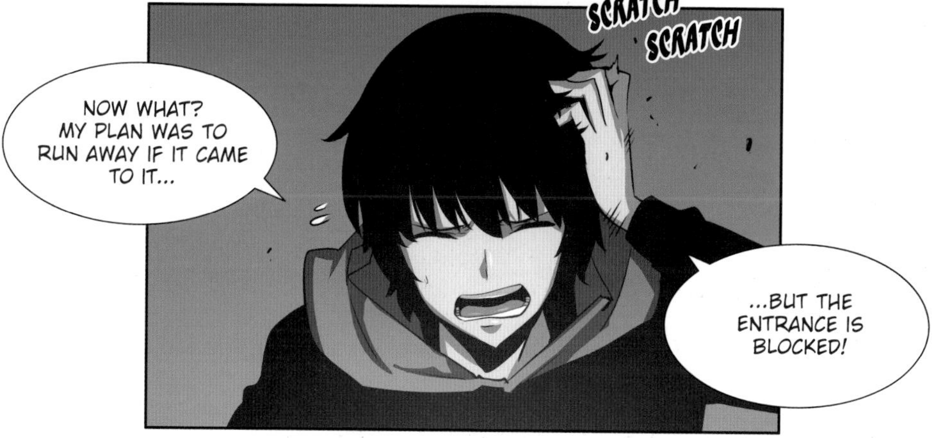
NOW WHAT? MY PLAN WAS TO RUN AWAY IF IT CAME TO IT...
SCRATCH
SCRATCH
...BUT THE ENTRANCE IS BLOCKED!

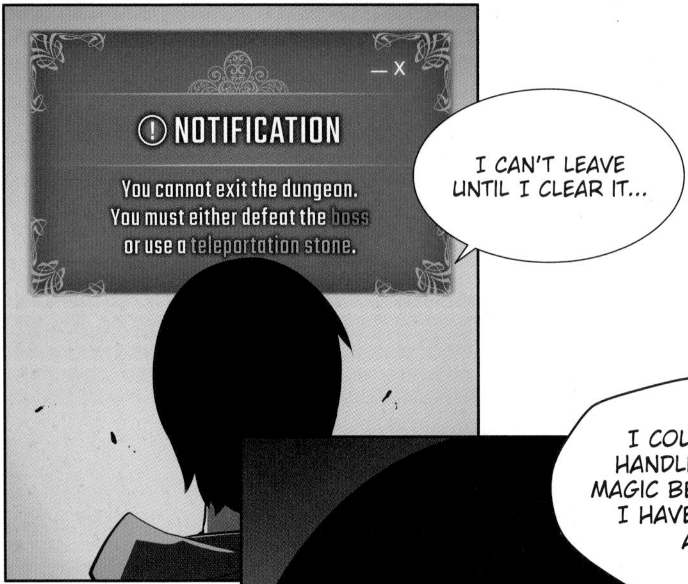
NOTIFICATION
You cannot exit the dungeon. You must either defeat the boss or use a teleportation stone.
I CAN'T LEAVE UNTIL I CLEAR IT...

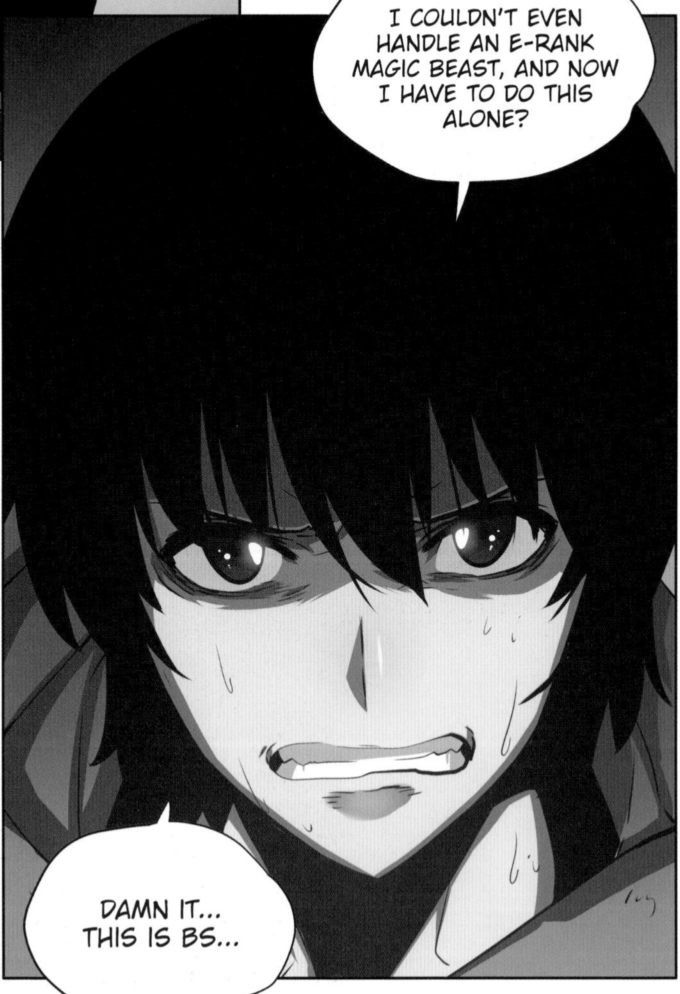
I COULDN'T EVEN HANDLE AN E-RANK MAGIC BEAST, AND NOW I HAVE TO DO THIS ALONE?
DAMN IT... THIS IS BS...

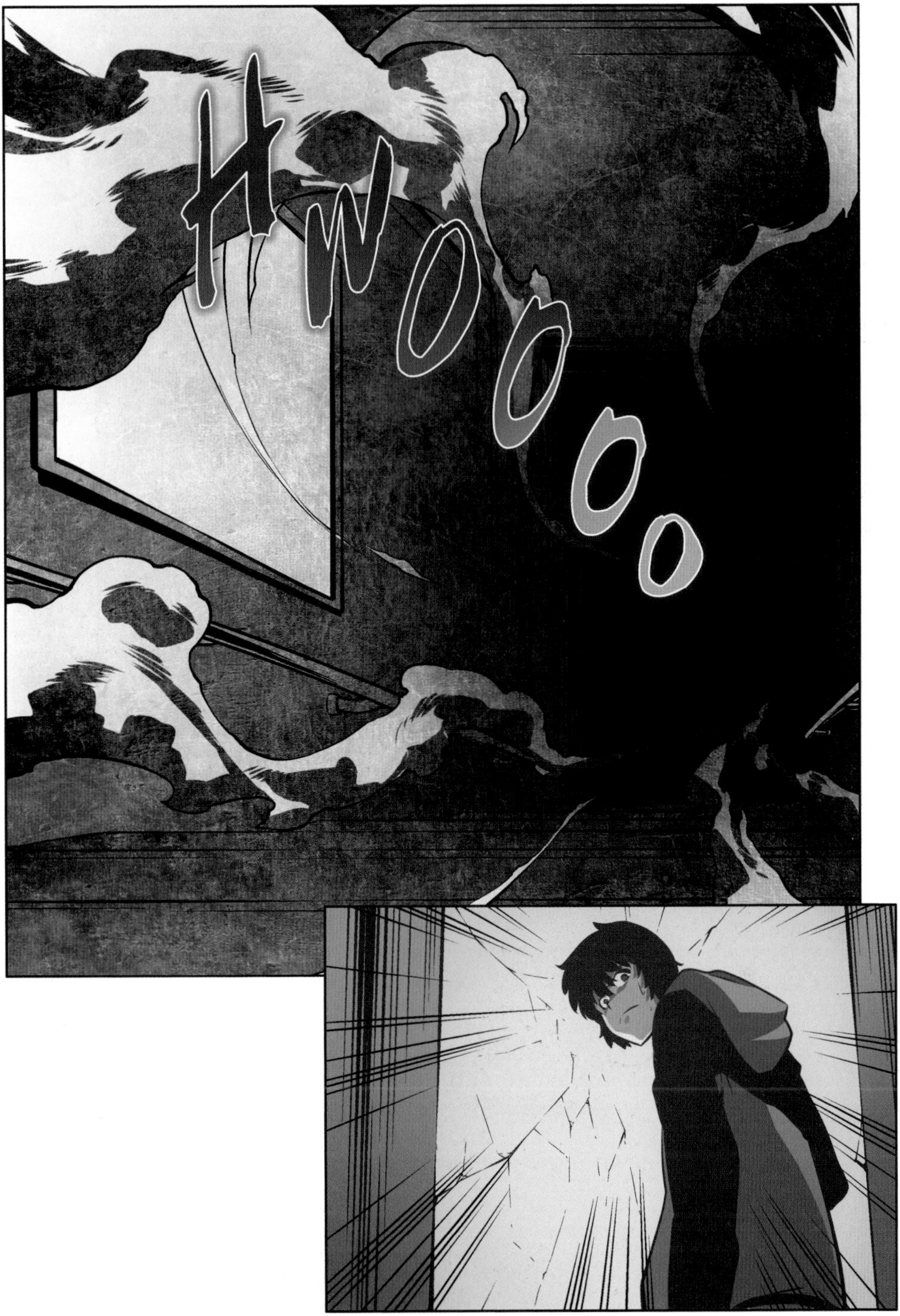
HWOOOO

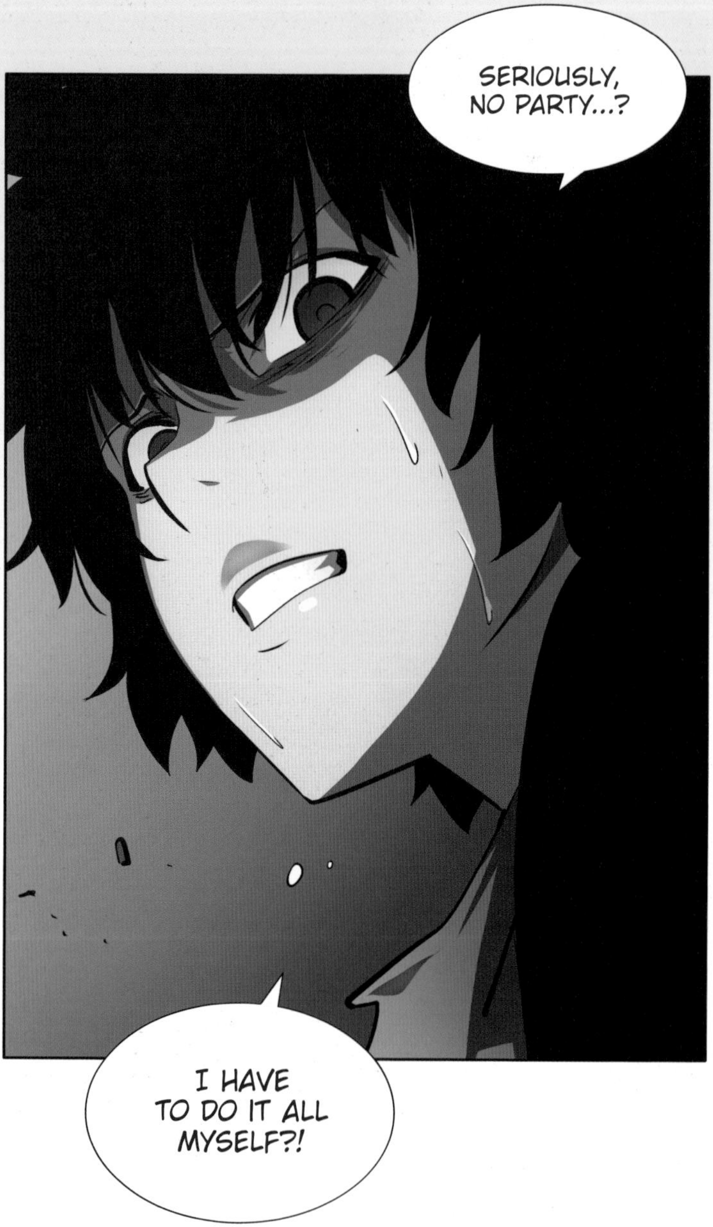
SERIOUSLY, NO PARTY...?
I HAVE TO DO IT ALL MYSELF?!

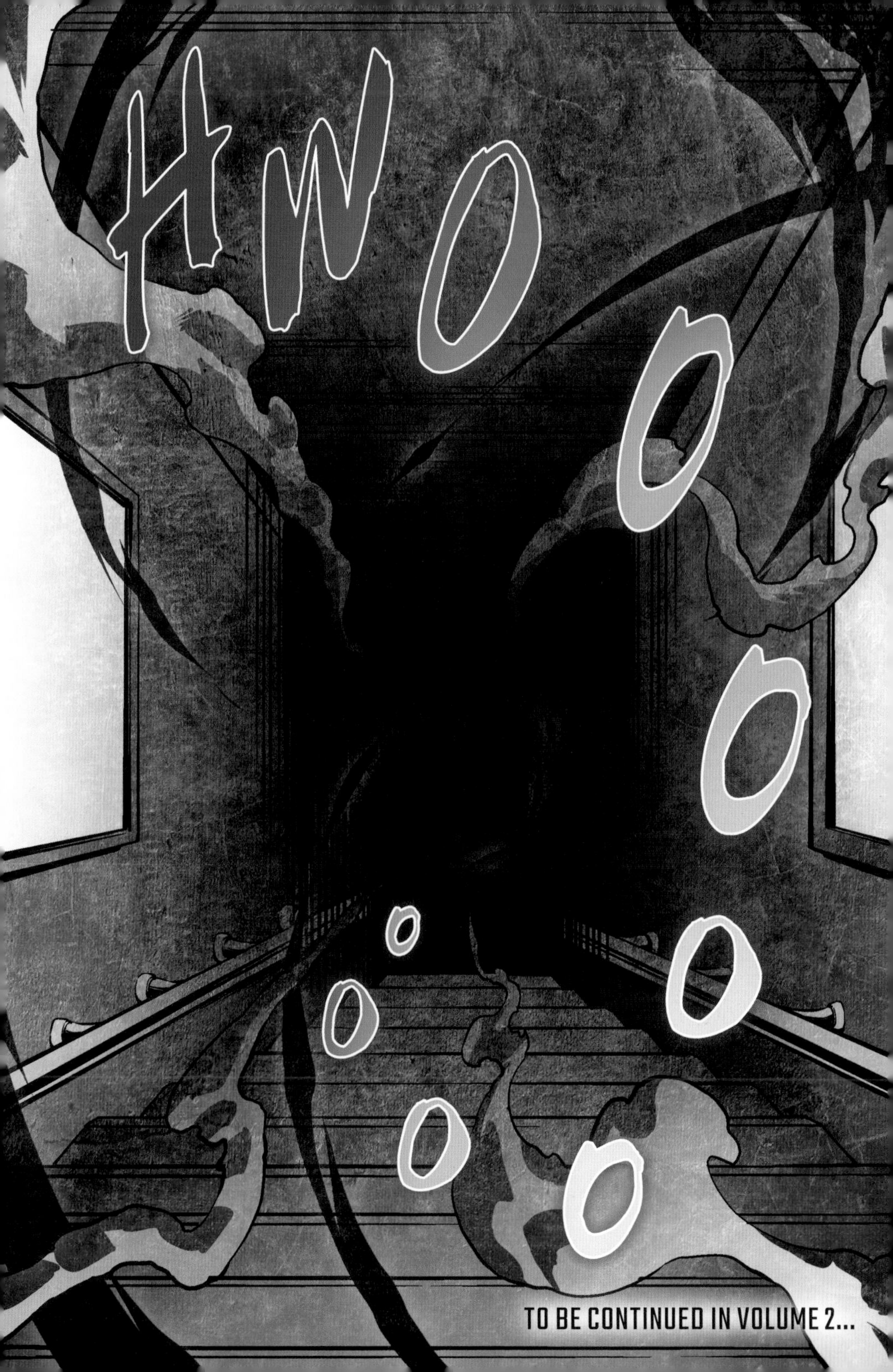
HWOOOOOOOO
TO BE CONTINUED IN VOLUME 2...

"If it means I'll get stronger, then I can play by these BS rules!"

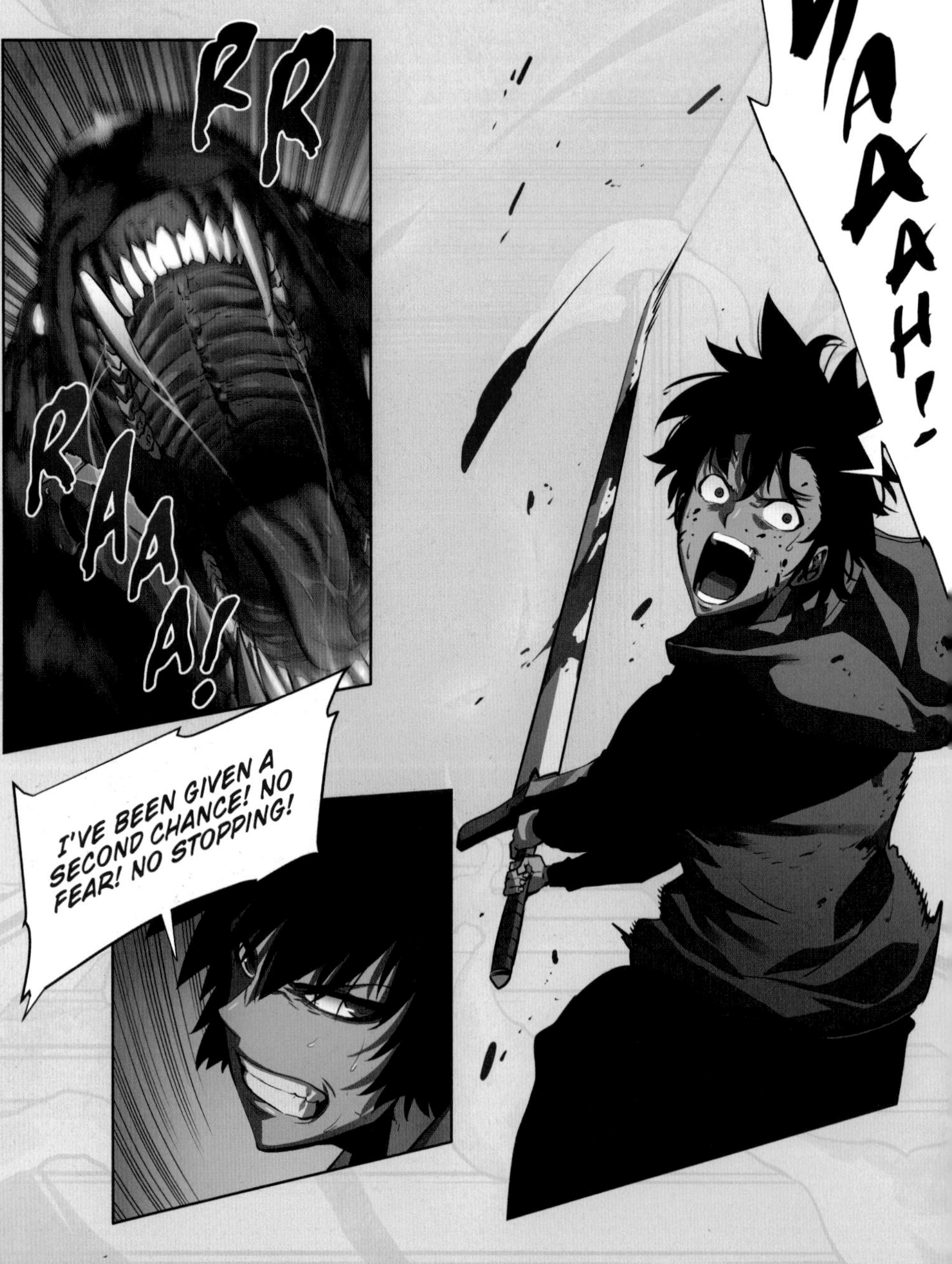
RRRAAAA!
I'VE BEEN GIVEN A SECOND CHANCE! NO FEAR! NO STOPPING!
NAAAAH!

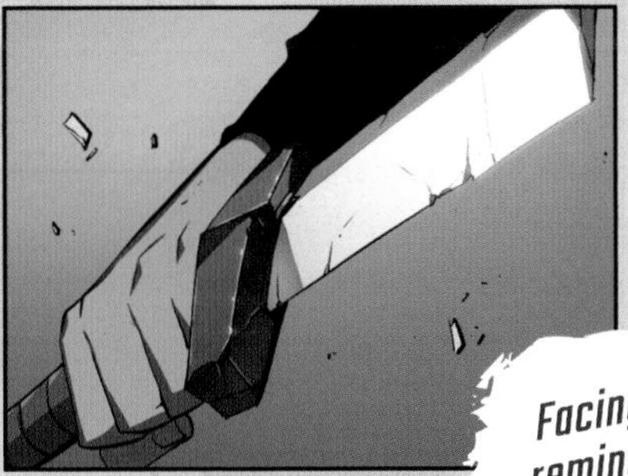

"How strong do I have to get...
to escape my powerless past?!"

Facing the danger alone...
reminds him of the double dungeon...
NONSTOP SOLO LEVELING!

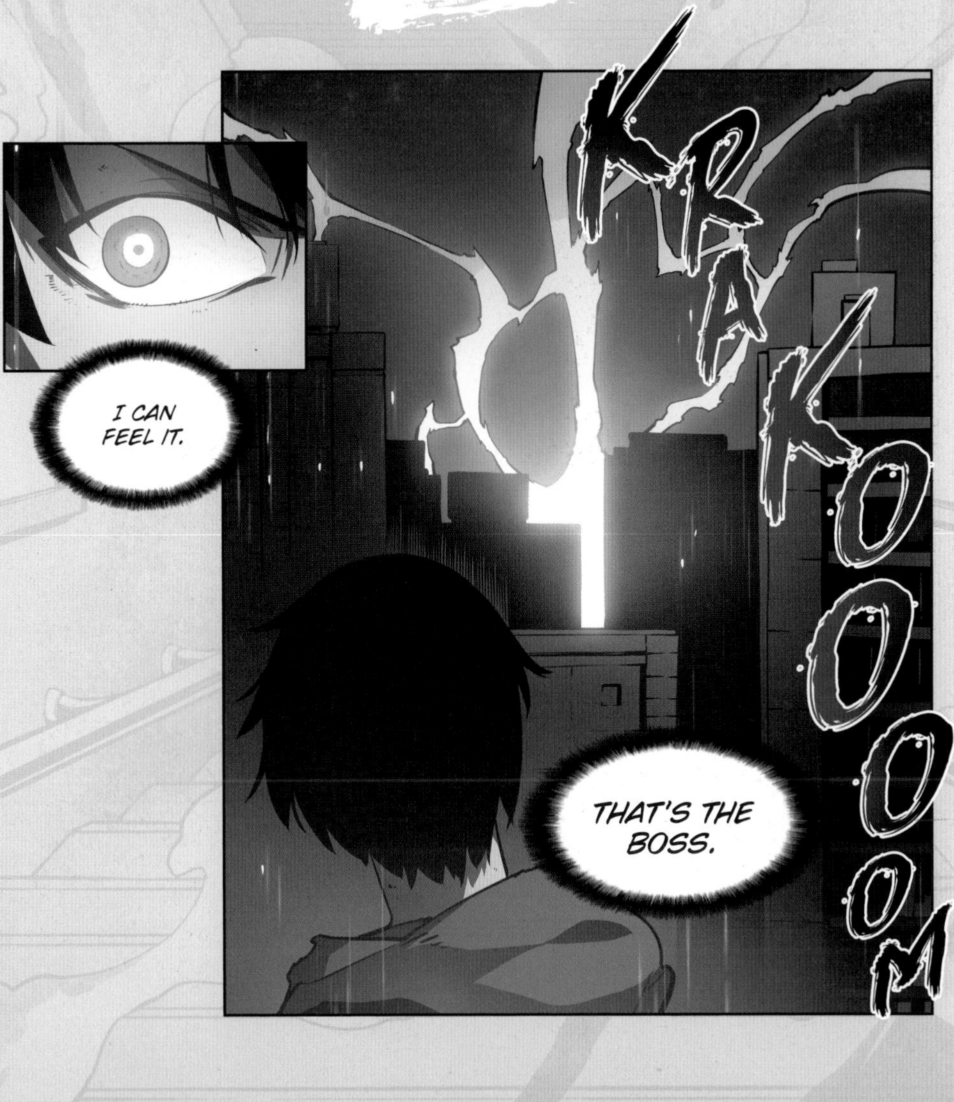
I CAN FEEL IT.
KRAKOOOOOM
THAT'S THE BOSS.

READ THE NOVEL WHERE IT ALL BEGAN!

© Chugong 2017 / D&C MEDIA

SOLO LEVELING

E-rank hunter Jinwoo Sung has no money, no talent, and no prospects to speak of—and apparently, no luck, either! When he enters a hidden double dungeon one fateful day, he's abandoned by his party and left to die at the hands of some of the most horrific monsters he's ever encountered. But just before the last, fatal blow...

PING!
[CONGRATULATIONS ON BECOMING A PLAYER.]

VOLUME 1 AVAILABLE WHEREVER BOOKS ARE SOLD!

Solo
Leveling

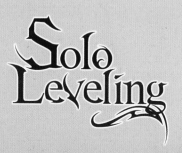

SOLO LEVELING

DUBU
(REDICE STUDIO)

I

ORIGINAL STORY
CHUGONG

Translation: Hye Young Im ◆ Rewrite: J. Torres ◆ Lettering: Abigail Blackman

SOLO LEVELING Volume 1
© DUBU(REDICE STUDIO), Chugong 2018 / D&C WEBTOON Biz
All rights reserved.
First published in Korea in 2018 by D&C WEBTOON Biz Co., Ltd.

English translation © 2021 by Yen Press, LLC

Yen Press
150 West 30th Street, 19th Floor
New York, NY 10001

Visit us at yenpress.com
facebook.com/yenpress
twitter.com/yenpress
yenpress.tumblr.com
instagram.com/yenpress

First Yen Press Edition: February 2021

Yen Press is an imprint of Yen Press, LLC.
The Yen Press name and logo are trademarks of Yen Press, LLC.

The publisher is not responsible for websites (or their content) that are not owned by the publisher.

Library of Congress Control Number: 2020950228

ISBNs: 978-1-9753-1943-4 (paperback)
978-1-9753-1944-1 (ebook)

10 9 8

TPA

Printed in South Korea